CONSTITUTIONAL DEMOCRACY

THE JOHNS HOPKINS SERIES
IN CONSTITUTIONAL THOUGHT
Sanford Levinson and Jeffrey K. Tulis,
Series Editors

CONSTITUTIONAL DEMOCRACY

Creating and Maintaining a Just Political Order

Walter F. Murphy

THE JOHNS HOPKINS UNIVERSITY PRESS
Baltimore

The Johns Hopkins University Press
2715 North Charles Street
Baltimore, Maryland 21218-4363
www.press.jhu.edu

Library of Congress Cataloging-in-Publication Data

Murphy, Walter F., 1929–
    Constitutional democracy : creating and maintaining a
just political order / Walter F. Murphy.
        p. cm. — (The Johns Hopkins series in constitutional
thought)
    Includes bibliographical references and index.
    ISBN 0-8018-8470-5 (hardcover : alk. paper)
    1. Democracy. 2. Constitutional law. 3. State, The.
4. Comparative government. I. Title. II. Series.
JC423.M83 2006
321.8—dc22   2006003550

A catalog record for this book is available from the
British Library.

For Terry, whose love conquers time.

Contents

Preface

Writing a long and substantial book is like having a friend and companion at your side, to whom you can always turn for comfort and amusement.

WINSTON CHURCHILL

Democracy became the great political buzzword of the closing years of the twentieth century. Its battle cry of freedom sounded in the East even as it rumbled in the West, not only in North and South America but also in Asia, Africa, Eastern Europe, the old Soviet Union, and, more faintly, in mainland China and Arab countries of the Near East. In 2001, George W. Bush, the first American president in more than twelve decades to receive fewer popular votes than his opponent, vowed to bring this political system to the Middle East—by force if necessary.

To talk about democracy that is stable is, in the modern context, to talk about constitutions. And to talk about constitutions implies, however falsely, an understanding of constitutionalism. Thus one may be led somewhat afield from the initial topic, for, as later chapters in this book stress, democracy and constitutionalism implicate norms that are in many ways alike but also in other ways different and in some ways opposed. To confuse democratic with constitutional—or, more accurately, constitutionalist—rule is to invite muddled thinking and disastrous public policy. The political systems of the United States and most so-called democracies in Western civilization are, in fact, constitutional democracies, resting on subtle blends of democratic and constitutionalist theories.

The chapters that follow seek to disassemble and then reassemble (much more civilized words than *disaggregate* and *reaggregate*) the components of constitutional democracy and examine them both separately and as a whole. This book is concerned, first, with the nature of that union and its sometimes schizoid norms. The next set of problems these pages address centers on the ways parts and whole of constitutionalism and democracy should and in many contexts do function: how to create a constitutionalist democracy, how to maintain it, and how to change it without destroying its integrity.

Throughout, I try to keep different concepts and processes analytically distinct. But as Lord Francis Bacon instructed us in Calvin's Case, "It is one

thing to make things distinct, another to make them separate." The real
world is not as neat as the scholar's study, even one as messy as mine. It is not
always clear, for example, when we are creating, when we are maintaining,
and when we are changing a political system. Thus, even though I frequently
call attention to the necessity of taking a systemic view, readers—and rulers—
must do so constantly.

One could, perhaps, make a useful study of constitutionalism through a
close examination of one or two countries.[1] Certainly such a work would be
easier to read. It might even have greater influence on public policy, because
public officials, especially judges, sometimes read scholarly writings that
have direct relevance to their own tasks. I began an earlier incarnation of this
volume under a contract with the Johns Hopkins University Press to write
precisely such a book on the United States and published several pieces from
that incomplete manuscript.[2] But as that work progressed, I became increasingly uncomfortable discussing, as if they were peculiarly American,
problems that occur throughout much of the world. I also became increasingly aware that, as Alexander Gerschenkron reminds us, insularity limits
understanding, even of the insular.[3] To understand the constitutional order
of the United States, it is necessary not only to realize how other peoples
have seen and tried to imitate that system but also to grasp that others have
coped in different ways with many of the same problems that Americans
have. Their solutions and efforts to justify their solutions may be quite
revealing of what we ourselves have been trying unsuccessfully to articulate.
"What is consistent from culture to culture," Walter Goldschmidt says, "is
not the institution; what is consistent from culture to culture are the social
problems. What is recurrent from society to society is solutions to these
problems."[4] And not all solutions—or, more accurately, efforts at solutions—
are likely to work across cultural and national lines. To differentiate what is

1. Gary Jeffrey Jacobsohn has masterfully done so in two books: *The Apple of Gold: Constitu-
tionalism in Israel and the United States* (Princeton, NJ: Princeton University Press, 1993) and *The
Wheel of Law: India's Secularism in Comparative Constitutional Context* (Princeton, NJ: Princeton
University Press, 2003).

2. See "Slaughter-House, Civil Rights, and Limits on Constitutional Change," 32 *Am. J. of
Jurispr.* 1 (1987); "The Nature of the American Constitution," James Lecture, Department of Politi-
cal Science, University of Illinois, Urbana-Champaign, 1988; "Privacy and the Constitution," in
Shlomo Slonim, ed., *The Constitutional Bases of Social and Political Change in the United States* (New
York: Praeger, 1990); and "The Nature of the American Constitution," in Tiziano Bonazzi, ed., *La
costituzione statunitense e il suo significato odierno, 1787–1987* (Bologna: Mulino, 1990).

3. *Economic Backwardness in Historical Perspective* (Cambridge, MA: Harvard University Press,
1962), p. 6. In displays of provincialism that are remarkable for intelligent and sophisticated men,
Judge Robert H. Bork dissents as does Justice Antonin Scalia. See esp. Bork, *Coercing Virtue: The
Worldwide Rule of Judges* (Washington, DC: American Enterprise Institute Press, 2003).

4. *Comparative Functionalism* (Berkeley: University of California Press, 1966), p. 31. Cf. Niccolò
Machiavelli: "In all cities and in all peoples there are the same desires and the same passions as there
always were." *Discourses*, ed. Bernard Crick (London: Penguin, 1970), 1.39, p. 207.

common from what is unique, what can be shared, imitated, or adapted from what must be avoided, is a daunting task; and, this book takes only a few teetering steps in that direction.

I have been driven in this project by the belief that the results of a broader exploration, while physically more formidable than those of a study of one or a few nations, could be more conceptually intelligible. Thus I have chosen the scholar's role of trying to increase understanding over the citizen's role of influencing public policy. Samuel Johnson claimed that only fools write for anything except money. On Dr. Johnson's or any other economic theory, scholars collectively qualify as fools, for typically they write to influence others and, perhaps more foolishly yet, each other.[5] I would be less than candid if I denied hoping that in the long run the message of studies such as this one will trickle down and become part of the intellectual heritage that scholars pass on to their students, including those who directly shape public policy.

One further note: This book concentrates on nation-states, only occasional mentioning supranational institutions such as the United Nations, the European Community, or the European Court of Human Rights. That focus does not reflect lack of appreciation for the work of such organizations or a belief that the nation-state is a higher or more desirable form of human political organization. But even if for more evil than good, nation-states are with us. Their organizations, functions, powers, obligations, and weaknesses may be fundamentally changing, but for generations to come they are likely to be the most important form of political organization.[6]

What follows offers tangible proof of the claim in Ecclesiastes that "the use of books is endless." This volume grew out of almost five decades of research, analysis, and worry. It began in 1956, when, as a graduate student at the University of Chicago and C. Herman Pritchett's research assistant, I sketched a long-term project as part of an application for a fellowship at the Brookings Institution. As broad as it seemed to my young mind, its scope was limited to the United States. The table of contents of the first edition of *Courts, Judges, and Politics* (1961) reflects that scheme, and some of my other

---

5. Former judge Robert H. Bork might prefer to label as charlatans academics and other members of what he terms "the intellectual or knowledge class," that is, those people who "work, however adroitly or maladroitly with words and ideas" and manage to spread constitutional "heresy." See his *The Tempting of America: The Political Seduction of the Law* (New York: Free Press, 1989), esp. the introductory chapter.

In a sense, scholars may be playing what Dr. Johnson would call a nonfoolish role insofar as they hope that officials of their institutions will at least note the writings' existence and reward the authors with those goods that academe bestows on the industrious in the hope that it is rewarding the creative.

6. See esp. Philip Bobbitt, *The Shield of Achilles: War, Peace, and the Course of History* (New York: Alfred A. Knopf, 2002).

work addressed specific topics within that framework.[7] Then in 1963, as part of teaching a summer session at the InterUniversity Consortium for Political Research at the University of Michigan, the late Joseph Tanenhaus and I decided to examine the field of public law in American political science. Our curiosity led us to write a slim volume on that topic[8] as well as to explore the sources of popular support for the Supreme Court of the United States. In the one unkind act he ever did to me, Tanenhaus died before we could complete our analyses. Still, we had made sufficient progress[9] to become aware of and fascinated by similar institutions in other polities.

Our efforts to replicate abroad our research in the United States were among the least notable and least mourned casualties of the war in Vietnam. Nevertheless, those attempts deepened our appreciation of the important roles that courts and constitutional texts play in many other nations. To spread that gospel, we published a volume of essays and annotated cases, *Comparative Constitutional Law*.[10] That book was, however, born before its time, attracting more attention (and selling more copies) in Europe than in the United States, where political scientists tended to view comparative studies of processes other than economic development, political parties, and voting as playgrounds rather than as arenas for serious scholarship.

After Joseph Tanenhaus's death in 1981, I continued to work in constitutional theory, sometimes in an overtly comparative fashion but usually, as in this book, concerned with interactions among general norms, more specific legal rules, and patterns of institutional behavior.[11] In 1987, Donald L. Rob-

---

7. Walter Murphy and C. Herman Pritchett, *Courts, Judges, and Politics* (New York: Random House, 1961). Related work includes esp. *Congress and the Court* (Chicago: University of Chicago Press, 1962) and *Elements of Judicial Strategy* (Chicago: University of Chicago Press, 1964).

8. *The Study of Public Law* (New York: Random House, 1971).

9. See, for instance, "Public Opinion and Supreme Court: The Goldwater Campaign," 32 *Pub. Op. Q.* 31 (1968); "La opinión pública y el Tribunal Supremo de los Estados Unidos," 11 *Revista Española de la Opinión Pública* 3 (1968); "Public Opinion and the United States Supreme Court: Mapping of Some Prerequisites for Court Legitimation of Regime Changes," 2 *L. & Soc. Rev.* 357 (1968), reprinted in Joel Grossman and Joseph Tanenhaus, eds., *Frontiers of Judicial Research* (New York: Wiley, 1969); "Constitutional Courts and Political Representation," in Michael Danielson and Walter F. Murphy, eds., *Modern American Democracy* (New York: Holt, Rinehart and Winston, 1969); with Daniel L. Kastner, *Public Evaluations of Constitutional Courts: Alternative Explanations* (Los Angeles: Sage, 1974); "Explaining Diffuse Support for the United States Supreme Court: An Assessment of Four Models," 49 *Notre Dame Lawyer* 1037 (1974); "Patterns of Public Support for the Supreme Court: A Panel Study," 43 *J. of Pols.* 24 (1981); and "Publicity, Public Opinion, and the Court," 84 *Nwn. U. L. Rev.* 983 (1990).

10. New York: St. Martin's, 1977.

11. In addition to three editions of *American Constitutional Interpretation*, the first with James E. Fleming and William F. Harris II, the second with Fleming and Sotirios A. Barber, and the third with Stephen Macedo joining the authors and editors (Westbury, NY: Foundation, 1986, 1995, and 2003), see "Civil Law, Common Law, and Constitutional Democracy," 52 *La. L. Rev.* 91 (1991); "Consent and Constitutional Change," in James O'Reilly, ed., *Human Rights: Essays in Honor of the Hon. Mr. Justice Brian Walsh* (Dublin: Round Hall, 1992); "Staggering toward the New Jurispru-

inson of Smith College wisely persuaded the Ford Foundation to celebrate the bicentennial of the Constitution of the United States by moving beyond American history to an investigation of constitutionalism as a general political phenomenon. Ford turned that project over to the American Council of Learned Societies, then headed by Stanley N. Katz. I was tangentially involved during Ford's planning stages and became a closer part of ACLS's effort.

The initial phase of the project under ALCS was a series of international conferences conducted in cooperation with various regional associations and institutes in the United States, Zimbabwe, Thailand, Uruguay, Berlin, and Hungary.[12] Scholars from these areas, as well as from Australia, the Soviet Union, and North America, attended. A small core of us ventured to all the meetings, but most people participated in only one or two sessions. A few journalists and public officials, including the ministers of justice of Hungary and Vietnam, also took part in one or more of these conferences. We convened first at Wingspread outside of Milwaukee, Wisconsin, then at Punta del Este (Uruguay), Chiangmai (Thailand), Harare (Zimbabwe), and West Berlin.[13] In November 1989, we returned to Princeton for what had been planned as a wrap-up session. But as we were meeting in the quiet of the Nassau Inn, the world turned upside down. The Berlin Wall was breached and the Soviet Empire began to crumble. To address these new crises, Ford and the Hungarian Academy of Sciences provided additional support to send our road show to Pecs, in western Hungary, where we joined scholars from China, the Federal Republic of Czechs and Slovaks, the Federal Republic of Germany, Italy, Norway, Poland, Turkey, and of course Hungary.

---

dence of Constitutional Theory," 37 *Am. J. of Jurispr.* 337 (1992); "Constitutions, Constitutionalism, and Democracy," in Douglas Greenberg, Stanley N. Katz, Melanie Beth Oliviero, and Steven C. Wheatley, eds., *Constitutionalism and Democracy: Transformations in the Contemporary World* (New York: Oxford University Press, 1993); "Excluding Political Parties," in Paul Kirchhof and Donald P. Kommers, eds., *Germany and Its Basic Law* (Baden-Baden: Nomos, 1993); "Creating Citizens of a Constitutional Democracy," in Tiziano Bonazzi and Michael Dunne, eds., *Cittadinanza e diritte nelle società multiculturali* (Bologna: Mulino, 1994); "What Is It Interpreters Interpret? A Response to Prof. Delperee," in Eivind Smith, ed., *Constitutional Justice under Old Constitutions* (The Hague: Kluwer, 1995); "Merlin's Memory: The Past and Future Imperfect of the Once and Future Polity," in Sanford V. Levinson, ed., *Responding to Imperfection* (Princeton, NJ: University Press, 1995); and "Can Constitutional Democracies Outlaw Political Parties?" in John Geer, ed., *New Perspectives on Party Politics* (Baltimore: Johns Hopkins University Press, 1998).

12. Zimbabwe: Southern Africa Political Science and Economic Series / African Association of Political Science, Southern Africa, P.O. Box MP111, Mt. Pleasant, Harare, Zimbabwe. Thailand: Law and Society Trust, 8 Kynsey Terrace, Colombo 8, Sri Lanka. Uruguay: Centro de Informaciones y Estudios del Uruguay, Juan Paullier 1174, Casilla de Correo 10587, Montevideo, Uruguay. Berlin: John F. Kennedy Insititut für Nordamerikastudien, Abt. Geshichte, Freie Universität Berlin (Z1 2), Landstrasse 7–9, 1000 Berlin 23, Federal Republic of Germany.

13. In Madison we were guests of the Johnson Wax Foundation. The Bank of Sweden Tercentenary Foundation, the Fritz Thyssen Stiftung, and the Volkswagen-Stiftung, along with the Ford Foundation, provided financial support for the meetings in Berlin.

H. W. O. Okoth-Ogendo of the University of Nairobi and I each wrote a general paper for four of the first five conferences, and many of the other participants gave a paper at one or another of these meetings. The regional associations have made all of these available, and ACLS has published a volume of selected essays, *Constitutionalism and Democracy: Transformations in the Contemporary World* (New York: Oxford University Press, 1993), edited by Douglas Greenberg, Stanley N. Katz, Melanie Beth Oliviero, and Steven C. Wheatley.

The ACLS project assigned Okoth-Ogendo and me an additional different task: each was to write a general volume on constitutionalism, he from the point of view of an African scholar, educated at Oxford and Yale as well as in East Africa and trained both in demography and law, I from the point of view of an American who had lived most of his life in economically developed constitutional democracies. This book constitutes my somewhat belated part of that arrangement.

Acknowledgments

Any book of this scope may have deeper roots in chutzpah than in wisdom. Still, such a study, as John Lewis Gaddis explains,[14] can also instill a great deal of humility, forcing the culprit to realize how much he or she owes to those who went before, such as Woodrow Wilson and Edward S. Corwin, as well as to those who are currently treading the same path. The pages that follow will demonstrate that I have accumulated a corps of debts. Indeed, a caustic reviewer might sneer that never has so little owed so much to so many. What follows is only a partial listing of debts.

Three deceased scholars, each a dear friend, were critically important in my work as well as my life: Joseph Tanenhaus, Alpheus Thomas Mason, and C. Herman Pritchett, my continual mentor and long-time coconspirator in *Courts, Judges, and Politics*. Each invested more of his time than he should have in trying to educate me. The late Rosemary Allen Little of Princeton's Firestone Library was, as with all work done in political science during her tenure at that university, a collaborator who could somehow locate the most esoteric of materials. Helen Wright, now retired after long service at Princeton University, scoured early drafts for errors, substantive as well as typographical; as usual, she found many glitches that less gifted mortals had missed. Sotirios A. Barber of the University of Notre Dame offered trenchant criticism, reasoned argument, and warm support. During this book's extended gestation, he performed an act of mercy by helping produce the second and third editions of *American Constitutional Interpretation* and yet found time while generating his own scholarship to read and criticize this

---

14. *The Landscape of History: How Historians Map the Past* (New York: Oxford University Press, 2002), p. x.

entire manuscript. One of my former graduate students, James E. Fleming, now a professor at Fordham Law School, took over leadership for the third edition of *American Constitutional Interpretation*, and he and Barber were joined by another former graduate student, Stephen Macedo of Princeton, to bring that rejuvenated project into the world.

Moreover, Barber displayed gentle patience with my fumbling slowness in completing the manuscript, as did Jeffrey Tulis of the University of Texas. Henry Tom, executive editor at the Johns Hopkins University Press, evidenced patience worthy of Job himself. Lee Epstein of Washington University at St. Louis, later joined by her colleague Jack Knight, took over most of the work for the fifth and sixth editions of *Courts, Judges, and Politics*.[15] She also managed to find time amid her constant scholarly projects to keep me informed about professional literature and to remind me of the standards that self-respecting scholars must meet.[16]

Gary Jeffrey Jacobsohn of the University of Texas and Douglas Verney, emeritus of York University, tried to teach me about matters Indian, as did Lawrence W. Beer, emeritus of LaFayette College, and Takeo Hayakawa, emeritus of Kobe University, about Japanese law and politics. Donald L. Robinson of Smith College assisted in that difficult endeavor. Time and again, Donald P. Kommers of the University of Notre Dame performed the same function with German law and politics. Jacobsohn and Martin Edelman, emeritus of SUNY at Albany, tried to repair my ignorance of the Israeli political system. Joanne Gowa of Princeton instructed me regarding war, peace, and democratic governance, while Robert P. Gilpin, emeritus of Princeton, frequently reminded me of the interrelations between domestic politics and foreign policy. Stephen Macedo of Princeton insisted that I conceptualize citizenship as life within a community. Robert P. George of Princeton and the noted moral theologian James Tunstead Burtchaell, C.S.C., often, occasionally sharply—with that edge softened by the former's selection of great wines and the latter's preparation of magnificent meals— reminded me of the centrality of moral philosophy to any normative theory of politics. One of Fr. Burtchaell's former students, James J. Owens, Esq., of Albuquerque, New Mexico, agreed to become executor of my estate so that my conscience would be free to continue this work.

I also benefited enormously from teaching and arguing with former colleagues at Princeton: Sotirios Barber, the late Harry H. Eckstein, M. Stanley Kelley Jr., Andrew M. M. Koppelman, Sanford Victor Levinson, W. Duane Lockard, Charles A. Miller, Jennifer Nedelsky, Jeffrey Tulis, and the late Clement E. Vose. My former teaching assistants who are now accomplished professional scholars—especially Mark Brandon of Vanderbilt Law School,

15. Boston: McGraw-Hill, 2002 and 2005.
16. See the devastating article she coauthored with Gary King: "The Rules of Inference," 69 *U. Chi. L. Rev.* 1 (2002).

Judith Lynn Failer of Indiana University, John E. Finn of Wesleyan University, James E. Fleming (here too) of Fordham Law School, William F. Harris II of the University of Pennsylvania, Suzette Marie Hemberger, Gregory C. Keating of the University of Southern California, Wayne Moore of Virginia Polytechnical Institute, Fred Morrison of the University of Minnesota, Noah Pickus of Duke University, and Anthony Sebok of Brooklyn College Law School—are all aware of the help they provided by refusing to allow me to pontificate. Other former graduate students, such as John Goldberg of Vanderbilt, Jacob Levy of the University of Chicago, and D. Grier Stephenson of Franklin and Marshall College, who over the years took Politics 515 or Politics 561, and also the faculty who grappled with the seminar on constitutional democracy sponsored by the National Endowment for the Humanities in 1996 will see some of their agony reflected here. So, too, will Princeton's undergraduates who endured "Con Interp" and (proudly, I hope) bear the scars of having survived one of the two most demanding courses offered at that university.

I had many research assistants at Princeton, especially Martin di Santos, '93, James Sigmund, '94, Judith Failer of Indiana University, and Monica Bhattacharyya, Esq., When they, too, were graduate students, Andrew Farkas of Rutgers University and Peter Barsoom managed to keep my mind, my computer, and WordPerfect in reasonable harmony. In Albuquerque, Thomas Olson and Marcia Kite took over that task, and Donna Price, with heroic effort, persuaded me that WordPerfect for Windows was somehow superior to the quiet elegance of WordPerfect 5.1 for DOS.

At ACLS, Stanley Katz supplied just the right—light—touch of leadership for the conferences, as did his two vice presidents, Douglas Greenberg and Steven C. Wheatley. Melanie Beth Oliviero and Rebecca Nichols organized and ran the various conferences. That participants were able to focus on ideas free from administrative concerns was a tribute to Melanie and Rebecca's graceful efficiency. At the Ford Foundation, Shepard Forman played the role of pastor for the project. With the able assistance of his deaconess, Lynn Walker, he led his flock into green pastures. At Princeton, the William Nelson Cromwell Fund provided constant support. The Center of International Studies, then under the directorship of Henry S. Bienen, who later retired to enjoy a life of mendicant opulence in the mansion of the president of Northwestern University, tapped the Peter B. Lewis Fund and the Boesky Family Fund to supplement the moneys provided by Ford and the Cromwell Fund. In addition, Princeton University's generous leave policy—its quid pro quo for practicing cannibalism on its faculty when they are not on leave—gave me several years free from most other responsibilities. The Center for the Study of the Ordinary Judiciary of the University of Bologna, under the directorship of Giuseppe Di Federico, offered its hospitality for those parts of this study that overlap with its own comparative work on courts and judges. TIAA-CREF, the U.S. Marine Corps's budget for retired officers, and the Social Security Administration subsidized the final phases of writing.

Colonel F. Brandon Carlon and Eleanor Carlon, roving residents of Pennsylvania, Florida, Hawaii, Maryland, New Mexico, Virginia, West Virginia, Midway Island, Laos, the Philippines, Romania, Thailand, Vietnam, Zaire, and much of the rest of the world, many times allowed my wife and me to invade their house high on a cliff overlooking the Atlantic on the island of Grenada. Their bright hospitality and magnificent views of water and mountains joined with warm, sunny weather in the middle of winters to allow me to write several chapters in serene comfort.

In Albuquerque, the University of New Mexico's libraries generously opened their resources, and Elias Frick of the UNM Class of 2003 was an indefatigable research assistant. Harry P. Stumpf, emeritus, and his wife Patricia Rodgers, and Albert Narath, retired director of the Sandia Laboratories and his wife Shanna, along with the Carlons in their New Mexican incarnation, supplied much needed friendship, encouragement, and excellent meals.

To all of these people and institutions I am profoundly grateful. Still, my greatest debt is as always to my wife, Terry, who put up with my living for weeks on 747s, my staring at screens displaying manuscripts (or NFL games) when I was home, and, not least, my frequent swearing that I had been foolish to undertake such a complicated project rather than write a new novel and multiply our financial assets. Never once did she raise objections based on constitutionalist or democratic principles, though on occasion she did allude to issues of rational choice.

An earlier version of Chapter Two appears in Sotirios A. Barber and Robert P. George, eds., *Constitutional Politics: Essays on Constitution Making, Maintenance, and Change* (Princeton, N.J.: Princeton University Press, 2001). For a study of the same general problem from a very different set of perspectives, see Richard Rose, William Mishler, and Christian Haerpfer, *Democracy and Its Alternatives: Understanding Post-communist Societies* (Baltimore: Johns Hopkins University Press, 1998).

An earlier version of the essay that now serves as Part II's introduction was published in 81 *Denver U. L. Rev.* 415 (2003).

Displaying enormous goodwill, even when wielding his hyperactive blue pencil, Sotirios A. Barber read all of the chapters of the present work, as did Jeffrey Tulis. For critical readings of drafts of specific chapters, I am indebted to Bernard Grofman and the late Harry H. Eckstein, both of the University of California, Irvine (Part I, Chapter Two); Robert P. George, Princeton University (Part I, Chapters One and Three); F. Brandon Carlon, Colonel, U.S. Marine Corps (Part I, Chapter Eleven); Ezra Suleiman, Princeton University (Part II, Chapter Twelve); Mark E. Brandon: James T.

Burtchaell; James L. Gibson, Washington University at St. Louis; Robert P. George, Princeton University; Dennis F. Thompson, Harvard University; and Christopher Yoo, Vanderbilt Law School (Part II, Chapter Thirteen); Donald P. Kommers, Notre Dame (Part II, Chapter Fourteen). For careful copy-editing of a sprawling manuscript, I thank Ruth Goring. My thanks go also to Michael J. Sullivan, who as a graduate student at Princeton checked many of the citations.

For the many errors of omission and commission that remain, I must, of course, take full responsibility. I shall do so, however, deeply disappointed in my friends, having expected them to be more adept at saving me from myself.

CONSTITUTIONAL DEMOCRACY

General Introduction

[I]n the right definition of names lies the first use of speech; which is the acquisition of science; and in wrong, or not definition lies the first abuse; from which proceed all false and senseless tenets. THOMAS HOBBES

To live in safety and pursue happiness, people need a political system to protect them from each other as well as from foreigners. "[I]t is to secure our just rights that we resort to government," Thomas Jefferson noted.[1] But as soon as a people have a state and a government, they need to be protected from Leviathan's officials. Thus any political system sensitive to the needs of its citizens and aware of the human propensity to sin has two objectives: to empower government and to limit government. As James Madison put it on the eve of the American Constitutional Convention:

> The great desideratum of Government is such a modification of the sovereignty as will render it sufficiently neutral between the different interests and factions, to controul one part of society from invading the rights of another, and at the same time sufficiently controuled itself from setting up an interest adverse to that of the whole Society.[2]

These needs are preventive, essentially negative; but in The *Federalist* No. 45, Madison spoke more positively about actions government could and should take: "[T]he public good, the real welfare of the great body of the people is the supreme object to be pursued and . . . no form of Government whatever, has any other value, than as it may be fitted for the attainment of this object." Two weeks later he added in *Federalist* No. 51 the simple but morally pregnant claim that "[j]ustice is the end of government. It is the end of civil society. It ever has been and ever will be pursued until it be obtained, or until liberty be lost in the pursuit."

Democracy offers one means to permit a people to live in safety and enjoy both liberty and justice. The people shall rule. As both governors and

---

1. To Mons. D'Ivernois, Feb. 6, 1795; in *The Writings of Thomas Jefferson*, ed. Andrew A. Lipscomb (Washington: Thomas Jefferson Memorial Association, 1903), 9:299.

2. "Vices of the Political System of the United States," reprinted in Marvin Meyers, ed., *The Mind of the Framer* (Indianapolis: Bobbs-Merrill, 1970), p. 267.

governed, they will advance the common good without oppressing themselves—or so the argument goes. Constitutionalists, however, believe that
"the people" seldom unite as a monolith; they are more likely to form a
congeries of different groups and thus, in a majoritarian political system, are
likely to be ruled by a coalition of potentially self-serving minorities. Constitutionalists are distrustful of "majority's" benevolence toward those who are
"different" from or compete against them. Lest a majority of any sort shrink
"the public good" into what is good for its own members, constitutionalists
offer another option: accept the necessity of government to advance and
protect the welfare of society, support popular government, but install institutional checks on the authority of all rulers, even the people themselves.
A third solution would marry these two forms of government into a hybrid:
constitutional democracy. It is this type of political order that is now common in Europe and North America and has spread to Australia, India,
Japan, and parts of Latin America.[3]

     This book focuses on that third solution: how and why to create a consti-
tutional democracy, how to maintain it, and how to adapt it to changing
circumstances. The chapters that follow seek to provide some arguments
about as well as insights into that political order. I begin with a set of definitions, not because I am so brash as to believe that this nomenclature will
become the standard vocabulary for political discussion. Efforts to impose
such dictionaries on the world often resemble the mating of a mare and a
jackass: the product is strong-headed but usually sterile. I do, however, hope
that defining critical terms will permit readers to understand, criticize, and
improve my analyses and so deepen our understanding of constitutional
democracy. (To avoid repetition, I shall use the term *polity* as the equivalent
of *constitutional democracy*, fully realizing that others have used that term in a
different sense.)

Definitions

In 1958, Albert Camus wrote that one of the roles of intellectuals is "to clarify
definitions in order to disintoxicate minds."[4] He was lamenting France's

---

3. Juan Rial speaks of "the myth of Latin America": "The Armed Forces and the Question of
Democracy in Latin America," in Louis W. Goodman, Johanna S. R. Mendelson, and Juan Rial,
eds., *The Military and Democracy: The Future of Civil-Military Relations in Latin America* (Lexington, MA: Lexington Books, 1990), p. 4. Throughout this book I frequently use the term "Latin
America," not as denominating a unified political culture or history but to indicate a geographic
region. I use "the Middle East" and "Africa," even "Sub-Saharan Africa," in a similar fashion but do
not include the Republic of South Africa in the latter.
     4. Marion J. Levy Jr., my late colleague at Princeton, used to put the matter sharply: "People
who can't define their terms don't know what they're talking about." Giovanni Sartori offered a more
positive, threefold justification for definitions: First, because they "declare the intended meaning of
words, they ensure that we do not misunderstand each other. Second, words are also . . . our data
containers. Therefore, if our data containers are loosely defined our facts will be misgathered. Third,

brutal efforts to strangle the Algerian revolution, but one can make a good case that much of American political and legal thinking has also been intoxicated by such beliefs as that *politics* is a dirty word, involving little more than partisan maneuverings and selfish jobbery; that the United States is a democracy; that the U.S. Supreme Court is (or should be) the ultimate constitutional interpreter, thus contradicting the system's democratic fundamentals; and that the American "constitution" is encapsulated in the document of 1787 as amended. These are shallow half-truths, lacking even the dubious status of noble lies. They deceive both public officials and private citizens, inhibit the formulation of wise public policy, and obfuscate moral as well as legal responsibility.

Politics

Many, perhaps most, journalists, judges, and even professional politicians themselves equate *politics* with partisanship, typically with adjectives such as *petty* or *personal* appended. The word, however, need not be so disdainfully defined. Aristotle claimed that "politics is truly the master art," describing efforts to achieve for a people the constitutional order that will best enhance the nobility of each citizen's character.[5] By that definition—the one I use and keep separate from *partisanship*—constitutional creation, maintenance, and adaptation (and therefore constitutional interpretation as well) are no less political in nature than are most other decisions by executive, legislative, and judicial officials and by private individuals acting in their official capacities as citizens. To an important extent, each such person is concerned with authoritatively determining a nation's goals and the means that society judges, or can be persuaded to judge, proper to achieve those ends—concerned, that is, with allocating costs and benefits, rights and duties.[6] These allocations often

---

to define is first of all to assign limits. . . . Hence the definition establishes what is to be included and conversely what is to be excluded by our categories." "Where Is Political Science Going?" 37 *PS* 785–86 (2004).

  5. *Nicomachean Ethics* 1094a-b; see also 1099b and 1102a. For other conceptions of politics, most different from and more elevated than the common journalistic image, see Seyla Benhabib, ed., *Democracy and Difference: Contesting the Boundaries of the Political* (Princeton, NJ: Princeton University Press, 1996), esp. the essay by Sheldon Wolin, "Fugitive Democracy," in which he defines politics as "the legitimized and public contestation, primarily by organized and unequal social powers, over access to the resources available to the public authorities of the collectivity." Wolin distinguishes that sort of activity from "the political," an "expression of the idea that a free society composed of diversities can nonetheless enjoy moments of commonality when, through public deliberation, collective power is used to promote or protect the well-being of the collectivity" (p. 31).

  6. I recognize, of course, that office holders do not always, indeed probably rarely, act solely out of concern for the public weal. As professionals they have their own career (and economic) interests, staying in office being the most salient. Professionals of different parties may realize they share certain interests quite distinct from, and perhaps in conflict with, those of their constituents. Writing before World War I, Roberto Michels claimed that in Britain Labour MPs had more in common with Tory MPs than with the trade unionists who had elected them. One reason that in the United

take place under conditions of cooperation, often under conditions of conflict, and almost as often under both. However intense the cooperation and/or conflict, these allocations may either stabilize or destabilize the political system. Felix Frankfurter's claim that constitutional interpretation is "applied politics,"[7] with *politics* defined in the broad sense used here, was exactly on target. The clauses of constitutional texts are typically general in nature; discovering their more specific meanings and applications to particular problems requires judgment and prudence as much as, and usually more than, linguistic and syllogistic skills.

Democracy

Democracy has become as much a theological as a political term. To many people around the world, it has come to signify all that is good in governance: individual rights and public officials attentive to the wishes of informed publics. In fact, however, political systems that call themselves democratic range from the ruthless "people's republic" that North Korean leaders brutally inflict on their countrymen to the gentle, Spirit-guided consensus of Quaker meetings.[8] Common sense and experience quickly dismiss the North Korean version as a mask for a determined, if clumsily inept, regime with totalitarian ambitions. And neither Friends nor consensus is so common as to make the Quakers' version feasible for other than small communities. Although data collected from survey research show that popular preferences are more accurately reflected in political units that employ referenda than in those that rely on refraction through representation, most serious arguments for democracy swiftly become arguments for representative democracy, perhaps a compliment to the persuasiveness of Madison's reasoning in *The Federalist* Nos. 10 and 39.[9]

States the Supreme Court's decisions regarding reapportionment produced a much smaller turnover in legislators than political analysts had expected was that Republican and Democratic incumbents realized they had a common interest against sudden wholesale unemployment. And it is unlikely that the United States will ever have effective limits on private contributions to election campaigns, at least as long as the rules of the national legislative process exclude the initiative and referendum.

7. "The Zeitgeist and the Judiciary," talk at the twenty-fifth anniversary of the *Harvard Law Review* (1912); reprinted in E. F. Pritchard and Archibald MacLeish, eds., *Law and Politics: The Occasional Paper of Felix Frankfurter* (1939; reprint New York: Capricorn Books, 1962), p. 6.

8. For a study of Quakers' decision-making processes, see Michael J. Sheeran, S.J., *Beyond Majority Rule: Voteless Decisions in the Religious Society of Friends* (Philadelphia: Philadelphia Yearly Meeting, 1983).

9. Preference for referenda: Bruno S. Frey and Alois Stutzer, *Happiness and Economics* (Princeton, NJ: Princeton University Press, 2002), ch. 8. The authors equate "better" with greater congruence between public policy and popular preferences. Their data, however, say nothing about the relative wisdom or effectiveness of policies, only about linkages among process, results, and public wishes. Despite the title of their book, Frey and Stutzer have a heavy interest in the influence of governmental institutions and processes on happiness.

Jean-Jacques Rousseau, of course, is the most famous democrat who opposed representative

Justice Hugo L. Black expressed a central tenet of representative democracy when he wrote for the U.S. Supreme Court: "No right is more precious in a free country than that of having a voice in the election of those who make the laws under which we, as good citizens, must live."[10] For theorists such as Joseph Schumpeter, the right of citizens to choose among competing elites—along with voters' rights to free discussion and association—pretty much captures the meaning of democracy.[11] Many democratic theorists, however, find Schumpeter's definition unacceptably deficient. They add that representative democracy requires wide deliberation, if not *by* the public, then *in* public by actual and aspiring officials as well as by journalists and putative intellectuals.[12]

When an analyst sorts through the writings of proponents of representative democracy, one element stands out as both common and crucial: "the people" should govern in the sense of periodically having before them a range of alternative public policies, candidates who advocate a bundle of

---

democracy, and Aristotle believed that popular election (as contrasted with choice by lot) of officials would lead to an aristocracy of orators. For an analysis of the literature produced by some recent theorists who believe that the modem can and should replace the ballot, with elected officials' main function reduced to setting agendas, see F. Christopher Arterton, *Teledemocracy* (Newberry Park, CA: Sage, 1987); for a defense, see Ted Becker, "Teledemocracy: Bringing Power Back to the People," *Futurist* 6 (Dec. 1981); for an attack, see James S. Fishkin, *Democracy and Deliberation* (New Haven, CT: Yale University Press, 1993), esp. ch. 3. Fishkin has constructed rather sophisticated means of directly measuring citizens' policy choices.

Robert A. Dahl is the most elegant theorist of representative democracy. See esp. his *Democracy and Its Critics* (New Haven, CT: Yale University Press, 1989) and *How Democratic Is the American Constitution?* (New Haven, CT: Yale University Press, 2001). Among other excellent discussions are Benjamin R. Barber, *Strong Democracy* (Berkeley: University of California Press, 1984); Patrick Deneen, *Democratic Faith* (Princeton, NJ: Princeton University Press, 2005); John Dunn, *Setting the People Free: The Story of Democracy* (New York: Grove Atlantic, 2005); Christopher L. Eisengruber, "Dimensions of Democracy," 71 *Fordham L. Rev.* 1723 (2003); Amy Gutmann and Dennis F. Thompson, *Democracy and Disagreement* (Cambridge, MA: Harvard University Press, 1996); George Kateb, *The Inner Ocean: Individualism and Democratic Culture* (Ithaca, NY: Cornell University Press, 1992); C. B. MacPherson, *Democratic Theory* (London: Oxford University Press, 1973); Gerry Mackie, *Democracy Defended* (New York: Cambridge University Press, 2004); J. Roland Pennock, *Democratic Political Theory* (Princeton, NJ: Princeton University Press, 1979); J. Roland Pennock and John W. Chapman, eds., *Liberal Democracy* (New York: New York University Press, 1983); Giovanni Sartori, *Democratic Theory* (New York: Praeger, 1965) and *The Theory of Democracy Revisited* (Chatham, NJ: Chatham House, 1987), 2 vols.; Ian Shapiro, *The State of Democratic Theory* (Princeton, NJ: Princeton University Press, 2006); and Yvres R. Simon, *The Philosophy of Democratic Government* (Chicago: University of Chicago Press, 1951).

10. Wesberry v. Sanders, 376 U.S. 1 (1964).

11. *Capitalism, Socialism, and Democracy,* 3rd ed. (New York: Harper and Brothers, 1950), chs. 21–22, esp. p. 269, where he says, "[T]he democratic method is that institutional arrangement for arriving at political decisions in which individuals acquire the power to decide by means of a competitive struggle for the people's vote." Rights to free discussion and association: ibid., esp. p. 272.

12. Dahl, in the works cited above, has been insistent on this point. See also Gutmann and Thompson, *Democracy and Disagreement* and *Who Deliberates?* and Barber, *Strong Democracy.*

each, and an opportunity to choose the most important framers of those public policies. Justifications for democratic rule ultimately rest on either or both of two foundations:[13] (1) the great and equal dignity of all men and women—the fundamental moral value of most theories of democracy—requires that every citizen share in making the rules that he or she must obey; (2) popular political participation increases stability and lessens the amount of force that government must use to maintain domestic tranquillity.[14]

For almost every democratic theorist, *processes* make governmental decisions morally binding—the processes of the people's freely choosing representatives to whom they delegate their rights to self-government; those representatives' proposing, debating, and enacting policies (and later standing for reelection); and then administrators' faithfully enforcing those policies. As Michael Walzer puts it: "The people's claim to rule . . . is most persuasively put . . . not in terms of what the people know but in terms of who they are. They are subjects of the law, and if the law is to bind them as free men and women, they must also be its makers."[15]

Constitutionalism

Constitutionalism is a normative political creed that endorses a special kind of political order, one whose principal tenet is as follows: Although government is necessary to a life that is truly human, every exercise of governmental power should be subject to important *substantive* limitations and obligations.[16] Constitutionalism agrees with versions of democratic theory that

---

13. The older mythical basis, *vox populi, vox Dei,* has gone completely out of favor with scholars, though not nearly so much with candidates who win elections. Losers tend to take the scholarly attitude.

14. This second justification borders on an economic argument for democracy that in substance, if not form, is at least as old as Herodotus: Because, in the long run, it is costly to govern a society in ways in which most members do not wish to be ruled, it requires, many analysts believe, fewer expenditures of scarce resources to allow members to take some part in governing themselves. Many rulers, of course, have found it worth the cost to govern without—indeed in violation of—the will of huge segments of the governed. For an introduction to the literature on the economic bases of democracy, see esp. Brian Barry, *Sociologists, Economists, and Democracy* (Chicago: University of Chicago Press, 1978); Robert A. Dahl, *A Preface to Economic Democracy* (Berkeley: University of California Press, 1985); Robert A. Dahl and Charles E. Lindblom, *Politics, Economics, and Welfare* (New York: Harper and Brothers, 1953); Anthony Downs, *An Economic Theory of Democracy* (New York: Harper and Brothers, 1957); John R. Freeman, *Democracy and Markets* (Ithaca, NY: Cornell University Press, 1989); Charles E. Lindblom, *Politics and Markets* (New York: Basic Books, 1977); Michael Novak, *The Spirit of Democratic Capitalism* (New York: Simon and Schuster, 1982); and Joseph Schumpeter, *Capitalism, Socialism, and Democracy,* 3rd ed., as well as the symposium on Schumpeter in 3 *J. of Democ.* (July 1992). For severe criticism of the efficacy of "markets" in politics as well as economics, see Robert Kuttner, *Everything for Sale: The Virtues and Limits of Markets* (New York: Alfred A. Knopf, 1997).

15. "Philosophy and Democracy," 9 *Pol. Theory* 379, 383 (1981).

16. The bibliography devoted to constitutionalism is almost as large as that explaining democracy. I have cited many of the better works in my "Constitutions, Constitutionalism, and Democ-

hold respect for equal human dignity, defined to include a wide degree of individual liberty, to be the fundamental value of any truly just society. All constitutionalists, however, agree that there are some things that government cannot do, no matter how exactly it follows procedures specified by a constitutional text and/or a larger constitutional order, even if those actions mirror the deliberate judgment of a charismatic leader, a benevolent junta, or the overwhelming majority of voters. Constitutionalists also agree that government should act so that its citizens can have opportunities to live decent lives. Obviously, this normative theory is at war with totalitarianism and is also incompatible with most forms of authoritarian government. Moreover, it coexists uneasily with its usual bed partner, representative democracy, which would impose few substantive limitations on the people's freely chosen representatives.

Just as there are several kinds of democratic theory so are there various versions of constitutionalism. For present purposes, the two most important are *negative constitutionalism*,[17] which comes close to endorsing the idea of the classical Liberals that restricted government to the role of night watchman, and *positive constitutionalism*, which contends that in a modern, tightly interconnected world, respecting human dignity imposes an obligation on government to assist its citizens in achieving good and just lives. This division represents more of a continuum than a dichotomy. Theorists aligned more toward the positive end of the scale argue that the public good that government must safeguard is a capacious concept, and thus government has a positive duty to act to advance the welfare of its citizens.[18] These lat-

racy," in Douglas Greenberg, Stanley N. Katz, Melanie Beth Oliviero, and Steven C. Wheatley, eds., *Constitutionalism and Democracy: Transformations in the Contemporary World* (New York: Oxford University Press, 1993), p. 20n. For a more recent analysis in the Civil Law tradition, see János Kis, *Constitutional Democracy*, trans. Zoltán Miklósi (New York: Central European University Press, 2003), and for a historical survey, see the two-volume work edited by Martin van Gelderen and Quentin Skinner, *Republicanism: A Shared European Heritage* (New York: Cambridge University Press, 2002).

17. For an unsystematic demonstration of this approach to constitutionalism, see Chief Justice William H. Rehnquist's opinion for the Court in Deshaney v. Winnebago County Dept. of Soc. Services, 489 U.S. 189 (1989). The Cato Institute is the most consistent of American organizations in pushing the cause of negative constitutionalism, and Richard Epstein is probably the most articulate American proponent of negative constitutionalism. See his *Takings: Private Property and the Power of Eminent Domain* (Cambridge, MA: Harvard University Press, 1985) and *Principles for a Free Society: Reconciling Individual Liberty with the Common Good* (Reading, MA: Perseus Books, 1998). Sotirios A. Barber has shown, however, that Epstein is less a negativist than he himself claims. By parsing Epstein's logic, Barber demonstrates that Epstein is a closet believer in positive constitutionalism. When he sees that the interests of property holders are at stake, he wants government to act protectively. His fear is governmental assistance to the less fortunate in society. Barber, *Welfare and the Constitution* (Princeton, NJ: Princeton University Press, 2003), pp. 147–51. For a defense of negative constitutionalism less simplistic than Epstein's, see Randy E. Barnett, *Restoring the Lost Constitution* (Princeton, NJ: Princeton University Press, 2004).

18. For an explication of a *positive constitutionalist* theory of governmental obligations and

ter theorists may have offered stronger reasoning to support their claims, but they may be outnumbered by their colleagues who drift toward the negative pole.[19]

All varieties of constitutionalists share representative democracy's dedication to process. Most constitutionalists, however, are more pessimistic about human nature than are democrats; they are concerned, sometimes obsessed, with humanity's propensity to act selfishly and abuse power. They fret about the human capacity to rationalize private gain as public good. In an unalloyed democratic system, Madison feared, the *"passions* . . . not the *reason* of the public would sit in judgment. But it is the reason, alone, of the public that ought to control and regulate the government. The passions ought to be controlled and regulated by the government."[20]

The nub of the dispute between constitutionalist and democratic theorists centers on two issues. The first is how best to protect individual rights. For democrats, the right to political participation is *the* fundamental right because is it "protective of all other rights."[21] The Thomas Jefferson who is the hero of democratic theorists claimed that the "mass of citizens, is the safest depository of their own rights."[22] Constitutionalists respect the right to political participation, but they—especially negative constitutionalists—are more apt to view "the right to be let alone" as equally, if not more, fundamental. As already noted, they believe that the "mass of the people" is likely to be a diversified conglomeration of social, economic, and ethnic groupings, each of which is sufficiently clever to oppress others without hurting its own rights. Thus the constitutionalist's hero is the Thomas Jefferson who wrote, "One hundred and seventy-three despots would surely be as oppressive as

---

authority, see Sotirios A. Barber, "Welfare and the Instrumental Constitution," 42 *Am. J. of Jurispr.* 159 (1997), and his *Welfare and the Constitution* (Princeton, NJ: Princeton University Press, 2003). He elegantly, and to me convincingly, demonstrates that once negative constitutionalists concede that government has a duty to advance the public welfare by policing the community, punishing fraud, and enforcing contracts (all necessary for a market economy to flourish), they have abandoned the philosophic field to positive constitutionalists. There is no principled argument to recognize government's duty or authority to spend the public's tax moneys to protect one group of citizens (those who own property and operate businesses) and deny that it has the duty or even the authority to spend tax moneys to do such things for the less well off as provide education, food, or medical care.

19. As Gary J. Jacobsohn has said: "The literature of modern constitutionalism makes clear what [its assumptions] are: protection of individual rights against collective power, a framework of public authority that is to be officially neutral with respect to competing social goals, and a philosophic commitment or at least predisposition to serving the interests of the individual or groups of individuals." *Apple of Gold: Constitutionalism in Israel and the United States* (Princeton, NJ: Princeton University Press, 1993), p. 46.

20. *The Federalist* No. 49, in *The Federalist Papers*, ed. Benjamin F. Wright (Cambridge, MA: Harvard University Press, 1961), p. 351. (Italics in original.)

21. Yick Wo v. Hopkins, 118 U.S. 356, 370 (1886).

22. Letter to John Taylor, May 28, 1816, in *The Works of Thomas Jefferson*, ed. Paul L. Ford (New York: Putnam's Sons, 1905), 11:527.

one. . . . An elective despotism was not the government we fought for."[23] Constitutionalists are apt to view democratic political processes as "at best regulated rivalry. . . . Political power rapidly accumulates and becomes unequal; making use of the coercive apparatus of the state and its law, those who gain the advantage can often assure themselves of a favored position."[24] Private funding of political campaigns aggravates these problems.

Constitutionalism, therefore, demands "a system of regularized restraints [beyond free elections] upon those who exercise political power."[25] A constitutional text with a bill of rights and judicial review are the two most visible but hardly the sole constitutionalist restraints. "Separate institutions competing for power"[26] and federalism are also typical constitutionalist weapons. Many constitutionalists, like most democratic theorists, also emphasize the importance of political culture, understanding that citizens' respect for the constitutional order's underlying values is essential to political stability. As Madison told the First Congress when he introduced the Bill of Rights:

> It may be thought that all paper barriers against the power of the community are too weak to be worthy of attention. . . . [Y]et, as they have a tendency to impress some degree of respect for them, to establish the public opinion in their favor, and rouse the attention of the whole community, it may be one means to control the majority from those acts to which they might otherwise be inclined.[27]

The second basic issue that divides the bulk of democrats from constitutionalists—again, especially from constitutionalists who align themselves toward the negative end of the scale—concerns what Madison called "energy in government."[28] Democrats tend to believe that government can legitimately act to advance the general welfare. (They are apt to disagree among themselves, however, about the wisdom of government's acting in a particular way in a particular situation.) In contrast, constitutionalists tend to look skeptically on governmental authority and to believe that rights generally trump powers. In this regard, democrats often speak of the "sovereignty of the people," while constitutionalists, perhaps remembering the use to which

---

23. "Notes on Virginia" (1784), in *The Writings of Thomas Jefferson*, ed. Andrew A. Lipscomb (Washington, DC: Thomas Jefferson Memorial Association, 1903), 2:163.
24. Johns Rawls, *A Theory of Justice* (Cambridge, MA: Harvard University Press, 1971), p. 226.
25. Carl J. Friedrich, *Transcendent Justice* (Durham, NC: Duke University Press, 1964), p. 17.
26. Charles Jones, "The Separated Presidency," in Anthony King, ed., *The New American Political System*, 2nd ed. (Washington, DC: American Enterprise Institute, 1990), p. 3. Jones was emending Richard E. Neustadt's famous claim that the American political system does not have a "separation of powers" but rather a regime of "separated institutions *sharing* powers." *Presidential Power*, rev. ed. (New York: Wiley, 1976), p. 101. The first edition was published in 1960, shortly before John F. Kennedy took over the White House and Neustadt became one of his aides.
27. Annals of Congress, 1:440ff. (1789).
28. *The Federalist*, No. 37.

Thomas Hobbes put the concept of sovereignty, are apt to regard it as dangerously fuzzy, full of mystery that threatens misery along with mastery.[29] They prefer a political system in which power is so dispersed that the supreme law-making power, if it exists at all, will be found only in the midst (and mist) of jealous interactions among popular and elitist institutions, where power is pitted against power and ambition against ambition, with both hemmed in by publicly accepted norms.

No nation has fully adopted either constitutionalism or democracy. Indeed, with its distrust of human nature and insistence on the primacy of individual rights, negative constitutionalism could make governance almost impossible. Certainly, as evidenced by the U.S. Supreme Court's reaction to the New Deal, negative constitutionalism would come close to outlawing energetic government. Similarly, unmodified democracy, at least a version based on unrestrained majority rule, could soon commit suicide by allowing today's majority to restrict the political rights of today's minority and tomorrow's new majority, in turn, to restrict tomorrow's minority (although it had been part of yesterday's majority), and so on until only a small junta or a single dictator were left. The operative principle would be "One person, one vote, one time."

Constitutional Democracy

Constitutional democracy, the most common arrangement in industrial societies, unites beliefs that, although the people's freely chosen representatives should govern, those officials must respect certain substantive limitations on their authority. Like most marriages, this one constantly suffers not only from flawed management and flawed human nature but also from tensions between the two basic theories.[30] And there is no guarantee against painful divorce, preceded by domestic violence.[31] As Anatol Lieven reminds us, constitutional democracy does not mark "the end of history," is not divinely ordained, and need not last forever.[32]

29. I am paraphrasing Carlo Cattaneo's critique of the concept. See Filippo Sabetti, *The Search for Good Government: Understanding the Paradox of Italian Democracy* (Montreal: McGill-Queen's University Press, 2000), p. 60.

30. The noted Hungarian philosopher János Kis has denied a real conflict between constitutional and democratic theory, but he does so by ranking the values of "liberalism," which he defines almost as I define constitutionalism, above those of democracy. See *Constitutional Democracy*, esp. pt. 2, ch. 2.

31. See John E. Finn, *Constitutions in Crisis: Political Violence and the Rule of Law* (New York: Oxford University Press, 1991); Mark E. Brandon, "Constitutionalism and Constitutional Failure," in Sotirios A. Barber and Robert P. George, eds., *Constitutional Politics: Essays on Constitution Making, Maintenance, and Change* (Princeton, NJ: Princeton University Press, 2001); and Brandon's book-length case study *Free in the World: American Slavery and Constitutional Failure* (Princeton, NJ: Princeton University Press, 1998).

32. *America Right or Wrong: An Anatomy of American Nationalism* (New York: Oxford University Press, 2004).

Yet this marriage can also produce much good and even happiness. The democratic elements of a political system make constitutionalists responsive to popular sentiments and constitutionalist elements lower the stakes of democratic politics. It is far easier for losers to accept the results of elections if they know that they will soon have other chances to gain governmental power and in the interim will retain their basic rights to life, liberty, and property. If democratic politics were played by the rules of the ancient Mayan version of basketball, which allowed the victors to eat the losers, each election would be followed by civil war.

The messages here are critically important as well as complex. First, limiting the stakes of elections is essential to the stability of a civil society. Second, these limitations must always be rooted in institutional competition and accepted norms of behavior rather than merely be encoded in the "parchment barriers" of constitutional texts. Public officials especially, but also the overwhelming majority of citizens, must internalize the norms of popular yet limited government. And third, the stakes of politics cannot be lowered to the extent that citizens feel no need to vote or engage in other forms of political participation. Popular government that is weak, unable to stir its people to act vigorously to promote the general welfare, is not likely to fulfill its basic functions. Moreover, a weak regime is likely to be replaced, perhaps violently, by another kind of political order that is neither constitutionalist nor democratic.

This book seldom if ever uses *Liberal* or *Liberalism* unless modified by an adjective such as *Classical*. Still, what I call constitutional democracy is very similar to what many other writers call liberal democracy.[33] I avoid that term because *liberalism* has more colors than Joseph's coat. It can refer to doctrines preaching governmental abstinence so as to allow individuals vast freedom as well as to doctrines advocating governmental action to foster certain rights by restricting individual choices. In a sense, Ronald Reagan and both Bushes were liberals, as, in another sense, were John F. Kennedy, Lyndon Johnson, and Jimmy Carter. Worse, in much of America *liberal* has become an epithet, the infamous L-word that supposedly disqualifies for public office men and women so branded. Thus I try to get along without the term.

Rule of law is another term that seldom appears in these pages. Certainly proponents of both constitutionalism and democracy are more comfortable

---

33. See, for example, Charles N. Quigley and John H. Buchanan, directors, and Charles F. Bahmueller, gen. ed., *Civitas: A Framework for Civic Education* (Calabasas, CA: Center for Civic Education. 1991). This volume, which came into existence because of Bahmueller's careful work, was the product of a series of conferences held in Washington, DC. The use of the term *liberal democracy* in place of *constitutional democracy* was largely due to the persuasive efforts of William F. Harris II. My objection to the use of *liberal* was based less on substantive grounds—we all generally agreed about the nature of the political system we wanted to explain—but on tactical grounds. *Liberal* made the volume, which was designed to help high school teachers offer instructions on American government, vulnerable to attack by people who thought of themselves as conservative.

with the rhetoric of a government of laws rather than that of men. But despite both ancient and recent discussions of these terms, precisely what they mean remains elusive.[34] At its core, a rule of law implies governance through regulations that apply not only to rulers and ruled but also equally among the ruled. Yet because human beings make laws, interpret laws, and apply laws, discretion and inequality are ubiquitous. (It was this truth that the little girl who wrote to Chief Justice William Howard Taft caught when she described the American system as "a government of lawyers and not of men.") At least equally important is the substantive content of laws, and that issue harks back to questions of positive versus natural law. In a common-sensical way, it is easy to say that a statute requiring all public officials and private citizens, including Jews, to kill Jews on sight hardly qualifies as what most people mean when they speak of the rule of law; nor, to use a less far-fetched example, would a statute allowing police to search all homes and offices, including those of fellow officers and other public officials, without outside supervision. Further, an analyst who thinks the rule of law is mainly concerned with procedures can make a strong case that reliance on juries damages the likelihood of evenhanded application of objective rules of criminal or civil law, assuming such exist. These kinds of issues are as important as they are fascinating, but this book explores enough snake pits to make it prudent to avoid this one.

A Constitutional Text and a Constitution

As Giovanni Sartori has said, every country has a constitution, most countries have a constitutional text, but very few have constitutionalism.[35] Yet almost all public officials claim to practice *constitutionalism*, thus proliferat-

---

34. Paul W. Kahn, *The Reign of Law: Marbury v. Madison and the Construction of America* (New Haven, CT: Yale University Press, 1997), attacks the myth that the rule of law is equivalent to rule by the people. Among the better of other recent studies are T. R. S. Allan, *Constitutional Justice: A Liberal Theory of the Rule of Law* (New York: Oxford University Press, 2003); David J. Danelski, "The Limits of Law," in J. Roland Pennock and John W. Chapman, eds., *The Limits of Law*, Nomos 15 (New York: Lieber-Atherton, 1974); James L. Gibson, *Overcoming Apartheid: Can Truth and Justice Reconcile a Divided Nation?* (New York: Russell Sage, 2004), ch. 5; Erik G. Jensen and Thomas C. Heller, *Beyond Common Knowledge: Empirical Approaches to the Rule of Law* (Stanford, CA: Stanford University Press, 2004); Ellen Kennedy, *Constitutional Failure: Schmitt in Weimar* (Durham, NC: Duke University Press, 2004); Gianfranco Poggi, *The Development of the Modern State: A Sociological Introduction* (Stanford, CA: Stanford University Press, 1978); Ian Shapiro, ed., *The Rule of Law* (New York: New York University Press, 1994), Nomos 36; Martin Shapiro, "The Success of Judicial Review," in Sally J. Kenney, William M. Reisinger, and John C. Reitz, eds., *Constitutional Dialogues in Comparative Perspective* (New York: St. Martin's, 1999); Roberto Unger, *Law in Modern Society* (New York: Free Press, 1976), pp. 47–86, 155–92; Robin L. West, *Reimagining Justice: Progressive Interpretations of Formal Equality, Rights, and the Rule of Law* (Burlington, VT: Ashgate, 2003); and Robert Paul Wolff, ed., *The Rule of Law* (New York: Simon and Schuster, 1971). (I am indebted to Kim Lane Scheppele and Peter Solomon for help in compiling these references.)

35. "Constitutionalism: A Preliminary Discussion," 56 *Am. Pol. Sci. Rev.* 853 (1962).

ing problems of nomenclature. In *The Politics,* Aristotle used several progressively broader definitions of a constitution. Book 3 referred to it as "the organization of a polis, in respect of its offices generally, but especially in respect of that particular office which is sovereign in all issues."[36] Early in book 4, his net widened: "'an organization of offices in a state, by which the method of their distribution is fixed, the sovereign authority is determined, and the nature of the end to be pursued by the association and all its members is prescribed.'"[37] Later in book 4, his concept of a constitution became sweeping: a "way of life"[38]—a definition that ensures competition between politics and religion unless the two are merged or, as in much of the contemporary Western world, religion becomes privatized.

One might, of course, reject Aristotle's lexical evolution and narrowly define a nation's *constitution* as a particular arrangement of public offices and powers as well as of individual and group rights. Even though Aristotle did not make the modern (and much revered as well as reviled) distinction between state and society[39]—a distinction generally credited to (or blamed on) John Locke, Thomas Hobbes, and Benedict de Spinoza—I prefer Aristotle's broader concept because it eliminates the confusion that results from conflating the political values and arrangements under which a people live with the values and arrangements that a constitutional document specifies. Despite the problems that viewing a constitution as a way of life creates for religion and politics, I shall use *constitution* interchangeably with what the Basic Law of the Federal Republic of Germany and the Constitutional Court refer to as the "constitutional order"[40]: the nation's constitutional text, its dominant political theories, the traditions and aspirations that reflect those values, and the principal interpretations of this larger constitution. These are all ambiguous terms that, I hope, will become less murky in the ensuing chapters. But it should be clear from the outset that neither the "constitution" nor the "constitutional order" need reflect constitutionalism, for neither may include any of constitutionalism's norms. The referent for

36. Ernest Barker, ed. and trans. (London: Oxford University Press, 1948), ch. 6 §1, 1278b.

37. Ibid., ch. 1, §9, 1288b.

38. Ibid., ch. 11, 1295a.

39. Revered because many theorists look on the distinction as the basis of individual liberty against government and most especially such freedoms as those of religious belief and practice; reviled by other theorists because it tends to isolate politics from many of the most important public issues. Feminists have been particularly vocal in their criticisms. See, among many, Benhabib, ed., *Democracy and Difference;* Joan B. Landes, ed., *Feminism: The Public and the Private* (New York: Oxford University Press, 1998); Carole Pateman, *The Disorder of Women: Democracy, Feminism, and Political Theory* (Cambridge, U.K.: Polity, 1986). For an attack from the male left, see Sheldon Wolin, *Politics and Vision: Continuity and Innovation in Western Political Thought* (Boston: Little, Brown, 1960), esp. ch. 9; from the male right, Harvey C. Mansfield Jr., *America's Constitutional Soul* (Baltimore: Johns Hopkins University Press, 1993), esp. ch. 8.

40. See, for instance, The Basic Law, Articles 2(1), 9(3), and 20(3) and (4). The Constitutional Court frequently repeats this term.

the constitution or constitutional order may vary from Iraq under Saddam
Hussein's rule or the Sudan under the ideology of Hassan al-Turabi, on the
one hand, to Australia, Canada, the Federal Republic of Germany, Norway,
or the United States.

In contrast to *constitution* or *constitutional order*, the term *constitutional
text* refers to the document (or set of documents) that supposedly spells out
some or most of the nation's basic political principles and goals, its institutional arrangements, its modes of selecting public officials, and the rights
and duties of private citizens. The authority of these charters varies widely.
At one extreme would be Josef Stalin's and Mao Tse-tung's constitutional
scripts, pious fig leaves whose main function was to impress foreigners, not
to serve as charters for governance. Toward the other extreme are the documents of constitutional democracies, whose terms public officials usually try
to follow.

Several points are important here. First, no constitutional text is completely authoritative. For example, the British North America Act of 1867,
which served as Canada's constitutional charter until it was dramatically
amended in 1981, explicitly says that the English monarch directly (or indirectly through a governor general) rules that country: "the Executive Government of authority of and over Canada . . . continue [to] be vested in the
Queen," who makes laws "by and with the Advice and Consent of the
[Dominion's] Senate and House of Commons." One can find only hints of a
prescription for or a description of the parliamentary system of government
that actually operates.[41] References to the monarchy offer a fiction, sym-
bolizing Canada's status first as a dominion of the British Empire and later as
an equal partner in the British Commonwealth of Nations.[42] In the United
States, of course, many clauses of the constitutional document have been
hortatory rather than mandatory.

Second, no constitutional document or set of documents long remains
coextensive with the constitutional order.[43] Michael Walzer's comment

41. For a fascinating use of this statement to protect freedom of the press more than forty years
before Canada had a constitutionally entrenched bill of rights, see the opinion of Chief Justice
Lyman Duff in Reference re Alberta Press Case, [1938] S.C.R. 100. Duff's reasoning is remarkably
similar to that in 2 of Harlan Fiske Stone's famous footnote 4 in United States v. Carolene Products,
304 U.S. 144 (1938). For some of the Court's internal documents and later scholarly commentary
relating to *Carolene Products*, see Walter F. Murphy, James E. Fleming, Sotirios A. Barber, and
Stephen Macedo, *American Constitutional Interpretation*, 3rd ed. (New York: Foundation Press,
2003), pp. 683–91. For another hint as to the power of Parliament rather than the queen to govern,
see also §91 of the British North America Act, discussed below.

42. One of the clearest clues to the establishment of a parliamentary system is located in the
preamble, which cites Canada's alleged desire to be governed by a "Constitution similar in principle
to that of the United Kingdom." See also the discussion in Chapter Fourteen, below.

43. Cf. Edward S. Corwin, "Constitution v. Constitutional Theory," 19 *Am. Pol. Sci. Rev.* 290
(1920); reprinted in Richard Loss, ed., *Corwin on the Constitution* (Ithaca, NY: Cornell University
Press, 1987), 2:183.

about religion applies equally to secular politics: Judaism "is not found in the text [of the Torah] so much as in interpretations of the text."[44] Typically, a constitutional document quickly becomes a palimpsest: the original words are soon overwritten by customs, usages, and interpretations, some crafted by one set of different interpreters, some by others. (Customs and usages are, of course, themselves interpretations, only less self-consciously, or perhaps even subconsciously, done.)

Third the existence of a constitutional text does not mean that the political system is a constitutional democracy or even a constitutionalist state. As one of Shakespeare's clowns put it: "[C]ucullus non facit monachum" (a cowl does not make a monk).[45] Labeling a document "the constitution" does not imbue it with any of the norms of either constitutionalism or democracy.

Constitutionism

I use an awkward neologism, *constitutionism,* to refer to adherence to the terms (and perhaps even the "spirit") of the constitutional text and the broader constitutional order. It may well be that most public officials, private citizens, journalists, and even professors equate fidelity to a constitutional text with constitutionalism.[46] Such, however, need not be the case. The basic values of both a constitutional order and a constitutional text can range from those of tight totalitarianism to loose libertarianism. Thus officials even of authoritarian governments, such as Chile's under Augusto Pinochet, may profess to be practicing constitutionalism while in fact they are only being true to a constitutional document or order that repudiates constitutionalism's values.[47]

It is possible that if the constitution is authoritative, that is, if public officials and private citizens take its terms seriously and try to act according to its norms, constitutionism could limit government. Nevertheless, limita-

---

44. *Exodus and Revolution* (New York: Basic Books, 1985), p. 144.

45. *Twelfth Night,* act 1, scene 5.

46. As far as I know, I coined the cumbersome term *constitutionism.* In the fall of 1988 at a conference in Uruguay financed by the Ford Foundation under the auspices of the American Council of Learned Societies under the presidency of Stanley N. Katz, I was confused when many of the Latin American scholars spoke of constitutions and constitutionalism. In 1989, at the invitation of the U.S. Department of State, John E. Finn of Wesleyan University, Solicitor General Designate Kenneth Starr, and I traveled to several Chilean universities, debating scholars who supported the regime of General Augusto Pinochet. These professors used the general's constitutional text as the touchstone not only for what was constitutional in Chile but also for what accorded with constitutionalism. At that point, the light (finally) went on. Even a scholar as able as János Kis conflates a constitutional text with constitutionalism when he writes that a democracy is constitutional if it has a written constitution that cannot be changed by simple majority vote of the legislature. *Constitutional Democracy,* p. xv.

47. I differ from Robert Barros, who argues that General Pinochet embraced constitutionalism: *Constitutionalism and Dictatorship; Pinochet, the Junta, and the 1980 Constitution* (New York: Cambridge University Press, 2002).

tions might not include respect for rights that most constitutionalists or democratic theorists consider fundamental. *Constitutionalism* differs from *constitutionism* in demanding adherence not to *any* given constitutional text or order but to principles that center on respect for human dignity and the obligations that flow from those principles.[48]

Constitutionalists judge the worth of constitutionism by the values that the particular constitutional text and/or constitutional order advance—and how closely government and society follow those norms. Constitutionalists evaluate "government by the people" according to similar standards. It is a means, not an end. Even if it is operational, the value of government's responsiveness to the popular will depends on what the people want. The "good" such a government will produce if "the people" want freedom and justice for themselves and all citizens will differ sharply from what that will ensue if, for example, an overwhelming majority of "the people" want religious conformity and try to force some of their number to change their religious beliefs, or if a similarly large majority want some of their numbers to live in luxury while forcing others to endure slavery to pay for that luxury.

Tyranny

Political analysts often speak of political systems such as that of Hitler, Stalin, and Mao as totalitarian. In fact, however, even those regimes only strived to achieve totalitarian rule without ever fully accomplishing their goal. It has also been popular to characterize as authoritarian political systems that deny many, if not most, inhabitants rights to vote and to personal freedom. To simplify very complex issues here, I shall lump all such regimes under the rubric *tyrannical,* fully understanding there are important gradations involved.

Creating, Maintaining, and Adapting Constitutional Democracy

Part I of this book examines the establishment of a constitutional democracy. These chapters differ in style from the rest of the book. They open with the birth of a fictional constitutional convention for a fictional country where fictional delegates—many of whose arguments track those of real-life political, economic, and legal theorists—debate a host of issues. First, these men and women argue among themselves about the public goods their new political system should protect and promote. After the majority has reached a fragile agreement, the delegates proceed to consider the likely costs and

---

48. H. W. O. Okoth-Ogendo has identified a version of constitutionism that he calls a "constitution with constitutionalism." In many African states, leaders do not even pretend to follow the terms of the constitutional text, a document they view, if they view it at all, as irrelevant. "Constitutions without Constitutionalism: Reflections on an African Paradox," in Douglas Greenberg, Stanley N. Katz, Melanie Beth Oliviero, and Steven C. Wheatley, eds., *Constitutionalism and Democracy: Transformations in the Contemporary World* (New York: Oxford University Press, 1993).

benefits of alternative governmental systems and, by a closely divided vote, *conditionally* opt for constitutional democracy.[49]

That condition is that such a political system be a practical option for their country. They next address some of the problems that the question of practicality raises: under what circumstances is constitutional democracy feasible, and does this fictional country's situation offer reasonable chances of success? After discussing "prerequisites" to constitutional democracy, a majority agrees that their country has a fair chance of making such a system work. The delegates then attack several interrelated problems concerning the design of appropriate institutions and processes, such as immediate drafting of a constitutional document versus either (1) the Israeli practice of rolling textual drafting or (2) the British practice of gradual accretions onto a (changing?) political culture, and whether their charter should have a sunset clause or aspire to perpetuity. With those matters uneasily settled, the convention turns to such subsidiary questions as a federal versus a unitary state; a parliamentary versus a presidential system; proportional representation (and if so, which form?) versus an Anglo-American "first past the post" electoral system; a more or less specifically worded bill of rights (with only negative or also positive rights?) versus a government whose authority is limited by rather specifically delegated powers (à la Hamilton's argument in *The Federalist* No. 84)[50] reinforced by a political culture operative through democratic checks; judicial review (and if so under which form and with how much authority?) versus legislative, executive, or electoral supremacy or some sort of shared testing of constitutional validity; and, far from least important, ratification of the constitutional charter by a legislative body versus popular referendum.

Part II returns to an expository analysis and deals with problems relating to constitutional maintenance, such as creating new citizens, rebuilding the state's administrative apparatus, determining the fate of officials of the former regime, establishing a viable economy, and interpreting the constitutional order so as to both maintain its basic principles and allow effective governance. Closely connected are constitutional adaptation and thus constitutional change. Custom, usage, political education, and constitutional interpretation all play important roles here.

The book's reprise attempts a brief summary of the arguments and a few concluding observations about the nature of constitutional democracy and constitutional politics. Its purpose is the same as that of the rest of the book:

49. For a short version of an early draft of this chapter, a version that does not use the Socratic technique, see my "Alternative Political Systems," in Sotirios A. Barber and Robert P. George, eds., *Constitutional Politics: Essays on Constitution Making, Maintenance, and Change* (Princeton, NJ: Princeton University Press, 2001).

50. "[T]he Constitution[al text] is itself, in every rational sense, and to every great purpose, a BILL OF RIGHTS."

to incite rather than to pontificate. Despite this seemingly neat division among the processes of creation, maintenance, and adaptation, one of the arguments running through these pages is that, in actual operation, these three processes bleed into one another. Because no institutional system can long survive in a changing world without itself changing, effective maintenance must include development, and change may add important elements to (or subtract equally important elements from) a constitutional system.

Formal amendments to the constitutional text provide the most obvious, though not the sole or even necessarily the most important, method of adaptation. Constitutional interpretation may precipitate changes in the structure and operations of the political system—or go so far as to create a different constitutional order.[51] Furthermore, if a successful political system needs a means for orderly change, it also needs some limits on change lest constitutional democracy regress into a radically different political order. Emergencies, for example, may move public officials to crush liberty in the name of security and convince the electorate that a "garrison state" is the price of such goods as domestic tranquillity and national survival.[52] In explicit terms, Articles 79 and 81 of Germany's Basic Law claim to impose limits on constitutional revolution.[53] Article V of the American constitutional document tries to outlaw a much narrower scope for change.[54] The British believe their customs and culture impose broad restraints. And some courts, such as those of Germany, India, Bangladesh, and California, have

51. "Precipitate" because in a constitutional democracy, one institution can seldom, if ever, accomplish major constitutional change. Other institutions must usually participate or at minimum acquiesce. And processes of constitutional change, even by formal amendment of the text, may take years, perhaps even decades, to achieve what seems to be their purposes. To use only American examples, for almost a full century the Fourteenth and Fifteenth amendments did precious little to advance the cause of black civil rights. So, too, although the Nineteenth Amendment, adopted in 1920, forbade official discrimination against women's voting, it was not until the 1960s that women voted in approximately the same numbers as men. Moreover, until that time the best predictor of how a married woman would vote was how her husband would vote. See Angus Campbell, Warren E. Miller, Philip E. Converse, and Donald E. Stokes, *The American Voter* (New York: Wiley, 1960).

52. Harold D. Lasswell popularized, if he did not actually invent, the term in a series of articles, the first of which was published in 1937: "The Garrison State Versus the Civilian State," 2 *China Q.* 543. Aaron L. Friedberg, *In the Shadow of the Garrison State: America's Anti-statism and Its Cold War Grand Strategy* (Princeton, NJ: Princeton University Press, 2000), p. 57, cites several of Lasswell's other articles using the term.

53. Article 81 disallows amendments and suspensions to the Basic Law proposed during officially declared states of emergency. Article 79.3 forbids amendments that would destroy federalism, remove the fundamental duty of the state to protect human dignity, or deny that all political authority emanates from the people, the democratic and social nature of the German political system, or the right of citizens to resist efforts to abolish the established "constitutional order."

54. "Tries" because Article 5 did not stop Congress's carving West Virginia from the state of Virginia. If the constitutional theory on which Lincoln justified fighting the Civil War was valid, Virginia never left the Union. Therefore, its act of secession was null and void *ab initio.* Virginia's acceptance during Reconstruction of its loss of territory hardly fits the kind of consent to which the constitutional document refers.

interpreted their constitutional orders as prohibiting amendments, even if adopted according to the procedures the text mandates, that alter the fundamental nature of the political system.[55] But the notion of limiting permissible constitutional change poses huge problems not only for the norms of constitutional and democratic theory but also for practical politics. In that respect, however, it does not differ from most other aspects of constitutional democracy.

55. Germany: Southwest Case, 1 BVerfGE 14, [1951], trans. and reprinted in part in Walter F. Murphy and Joseph Tanenhaus, eds., *Comparative Constitutional Law* (New York: St. Martin's, 1977), pp. 208ff. The court divided 4–4 on whether a constitutional amendment legitimating wiretaps was itself unconstitutional: Privacy of Communications Case, 30 BVerfGE 1, [1970], reprinted in *Comparative Constitutional Law*, pp. 659ff.

India: Golak Nath v. Punjab, [1967] A.I.R. 1643, was the first instance. It provoked a stream of criticism—some from scholars, for example, H. C. L. Merillat, *Land and the Constitution in India* (New York: Columbia University Press, 1970), but, more important, much from public officials. Because during the 1970s this, other rulings, and parliamentary opponents stymied Indira Gandhi's reforms, she declared a state of emergency, imprisoned parliamentary opponents, and pushed through a set of constitutional amendments that reversed *Golak Nath*'s doctrine. Eventually, the Indian electorate repudiated Gandhi's leadership. Although rejecting the basis of *Golak Nath*'s assertion of power to annul an amendment, the Supreme Court found new and stronger authority for this claim and invalidated some of Gandhi's amendments. Kesavananda Bharati's Case, [1973] S.C.R. 1 (Supp.) (Ind.), especially the separate opinion of Justice H. R. Khanna, and Minerva Mills v. Union of India, [1980] S.C.R. 1789. See the commentary in Upendra Baxi, *Courage, Craft, and Contention: The Indian Supreme Court in the Eighties* (Bombay: Tripathi, 1985); Lloyd and Suzanne Hoeber Rudolph, *In Pursuit of Lakshimi* (Chicago: University of Chicago Press, 1987), especially ch. 3, and H. M. Seervai, *The Constitutional Law of India*, 3rd ed. (Bombay: Tripathi, 1983), vol. 1, ch. 3 and vol. 2, chs. 14 and 28.

Bangladesh: I am doubly embarrassed not to have a citation here. I was gleefully told by a constitutional scholar from Bangladesh that his country's highest court had invalidated a constitutional amendment, citing my work as its authority. His glee was not generated solely by our friendship. He said the true authorities were the decisions of the Indian Supreme Court, listed in the previous note, but no self-respecting judge in Bangladesh could cite Indian case law as authoritative, so the court cited my analysis of the Indian cases as authoritative. Despite heroic efforts by several law-school librarians, I have not been able to gain access to the reports of Bangladesh's courts.

California: Raven v. Deukmejian, 801 P. 2d 1077 (Cal. 1990).

I

CREATING
A CONSTITUTIONAL
DEMOCRACY

Introduction

The general introduction explained the objectives of this book, discussed some of its principal terms, and outlined the central problems to be addressed. Part I targets one of those problems, the founding of a constitutional democracy, a task that not only confronts tight knots of substantive difficulties but also imposes a dilemma that is partially analytical, partially literary. Speaking in abstract terms allows an author to examine general theories, but testing theories requires tons of data. And there are too few nation-states that have converted to constitutional democracy to allow meaningful statistical testing. Even demonstrating that a theory is plausible involves producing waves of "for instances." Focusing on concrete situations entails either concentrating on a few highly detailed case studies, from which generalization is seldom possible,[1] or offering many case studies whose nuances can only be cursorily described, thus presenting what Alfred, Lord Tennyson called "a wilderness of single instances," equally unlikely to gestate broad understanding.

To avoid these difficulties and also to vary the pace of this lengthy tome (Part II returns to more conventional analysis), I have created a mythical nation, Nusquam, that is emerging from a long period of authoritarian rule by a dictatorial junta of military officers and wealthy civilians.[2] Many of this country's difficulties have been quite common during the last several centuries of Western, and now Eastern, political history: how to cope with competing economic interests and sometimes antagonistic ethnic groups while educating a population that has almost no firsthand experience with the norms of either democratic or constitutionalist rule. In sum, although Nusquam is not without impressive resources, it badly needs not only economic but also civic development to encourage a culture conducive to governance based on popular participation but also limited in power. Those sorts

---

1. Case studies can, of course, suggest theories (or at least hypotheses) and, carefully chosen, can allow analysts to test theories. See Harry H. Eckstein, "Case Study and Theory in Political Science," in his *Regarding Politics* (Berkeley: University of California Press, 1992).

2. For a study of the same general problem from a very different set of perspectives, see Richard Rose, William Mishler, and Christian Haerpfer, *Democracy and Its Alternatives: Understanding Postcommunist Societies* (Baltimore: Johns Hopkins University Press, 1998).

of needs have faced and most likely will continue to face people who wish to establish a civil society.

Members of what is, in effect, a constitutional convention will debate among themselves as well as with professional scholars who will address problems at a more general level than most of the delegates. Some members of the caucus will also speak as sophisticated political analysts. For example, one, who in his youth did graduate work at Yale, will push Robert A. Dahl's ideas, while another, a product of the University of Chicago, will reflect Richard A. Posner's economic interpretation of the roles of law. All of these people, however, will debate as practical, intelligent, and educated men and women who are deeply concerned about the long-range future of their nation and its political system. Some may be wrongheaded, insensitive, acerbic, or even rude, but each will be a patriot according to his or her own lights.

I hope this device will allow easy intellectual access back and forth between broad principles and concrete circumstances and so sharpen understanding of the nature and scope of many of the obstacles that confront founders of a new constitutional order. Perhaps this literary mode will also silhouette ways of coping with, if not removing, barriers to governance that is based on popular support, furthers justice, and protects what have become known as fundamental human rights.

Nusquam
The Political Setting

Nusquam is a medium-sized nation with a population of forty million. For seven decades, it was ruled by a coalition of military officers and prosperous landowners, merchants, and entrepreneurs. Juan J. Linz and Alfred Stepan would classify that regime as authoritarian rather than totalitarian or post-totalitarian.[3] Amos Perlmutter would characterize Nusquam's governance as close to classic "authoritarian praetorian," that is, "a coalition of military and civilian governing with little or no external political control."[4] In keeping with the simpler classification explained in the general introduction, I shall refer to this regime merely as tyrannical.

POLITICAL CENTRALIZATION AND SOCIAL PLURALISM. Political parties had not been tolerated. Despite operating branches in every city and hamlet in the country, the National Alliance of Nusquam, the junta's po-

---

3. *Problems of Democratic Transition and Consolidation* (Baltimore: Johns Hopkins University Press, 1996), ch. 3.

4. *The Military and Politics in Modern Times: On Professionals, Praetorians, and Revolutionary Soldiers* (New Haven, CT: Yale University Press, 1977), p. 95. I say "coming close to" rather than exactly meeting Perlmutter's criteria because his ideal model would have pictured the civilians in the junta as "bureaucrats, managers, and technocrats" but would not have included businessmen.

litical organization, was small, elitist, and structured so that all authority flowed from the top to the bottom. Its members were carefully chosen and local officials appointed from above. The five hundred delegates to the so-called parliament were chosen by the central government. People who publicly criticized the government were fined, imprisoned, or exiled. All television and radio stations, newspapers, magazines, and publishing houses were owned by the Ministry of Education. Dissidents' writings, however, were published by underground or foreign presses, and several radio stations broadcast to Nusquam from nearby countries. More effective were notices posted on websites located in Asia and Europe and e-mails sent by reformers through cleverly disguised networks of ISPs.

Although the junta tried to eliminate political dissent, it allowed some social and much economic pluralism. The junta never persecuted any religious group, but it did restrict religious organizations. For instance, it was a crime for any person to contribute money or any other thing of value to a church, temple, mosque, or other religious institution or person. The Ministry of Religious Affairs published a list of "approved" sects and paid an annual stipend to a small number of clergy whom each such group designated. In addition, the government allocated funds to construct and maintain church buildings, but no new buildings could be put up without the ministry's financing. No permit was issued until after an existing building had been razed.

Legally, churches, mosques, and synagogues could be used only for religious rituals; they could not be the site of men's or women's social-religious associations or even Sunday or Shabbat schools. The junta also monopolized the charitable and educational activities that such organizations typically undertake. Every hospital, hostel, home for the elderly, daycare center, and orphanage was run by the Ministry of Human Resources. Medical personnel and social workers were employees of the government. The government operated a national health plan and a system of social welfare that, the junta claimed, took care of all citizens.

Schools, from kindergartens to universities, were operated by the Ministry of Education, which also ran a program that financed graduate study abroad for a limited number of students. Mostly "hard scientists," these people were thoroughly vetted for loyalty to the regime. Indeed, more than three-quarters of those admitted to the program were relatives of members of the junta.

The junta encouraged accumulation of wealth and treated private property as quasi-sacred. Most commercial operations were in private hands, but the government tightly controlled unions, appointing officers, forbidding strikes, and requiring any labor disputes to be subject to arbitration by public officials. Private trade associations flourished, but they were also closely regulated. Each was chaired by a public official. The legal system modeled its provisions for sales, contracts, and liabilities on Spain's version of the Civil Law.

Formally, at least, professional associations did not exist. There were no bar associations. The most gifted of graduates of law faculties who passed the professional examinations were drafted into public service, serving as magistrates (judges and procurators), as advisers to various state agencies, or as officials whose main task was to negotiate with foreign corporations. Private citizens accused of "normal" crimes could engage an attorney at their own expense, but the state provided no legal assistance. Furthermore, there was no right to counsel in cases involving national security. All such charges were tried before military tribunals, behind closed doors. Corporations and private citizens could hire lawyers for advice and for suits against one another, but there was no right to sue the government or any of its agencies.

LEADERSHIP. When "the Great Revolution" occurred in 1936, its leader was a charismatic general. For almost six years he ruled as head of a troika; the other two were an admiral and a banker. During World War II, the general accused these two of treason, executed them, and graciously acceded to Parliament's bestowal of the title "President General for Life." The reign of terror that followed seemed directed as much at friends as at foes among the economic elite. Fortunately for these people, in 1950 the president general died from a strange case of food poisoning, and a new, more broadly based leadership, which included representatives from all four branches of the armed services as well as industry and finance, initiated "the Second Revolution," this one peaceful. Officially, neither governmental organization nor public policies changed; but rule became more bureaucratized, and an efficient method of cooption into and "retirement" from the junta operated. Never again was a member of the junta executed or imprisoned.

IDEOLOGY. What ideology the junta professed loosely resembled an authoritarian form of Franklin D. Roosevelt's First New Deal. Governmentally coerced cooperation among all sectors of the economy was the centerpiece of economic policy, and monopoly of power was the core of its political operations and organization. Opponents labeled the regime fascist, but that charge was exaggerated. Although the junta was quite ready to use brute force against citizens to maintain its political power, after 1950 it relied not on terror but on harsh and explicit rules enforced by zealous procurators and judges. Long prison terms and capital punishment were common penalties. Although Nusquam's domestic policies discriminated against Muslims, Sephardic Jews, blacks, Gypsies, and recent immigrants of any genre, official propaganda exhibited neither racism nor belligerent nationalism. The absence of the latter was due more to realism than to idealism: Nusquam's economy had not allowed it to acquire much modern military equipment.

MOBILIZATION. High among the junta's goals was an obedient and economically productive nation, but the regime was more successful in achieving docility than productivity. Not until its final days did the government try to organize mass, enthusiastic support. Fearing that involving citizens in political activities would threaten the system, the junta had been content with the acquiescence of a passive population.

The Economic Setting

Nusquam's neutrality during World War II earned some prosperity, but peace brought a competition that squeezed the country out of many foreign markets. Only steel manufacturers were able to compete effectively with foreign firms. Because a large share of the land is fertile and receives about forty-eight inches of rain a year, agricultural production meets domestic demands. Ranching and fishing do well and provide exports that bring in welcome foreign currency.

At one time, Nusquam had small but rich petroleum deposits. Then, during the embargo that followed the Yom Kippur War of 1973, the government encouraged its oil barons to produce and sell as much as they could. The result was an immediate windfall of profits but also a quick exhaustion of reserves. Thus, when the second embargo came in 1979, the country was economically devastated. Beginning in 1989, however, the junta began to use tax policies to encourage research in electronics and also created a legal environment friendly to the less savory aspects of "offshore" banking, making Nusquam attractive to foreigners. Although the country has never known anything like the prosperity of Germany, Italy, or Singapore, Nusquam's per capita income is higher than Turkey's but lower than that of Greece. Still, the distribution of income is badly skewed, with one-fifth of families living on incomes below the poverty level. And since 1979, unemployment has usually hovered between 18 and 20 percent.

In 2000, the junta announced its New Economic Program, essentially a modification of extant policies. It completely deregulated banking and guaranteed absolute confidentiality to all depositors and investors with foreign passports and also encouraged trade in arms by exempting transshipments of such "goods" from all customs inspections and import and export duties. Arms merchants would only pay a transactional fee. Needless to say, some of the uninspected crates included cocaine and heroin as well as guns.

The Social Setting

One of the happier aspects of Nusquam's history is that early in the nineteenth century its government began to take education very seriously and established an excellent system of primary and secondary schools. Realizing that few people outside of the country spoke Nusquam's language or felt any need to learn it, officials required that English be taught from the second grade onward. Thus, by the time of the junta's collapse, most of the people were fluent in English, and the well educated were likely to be truly bilingual. Nevertheless, the country's economic problems caused drastic reductions in spending for education, with a consequent drop in quality.

Even had educational standards remained high, the country's ethnic fissures would have complicated transition from authoritarian rule. The last census reported that 80 percent of respondents listed a religious affiliation: about one-quarter of these people claimed to be Catholics, and 8 percent said they were Jews, a slightly larger proportion than identified themselves as Muslims. Most of the remainder claimed to be Protestants of various denominations. Several thousand said they were Buddhists. Most Jews are Ashkenazim whose roots run back several centuries in Nusquam's history. Almost a third, however, are ultra-orthodox Sephardim, whose families migrated from North Africa and the Persian Gulf.

Most Protestants in Nusquam are white, native-born citizens, but about a hundred thousand are blacks whose ancestors escaped from slavery in the United States and the Caribbean two centuries ago. Catholics are divided into four groups. A majority are from old families; about 20 percent are relatively new immigrants from Central America; a group of seventy-five thousand Catholics are Vietnamese émigrés and their children from the years 1978–1981; and last is a group of about twenty-five thousand Armenians whose great-grandparents had fled Turkey after World War I. Nusquam also has about sixty thousand Gypsies and about twice that number of Chinese, whose families arrived near the end of the nineteenth century. Nonbelievers are spread rather evenly across the spectrum of ethnic groups except Hispanics and Vietnamese, almost all of whom are Catholic.

White Protestants have the highest incomes, followed by Chinese, Ashkenazim, Vietnamese and other non-Hispanic Catholics, Muslims, Sephardim, black Protestants, Hispanics and, far behind all, the Gypsies. Ashkenazim have attained the highest educational levels, closely followed by non-Hispanic Catholics. Gypsies receive the least schooling; few of them have graduated from the equivalent of grade school. Only eighteen of those interviewed in the last census said they had attended a university, and of these only four were graduates.

Hostility within and among these groups is rife. Sephardic Jews tend to scorn the Ashkenazim for having assimilated into Nusquam's general culture. In turn, Ashkenazim are apt to look on Sephardim as ignorant urban peasants. Although a significant minority of Muslims are descendants of Turks who came to work in the steel mills, the majority are first- and second-generation exiles from Palestine, and some emigrated from Pakistan and

Indonesia. Most of Nusquam's Muslims are Sunni. Nevertheless, they hold diverse religious and political attitudes. About 150 are members of the Wahhabi sect, the fundamentalist group who spawned Osama bin Laden. They despise Nusquam's other Muslims as hypocritical atheists. In turn, more educated Muslims fear the Wahhabites as fanatics who are looking for excuses to murder Muslims whom they deem apostates.

For their part, white Protestants and Catholics have never been warm toward each other, and both have evidenced distrust of all immigrant groups of whatever religion or ethnicity. Moreover, relations between Turks and Armenians as well as between Sephardic Jews and Palestinian Arabs have several times fired riots. No group has fully accepted the Hispanics, and most citizens openly say they despise Gypsies, though few claim to know a Rom personally. The result has been a large amount of self-imposed segregation. Gypsies tend to live nomadic lives, and most Hispanics work as hired laborers on farms, while poorer members of other minority groups typically cluster together in urban ghettos. Because of this separation, immigrants and many of their children continue to use ancestral languages for day-to-day living.

The Junta's Demise: "The Third Revolution"

The junta collapsed more from corruption and a failure of will than from violent overthrow. Although there had been some uncoordinated acts of terrorism, the secret police and the Special Guards, an elite military force, had been efficient in squelching organized dissident groups. The first of what proved to be fatal cracks began to appear less than three months ago, when the first five years of the highly touted New Economic Plan succeeded in raising the gross domestic product by 1.6 percent but without significantly improving maldistributions of income or lowering the unemployment rate below 17 percent. According to widespread rumors, most of the gains were going into the Swiss bank accounts the ruling elites maintained. Hitherto docile unions started a series of illegal strikes that escalated in seriousness; the last of them left the capital without either electricity or public transportation for several days. University students began taking to the streets, protesting that while tuition was being raised, there were no jobs for them after graduation.

The government's first reaction was to try to break the strikes; but when officials realized how quickly unrest was spreading, they began to make sympathetic noises. "We feel your pain," the junta's president said on television. "Let us sit down together and discuss how we can make Nusquam a happier place." To provide a facade for that discussion, he announced that the government was installing a licensing system to grant autonomous status to some groups. Within a week of the announcement, more than three thousand embryonic organizations were seeking permits. During that time, the junta's leaders used a combination of threats and bribery to try to co-opt leaders of the new dissidents. These efforts produced little success.

Meanwhile, in the capital, students at the National University ignored the licensing option and again took to the streets. Changing course from their previous protest, they now had a single demand: the junta must resign. One afternoon, during a particularly raucous demonstration by women students in front of the presidential palace, secret police fired on the crowd, killing six of the women and wounding several dozen more. The next morning, the Presidential Plaza was filled with more than thirty thousand women from all around the country, shouting for the junta's resignation. The general president ordered a regiment of marines, led by Colonel Nestor Martin, to disperse the demonstrators. By the time the regiment arrived, the protesters had established a tent city in front of the palace and were being fed by the capital's inhabitants.

Colonel Martin met with the students' self-selected leaders, listened to their arguments, and suggested that they go back to their homes. They refused. The president then commanded Martin to use force to disperse the group. Instead, the colonel announced that he found the students' case persuasive and their sole demand reasonable. He immediately deployed one of his battalions around the palace and placed the other two in defensive positions in the city. The junta then ordered a tank battalion of Special Guards and a mechanized division from the regular army to attack Martin and crush the rebellion. As the seventy-two tanks of the Special Guards were strung out along a mile-long bridge in the city's center, Marine demolition experts blew all four spans, sending the bridge and sixty tanks into the river.

As the mechanized division was entering the capital, the colonels commanding the three infantry and one artillery regiment declared their solidarity with Martin and surrounded the central barracks of the secret police. Around the country, a dozen army and air force units began to move to relieve the government but were met by still other units. The fighting was sporadic, largely because desertions depleted most of the loyal forces before they could engage the rebels. Lacking the courage for a sustained civil war and fearing a fate like that of Romania's Nicolae Ceaușescu and his wife Elena, the junta speedily negotiated a settlement with Martin and the four army colonels: The leaders and their families got safe passage out of the country. Left behind were all their minions, including the chief of the secret police and the commander of the Special Guards. Both men and their staffs were quickly arrested and imprisoned along with several dozen judges and procurators.

The Colonels (now capitalized) prorogued the junta's sham parliament and took control of the government. To the surprise of the population and foreign diplomats, these officers immediately issued a proclamation:

We, officers and men of the armed forces loyal to the nation of Nusquam, have wrenched command of government from the hands of despots. As soon as public order and safety permit, we shall surrender that power to lawfully constituted civilian officials. But the nation's political health cannot be restored merely by removing a single nest of tyrants. Without new and vibrant political institutions and processes that both promote justice and reflect the wishes of our citizens, Nusquam is doomed to further cycles of oppressive rule by small cliques. Thus our nation has an urgent need for a system of governance that will help our people live in peace, justice, order, liberty, and prosperity. To speed the day when we can in good conscience return to our dedicated careers, we summon a Caucus for a New Political System to propose a fresh constitutional order for our nation.

As convened, the caucus consists of twenty-five members, mostly civilians, and is authorized to meet for as long as necessary and to do so in splendid isolation in the presidential villa on Lake Lakshmi. The Colonels have also specified that the caucus can draft as research assistants any or all members of the faculties of Nusquam National University. In addition, the Colonels have made money available so that the caucus, as the Estonian constitutional convention of 1991–92 did, can invite such foreign consultants as it might deem helpful to its deliberations.

The Caucus for a New Political System

The ideal founders of a constitutional order would be, as Socrates understood, both philosophers and statesmen. Such paragons, however, are rare, and none of them was selected as a member of this constitutional convention. Still, the chosen people are all intelligent and have a variety of experiences. To some extent, their diversity represents Nusquam's population, though their educational level is far superior to that of most citizens. Some had been officials under the old regime, some are academics; others journalists; several are labor leaders who had struggled for independence from governmental domination; still others had been leaders of dissident groups; one is a banker; one is a Jesuit; two are Protestant ministers; and one of the Jewish members is president of his temple. Two members are Muslims, one is of Chinese descent, one is Hispanic, and yet another is a Gypsy. Pointedly absent from the group are people who had been sympathetic to the junta.

Only two founders are currently in the military. One is a mathematician who teaches at the country's naval academy; he has the official rank of commander, though he has never served aboard a combat vessel. The other is Nestor Martin himself. He probably owes his stiff-backed posture and penchant for short, brush-cut hair (now steel gray) to his family's genes. The patriarch of that clan was an Irish officer who, after Wolfe Tone's failed rebellion in 1797, emigrated to Nusquam. Standing first in his class at the naval academy, Martin had opted for a Marine commission, realizing that being built like a linebacker on a American football team would be an asset in an organization that valued physical strength as much as, if not more than, intelligence. After four years of service, he resigned and became a soldier of fortune, fighting in the Sudan for the rebels, again for the rebels in East Timor, and then for Croatian Muslims against the Serbs. After the Dayton Accords, he returned to Nusquam, exuding gravitas, and because of his unique combat experience was reinstated in the Marine Corps with the rank of lieutenant colonel. He was promoted to colonel shortly before the women took to the streets. His reputation as a soldier of fortune and dramatic action against the junta made him the most prominent of the Colonels, the one to whom the others looked for leadership. Foreign journalists who had covered coups in Latin America refer to him as "El Jefe," and unconfirmed rumor has it that he wrote the statement convening the caucus and personally selected its members. Whatever the truth of these reports, at its first meeting the caucus prudently elects him chairman.[5]

Despite the presence of academics, most members, even the clerics, are reputed to be practical men and women concerned about the real-life consequences of their choices. (The Colonels, as reporters were quick to note, did not appoint a professional philosopher to the group.) Because of Nusquam's jagged sectarian divisions, most members believe it would be wise to avoid using theological arguments to justify decisions. Nevertheless, many of them also realize that some of their own politically relevant values rest on religious convictions and that sooner or later they must face up to the impact of these potentially divisive norms within the caucus as well as within the nation as a whole.[6]

Dramatis Personae

Of the twenty-five members of the caucus, the chair, Colonel Martin, and the following delegates will play particularly active roles in debate:

Ibrahim Ajami: A Sunni Muslim who is a professor of Islamic Studies at the National University. Learned in the Qur'an, the Shari'a (literally the

---

5. Colonel Martin's biography shows marked similarities with that of Colonel (later President) Lucio Gutiérrez of Ecuador. Here, however, life followed art (at least temporally), for I wrote the original draft of this chapter in 1997, some three years before Gutiérrez launched his political career by joining forces with a populist insurrection.

6. For John Rawls's development of the concept of "public reasons," see esp. his "Kantian Constructivism in Moral Philosophy" and "The Idea of Public Reasons Revisited," both in *John Rawls: Collected Papers*, ed. Samuel R. Freeman (Cambridge, MA: Harvard University Press, 1999). For critical analyses, see Robert P. George, *The Clash of Orthodoxies: Law, Religion, and Morality in Crisis* (Wilmington, DE: ISI Press, 2001), pp. 45–55; and the articles by Samuel R. Freeman, Dennis F. Thompson, Abner S. Greene, David A. J. Richards, and Michael Baur in "Symposium: Rawls and the Law," 72 *Fordham L. Rev.* 2021 (2004).

path to the watering place), and the theology implicit and explicit in both, he has the honorary title Mufti.[7] His scholarly reputation, enhanced by his gaunt, saintly appearance and the long white beard that droops almost to his waist, has given him the status of a wise and holy man. Non-Muslims sometimes (mistakenly) refer to him as "Imam." He must struggle constantly to differentiate the Muslims with whom he works from the Wahhabites, who regard him as an atheist.

Anita Baca: A twenty-five-year-old Hispanic graduate student in sociology from National University. Short, dark haired, and noted for a fiery temper and cold courage, she had nominated herself to be leader of the women demonstrators and had been accepted by acclamation. Although wounded in the first volleys against the women, she had refused hospitalization and had presented to Colonel Martin the women's demand for the junta's departure. Her imprimatur on a new constitutional order would, in the minds of many women, confer legitimacy on the political system.

Rudolf Glückmann: A Lutheran pastor who at first glance seems meek and unimposing, a heavy, balding Caspar Milquetoast. Yet he had used his pulpit to call for the junta to show greater respect for human rights. In keeping with its policy of not directly confronting religious leaders, the government pretended to ignore him. His church, however, had mysteriously burned down, and his congregation was denied a permit to rebuild. In the meantime, the state cut off his salary.

Atilla Gregorian: A Jesuit who, with his provincial's permission, had gone to the steel mills as "a worker priest." There, he built up support among the steelworkers, publicly called for democratic elections to Parliament, and offered himself as a candidate. The junta's initial reaction was to imprison him on trumped-up charges of sedition, but later the leaders traded his freedom for a promise to stay out of electoral politics. Instead, with the cooperation of his provincial and a local bishop, he began preaching in churches around the country. A short, dapper man who wears his silver hair tied in a ponytail that reaches halfway down his back, he was fiercely eloquent, a master at criticizing the junta through sarcastic allegory. His most famous punch line was that the members of the junta were true Christians who meticulously followed Christ's admonition "to make friends with Mammon." Gregorian is a humble man who interprets God's giving Nusquam a priest as wise and holy as he to be a sign of divine love for humanity.

Jessica Jacobsohn: A former professor of comparative constitutional law on the faculty of Nusquam's National University. She had been fired because of telling her classes that Nusquam urgently needed sweeping constitutional reform. Once considered attractive and well dressed, she appears to have

---

7. For brief descriptions of the titles and roles (usually unofficial or quasi-official) of those who perform Muslim religious functions, see Leon Carl Brown, *Religion and State: The Muslim Approach to Politics* (New York: Columbia University Press, 2000), esp. chs. 1–3.

aged a decade during the past several years. Having had to earn her living as a helper in a flower shop, she can no longer afford stylish clothes.

Jon Kanuri: An economist whose ancestors had escaped from slavery in West Africa. Six feet four inches tall and weighing 245 trim pounds, he is blessed with a physical appearance that adds force to his words. For a time, when he was preaching that an authoritarian state was useful for economic development, he had been the darling of the junta. Appointed minister of finance, he had quickly embarrassed his patrons by charging that a large part of the nation's wealth was being siphoned off into Swiss bank accounts. Shortly after his accusations, an auditor found "errors" in the minister's own accounts, and when the Colonels revolted, he had been awaiting trial for fraud.

Tuncer Kirca: A Turkish émigré who had come to Nusquam in 1980 as an unskilled worker in the steel industry. Later, he secretly organized other Turkish laborers and tried to found a labor union independent of the government's control. Short, muscular, and strong, he had several times man-handled goons whom the government sent to harass him. Indeed, on one occasion he broke the arm of one such worthy and cost another three teeth and a serious concussion. For that crime, he spent four years in prison; he was released after the Colonels' revolt. Kirca is acutely sensitive to the prejudice directed against Muslims in Nusquam and places much of the blame for the continuation of such bias on the rantings of the Wahhabi.

Václav Pilsudski: At the fall of the junta, he was still minister of justice. He had been a distinguished professor of criminal law at the National University. Thinking that he would lend legitimacy to the government and, at the age of seventy-six, would be politically tame, the junta had appointed him to the cabinet. Once in office, however, he initiated disciplinary actions against several procurators and judges who had been draconian in enforcing the junta's policies. Fearing loss of much-needed public support, the leaders did not fire him; instead, they surrounded him with hacks who sabotaged his policies. With a flowing mane of white hair, he looks like Walt Disney's animation of Pinocchio's father.

Demos Pyknites: Nephew of an immensely wealthy Greek shipping magnate who was a member of the junta, Demos became a famous—and famously tall, slim, and handsome—television commentator. A graduate of the National University, he had been allowed to pursue graduate study for three years at Yale, where he completed the coursework and passed the examinations required for a Ph.D. in political science. He did not, however, finish his dissertation. A decade after returning to Nusquam, he was imprisoned when the secret police discovered he was the author of a series of tracts attacking the junta. He, too, had been freed only after the Colonels' revolt.

Federika Strega: After graduating first in her class from the law faculty of

National University, she joined the civil service and quickly earned promotion. She was one of the few people selected for study abroad who were not related to a member of the junta. At the University of Chicago, she studied law and economics. Although endowed with a husky voice, soulful brown eyes, and silky black hair, she was better known for her keen intelligence and a tongue that cracked like a bullwhip. While still a middle-level bureaucrat, she had persuaded the junta to subsidize the electronics industry and to change the legal system to make foreign bankers welcome. Last year, at thirty-six, she became deputy minister of finance. In that post, she was trying desperately to improve Nusquam's rickety system of health care. Throughout her career, she had managed to stay out of the beds, ideological as well as recreational, of all members of the junta.

Minxin Wei: A member of a wealthy family of bankers and now CEO of Nusquam's largest bank. Some people view him as tightly self-contained, others as arrogant, perhaps because his pencil-thin mustache gives him a sneering look and his use of traditional Mandarin robes indicates disdain for the dominant white culture. Nevertheless, all people with whom he deals recognize him as a brilliant financier, and the junta had courted him and his family because of their links to financial institutions around the world. It had seemed that he had no contact with politics other than to facilitate the government's revised banking policies. After the Colonels' revolt, however, it became evident that he and his family had been using their connections abroad to help finance the dissidents.

Ion Zingaro: The only Gypsy in the group, he is a dark, diminutive man whose deep brown eyes warn that he does not tolerate intimacy. As a teenager, he had followed his father as an itinerant tinker. Convicted twice for larceny, he learned to read and write while in prison and, during his second three-year term, discovered that he had a talent for serious poetry, both in Nusquam's ancient language and in Shelta, the Gypsies' dialect. Several members of the junta adopted him as their tame dissident and, perversely, seemed to enjoy the sarcastic barbs his poems hurled at them. Later he learned English as well as French and Spanish but could never write poetry in those languages.

CHAPTER ONE

Values, Interests, and Goals

Before we can undertake properly the investigation of our next theme, the nature of the ideal constitution, it is necessary for us first to determine the nature of the most desirable way of life.   ARISTOTLE

The twenty-five members of the Caucus for a New Political System assemble at the presidential villa along Lake Lakshmi. Each has his or her own desk, a laser printer, and a laptop computer connected to a database containing the texts of papers that various presenters will give as well as dozens of books and articles that might be relevant to discussions. Down a corridor, jury-rigged cubicles house the two research assistants from the faculty of the National University chosen for each member. In addition, the Colonels have invited a parliamentarian from Westminster to offer procedural advice. Besides these people, a staff of navy stewards and several teams of secretaries and technicians who will record the proceedings on videotape are in attendance. Various foreign experts will come and go; all have been invited to remain as long as they wish and participate—without a vote—in discussions. Marines stationed around the property ensure that no one except invited guests and librarians bringing books from the university can enter or leave the grounds.

After the caucus elects Colonel Nestor Martin as its chair and settles a few preliminary procedural matters, he proposes that the founders take a week to study, reflect, and get to know each other. The suggestion barely carries. Although many members are anxious to begin their work, a majority agree that they need to do some serious reading and to meditate on the task before them. One of the items on the list of strongly recommended readings is a longer version of the general introduction of this book.[1] Thus members begin with some understanding of the nature of constitutional and representative democracy and the differences between them.

---

1. "Constitutions, Constitutionalism, and Democracy," in Douglas Greenberg, Stanley N. Katz, Melanie Beth Oliviero, and Steven C. Wheatley, eds., *Constitutionalism and Democracy: Transformations in the Contemporary World* (New York: Oxford University Press, 1993)

On the eighth day, the chair opens the formal sessions with a brief speech whose humble tone masks an indirect style of leadership:

Daniel Bell said that the real problems arise the "day after the revolution."[2] He was correct. Bringing down an old political order is much easier than building a new one. Our basic task is to design a political system that is strong enough to govern effectively yet also sufficiently constrained as not to oppress our people. I will do all I can to facilitate that work, though I come to this mission "like a skittish horse to a brass band,"[3] fully realizing my limited knowledge, wisdom, and vision. My hope is that our combined goodwill, intelligence, and experience will prove sufficient. Trying to master the craft of war has left me ignorant of the craft of state; but with your patient help I will learn. Because we are a group unique in Nusquam's history and this is the first time I have presided over civilians, our parliamentarian has suggested that we proceed as informally as is compatible with orderly discussion. He promises to intervene if we threaten to commit mortal sin against parliamentary standards.

Furthermore, like all of you, I am acutely aware that what we want, what we can persuade each other to endorse, and what we can convince people outside this caucus to accept may differ. Although constitutional democracy may seem the obvious choice to much of the world, it could bring heavier burdens than our people are willing—or able—to bear. Therefore, the very first question we must address concerns the kind of constitutional order we want to create. To answer that question, we must consider alternative systems.

Rudolf Glückmann, the Lutheran pastor, interrupts: "You have skipped a step, Colonel. We cannot weigh alternative political systems until we identify goals and thus the values we want our new regime to promote. That identification must be the first item on our agenda."

Demos Pyknites, the dissident journalist, interrupts the interruption. "With all due respect to the Pastor, we sit here as practical men and women. We have already wasted seven days in indolent reading. And as the Pastor would surely remind us, the Almighty needed less time to create the universe. We must move quickly. Soon the Chair's military colleagues will

---

2. *The Cultural Contradictions of Capitalism* (New York: Basic Books, 1978), p. 29.

3. Chief Justice Charles Evans Hughes's comment on opening the Supreme Court's conference on the First Flag Salute Case, Minersville School District v. Gobitis, 310 U.S. 586 (1940), as reported in the papers of Justice Frank Murphy, University of Michigan. Although Hughes's remark has a nice military ring, Colonel Martin would not be familiar with American constitutional history. Still, authors of fiction may legitimately exercise omnipotence over matters imaginary.

become accustomed to ruling and decide to take up permanent residence in the palaces of power. We have been extraordinarily fortunate in that the Colonels have asked us to construct the framework for a new political system. We can think of Pinochet in Chile, who surrendered power only bit by bit, protecting himself and his henchmen from prosecution for their crimes and keeping himself and many of his friends in office in the army, Senate, and courts long after his defeat at the polls. One could recite similar actions by the military in Argentina and Uruguay, though in those latter two countries the military were more concerned to protect themselves from criminal prosecution than to shape general public policy. A group as diverse as we will never agree on a blueprint of values. And while we wrangle, our Colonels will wonder about their wisdom in convening a squabbling body of civilians and succumb to the praetorian temptation."

"We best do our job," Atilla Gregorian, the Jesuit priest, puts in, "when we try our best to do our job, and that 'best' must include frank discussions of the values the new political system should establish. If the Colonels disagree, they have the power to kill—and I use that word deliberately—this caucus. But let us do our job and let the Colonels answer to their own consciences, which have so far been rightly formed. Now, as to the merits of our discussion, perhaps we can't agree on 'a blueprint of values,' but we might follow the advice of C. S. Lewis and seek agreement at the core rather than at the edges.[4] Our unhappy history allows us agree on a core value: the necessity that the state, society, and all individual citizens respect the innate worth and dignity of every human being."

"I doubt we can agree even on core values," Pyknites says. "The scope and content of 'human dignity' are hotly contested issues, usually immersed in religious debates. And we must build a civic, not a religious, culture. We should not justify our choices by appeals to religious values that are not shared by all of our people, now or in the future. We must appeal only to reason and evidence that people can accept or reject regardless of their adherence to or rejection of religion. Our arguments must be *public*, not sectarian."

"You would exclude arguments that proceed from religious principles?" Pastor Glückmann asks. "If you want to tear a country apart, you've hit on an effective method."

"Let me clarify," Pyknites protests. "My research assistant has provided a statement by an eminent Princeton professor that succinctly expresses what I mean: 'The point is not to exclude appeals to religious authority per se, but to exclude appeals to *any* authority impervious to critical assessment from a variety of reasonable points of view. For public power is held in common by us all, and we should exercise it together based on reasons and arguments

4. *Mere Christianity* (New York: Macmillan, 1943), p. viii.

that we can share in spite of our differences. The authority that remains is the authority of reasons that we can share in public as fellow citizens.'[5] I fear that what you call values will have a strictly sectarian basis."

"That's not necessarily true," the Mufti puts in. "The noted philosopher Anthony Appiah has written about certain 'basic resources' that every person needs, such as freedom to pursue a plan of life, and to be accorded respect.[6] These are practical, not theological, concepts."

"Perhaps, but they will seem theological," Pyknites says. "We should proceed in a more frugal fashion: construct a law for the election of a new parliament that can begin democratic governance and encourage a lasting political system to develop. Our mandate is to propose a means of allowing the military to turn over power to a civilian regime that can promote the common good. Battles over values can be fought in Parliament as issues cry out for solutions. We needn't, we can't, impose a set of overarching values on our people. Drafting an electoral law is challenge enough."

"But," Jessica Jacobsohn, the former professor of constitutional law, objects, "if we follow Mr. Pyknites's proposal we will have, without deliberation, proposed a representative democracy."

"Possibly," Pyknites agrees, "but the new parliament could itself draft a constitutional text either at once or over a long period, as the Israeli Knesset has been doing.[7] We shouldn't try to guess what sort of system would emerge."

"MPs would vote themselves out of office?" Federicka Strega, the deputy minister of finance, scoffs. "Believe that and you believe the Easter Bunny is a hard datum. But Professor Jacobsohn is right. Mr. Pyknites's suggestion means that we adopt a form of representative democracy that will give enormous power to Parliament. If they draft a charter, the MPs will have a conflict of interest, and self-interest always trumps the general good. Besides, I, for one, do not want representative democracy, at least not now. And more generally, we shouldn't adopt any political system without serious reflection and debate. Nevertheless, I agree with Pyknites's main point: we should not waste time discussing airy-fairy concepts like values."

"Forgive an ignorant soldier's intervention," Colonel Martin says. "Mr. Pyknites may have proposed the wisest course. But shouldn't we reach that decision only after carefully weighing our options? Let's continue discussion,

5. Stephen Macedo, *Diversity and Distrust: Civic Education in a Multicultural Democracy* (Cambridge, MA: Harvard University Press, 2000), p. 172. Macedo is here expressing his agreement with John Rawls, *A Theory of Justice* (Cambridge, MA: Harvard University Press, 1971), and Amy Gutmann and Dennis F. Thompson, *Democracy and Disagreement* (Cambridge, MA: Harvard University Press, 1996).

6. Kwame Anthony Appiah, *The Ethics of Identity* (Princeton, NJ: Princeton University Press, 2005).

7. See Martin Edelman, "The New Israeli Constitution," 36 *Middle Eastern Studies* 1 (2000), and sources cited.

remembering we have a program of speakers on various kinds of regimes. Father Gregorian, you were making a point?"

"I believe I made it, Mr. Chairman. We can agree on a statement of equal human dignity and not merely because of our religious beliefs. Why else do we want a political system that protects the individual rights of all our citizens?"

"It's enough," Strega responds, "that we want freedom for ourselves. I'd be delighted to have total and absolute power, with the rest of the world having none whatsoever. But I know that other people would object to that ideal arrangement, so I must compromise to maximize my own power—and security. Which doesn't mean I want either representative or constitutional democracy. We need only justify our new regime as serving the interest of most of our people. Talking about 'values' and 'human dignity' opens the door to religious acrimony. We'd have to define 'human being' and get into endless wrangles about such issues as planned cessation of gestation."

"Planned what?" Ibrahim Ajami, the Mufti, asks.

"Abortion."

"Jesus, Mary, and Joseph!" Gregorian says, only half in prayer.

Strega continues: "See, the A-word rouses hypocritical males who use religion to force women to bear their children. Let's get on with constructing a workable political system."

"Thank you," Pyknites says.

"Don't thank me," Strega continues. "I think we should discuss the form of government that helps the greatest number of citizens enjoy the greatest happiness."

"Absurd!" Gregorian retorts. "Patently absurd!"

"You find happiness absurd? Were you castrated when you took your vows?"

Martin raps his gavel. "The minister will be civil."

"I'll try," Strega says, "but government is concerned with this life, with maintaining peace and decreasing unhappiness in the here and now."

"You complain," Gregorian notes, "about the vagueness of 'values.' What about happiness? Now there's a smoky concept. 'Hannibal the Cannibal' Lecter, the villain of Thomas Harris's novels, found happiness in eating people alive. 'He did it,' another character explained, 'because he liked it. . . . Dr. Lecter is not crazy, in any common way we think of as being crazy. He does some hideous things because he enjoys them.'"[8]

"Don't trivialize my argument with allusions to popular novels. No political system need pander to sociopaths."

"Fair enough," Gregorian says. "Let's look at what 'normal' people think

8. *Red Dragon* (New York: Dell, 1981), p. 68.

about happiness.[9] 'If you don't like novelists, how about a musician? 'Happiness is not something you experience, it's something you remember.' That's Oscar Levant. Or poets? 'Count no one happy until dead,'[10] Euripides said. Or an American who wrote about a handsome young man 'who was richer than a king—And admirably schooled in every grace':

> In fine, we thought that he was everything
> To make us wish we were in his place.
> So on we worked, and waited for the light,
> And went without the meat, and cursed the bread;
> And Richard Cory, one calm summer night,
> Went home and put a bullet through his head.[11]

"We don't know what brings happiness. Money won't do it, at least not by much or for very long. 'Within an industrialized country,' Steven Pinker reports, 'money buys only a little happiness: the correlation between wealth and satisfaction is positive but small.' I would hope happiness would be found in helping one's fellow man, but I fear many people enjoy seeing or reading about other people's suffering. And we must never forget, envy is part of human nature. You recall Shakespeare's line in *As You Like It:* 'But, O! how bitter a thing it is to look into happiness through another man's eyes!' The easiest way to achieve your goal would be to put Prozac in the water."[12]

"Forget about happiness as an abstract concept," Strega snaps. "Talk about the conditions under which most people can pursue their private conceptions of happiness in *this* world, not some other. You quoted Pinker, but he admits that '[w]e are happier when we are healthy, well fed, comfortable, safe, prosperous, knowledgeable, respected, non-celibate and loved.'[13] Government can't make people respected, but it can help them become healthy, well fed, and prosperous."

"Colleagues," Pyknites puts in, "let's not entangle ourselves in an endless debate about insoluble problems. I repeat my proposal: establish a political system that allows the people's government to pursue a variety of goals, even

---

9. For discussions of happiness, see Steven Pinker, *How the Mind Works* (New York: W. W. Norton, 1997), pp. 389ff. I have drawn several of these examples from those pages. See also Robert Lane, *The Loss of Happiness in Market Democracies* (New Haven, CT: Yale University Press, 2000), esp. chs. 5–6.

10. *Daughters of Troy*, line 729, trans. Mark Rudman and Katharine Washburn, in David R. Slavitt and Palmer Bovie, eds., *Euripides* (Philadelphia: University of Pennsylvania Press, 1998), 3:94.

11. "Richard Cory," in *Collected Poems of Edward Arlington Robinson* (New York: Macmillan, 1948), p. 82. Reprinted with permission of Palgrave Macmillan.

12. See Richard Posner, "The Problematics of Moral and Legal Theory," 111 *Harv. L. Rev.* 1637, 1659 (1998).

13. *How the Mind Works*, p. 389.

to decide from time to time what are the system's basic values and/or what makes the people happy, if either term has any real meaning."

Pastor Glückmann starts to speak, but the Jesuit is quicker. "We have been less than charitable toward Gypsies—and Muslims and Hispanics and Vietnamese and blacks—in short, toward one other. That is precisely why we should explicitly acknowledge the centrality of human dignity and equality."

Again the pastor tries to speak, but Gregorian continues: "And Minister Strega has made an important point: philosophers will endlessly debate definitions of human dignity and all other values most of us cherish. But as Mr. Pyknites has cogently pointed out, we are practical men and women. At a general level, we can agree on certain concepts such as human dignity and leave it to other people at other times to translate those concepts into specific public policies. I repeat: we share a set of *politically relevant values*, and we can articulate them in strictly secular terms."

"For Islam," Ibrahim Ajami cuts in, "the Prophet himself, peace be upon him, spoke with clarity. A well known hadith says that Man is created in the image of Allah the all-merciful. And 'Man' is a generic word that refers to males and females of all races and religions. Allah has given Man dominion over the earth; he is Allah's *khalif,* His representative.[14] Thus for an observant Muslim, equal human dignity is at least as central as it is for a Christian."

"And Christians and Muslims got that from us Jews," Jacobsohn adds. "Deuteronomy commands us to love strangers as well as neighbors. Believing Jews—Orthodox, Conservative, or Reform—must respect the equal dignity of all human beings."

Pyknites looks around. "Now I understand how Jesuits got their reputation for organizing conspiracies. As much as I admire Father Gregorian's rhetorical and organizational skills, the religious spin he and his fellow clerics have put on the problem confirms its religious nature."

Colonel Martin speaks up. "It seems to me that Mr. Pyknites is correct. We must base our work on civic reasoning, not moral theology. But questions of legitimacy in politics ultimately pose moral questions, and morality is central to religion. We can do a fair job of separating church and state, but we cannot separate religion and politics. We must rely on civic, secular reasons, but we must realize that we are also thereby raising religious issues. The only alternatives, other than burying our heads in the sand, are to emasculate either religion or politics, or both."

"We're debating whether to debate. A waste of time," Pyknites says. "Even though the Pastor is putting the wrong issue before us, I agree to

14. Quoted in William Soliman Kilada, "Christian-Muslim Relations in Egypt," in Kail C. Ellis, ed., *The Vatican, Islam, and the Middle East* (Syracuse, NY: Syracuse University Press, 1988), p. 245.

discuss it. In return, I ask the chair to limit debate and then call for a vote on a specific proposal—if we ever have one."

"Very well," the chair replies. "Let me retreat in order to advance. The Pastor is correct: I rushed the cadence. A choice among ends presupposes a choice among values against which to gauge those ends. I pray that Father Gregorian is correct, but I fear that Mr. Pyknites and Minister Strega are also correct. We face a very long battle. My solution is to ask unanimous consent to docket the Pastor's proposal but also to limit discussion of our choices and definitions of values to the remainder of today and tomorrow morning's session." Martin looks around the room, then raps his gavel. "Hearing no objection, it is so ordered. . . . Professor Pilsudski?"

"I hate to complicate our lives further," the minister of justice begins, "but as we discuss human dignity, we must also keep a mind a cognate right, autonomy. The term reflects a compound Greek word: *autos*, meaning 'self,' and *nomos*, meaning 'law'—thus 'self-rule.' None of us can be fully autonomous. Even Rousseau conceded that '[s]ocial man is too weak to do without others; he is in all ways needy from the moment of his birth to the moment of his death and, rich or poor, could not survive if he received nothing from others.'[15] Nevertheless, we should strive for a wide angle of freedom within a life of interdependence. Autonomy demands that we, as individuals, be as free from the control of others, including government, as we wish, within the necessary restraints of a complex society. We should be able to speak, read, and write as we prefer, to choose among a variety of lifestyles, professions, friends, and mates, to worship or not worship as we see fit—in short, to have legal as well as moral control over aspects of our lives whose orbits do not restrict equal independence of others. That last, I admit, entails limitations as huge as they are amorphous."

"As a personal matter," Pyknites says, "I agree with you both about the importance of autonomy and its practical limitations; but for all the reasons I have stated, I urge that we leave these questions to the people in Parliament."

Anita Baca, the graduate student, gains recognition. "As the youngest member of this group, I should probably be silent, right? But, like, I must share how troubling I find the Minister's comments. He is insisting on a male constitutional jurisprudence, denying feminine values."

"How does gender enter here?" Father Gregorian asks.

"In modern jurisprudence, autonomy is a masculine concept," Baca explains. "It assumes that what separates us is morally and historically prior to

---

15. The excerpt is a letter that Rousseau wrote in 1757. It has seldom been included in collections of his writings but has recently been translated into English by Jean Starobinski and published as "Letter on Virtue, Individualism, and Society," *N.Y. Rev. of Bks.*, May 15, 2003, pp. 31-32. Among recent critiques of the concept of autonomy is John F. Kavanaugh, "The Ambiguities of Autonomy," *America*, Dec. 5, 1998, pp. 22ff.

what connects us.[16] Even though writers who follow Hobbes and Locke did not use 'the state of nature' as an historical account, the idea that the natural human state is to live alone has had widespread, if unthinking, acceptance."

"Get to the point," Strega interrupts.

The chair taps his gavel against the rostrum. "Order! Please continue, Ms Baca."

"I'll try to be brief, right? I have, like, three concerns to share with you. First, males want to have sex with as many women as possible, which means they compete with each other. Some of them are bigger, stronger, and more willing to kill than others. So males grow up in an often violently competitive psychological atmosphere. They feel threatened by other males and fear being denied access to women, dominated, or even annihilated. Hobbes's state of nature totally maps the typical male psyche. Fearing violent death, they try to create a hierarchy to control others; when they can't, they seek a secure niche in an existing hierarchy as protection against other predatory males. Modern males, unable to create new hierarchies and unsure of traditional hierarchies, try to create a governmentally enforced 'rights culture' to protect themselves. The basic right of that culture is autonomy; but it's *the* basic right only for males. More than half of humans are women; we don't, you know, share all of men's fears and values. Instead, being biologically and psychologically more connected to life and nurturing, we see harmonious communal life as the chief civic goal. Often intuitively rather than intellectually, we sense our 'connectedness,' we value rather than dread intimacy. We know that what males call autonomy is really a denial of community, a denial of obligations to mates, children, and neighbors, a denial of connectedness, the relationship that for women is 'prior.' What males call 'rights protection' often does not apply to us—indeed, is often aimed at us—and does not guard either our physical or our psychological integrity."

"I'm not sure I understand," the chair confesses.

Baca smiles. "Because you're not a cultural feminist. As Robin West says: 'Women's concept of value revolves not around the axis of autonomy, individuality, justice and rights, as does men's, but instead around the axis of intimacy, nurturing, community, responsibility and care. For women, the creation of value, and the living of a good life, therefore depend upon relational, contextual, nurturing and affective responses to the needs of those who are dependent and weak, while for men the creation of value, and the living of the good life, depend on the ability to respect the rights the rights of independent co-equals, and the deductive, cognitive ability to infer from those rights rules for safe living.' "[17]

16. Michael Sandel, *Liberalism and the Limits of Justice* (New York: Cambridge University Press, 1982), p. 133.

17. "Toward a Feminist Jurisprudence," 55 *U. Chi. L. Rev.* 1, 28 (1988). West continues this

"To use a metaphor that should appeal to Ms Baca," Strega says, "she's in the right church but the wrong pew. Cultural feminism is watered-down feminism. It overlooks three facts. First, women may naturally be more caring and sensitive than men, but we're just as tough, just as smart, and, if we want, just as competitive and aggressive as men. We shouldn't hide behind 'culture'; we should assert our claims."

"You're so yesterday!" Baca breaks in.

"No, I'm today!"

The chair taps his gavel on the dais. "Ladies!"

"*Women* is the operative word!" Strega snaps. "My second point is that the way you and others here use the concept of rights is misleading. People do not have rights because they are human beings. No norms flows from the fact that we're animals who have language and opposable thumbs. Rights are social constructs, one person's claims that some governmental authority will enforce against other persons. Society creates them or not, modifies them or not, and abolishes them or not. Those 'rights' are not transferable from one society to another. They owe their existence to physical power. What you simple-mindedly believe are 'human rights' depend on the capacity and willingness of the state to enforce particular claims. And there's a good reason: real 'rights' exist for the good of society, at least for the good of those who control society and its government."

"That's fascism!" Baca hisses.

"Fascism? No, good American constitutional law! You ultraliberals stupidly worship that American jurist Oliver Wendell Holmes, but he once wrote that 'a right is only the hypostasis of a prophecy—the imagination of a substance supporting the fact that the public force will be brought to bear upon those who do things to contravene it. . . . The most fundamental of the supposed preexisting rights—the right to life—is sacrificed without a scruple not only in war, but when ever the interests of society, that is, of the predominant power on the community, is thought to demand it.'"[18]

"You don't believe that women have rights?" Baca asks. "You'd betray your own gender?"

"No. And the correct word is *sex,* not *gender.* Nouns have gender, people have sex."

"Not all the time," the chair muses. Several men smile, and Father Gregorian nods approvingly.

"See what I mean?" Strega asks. "Women have to put up with this sort of crap because the state doesn't recognize our having equal 'rights' and, even

argument in *Re-imagining Justice: Progressive Interpretations of Formal Equality, Rights, and the Rule of Law* (Burlington, VT: Ashgate, 2003).

18. "Natural Law," 32 *Harv. L. Rev.* 40 (1918); reprinted in Richard A. Posner, ed., *The Essential Holmes: Selections from the Letters, Speeches, Judicial Opinions, and Other Writings of Oliver Wendell Holmes Jr.* (Chicago: University of Chicago Press, 1992), p. 180; the quotation is from p. 182.

when it does, won't enforce them. Therefore we have no rights. We have only claims the state won't enforce. Men have 'rights.'"

"And so you come around in a circle? We have no rights—no right not to be raped, no right to equal opportunities for education, employment, or promotion—because the state won't enforce our claims. That's so male chauvinist!" Baca protests.

"You miss the point. What I mean is that women are as smart as men and at least as tough. We have to fight to force the state—now run by men—to enforce *our* claims, to turn them into legal, meaningful rights. We need power, not moral arguments about gauzy rights."

"I agree we need power, but power based on firm moral claims," Baca answers.

"I wouldn't expect anything more intelligent from you," Strega continues. "The third fact: What men call a right to 'autonomy' really means the freedom of males to oppress women, to use them as sexual objects and turn them into drudges to do the hard, dull, and dirty work of breed cows to perpetuate the race while males live 'autonomous' lives. 'Autonomy' is like 'dignity,' a hypocritical deception to mask exploitation. Nobody deserves any more dignity or autonomy than she is willing to fight for, tooth and claw."[19]

"Well," Mufti Ajami notes, "male efforts at domination certainly haven't succeeded with our beloved minister, peace be upon her."

"For once you got something right," Strega snaps.

There are a few moments of awkward silence, then the chair intervenes: "I believe Ms Baca said she had three points."

"Yes, but first, I want to stress that I think that all humans have rights. We are children of God, and because we share in Her divine nature we are to some degree sacred."

"We've already heard that line from your clerical masters," Strega says.

Once again the chair raps his gavel. "Please!"

Baca waves her hand. "The second concern I wanted to share with you also involves community, but in a different way. As I said, the whole notion of individual autonomy—male autonomy—presumes that separation is the 'normal' state. But what are the data? When or where have individuals ever, like, lived alone? Human beings are 'social animals,' 'political animals,' as Aristotle said. None of us can be autonomous; even Robinson Crusoe had his man Friday. We live together, we interact constantly, we relate constantly. Every culture has its rituals to celebrate together as a community: birth, puberty, marriage, and even death. We are essentially connected, in life as well as in death. However men and women differ in psychology, women are

19. For a discussion of "radical feminism," see West, "Toward a Feminist Jurisprudence," esp. pp. 29ff.

empirically correct. We, men as well as women, form communities, right? Autonomy is basically a male concept."

"I wonder," the chair intervenes. "I've long been an admirer of Homer. but in *The Iliad*, even Achilles, who is surely a savage brute, is not autonomous. When he sulks in his tent at Agamemnon's mistreatment and threatens to go home—to a home, incidentally, where his father will choose Achilles' bride—we know it won't happen. Achilles is a great warrior, 'the most violent of men,' a prince in his own right and chief of a band of pirates; but he is bound to his fellow Greeks, He sulks because of Agamemnon's affront to his dignity, but he cannot abandon his comrades. He gives instructions to be called if the Trojans break through to the ships. And when Hector kills Patroklos, Achilles feels morally bound to avenge his dear friend. Moreover, Julian Jaynes—I do not pretend to be a literary scholar, only a lover of Homer—points out that at almost every crucial point in the *Iliad*, a god intervenes and takes over. These mortals are not self-determining beings. Even the gods are not autonomous. One god sometimes needs another god's help, and on occasion they work against each other as patrons of Paris, Achilles, or Hector. Furthermore, Zeus, though hardly omniscient or omnipotent, can almost always exercise some limited control over the other gods."[20]

"I don't understand your point," Strega says, "and I'm no defender of this phony concept of autonomy, but in *The Odyssey*, Odysseus is much more like the free-choosing modern male."

"True," the colonel replies, "but still the gods are at work. Even he, the wily Odysseus, sneaky, pillaging 'sacker of cities' that he is, is far from autonomous."

"I grant all that. But what are you getting at?" Strega asks.

"I was only musing out loud about Ms Baca's claim and, I guess, yours."

"I asked Baca what she was getting at, not you."

"My point is, dignity does not mean separation," Baca responds. "If it did, then no one could have dignity, for we must live together. If we stress autonomy and separateness over connectedness, we weaken the sense of community that unites us. We 'privatize' what should be a public virtue, publicly shared: a commitment to each other and to the common good."

"Your point, *please*?" Strega asks.

"To urge that we, like, consider as our basic value not individual dignity that includes the stale, standard version of autonomy, but equal dignity and 'connected' individualism within a harmonious human community. Thoughtlessly, we're about to hallow the atomistic individualism, what Harvey Mansfield Jr. calls a disease.[21] If we do, by implication we'll be approving

20. *The Origin of Consciousness and the Breakdown of the Bicameral Mind* (Boston: Houghton Mifflin, 1976).

21. *America's Constitutional Soul* (Baltimore: Johns Hopkins University Press, 1991), p. 209.

the continued subjugation of women. We must become a community of individuals with different tastes and lifestyles, but individuals within a community nevertheless, right?"

"May I ask," Father Gregorian intervenes, "what sort of community Ms Baca is talking about. I suspect that she, as a Catholic, has a deeper sense of community than Minister Strega."

"What are we," Strega asks, "pious pupils in a parochial school talking claptrap about how God made us and loves us so we must love another and be part of the communion of saints, struggling on earth, suffering in purgatory, and triumphant in heaven? This caucus is trying to build a political system that will survive in a real and ugly world, not please holy nuns. Life *is* a struggle. Hobbes was right, right for the seventeenth century, right for the twenty-first. Some specific rules have changed but not the fact of constant struggle for power, now by women as well as men. We women want autonomy, too; males want it only for themselves, not for us. If this caucus truly wants a community, we need a strong political system to create it and maintain it—maintain it by harnessing aggression and insecurity and channeling them, not by denying them or trying to bottle them up. Peace is not something that comes by itself. Neither is prosperity."

"There are worse things," Ajami says, "than acknowledging we are all Allah's children, sharing a heritage left by those who have died and that we must pass on to those who come after."

"I suggest," Pilsudski says, "that Ms Baca and I are not very far apart. I even hear a hint of agreement in Minister Strega's gentle comments. If the proposition is that not only Nusquam's authoritarian political system but also the political systems of most so-called democratic nations have denied women full equality—if that is the proposition, I concur. I admit, too, that in most other countries autonomy has meant male autonomy. Still, granting all that, I think we can create a political system that is not hypocritical, that does recognize both diversity and community and the full legal and moral equality of men and women."

"But I want more," Baca answers. "I want us to, you know, explicitly acknowledge our connectedness, not our separateness."

"So do I," Pyknites says, "but the role of this caucus is limited. First we got off on a sectarian debate between the religious and the irreligious; now we're debating various versions of feminism. I suspect that this debate is also about religion."

"I leave it to the ladies," Gregorian says, "to instruct us about feminism, but we should recall that Minister Strega introduced the term 'communion of saints,' not Ms Baca, or the Mufti, or I."

"Yet Ms Minister's description is not inaccurate," Pyknites continues. "Ms Baca's feminism does have a very Catholic resonance. We can't *impose* such a system on a religiously divided nation. I share Ms Baca's and Minister Pilsudski's desire for a system that respects individual diversity within a shared sense of community. That's precisely what a democratic political culture should do. Our best hope for such a system is to set a representative democracy into motion."

"We'd just change political institutions, perpetuate the old social system, and so sabotage the new constitutional order," Professor Jacobsohn counters.

"Colleagues," the chair intervenes, "we have strayed off course. We are discussing political systems rather than values. Perhaps we are all tired. It is 1800 hours. Ms Baca had three points, but we have allowed her to make only two. Before we adjourn, we should let her complete her presentation. Ms Baca?"

"Thank you. My third point follows from the second. Some of you asked what kind of community I had in mind, right? Minister Strega was partially correct: as a Catholic, I do think all of us—even Minister Strega—are members of the communion of saints."

"Oh, Christ," Strega mutters.

"Him, too," Baca says smilingly, then waits for the laughter to die down. "I agree that in a country as religiously divided as ours, we should explicitly or implicitly endorse theological concepts. I mention my beliefs only so you'll know where I'm coming from, right?"

"Mr. Chairman," Strega asks, "could you direct our graduate student to stop asking us if she's right? The answer is 'hardly ever.' And please also ask her to make her point during our lifetime."

"Please go on, Ms Baca," the chair says.

"I apologize," Baca replies. "Now that I look carefully at Minister Strega, I see that I must hurry." After another pause to allow the chuckles to die down, Baca continues: "Let me talk, then, about the community I envision. The nation-state is almost dead, morally if not legally, right? As Václav Havel has pointed out, soon everything that affects one people will affect every people. 'In such a world,' Havel says, 'the idol of state sovereignty must inevitably dissolve.'"[22]

"You want us to vote to dissolve Nusquam?" the chair asks.

"No, not yet. We are talking as if the nation-state were itself a critically important value in and of itself. On the contrary, many European writers, such as Jürgen Habermas, have been speaking for some years about the 'development of postnational society.'[23] We should look on the nation-state

---

22. "Kosovo and the End of the Nation-State," speech given to a joint session of the Canadian Parliament, Apr. 29, 1999; reprinted in *N.Y. Rev. of Bks.*, June 10, 1999, pp. 4–6. The quotation is from p. 4.

23. "Citizenship and National Identity: Some Reflections on the Future of Europe," in Ronald Beiner, ed., *Theorizing Citizenship* (Albany: State University of New York Press, 1995), p. 256.

as terminally ill and search for alternative arrangements. For example, we could say that we look forward to the day when Nusquam surrenders its 'sovereignty' to the United Nations."[24]

Baca sits down to crushing silence. "Even I am struck dumb," Strega comments.

After several awkward moments, the chair says, "Let us recess until tomorrow at 0930. The bar will be open until 2300—that's eleven p.m."

At the next morning's session, the chair first recognizes Demos Pyknites.

"We're no closer to agreement than when we began. Terms like *justice* and *human dignity* sound wonderful; but without clear definitions they are vapid slogans. I heard no clear definitions that more than two or three people could agree on, and introducing sub- or coordinate concepts like 'autonomy' further divides us. I like my values and you like yours. I can't prove that my values are better than yours or even that my values defined my way are better than if they were defined your way. Our values and the definitions we give them are choices, prerational, perhaps even extrarational. There is only one truth: there is no ultimate truth. Religion, itself a cultural artifact, further complicates matters. No person can stand outside of a system of belief rooted in faith in a divine being and fully understand, much less rebut, other systems of belief.[25] There is no objective scale of values against which we can measure values, norms, likes, and dislikes. Therefore we should end this discussion, propose an electoral law for a parliament, and let the national community, if there be one, identify and define the values it, from time to time, wants to endorse."

Zingaro speaks out. "Yesterday Father Gregorian quoted Euripides; let me do so today:

If wisdom and truth were the same for all,
men would not fight one another.
But 'justice,' 'equal rights'—these are mere words,
names, that have no palpable meaning."[26]

"It's good to be in such famous company, especially Greek company," Pyknites says. "At graduate school at Yale, I studied under proponents of a 'procedural republic.' Robert A. Dahl reminded us that within a given culture, procedures are pregnant with moral significance. '[G]iven certain assumptions, the democratic process itself is a form of justice: It is a just

24. The preamble to Germany's Basic Law lists among its objectives serving "the peace of the world as an equal partner in a united Europe."

25. See the debate between Stanley Fish, "Why We Can't All Just Get Along," *First Things*, Feb. 1996, p. 18, and Richard John Neuhaus, "Why We Can Get Along," in the same issue, p. 27.

26. *The Phoenician Women*, lines 535–38, trans. Richard Elman, in Slavitt and Bovie, eds., *Euripides* (Philadelphia: University of Pennsylvania Press, 1998), 3:164.

procedure for arriving at collective decisions.'[27] That's as close to justice, to protecting human dignity, as fallible men and women are apt to get."

Several members continue to seek recognition, but the Jesuit speaks even before the chair formally recognizes him. "Mr. Pyknites has contradicted himself. The claim that there are no absolutes is itself an absolute claim. To assert that all truth is relative is to assert a truth that is not relative. To assert that no other truth is absolute is an additional absolute. Further, he absolutely claims that the rest of us can know no other absolutes, a sweeping claim about others' intellectual incapacities. If he can know, we can know; if he can know some absolute truths and we can't, then he must also claim to know us absolutely. His assertion that no one can stand outside his religious beliefs is equally contradictory, for to claim validity for that statement he has to stand outside his own religiously nonreligious beliefs and analyze *and* understand other systems of belief, precisely what he says humans can't do.[28] He is embracing intellectual nihilism, quite different from skepticism. We can understand skepticism. At times we all doubt our senses as well as our reason, even, God help us, our faith. To place the burden of proof on those who claim to 'know' something is not the same as to deny that we can know anything."

"Now that," Strega interrupts, "is pure Jesuitical reasoning. It is Thomistic, eminently Catholic. And because it is sectarian, it can only fracture our people."

"Thomas," Gregorian answers, "was a Dominican, not a Jesuit, and his philosophy is not sectarian. He borrowed it from Aristotle, and it is reflected by modern philosophers such as Thomas Nagel[29] who have no connection to Catholicism. Indeed, Nagel avows that he is a nonbeliever."

Pyknites responds: "I do not contradict myself. You believe 'truth' is 'out there' waiting to be defined or found. My view is more like that of John Dewey and Oliver Wendell Holmes. Truth does not lie 'out there.' As 'all life is an experiment,' so, too, our search for truth and justice is experimental. 'Certainty generally is an illusion,' Holmes said.[30] Our best hope is to follow procedures that most efficiently help us discard useless ideas and refine useful ones. That quest never ends; therefore, we should focus on procedures in science, on processes in politics, that is, on open processes of discussion and debate, on free choice. Discussion and debate do not, however, end when we make a choice. That choice must always remain open to reexamination in the

---

27. Robert A. Dahl, *Democracy and Its Critics* (New Haven, CT: Yale University Press, 1989), p. 164.

28. See Neuhaus, "Why We Can Get Along," p. 29.

29. *The Last Word* (New York: Oxford University Press, 1998).

30. "The Path of the Law," 10 *Harv. L. Rev.* 457, 466 (1897). "I detest a man," he wrote to Harold Laski thirty-three years later, "who knows that he knows." In *The Holmes-Laski Letters,* ed. Mark DeWolfe Howe (Cambridge, MA: Harvard University Press, 1953), 2:1291.

light of new evidence or new arguments. That quest is what representative democracy is all about."[31]

"Are you claiming," the chair asks, "that truth and justice are foolish illusions?"

"I'm talking about the status of our *beliefs* about truth and justice. Often what we *think* are truth and justice are merely illusions, and sometimes dangerous ones. We can have ideals, but they will be what Justice Holmes called 'can't helps,' not propositions we can prove in any final way. Our most reasonable hope lies in constructing processes that allow free discussion so that the ideals we affirm will, in fact, be those that our society accepts. To quote Holmes again: 'The best test of truth is the power of that thought to get itself accepted in the market [of ideas].'[32] I'd say the same thing about concepts like justice or any other political ideal."

The colonel frowns; but before he can speak, Pastor Glückmann intervenes: "Two points: First, you do contradict yourself. You are defining truth and justice as products of popular consensus, regardless whether there is a popular consensus about the legitimating power of popular consensus. Thus you claim to define truth, albeit indirectly. Second, my Jesuit colleague is not being sectarian, at least in a religious sense. His reasoning does not contradict itself, and that quality is essential. If, however, Mr. Pyknites is saying we should come down from the level of philosophic abstractions, a level to which he himself has lifted us, I agree. So I ask a mundane question: Do you really think that all values are relative? Do you believe the values of a rapist or a murderer are no better than those of his victims?"

"There are no 'true' values, no 'human' rights," Strega interrupts, "only what a group can persuade the state to enforce."

"I thank the noble minister," Glückman says, "but I asked the question of Mr, Pyknites."

"*I* don't believe all values are equal," Pyknites responds. "I think it was Joseph Schumpeter who said that 'to realize the relative validity of one's convictions and yet stand for them unflinchingly, is what distinguishes a civilized man from a barbarian.' Throughout my life, I have stood for my convictions as best I could. But I understand that *my* conviction that a proposition is just or true is not proof that it is just or true. Justice and truth are not like mass and velocity, existing independently of human perception. They are social constructs. Societies, even individuals, create these concepts and give them meanings, and those meanings change from society to society and over time within a single society. We can't intellectually persuade rapists

31. For a discussion of this sort of approach to problems of knowledge in science and jurisprudence, see Lous Menand, *The Metaphysical Club: A Story of Ideas in America* (New York: Farrar, Straus and Giroux. 2002), esp. ch. 15.

32. Abrams v. United States, 250 U.S. 616, dis. op., 630 (1919).

or murderers that they are wrong. We can offer our reasons, and if we convince our society that we are right, we can severely punish rapists and murders. We have the moral authority to do so because these people have violated our community's values, not because there is a universal law against rape and murder. Like values, 'morality is local.'[33] In some communities, acts we view as horrendous have been hailed as laudable. In the American West, the Comanches saw torture of prisoners as manly and rape of captured women as a brave's fundamental right. In sixteenth-century Europe, Catholic and Protestant clergy both thought it their duty to burn, disembowel, or behead people whom they knew an all-loving God hated. Those acts don't reflect our values; but using reason alone, we could not have persuaded a Comanche in 1850 that it was better to love one's enemy than to roast him slowly on a spit while savoring his screams of agony. Nor could we have persuaded Catholic and Protestant inquisitors during the sixteenth century. These people grew up in cultures that revered as virtuous acts that we deem monstrous. They were behaving morally, as they understood morality."

"Your case is even stronger," Strega interrupts, "if you cite *The Iliad.*"

"What about *The Iliad*?"

"You don't understand Homer's plot. Achilles is furious at Agamemnon because he's taken as his kingly prize Briseis, Achilles' concubine whom he kidnapped from a village he plundered. No one among the Greeks or Trojans thought it was wrong for Achilles to kidnap Briseis and bed her. Homer didn't think it was worth noting whether or not she consented; her consent was irrelevant. On the other hand, most of the Greeks agreed that it was wrong for Agamemnon to steal her from Achilles: she was his property."

Strega pauses. "I am supporting your case, Mr. Pyknites, so I quote Oliver Wendell Homes: 'Men to a great extent believe what they want to—although I see in that no basis for a philosophy that tells us what we should want to want.' What our pious colleagues call morality is nothing more than ideas they grew up with. They think that because those ideas are theirs, those ideas are correct and bind the rest of us."

"I take it, then, Mr. Pyknites," the pastor says, ignoring Minister Strega, "that you had no justification to oppose the junta other than that they displeased you for reasons that other decent, intelligent men and women need not have shared. If all values were relative, there would have been no way you could have persuaded us that it was *wrong* for one group of people to do to others what inquisitors did to heretics, Comanches did to prisoners, or the junta to us. Your only logically consistent appeal must have been that it is less painful to hurt than to be hurt. It is better to be an inquisitor, a Comanche, or a member of a junta than one of their victims."

33. Posner, "Problematics of Moral and Legal Theory," p. 1640.

"You twist my argument," Pyknites replies. "My point was both more subtle and more far ranging: the terms *justice, fairness,* and *decency* have no meaning outside of a specific culture."

"Not subtle at all," Ibrahim Ajami interjects. "Claiming all values are relative attacks morality with a sledgehammer. Why did 'correct' processes not stop the junta's savagery?"

"Because," Pyknites replies, "the open processes I advocate were not followed. The junta, with my good uncle's cooperation, used brute force, not reason."

Strega looks around and smiles. "Give it up, Demos. You'll never convince these people. We're surrounded by hostile clerics. Thank God we don't have a rabbi here."

"Just a moment, please," Minxin Wei interrupts. "I am a mere banker and what Christian missionaries called a pagan; but it seems to me that the dispute is not theological. Heathen that I am, I want equal human dignity to be the central value of any political system in which I live."

"I'm glad that our lines of division cut across religious groupings—a healthy sign for a society that wants to become democratic," Pyknites answers. "I do not attack morality at all. I do not say that all values are idiosyncratic; I do not say that we cannot share many of them; I do not say a community may not punish someone who violates its beliefs about right and wrong. What I do say is that those beliefs aren't universal and they don't have to be universal. They are culturally based. Had you and I been mid-nineteenth-century Comanches or plantation owners in the American South, we would have had attitudes toward torture and slavery very different from our own. As for the junta, as much as I detested what they were doing, there was no way to rationally persuade them that their values were 'wrong'— a word I put in quotes. And, believe me, I tried with my uncle, who was a very intelligent man. What I did was to explain to our people that the junta's values and interests were not ours. I did not make universalistic claims, except as a rhetorical device."

Gregorian intervenes: "You are thus left with the proposition that what Comanches, plantation owners, and the junta did was morally legitimate as long as the community tolerated it."

"It is important that *we* didn't continue to tolerate what the junta was doing."

"And that was what made their actions wrong, that we stopped tolerating it?"

"By my personal scale of values, no. I opposed those people and went to jail for my actions. But, I repeat, we have no objective scale that registers our values as higher than theirs. Our triumph allows us to enforce values until the people throw us out."

"Forgive me," the chair says, "but I suspect my reactions mirror those of many of us inside as well as outside this villa. Mr. Pyknites's clarity and candor are both enormously enlightening and enormously troubling. As a Marine officer, I have believed that my duty to serve my country was absolute, although I may have also thought all other values were relative. I never tried to reconcile those two beliefs or even lifted them to the level of conscious scrutiny. Perhaps we all treat one or two of our own values as absolute and look on those that others endorse as relative. I'm not sure where that confession leaves me or, more importantly, us."

"In need of absolution," Gregorian mutters under his breath.

"The Chair," Pyknites says, "has put his finger on the problem. Our most cherished values are absolute. Each of us has what Holmes called 'a fighting faith.' But we also see other people's values as relative. And we cannot always persuade others by reason,[34] though we may occasionally 'convert' them through threats, bribery, or emotional appeals."

"If deliberations are senseless," the chair asks, "then why do you want open political processes? Why shouldn't we just enjoy a brief vacation and report back to my colleagues that they should stay in power until public opposition imposes costs they are not willing to bear?"

"Because we *know* the costs military dictatorship imposes. We need to quickly establish an efficient civilian government. Our situation is hardly hopeless. Discussing values attacks the wrong question. We should be discussing 'interests,' which ones we share and how best to protect them. All humans have a fundamental interest in their lives. And from that other interests flow, to autonomy for all adults, not merely males, to property to protect that autonomy, to peace and security, and so forth. We can try to construct processes that will offer the best chance of generating institutions that will protect every citizen's life, freedom, and property. We need not and should not appeal to amorphous concepts like human dignity, but to *interests,* hard and tangible."

"I want to hear more," Strega comments.

"Thomas Hobbes said it all four centuries ago," Gregorian hisses.

Pyknites smiles. "Every human being shares basic interests. Reluctantly, I'd even call them secular values if that's the sense of the caucus. It is, however, crucial that we set as the political system's initial goals the furthering of interests we share and also establish processes our society thinks fair to settle differences when our interests compete. Those goals would unite rather than divide us and provide a viable, practical basis on which a constitutional order could grow."

"I don't see how talking about interests solves anything," Jacobsohn says. "Human beings are not input-output machines for whom claims of interest

---

34. For an interesting argument about the restricted reach of reason not only among judges but also among intelligent human beings generally, see Martin Shapiro, "Can Judges Deliberate?" Third Annual Walter F. Murphy Lecture, James Madison Program, Princeton University, Apr. 29, 2003.

automatically produce moral or political judgments. We may well decide that what advances our personal economic or social interest will cause us to hate ourselves. Besides, there are many interests. Saying we share interests in life, autonomy, and property doesn't move us any further along than saying we share the value of equality. Interests usually compete and often clash. My right to property may conflict with your freedom. Young men who have been drafted into armies to risk their bodies in war might have a very strong preference that rich, older folk use their property to buy the enemy off. Accurate interpersonal comparisons of utilities are impossible.[35] If we can't compare one person's utility in her interest against another person's utility in his interest, we can't justify the choices we make for society. Saying we should protect some interests, without endorsing a set of values that underlie those interests, means the best hope to reduce conflict is to vote. The solution would be something like, My interest in property wins ten votes, your interest in life has five; therefore my interest in property trumps yours in life. I keep my property, and you go to war and lose your life."

"I addressed that issue," Pyknites replies. "First, we are united in an interest in peace and order and so in establishing and following procedures to settle nonviolently our disputes about interests that divide us. We can specify a rough hierarchy of interests, agree on those that unite us, and agree to differ, within bounds, about those that divide us. And we can, in a parliamentary democracy, debate those differences and, if not finally settle them, compromise them."

"But," Jacobsohn persists, "how can you weigh on any scale of justice money versus a young man's life or legs? If we can't specify a hierarchy of values, how can we judge the relative importance of interests that cut across the population? Your insistence on the relativity of all judgments must include decision makers' judgments about interests."

"Yes," Pyknites responds. "We cannot settle disputes about ultimate values, about issues of principle, by voting. On the other hand, if trade-offs are possible, we can settle some disputes about clashes of interests by voting. You ridiculed voting as a means to resolve conflict; but it is the safest way and more likely than any other to produce results that most of our people will think just—providing, of course, it is surrounded by free and open debate. If people later change their minds about a particular solution, they can change the policy and do so peacefully."

"Wait," Jon Kanuri, the black economist, breaks in. "If a majority thinks some people's skin color makes them inferior, that majority may satisfy its economic interests by enslaving these people? If the test of justice and moral-

35. This idea is usually attributed to Kenneth Arrow. See his *Social Choice and Individual Values* (New York: Wiley, 1951), and "Values and Collective Decision Making," in Peter Laslett and W. G. Runciman, eds., *Philosophy, Politics, and Society* (New York: Barnes and Noble, 1967).

ity were the number of votes, that enslavement would be both just and moral. And free speech wouldn't liberate the slaves; only violence could do that. 'Numbers make right' is not much less odious than 'might makes right.'"

"No!" Pyknites shouts. "I offer a full explanation tomorrow. Let me say now that if public choices were surrounded, *in our society,* by free and open debate and if citizens and representatives took their roles seriously, the morality of those choices, as our society understands morality, would be laid bare. The people and their representatives would be informed and their consciences seared."

"As in the American South before the Civil War?" Kanuri asks.

"There were no free elections and no open debates there. Slaves could neither speak nor assemble in public, except in work gangs, and they certainly could not vote. Whites who spoke against slavery were often tarred and feathered and sometimes lynched—and not only in the South. Elijah Lovejoy, the abolitionist editor, was murdered by a mob in Illinois, not Mississippi. The U.S. Post Office wouldn't even deliver abolitionist literature."[36]

"Our job, I remind you," Strega says, "is to design a system of governance, not morality."

"And as our chair has also reminded us," Father Gregorian replies, "we can't separate morality and politics. Almost everything government does and much that it doesn't do touches on moral issues. That's why Hobbes—as relentless an exponent of utilitarian ethics as ever lived—claimed that a true sovereign had to be chief of religion as well as head of state. To construct a constitutional order is to construct a moral order. We need a dual order that will gain the allegiance of our different religions without alienating the nonreligious. Hobbes and Rousseau talked about a civil religion,[37] and in a sense—not quite theirs, I hope—we must search out intellectually defensible moral beliefs to undergird our constitutional order. Saying we favor the interests of those who can command a majority of the votes provides no moral basis at all."

"I don't know whether to be comforted or terrified," Kanuri says with a loud sigh.

"Neither do I," Strega puts in. "I suggest that our humble Jesuit read *The Federalist.* Those articles flogged the American constitutional text of 1787 as a framework to resolve conflicts among interests. Publius didn't talk about the moral basis of the new constitutional order or its capacity to reform public or private morals. He lauded the new text's fit with the history and needs of the

36. The story is beautifully detailed in Michael Kent Curtis, *Free Speech, the People's Darling Privilege: Struggles for Freedom of Expression in American History* (Durham, NC: Duke University Press, 2000), chs. 5–13.

37. Thomas Hobbes, *Leviathan,* ch. 18 and pt. 2 generally, esp. chs. 39–42. Jean-Jacques Rousseau, *The Social Contract,* bk. 4, ch. 8.

American people and its practical promises of producing peace, security, and prosperity for a commercial republic. That system seems to have survived."

"The price of ignoring morality was the horror of slavery for another seventy-five years, not to mention a civil war," Kanuri says. "That shows one serious problem with focusing on interests to the exclusion of values—interests not adequately represented lose, and they may lose terribly."

Strega cuts in: "Losing is always a risk. Listen to what Adam Przeworski says: '[U]nder a democracy no one can be certain that their interests will ultimately triumph.'[38] If you haven't got the courage to take political risks, move to a South Pacific island, wear a grass skirt, eat coconuts, and live by yourself." She waves her hand dismissively, then continues: "Mr. Pyknites and I are cast in the role of being against morality. That's the punishment hypocrites always heap on the honest. Mustering all my diplomatic skills, I shall try to explain the truth of the matter."

"How can a relativist speak about 'the truth of the matter?'" Gregorian asks.

Strega continues. "That I lack faith in a divine being who gives a damn about humanity doesn't mean I'm immoral. We are framers of a political system, not evangelists. We work within our society's standards. We're realists, not rosy-cheeked seminarians who think that if only we mouth pious words, Jesus, Allah, Buddha, or the Great Ju-Ju will save our country. When there's a scramble for power—and just as the junta's collapse marked the end of one scramble for power, it also marked the beginning of another—all that matters is force, not ideals. Only when we act on that harsh fact can we hope to mold a tolerable political system. We're not creating a Brave New World. 'All a statesman should hope for is that his policy will not diminish human happiness.'"[39]

"Let me try," Pilsudski offers, "to reconcile two arguments that, however distant philosophically, are really rather close practically. I think we all accept certain basic *political* values; it is in our *interest* and the nation's *interest* that we do so. We agree that the state, society, and each of us should treat all human beings as equally deserving of respect. But some of us fear that such a statement will embroil the nation in sectarian debates about what that concept means. Others fear that stressing only interests will leave the new political system devoid of a moral basis, unable to judge good from bad except as choices that affect selfish interests. There is much to be said for both sides. I agree that we can't act like starry-eyed idealists. Still, we must take values, others' as well as our own, into account. Mr. Pyknites's remarks about open

38. "Democracy as Contingent Outcome of Conflicts," in Jon Elster and Rune Slagstad, eds., *Constitutionalism and Democracy* (New York: Cambridge University Press, 1988), p. 62.
39. Noel Annan, "The Death of the Cold War," *N.Y. Rev. of Bks.*, Nov. 19, 1998, p. 17.

debate plead for a system that will strengthen a public conscience and create a civic culture in which duties and rights are 'correlative, mutualist,'[40] rather than antagonistic."

Pyknites shakes his head; Strega stares up at the ceiling.

Pilsudski continues: "During our week of contemplation, I read a lot about the necessity of 'government by consent.' I read those arguments as more than appeals to power and interests. I understood them as moral appeals. Today, the belief is widespread that the people have a *right* to self-government. If we accept an argument for a political system based solely on power, we must accept as legitimate a popular constitutional order that is equally ruthless as the junta's. But acceptance of people's *right* to self-government assumes people have some special quality. That quality must be their nature as human beings, not their numbers, not their access to instruments of violence, and most assuredly not their individual or collective wisdom. What we then are talking about is expressed by the term *human dignity* as well as by any other. But let us use Mr. Pyknites's word and call protection of human dignity a 'goal' rather than a value."

"Let me switch roles," Gregorian intervenes, "and reinforce your moral argument with a prudential concern. I quote the text Ms Strega suggested I read. In the fortieth *Federalist*, James Madison wrote that a constitution is of 'no more consequence than the paper on which it is written unless it be stamped with the approbation of those to whom it is addressed.'"

"At last an intelligent remark from our holy father," Strega says. "But I'd prefer we do good rather than talk about good. Does our minister of justice have anything specific to suggest?"

Pilsudski quickly answers: "Yes, he does. As a starting point for discussion, I offer the following set of goals for our new political system:

1. Maximize the chances of the nation's existing in peace and honor with its neighbors;
2. Provide political stability so that citizens can enjoy domestic tranquillity;
3. Recognize and protect the great and equal dignity of each citizen;
4. Prevent public officials from oppressing any citizen or group of citizens in exercising rights to life and ordered liberty, while also protecting citizens against rapacious neighbors;
5. Foster a civic culture that recognizes that citizens have both rights and duties; and
6. Promote an economic environment in which citizens can meet the material needs of themselves and their families.

40. Lawrence W. Beer, "Human Rights and 'Freedom Culture' in Eastern Asia," in A. Anghie and G. Sturgess, eds., *Legal Visions of the 21st Century* (The Hague: Kluwer, 1998), p. 159.

On these goals, we can construct a viable political system and justify to ourselves and other preferring some interests over others."

Before either Pyknites or Strega can reply, Pastor Glückmann intervenes: "The minister has put the matter very well in secular terms. But there is a prior and higher ground for human dignity. We are all, as the Mufti Ajami has reminded us, children of God. We owe each other love and respect because we are made in the image and likeness of God. We must recognize in all our brothers and sisters—not only in our fellow citizens— that same divine spark we ourselves have. Without that recognition, we cannot hope to construct a just political or social order."

"Hear, hear!" Gregorian and Ajami shout out.

"Minister Pilsudski had almost convinced me," Pyknites says, "but then the choir chanted. I keep repeating that our task is to further a truly civic culture, a secular culture, not to divide the nation by sectarian rhetoric."

"I'm not sure I was ever saved," Strega adds, "but I'm sure that now I am lost. We can't legislate for all human beings. Our ethnic divisions make it difficult enough to talk about 'fellow citizens.' If we were even to imply that we would recognize the equality of every beggar in Africa and Asia, we'd anger a lot of our fellow citizens. Then, if that debate quieted, we'd be back to the question of who among us is a human being and raise issues of abortion and euthanasia, which would tear us apart."

"I disagree," Pastor Glückmann responds. "We *can* put those important but divisive issues aside. All we need do for now is to outline a just political order."

"A 'just political order'? Absurd! The most we can hope for is a system that guarantees public peace and is markedly less oppressive than the last. The term *civic culture* is silly; still, if it helps, I'll accept it. But whatever rhetoric we spread to grease popular approval, we should keep firmly in mind that there was no Eden, there is no Eden, and there will be no Eden."

At that point the chair intervenes. "It seems to me that Minister Pilsudski has found a workable compromise. His aims are expressed in secular terms, which should gratify those who fear religious divisions as well as those who fear a normless state. At any rate, the language is understandable to any intelligent person regardless of religious belief or lack of belief. Believers can support this sort of statement in the hope that it will lead to a broader concept, and nonreligious can accept it because it does not foreclose the moral issue. I suggest that we vote on the Minister's proposal. He has written it down; the clerk will scan it and send it to you so we can be clear on the issue before us. Is there a second?"

Jacobsohn raises her hand, while Strega tries to gain recognition. The chair looks past her and nods at Jacobsohn. "I second the motion," she says. "And because we are voting only on guidelines, I see no reason to worry about exact phrasing at this time. It is important, as Mr. Pyknites reminds us, to move on. So let us vote the proposal up or down. If it loses, we can consider refining the language or even substituting new goals."

There is some grumbling from members who want to settle on specific language before a vote; but when the hands are counted, the supporters win 18–6.

"Let us now," the chair says, "use these goals as benchmarks against which to measure alternative systems. The time is now 1252. I was going to propose that we take a sixty-eight-minute recess for lunch, but our first speaker suggests that we recess until 1600—sorry, four p.m.—to allow members not only to eat but also to siesta. He says that the only thing worse than having to listen to a lecture immediately after lunch is to give a lecture then. . . . So ordered."

To serve as a general adviser, the caucus has invited Retlaw Deukalion, a retired member of the faculty of Princeton University. Although he is well beyond his intellectual prime, he had written extensively about problems of establishing a new constitutional order and helped educate a stable of brilliant scholars. Promptly at four p.m., the chair introduces Deukalion. He walks to the dais, adjusts his glasses, and begins.

Unlike the members of this body, I operate not by reason of my competence but by force of my commission,[41] which instructs me to offer academic knowledge about creating a new constitutional order. I can tell you little of importance that you do not already know, but I may be able to help you look at your own experiences from a different perspective. If I can accomplish that much, I shall have fulfilled my mandate. With that apologia, I begin.

In the beginning, Genesis says, chaos reigned: "the earth was without form and void, with darkness over the face of the abyss, and a mighty wind that swept over the face of the waters." Operating at a macrolevel, the Deity needed only six days to sculpt from that turmoil a planet for human habitation. But Yahweh was not into micromanagement. A million millennia later, we mortals are still trying to cope with residual chaos and impose order on our world, to calm the mighty wind of passion that constantly threatens to sweep us away.

The chaos with which nature menaces us is real enough: floods, earthquakes, tidal waves, droughts, and epidemics pose frequent danger. Nevertheless, the menaces posed by human beings are more perilous. The most obvious way to prevent injury from other humans is for people

---

41. Here Deukalion is, of course, paraphrasing Justice Robert H. Jackson's response, famous to Americans but probably unknown to most citizens of Nusquam, to Justice Felix Frankfurter's protest that judges were not competent to deal with complex educational issues involving patriotism and religion. West Virginia v. Barnette (the Second Flag Salute Case), 319 U.S. 624 (1943).

to band together into units that we would call political, to exchange some freedom for greater security against predators, aid in times of natural disaster, and benefits that come from cooperative action. The "dark side," as Obi-Won Kenobi would say, of this exchange is that political officials are as vulnerable to temptation as are the rest of humanity. Thus we both need government and fear government. However various peoples have tried to cope with this dilemma, in the opening years of the twenty-first century, almost all of us live in organizations called nation-states. Their collective history has left a trail of bloody suffering; but until we devise a better organization to control human passions, the nation-state remains necessary, even if only a lesser evil. As the paper you read on constitutionalism and democracy pointed out, founders have three objectives that are difficult to reconcile: to hold up a people's ideals as goals, to empower government, and to limit government. Now, of course, the need for government to keep one part of society from invading the rights of another, as Madison put it in *The Federalist* No. 10, has become far more complicated, as have the ways in which one part of society can invade the rights of another. In a parallel fashion, modern industrial societies have also made the positive goals of government more necessary as well as more complicated. Securing the public welfare now means much more than protecting society from foreign invaders or killers, rapists, and burglars.

Effective leadership of a revolution means transformative leadership, changing a people, not merely their institutions but also their souls. You want to change your people, not as Adolf Hitler did, to become brutes, but to become more truly human, concerned for others besides themselves. I encourage you, however, not to construct a political system that depends on heroic leadership. That virtue is too rare. As Madison noted: "Enlightened statesmen will not always be at the helm."[42]

Let me make a few more preliminary points. First, your work involves at least four dimensions: idealism, practicality, partisanship, and civic understanding. You want to create the best political system, that is, a system that best protects your values—though I've heard that word causes some dissent among you—and the best must be possible. You are subject not only to the future's uncertainty but also to current economic, military, geographic, and social forces. Different groups of citizens retain different collective memories and will read your proposals differently. You must, therefore, be attentive to varied "inclinations, riches, numbers, commerce, manners, and customs."[43] William Graham Sumner

---

42. *The Federalist*, No. 10.
43. Montesquieu, *The Spirit of the Laws*, trans. Thomas Nugent (New York: Harper, 1949), bk. I, §3, p. 6.

was wrong when he said state ways cannot change folkways; but only violence can quickly create a new public "genius." Your people have endured enough violence.

I mentioned partisanship. Few, if any, of us can continuously act selflessly. You are not like John Rawls's "free and rational persons" operating behind a veil of ignorance. You know who you are and hope to become, where and when you live, and at least some of your general values and specific interests. You also know, if not fully understand, the ambitions you harbor for yourselves and your children. This awareness forms a third and possibly corrupting dimension to your work.

The fourth dimension I have called civic understanding, an understanding that agreement on the broad principles of constitutional democracy does not preclude serious disagreement about constitutional meaning as well as specific public policies. You have ended one era of politics only to enter a new one. Under the old regime, the locus of politics was within the junta's five members and their not always identical interests. Competition, friction, and division must have occurred. I read reports that the army believed that when it came to allocating money, the general president gave undue preference to the Special Forces. The political relationship between the junta and the people was essentially that of patron and peasants.

There was another political arena, that among the people themselves. By removing the junta, "the them," the Colonels removed much of the social glue that held the people together as an "us." Now that your common enemy is gone, ethnic divisions will fester. So, too, economic and social fissures will widen. Ranchers, unions, entrepreneurs, managers, bankers, white-collar workers, and fishers will support somewhat contradictory public policies; the medical professions will clash with governmental bureaucrats; the sick and the well will disagree about how heavily the government should subsidize health care; younger and senior citizens will dispute about how much public money should assist the elderly; the rich will oppose steep gradations in income taxes while the poor will support them; women will demand governmental help in securing full equality with men; gays and lesbians will insist on legal recognition of their equal legal and moral status with straight people, a claim that will cause many of the latter to feel their "family values" are being threatened. All these and more groups will want the political system to provide different goods and services that compete for scarce public resources.

Your revolution will consist in reinventing politics.[44] Much of that

---

44. For applications of this concept to Eastern Europe, see Vladimir Tismaneanu, *Reinventing Politics: Eastern Europe from Stalin to Havel* (New York: Free Press, 1992).

reinvention will involve creating processes that will strengthen the norms in which your people will need to believe if they are to change from oppressed subjects into functioning citizens. Those norms must include accepting as legitimate inevitable differences about public policies. You differ sharply among yourselves. You should expect equally sharp, if less reasoned, differences to fracture your citizen body. In Central and Eastern Europe, especially in the Czech and Slovak Republic, the leaders of the old opposition were unprepared for a new politics. They had courageously dissented against their oppressors. That, after the Berlin Wall fell, others would dissent against them, the righteous, not only was unexpected but seemed a betrayal. That attitude promised either an authoritarian democracy like that of the old Russian Sobornost or a series of painful conflicts followed by equally painful relearning.[45]

Among your more important jobs will be keeping disagreements civil, treating them, even when they aren't, as honest differences that must be respectfully addressed. If your citizens regard most of these differences as basically moral, your polity will collapse.[46] To be sure, some disagreements will involve moral issues, but most will reflect differences in outlook and interest. You must create a political culture, as well as institutions, that impel leaders of competing interests to work together in mutual acceptance of the legitimacy of the goals you have outlined and the processes you have created.

My second and closely related preliminary point is that experience with harsh authoritarian rule has made most of you rank personal security against government high among your goals. I do not criticize that judgment, but it raises serious practical issues. Preserving freedom *from* government is not enough. If such a system allows criminals to prey on law-abiding people, it is likely to be despised. One of Hitler's great appeals was a promise to restore order to German life. But as necessary as it is to keep public peace, government must do more. Our lives have become so entangled that energetic government is also essential, especially if human dignity is to be central to your political system. That value may require government to allow some citizens to adopt a lifestyle that

---

45. For a discussion of the Sobornost, see Victor Sergeyev and Nikolai Biryukov, *Russia's Road to Democracy: Parliament, Communism, and Traditional Culture* (Brookfield, VT: Elgar, 1993), esp. ch. 2.

46. One can see something of the "painful conflicts" in Pope John Paul II. Unity and solidarity within the Polish Church (and much of Polish society) against the communist government may have been necessary for survival. When he moved to Rome, he found a church divided among itself on many issues; unable to appreciate (or perhaps understand) the concept of a loyal opposition, he often struck out against those who dissented *within* the faith as if they were dissenting *against* the faith. His efforts to settle honest disagreements about such issues as birth control and the ordination of women by fiat and his appointing of bishops who mindlessly followed his directives but were untroubled by pedophiliac priests only exacerbated dissent.

leads them to starvation; but respect for human dignity also requires government to ensure that their children do not also starve. Compounding difficulties, many people will transfer their distrust of the junta to the new government. Few adults in Nusquam can remember a regime that did not oppress them. They may be loyal to their country, but patriotism does not automatically bond citizens to a particular constitutional order, even one that promises liberty. During the lifespan of the United States, France has endured two royal regimes, several emperors and dictators, five republics, and more than a dozen constitutional texts. Germany, Japan, Poland, and Russia have somewhat similar histories. Your new political system must earn its citizens' trust and devotion, not only because of what it does not do but also because of what it does do. Nations have reservoirs of "diffuse support" that keep them going through crises, but a regime must work to build up reserves to survive its crises. New governmental structures also need "specific support," the backing citizens offer in return for recent or immediately expected benefits.[47]

In sum, most of your people are likely to take an instrumental rather than a reverential view of the new constitutional order. They are apt to be ready to replace any particular institution or even an entire system they deem inefficient.[48] Thus I suggest that you give heavy weight to your regime's ability both to establish "domestic tranquillity" and to spur economic growth.[49] Although Alexis de Tocqueville's claim that "[t]he man who asks of freedom anything other than itself is born to be a slave" may seem like gospel to "a people of plenty,"[50] where poverty is rife, hungry citizens are apt to judge that message and leaders who preach it to be horribly wrong.

Still, as Gigi complained about a different fixation, "there must be

47. David Easton's *A Systems Analysis of Political Life* (New York: Wiley, 1965) is the seminal work on diffuse and specific support; he revised his definition somewhat in "A Re-assessment of the Concept of Political Support," 5 *Br. J. Pol. Sci.* 435 (1975). Joseph Tanenhaus and I coauthored a series of articles about public opinion and the U.S. Supreme Court that modify and operationalize those two concepts. We list the citations in "Publicity, Public Opinion, and the Supreme Court," 84 *N'wn. U. L. Rev.* 985 (1990).

48. See Juan Linz, *The Breakdown of Democratic Regimes* (Baltimore: Johns Hopkins University Press, 1978), p. 11; *The Federalist*, No. 45. The United States since the end of the Civil War, but surely not before, might be seen as an exception to this claim. The constitutional text and the United States appear inseparable, though one suspects that few Americans have a deep understanding of the former.

49. See generally Gerald W. Scully, *Constitutional Environments and Economic Growth* (Princeton, NJ: Princeton University Press, 1992).

50. "Born to be a slave" is from *The Old Regime and the French Revolution*, trans. Stuart Gilbert from 4th ed. of 1858 (New York: Doubleday, 1955), p. 169. The phrase "a people of plenty" is also Alexis de Tocqueville's; see David M. Potter's superb study *People of Plenty: Economic Abundance and the American Character* (Chicago: University of Chicago Press, 1954).

more to life than this." How much and what more pose questions that complicate your work. Your goals are not easily reconciled. Achieving and reconciling them are political tasks, choosing among interests and values, privileging some over others. Constructing and operating a constitutional order are integral parts of a never-ending struggle for power.[51] No governmental institution, not even a constitutional court or a central bank, can long remain "above politics," for politics "is concerned with the authoritative processes that determine the goals of a society, mobilize its resources to achieve these goals, and distribute rights, duties, costs, benefits, rewards, and punishments among members of that society."[52]

Governments are both created by and creators of political culture. Whatever else you do, you cannot establish principles, processes, or institutions that are neutral in setting the norms that men and women cherish or the tangible goods they desire. By definition, principles cannot be neutral; they offer general means of distinguishing good from evil, or, if you prefer, between what a society accepts and rejects.[53] Institutions seldom come into existence merely because of some overarching sentiment regarding a common good; they are created by people who have the skill and resources to act effectively to enshrine and enforce certain principles.

Any policy-making process you can invent will inescapably give preference to some claims and claimants to tangible goods. Because an elite's seizure of control over the brute force of the military and secret police produces evil, it does not follow that democratic political processes will be benign or offer equal opportunities. Open debate favors those who are articulate and quick witted over those who may be more thoughtful but slower of tongue. Those of us who are less verbally gifted seldom fare well in debate, though our common sense may yield more wisdom than do the honeyed words of the serpentinely eloquent. And, of course, modern democratic electoral systems confer great advantages on the wealthy, who can buy access to mass media, hire lobbyists, and make what are euphemistically called campaign contributions, just as negative constitutionalist processes give an edge to those who can afford clever lawyers to block rather than foster governmental action.

51. For an empirical study of Russian constitutional "reform," see Aleksei Pushkov, "Constitutional Reform as a Struggle for Power," 7 *East Eur'n Con'l Rev.* 77 (Fall 1998).

52. Michael N. Danielson and Walter F. Murphy, *American Democracy*, 10th ed. (New York: Holmes and Meier, 1983), p. 3.

53. See the discussion in Arthur Selwyn Miller and Ronald F. Howell, "The Myth of Neutrality in Constitutional Adjudication," 27 *U. Chi. L. Rev.* 661 (1960), responding to Herbert Wechsler, "Toward Neutral Principles of Constitutional Law," 73 *Harv. L. Rev.* 1 (1959). Wechsler conceded the point in his *Principles, Politics, and Fundamental Law* (Cambridge, MA: Harvard University Press, 1961) and said what he meant to advocate was neutral application of principles, not principles that were themselves neutral among values and policies.

My final preliminary point is that a search for appropriate models reveals an embarrassment of riches. Rather than revealing a unique solution to your problems, this long menu may only provide a variety of answers that, for you, are either partially correct or wholly incorrect. As Publius warned, the practices of other nations can "furnish no light other than beacons, which give warning of the course to be shunned, without pointing out that which ought to be pursued."[54]

Your most vexing fact is that, at best, your informed judgments are fallible, products of your reason and imagination, not of scientific calculations. Furthermore, the system you create is unlikely to long remain the system you intended to create, if indeed any group of founders have had a common "intent." Whatever institutions and processes you initiate will soon take on lives of their own, pushed by interests seeking special benefits and officials trying to further their own ambitions. From your concepts, intelligent, honest, and self-reflective men and women will deduce conceptions that will often surprise you. If you are successful in constructing a lasting constitutional order, you will live out the joke American historians tell about their system: "If James Madison were alive today, he'd be turning over in his grave."

Fortunately, the goals you have chosen shorten the list of candidates for a new constitutional order. The junta ruled in a brutal way that some have called "fascist." Whether that description is accurate, all fascist systems, semi-, quasi-, or otherwise, have so badly failed the test of personal freedom that you have dropped them from discussion. You have also eliminated Soviet and Chinese styles of Marxism as equally failing your goals. Plebiscitary democracy, which is where the junta began, is likely to eventually restore another junta or single dictator. I urge you to drop that one as well. To my mind, that leaves only five, not mutually exclusive, options: constitutional democracy, representative democracy, consociational democracy, coercive capitalism, and a perfectionist state.

"It is now," the chair says, "eleven minutes after five. Let us break for exactly nineteen minutes, during which espresso should liberally flow. Then Professor Deukalion will make an argument for constitutional democracy. After, our own Demos Pyknites has asked to make the case for representative democracy. Reassembly is at 1730."

54. *The Federalist*, No. 37.

CHAPTER TWO

Alternative Political Systems

The great tides and currents which engulf the rest of men do not turn aside in their
course and pass the judges by.   BENJAMIN N. CARDOZO

Much to Colonel Martin's annoyance, the recess lasts twenty-one minutes;
then Professor Retlaw Deukalion continues.

Your reading "Constitutions, Constitutionalism, and Democracy"[1]
has reminded you that blending constitutionalism and democracy poses
huge difficulties of political engineering. This mixture sometimes produces cacophony rather than harmony. But the promises, too, are huge: a
fair chance for citizens to work peacefully together for a good life for
themselves and their families within a just society.

Freedom from governmental oppression, equality before the law, and
the right to political participation allow citizens to enjoy far better lives
than under authoritarian regimes. But constitutional democracy's record
is far from perfect. Americans' oft-proclaimed love of liberty was long
accompanied by slavery as well as rejection of the social, legal, and political equality of women and people who have different-colored skin.[2]
Today, their so-called Patriot Act allows police to obtain secret war-
rants to search citizens' homes when they are absent, and their president
claims authority to listen in, without a warrant, on their telephone conversations. So, too, when constitutionalism does focus on protection
against governmental oppression, it often exposes some individuals'
rights to abuse by private citizens and corporations. One might even
argue, as Rousseau did, that elections restrict the people's right to self-
government.

There is some truth in Lee Juan Yew's comment that the American

1. In Douglas Greenberg, Stanley N. Katz, Melanie Beth Oliviero, and Steven C. Wheatley,
eds., *Constitutionalism and Democracy: Transformations in the Contemporary World* (New York: Oxford University Press, 1993).

2. For an excellent survey, see Rogers M. Smith, *Civic Ideals: Conflicting Visions of Citizenship in
U.S. History* (New Haven, CT: Yale University Press, 1997).

political system, which spends about as much public money for prisons as for higher education, is menaced by "guns, drugs, violent crime, [and] vagrancy."[3] Nor is this situation unique to the United States. Crime "has become an obsession in the new South Africa,"[4] with a murder rate seven times that of America. In Russia, "[t]he terror of a police state is gone," a reporter wrote in 1995, "but it has been replaced by a fear of gangsters and corrupt police officers."[5] The rate of violent felonies there more than doubled between 1987 and 1992, and within a decade some estimates claimed that criminal activities accounted for as much as 40 percent of the national economy. The Russian Mafia now operates in New York and London as well as in Moscow and St. Petersburg. In Eastern Europe generally, the *Economist* claims, a similar pattern of official corruption combined with privatized gangsterism prevails: "Much of the wealth has stealthy origins, corruption is endemic, and the quality of Central Europe's politicians, civil servants and judges is poor to dire. . . . Anger bubbles up."[6] In Afghanistan, American occupation coincided with an increase in the opium trade. In Iraq, the situation remains so muddled by civil war that it is difficult to separate exploding terror, peacekeeping fire, and official corruption.

To be fair, although political liberalization has typically been accompanied by a rise in crime, connections between crime and freedom are complex. Under dictators, as in Haiti, Iraq, Kenya, North Korea, Paraguay, Syria, or Zaire, violent crime was or is common. One cause of the apparent increase in crime in the former Soviet bloc lies in the fact that much criminal activity that was once a monopoly of government is now privatized. Another cause may be that the old regimes failed to generate civic virtue. A third may be that increased liberty and decreased probability of being punished do encourage crime. Edward S. Corwin sketched the dilemma: "[W]e enjoy *civil liberty* because of the restraints which government imposes upon our neighbors in our behalf." Freedom,

3. Quoted by Fareed Zakaria, "Culture Is Destiny: A Conversation with Lee Kuan Yew," 73 *For. Affrs.* 109, 111 (Mar./Apr. 1994).

4. *Economist,* Aug. 10, 1996, p. 30, and May 31, 1997, p. 43. For more general analyses, see the pair of articles by Mark Shaw and Peter Gastrow: "Stealing the Show? Crime and Its Impact in Post-apartheid South Africa," 130 *Daedalus* 235 (2001), and "In Search of Public Safety: Police Transformation and Public Responses in South Africa," 130 *Daedalus* 259 (2001).

5. Alessandra Stanley, "Gorbachev's New Battle: Overcoming His Legacy," *N.Y. Times,* Mar. 10, 1995. See more generally and more recently David Satter, *Darkness at Dawn: The Rise of the Russian Criminal State* (New Haven, CT: Yale University Press, 2003).

6. "Special Report: Eastern Europe," Oct. 26, 2002, pp. 24–25. See, more generally, Avinash K. Dixit, *Lawlessness and Economics: Alternative Modes of Governance* (Princeton, NJ: Princeton University Press, 2004). In 2005, the *Economist* was still reporting that "corruption in Russia is everywhere." "Corruption in Russia: Blood Money," Oct. 22, 2005, p. 53.

he added, "may be infringed by other forces as well as by government; indeed, [liberty] may require the *positive intervention* of government against these other forces."[7]

On your second goal, peace, constitutional democracy's record is also mixed. "Democratic Republicanism," said Sam Adams, the American revolutionary, would bring the world "perfect Peace and Safety till time shall be no more."[8] He was overly optimistic. A nation may want peace, but aggressors are not noted for respecting others' wishes. Moreover, as founders you must worry about the systemic proclivities of the governmental structures you establish: during the period 1813–1980, democracies were no less likely than other kinds of regimes to wage war.[9]

Scholarship offers no help in choosing between constitutional and representative democracy on this count. Most relevant studies analyze the records of *democracies,* not *constitutional democracies.* For democratization, scholars rely on Ted Robert Gurr's ranking of nations across almost two centuries and, for war, on the Correlates of War Project directed by Melvin Small and J. David Singer.[10] In defining democracy, Gurr specified such elements as institutionalized protections of individual rights. On the other hand, his "operational indicator" of democratic rankings includes only a small portion of these elements.[11] Hence, although research relying on Gurr's rich database has great utility for many purposes, it cannot be conclusive for this caucus.

The claim that democracies are not apt to fight each other did not hold up in earlier eras. Between 1817 and World War I, there was "*no* significant relationship" between types of regimes that went to war with each other.[12] Furthermore, "militarized interstate disputes"[13] in which

7. *Constitutional Revolution, Ltd.* (Claremont, CA: Claremont College Press, 1941), pp. 7, 67 (italics in original). Jack Knight puts it more formally: "[I]f self-interested individuals want institutional arrangements that favor them as individuals, they will prefer institutional rules that constrain the actions of others with whom they interact. . . . [B]ut they are faced with the fact that social institutions constrain the choices of all actors in some ways." *Institutions and Social Conflict* (New York: Cambridge University Press, 1992), p. 64.

8. Quoted in Pauline Maier's review of Gordon S. Wood, *The Radicalism of the American Revolution, N.Y. Rev. of Bks.,* Mar. 1, 1992.

9. Henry S. Farber and Joanne Gowa, "Polities and Peace," 20 *Int'l Security* 123 (1995) and, more generally, their *Ballots and Bullets: The Elusive Democratic Peace* (Princeton, NJ: Princeton University Press, 1999).

10. *Resort to Arms: International and Civil Wars, 1816–1980* (Beverly Hills, CA: Sage, 1982).

11. Gurr's exact wording is important: "our operational indicator of democracy is derived from codings of the competitiveness of political participation, . . . the openness and competitiveness of executive recruitment, . . . and constraints on the chief executive." *Polity II: Political Structures and Regime Change, 1800–1986,* electronic manuscript, Center for Comparative Politics, Boulder, 1989, distributed by Inter-university Consortium for Political Research, Ann Arbor, MI, p. 38.

12. Farber and Gowa, "Polities and Peace," pp. 141–42 (italics in original). For a contrary conclusion, see Spencer B. Weart, *Never at War: Why Democracies Will Not Fight One Another* (New Haven, CT: Yale University Press, 1998).

violence is overtly threatened, as in the Cuban missile crisis, or occurs at a low level, as in various American retaliations against Iraq between the Gulf War and the invasion in 2003, have been far more common than full-fledged wars. Before 1914, democracies were more likely to engage in such disputes with each other than were other types of regimes.[14] Since then, and especially since the close of World War II, the pattern has changed dramatically. "Mature" democracies are apt to retreat from strategic overcommitments, seldom battle each other, and rarely fight "preventive wars."[15] When democracies do wage war, they are likely to win, as Saddam Hussein and Slobodan Milosevic learned.[16] We should be wary, however, of labeling democratization as the sole or even primary cause of the paucity of intrademocratic wars since 1945. Europeanization and the dominance in the free world of the United States were probably equally, if not more, important.[17]

But even if there is a democratic tendency toward peace, becoming a representative or constitutional democracy is seldom a sudden event. Edward D. Mansfield and Jack Snyder looked at 150 years of data and concluded that during the early stages of democratization "countries become more aggressive and war-prone, not less, and they do fight wars with [more mature] democratic states."[18] Furthermore, during that period, states that had recently become more democratic were "much more war-prone" than those that underwent no change, and they were "somewhat more war-prone" than those that became more autocratic.[19] Worse, rapid passage did not lower the risks of war. Comparing changes from autocracy to a mixed democratic-autocratic regime with those from autocracy directly to democracy, Mansfield and Snyder discovered that the latter had been "more likely to promote wars."[20]

It is fair, then, to conclude that although the long-term record is mixed, recent history shows that democracies' promise of peace is realistic.[21] On the other hand, the caveat about belligerence and youth is

13. Charles S. Gochman and Zeev Maoz, "Militarized Interstate Disputes, 1816–1976," 28 *J. of Conflict Resolution* 585 (1984).

14. Farber and Gowa, "Polities and Peace," p. 143.

15. George W. Bush's invasion of Iraq in 2003 to protect the United States against nonexistent weapons of mass destruction is a famous exception.

16. Edward D. Mansfield and Jack Snyder, "Democratization and the Danger of War," 20 *Int'l Sec.* 5 (1995).

17. See Sebastian Rosato, "The Flawed Logic of Democratic Peace Theory," 97 *Am. Pol. Sci. Rev.* 585 (2003).

18. Mansfield and Snyder, "Democratization and the Danger of War," p. 8.

19. Ibid., p. 8. Snyder has amplified this point in *From Voting to Violence: Democratization and Nationalist Conflict* (New York: W. W. Norton, 2000), arguing that in the early stages of democratization, nations are often beset by fits of belligerent nationalism.

20. Mansfield and Snyder, "Democratization and the Danger of War," p. 17.

21. Colonial wars constitute another savage form of combat, but one in which two nation-states

relevant. Like human beings, democracies would be better off if they could skip adolescence.

Next is the economy. Everyone agrees that your new system must foster prosperity. But, again, directly relevant studies of political economy make no distinction between constitutional and representative democracies. In addition, democracy grew up with capitalism, with proponents of each offering similar justifications.[22] And despite persistent affairs with mild forms of socialism and continuing efforts to dull capitalism's crueler edges, all representative and constitutional democracies have retained some version of that economic system. Thus it is difficult to sort out how much of their economic achievements is due to capitalism, how much to political structure, how much to habits of heart and purse that each encourages, and how much to accidents of time and place. You must somehow crank this complication into your calculations.

Worse, the situation does not become crystalline when you look at other kinds of regimes. Comparing economic performances of constitutional democracies and fascist systems is difficult because we have few full-blown cases of the latter and each was short lived: the Thousand-Year Reich began well but lasted a mere dozen years, Benito Mussolini's poverty-plagued Roman Empire barely twenty,[23] and Francisco Franco's reign only about twice that long. Moreover, none consistently gave priority to economic theory over political domination.[24]

Anita Baca, the graduate student who had led the demonstrations against the junta, interrupts: "May I ask a factual question? Wasn't it Kurt von Schleiser, Hitler's predecessor as chancellor, who authorized the cool public works program that led Germany out of the Depression?"

---

are not directly involved, so they are not included in many studies. For example, one of the most systematic studies of relationships between war and democracy limits its scope to "conflicts between two independent states": David L. Rousseau et al., "Assessing the Dyadic Nature of the Democratic Peace, 1918–1988," 90 *Am. Pol. Sci. Rev.* 512n1 (1996). Nevertheless, a plague of such conflicts afflicted constitutional democracies well into the second half of the twentieth century.

22. See Albert O. Hirschman, *The Passions and the Interests: Political Arguments for Capitalism before Its Triumph* (Princeton, NJ: Princeton University Press, 1977).

23. For studies of Mussolini, see R. J. B. Bosworth's work: *Mussolini* (New York: Oxford University Press, 2002); *Mussolini and the Fascist Destruction of Liberal Italy* (Adelaide: Rigby, 1973); and *The Italian Dictatorship: Problems and Perspectives in the Interpretation of Mussolini and Fascism* (London: Arnold, 1998). Nicholas Farrell, *Mussolini: A New Life* (London: Weidenfield and Nicolson, 2003), is less critical.

24. Among the best political analyses of fascism are Michael Mann, *Fascists* (New York: Cambridge University Press, 2004), and Robert O. Paxton, *The Anatomy of Fascism* (New York: Alfred A. Knopf, 2004). For studies focusing on economic policies, see Avraham Barkai, *Nazi Economics: Ideology, Theory, and Policy*, trans. Ruth Hadass-Vashitz (New Haven, CT: Yale University Press, 1990); Dan P. Silverman, *Hitler's Economy* (Cambridge, MA: Harvard University Press, 1998); and, generally, Ronald Wintrobe, *The Political Economy of Dictatorship* (New York: Cambridge University Press, 1998).

Certainly Henry Ashy Turner claims that von Schleiser approved this plan before Hitler assumed power.[25] But the Nazis deserve credit for, before John Maynard Keynes's *General Theory of Employment, Interest, and Money*[26] was published, operationalizing such an innovative strategy.

Whoever created that public works program, Hitler's megalomania soon produced total war and near-total destruction. After 1936, El Caudillo tried to create a fascist economy; but like his mentors, Franco subordinated economic theory to personal power.[27] Furthermore, by the mid-1960s, Spain was drifting toward a capitalist system more in accord with the rest of Western Europe. Asia's Tiny Tigers have done well, but most authoritarian governments have sad records. The military regimes of Sub-Saharan Africa have coexisted with gross poverty. So, too, except in Pinochet's Chile, Latin American dictatorships have not provided models of growth and prosperity, despite what the World Bank claimed to believe in the mid-1980s.[28] And your own junta had only slight economic success.

As for Marxist regimes, the Soviet Empire often teetered on the brink of poverty.[29] Famines in Mao's China took somewhere between thirty and fifty million lives, and North Korea has suffered catastrophic famines. Meanwhile, most constitutional democracies have dramatically raised their standards of living. Yet the correlation is not perfect. According to the World Bank, soon after Beijing eased Mao's controls, the average Chinese was almost twice as likely as the average citizen of

25. *Hitler's Thirty Days to Power: January 1933* (Reading, MA: Addison-Wesley, 1996).

26. 1936; reprint New York: Harcourt, Brace, 1964.

27. Whether Franco was merely an old-fashioned military dictator who exploited fascist ideology or was a true fascist is contested. See Robert O. Paxton, "The Uses of Fascism," *N.Y. Rev. of Bks.*, Nov. 28, 1996, 48, 51; Robert O. Paxton and Stanley G. Payne, *A History of Fascism, 1914–1945* (Madison: University of Wisconsin Press, 1996); Walter Laqueur, *Fascism: Past, Present, and Future* (New York: Oxford University Press, 1996); and George L. Mosse, *The Fascist Revolution: Toward a General Theory of Fascism* (New York: Fertig, 1998). For discussions of Franco's economic policies, see Victor M. Pérez-Diaz, *The Return of Civil Society: The Emergence of Democratic Spain* (Cambridge, MA: Harvard University Press, 1993), chs. 1, 4; Howard J. Wiarda, *The Transition to Democracy in Spain and Portugal* (Lanham, MD: American Enterprise Institute for Public Policy Research, 1989), chs. 1, 8; and Phillipe Schmitter and G. Lehmbruch, eds., *Trends toward Corporatist Intermediation* (Beverly Hills, CA: Sage, 1979). For the transition from fascism to constitutional democracy, see Arvid John Lukauskas, *Regulating Finance: The Political Economy of Spanish Financial Policy from Franco to Democracy* (Ann Arbor: University of Michigan Press, 1998).

28. See Karen L. Remmer, "Democracy and Economic Crisis: The Latin American Experience," 42 *World Pols.* 315–16 (1990). For a broader study, see Morton H. Halpern, Joseph T. Siegle, and Michael M. Weinstein, *The Democracy Advantage: How Democracies Promote Prosperity and Peace* (New York: Routledge, 2004).

29. For a study of the systemic problems with the Soviet economy, see Paul R. Gregory, *The Political Economy of Stalinism: Evidence from the Soviet Secret Archives* (New York: Cambridge University Press, 2003).

India's constitutional democracy to be literate and could expect to receive a larger income, live five years longer, and have healthier children. And China's GNP has continued to grow faster than India's.

The story is not unmixed, but the economic records of constitutional and representative democracies have tended to be much better than those of Marxist, fascist, or military dictatorships. The real rival here is coercive capitalism, but even its performance has not been constantly positive, and its growth has come at a high price in personal freedom.

Your goals include political stability, and here constitutional democracies score high. Although they frequently rotate ruling parties and sometimes alter particular governmental structures, the basic political system has endured. Even Italians, who changed governments fifty-eight times during the Republic's first fifty years, have remained staunch constitutional democrats. France might also seem an exception, but it has had only one major change of regime since World War II, and that added constitutionalist elements to democratic processes. Many of the less sweeping changes since, notably the Conseil Constitutionnel's decision that it could enforce the Declaration of the Rights of Man of 1789,[30] have further augmented the system's constitutionalist elements.

A common explanation for this stability stresses the legitimating power of public opinion. As David Hume noted, all governance rests on public acceptance, and more than any regime except representative democracy, constitutional democracy involves citizens in peaceful politics. Within broad limits, the electorate can even revise the rules of the political game. Another explanation relates to the putative legitimizing effect of judicial review. Public policies often raise questions not only of wisdom but also of congruence with the polity's basic principles. At least in Australia, Germany, Ireland, Japan, and the United States, judicial review much more often than not sustains the validity of challenged policies.[31] Such decisions may quiet doubts among losers as well as neutrals.[32]

---

30. Decision of Jan. 16, 1982; reprinted in part in Louis Favoreau and Loïc Philip, *Les grandes décisions du Conseil Constitutionnel*, 6th ed. (Paris: Sirey, 1991), pp. 470ff. For a discussion of this decision, see Alec Stone, *The Birth of Judicial Politics in France: The Constitutional Council in Comparative Perspective* (New York: Oxford University Press, 1992), esp. pp. 80–86.

31. See Robert A. Dahl, "Decision-Making in a Democracy: The Supreme Court as a National Policy Maker," 6 *J. of Pub. L.* 279 (1957); and Charles L. Black, *The People and the Court: Judicial Review and Democracy* (New York: Macmillan, 1960), esp. ch. 3. The Japanese Supreme Court had, as of 2000, invalidated only a half-dozen of several hundred challenged statutes. Lawrence W. Beer and Hiroshi Itoh, *The Constitutional Case Law of Japan, 1970 through 1990* (Seattle: University of Washington Press, 1996), p. 24. Irish judges are less agreeable to the government than the Japanese but have been more likely to sustain than invalidate a statute. In its first few decades, the German Constitutional Court invalidated more statutes than the U.S. Supreme Court had in its first century; nevertheless, the German judges have upheld the validity of more than two thousand challenged governmental acts.

Obviously, constitutional democracy is not always successful, but neither is representative democracy. Latin America and Sub-Saharan Africa have opened yawning graveyards for democratic regimes, and the records of Greece, Pakistan, the Philippines, South Korea, and Turkey are checkered. Alas, we have few representative democracies to compare with the many (efforts at) constitutional democracies. New Zealand stands out, but even the United Kingdom, for centuries the case par excellence, has taken on many of constitutional democracy's institutionalized protections of rights through its membership in the European Union and its many treaties. In any event, the most you can expect of any form of democracy is that it will facilitate political stability, *if* it takes root—a huge if.

Your goal of a civic culture that demands respect for duties as well as rights is also enormously difficult to achieve. Both Britain and the United States illustrate the problems you face. During the 1920s, when Britain's regime more closely conformed to the Westminster model, critics such as Beatrice and Sidney Webb and R. H. Tawney attacked their country for fostering selfishness and greed. Furthermore, an influx of immigrants from Pakistan, India, East Africa, and the Caribbean has brought out the same charges of bigotry that have bedeviled the United States.[33] That the United States as a constitutional democracy has not fully lived up to its supposed societal norms has been charged not only by right-wing candidates trumpeting "family values" but also by eminent scholars such as Daniel Bell, Robert N. Bellah, Mary Ann Glendon, and Michael J. Sandel.

Two kindred beliefs underlie these critiques. The first is that capitalism facilitates a culture committed to "ceaseless change," accepts inequality, and works synergistically with Liberalism to create an "acquisitive society." The real norms become those of the competitive market of "possessive individualism."[34] The second belief is that these characteristics make it very difficult to maintain a sense of community and civic obligation. In its American incarnation, constitutional democracy has come to be defined less in terms of such public purposes as concern for social justice and more in terms of protecting individual rights. A negative form of constitutionalism has joined with capitalism to produce a

32. For citations of some of the relevant literature, see Walter F. Murphy and Joseph Tanenhaus, "Publicity, Public Opinion, and the Supreme Court," 84 *Nw'n. L. Rev.* 985, 989n17 (1990). Our findings do not lend strong support to the basic hypothesis.

33. See, for example, the *Economist*'s editorial "Racism in Britain's Police," Feb. 29, 1999, p. 18.

34. Daniel Bell, *The Cultural Contradictions of Capitalism* (New York: Basic Books, 1976); R. H. Tawney, *The Acquisitive Society* (New York: Harcourt, Brace, 1920); C. B. McPherson, *The Political Theory of Possessive Individualism: Hobbes to Locke* (New York: Oxford University Press, 1962).

public philosophy that venerates "the unencumbered self,"[35] free from all obligations not personally chosen. The notion that some duties and values are inherent in the human condition and thus shared not only with members of the current but also with past and future generations— Bellah's "community of memory"[36]—has been succeeded by atomistic individualism and moral relativism. What has emerged is a double caricature: of Karl Marx's view of a bourgeois state built "upon the separation of man from man"[37] and of a Protestant image of a society that has privatized and thereby marginalized not only institutional churches but also religious values.[38]

"Some of us," Federika Strega interrupts, "think that individualism, moral relativism, and marginalization of religion are politically healthy." "I heard," Deukalion replies, then continues.

In politics, Sandel says, this culture has spawned a "procedural Republic"—Mr. Pyknites referred to that concept earlier—whose public philosophy is concerned less with the substance of decisions than with the processes of decision making.[39] In fact, however, procedures shape substantive outcomes. And when substantive choices are hidden behind a procedural screen, they seldom need to be justified. Liberalism's demand for governmental neutrality among individual choices is usually either self-deceptive or hypocritical. Even government as "night watchman" supports current distributions of economic, social, and political power, as Sotirios Barber has devastatingly demonstrated.[40] From a different perspective, Mary Ann Glendon complains that individualistic "rights talk" poisons "the principal seedbeds of civic and personal virtue," impoverishes political discourse, enlarges social conflict, and inhibits dialogue that might lead to discovery of common ground among individuals and groups.[41] Amy Gutmann and Dennis Thompson are less pessimistic, but they, too, label the public discourse of interest-group politics

35. Michael J. Sandel, "The Procedural Republic and the Unencumbered Self," 12 *Pol. Th.* 93 (1984), and *Democracy's Discontent* (Cambridge, MA: Harvard University Press, 1996).

36. Robert Bellah et al., *Habits of the Heart: Individualism and Commitment in American Life* (New York: Harper and Row, 1985), pp. 152–55.

37. "On the Jewish Question," reprinted in *The Marx-Engels Reader*, ed. Robert C. Tucker (New York: W. W. Norton, 1972), p. 40.

38. See Stephen L. Carter, *The Culture of Disbelief: How American Law and Politics Trivialize Religious Devotion* (New York: BasicBooks, 1993).

39. For a defense of a focus on procedure, see Stuart Hampshire, "The Reason Why Not," a review of T. M. Scanlon, *What We Owe to Each Other* (Cambridge, MA: Harvard University Press, 1999), *N.Y. Rev. of Bks.*, Apr. 22, 1999, pp. 21–23.

40. *Welfare and the Constitution* (Princeton, NJ: Princeton University Press, 2003), esp. ch. 2.

41. *Rights Talk: The Impoverishment of Political Discourse* (New York: Free Press, 1991), p. 14.

"impoverished."[42] As founders, you must ask if these critics are merely attacking transient manifestations of "American exceptionalism" or have identified deficiencies inherent in constitutional democracy and perhaps in representative democracy as well.[43]

Data from other constitutional democracies are mixed. Italy, especially the south, suffers from individualistic difficulties of greater proportions than does the United States.[44] On the other hand, Canadian, German, and Irish versions of constitutional democracy operate in cultural settings quite different from those of the United States and the Mezzogiorno. While the broader American constitutional order stresses individual liberty, Donald P. Kommers argues, the broader constitution of Canada underscores "fraternity" and community, though not necessarily between Anglo- and Francophones. The German constitutional order emphasizes dignity, the incalculable worth of each human being, demonstrated through not only rights but also duties.[45] In Japan, "self-realization," Lawrence W. Beer says, is "achieved *within* rather than against or separate from the community, the family, or the in-group. Individual obligations are correlative, mutualist."[46] At first glance it seems that Ireland is stumbling along the American path. Irish culture is now far less pietistic than when James Joyce wrote, "O Ireland, my one and only love, where Christ and Caesar are hand in glove"; indeed, as the country has become more prosperous, its people have also become less formally religious. Moreover, the Irish Church has been shaken by scandals, and its opposition to divorce, birth control, and even abortion has become far less effective.[47] Nevertheless, Ireland's constitutional order

42. *Democracy and Disagreement* (Cambridge, MA: Harvard University Press, 1996).

43. Some scholars argue that American culture was once much more civic-republican than it now is: e.g., Sandel, *Democracy's Discontent*, chs. 5–8; and Barry Alain Shain, *The Myth of American Individualism: The Protestant Origins of American Political Thought* (Princeton, NJ: Princeton University Press, 1994).

44. See Robert D. Putnam, *Making Democracy Work: Civic Traditions in Modern Italy* (Princeton, NJ: Princeton University Press, 1993). See also Edward Banfield, *The Moral Basis of a Backward Society* (Glencoe, IL: Free Press, 1958); Ann Cornelisen, *Torregreca* (New York: Holt, Rinehart and Winston, 1969), and *Strangers and Pilgrims: The Last Italian Migration* (New York: Holt, Rinehart and Winston, 1980); and, of course, Carlo Levi, *Christ Stopped at Eboli* (New York: Farrar, Straus, 1947). Despite southern Italians' lack of attachment to the state, their commitments to family, neighborhood, and even city appear strong. For an analysis that challenges Putnam et al. and stresses institutional design and misdesign, see Filippo Sabetti, *The Search for Good Government: Understanding the Paradox of Italian Democracy* (Montreal: McGill-Queen's University Press, 2000).

45. "Freedom of Speech, Democracy, and Constitutionalism: United States, Germany, and Canada," inaugural lecture for the Robie Chair, University of Notre Dame, Oct. 1994.

46. "Human Rights and 'Freedom Culture' in Eastern Asia," in A. Anghie and G. Sturgess, eds., *Legal Visions of the 21st Century* (The Hauge: Kluwer, 1998), p. 159. For a fascinating study of change and stability in Japanese culture, see Paul Garron, *Molding Japanese Minds: The State in Everyday Life* (Princeton, NJ: Princeton University Press, 1997).

47. James F. Clarity, "Scandals and New Beliefs Changing Ireland's Church," *N.Y. Times*,

still reflects the social teachings of papal encyclicals: men and women exist, as fully human, only within society; an objective morality binds every person in public as well as private affairs; and all people have a duty to take care of each other. The Irish continue to believe we are our brothers' keepers.

A new constitutional order must help build a new political culture. In your case, you must also replace parts of your old culture. Each of these tasks is daunting. Culture can suffer from inertia of rest as well as of motion. And to what extent does the kind of civic cohesion you want to create depend on religiously rooted beliefs?[48] Can a purely secular political theory provide the necessary civic glue? I am not sure of the answer here. Indeed, I suspect humanity will be debating these questions centuries after all of us have joined that Great Caucus in the Sky.

I believe that your objectives may be easier to attain under constitutional than representative democracy. By providing a web of institutional checks on governmental power, you provide institutional protections for rights of people who are religiously, culturally, and economically divided. If life, liberty, and property depended on the outcome of the next election, thoughtful citizens might be reluctant to accept that decision-making process. Constitutional democracy increases trust in the political system not only because it protects the rights of diverse groups but also because it is seen to do so by guarding substantive rights and by ensuring that procedural rules are followed in official decision making. And I

June 13, 1999. Clarity also speaks of increased anticlericalism. Similarly, Mary Kenny writes: "The church has been rocked; society is more secularized; prosperity is altering culture; Catholic power has receded." *Goodbye to Catholic Ireland: A Social, Personal, and Cultural History from the Fall of Parnell to Mary Robinson* (Springfield, IL: Templegate, 2001). Changes in Irish religious devotion are difficult to measure, given the scarcity of accurate public-opinion polling in earlier periods. It is important, however, to distinguish among being anticlerical, anti-Church, and antireligion. Anticlericalism has long flourished in Ireland. In the nineteenth century when the British, with some success, tried to enlist the Vatican to help keep the Irish in political and economic subjection, a popular battle cry sounded the theme: "We get our religion from Rome, but our politics from home." In the 1920s, during the civil war, Irish bishops excommunicated leading members of the rebel Irish Republican Army, a decree that had little effect, in part because many priests were sympathetic to the IRA and continued to administer the sacraments to those supposedly excommunicate. One long-term result of the bishops' action was that Fianna Fail, De Valera's party and the one that has since 1932 usually had at least a plurality of seats in Parliament, has been noted for its anticlericalism but also for its devotion to the Catholic religion and the Catholic Church as a concept, if not to its hierarchy. When they reject religion and not merely the historic narrowness of their bishops, the Irish are among the most eloquent and pious of atheists.

48. Carl J. Friedrich believed that constitutional democracy was "rooted in Christian beliefs." *Transcendent Justice: The Religious Dimension of Constitutionalism* (Durham, NC: Duke University Press, 1964), p. 17, and ch. 1 generally. If he is correct and if those roots can grow only in Christian soil, most Africans and Asians should not seriously consider constitutional democracy. The experience of Japan and India offers hope, however.

mean the rights of the majority as well as the minority. In representative democracies, where restrictions on power are typically functions of the conscience of a civil culture, public policies are often determined by shifting coalitions of minorities rather than by a single, unified majority. The ephemeral nature of such coalitions increases temptations to cannibalism. Furthermore, even a majority may sometimes shoot itself in the foot. Constitutional democracy can't prevent that mistake, but it does make it more difficult for the majority to shoot itself in the head.

In sum, constitutional democracy has done pretty well in achieving the goals you have adopted. Its record of freedom under law is impressive though uneven. Constitutional democracy's greatest attraction is that it lowers the stakes of conflict. Different groups whose interests conflict can be assured of basic protections to their life, liberty, and property. South Africa offers a classic case for constitutional democracy. Not only did whites dread the revenge that a majoritarian government dominated by blacks might wreak, but some black groups, especially the Zulus, feared rule by the coalition of other black groups under the African National Congress, whose leadership was largely Xhosa. "Coloureds," a legal classification under apartheid that included persons of mixed race and Malays, also had cause to worry about such a regime. And, of course, Indians, remembering not only the results of black rule in Kenya but also the riots against them in Durban in 1949 and several near-riots after, feared for their status under parliamentary supremacy.[49] On the other hand, the leaders of the ANC wanted wide room to dismember apartheid's effects and create a less unjust society. Constitutional democracy provided the obvious—perhaps the only practical and peaceful—solution.[50]

My analysis has two important implications for this caucus. First, for a divided society constitutional democracy offers a greater promise of success than does any other system. Second, to fulfill that promise you must design institutions and processes with a mixture of bold imagination and exquisite care.

As Professor Deukalion finishes his formal presentation, the chair speaks: "I suggest that we postpone questions and debate until we hear from all of

49. For ethnic divisions and conflicts in South Africa before adoption of constitutional democracy, see esp. Donald L. Horowitz, *A Democratic South Africa? Constitutional Engineering in a Divided Society* (Berkeley: University of California Press, 1991).

50. For the decision-making processes that led to South Africa's decision to adopt constitutional democracy, see Heinz Klug, *Constituting Democracy: Law, Globalism, and South Africa's Political Reconstruction* (New York: Cambridge University Press, 2000); for developments since 1996, see symposium, "Why South Africa Matters," 130 *Daedalus* 1. (2001), and James L. Gibson and Amanda Gouws, *Overcoming Intolerance in South Africa: Experiments in Democratic Persuasion* (New York: Cambridge University Press, 2003).

our presenters." The colonel looks around, but no one speaks. "Very well, so ruled. Next, our colleague Demos Pyknites has asked that he be allowed to make the case for representative democracy. No one in this country is better qualified." Pyknites comes up to the rostrum.

I admire the learning that underpins Professor Deukalion's epithalamion for constitutional democracy. I do not challenge his judgment regarding the potential of constitutional and representative democracy to facilitate peace, prosperity, and stability. He honestly concedes that arguments for constitutional and representative democracy are equally strong on those points. What I challenge is his relative evaluation on the goals of protecting rights and fostering a civic culture. I shall make the case for the genus of representative democracy, which answers the question "Who governs?" very simply: The people, through free, open, and periodic elections. For now, I leave open the relative merits of particular species of that political genre.

The most obvious advantage of representative over constitutional democracy is that it can achieve our goals without infringing what I believe is a people's most fundamental interest, to govern themselves. In representative democracy, officials, chosen for limited terms, enact public policies without such institutional restrictions as judicial review. At elections, the voters know whom to hold responsible for enacting or not enacting public policies. Candidates can blame opponents, but no one can transfer responsibility to officials of another institution. Individual delegates and their parties must take full credit or blame for public policies or for their opposition to the government's plans.

The critical difference between constitutional and representative democracy lies in the means each uses to protect substantive rights. Constitutional democrats want to lower the stakes of politics. They would fracture governmental power, entrench a bill of rights, and confer much of the authority to interpret those rights on officials who are not directly responsible to an electorate. In contrast, representative democracy leaves it to the people's freely chosen representatives to formulate public policy as well as to determine that policy's legitimacy. It thus allows the people to govern themselves. The basic question representative democracy poses to constitutional democracy is, Whom do we trust to rule? Those who contend that elites should be able to block putatively unconstitutional policies or that elite guardians should have the functional equivalent of a veto over public policies that directly touch on the interests of minorities are really contending that these guardians are better qualified to rule than are the people as a whole. Robert A. Dahl puts it this way: "In an ideal system of guardianship, only the guardians can exercise the most fundamental of all freedoms, the freedom to participate in the making of laws that will be binding on oneself and one's community. But in an ideal democracy, the whole people enjoy that freedom."[51]

Constitutionalists typically make the moralistic argument that every human being has equal worth and dignity. Yet most constitutionalists contend that elites are better able to judge whether certain popular public policies accord with basic goals or harm interests of minorities that government should respect. The response of representative democrats is that this conclusion does not logically follow. If we agree that each of us possesses equal worth, how can the moral judgment of a minority be privileged on a matter to which a majority of the adult population has given careful consideration? The answer that the elite are more intellectually or morally capable contradicts the premise of equal worth.

Of course, some adults are mentally handicapped or politically indifferent. The obvious response is that it is difficult, but not impossible, to restrict the ballot to those who are not mentally ill and, if political institutions and processes are carefully constructed, to minimize the number of indifferents so that they do not decisively affect public policy.

The second basis of an argument for guardianship rests on a claim of the intellectual or technical superiority of a group of "optimals."[52] An honest representative democrat must concede that some people are smarter, more educated, better technically trained, more industrious, more informed about, and more concerned with, politics than are others. But identifying these people by objective criteria and placing them in public office defied even Socrates. Look at the U.S. Supreme Court. Some of the justices have been brilliant; some have been dumb; most have been people of much, but not great, intellect. I would ask Professor Deukalion if he could imagine—I mention only the dead—Peter V. Daniel, John McClean, Morrison Waite, Rufus Peckham, Pierce Butler, Edward T. Sanford, Frank Murphy, Sherman·Minton, Harold Burton, Fred Vinson, Tom Clark, Charles Whittaker, or Warren Earl Burger getting tenure at Princeton.

Smiling, Deukalion shakes his head.

No evidence supports a claim that elites like judges better understand the needs and interests of the whole people than do the people them-

---

51. *Democracy and Its Critics* (New Haven, CT: Yale University Press, 1989) , p. 78.

52. Edmund S. Morgan, *Inventing the People: The Rise of Popular Sovereignty in England and America* (New York: W. W. Norton, 1988), p. 103, credits Anthony Ashley Cooper, Earl of Shaftesbury, with using the term *the optimacy* in 1675 to describe the English nobility, through whom, he thought, the king should rule. If Morgan did not himself invent the term *optimals*, he still deserves credit for reviving the notion. For a argument that judicial review aids democracy, see Tom Ginsburg, *Judicial Review in New Democracies* (New York: Cambridge University Press, 2003).

selves. The people are often wrong, and so are their representatives, but so, too, are judges. Charles Evans Hughes, later chief justice of the United States, wrote about the Supreme Court's "self-inflicted wounds"[53] and the grievous harm that court had done itself and the nation. Over the long haul, the majority of the people are the best judges of their own interests—the best protectors, Jefferson said, of their rights.[54]

Even if it could be shown that a group of optimals are politically more astute than the rest of us, does it follow that they would not be swept along by the passions of the day? During World War II, the Supreme Court joined racist hysteria against American citizens of Japanese ancestry.[55] In 1961, the German Constitutional Court displayed paranoia about a free, if somewhat scurrilous, press.[56] These are not isolated incidents. Furthermore, why should we believe that optimals will not be influenced by their own interests or those of the class from whom they have been drawn? American constitutional history certainly shows that justices of the Supreme Court have often read their biases into the constitutional text.

My second challenge to Professor Deukalion concerns achieving a civic culture in which duties and legal rights are correlatives rather than competitors. Like constitutional democracy, representative democracy can function only in a hospitable culture; but political institutions and processes can help push, change, or even create such a culture. It is, I think, precisely because the political system of the United States has lowered the visible stakes of politics so much that Americans are so bored by politics that usually only half of them bother to vote, that campaigns are characterized by "sound bites" rather than by intelligent debates about real issues.[57]

In contrast, representative democracy makes the stakes of politics seem to be what they are: matters of utmost seriousness for all citizens. It

---

53. *The Supreme Court of the United States* (New York: Columbia University Press, 1928), p. 50.

54. After a magisterial analysis of the development in the United States of the rights to freedom of speech, press, and petition until the end of the Civil War, Michael Kent Curtis concluded that "courts provided little protection. . . . [J]udges sentenced political critics of John Adams to jail. Likewise, no Southern court struck down bans on antislavery speech as a violation of a state's constitution. . . . Nor did the United States Supreme Court ever void any Southern statute banning antislavery speech. . . . During the Civil War, a federal court refused to issue a writ of habeas corpus to free Clement L. Vallandigham, who faced a military trial for making an antiwar speech in Ohio." *Free Speech, the People's Darling Privilege: Struggles for Freedom of Expression in American History* (Durham, NC: Duke University Press, 2000), p. 416.

55. Hirabayashi v. United States, 320 U.S. 81 (1943), and Korematsu v. United States, 323 U.S. 214 (1944).

56. Schmid-Spiegel Case, 12 BVerfGE 113, trans. and reprinted in part in Donald P. Kommers, *The Constitutional Jurisprudence of the Federal Republic of Germany*, 2nd ed. (Durham, NC: Duke University Press, 1997), pp. 369ff.

57. Cf. E. E. Schattschneider, *The Semisovereign People: A Realist's View of Democracy in America* (New York: Holt, Rinehart and Winston, 1960).

encourages them to learn about politics, to worry about politics, and to act in politically meaningful and responsible ways. At the core of democratic theory, Joseph Tussman has written, is "the faith that all men can, if encouraged and given the opportunity, develop the arts, the skills and habits necessary for a life of responsible deliberation and decision making. Democracy seeks to universalize the parliamentary state of mind."[58] Similarly, Dahl claims that life in a representative democracy is itself a form of political education toward that mental state. No more than any other form of education does representative democracy guarantee happy outcomes: "The democratic process is a gamble on the possibilities that a people, in acting autonomously, will learn how to act rightly."[59] Carefully crafted political institutions greatly increase the odds here.

As Pyknites takes his seat beside Deukalion, Colonel Martin taps his gavel on the block. "It is now almost half-past six. We have had serious discussion among ourselves and heard two stimulating talks. Let us recess until tomorrow at 0930 and allow these ideas to percolate through our brains." He looks around the room. "Hearing no objection, it is so ordered."

At forty-two seconds after 0929, the colonel begins to tap his gavel on the dais. "We now," he says as the minute hand of the clock touches 6, "turn to another hyphenated democratic regime, consociational democracy. Hans Hendrik Smitskamp, Gordenker Professor of Political Science at Columbia University, will explain that system to us." Smitskamp is a tall, graying, middle-aged man with a gait that, compared to Deukalion's shuffle, seems athletic. He looks around the room, smiles sheepishly, then begins speaking in a flat, staccato tone.

Consociationalism attempts to cope with volatile ethnic or religious divisions that stifle a sense of common citizenship. In some societies, members of different groups see each other as aliens or even enemies. Consociational regimes utilize agreements among leaders of these groups to enable the state to function peacefully. Many such regimes display constitutionalist and/or democratic elements, yet a consociational political system need be neither.[60] When Austria became consociationalist, it already had judicial review and a bill of rights along with free elections.[61]

---

58. *Government and the Mind* (New York: Oxford University Press, 1977), p. 143.
59. *Democracy and Its Critics*, p. 192.
60. Hans Daalder, "The Consociational Democracy Theme," 26 *World Pols.* 604, 617 (1974).
61. But, according to one Austrian writer, before 2000 and Jörg Haider's joining the ruling coalition "[w]e were a predemocracy, a state without opposition, nestled by the Iron Curtain, where only stability counted." Quoted by Roger Cohen, "A Haider in Their Future," *N.Y. Times Mag.,* Apr. 30, 2000, p. 5 of Internet version.

The Netherlands had only democratic processes. On the other hand, under Tito, Yugoslavia had a harshly authoritarian consociational regime. Malaysia, a consociational, coercive capitalist state, has only the trappings of free political processes and little constitutionalism. When linked with democracy, consociationalism seeks to maintain at least a mask of popular government. Like constitutionalism, consociationalism tries to lower the stakes of politics. Its essential mark is cooperation among leaders of hostile groups. They agree to govern through a benign conspiracy.[62] Political parties may campaign on platforms that are mutually threatening, but leaders agree, like principals in a cartel, to settle most divisive issues through consensus among themselves. These regimes, Arendt Lijphart notes, usually have four characteristics:

> (1) grand coalition governments that include representatives of all major linguistic and religious groups, (2) cultural autonomy for these groups, (3) proportionality in political representation and civil service appointments, and (4) a minority veto with regard to minority rights and autonomy.[63]

Many aspects of consociationalism are attractive to multicultural nations. Although ethnic enmity seldom reaches levels seen in Rwanda, the shards of Yugoslavia, or post-Saddam Iraq, it often imperils public peace. I cite only Canada and South Africa. To dampen such antagonisms, constitutionalists protect minority rights by listing safeguards in a constitutional text. Elected officials typically augment these provisions with less formal arrangements. The give-and-take of pluralist politics in the United States displays some consociational features, as in "affirmative action" and appointments of members of minorities to important public offices. Canada provides clear examples of such efforts: French is an official language along with English; the constitutional text allows public support of religious schools (in fact, mostly Catholic); by custom,

---

62. In a consociational system with democratic ambitions, Daalder says, "elites must consciously eschew the competitive practices which underlie the norms of British-style democracy. Instead, they must regulate political life by forming some kind of elite cartel." "Consociational Democracy Theme," p. 607.

63. "The Puzzle of Indian Democracy: A Consociational Interpretation," 90 *Am. Pol. Sci. Rev.* 258, 258 (1996), citing much of the literature on consociationism, including Lijphart's earlier work: *The Politics of Accommodation: Pluralism and Democracy in the Netherlands*, 2nd ed. (Berkeley: University of California Press, 1975); "Consociational Democracy," 21 *World Pols.* 207 (1969); *Democracy in Plural Societies* (New Haven, CT: Yale University Press, 1977); *Democracies: Patterns of Majoritarian and Consensus Government in Twenty-one Countries* (New Haven, CT: Yale University Press, 1984). Hans Daalder has also been important in this field: "Consociational Democracy Theme," and "On Building Consociational Nations," 23 *Int'l Soc. Sci. J.* 355 (1971). See also G. Bingham Powell Jr., *Conflict Resolution in Divided Societies* (Stanford, CA: Stanford University Press, 1970).

three of the nine justices of the Supreme Court are from Quebec; that province retains its French Civil Code; and the Liberal and Conservative parties take pains to promote Quebeçois to influential positions. Not infrequently, prime ministers have been Francophones; Pierre Trudeau and Jean Chrétien are only the most recent in this line.

Fully consociational states are few in number and relatively recent in operation. Thus it is difficult to compare their records on peace, prosperity, and stability with those of other political systems. Only India, a consociational constitutional democracy, has waged a war of conquest. The others have been too small or weak to do so or even to defend themselves if attacked by a major power. Economically, Malaysia did extremely well for several decades, toppled into a recession in 1997, and, then recovered quickly. India, despite impressive economic growth in recent years, remains mired in poverty. The Netherlands, when it was a consociational state, ranked among the wealthiest nations.

Domestic stability and tranquillity are consociationalism's great promises, and it has often delivered on those pledges. Its peculiar form of power sharing certainly helped preserve peace and national unity in Austria, Belgium, Switzerland, and the Netherlands. On the other hand, Lebanon erupted in civil war, though largely because of Arab-Israeli conflicts in which it was an unhappy pawn.[64] India presents a more troubling case. The scale and frequency of its interethnic violence demonstrate that consociationalism does not always result in full domestic peace.[65]

As far as freedom from government is concerned, consociationalism presents three problems. First, when constitutionalist controls are lacking, the only minorities who can demand close protection are those represented in the grand coalition. That alliance shields only groups and rights that leaders have agreed to protect.[66] Political culture might function as constitutionalist checks, but it is the absence of such a culture that argues for consociationalism. A related difficulty is that while autonomy for particular minorities may ease certain problems, it may also leave some members of those minorities without equal rights. India, for example, allows Muslims to be governed in many respects by Islamic law. Thus Muslim males can deny their divorced wives alimony and custody

---

64. For an analysis of Lebanon's troubled politics, see esp. Farid El Khazen, *The Breakdown of the State in Lebanon* (Cambridge, MA: Harvard University Press, 2000).

65. Whatever the arguments for viewing Colombia as a failed, or at best only minimally successful, consociational democracy, its constant and murderous civil strife is, in large part, a byproduct of drug cartels. See Lijphart, "Puzzle of Indian Democracy," for bibliography on which nations might be accurately categorized as consociational.

66. Jacob Levy, "Consociationalism as a Substitute for Constitutionalism?" seminar paper in Politics 561, Princeton University, 1995.

of their children. Canada has also had problems with equal rights between men and women within indigenous groups.[67]

Consociationalism's third problem: insofar as it operates through an
informal cartel of elites, it "inevitably reduces the importance of elections
and even of the direct accountability of leaders . . . presuppos[ing] that
the electorate on the whole plays a rather passive role as both a condition
for and a consequence of stable politics in divided societies."[68] This arrangement strikes at representational democracy's central norm: The
people govern through the officials they elect.

Consociationalism's record on freedom has been better than these
problems indicate. The liberties of Belgians and Dutch—and Austrians
even when Jörg Haider's NeoNazi Freedom Party was part of the government—have not been much different from those of Germans, Irish,
and Americans. On the other hand, some consociational states have had
major problems. Although Indira Gandhi's attempt to institute a dictatorship was an aberration, India's subjugating the rights of Muslim
women seems permanent. Moreover, India has been quick to use troops
to quell ethnic violence and slow to return affected regions to civilian
rule.[69] And at the hinge of the twenty-first century, when the Hindu
Nationalist Party ruled, government sometimes failed to protect religious minorities like Sikhs and Christians from mobs of Hindus. Worse,
the threat of returning to a legally sanctioned caste system hung in the air.
Ethnic differences in Malaysia have also occasionally exploded into mob
violence, an excuse the government uses for its affirmative action to
equalize wealth between the Chinese and Malays. The result has been a
fragile modus vivendi between what Lucian W. Pye calls "two incompatible cultures."[70] To keep that peace—and, not incidentally, themselves in
power—Malaysia's rulers have cracked down hard on dissent: "Indefinite

67. Freedom of religion also poses difficult problems for Canada. To protect the religious beliefs
of indigenous peoples, James Youngblood Henderson, in John McLaren and Harold Coward, eds.,
Religious Conscience, the State, and the Law (Albany: State University of New York Press, 1999), has
proposed that the government forbid "Eurocentric evangelization" that targets these groups. Regardless of whether such a policy would protect native religions, it would certainly interfere with the
religious freedom of other Canadians as well as with the religious freedom of indigenous people who
wished to learn about or convert to so-called Eurocentric faiths. For a fuller discussion of the
problems of rights that minority groups accord their own minorities, see Will Kymlicka, *Multicultural Citizenship* (New York: Oxford University Press, 1995), esp. pp. 163–70. For a more general
analysis of the problem of minorities within minorities, see James Madison, *The Federalist*, esp. No.
10; Russell Hardin, "The Fallacies of Nationalism," in Ian Shapiro and Stephen Macedo, eds.,
Designing Democratic Institutions, Nomos 42 (New York: New York University Press, 2000).

68. Daalder, "Consociational Democracy Theme," p. 608.

69. See the discussion in Stephen P. Cohen, "The Military and Indian Democracy," in Atul
Kohli, ed., *India's Democracy* (Princeton, NJ: Princeton University Press, 1988).

70. The title of ch. 9 of his *Asian Power and Politics* (Cambridge, MA: Harvard University
Press, 1985).

detention; rallies only by permission; no real opportunity to criticize."[71] Cultural norms against open disagreement with authority reinforce governmental intolerance of opposition.

I summarize: The great benefits of consociationalism are domestic peace and autonomy of diverse ethnic groups. Its great costs are electoral unaccountability and uneven protection of individual rights. Where secession, civil war, or ethnic violence is a clear and present danger, consociationalism offers an attractive alternative.[72] Still, although some consociational measures are often necessary for all multicultural societies, India is the sole large nation that has heavily deployed consociational arrangements. This singularity and India's checkered record may indicate that full-scale consociationalism is an optimal option only for small states. More significantly, there is no assurance that consociational governments will remain benevolent over the long haul. History offers scant hope that rulers who can ignore their own citizens will habitually use power benignly. The danger here is of oligarchic wolves camouflaged in clothing sheared from the sheep.

A more ominous threat to consociational democracy, indeed to all political systems in multicultural states, may be lurking in "a clash of civilizations," which, as Samuel P. Huntington argues, is replacing the old rivalry between superpowers: "the most pervasive, important, and dangerous conflicts will not be between social classes, rich and poor, or other economically defined groups, but between people belonging to different cultural entities. Tribal wars and ethnic conflicts will occur within civilizations."[73] To the extent that he is correct, consociationalism may be dysfunctional. By encouraging divergent groups to continue their solidarity—to identify as Hindus or Sikhs rather than as Indians, as Chinese or Malays rather than as Malaysians—consociationalism could hasten the breakdown Huntington predicts. Its homeopathic remedy for a society's divisions could stunt the growth of an inclusive national identity. If such a movement would create a congeries of small, tolerant countries, we might be satisfied. But there is little evidence that political systems dominated by a single culture moderate either rapacity or bigotry.[74]

---

71. Editorial, "The Shaming of Malaysia," *Economist*, Nov. 7, 1998, p. 16. See, more generally, Edmund Terence Gomez and K. S. Jome, *Malaysia's Political Economy: Politics, Patronage and Profits*, 2nd ed. (New York: Routledge, 1999), and R. S. Milne and Diane K. Mauzy, *Malaysian Politics under Mahathir* (New York: Routledge, 1999).

72. See Timothy Sisk, *Power Sharing and International Mediation in Ethnic Conflicts* (Washington, DC: U.S. Institute of Peace, 1998).

73. *The Clash of Civilizations and the Remaking of the World Order* (New York: Simon and Schuster, 1996), p. 28.

74. One could cite Catholic Ireland as providing positive evidence here. It has not engaged in any foreign war, and, although dominated by Catholic culture for much of its first fifty years as a republic, it has been very sensitive to the interests of its Protestant and Jewish citizens, even ensuring

As I hope you can tell, I came to explain, not to convert. Yet all I have read and heard here makes me believe you must think very seriously about adapting some of consociationism's institutions and processes. Certainly, some promises of mutual respect should be included in informal agreements among groups, of which Professor Giuseppe Di Palma so eloquently spoke.[75] You must share power with each other—and be seen by each other to be sharing.

Smitskamp leaves the podium, and Colonel Martin stands up. "The professor was mercifully brief, a rare virtue in this hall. Let us take a coffee break for fifteen minutes—today, ladies and gentlemen, let fifteen equal fifteen, not seventeen or even sixteen—and reassemble to hear our colleague Federika Strega present the case for coercive capitalism."

Eighteen minutes later, Strega walks slowly to the podium, places a manuscript in front of her, and looks down at the caucus.

Unlike Professor Smitskamp, I do advocate a particular kind of political economy, but first I must correct our chair and two previous speakers. Their references to "coercive capitalism" are ideologically loaded. They probably got that term from a misleading article by an American whom the late Justice C. Bradley Walker of the U.S. Supreme Court charitably described as "vulgar."[76] "Guided capitalism" more accurately describes this regime, an alliance between economic experts in government and business. The state leads the economy, steers investment, and induces business and labor to work together. Just as war is too important to be left to generals, economic development is too important to be left to individual greed or impersonal markets. Public officials, primarily concerned for the national good, guide entrepreneurs, managers, and investors to put their resources where they will not only earn a fair return but also benefit the country as a whole.

We face a double crisis, economic as well as political, but we must find a single solution. We need to establish a regime that will maintain civil peace while fostering economic growth. Those objectives are closely

---

in a consociational fashion that each would hold political offices in excess of what a random distribution would provide. In addition, since the 1920s there has been agreement that both the Supreme Court and the High Court would include at least one Protestant jurist, allocating to 3 percent of the population about 16 percent of important judgeships.

75. *To Craft Democracies* (Berkeley: University of California Press, 1990).

76. Walter F. Murphy, "Alternative Political Systems," in Sotirios A. Barber and Robert P. George, eds., *Constitutional Politics: Essays on Constitution Making, Maintenance, and Change* (Princeton, NJ: Princeton University Press, 2001). Walker's "vulgar" is quoted in Walter F. Murphy, *The Vicar of Christ* (New York: Macmillan, 1979), p. 174.

connected. Our current economic situation is an incitement to civic conflict. How much happier any particular increment of real income makes people is not our concern. They should have a chance to live in peace with as many tangible goods as they can lawfully amass. Those are the state's concerns, its sole concerns: the peaceful, material well-being of its citizens.[77] To accomplish that goal, we need a regime that protects, while closely regulating, rights of property.[78] Under this system, public officials —economic technocrats, if you prefer—not merely support growth but lead the economy in directions that will be most beneficial to the nation as a whole.

We do not need a political system that reflects our pious clerics' naive visions of divine justice but one that will generate material well-being. There is a connection here that should move us all to be wary of equating economic growth with what some people portray as crass materialism. A brilliant economist has demonstrated that prosperity also shapes— according to our religious colleagues' views, improves—the moral lives of a people: they become more sharing, more tolerant of diversity, and more favorably disposed toward democratic governance. Whatever our theology, or lack thereof, these developments would further the goals this caucus has endorsed.[79]

I concede that the political records of states have not all yet—I stress *yet*—fully met these expectations. Even the World Bank, hardly a friend to civil liberties, concedes that guided capitalist governments have often been "authoritarian or paternalistic."[80] In punishing words or deeds officials consider threatening to public order, these officials have sometimes confused domestic peace with personal tenure in office. In Malaysia, Mahathir Mohamad ran a tight ship, going so far in 1998 as to arrest his

77. Those interested in medieval political theory will note that Deputy Minister Strega is offering her listeners a version of the argument of Marsilius of Padua. See *Marsilius of Padua*, Alan Gewirth's two-volume study of Marsilius, the first an analysis of his political thinking and the second a translation of the *Defensor Pacis* (New York: Columbia University Press, 1951–1956).

78. See esp. Alasdair Bowie and Danny Unger, *The Politics of Open Economies: Indonesia, Malaysia, the Philippines, and Thailand* (New York: Cambridge University Press, 1997); W. G. Duff, *The Economic Growth of Singapore* (New York: Cambridge University Press, 1997); Robert Wade, *Governing the Market: Economic Theory and the Role of Government in East Asian Industrialization* (Princeton, NJ: Princeton University Press, 1992); and Edmund Terrence Gomez and K. S. Jome, *Malaysia's Political Economy*, 2nd ed. (New York: Cambridge University Press, 1999).

79. Benjamin M. Friedman, *The Moral Consequences of Economic Growth* (New York: Alfred A. Knopf, 2005).

80. World Bank, *The East Asian Miracle: Economic Growth and Public Policy*, Policy Report (New York: Oxford University Press, 1993), p. 13. As a senior adviser to Human Rights Watch described Soeharto's Indonesia, citizens were "expected to refrain from political activity, except for once every five years when, in what the government calls 'a festival of democracy,' they [re]elect the sitting parliament." Jeri Laber, "Smoldering Indonesia," *N.Y. Rev. of Bks.*, Jan. 9, 1997, p. 40. For a critique of East Asian politics that is sensitive to cultural differences, see Daniel A. Bell, *East Meets West: Human Rights and Democracy in East Asia* (Princeton, NJ: Princeton University Press, 2000).

chief deputy when he dared display independent judgment.[81] Singapore does not suffer dissent gladly. Critics are seldom jailed; more likely, they are sued for libeling a public official. During Korea's long military rule, the government ostensibly tolerated some political dissent; in fact, however, the generals paid tame opponents to act out a charade.

But we need not blindly follow these patterns. If harsh restrictions on political and personal liberty were necessarily permanent parts of guided capitalism, I would oppose it. But they are not. Some restrictions are necessary, but not of the sort that rulers like Suharto,[82] Mahathir, and Lee imposed. Let me explain more about the system and then return to this point.

Although the seven Tiny Tigers—Hong Kong, Indonesia, Malaysia, the Republic of Korea, Singapore, Taiwan, and Thailand—had or still have guided capitalist regimes, Singapore presents the paradigm. In the 1950s, as colonial rule was ending, Lee Kuan Yew helped organize the People's Action Party and, by allying with the communists, won control of the new government. He then ousted all and imprisoned many of his erstwhile allies and used his police to keep labor unions in check.[83] His program was ambitious, his economics brilliant. Success brought enormous charisma: as we sit, Lee continues to personify the city-state, even though he formally stepped down from office in 1990. For the sake of prosperity, he has unapologetically controlled his subjects' lifestyles: "I say without the slightest remorse, that . . . we would not have made economic progress if we had not intervened on very personal matters—who your neighbor is, how you live, the noise you make, how you spit, or what language you use. We decide what is right. Never mind what the people think."[84]

The police keep the streets clean, quiet, and safe. The buses run on time. The government operates some large enterprises and others as joint ventures with foreigners; serves as the nation's largest employer; provides public utilities and port and airport facilities; censors the media; sets wages; and owns most of the land. While respecting private property, Singapore steers reinvestment of corporate profits into new technology and, building on its historic role as trader and banker, into other countries as well. Public officials court foreign corporations; they *direct* firms

81. Michael Pinches, ed., *Culture and Privilege in Capitalist Asia* (New York: Routledge, 1999).
82. Michael R. J. Vatikiotis, *Indonesian Politics under Suharto*, 3rd ed. (New York: Routledge, 1999).
83. For details, see Lee Kuan Yew, *The Singapore Story: Memoirs of Lee Kuan Yew* (New York: Prentice-Hall, 1998), and *From Third World to First: The Singapore Story, 1965–2000* (New York: HarperCollins, 2000); Christopher Tremewan, *The Political Economy of Social Control in Singapore* (New York: St. Martin's, 1994), ch. 1.
84. Speech at National Day Rally, 1986; quoted in Tremewan, *Political Economy of Social Control in Singapore*, p. 4.

TABLE 1. Average annual real per
capita growth in GDP, 1980–1994

Country	1980–1990 (%)	1985–1994 (%)
Singapore	5.2%	5.9%
Germany	2.1%	2.1%
United States	1.7%	1.6%

Source: James Gwartney, Robert Lawson, and
Walter Block, *Economic Freedom of the World,
1975–1995* (Washington, DC: Cato Institute,
1995), pp. 145, 167, 197, 221.

based in the city-state. Public officials levy low taxes, encourage foreign
investment, establish compulsory savings for citizens, help secure foreign
markets, tolerate monopolies, and create a tame, disciplined labor force
that is increasingly well trained. (In 2003, an international mathematics
and science study ranked Singapore's students as best in the world, far
ahead of American students.)[85]

The mass of Singapore's citizens share in this boom, though Malays
less than Chinese.[86] (The former make up only 14% of the population,
the latter about 77%.) The law requires that workers be well compensated, and they are protected by a form of social security.[87] Among Lee's
most visible accomplishment has been construction of public housing for
more than 85 percent of the population. Soon after independence, the
city state's per capita income exceeded that of the United Kingdom;
although the Brits have regained the lead, Singaporeans' incomes are
still impressive. Moreover, the average annual growth in real per capita
gross domestic product has often been far higher than that of the United
States or Germany, as Table 1—which is now on your computer screens—
demonstrates. You might think these data are dated, but their time frame
is critical for us, because it shows that guided capitalism quickly brought
and long sustained real economic growth.

85. But only about 75 percent of Singapore's children attend secondary school.
86. Lily Zubaihad Rahim, *The Singapore Dilemma: The Political and Educational Marginality of
the Malay Community* (New York: Oxford University Press, 1999).
87. In 1995, the hourly cost for labor was $7.28 in Singapore, $31.88 in Germany, $17.20 in the
United States, 71 cents in the Philippines, 60 cents in Russia, and 25 cents in China and India
(*Economist*, Nov. 2, 1996, p. 77). Worker and employer in Singapore each contribute about 20 percent
of salary to the Central Provident Fund, in which each worker holds several kinds of accounts to pay
for items like life and medical insurance, education, and pensions. Meanwhile, the government can
use these billions of dollars (Tremewan, *Political Economy of Social Control in Singapore*, pp. 53-55).
For a succinct description of the Fund, see "Fiscal Providence, Singapore-Style," *Economist*, Jan. 13,
1996, p. 38.

Until mid-1997, guided capitalism richly fulfilled its promise of prosperity for the Tiny Tigers. Furthermore, in these states, the distributions of wealth, as shown by the Gini coefficient, one of the standard statistical measures for such allocations, were becoming more equal. The World Bank's accolade "the East Asian Miracle"[88] was fitting. Then, in 1997–1998, guided capitalism's economic record was tarnished. The surge that had produced thirty years of plenty for the Tiny Tigers was followed by crashes that shook the world. Only Taiwan's economy continued to yield substantial growth. But let us carefully examine the data from Singapore: In late 1998, the city's reserves of foreign currency were one and half times what they had been in 1993—hardly a sign of insolvency. In late 1998, growth did slip to 1 percent and unemployment rose to 4.5 percent.[89] Awful! How many years here in Nusquam have we had negative growth? Look back at Table 1. From 1980 through 1994 the United States averaged a growth rate of less than 1.7 percent. Next, look at unemployment. Four and a half percent would have seemed glorious that year in South Africa, where almost a third of workers were out of jobs, and wonderful in Germany, France, and Italy, where about 11 percent of the work force were unable to find employment.[90] Singapore's is the sort of bust that most people in the world love to enjoy.

"Order," Colonel Martin angrily raps his gavel to silence the snickers of several members. "Please proceed, Ms Strega." She looks stonily around the room, then continues:

It is critically important that by late 1998 the Tiny Tigers' economies were again thrusting ahead. Every economic order has recessions, even depressions, but few produce decades of continuous, dramatic growth in real wealth, suffer a major collapse, and then bounce quickly back.[91] Lest

---

88. *East Asian Miracle.*

89. Fareed Zakaria, "Op Ed: Will Asia Turn against the West?" *N.Y. Times,* July 10, 1998. Other analysts gauged lesser but still serious declines: "Still Sick and Gloomy, Now Rebellious," *Economist,* July 11, 1998, p. 41. In its weekly tables of "Emergent Market Indicators," that magazine chronicles the Tigers' rise, fall, and resurrection.

90. *Economist,* Oct. 24, 1998, p. 86, reports data from national statistics offices.

91. There had been early rumblings of trouble: "States of Denial," *Economist,* Aug. 10, 1996, pp. 56–57, that journal's editorial "Wobbly Tigers," Aug. 24, 1996, pp. 13–14, and "Emerging Asia's Sombre Era," same issue, pp. 55–56. Economists have heatedly disputed the causes of the Tiny Tigers' crash. The most plausible explanation for the collapse is that greedy speculation by bankers in those countries, as well as in the United States, Western Europe, and Japan, led them to make very risky loans. When debtors were unable to make good, something close to panic ensued. The easy and nearly instantaneous means of moving capital across national boundaries meant that bankers and other investors could rapidly withdraw funds. For more developed explanations, see World Bank, *Global Economic Prospects and the Developing Countries,* *1998*/99 (Washington, DC: International Bank for Reconstruction and Development / World Bank, 1998). This report tactfully

you reply, "Western Europe's more traditional marriage of democracy and capitalism," I remind you that the United States jump-started those economies with the equivalent in current currency of hundreds of billions of dollars from the Marshall Plan. It would not be prudent for us to count on similar charity.

That Asian miracle also unfolded in more human terms, such as life expectancy, as Table 2 indicates. It should appear on your screens. During this same period, lifespan also rose in other low-income nations from thirty-six to forty-nine years, while in Russia it decreased from seventy to sixty-four years between 1989 and 1994, with similar declines during those years in other former socialist states.[92]

Table 3, which will appear on your screens in a moment, displays the most recent data from the CIA's *World Factbook*, available at the agency's website.

Singapore experienced another hiccup that lasted from the summer of 2001 until the summer of 2002; but soon its growth rate was again exceeding that of the United States. We can assume there will be other bumps along the economic road, but the direction is likely to be generally—and steeply—upward. A study by the World Economic Forum reported that in 2004–05, Singapore, not the United States, was the country best positioned to exploit informational and communication technologies. Overall the forum ranked Singapore as the seventh most competitive country in the world, ahead of Japan, Switzerland, and Australia.[93]

I warn, I repeat, I stress: we need economic growth, and we need a political system that will facilitate economic growth. Our people were miserably poor under the junta. Six months ago, unemployment had again reached 17 percent. When I left the ministry two weeks ago, that

---

refrained from naming either the United States or the IMF. See also David E. Sanger, "U.S. and I.M.F. Made Asia Crisis Worse, World Bank Finds," *N.Y. Times*, Dec. 3, 1998; Nicholas D. Kristof and David E. Sanger, "How U.S. Wooed Asia to Let Cash Flow In," *N.Y. Times*, Feb. 16, 1999; Pierre-Richard Agénor, David Vines, Marcus Miller, and Axel A. Weber, eds., *The Asian Financial Crisis: Causes, Contagion, and Consequences* (New York: Cambridge University Press, 2000); Gregory W. Noble and John Ravenhill, *The Asian Financial Crisis and the Architecture of Global Finance* (New York: Cambridge University Press, 2000), and Paul Krugman, "What Happened to Asia?" http://web.mit.edu/krugman/www/DISINTER.html, Jan. 1998. John Gray, *False Dawn: The Delusions of Global Capitalism* (New York: New Press, 1999), and Thomas L. Friedman, *The Lexus and the Olive Tree* (New York: Farrar, Straus, and Giroux, 1999), offer more general critiques of global capitalism.

92. See the data reported in *Economist*, Aug. 3, 1996, pp. 45–46. For Russian males, the decline was even more dramatic, from sixty-five in 1989 to fifty-eight in 1995: *Economist*, Sept. 21, 1996, pp. 53–54.

93. See *Global Information Technology Report, 2004–2005*, summarized by *Economist*, Mar. 19, 2005, p. 104; and *Global Competitiveness Report, 2004-2005*, summarized by *Economist*, Oct. 16, 2004, p. 98. Both reports are available through the forum's home page at its website.

TABLE 2. Life expectancy at birth

	1960	1990
Guided capitalist states		
Hong Kong	64	78
Indonesia	46	59
Korea	53	72
Malaysia	58	71
Singapore	65	74
Thailand	52	68
Other		
India	47	58
China	43	69

Source: World Bank, *The East Asian Miracle: Economic Growth and Public Policy,* World Bank Policy Report (New York: Oxford University Press, 1993), p. 34.

figure had risen beyond 20 percent. Medical care has been bad; it will get worse in the next months. People will have less money and pay less taxes; many citizens are apt to use the current political confusion to hide the fact that they've stopped paying any taxes. Our system of social welfare in which we have great pride is threatened with bankruptcy. A huge segment of our population is sliding from bare subsistence to want. People out of work and without public welfare will go hungry. Without our medical coverage they will die sooner—or revolt against a "just" but inefficient economic system.

Our economic history and our immediate future, like those of Poland and Hungary in 1989, have left our people "highly materialist, atomized, and cynical."[94] They support the Colonels' coup primarily because they are tired of being poor, and only secondarily, if at all, for political reasons. As Bill Clinton's staff repeatedly said during his presidential campaign of 1992, "It's the economy, stupid!" We are on the brink of disaster. Our only hope for the new system's being accepted by the people is that it quickly bring them a real measure of material well-being. Well-being requires peace but also money, and money requires economic growth that will dramatically lower unemployment and help refinance tottering systems

94. Adam Przeworski, *Democracy and the Market: Political and Economic Reforms in Eastern Europe and Latin America* (New York: Cambridge University Press, 1991), p. 2. For a more general study of the complex relationships between political systems and economic development, see Adam Przeworski, Michael E. Alvarez, José Antonio Cheibub, and Fernando Limongi, *Democracy and Development: Political Institutions and Well-Being in the World, 1950-1990* (New York: Cambridge University Press, 2000).

TABLE 3. Social and economic life, 2003–2004

Country	Infant mortality rate[1] (per 1,000)	Life expectancy (years)	Per capita GNP* (dollars)	Inflation (%)	Unemployment (%)
Singapore	2.28	81.5	23,700	0.5	4.8
Germany	4.2	78.5	27,600	1.1	10.5
United States	6.6	77.4	37,800	2.3	6.0
United Kingdom	5.22	78.3	27,700	1.4	5.0

*Purchasing power parity.

of medical and social welfare. Economic growth, in turn, requires—and guided capitalism provides—more and closer governmental regulation, more order, more discipline, than constitutional democracy's protections of individual liberty or representative democracy's frequent recurrence to a myopic electorate would permit.[95]

Singapore and the other Tiny Tigers did well on several other indices important to us. Like consociational regimes, guided capitalist countries have usually been too weak to be aggressors. Only Taiwan and Korea have been involved in serious international conflicts, and both were threatenees rather than threateners. In 1975, Indonesia provoked what could have become a war by seizing East Timor, but the Portuguese offered no military opposition.

Stability in Singapore has been close to perfect. Its political system, governing party, and even de facto leader have not changed since independence in 1965. Korea and Indonesia lie near the opposite extreme. Korea has had six republics since World War II, and Indonesia has undergone spells of rioting against peaceful Chinese merchants and near civil war.[96] With the largest Muslim population of any nation in the world, the islands remain vulnerable to Islamic fundamentalism's demands for a religiously orthodox state. Like Malaysia, Indonesia has

95. See Jon Elster, "The Necessity and Impossibility of Simultaneous Economic and Political Reform," in Douglas Greenberg, Stanley N. Katz, Melanie Beth Oliviero, and Steven C. Wheatley, eds., *Constitutionalism and Democracy: Transformations in the Contemporary World* (New York: Oxford University Press, 1993).

96. See Adam Schwartz, *A Nation in Waiting: Indonesia in the 1990s* (Boulder: Westview, 1994); Daniel Lev, "Social Movements, Constitutionalism, and Human Rights," in Greenberg et al., *Constitutionalism and Democracy*; Donald K. Emmerson, ed., *Indonesia beyond Suharto* (Amoronk, NY: Sharpe, 1999); Damien Kingsbury, *The Politics of Indonesia* (New York: Oxford University Press, 1999); Theodore Friend, *Indonesian Destinies* (Cambridge, MA: Harvard University Press, 2003), and Charles P. Corn, *Distant Islands: Travels across Indonesia* (New York: Viking Penguin, 1991). For a brief account of the rioting, see "Indonesia: Terror in the Spice Islands," *Economist,* Mar. 6, 1999, p. 38.

additional problems stemming from differences in wealth and work ethic between Malaysian majorities and Chinese minorities.[97]

Between lie Taiwan, Thailand, and Malaysia. Taiwan suffered bloodily after Chiang Kai-shek fled the mainland in 1949. A cowering rabbit before Mao's soldiers, the Generalissimo was a raging lion before unarmed Taiwanese, murdering thousands of potential as well actual opponents. Jonathan Mirsky described Taiwan of the late 1950s as "a Leninist state propped up by secret police, infamous for the torture, imprisonment, and murder of dissidents—most of them Taiwanese—and with a captive press."[98] After several decades, however, Chiang's successors and the Taiwanese arrived at a trade-off. One side retained public office, the other money. The Kuomintang's children controlled the military and civil service, while the Taiwanese had a near monopoly on commerce. By the mid-1980s, the government began easing authoritarian rule and allowed serious political competition and relatively free elections.[99] Then, at the next free election in 2000, the Kuomintang's party (KMT) lost and peacefully surrendered office. And although the new regime has not gained full control of the bureaucracy, Mirsky still concludes that the island has "been transformed since 1949, and Americans can feel proud that the island is indeed a triumph of economic and democratic development."

Thailand has staggered toward political democratization. Several decades ago, the military frequently intervened to restore its conception of order. In recent years, however, the army has remained strongly committed to capitalism guided by civilians, even during the economic turmoil of 1997-1998.[100] Hong Kong's retreat from the democracy the British belatedly initiated in the 1990s[101] is a result of Beijing's refusal to tolerate restrictions on its power, not of local decisions. Mahathir Muhamad's twenty-two-year rule of Malaysia, which ended peacefully in 2003, was never democratic in any meaningful sense of that term. His successor has instituted a series of reforms, but it is not yet clear how soon these will allow vigorous political opposition.

97. See Lee Kam Hing and Tab Chee Beng, eds., *The Chinese in Malaysia* (New York: Oxford University Press, 2000).
98. "Taiwan Stands Up," *N.Y. Rev. of Bks.*, June 29, 2000, p. 37.
99. See John F. Cooper, *The Taiwan Political Miracle* (Lanham, MD: University Press of America, 1997); Bruce J. Dickson, *Democratization in China and Taiwan: The Adaptability of Leninist Parties* (Oxford: Clarendon, 1998); and Linda Chao and Ramon H. Myers, *The First Chinese Democracy: Political Life in the Republic of China on Taiwan* (Baltimore: Johns Hopkins University Press, 1998).
100. See Danny Unger, *Building Social Capital in Thailand: Fibers, Finance, and Infrastructure* (New York: Cambridge University Press, 1998).
101. See Alvin Y. So, *Hong Kong's Embattled Democracy: A Social Analysis* (Baltimore: Johns Hopkins University Press, 1999).

On personal freedom, guided capitalism's grades are mixed. Western notions of due process have not flourished. Certainly mainland China's control will not further civil rights in Hong Kong or elsewhere. On the other hand, in Singapore freedom from oppression by fellow citizens is much greater than in the West. Violent crimes occur there far less frequently, and abuse of narcotics is uncommon, though the city state's location makes it a hub for the international drug trade. Moreover, Korea's Sixth Republic seems firmly committed to constitutionalism.[102]

Opponents assert that official corruption is one of guided capitalism's costs. I make three observations: First, long before guided capitalism, bribery was a way of life in most of Asia; and it remains a serious problem, even in mainland China.[103] Nevertheless—my second observation— Lee turned Singapore's political economy into one of the most open and clean in the world. According to a leading "opacity index," which measures such factors as corruption and clarity of regulations, Singapore continues to rank near the top, well ahead of Britain and the United States.[104]

Third, corruption is no stranger to constitutional democracy. In Japan, bribery is a normal part of business-government relations.[105] In India, bribery of officials is so common that only the grossest forms stir public attention, In Italy during 1992–1993, half the members of the Italian parliament were under criminal investigation for corruption, and shortly before, Bettino Craxi had been convicted of accepting bribes when he was prime minister. In 1998, Ireland was shaken by the revelation that a former prime minister had accepted a gift worth about $3 million and a relative of the sitting prime minister had ruled for the government that the gift was not taxable. In 1999, a similar scandal involved an Irish delegate to the European Community and gifts to the prime minister's party. Later that year, scandals involving Germany's Christian Democrats flared up, touching even the venerable Helmut Kohl.

In Washington, everyone knows that "campaign contributions" unlatch many locked doors. Political action committees regularly give dozens of millions of dollars to promote or block legislation.[106] Even presi-

---

102. James M. West and Dae-Kyu Yoon, "The Constitutional Court of the Republic of Korea: Transforming the Jurisprudence of the Vortex?" 40 *Am. J. of Comp. L.* 73 (1992).

103. See, for example, Julia Kwong, *The Political Economy of Corruption in China* (Amoronk, NY: Sharpe, 1998).

104. Transparency International's Report for 2005, summarized in *Economist*, Oct. 22, 2005, p. 114; a more detailed account is available on Transparency's website. Earlier, the Kurtzman Group's *Opacity Index, 2004,* summarized in *Economist*, Sept. 18, 2004, p. 106, and available at the Kurtzman Group's website, had similar rankings.

105. Jacob Schlesinger, *Shadow Shoguns: The Rise and Fall of Japan's Post-war Political Machine* (New York: Simon and Schuster, 1997).

106. For studies of campaign contributions' corrupting influence on American politics, see esp.

dents may respond warmly to gifts. Bill Clinton opened the White House to donors, inviting the more generous to social affairs, photo ops, and nights in the Lincoln bedroom. During George W. Bush's reign, the federal government awarded, without competitive bidding, a multibillion dollar contract to Halliburton, Vice President Dick Cheney's former company, to help rebuild Iraq. Although the White House denied any favoritism or collusion, an e-mail from within the Pentagon indicated that the terms of the contract had been cleared with Cheney. And to no one's surprise, auditors soon found that Halliburton had overcharged the government by many millions of dollars.

Anita Baca interrupts: "If economic growth is your object, why not cite the People's Republic of China? That country's economic development has been, like, awesome. No one in the Third World, including Singapore, even comes close. In fact, when we talk about economic growth, Singapore has become so yesterday."

"I agree about China's growth, but the price has been too high. As a feminist, I favor abortion and birth control, but a police state and *forced* abortions offend me," Strega replies.

"A police state offends you?" Baca asks. "You who deny that human rights exist?"

The chair raps his gavel on the dais. "Please. Ms Minister is making her presentation. We shall soon have an opportunity to discuss all the alternatives. Please continue."

"Please," Baca continues, "just one more question: what about Ireland? It endured decades of poverty from its birth until the 1990s, when the so-called Whittaker Plan for economic development finally kicked in. By the mid-1990s, Ireland's per capita income was second only to Luxembourg's in Europe, and Galway was the fastest-growing city in the European Union. And all that time, through poverty and plenty, the Irish remained staunch constitutional democrats. They rejected coercive or, if you prefer, guided capitalism."

"One swallow does not a spring make, even if in Ireland that swallow is likely to be a gulp of whisky," Strega replies.

Martin wags his finger at the minister. "Please continue your presentation."

Herbert E. Alexander with Anthony Corrado, *Financing the 1992 Election* (Armonk, NY: M. E. Sharpe, 1995); Elizabeth Drew, *The Corruption of American Politics: What Went Wrong and Why* (New York: Birch Lane, 1999); Thomas Byrne Edsall, *The New Politics of Inequality* (New York: W. W. Norton, 1985); William Greider, *Who Will Tell the People? The Betrayal of American Democracy* (New York: Touchstone, 1993); Brooks Jackson, *Honest Graft: Big Money and the American Political Process*, rev. ed. (Washington, DC: Farragut, 1990); and the review article by Lars-Eric Nelson, "Undemocratic Vistas," *N.Y. Rev. of Bks.*, Aug. 12, 1999, pp. 9–12.

I thank the Chair. Of course, each of us would like complete personal freedom for herself, but we know that can't be. If political rights get far ahead of economic development, a coup is likely to turn the regime authoritarian. So let's approach the problems from the other side. Although individual rights do not promote, and may even retard, prosperity, prosperity tends to promote individual rights. Robert J. Barro, for example, views political freedom as a luxury: "Rich places consume more democracy because this good is desirable for its own sake and even though the increased political freedom may have a small adverse effect on [economic] growth."[107] We urgently need economic growth, and only a political system run by economic experts not immediately answerable to the electorate can make the hard, immediately unpopular decisions that are required. While representative democrats worry about voters' short-term reactions and constitutionalists worry about legal niceties, economists cut to the heart of the matter: how to allocate resources most efficiently. Thus they lay the foundations necessary for a kinder and gentler political system.

As for political and personal freedoms, guided capitalism can immediately provide some of those "goods." Later, as we enjoy economic growth, government can offer more. Historically, this has been more than a vague hope. Capitalism, Gabriel Almond tells us, has historically been "positively linked with democracy, shares its values and culture, and facilitates its development."[108] And recently, guided capitalism's initial opposition to both constitutionalism and democracy has eased in several nations. After economic successes, Korea, Taiwan, and Thailand moved toward democracy as well as constitutionalism. So did Hong Kong before its reabsorption into China. Even Soharto's successors in Indonesia have been acting more democratically; they have negotiated a form of political autonomy for East Timor and accepted, albeit reluctantly, that the opposition won the presidency in 1999. In turn, a different opposition won the elections of in 2004.

What would the political system I propose look like? Let us look first at the policies needed for growth: controls on wages, on prices, on the movement of capital; tight regulation of banks and similar financial institutions; governmental ownership of some of the means of production; restrictions on imports; and compulsory saving. We shall also need to direct labor, possibly to require certain kinds of training and certainly to

107. *Getting It Right: Market Choices in a Free Society* (Cambridge, MA: MIT Press, 1997), p. 11. For contrary views about authoritarian economic advantages, see Remmer, "Democracy and Economic Crisis"; José Maria Maravall, "The Myth of the Authoritarian Advantage," and Barbara Geddes, "Challenging the Conventional Wisdom," both in Larry Diamond and Marc F. Plattner, eds., *Economic Reform and Democracy* (Baltimore: Johns Hopkins University Press, 1995).
108. "Capitalism and Democracy," 24 *PS* 467, 468 (1991).

forbid strikes. The government may have to assign students to educational programs that best suit their talents and national needs. Perhaps we shall need the equivalent of a peacetime draft to assure that labor goes where the general interest requires it. All these and similar policies inevitably restrict choices, but they lay the economic foundation for freer political system.

Only a government run by economic experts could formulate and execute such a program. To facilitate that rule, our Colonels should remain in power under the tutelage of professional economists. To quell fears of continued despotism that many citizens and foreign investors may share, the Colonels should make it clear that their regime is transitional, aimed toward the ultimate goal of a democratic and, perhaps, constitutionalist state—but only after they have built a firm economic base. To show their seriousness about the regime's eventual reconstitution, the Colonels should legislate fair procedures in criminal and civil matters, establish truly independent courts, limit the police, and guarantee rights to property and some degree of privacy.

As Strega sits down, both Minxin Wei and Jessica Jacobsohn leap to their feet, shouting for recognition. The chair, however, stares at the ceiling and says sternly: "I remind my colleagues that we agreed to hold questions until after all of our presenters have addressed us. Besides, it is time for dinner. Let us take ninety minutes and return to this hall at nine p.m. To encourage attentive listening, I have directed the staff to keep the bar closed until we have finished tonight's session." Grumbling, the members file out.

Precisely at nine, Colonel Martin announces, "Our next guest is Rheaux von Whaide, Singer Professor of Ethics and Public Policy at the Devlin School of Government of the Australian National University. He will tell us about the perfectionist state. Professor Whaide."

A young man of thirty-five with long black hair that trails below his shoulders, Whaide strides rapidly to the podium.

As did Ms Strega, I begin by commenting on the title of my talk. The term *perfectionist* is often one of derision, tossed about as if its proponents were Leibnizian optimists who believe the state can perfect human beings. But if neither religion nor mothers have yet been able to do so, surely the state cannot. Perfection, Muslims say, belongs only to Allah. Certainly, the state cannot impose on its people the sort of Judeo-Christian-Islamic morality most of us have in mind. Law, standing alone, a Jesuit scholar tells us, is a feeble moral instrument.[109] But we

109. See Robert F. Drinan, "Will Religious Teachings and International Law End Capital Punishment?" 29 *St. Mary's L. J.* 957 (1998).

should not give up. As a Jewish jurist pointed out, "Government is the potent, the omnipresent teacher. For good or ill, it teaches the whole people by its example."[110] In short, a perfectionist state does not refer to a utopian form of government but to one in which government tries to help, because it should help, its citizens to improve the moral character of their lives, realizing that the process of human moral improvement is asymptotic.

Had I participated in your debate, I would have sided with those who argued for the existence of objective moral truths and the capacity of human beings to discover many of those truths. I do not, however, contend that we can know all truths or that some of us can know much truth at all. Certainly many human beings are intellectually retarded or mentally ill. Hobbes also recognized the futility of using reason with "glory seekers" and religious fanatics. Russell Hardin would also exclude "skin heads."[111] I assume that means political fanatics. But what is left is the vast majority of adults.

I do not claim that any of us can know truth perfectly. We can argue, should argue, with one another; we can learn, should learn, from each other; and we can improve, should improve, imperfect reasoning. And we need not, should not, avoid critical questions of morality, public or private, simply by saying either "We have fair procedures, so what they produce must be good" or "I have my opinion; you have yours; and we cannot judge between them." Very often, we *can* judge. At its best that decisional process is Socratic, but it should always be alembic, moving us toward keener understanding. I admit that there may be occasions when reason runs out, or when it is unclear which (or even whether) reasons supporting one position are superior to those supporting a contrary position. When this condition obtains, it is usually because there are many human goods as well as many morally permissible ways of achieving those goods. But to conclude that two opposing arguments are each morally worthy of choice, we must first acknowledge the primacy of reason—of judgment based on reason, not on self-interest, cultural biases, or class, familial, or partisan allegiance. We must fully utilize our capacity to reason and rigorously test our conclusions against available evidence, always realizing that our reason is human, not divine. Equally important, we must realize that the variety of human goods and the diversity of moral means to achieve those goods are themselves good: a society without some forms of diversity would be dull indeed.

What distinguishes people like me—the "like me" includes Aristotle,

<hr>

110. Justice Louis D. Brandeis dissenting in Olmstead v. United States, 277 U.S. 438, 485 (1928).
111. *Liberalism, Constitutionalism, and Democracy* (New York: New York University Press, 1999), p. 151.

Aquinas, and Maimonides, as well as many moderns[112]—from our critics is that we reject the notion that the state should act as if all values and forms of moral reasoning are either equally acceptable or equally unprovable. Justice does not require law to be neutral between claims of what contributes to or detracts from a morally worthy life. Indeed, it is impossible for the state always to be neutral. Even the claim that all values are equally acceptable is itself a powerful and consequential value judgment.

Ronald Dworkin has claimed that the notion of basic human equality, with its foundation of equal human dignity, commands governments "not [to] constrain liberty on the ground that one citizen's conception of the good life of one group is nobler or superior to another's."[113] That assertion is flatly wrong for at least two reasons. First, it leads to anarchy. Are we to say that a pedophile's notion of the good life is as noble as that of a parent who would defend his or her child against rape? True, we can insert the notion of harm to children. But how can a neutral state give no weight to the harm to the pedophile who asserts—and deeply feels—a right to full development of his personality denied by laws against adults' having sex with children? The North American Man-Boy Lovers Association, among other groups, makes a claim to exactly that right. Government must make a moral judgment here, a judgment between the nobility of the competing conceptions of a good life entertained by practicing pedophiles, targeted children, and their parents.[114] A public official's assertion that enacting a statute or refusing to enact a statute merely reflects the will of the people does not remove moral judgment; it only shifts the locus of decision making—and typically does so in a cowardly way.

Second, criminalizing pedophiliac acts does not deny the equal dignity of pedophiles. Indeed, a carefully crafted law should accomplish precisely the opposite result. The criminal law is one way, perhaps

112. See, for example, John Finnis, *Natural Law and Natural Rights* (New York: Oxford University Press, 1980), and "Legal Enforcement of 'Duties to Oneself': Kant v. Neo-Kantians," 87 *Colum. L. Rev.* 433 (1987); Hadley Arkes, *First Things: An Inquiry into the First Principles of Morals and Justice* (Princeton, NJ: Princeton University Press, 1986); George Sher, *Beyond Neutrality: Perfectionism and Politics* (New York: Cambridge University Press, 1997); and Joseph Raz, *The Morality of Freedom* (Oxford: Clarendon, 1986). T. M. Scanlon's argument in *What We Owe to Each Other* (Cambridge, MA: Harvard University Press, 1999) implies a universality of reason that, by definition, transcends time and culture. See also Thomas Nagel, *The Last Word* (New York: Oxford University Press, 1997). [The gentle reader will note that, in many respects, Whaide's arguments parallel those of Robert P. George: *Making Men Moral: Civil Liberties and Public Morality* (Oxford: Clarendon, 1993); *In Defense of Natural Law* (Oxford: Clarendon, 1999); and *The Clash of Orthodoxies: Law, Religion, and Morality in Crisis* (Wilmington, DE: ISI Books, 2001). For George, Whaide, and Mufti Ajami, "men" is a synecdoche, standing for human beings.]

113. *Taking Rights Seriously* (Cambridge, MA: Harvard University Press, 1977), p. 273.

114. Prof. Whaide adds: I do not discuss the interest of the targeted child, though I believe it is stronger than that of a loving parent, because it is quite possible that a small child has not yet developed a coherent conception of a good life.

not the most effective way but certainly a permissible way, of instructing those with pedophiliac proclivities that acting on such desires is
wrong.[115] Public policy should recognize that criminals possess intelligence as well as dignity and deserve respect as human beings who can
learn that certain actions are morally as well as legally wrong. A criminal
law that punishes pedophiles (or sociopaths or alcoholics or drug addicts)
merely for their mental states, over which they may have little or no
control, would violate equality and human dignity. A statute that punished only deeds would not.

More positively put, a perfectionist believes that democratic or constitutionalist principles of autonomy, dignity, and equality allow government to act upon a view, arrived at through careful reasoning, of what
constitutes morally acceptable ways of life. I insert an important caveat
here: precisely because government need not, should not, surrender to
nihilism when facing moral problems, so it need not, should not, deduce
moral judgments merely from a country's past or current opinions. And,
I again stress, because of the diversity both of human goods and morally
acceptable ways to attain those goods, the state should not try to impose a
single culture or lifestyle upon its people. Not only were the mullahs in
Iran, the Taliban in Afghanistan, and the Puritan divines in colonial
New England fanatics, they were ignorant, narrow-minded fanatics.
There is a wide range of morally good ways of life, but that width is not
infinite: some people deliberately choose bad ways of life.

Perfectionists do advocate government's enforcing morality, but a
morality arrived at through reasoned judgment, not through fiat, divine
or otherwise. I also remind you that most liberals proclaim a fundamental moral precept that *they* want the state to enforce: it is wrong to harm
another human being except in self-defense or in defense of an innocent
third person. I agree with that claim, as far as it goes, though I cannot
forbear using against my opponents their own argument: that principle
has not been accepted by all societies nor by all members of all societies
that have officially accepted it. Thus, to defend this precept adherents
must either seek universalistic arguments for its validity or by saying
something like "Some people and some societies believe murder is morally permissible, others do not. Most people in our society believe that
murder is wrong, and so we will punish it. But we recognize that it is
morally permissible for those who disagree with us to murder, though
only within those jurisdictions that share their disagreement." This assertion leads to the conclusion that if Nazis thought it was moral to
exterminate Jews and Serbs deemed it moral to murder Muslims, then

115. See the argument of John Finnis: "Legal Enforcement of 'Duties to Oneself': Kant v. Neo-
Kantians."

the Holocaust and the "ethnic cleansing" in Kosovo were not immoral, however much we might find them personally revolting.[116] Richard A. Posner is one of the few jurisprudes with the courage to make such an argument in public.[117]

Many people who call themselves liberals also endorse a corollary precept, that the "good, either physical or moral [of an actor], is not a sufficient warrant" for government to restrict his actions. "In the part [of his conduct] which merely concerns himself, his independence is, of right, absolute."[118] Together these two precepts form John Stuart Mill's famous "harm principle." And he made an equally famous exception to it: The state may prevent a man from selling himself into slavery because, "by selling himself for a slave, he abdicates his liberty. . . . The principle of freedom cannot require that he should be free not to be free."[119] But the logic that justifies the exception savages the principle, which must also allow the state to prevent a person from inflicting other harms to himself that destroy his freedom, addiction to drugs or alcohol being the most obvious. Although Mill himself thought of this reasoning and rejected it, the logic of his argument makes his rejection illogical. Slavery to chemicals is no less slavery than to another human being. At very least, the exception and its justification throw open debate about what other self-harms the state might legitimately prevent.

Even without Mill's intellectual self-mutilation,[120] his analysis would not exhaust the moral reasons on which a state dedicated to the common welfare may legitimately act. All of us here value freedoms such as those

116. For discussions of the extent to which the Holocaust was congruent with or aberrant from German culture, see Daniel Jonah Goldhagen, *Hitler's Willing Executioners* (New York: Alfred A. Knopf, 1996); Norman G. Finkelstein and Ruth Bettina Birn, *A Nation on Trial: The Goldhagen Thesis and Historical Truth* (New York: Holt, 1998); Peter Gay, *My German Question* (New Haven, CT: Yale University Press, 1998); and Richard Breitman, *Official Secrets: What the Nazis Planned, What the British and Americans Knew* (New York: Hill and Wang, 1999). Less innocently than Colonel Martin, many legal theorists would like to have it both ways: they proclaim the inevitable relativity of most legal standards, but the absoluteness of principles they hold most dear. I do not object to the proposition that many if not most legal rules, and perhaps even legal principles as well, can serve as moral imperatives only within particular cultures. What I do object to is the assertion that legal principles are intrinsically so restricted.

117. "The Problematics of Moral and Legal Theory," 111 *Harv. L. Rev.* 1637 (1998). He repeated his conclusion in an exchange with Ronald Dworkin in *N.Y. Rev. of Bks.*, Apr. 27, 2000, p. 60. Linking his position to that of Richard Rorty, Posner writes, "[W]e simply believe that there is no reliable *external* perspective from which to evaluate conflicting moralities." I believe one can make a strong case that, at root, Dworkin does not disagree with Posner on this issue.

118. John Stuart Mill, *On Liberty*, ed. R. B. McCallum (original 1859; Oxford: Blackwell, 1948), p. 8 and chs. 4–5.

119. Ibid., p. 92.

120. Prof. Whaide also says: I put aside his heavy reliance on consequentialist reasoning. Although any person who wishes to act ethically must consider the consequences of his or her acts, consequentialism offers a very shaky foundation for any ethical system.

of expression and religion; we also value the right to enjoy our own lifestyles. But these are all instrumental rights, not ends in themselves. Properly used, they enable us to enjoy more basic goods such as a fully human life, which, in the modern world, can be lived only in a political community. Improperly used, of course, these putative rights can become instruments of destruction. As Aristotle said, "[A]ny polis which is truly so called, and is not merely one in name, must devote itself to the end of encouraging goodness. . . . What constitutes a polis is an association of households and clans in a good life, for the sake of attaining a perfect and self-sufficing existence. . . . The end and the purpose of a polis is the good life, and the institutions of social life are means to that end."[121] But a nation cannot nurture a good life for its citizens if its jurisprudence takes the line "Some people freely choose to destroy their minds and bodies with drugs or rent their bodies for others' sexual gratification, while others don't. Society cannot judge who is morally right here. Therefore, as long as such transactions are voluntary, they are legal; their morality is not a matter of public concern."

I do not say government must always or even should ever criminalize such behavior. Many prudential considerations come into play, such as the extent to which criminal penalties might discourage rehabilitation or lead to official corruption. But a society that wants a good life for its citizens cannot treat activities like prostitution or abuse of narcotics merely as "alternative lifestyles."

I agree that a group of people cannot long live together without a common sense of morality, but I do not ground my arguments on this assertion. Of itself, social cohesion cannot be a compelling reason for moral legislation. As we saw in Germany and Japan before and during World War II, social cohesion is not good in itself. (That there was much less cohesion in those societies than the rest of the world then thought doesn't change the argument.) Social cohesion is an instrument that may further goals that are beneficent or horrendous. Rather, I argue that if society's shared sense of morality is indifferent toward such matters as drug abuse, pedophilia, and prostitution or offers only a feebly reasoned moral defense of its opposition, it will destroy what you—and I—call a civic culture. On the other hand, a civic culture that facilitates virtue not only helps individual citizens form good moral character but also helps society pursue values such as justice, mutual respect, and a sense of obligation not only toward members of this community but toward all humanity.[122]

---

121. *The Politics*, trans. Ernest Barker (London: Oxford University Press, 1946), bk. 3, ch. 9, §9, 1280b. He added: "It is therefore for the sake of good actions, and not for the sake of social life, that political associations must be considered to exist."

122. See George, *Making Men Moral*, esp. pp. 71–82.

Now, what specific institutional arrangements do I argue for? Perhaps a constitutional democracy, or a representative democracy, or some hybrid cross-bred with consociationism. I concede, though I am nervous about it, that what I urge might even be compatible with guided capitalism. But whatever the institutional arrangements, they would have to enforce broad freedoms to speak and write as well as an obligation of all public officials to listen to and engage in such discussions. Arguments, in a context of mutual respect for persons holding positions with which we disagree, are essential to making moral judgments in which we can reasonably have confidence.[123]

Once again, note that I did not say respect for the "positions," only for the persons. My argument for free discussion goes beyond, though it certainly includes, reasons of prudence. For instance, I accept social scientists' finding that people are more apt to be content with decisions in whose making they played a role than with those, equally beneficial, imposed from above. What I also contend is that communication in general and speech in particular are essential to cooperation, and cooperation with other men and women for morally worthy ends is itself a good, one that a just state must promote.[124]

I urge that you not create a political system that is morally constipated. I am not arguing for a constitutional order that protects freedom in general or specific freedoms as if they were ends in themselves and thus absolute or nearly so. They are merely instrumental goods. Neither do I argue for these freedoms because they are functional for a particular regime. I do not object to that reason; indeed, I might often support it. But there is a better and deeper reason to protect freedom: to help fulfill the basic purpose of the state, to enable citizens to live truly human lives.

The political system I advocate looks on civil liberties as instruments that, directed toward morally worthy goals, are necessary for a people's living moral, fully human lives. And those ends allow restrictions on "rights" under some circumstances and under others forbid restrictions on them. Conclusions of the U.S. Supreme Court holding that legislatures cannot look at the content of speech in deciding whether to regulate it may be congruent with American constitutional law and reflect American notions of individualism as including all persons' right to be, do, and

---

123. To this extent, Prof. Whaide agrees with Gutmann and Thompson's claims for "deliberative democracy" in *Democracy and Disagreement*. I wish, however, that they had displayed greater understanding of and respect for some of the reasoning with which they disagree, such as that offered by those who oppose abortion. See Robert P. George, "Book Review: Law, Democracy, and Moral Disagreement," 110 *Harv. L. Rev.* 1388 (1997).

124. See Lon Fuller, *The Morality of Law* (New Haven, CT: Yale University Press, 1964); and George, *Making Men Moral*, ch. 7.

say almost anything that pleases them.[125] As an Australian, I do not have an informed judgment on that issue. But such rulings are intellectually vapid, morally empty, and at war with the notion of establishing justice—which, in my ignorance, I had thought the Preamble to the American constitutional text listed as one of the system's basic goals.

Citizens are moral beings. Both in protecting and in regulating what we deem to be civil liberties, the lodestar must be aiding citizens to live fully human—that is, moral—lives, to enable them to live in justice and peace with themselves, their neighbors, and their community. No matter how much we might wish it otherwise, soulcraft is a necessary part of statecraft.

As Whaide leaves the podium, Colonel Martin speaks in a firm voice: "It is now 2300 hours. We are in recess until tomorrow at 1000."

125. See, for example. R.A.V. v. St. Paul, 505 U.S. 377 (1992).

CHAPTER THREE

Alternative Political Systems
The Debate

The most perfect machinery of government will not keep us as a nation from destruction if there is not within us a soul. No abounding of material prosperity shall
avail us if our spiritual senses atrophy   GEORGE GRANT

Just before ten, as the members of the caucus are milling about the meeting
room, Colonel Martin walks to the podium and raps his gavel three times.
"We convene in exactly one minute and eighteen seconds. I suggest members take their seats."

As the minute hand of the clock touches 12, Martin raps his gavel again.
"So that our debate may have some semblance of order, questions should be
first directed to Professor Deukalion and Mr. Pyknites. We should focus on
their talks, then move to the other speakers. To facilitate discussion, let us
make two exceptions: first, any of the speakers may respond to any question
to or answer by any other speaker; second, any member of the caucus may ask
the views of any speaker on any relevant issue. I will give notice when I think
we should move from one speaker to another. Any questions about procedure? Hearing none, we move to substance. Mr. Zingaro?"

"I'm a poet and know little about politics, but I don't see any basic
difference between constitutional and representative democracy. Can anyone name a representative democracy? Aren't we really talking about one
system that offers a range of institutional arrangements, stretching from the
simple Westminster model to the tangled webs of the United States?"

Pyknites responds: "New Zealand is the paradigm case; and if we exclude
the limited constitutionalist checks of the European Union and the Convention on Human Rights, we would include Britain, the Netherlands and, de
facto, Sweden, Denmark, and Finland."

"Luxembourg, Andorra, Liechtenstein, Monaco, San Marino, and the
Vatican City State," Deukalion adds, "don't have judicial review either, but
you might not classify them as democracies."

Pyknites continues. "We shouldn't seek representative democracy for the
purpose of imitating anyone but because by relying on political culture to
protect substantive rights, representative democracy forces us to realize that
civic education is the most important function of free government. There

citizens learn by doing, by participating in governing themselves under democratic principles."

"My question," Zingaro repeats, "was whether the two are not versions of one basic regime."

"We could see constitutional and representative democracy," Pyknites replies, "as falling along a single spectrum. But there is a point where the differences become critically important. We reach that divide when we allow an institution not directly responsible to the people to invalidate substantive policies the popularly elected legislature has enacted, when, that is, we have judicial review or a functional equivalent that goes beyond protecting open political processes."

"Functional equivalent?"

Pyknites smiles. "I apologize for the jargon. Let me offer a few examples. For a time in 1976, the Portuguese Council of the Revolution, controlled by the military, exercised constitutional review over the new legislature. De facto, so have the military in Turkey and some Latin American countries. Currently, Iran has the Council of Guardians, which protects the Islamic constitutional order. More consonant with theories of constitutionalism, the French Conseil Constitutionel, though not formally a court, can declare proposed legislation unconstitutional."

"I agree with Mr. Pyknites about the differences between the two regimes," Deukalion adds, "but I wouldn't count as constitutionalist a regime that allowed the military or the clergy to exercise constitutional review over elected officials. I also disagree with his ranking of constitutional and representative democracy. If you had a democratic culture and a history of ethnic harmony, the choice between the two might be a matter of taste. But Nusquam lacks a democratic culture; you do not have a history of popular rule or limited government or ethnic harmony. Thus, constitutional democracy offers you a much better chance. It augments cultural checks with institutional limitations. In Madison's terms, it gives officials vested interests in restricting each other, pitting power against power, ambition against ambition."

"But," Zingaro persists, "why then aren't there more representative democracies?"

"I could simply rest my case on that observation, but I won't," Deukalion answers. "One reason may be imitation of political success. Latin American nations have often followed the United States; Argentina's constitutional document of 1853 even instructed interpreters to follow the U.S. Supreme Court's constructions of its own text. The Australians, Canadians, Irish, and Norwegians also opted—the Japanese had no choice, though the Germans had some latitude—to modify their parliamentary systems with entrenched bills of rights and American-style judicial review. Like Spain and Portugal, Eastern Europe followed the German model, which, as did the Italian, used Hans Kelsen's design of the Austrian Constitutional Court. Founders or reformers in other nations, such as Belgium, Greece, and even Russia, chose to modify representative democracy with constitutionalist checks. They lacked a political culture that could limit power, just as you do, or, as in Belgium, Canada, and South Africa, feared that ethnic minorities would believe that the ethnic majority was abusing its power. I might also add the example of the European Community's using the American model of a Supreme Court to mute nationalism and supervise a quasi-federal system."

Before Pyknites can comment, Federika Strega cuts in. "Please! Political culture is a vast vat of viscous verbiage. Besides, neither constitutional nor representative democracy can *now* provide us with a viable political system. Neither can create sufficient prosperity to build allegiance to the regime, at least not in our lifetimes. Furthermore, we need ethnic peace unless we want to become like Yugoslavia after Tito. Unlike the Serbs, Croats, Bosnians, and whomever, we don't have a history of mutual murder; but neither do we have a history of mutual love. We need a political system that can impose peace until our various peoples can learn to live together as citizens of one nation. And note I said 'impose,' not negotiate."

Colonel Martin taps his gavel. "Minister Pilsudski."

"Professor Deukalion, Mr. Pyknites made a much stronger case for representative democracy than you did for constitutional democracy. You buttressed your argument for limiting the state, as well as the power of a majority to control the state, with the example of South Africa. But as sorry as our ethnic problems are, they are substantially different from those of South Africa. The junta—and, to our shame, probably society as a whole—discriminated against Gypsies, Muslims, Hispanic immigrants, blacks, and Sephardic Jews. My point is that these ethnic groups, taken together, are a minority. On the other hand, in South Africa, blacks are a large majority. The white minority, who also controlled most of the nation's material wealth, had good reason to fear revenge from a black majority. This fear was exacerbated by the links that had existed before 1990 between the African National Congress, the old Soviet Union, and various other communist movements. The violent ways in which many ANC leaders, such as Winnie Mandela, dealt with foes within their own organization certainly did not inspire confidence about peaceful coexistence. Here in Nusquam we whites don't need to fear open elections, even though we also control most of the country's wealth. It is the ethnic minorities who need to fear *our* bigotry."

Deukalion pauses for a few moments before responding. "Your question is complex. Let me try, as economists would say, to disaggregate it. First, the two presentations: Mr. Pyknites's was neater than mine because he painted an idealized picture of representative democracy, while I described constitutional democracy warts and all. Next South Africa: Your situation is obviously different, but it is similar. You put your finger on that difference when you said your ethnic minorities had to fear the bigotry of the whites while it was whites' fear of black revenge that was one of the biggest issues in South Africa.[1] But here as there, sizable ethnic groups do not trust one another. That's why I stressed that if you're going to build up confidence in the political system, you will have to limit the stakes of conflict. Each of your ethnic groups, except white Protestants, has some memory of being oppressed by one or more of the other groups either here or in the old country. Mr. Pyknites speaks, and properly so, of the importance of a civic culture to any system of free government."

"What about a civic culture?" Pilsudski asks.

"Constitutional democracy fosters a civic culture by allowing people to come together knowing that they will often lose in political processes but that their basic rights to life, liberty, and property will be respected. Government won't oppress the losers, and majorities will have wide, though not full, room to rule."

"But," Pilsudski asks, "what about Mr. Pyknites's point about constitutionalist checks' undermining the norm of equal human dignity?"

"To say you need checks on popular government no more implies unequal dignity than a parliament's ability to make laws that bind citizens implies that legislators have greater dignity than ordinary citizens. Complex societies need complex governmental institutions staffed by people with special skills in formulating and securing agreement about public policies. Inevitably, those men and women will sometimes see things differently from ordinary citizens. Government by public opinion poll, electronic or otherwise, is government without deliberation; and government without deliberation is government by momentary passion. I won't rehearse the usual arguments for representative rather than direct democracy. Madison made the strongest case in *The Federalist*.[2] I believe Mr. Pyknites agrees on this point."

Pyknites nods his head.

"But there is much more," Deukalion goes on. "To repeat my mantra, constitutional democracy lowers the stakes of conflict and thus of politics. Conflicts among ethnic groups may be the most obvious, but you also have social and economic divisions. Although not as cleanly as in South Africa, these tend to follow ethnic fault lines and so reinforce distrust among groups. All those groups whom Minister Pilsudski mentioned as victims of discrimination also tend to be the least well off. They will press for more generous welfare programs, for redistributions of wealth. All sides need to be reassured that the new political system will respect basic rights, whatever specific policies take shape.

---

1. For a snapshot and analysis of public opinion shortly after the birth of constitutional democracy there, see James L. Gibson, *Overcoming Apartheid: Can Truth Reconcile a Divided Nation?* (New York: Russell Sage, 2004); and James L. Gibson and Amanda Gouws, *Overcoming Intolerance in South Africa: Experiments in Democratic Persuasion* (New York: Cambridge University Press, 2003).

2. Esp. Nos. 10 and 57.

"More specific is the danger that representatives will sometimes blindly follow popular passion. 'Wherever there is an interest and a power to do wrong,' Madison claimed, 'wrong will generally be done, and not less readily by a powerful and interested party than by a powerful and interested prince.' In the American system, he added, 'the real power lies in the majority of the Community, and the invasion of private rights is *chiefly* to be apprehended, not from acts of Government contrary to the sense of its constituents, but from acts in which Government is the mere instrument of the major number of its constituents.'[3] Mr. Pyknites says judges at times also succumb to popular passions, and he's right. But the example he cited of the Japanese-American cases from World War II involved the Supreme Court's sustaining legislation enacted by a popularly elected Congress and signed into law by a popularly elected president. I agree that constitutional courts cannot always remain above partisan struggles. Nevertheless, constitutionalism tries to insulate judges from such conflicts. It has not always been successful, but it has been more successful than representative democracy has been in insulating elected officials from popular prejudices.

"There is also a quite different danger," Deukalion continues. "Most citizens have limited political knowledge and few serious political interests. This situation allows representatives, out of the sight of most of their constituents, to form coalitions and bargain among themselves about public policy, processes that should ignite the democratic criticism of consociationism: voters don't have much voice in or even knowledge of what their representatives are doing. Douglass C. North, the Nobel laureate, argues, 'Not only could the voter never acquire the information to be vaguely informed about the myriad bills that affect his or her welfare, but there's no way the constituent (or even the legislator) could ever possess accurate models to weigh the consequences.'[4] Adam Przeworski makes a complementary point: representative democracy 'generates outcomes that are predominantly a product of negotiations among leaders of political forces rather than of a universal deliberative process.' The function of the electorate, he says, 'is to ratify these outcomes or to confirm in office those who brought them about.'[5]

"Moreover," Deukalion adds, "coalitions do not always quickly dissolve, and they may impose heavy costs on smaller groups. I cite only the American example of the conservative Republican–southern Democratic alliance that

3. To Jefferson, Oct. 17, 1788, italics Madison's; reprinted in Marvin Meyers, ed., *The Mind of the Framer* (Indianapolis: Bobbs-Merrill, 1973), pp. 206–7. In *The Federalist* No. 51, Madison asked: "But what is government itself, but the greatest of all reflections on human nature? If men were angels, no government would be necessary."

4. *Institutions, Institutional Change, and Economic Performance* (New York: Cambridge University Press, 1990), p. 109.

5. *Democracy and the Market: Political Consequences of Economic Reforms in Eastern Europe and Latin America* (New York: Cambridge University Press, 1991), p. 13.

for three-quarters of a century strangled efforts to enact federal civil rights legislation that blacks desperately needed for protection against combined state and private action denying them equal citizenship."

"Let me follow up," Pilsudski says. "I agree that few people are attentive to politics. 'Given their obstinate lack of interest in the subject,' an American newspaper editor wrote, 'asking a group of average Americans about politics is like asking a group of stevedores to solve a problem in astrophysics.'[6] Representative democracy often operates undemocratically."

"Wait," Pyknites interrupts. "It's not fair to generalize from the United States. Their constitutionalist checks have brought about precisely what Professor Deukalion says is constitutional democracy's main benefit. They have lowered the stakes of politics to the point where it often seems to be a trivial game. In a true representative democracy, people could see how Parliament was affecting their interests and how they could hold representatives responsible."

"I wasn't trying to get into that discussion," Pilsudski continues. "I wanted to ask Professor Deukalion: How could constitutionalism have helped American blacks? I thought constitutionalist checks check, not spur, governmental action."

"In part, you're right," Deukalion answers, "but constitutionalism is not merely negative. Insofar as it recognizes that every human being possesses great and equal dignity, it implies that government must do more than passively watch injustice and so has a positive dimension. Even negative constitutionalists believe that government is obliged to keep order, protect human life, safeguard private property, and enforce contracts.[7] And in both incarnations constitutionalism helped American blacks. By invalidating some of the most flagrantly discriminatory state statutes, the Supreme Court played an educational role. By reminding Americans of their basic values, most critically that of equality before the law, the Court also educated citizens. It seared the consciences of whites. A few weeks after *Brown v. Board of Education,* hundreds of clergy of all denominations, in the South as well as in the North, suddenly began preaching the gospel according to Earl Warren: God Almighty had forbidden segregation through all eternity. The Court also increased awareness among Afro-Americans. Leaders as diverse as Eldridge Cleaver and Martin Luther King Jr. exploited this new consciousness. Racial discrimination, Cleaver said *Brown* taught him, was not merely immoral, it was also unconstitutional.[8] 'Any law that uplifts human personality is just,' the Reverend King wrote in his 'Letter from a Bir-

6. Andrew Ferguson of the *Weekly Standard,* quoted in Joan Didion, "Uncovered Washington," *N.Y. Rev. of Bks.,* June 24, 1999, p. 78.

7. See esp. Sotirios A. Barber, *Welfare and the Constitution* (Princeton, NJ: Princeton University Press, 2003).

8. *Soul on Ice* (New York: McGraw-Hill, 1968), pp. 3–4.

mingham Jail.' 'Thus it is that I can urge men to obey the 1954 decision of the Supreme Court, for it is morally right; and I can urge them to disobey segregation ordinances, for they are morally wrong.' That realization spurred African-Americans to help themselves through the political as well as legal processes. Constitutionalism and democracy operated synergistically, generating the civil rights movement. Congress, which had not enacted any civil rights legislation since 1877, birthed a spate of statutes protecting ethnic minorities, women, and the handicapped."[9]

"An interesting interpretation," Pilsudski remarks. "You have more?"

"Yes," Deukalion says. "Most defenses of representative democracy assume that when the people are informed about political issues, their views 'will aggregate into a common view.'[10] This assumption, however, seldom holds in the real world. When they're well informed about most kinds of issues, 'the people' divide as often as they coalesce. On the other hand, most of the time most of the people are not well informed. On many issues of public policy there is no 'voice of the people,' only multiple voices from a few minorities. The policy choices that result are typically products of bargains among leaders, and very often 'the people' do not know what is being swapped for what. And the goods being swapped are often financial.

"Bargaining may often be functional, but its result can be a far cry from Mr. Pyknites's ideal of the people's governing themselves through representatives who reflect their preferences. This system of government meets democratic criteria only if we define democracy as Joseph Schumpeter did: the people choose their rulers in a free election, then retire until the next election."

"I disagree," Pyknites says. "In a representative democracy, representatives are chosen by the people after full and free debate and remain responsible to the people through periodic reelections. The key word here is *responsible*. Representatives offer themselves up to the people's judgment. Should we *force* people to be more politically attentive and knowledgeable than they wish to be? Isn't it enough that they can be as knowledgeable as they wish to be and that the political system encourages them to be politically attentive and knowledgeable? By raising the stakes of politics, representative democracy encourages the people to acquire and use political knowledge."

"How can the voice of the people be intelligible," Deukalion responds, "if the people have neither knowledge of nor concern for what's happening? As North would later, Schumpeter contended that the people simply do not,

9. Gerald N. Rosenberg, *The Hollow Hope* (Chicago: University of Chicago Press, 1991), misses the whole point of the massive moral and psychological change the Supreme Court initiated.

10. Russell Hardin, *Liberalism, Constitutionalism, and Democracy* (New York: Oxford University Press, 1999), p. 154, attacks this assumption.

perhaps cannot, act as Mr. Pyknites postulates.[11] He makes several contrary-to-fact presumptions: the people usually have specific policy wishes, representatives will reflect those wishes, and, most significant, the will of a majority, either of the voters or of elected officials, is the will of the people. As Schumpeter pointed out, the people form 'a mosaic that [the majority] completely fails to represent.' Mr. Pyknites uses definitions, not data, to translate his assumptions into reality. What those definitions yield—at very best—is government by popular acquiescence, a thin form of consent, not government by the people's active will expressed through their representatives' actions."

Pyknites replies: "I reject that argument."

"Of course," Strega cuts in, "all most people ever do is acquiesce—or revolt. If government gives the people peace, order, and prosperity, most of them will happily forgo voting and the other frills you two are debating. They have families to clothe and feed and medical bills to pay. For them, politics is a silly game that takes their money in taxes. Besides, when they do take politics seriously, voters consider only their short-term interests, as James M. Buchanan has shown.[12] They want low (or no) taxes along with massive spending for services they think they need."

"You exaggerate Buchanan's arguments," Deukalion replies, "and even if you didn't, Mr. Pyknites's response is still valid. As much as I respect Buchanan, he makes an abstract rather than an empirical argument. Besides, you're absolutely wrong to call due process of law a frill."

The chair raps his gavel against the dais. "We've moved afield. Mr. Pyknites has the floor and was trying to respond to Professor Deukalion. Please continue, sir."

"Thank you. I started to say that when people vote, they vote for a person and/or a platform. Americans may look on candidates as solo performers and platforms as gimmicks. So be it. Still, they choose a candidate whose discretion all voters with two digits in their IQ know will be wide, and they can hold that person responsible at the next election. In Europe, Australia, Canada, India, and Japan, parties are much more disciplined and programmatic; they tend to take clear positions that their candidates will support. Knowledgeable voters experience some, but rather few, surprises, usually because unforeseen problems arise. Nor does the concept 'representation' mean that legislators are merely their constituents' mouthpieces. The proper

11. Joseph A. Schumpeter, *Capitalism, Socialism. and Democracy,* 3rd ed. (New York: Harper and Brothers, 1950), ch. 21, esp. p. 272. For an excellent study that claims Schumpeter's early theory of democracy was also elitist, see John Medearis, *Schumpeter's Two Theories of Democracy* (Cambridge, MA: Harvard University Press, 2001).

12. It is often difficult to judge exactly what Minister Strega has in mind, but here she is probably referring to James M. Buchanan's *Democracy in Deficit: The Political Legacy of Lord Keynes* (New York: Academic Press, 1977), and *The Economics of Politics* (Lancing, UK: Institute of Economic Affairs, 1978).

relationships between representative and represented are contested, but no one in his or her right mind expects members of a parliament to be ciphers."

"I'm familiar," Deukalion responds, "with some of the literature about the proper role—or roles, as I prefer—of representatives.[13] I would not want legislators to habitually act as closely instructed agents. Indeed, I come close to Edmund Burke on this issue, though not in his view of the people as a 'swinish multitude.' My concern is not discretion per se but misuse and abuse of discretion while cloaking actions with hypocritical claims to be speaking with the voice of the people."

"My concern lies there as well," Pyknites says. "That's why I favor representative democracy's requiring legislators to stand for periodic reelection. If they have misused or abused their discretion, the voters can turn them out. What you overlook is that voting is an iterative process. When issues are important to voters, they can and will remember what their representatives have done and hold them responsible at the next election. Retrospective voting is documented by scholars[14] and feared by politicians. They have to keep looking over their shoulders."

"Some voters do factor officials' earlier behavior into choices," Deukalion admits, "but many do not; and most of those who do, do so only on a few issues. Public attention span is notoriously short, and the lapse between parliamentary votes and elections is usually years, not weeks. Furthermore, a voter's cost of obtaining accurate information about candidates is large, and the impact of a single vote is tiny. I repeat: the interests of legislators sometimes have little to do with those of their constituents, and sometimes the two conflict. But it is from being popularly designated agents that legislators get their legitimacy. As that linkage weakens, the justification for representative over constitutional democracy weakens. It is inevitable that that linkage will fray."

"Of course no two human beings can have identical interests in all things," Pyknites asserts. "But elected representatives' interests will be closer to their constituents' than those of appointed officials, because elected officials must stand for reelection. They individually and their parties collec-

---

13. For empirical studies, see, *inter alia,* Warren E. Miller and Donald E. Stokes, "Constituency Influence in Congress," 57 *Am. Pol. Sci. Rev.* 45 (1963); John C. Wahlke, Heinz Eulau, William Buchanan, and LeRoy C. Ferguson, *The Legislative System: Explorations in Legislative Behavior* (New York: Wiley, 1962). See also Roger H. Davidson and Walter J. Oleszek, *Congress and Its Members* (Washington, DC: Congressional Quarterly Press, 1981); Clem Miller, *Member of the House,* ed. John Baker (New York: Scribner's, 1962); Charles L. Clapp, *The Congressman: His Work as He Sees It* (Washington, DC: Brookings Institution, 1963); Richard Fenno, *Home Style: House Members in Their Districts* (Boston: Little, Brown, 1978); and John W. Kingdon, *Congressmen's Voting Decisions,* 3rd ed. (Ann Arbor: University of Michigan Press, 1989), esp. ch. 2. For discussions of the concept of "role," see Wahlke et al., *Legislative System,* and Walter F. Murphy and Joseph Tanenhaus, *The Study of Public Law* (New York: Random House, 1972), pp. 140–44.

14. See, for example, Morris Fiorina, *Retrospective Voting in American National Elections* (New Haven, CT: Yale University Press, 1981).

tively want to retain their posts. Thus, they will do their best to serve voters' interests. Moreover, a lot of information is free. That's what political campaigns are all about."

"My counter," Deukalion says, "is that parties and legislators are concerned about constituents' interests only to the extent they deem it necessary for reelection.[15] Your argument about responsibility and the iterative nature of elections concedes that point. Furthermore, political campaigns are all about puffing up one's own image and tearing down opponents'. Truth is only tangentially related to what's broadcast. And except on election day, a constituency is a fiction. On all other days, every representative has several, perhaps several dozen, constituencies; these vary in awareness and resources and thus in importance to political parties and individual representatives, My principal point holds: the interests of legislators and their parties often diverge from those of most of their constituents and much more often from those of sizable minorities among voters. Robert R. Palmer, one of the great modern political historians, spoke of 'the folly of identifying the deputies with the deputizers.'[16] Of necessity, politics is a profession. Pros run the game. And they have interests as professionals. Remember Roberto Michels's comment that in Britain a Labour MP had more in common with a Conservative MP than with members of the unions who elected him. In the 1960s, Americans gained much less from reapportionment than expected because, rather than risk massive changes, leaders of the two parties often acted like risk-avoiding oligopolists: they carve up markets to manage competitiveness. Professionals know how to manipulate rules—and news—to advance their own interests and conceal bargains from the mass of voters."

"You underestimate journalists and overestimate politicians. But more basically, are you arguing for more democracy?" Pyknites asks.

"I have a double argument," Deukalion responds. "First, not only do most citizens typically care very little about politics, but just as typically, legislators act first and foremost to advance their own careers, which often include jobs with large corporations or labor unions after they leave electoral politics. These interests, where such matters as campaign finance are concerned, may sharply conflict with their constituents' interests."

"We disagree," Pyknites puts in, "on how frequently those conflicts occur and on how often journalists sniff them out and the electorate votes representatives out."

"Yes, but, as George W. Bush's staff did, politicians can pay supposedly independent journalists to plug pet policies. My second argument is that when legislators do faithfully respond to public opinion, it is frequently to discriminate. A majority is not 'the people.' Representative democracy al-

15. See David R. Mayhew, *Congress: The Electoral Connection* (New Haven, CT: Yale University Press, 1974).

16. *The Age of Democratic Revolution* (Princeton, NJ: Princeton University Press, 1959), I, 221.

lows a party or coalition that controls Parliament to enact whatever policies it wants, providing it does not interfere with free political processes. (I leave aside the question of what will happen if those who dominate Parliament decide to continue their domination by gerrymandering, selective disfranchisement, or some other means of tilting the electoral scales because you, like Robert Dahl and Michael Walzer, would allow judicial intervention under such circumstances.[17]) A. V. Dicey may have exaggerated when he wrote that the British Parliament had authority 'to make or unmake any law whatsoever,'[18] but he was in good company: Benjamin Franklin noted that the British Parliament claimed 'omnipotence without omniscience.'[19] Both Dicey and Franklin came close to the truth for a pure representative democracy. And here I return to my earlier point: such a system entrusts civil liberty to political culture as perceived by a parliamentary majority, responsible only to active, informed voters—in sum, to a minority, a minority whose interests will often be deeply antagonistic to those of other minorities. Such a faith is risky in many political systems; in yours it would be perilous. For its part, constitutionalism, when alloyed with democracy, reinforces a civic culture by building up trust; it does not rely on culture alone or even on culture fortified by campaigns and elections. It uses these, but as parts of a larger network of institutions and processes that increase the chances that other political actors—who, incidentally, also read newspapers and watch television—will have interests in perceiving and curbing each other's abuses."

"Yes," Pyknites says, "legislative abuses should be curbed, indeed prevented. But I would let an informed public perform that function and the threat of that reaction—ignited by ambitious journalists and self-interested members of the parliamentary opposition—stop abuses before they occur. This sort of system will reinforce, and in the beginning help create, a democratic culture in which politicians operate at their peril. There is another aspect to this problem. The professor has alluded to the possibility of the tyranny of the majority open under representative democracy; but under constitutional democracy tyranny of the minority is an equal possibility. Ran Hirschl makes a convincing argument that much of the support for constitutionalist checks comes from elites who fear democracy.[20] Constitutionalism allows them to prevent the people from governing by preventing government's taking positive action to protect both the people as a whole and

17. Robert A. Dahl, *Democracy and Its Critics* (New Haven, CT: Yale University Press, 1989), p. 191; Michael Walzer, "Philosophy and Democracy," 9 *Pol. Th.* 379, 397 (1981).

18. A. V. Dicey, *Introduction to the Study of the Law of the Constitution*, 6th ed. (London: Macmillan, 1903), p. 38.

19. Franklin's letter of Apr. 11, 1767, to Lord Kames; reprinted in Alpheus Thomas Mason, *Free Government in the Making*, 3rd ed. (New York: Oxford University Press, 1965), pp. 90–93; the quotation is at p. 91.

20. *Towards Juristocracy: The Origins and Consequences of the New Constitutionalism* (Cambridge, MA: Harvard University Press, 2004).

specific minorities not included in the blocking alliance.[21] Inaction, as Mr. Zingaro has reminded us, can be as damaging to civil liberties as action. As Father Gregorian would instruct us, the prayer that opens every Mass asks forgiveness for 'what we have done and what we have failed to do.'"

"Every representative system," Deukalion replies, "interferes with a majority's ability to rule, as do proportional representation, bargaining among parliamentary leaders, a bill of rights, and a host of other institutional arrangements. Constitutional democracy differs only in making it clear that certain actions fall beyond the pale of proper governance and in setting up institutional structures to enforce those boundaries."

The chair taps his gavel against the dais. "Both gentlemen have stated their arguments fully. Let us move on to Professor Smitskamp. The chair recognizes Ms Baca."

"Before we move on, I must, like, share with you my deep disappointment at what both Mr. Pyknites and Professor Deukalion have said. They accept the conventional view of how best to choose representatives, right? And the Professor has contemptuously dismissed such modern devices as electronic voting. Lenin would have thought this debate was cool. He wrote that representative government is only a means to 'decide every few years which member of the ruling class is to repress and oppress the people.'[22] But Bernard Manin has shown that other methods than election are very possible and very possibly more democratic.[23] We should, you know, remember that Aristotle thought elections produce not democracy but oligarchy.[24] Montesquieu and Rousseau agreed that selection 'by lot is natural to democracy; as that by choice is to aristocracy.'[25] Elections are a substitute for democracy. At best they, like, produce an aristocracy of orators, at worst an oligopoly of rich, politically ambitious people."

"Are you suggesting," Pyknites asks, "we choose representatives by lot?"

"That would be fairer, and it's actually practical. Let me show you how. The Athenians, Romans, and Italian city-states chose some of their officials that way.[26] Today, machines randomly choose winners of national lotteries. We could allow anyone who wanted to be a representative to pick up a ticket and have a drawing every few years. What you two call representa-

21. See Robert A. Dahl's *A Preface to Democratic Theory* (Chicago: University of Chicago Press, 1956), pp. 131–32, and *Democracy and Its Critics*, chs. 4, 5, 11, 23.

22. *State and Revolution* (New York: International, 1932), p. 40.

23. *The Principles of Representative Government* (New York: Cambridge University Press, 1997).

24. *Politics*, bk. 4, chs. 8–9, 1294a-b.

25. Montesquieu, *The Spirit of the Laws*, trans. Thomas Nugent (New York: Hafner, 1949), 2.2; Jean-Jacques Rousseau, *The Social Contract*, trans. Frederick Watkins (London: Nelson, 1953), 4.3, quotes Montesquieu and says, "I agree."

26. For an excellent study of Athenian politic structures, see Mogens Herman Hansen, *The Athenian Democracy in the Age of Demosthenes: Structure, Principles, and Ideology* (Norman: University of Oklahoma Press, 1999).

tive and constitutional democracies are not democracies at all, but oligarchies. The oligarchs rotate in office, but they're still oligarchs. Lenin wasn't far wrong."

"The concept of representation," Pyknites says, "has changed since Aristotle and even since Montesquieu. We now also have the equally powerful concept of consent of the governed."

"Consent? Then why can't the people consent to choose representatives by lot rather than election? 'Government by consent' doesn't mean government by election. It doesn't even necessarily mean democratic government. The people can consent to all sorts of arrangements, right?[27] In many countries, the military depend on enlistments, not a draft. In neither case do young men enter an organization that has a hint of democracy about it and very little constitutionalism.' "

"Two responses," Pyknites counters. "First, your idea of consent is too limited. You rely on Manin, so let me quote him:

> However lot is interpreted . . . it cannot possibly be perceived as an expression of consent. . . . Under such an arrangement, the power of those selected for office at a particular time would be ultimately founded on the consent of the governed. But in this case, legitimacy by consent would only be indirect: the legitimacy of any particular outcome would derive exclusively from the consent to the procedure of selection. . . . Under an elective system, by contrast, the consent of the people is constantly reiterated.[28]

Second, consent is now also tied to the notion of official responsibility to the people. Choosing representatives by lot means those so selected don't have to face the people again.

"No, Manin is, you know, wrong on this particular point. In almost all truly democratic elections, the number of people who vote against a candidate or party is huge. And you commit the fallacy that Schumpeter identified: you conflate a majority with the people as a whole. What happens when a candidate or a party wins only a plurality? In the United States, Abraham Lincoln in 1860 and Woodrow Wilson in 1912 won only a plurality of the popular vote, as did Bill Clinton in 1992 and 1996. The Republicans denied the legitimacy of Clinton's claim to office, but they were very quiet about George W. Bush's actually losing the popular vote in 2000. Moreover, you and Manin are assuming that all citizens vote. They don't, even where the

27. Some scholars would doubt that human beings can in any morally meaningful way "consent" to be subjects of a totalitarian system. See Walter F. Murphy, "Consent and Constitutional Change," in James O'Reilly, ed., *Human Rights and Constitutional Law: Essays in Honour of Brian Walsh* (Dublin: Round Hall, 1992); and below, Chapter Fifteen. Scholarly as well as partisan literature on consent is somewhat confused. Russell Hardin summed it up best: "Perhaps there is no part of the political vocabulary that is more subject to the distortions of hortatory and self-boosting rhetoric than the vocabulary of consent." *Liberalism, Constitutionalism, and Democracy*, p. 142.

28. P. 85.

law requires them to, as in Australia. Worse, less than half of eligible voters turn out for American off-year congressional elections, and only a bit more do so in most presidential elections. What makes that sort of choice democratic? As for responsibility, if we used lottery, officials could be prosecuted for malfeasance in office as they often were in Athens, and after leaving office they would have to live under the laws they had made, right?[29] But your question totally misses the whole point: representatives selected by lot would be the people in microcosm. Elected representatives really aren't."

"Four hundred people," Deukalion intervenes, "can't accurately mirror forty million."

"Maybe in a statistical sense, but lot offers a better chance of real representation. In America, both the Federalists and the Anti-Federalists understood that election would mean that 'notables' would form the bulk of candidates. Few people who work for wages, professionals such as schoolteachers and doctors, or stay-at-home mothers who aren't wealthy can take the time off to campaign or even to raise the money needed. Madison and the other Federalists thought that having an elite govern would be a good thing. *The Federalist* Nos. 10 and 57 reek of elitism, of the superiority of the elected over the electors. The elected will supposedly be the 'men who possess most wisdom to discern, and most virtue to pursue' the common good.[30] Many others, perhaps Madison himself, saw that the rich, the leisured, and, of course, the professional politicians would run government for themselves but in the people's name. One Anti-Federalist protested that '[i]t is deceiving the people to tell them they are electors, and can chuse legislators, if they cannot in the nature of things, chuse men among themselves, and genuinely like themselves.'[31] And that's, like, the crux of the matter: representatives chosen by lot are 'genuinely like' their people. If we have elections, representatives will soon become professionals. If our system develops as it has in the United States, they'll be mostly toadies—*ward heelers* is the term, I believe— who suck around the edges of power until their turn to run comes around, or they'll be rich lawyers who can take time off from their practice and even

29. Madison listed this requirement as a check on elected legislators (*The Federalist*, No. 57). In reply to his own question of what would keep the legislature—in context, the House of Representatives—from discriminating in favor of the interests it represents, he wrote: "the genius of the whole system; the nature of just and constitutional laws; and, above all, the vigilant and manly spirit which actuates the American people—a spirit which nourishes freedom and in return is nourished by it."

30. *The Federalist*, No. 57. As would be expected, Hamilton foresaw (and approved of) even greater differences between electors and elected than did Madison. See *The Federalist*, No. 35. And Madison's own elitism was an integral part of his political outlook. See the analysis in Richard K. Matthews, *If Men Were Angels: James Madison and the Heartless Empire of Reason* (Lawrence: University Press of Kansas, 1995).

31. Letters from *The Federal Farmer*, No. 7, reprinted in Herbert Storing, ed., *The Complete Anti-Federalist* (Chicago: University of Chicago Press, 1981), 2:266. (The identity of the author is still disputed, though at one time most scholars believed him to be Richard Henry Lee. See ibid., 2:215–16.)

gain clients through the publicity they get. If our system develops in the European way, we'll get mostly the first sort. In either case, we'll get professionals who are not like us."

"I'm not a proponent of representative democracy," Deukalion says, "but you paint too bleak a picture. Furthermore, representation is a multiflavored word. You're using that word to mean 'chosen from.' That connotation is legitimate and is reflected in consociationalism. But today representation more often means 'chosen by.'[32] That's how Mr. Pyknites and I were using the term."

"You can't escape through semantics," Baca continues. "Each of you two, like, wants an oligarchy; you only disagree about what kind of oligarchy. Constitutionalists, at least, are honest about wanting a judicial oligarchy to curb the people's power. Mr. Pyknites's oligarchic representation denies an important aspect of the democratic equality it purports to promote by setting up a barrier to free entry into politics. The paper we read in our first week said that, in a democracy, not only was voting a right but so was running for office. But for most of us, representative democracy makes a mockery of that second right. To have a fighting chance of electoral success, a candidate must be rich, have access to lots of money, or have patrons in power—or possibly all three. This way your system denies most citizens a fair opportunity for political office. That sort of equality was dear to Athenians, and it should be dear to us if aspire to be democratic. If we endorse what Peter Singer, hardly a religious sectarian, calls 'the principle of equal consideration of interests,'[33] we would give equal weight to the interest of each person affected by a decision. And we all have an interest in governing as well as in being governed, right? Your system of representation privileges the interest in governing held by those who are, like, rich and/or have rich and powerful friends."

"This is sophistic," Strega says. "Elites govern. Period! The only question is which elite. Look around. We're not average men and women. We're all talented, educated people who have made something of our advantages. As a graduate student, Ms Baca, you are a member of an intellectual elite. As a leader of the students' revolt, you're a member of a political elite. And you weren't chosen for either role by lot but because of your talent. Still, you want us to choose representatives by lot as if we were a pack of Greeks living twenty-three hundred plus years ago?"

"This isn't about me or even all of us here. It's about our country. Mr. Pyknites wants to change the classic notion of citizenship. Aristotle described a citizen as one who alternately governs and is governed. Election fixes it so only a few can govern. And this is no accident. Manin describes

32. See Murphy and Tanenhaus, *Study of Public Law*, pp. 37–38 and ch. 3.

33. *Practical Ethics*, 2nd ed. (New York: Cambridge University Press, 1997), p. 21. This principle makes, as Singer admits, a minimal claim. "What the principle really amounts to is this: an interest is an interest, whoever's interest it may be."

how the British and the French tried to rig their electoral systems so that only members of elites could compete for office. And only a few years ago, a noted scholar described electoral politics as 'the most protected industry in the United States.'"[34]

"What I want to know," Pyknites puts in, "is exactly what Ms Baca is proposing. Is she suggesting direct democracy or a different scheme of representation?"

"I want to share with you a different representational system, one that, while not perfect, is better than yours.[35] We could establish a system of representation by lot augmented by electronic referenda. We could divide the country into legislative districts, each entitled to multiple members to allow proportional representation. Each representative after the first parliament would serve for six years; members of the first parliament would, as did the first American senators, divide into groups—again chosen by lot—to serve, two, four and six years so that a new selection would take place every two years, so we would have, you know, both experience and new ideas."

"Fascinating," Gregorian says, with only a trace of irony.

"Actually, it's cool. Each citizen over twenty-five who wished to take part in the lottery could obtain a free ticket. Winners would be chosen as in national lotteries now. There would be no campaigns, no need for candidates to mortgage their integrity to pay for television and travel."

"May the chair inquire how electronic referenda enter in?"

"When issues come up in Parliament," Baca explains, "they would be posted on the Internet for one week, along with summaries of the arguments for and against. At the end of that time, every citizen in each district could, you know, instruct his or her representatives how to vote. The delegates from each district would then vote according to the proportion of their constituents' wishes: If there were five delegates from a district and the constituency divided 60–40, three delegates would vote for the proposal and two against."

"What would be the point of choosing representatives, by lot or otherwise?"

"There will be much work to do within Parliament, such as formulating issues, agreeing on exact language for legislation, and drawing up arguments for and against—full-time work. But what we would ensure is that representatives closely represent their constituents. To the extent that Professor

---

34. Adam Przeworski, *Democracy and the Market: Political and Economic Reforms in Eastern Europe and Latin America* (New York: Cambridge University Press, 1991), p. 91.

35. Before gentle readers dismiss Baca's suggestion as silly, they might note that Akhil Reed Amar has concluded: "Enormous logistical, political, and psychological questions surrounding lottery voting remain to be explored. . . . But like the microeconomist's model of an economy without transaction costs, or the philosopher's model of the perfectly just republic, the lottery model can also serve as a potent heuristic device." "Note: Choosing Representatives by Lottery Voting," 93 *Yale L. J.* 1283, 1308 (1984).

Deukalion and Mr. Pyknites are right, their arguments, like, prove that we should abolish the traditional system of representation."

"If I may steal from another poet," Zingaro chimes in: "'Though this be madness, yet there is a method in 't.' I was an insider as far as prison was concerned, but otherwise I have been an outsider in this society. As I see it, elections pose a conflict between freedom and equality. The costs of campaigning give great advantages to the rich and famous. And then there's prejudice.[36] If people can vote for whomever they wish, a majority of voters may oppose candidates whose race, ethnicity, gender, physiognomy, or geographical origin they don't like. So it's probable that successful candidates will not include any of those who run afoul of the majority's prejudices, even though those excluded may be the best qualified by all the objectively relevant criteria such as intelligence, integrity, and energy. Thus, as a member of a despised minority, I can't dismiss choice by lot as foolish, though I concede it would be difficult to persuade our citizens to accept."

"Interesting," the chair says. "Ms Baca has given us an intellectual banquet."

"A Barmecidal feast, you mean," Strega injects.

The chair ignores the minister. "Ms Baca has offered an interesting idea. We shall need time to digest it. Perhaps we can take up her suggestion when we talk in a few days about electoral systems. Let us turn, for the time being to Professor Smitskamp. The Mufti has the floor."

"I agree with the Chair, peace be upon him, and also, as member of another despised minority, share some of Mr. Zingaro's concern, peace be upon him as well. But I need to think about what Ms Baca, for whose welfare we all pray, has proposed. Now, let me ask Professor Smitskamp, may Allah give him peace: if all democratic systems have heavy elements of consociationism, how does it help to talk about it as a separate genre?"

"Speaking separately of consociationism reminds us of the many peaceful ways of coping with ethnic divisions."

"All right. Then which democratic system does consociationism better fit?" Ajami asks.

"Both equally well."

"I'm less sure," Pyknites injects. "Professor Smitskamp has mentioned the problem that cartels of elites pose for democratic values."

"But," Deukalion counters, "Mr. Pyknites admits that representative democracies have such cartels; he just doesn't call them cartels."

The chair interrupts. "We've crossed that terrain. Something new, Father Gregorian?"

"You spoke, Professor, about consociationism's record on civil liberties

---

36. Zingaro is following Bernard Manin, *The Principles of Representative Government* (New York: Cambridge University Press, 1997), ch. 4, esp. pp. 136–38.

as quite good. But you mentioned the riots in India, not only against Sikhs but also against Christians. The government did a poor job of protecting both. And in 1999 Chief Minister Keshunhai Patel of the Hindu nationalists, the Bharatiya Janata Party, who then controlled the government, made accusations against missionaries that increased the probability of such riots."[37]

"Yes," Smitskamp says. "Consociationism gives strongest protection to groups in the ruling coalition, and Indian Christians are too small a minority to have their own party. I should add that the Bharatiya Janata Party's assertion that India is a Hindu state reverses the historic secular policies of Mohandas Gandhi, Jawaharlal Nehru, and the Congress Party and threatens not only to unravel the whole fabric of India's consociationism but ultimately to encourage interethnic violence."[38]

"Professor Jessica Jacobsohn?"

"I share Father Gregorian's concern. I'm also worried about minorities among minorities where those groups have some autonomy. Specifically, I'm thinking of women among indigenous peoples in Canada and of Muslim women everywhere. The most terrible offense is mutilating women. To call that process 'female circumcision' is like saying Lorena Bobbitt performed a *bris* on her husband.[39] How can consociationism ensure that minorities among minorities have basic rights and still give groups a real measure of control over public policies that directly touch on their traditions?"

"Again," Smitskamp answers, "I mentioned both in my presentation."[40]

The mufti interrupts: 'I must have said it before, but the Qur'an speaks of men and women as equal, and genital mutilation of women is not among Islam's precepts. It's tribal, not religious, a cruel, crude custom of many groups within and outside of the Muslim world, especially in Africa. Even in India, some Borahs—certainly not Muslims—mutilate women.'[41]

---

37. See Celia W. Dugger's articles in the *N.Y. Times*, Feb. 19 and Mar. 19 and 23, 1999.
38. For general analyses of the policies of the BJP Party, see Thomas Blom Hansen and Christophe Jaffrelot, *The BJP and the Compulsion of Politics in India* (New York: Oxford University Press, 2000).
39. Without realizing it, Jacobsohn is quoting a remark by Steven Pinker, *How the Mind Works* (New York: W. W. Norton, 1997), p. 447.
40. For more complete critiques of consociationism, see Hans Daalder, "The Consociational Democracy Theme," 26 *World Pols.* 604 (1974), and Donald L. Horowitz's two articles "Constitutional Design: An Oxymoron?" and "Provisional Pessimism: A Reply to Van Parijs," both in Ian Shapiro and Stephen Macedo, eds., *Designing Democratic Institutions*, Nomos 42 (New York: New York University Press, 2000). For analyses of the more specific problem of the group rights of minorities and individual rights in constitutional and representative democracies, see D. L. Sheth and Gurpreet Mahajan, eds., *Minority Identities and the Nation-State* (New York: Oxford University Press, 2000).
41. The mufti's unacknowledged source is Chiranjivi J. Nirmal's concluding essay, "Setting an Agenda," in a book he edited: *Human Rights in India: Historical, Social, and Political Perspectives* (New York: Oxford University Press, 2000).

"If you were in our shoes, how would you handle that problem?" Jacobsohn asks.

Smitskamp hesitates. "Were the choice mine, I would try to persuade Parliament to mandate fair employment opportunities and equal treatment in matters like ownership of group property, divorce settlements, and custody of children. Within that framework, I would give groups a veto over most policies directly affecting their customs, but not including genital mutilation."

"But," Jacobsohn persists, "are we likely to get such civil rights legislation from a legislature that has consociational checks built into it?"

"It would be difficult," Smitskamp admits.

"The problem that granting semiautonomy to some groups raises for women's equality has been duly noted," the chair says. "I don't know what more we can say. Let us move on. Mr. Pyknites?'

"I'll have more to say when we discuss specifics like electoral systems, but I must note a general point here: consociationism tends to institutionalize ethnic divisions—unhealthy for representative democracy and, I would assume, for constitutional democracy as well.[42] We need political arrangements that dull, not sharpen, ethnic divisions."

"I don't hear," the chair says, "any great move toward adopting a full-scale consociationist system." The colonel looks around the room. "No one else asks to be recognized, so I assume that Professor Smitskamp's presentation is clear. I would add that it has also been very helpful to me. As an ignorant soldier, I had never thought about such matters. I seem to recall from my youth a biblical saying to the effect that he who adds to knowledge adds to sorrow. Let us take a fifteen-minute break for coffee and then question Deputy Minister Strega."

As the members take their seats, the chair begins: "Ms Minister, how does your system of guided capitalism differ from fascism, which we agreed to exclude?"

"There are several obvious differences. First, guided capitalism neither needs nor wants a charismatic *führer, duce,* or *caudillo* in command. No more nor less than any other political system, it may require a charismatic leader to initiate it, but operating it requires quiet, efficient economic experts, not demagogues. There, in Chalmers Johnson's famous phrase, politicians reign, but bureaucrats rule.[43] Second, the only ideology guided capitalism proclaims is that it is better to be rich than to be poor. Third, guided capitalism does not imply ethnic or racial superiority, focus on territory *irredenta,* or

42. For a fuller critique of consociationism, see Horowitz, "Constitutional Design."

43. Quoted in Steve Chan, "Democratic Inauguration and Transition in East Asia," in James F. Hollifield and Calvin Jillson, eds., *Pathways to Democracy: The Political Economy of Democratic Transitions* (New York: Routledge, 2000), p. 185.

hark back to a *volk*'s lost empire.[44] Its spirit is pragmatic, not euphoric. Its stance is pacific, not belligerent. It tries to build society on a rational, commercial model rather than a military one. As such, it respects the rule of law; terror in any form is taboo. Is that response adequate?"

"Yes, thank you," the chair replies. "Mufti?"

"A questions still gnaws at my ignorant mind: How does the system she advocates differ from the one from which we were so recently rescued?"

Strega sighs. "That answer is also obvious. First, the members of our junta were corrupt; whatever their early ideals, those men quickly yearned only for more power and more money. Guided capitalism is less likely than most regimes to be corrupt, because public servants must meet clear standards. It is, of course, possible that we could see venal arrangements between officials and firms such as those that developed under Soharto in Indonesia. If, however, we are careful, we can establish a regime like Singapore's, where corruption is about as low as it gets in any governmental system. Second, the purpose of public policies will be to improve the economic status of the country as a whole, with benefits spread as widely across the citizenry as is compatible with economic efficiency. Third, although the new regime will not immediately institute full democratic and constitutionalist arrangements, its leaders will pledge to move in those directions as soon as the economy is functioning smoothly. Indeed, as gestures of good faith, they might well initiate some of those arrangements rather promptly. They might, for instance, dissolve the secret police and Special Forces and end governmental control of private associations. On the other hand, they might continue the ban on strikes and even draft workers for particular segments of the economy, and negotiations between labor and management would be supervised by public officials who have the twin objectives of economic efficiency and wide distribution of wealth. I look forward to immediate publication of regulations to which all citizens would be subject, fairly administered by public officials, with cases to be tried before impartial judges."

Colonel Martin nods toward the center of the hall. "Father Gregorian, the floor is yours."

"Minister, I sensed that your system would place economic growth above all else."

"If you would add peace to prosperity, you would be correct. Without domestic peace, we cannot have prosperity; without prosperity, we cannot have either political stability or freedom. Our people will not accept a governmental system that leaves them mired in poverty. Without prosperity, constitutionalism and democracy are doomed, while prosperity often begets liberty."

44. See Aristotle Kallis, *Fascist Ideology: Expansionism in Italy and Germany, 1922–1945* (New York: Routledge, 2000).

"Many political scientists disagree," Gregorian goes on, "and do so with hard data."

"Then let me also cite a political scientist, Russell Hardin," Strega interrupts. "He attributes much of the American political system's success to the fact that when that constitutional order began in 1788, the country was already so 'firmly coordinated on most of what matters . . . that politics [could] mainly deal with the chaff at the margins.'[45] And 'what matters' has been the economic arrangements that have fostered prosperity."

"Thank you. As I was saying, Juan Linz and Alfred Stepan say that putting prosperity before stable democracy—they seem to mean constitutional democracy—turns upside down 'the legitimacy pyramid,'[46] if you'll forgive the literary barbarism. They cite public opinion polls from Spain after 1975, Argentina after 1983, and Eastern and Central Europe after 1989 to show that people do differentiate governmental from economic systems. Although respondents tended to be dissatisfied with their economic lot, they also tended to support their hyphenated democratic regimes. If you want a concrete example of the problems of putting economic before political reform, look at the Russians. Those people teeter on the brink of economic and political disaster."

"I've read Linz and Stepan. Once they get off their pet hobbyhorse of the superiority of parliamentary over presidential systems, they make plausible arguments. But their data cover a short time span, and later surveys reported by the *Economist* show unhappiness with democracy in much of Latin America.[47] Support for any political system that replaces a harshly oppressive regime is likely to have a certain stickiness, thickened by the uncertainties of another shift in regime. But we can't count on that support's enduring for many years. 'Giving up wealth and income for other values is one thing in the face of a common and hated oppressor,' Douglass North says, 'but the value of the trade-off changes as the oppressor disappears.'[48] Let's see what happens in Eastern Europe during the next few decades. As for Russia, a quarter-century of Stalinist terror, followed by an even longer period of corrupt authoritarianism, doomed that country to economic, political, and social disasters. Besides, the Russians went about reform in a predictably backward fashion. First they tried political liberalization; then, with discipline shattered, they attempted economic reform. Mikhail Gorbachev's advisers conceded they had made 'a horrible mistake.'[49] They produced a

45. *Liberalism, Constitutionalism, and Democracy,* p. 30.

46. Juan J. Linz and Alfred Stepan, *Problems of Democratic Transition and Consolidation* (Baltimore: Johns Hopkins University Press, 1996), pp. 129, 195, 222–23, 225–30, and ch. 21.

47. "Democracy's Low-Level Equilibrium," Aug. 4, 2004, pp. 35–36.

48. North, *Institutions, Institutional Change, and Economic Performance,* p. 90.

49. Samuel P. Huntington, "What Cost Freedom: Democracy and/or Economic Reform?" 15 *Harv. Int'l Rev.* 8, 12 (1992–93), reports his conversations in 1989 with Gorbachev's aides.

state that couldn't govern and an economy run by gangsters. You must remember that, under Moses, the ancient Israelites' transition from slavery to independence required a generation to die off. The Russians will have to suffer the same fate, but probably for two generations. But we don't need to endure such chaos. We can enjoy decent, efficient government if we opt for guided capitalism."

"But if Linz and Stepan are right . . ." Gregorian begins.

"The issue is not which group of closet scholars is right. We have a weak society. We need a strong state to compensate."

"I would like," the mufti says, "to inquire into what seems to me to be implicit in the Minister's presentation: a high level of economic development will tow a democratic and/or constitutionalist regime in its wake. I first encountered this reasoning as justifying America's giving China 'most favored nation' status in trade despite that country's systematic violations of human rights. That argument was not persuasive in the Sino-American context; it is less so in ours."

"My dear sir," Strega interrupts, "you are not an economist but a theologian. Had you studied economics, you would know that long ago Frederick Hayek, Milton Friedman, and Joseph Schumpeter[50] linked individual liberty to the development of capitalism."

"But I am still troubled," Ajami replies. "My research assistant has provided me with an article by Thomas Carothers, who says that of the hundred or so supposedly transitional regimes, only about twenty have moved toward a truly open society.[51] That pattern does not encourage me to link economic development with free government. And the history of Weimar Germany frightens me. Although it had endured grievous economic problems from 1920 to 1930, it was the most technologically and culturally advanced European society. Yet when the Nazis came to power, the overwhelming majority of those Germans accepted brutish racist rule not only as fully legitimate for themselves but as one that should murderously conquer the rest of Europe. Given this history, why should we believe guided capitalism will follow a 'virtuous cycle' and produce civil government?"[52]

'You misunderstand me. I am not promising utopia. I repeat: neither politics nor economics offers guarantees. I do not claim that some sort of democratic regime will follow as night the day from economic development,

50. Hayek, *The Constitution of Liberty* (London: Routledge and Kegan Paul, 1960); Friedman, *Capitalism and Freedom* (Chicago: University of Chicago Press, 1962); and Schumpeter, *Capitalism, Socialism, and Democracy.*

51. "The End of the Transition Paradigm," 13 *J. of Democ.* 5 (2002).

52. Lucian Pye recites some of these arguments: "Democracy and Its Enemies," in James F. Hollifield and Calvin Jillson, eds., *Pathways to Democracy: The Political Economy of Democratic Transitions* (New York: Routledge, 2000); see also, in the same volume, the chapters by Cal Clark, "Modernization, Democracy, and the Developmental State in Asia: A Virtuous Cycle or Unraveling Strands?" and Steve Chan, "Democratic Inauguration and Transition in East Asia."

only that without economic development we are apt soon to revert to another junta-ish system. If we must bet—and we do—I'd put my money on Hayek and Friedman rather than on a few ignorant political scientists. Guided capitalism offers our best chance, because it offers the discipline that other more or less democratic regimes cannot. Democratic government always panders to what voters believe are their immediate interests; long-term interests demand too much sacrifice for such political arrangements."

"I agree," Pyknites puts in, "that we need a strong government, and, if not absolutely essential, prosperity increases the odds for stability. I disagree with the Minister's solution. Representative democracy can produce a government as strong as we need and do so without damaging the people's freedoms and their right to change their political system."

"Plato," Strega replies, "said that democracy was a 'charming form' of government. I want a political system that will not charm us but bring us prosperity so some day we can be truly free."

"Let's go back to Linz and Stepan," Minxin Wei, the banker, cuts in. "Since their book came out in 1995, of Eastern and Central European countries outside the old Soviet Union only Romania has seriously flirted with authoritarianism. Equally important for us, although most of these countries have made economic progress, only the Czech Republic and Hungary have made dramatic strides."

"I repeat," Strega says, "we have only data from the short run; and second, even if those countries can remain poor and not revert to oppressive government does not mean *we* can."

"Yes," Wei concedes, "but Linz and Stepan offer a more general argument: democracy can cope with economic adversity better than authoritarian systems, because the latter's legitimacy depends on economic success. When bad times come, those regimes have only shallow reservoirs of legitimacy. On the other hand, democratic governments of either form carry their own legitimacy. Moreover, the fact that elections are regularly imminent opens the possibility that a new government can peacefully correct current failures."

"Plausible," Strega concedes, "but our revolution was more about economics than politics. The junta stirred up people's hopes that their lives would get better, that they could live, if not like Germans or Swedes, at least like Spaniards. When those hopes collapsed, the people began to resist. We can't let that frustration continue to fester."

"The causes of our revolt are more complex than you assert," Wei says. "Economic deprivation made people restless, but political oppression—and knowledge that others had thrown off similar oppression—made them ready to rise up. We had almost had our own Tiananmen Square, but our armed forces had the courage and decency that Chinese officers lacked."

Colonel Martin seems to blush. "Let us move ahead," he says. "Minister Pilsudski?"

"You quote, among others, Douglass North. But wasn't the whole thesis of his book that the political system determines the institutional framework within which economics operate?[53] If he is correct—and it is worth noting that Josef Stalin made a similar argument in 1950[54]—you are focusing on the wrong problem. Doesn't political reform have to come first?"

"What do you think I've been talking about?" Strega exclaims. "I want us, a political body established to create political institutions, to set up a political system that will allow guided capitalism to function so it can bring our people material happiness. After we do our political work, economists can do their work of bringing prosperity; then the next round of politicians can, if they want, change the political and economic systems."

"Yes, Dr. Kanuri?"

"I would ask the Deputy Minister if she has read the book by Bruno S. Frey and Alois Stutzer on happiness, economic advancement, and rights of political participation."[55]

"I have not."

53. *Institutions, Institutional Change, and Economic Performance.*

54. "Concerning Marxism in Linguistics" (1950), in Josef Stalin, *Marxism and Linguistics* (New York: International, 1950), esp. p. 50, where he wrote that although the "superstructure" of a society is the product of the economic base—orthodox Marxism—"this does not mean that it merely reflects the base, that it is passive, neutral, indifferent to the fate of its base, to the fate of the classes, to the character of the system. On the contrary, no sooner does it arise than it becomes an exceedingly active force, actively assisting its base to take shape, to consolidate itself, and doing everything it can to help the new system." For analysis of this essay, which turned Marxism on its head, see Vernon V. Aspaturian, "The Contemporary Doctrine of the Soviet State and Its Philosophical Foundation," 48 *Am Pol. Sci. Rev.* 1031 (1954).

55. *Happiness and Economics* (Princeton, NJ: Princeton University Press, 2002). There is a growing body of literature on possible connections between money and what people call happiness. See, for example, Richard A. Easterlin, "The Economics of Happiness," *Daedalus*, Spring 2004, who says at p. 31: "To judge from survey responses, most people certainly think [there is a connection], although there is a limit." When asked how much more money is needed to make them happy, most say about 20 percent. But health seems more important than income. Although income tends to increase with age, happiness does not, perhaps because problems with health also increase. Divorce and death of spouse also decrease happiness markedly. Easterlin concludes: "Most people could increase their happiness by devoting less time to making money and more time to nonpecuniary goals such as family life and health" (p. 33). See also Easterlin, "Does Economic Growth Improve the Human Lot?" in Paul David and Melvin Reder, eds., *Nations and Economic Growth: Essays in Honor of Moses Abramovitz* (New York: Academic Press, 1974), and "Will Raising the Incomes of All Increase the Happiness of All?" 27 *J. of Econ. Behav. and Org.* 35 (1995). In these articles, Easterlin argues that a change in relative income is more important that the size of income. Some decades earlier, W. G. Runciman arrived at a rather similar conclusion: *Relative Deprivation and Social Justice: A Study of Attitudes to Social Inequality in Twentieth-century England* (Berkeley: University of California Press, 1966). Using some of the same data as Easterlin, Robert H. Frank, "How Not to Buy Happiness," *Daedalus*, Spring 2004, pp. 69ff., suggests that happiness does not increase with absolute gains in income but with how people spend their money.

"Allow me to give a quick summary that does not do justice to the book's richness. These two economists use data from interviews of six thousand respondents in all twenty-six Swiss cantons, ranked according to the degree of direct democracy they allow. Frey and Stutzer found that even with such factors as age, sex, and income controlled, small increases in political rights generally produced much greater increases in what respondents said was their level of happiness than did comparable amounts of money. In contrast, more income did not produce statistically significant increases in subjective evaluations of happiness except among respondents at the upper levels of income."

"So?"

"So these data support Linz and Stepan and indicate that people highly value political freedom and are willing to sacrifice some economic advantage for political rights."

"To some extent your information is relevant," Strega admits, "but how relevant for how long? I wouldn't extrapolate from the views of middle-class Swiss, who're rich by our standards, to those of our poor citizens."

Minxin Wei speaks: "I have another question. Both you and Professor Deukalion talk about the serious problems money presents for representative democracy, whether through campaign contributions or through less subtle bribery. How would your system cope with these problems? Surely bureaucrats would be targets for special interests, including bankers like me."

"Of course, but that danger lurks in any political system. It is less likely under guided capitalism. First, civil servants needn't run for election and so don't need big campaign chests. Second, because the salaries of civil servants are matters of public knowledge, conspicuous consumption would be obvious. Third, once the bureaucracy is established, an esprit de corps builds up and officials will want their colleagues' respect, just as soldiers do. Napoleon, after all, claimed he could keep an army together with a few pieces of ribbon. Last, I remind you that Singapore's government is among the cleanest in the world.'

"Anything further?" Colonel Martin asks. "Very well, then, we turn to Professor Whaide.

Pyknites speaks first: "Professor, what you preach is essentially Catholic moral philosophy, modernized Thomism. Won't your 'perfectionist state' quickly become a confessional state and exacerbate existing distrust among our Protestants, Jews, Muslims, agnostics, and atheists?"

"Why should it?" Pastor Glückmann interrupts. "Without rehashing our earlier debate, there is a core of morality that all people of goodwill accept. Professor Whaide urges us to construct a political system whose public policies frankly confront moral considerations. As a Lutheran, I did not find his approach sectarian, though our answers to particular questions might differ. He advocates our confronting the fact that important public policies raise moral problems. Minister Strega has made negative remarks about our interest in morality, but her efforts to reform our medical system were not solely aimed at quieting public unrest. I believe she recognized that it was morally wrong that infants were dying from lack of medical care, that sick children and adults were going without treatment, and she tried to right those moral wrongs. Ms Strega is a better person than she would like us to believe."

"Possibly, Pastor," Strega says. "But you and I are the only two who believe it."

"I doubt that, Ms Minister, but regarding Professor Whaide's larger message: we are all moved by moral considerations to advocate or oppose certain public policies. We deceive others when we conceal that motivation. Worse, we deceive ourselves. Our new political system should encourage open discussion of moral judgments, try to convince us to convince others we are right, and encourage others to try to persuade us of our being wrong."

"How," Strega asks, "would the Pastor handle a situation in which, for example, after full and fair debate the legislature forbade medical treatment to infants with spina bifida, beyond coping with any pain they might have?"

"I don't know, I honestly don't."

"Fair enough. Then let me ask the question of our Jesuit. How would he react?"

"I would fight such legislation. If we were facing a crisis in which disease were rampant and medical facilities overwhelmed, I might merely weep. Triage is sometimes a harsh fact of life. During battle, it is certainly moral for doctors to give priority to the wounded who have the best chances of survival. But as poor as we are, we are not at that stage.'

"We most certainly are at that point," Strega says tartly, "and so is every other nation in the world. Even the United States can't support research to the extent needed to develop cures for AIDS, coronary disease, cancer, multiple sclerosis, and strokes, to mention only the most obvious illnesses. Instead, the American Congress throws enough money at each to placate powerful lobbies but not enough to find a cure for any one of these diseases. And you still haven't answered my question."

"I didn't because, like the Pastor, I don't know what I would do. I hope I would try to persuade medical personnel to disobey the law."

"Even though treating ten infants with spina bifida might mean that a hundred children with other diseases would die because scarce resources went to the first group?" Strega asks.

"Again, if we were facing a crisis . . ." Gregorian begins.

"But every nation faces a continuous medical crisis," Strega cuts in. "Thousands of infants and adults die daily from diseases for which adequately funded research could soon discover cures. As long as resources are scarce, every allocative choice we make has negative as well as positive consequences. To weigh each option on a moral scale invites paralysis, a result that has only negative consequences. We should weigh our options on a utilitarian scale: which choice yields the greatest good for the greatest number of people? That scale is not as finely calibrated as we'd like; but by using as our prime criterion for politics the arrangements that are likely to produce the greatest prosperity, we allow citizens to make the choices they want. To me, that's freedom, that's respecting what you clerics call human dignity."

"We had been straying off target," the chair intervenes, "but the Minister has brought us back: the extent to which our new political system should push government to confront moral problems, debate moral alternatives, and make morally justifiable choices."

"If prosperity and good health would necessarily follow from sacrificing immediate freedom and risking that freedom over the long haul," Professor Jacobsohn says, "I'd join Ms Strega, but that just isn't so. For the moment, I'd like to question Professor Whaide. Sir, I both sympathize with and worry about your suggestions. Let's take abortion. I infer you're opposed."

"That inference would not be unjustified."

"Yes. And I assume you have strong arguments to support your strong feelings?"

"That's a fair assumption."

"I believe it," Jacobsohn says. "But I, too, have strong moral arguments that a woman should have control over her own body."

"Even to the point of killing the human life she bears?" Whaide asks.

"Yes," Jacobsohn admits. "And I know the response: If a woman has control over her body, why doesn't a man have control over his? If a woman can kill her fetus, why can't she kill other people, too? I answer that until viable outside the womb, a fetus is only potentially human—which means, incidentally, that I think late-term abortion is tantamount to homicide."

"That concession aside," Gregorian interrupts, "why doesn't the father have an equal right to order an abortion before the fetus is viable?"

"Because the father's connection to the fetus is too distant. To use a nautical trope, he's present at the keel laying but not during the building. . . . Never mind; we can endlessly debate the morality of abortion without changing each other's minds. I ask Professor Whaide a more general question: how would a perfectionist state resolve the sort of conflict you and I have?"

"Mr. Chairman," Pyknites puts in, "that's an excellent way of focusing discussion. Let's compare how different regimes have coped with this difficulty. A deliberative version of representative democracy provides the best solution: After full and fair debate, we settle the issue by judging the weight not only of the conflicting interests but also of the moral arguments. A compromise, which we can revise as we gain additional information or wisdom, would become binding public policy, perhaps something along the

German pattern, in which, to be eligible for a legal abortion, a woman twelve weeks or less pregnant agrees to counseling at a special center.[56] There she is informed of differing views about when human life begins and about alternatives to terminating pregnancy; only after presentation of a certificate that she has attended such counseling may she lawfully choose to abort the fetus."

"Why," Jacobsohn asks, "is that solution peculiar to representative democracy?"

"Such solutions are not 'peculiar' to representative democracy," Pyknites admits, "but issues are more likely to be handled in this way in that system. Problems can be settled by men and women who can adjust, negotiate around legal rules, or even create new legal rules. Representative democracy, as Walter Bagehot said, is 'government by discussion.'[57] In contrast, constitutional democracies tend to announce moral principles and produce either-or decisions on such terrible issues. American and Canadian judges have come close to holding that a woman has a right to demand an abortion, and Ireland tries to block all abortions, except to save the life of the mother."[58]

"It's peculiar," Jacobsohn muses out loud, "that Mr. Pyknites uses Germany as a model of the way representative democracy would handle abortion. He must have forgotten that Germany is a constitutional democracy. He must also have forgotten that the German Parliament at first passed a very permissive abortion statute, but the Constitutional Court struck it down as not respecting human life and dignity and kept in force the old antiabortion law until Parliament enacted the statute that Mr. Pyknites admires, a statute incidentally whose validity the Constitutional Court has sustained.[59] What Mr. Pyknites has actually provided is an instance of con-

---

56. Prior to 2000, the German Catholic bishops operated about 270 such counseling centers. They hoped to dissuade women considering abortions. Consonant with the law, however, these, like all counseling centers, issued certificates to all women who attended, stating that they had fulfilled that part of the statute's requirement. In September 1999, the pope sent the German bishops a sharply worded letter demanding that they stop such activities. Reluctantly, the bishops ordered their centers to stop issuing certificates "in the course of the year 2000." See Alessandra Stanley, "Pope Lectures German Bishops on Abortion," *N.Y. Times*, Nov. 21, 1999; Roger Cohen, "German Bishops to Halt Abortion Certificates," *N.Y. Times*, Nov. 24, 1999.

57. Walter Bagehot, *The English Constitution*, 2nd ed. (original 1872; Garden City, NY: Doubleday, n.d.), p. 59. Actually, Bagehot said all first-rate states must have government "by discussion," but he was also claiming that the only serious choice was between presidential and parliamentary regimes.

58. The basic U.S. case, of course, is Roe v. Wade, 410 U.S. 113 (1973). For Canada, compare Morgentaler v. the Queen, [1975] 20 C.C.C. (2nd) 449, decided before the adoption of the Canadian Charter of Rights and Freedoms and its entrenchment of judicial review, which sustained provisions of the federal criminal code that regulated but did not forbid abortions, with Morgentaler v. the Queen, [1988] 1 S.C.R. 30, which invalidated those same provisions after adoption of the charter. For a history of the cases, see F. L. Morton, *Morgentaler v. Borowski: Abortion, the Charter, and the Courts* (Toronto: McClelland and Stewart, 1992).

59. For the permissive law, see Abortion Case, 39 BVerfGE 1 (1975), trans. and reprinted in part in Walter F. Murphy and Joseph Tanenhaus, eds., *Comparative Constitutional Law* (New York: St.

stitutionalism and democracy's acting synergistically to bring about a result he considers laudatory."

"Perhaps," Pyknites concedes, "but three other constitutional democracies, Canada, Ireland, and the United States, made a mess of the problem, which could have been far better, if not perfectly, solved by a deliberative representative democracy."

"Well," Jacobsohn replies, "let's look more closely at how Ireland handled abortion—quite differently from the way you believe.[60] In 1983, the two largest parties—disciplined, as you would expect, since it was the Irish under Charles Stewart Parnell who, in the 1880s, taught the English about the power of disciplined parties[61]—agreed that an amendment to the constitutional text was needed to prevent an American-style solution. The Dail approved a compromise measure and, as required, submitted it to a referendum. It was subjected to vigorous discussion and won handily, becoming Article 40.3.3°:

> The State acknowledges the right to life of the unborn and, with due regard
> to the equal right of the life of the mother, guarantees in its laws to respect,
> and, as far as practicable, by its laws to defend and vindicate that right.

These words are less than clear, but they recognize that the mother need not continue a pregnancy that threatens her life. The controversies since have concerned the right of organizations to refer women to places outside of the country for abortions. Although Irish courts initially ruled against such a right, in 1992 the European Court of Human Rights at Strasbourg interpreted the European Convention on Human Rights to permit such agencies to operate, a conclusion the European Court of Justice had earlier indicated was also required by the Treaties of Rome.[62]

"During 1992 several other events took place. First, as a condition to its signing the Treaty of Maastrict, Ireland obtained a protocol exempting it from any law of the European Union that allowed abortions. Second, in the famous X Case,[63] a young, unmarried woman said she was suicidal because of her pregnancy and was going to England to have an abortion. The government obtained an injunction against her leaving. The Supreme Court,

---

Martin's, 1977), pp. 422ff., and Donald P. Kommers, *The Constitutional Jurisprudence of the Federal Republic of Germany,* 2nd ed. (Durham, NC: Duke University Press, 1997), pp. 336ff. For the later law, see Abortion Case II, 88 BVerfGE 203 (1993), reprinted in Kommers, *Constitutional Jurisprudence,* pp. 349ff.

60. For a brief summary of these events, see *Report of the Constitution Review Group* (Dublin: Stationery Office, 1996), pp. 273–79.

61. See Connor Cruise O'Brien, *Parnell and His Party, 1880–90* (Oxford: Clarendon, 1957), esp. chs. 4, 8.

62. Open Door and Dublin Well Woman v. Ireland, 64/1991/316/387-388 (1992). See vol. 246 of ECHR reports (1991) ECR.

63. Attorney General v. X, [1992] 1 I.R. 1.

however, ruled that (1) Article 40.3.3° recognized a mother's right to travel abroad to obtain an abortion when continuing a pregnancy threatened her life, and (2) a real danger of suicide constituted a constitutionally cognizable threat to the mother's life. Thereafter, following much debate, the Dail proposed new amendments to the constitutional text. The first would have eliminated risks to the mother's health—as contrasted to her life—and threats of suicide as allowing abortions. After a bitter parliamentary and public battle, this proposal was defeated at referendum by a vote of almost two to one. Two other amendments were adopted and added to 40.3.3°. They come close to entrenching the holdings of the X Case and of the Court of Human Rights:

> This subsection shall not limit freedom to travel between the State and another State.
>
> This subsection shall not limit freedom to obtain or make available, in the State, subject to such conditions as may be laid down by law, information relating to services lawfully available in another state.

"I apologize for speaking at such length," Jacobsohn concludes. "But it is critical to understand that neither Ireland nor Germany followed a rigid moral or legal course. Rather, these constitutional democracies acted through thoughtful deliberations in which judges were helpful participants. Furthermore, those processes produced compromises far more respectful of competing moral arguments than did the British Parliament in 1967, when it was free of most constitutionalist restraints. The United Kingdom rejected arguments that a fetus should have a legally protected right to life against the combined wishes of the mother and the judgment of two physicians. As a feminist, I mostly approve of the outcome, but I can't cite it as a product of thoughtful democratic deliberation."[64]

"The British solution sounds good to me," Strega comments, "much better than that wonderful Irish compromise recognizing a right to travel abroad!"

"More wonderful than you imagine. Ulster is contiguous to the Republic, and no part of the country is farther from the border than a few hours' drive—considerably less for most of the population. And, you of course

---

64. The Abortion Act of 1967, sec. 1 (1), provides that abortions are lawful if two physicians in good faith believe

(a) that the continuance of the pregnancy would involve risk to the life of the pregnant woman, or of injury to the physical or mental health of the pregnant woman, or any existing children of her family, greater than if the pregnancy were terminated; or

(b) that there is a substantial risk if the child were born it would suffer from such physical or mental abnormalities as to be seriously handicapped.

Subsection 2 allows the examining physicians to consider "the pregnant woman's actual or reasonably foreseeable environment" when judging potential injury to herself and/or her other children.

remember, the Irish do not need passports to travel to the United Kingdom; the British like to pretend that Ireland never left the Commonwealth."

"I confess that the situation is better than I thought," Pyknites says, "but amending a constitutional text is cumbersome. In a representative democracy, you need only a shift in public sentiment and . . ."

"As on gun control in the United States?" Jacobsohn asks.

"That constitutional democracy," Pyknites answers, "allows enthusiasts to quote only half of the relevant clause in an eighteenth-century constitutional text, adopted when muskets and pistols were single-shot weapons needed for defense against wild beasts and hostile Indians, and transfer that half-truth to automatic weapons with armor-piercing ammunition."

"You left out several facts," Deukalion interrupts. "First, the U.S. Supreme Court has interpreted the Second Amendment exactly as you do, only to guarantee states the authority to maintain militias, not individuals' right to own guns.[65] Second, the gun lobby falsifies history. Most Americans in the late eighteenth century did not own guns, and states limited who could join the militia.[66] Third, you do not mention that gun manufacturers and the National Rifle Association offer tons of money to legislators to help them get reelected if they support an open market in deadly weapons. These same worthies also threaten to spend larger sums to defeat representatives who oppose allowing anyone with enough cash to buy an assault rifle. Legislators' interests in funding their next campaign takes precedence over the safety of their constituents—and their children."

"And you," Pyknites responds, "omit at least one important fact: large segments of the American public love guns in a way that strikes outsiders as a dangerous worship of phallic symbols. Those people encourage legislatures to keep open their own access and their children's access to deadly weapons. If arms manufacturers and their front, the National Rifle Association, are in effect bribing legislators, they're wasting money. Most legislators who oppose strict gun controls are merely following their constituents' wishes."

"Views the NRA represents?" Deukalion replies. "If so, you've made my point about representative democracy. But most Americans are more intelligent than you believe, though I agree that many leaders of the NRA pimp

65. See, inter alia, United States v. Cruikshank, 92 U.S. 542 (1876); Presser v. Illinois, 116 U.S. 252 (1886); and United States v. Miller, 307 U.S. 174 (1939).

66. Sanford V. Levinson opened the scholarly debate with an article suggesting that the historical context of the Second Amendment raised serious constitutional problems for gun control legislation. "The Embarrassing Second Amendment," 99 *Yale L. J.* 637 (1989). For responses that argue the contrary, see esp. Saul Cornell, "Commonplace or Anachronism: The Standard Model, the Second Amendment, and the Problem of History in Contemporary Constitutional Theory," 16 *Con'l Comm.* 221 (1999); Michael A. Bellesiles, "Suicide Pact: New Readings of the Second Amendment," 16 *Con'l Comm.* 247 (1999); Don Higgenbotham, "The Second Amendment in Historical Context," 16 *Con'l Comm.* 263 (1999); and Robert E. Shalhope, "To Keep and Bear Arms in the Early Republic," 16 *Con'l Comm.* 269 (1999).

for the gun industry. Public opinion polls consistently show that a huge majority of voters favor stringent gun controls."[67]

"Our disagreement is about who governs. My basic argument for representative democracy is that a shift in public sentiment can shift parliamentary majorities, and you can easily have a new statute that better serves current moral evaluations."

"I recall," the chair intervenes, "that Professor Jacobsohn had put a question to Professor Whaide. Mr. Pyknites's spirited intervention has undoubtedly given the Professor time to gather his thoughts."

"Thank you," Whaide says. "Mr. Pyknites adumbrates what could be a sound moral algorithm when he speaks of how deliberative democracies could handle problems like abortion."

"With Professor Whaide's permission," Deukalion breaks in, "I must again point out that Mr. Pyknites spoke of how a representative democracy *should* handle problems like abortion; he did not tell us how any representative democracy *did* handle such problems. He also ignored what other constitutional democracies, such as France, Italy, and Spain, have done.[68] That's not a good argument."

"I think the professor knows," Pyknites interrupts, "that I was referring to representative democracies that are also deliberative democracies."

"Please, explain to a dumb professional soldier the distinction," the chair asks.

"I mean a representative democracy in which decision markers look at every side of a problem and protect as best they can the moral and economic interests of all parties."

"Of course," Deukalion says, "all of us here want that kind of deliberation, but even long-established democratic systems seldom get it. And the problem goes beyond elected officials who're looking over their shoulders to what a majority of their constituents want. When discussing abortion, Amy Gutmann and Dennis Thompson, two eloquent and talented proponents of deliberative democracy, do not offer the sort of deliberative example they advocate for others. They convincingly argue that decision makers should look at every side of a problem and protect as best they can the moral interests of all parties. Yet they evince small understanding of arguments for

67. According to Tom W. Smith, director of the General Social Survey of the National Opinion Research Center at the University of Chicago, three annual pollings of national samples showed that even before the tragic shootings in Littleton, Colorado, in 1999, "majorities of up to 90 percent back all [regulatory] measures except those that call for the outright outlawing of guns or restricting them only to police officers and other authorized persons." Smith, "Gun Control Support Nearly Universal," *Albuquerque Journal*, July 18, 1999 (reprinted from *Washington Post*). The full report of the results of the survey by the National Opinion Research Center can be found online at www.norc.uchicago.edu/online/gunrpt.pdf.

68. See Mary Ann Glendon, *Abortion and Divorce in Western Law: American Failure, European Challenges* (Cambridge, MA: Harvard University Press, 1987).

the fetus's right to life and ignore respected scholars who make such arguments—though they concede that these unexplored arguments are strong enough to deadlock the debate about abortion, at least for now."[69]

"Professor Whaide, would you continue?" the chair asks.

"Yes. I don't expect my reasoning always to triumph. Reason has limits, but David Hume was self-contradictory. If reason is a slave to the passions, why did he spill so much ink trying to reason with his readers? A public temper tantrum would have been more logically consistent with his claim. Even an appeal to self-interest is an appeal to an important form of reason, cost-benefit analysis. Reason isn't *always* a slave to passion, only sometimes. True, debate can be phlogistonic rather than intellectually persuasive. Even the brightest among us may be unable to convince others of anything beyond our own sincerity. I don't think the German and Irish solutions to abortion are ideal, but they're better than the American and Canadian."

"Let's move on," the chair says. "Minister Pilsudski?"

"Professor Whaide, are you familiar with Arthur Miller's play *The Crucible*?"

"The one about witch trials in Puritan New England, literary surrogates for congressional investigations during the McCarthy era? Yes, of course. I've seen it performed on the stage and in cinema. I also assign it in my graduate seminar."

"Then you know what I'm going to ask?"

"Yes. Uniformity is not among perfectionism's goals. Citizens as well as officials should confront and decide moral issues on moral grounds. As the Pastor said, every society tries to solve moral problems. A decision for abortion on demand offers a solution. That this solution does not confront the moral issues or even competing interests does not make it any less a solution. Perfectionism encourages a sense of social and moral responsibility; it pushes citizens and public officials to confront the moral problems that public policies raise. Solutions will be less imperfect if political actors candidly admit they must make moral choices, truly listen to moral arguments on all sides, openly debate on moral terms, honestly make their decisions on what they judge are the most compelling moral principles, publicly justify their decisions on those grounds, and yet realize that agreement and self-satisfaction with that agreement do not mean they have reached the perfect solution. I do not doubt that many public officials are willing so to act. What I do doubt is that many officials will so act unless the political system rewards them for doing so."

69. See Robert P. George, "Law, Democracy, and Moral Disagreement," 110 *Harv. L. Rev.* 1388 (1997), who makes similar points. For an even more searing critique of the one-sidedness of Gutmann and Thompson's argument—and from a judge who boasts of his moral relativism—see Richard A. Posner, "The Problematics of Moral and Legal Theory," 111 *Harv. L. Rev.* 1637, 1677 (1998).

"Are you advocating," Pastor Glückmann asks, "Mr. Pyknites's deliberative democracy?"

"Partly," Whaide admits. "What is missing in Gutmann and Thompson as well as in Mr. Pyknites's remarks is an affirmation that objective moral principles exist and that we can often approximate them, not merely compromise moral concerns through mutual sensitivity."

"You are asking for a great deal," Strega asserts. "What sort of institutional arrangements would reward public officials for frankly confronting moral problems?"

"As a philosopher," Whaide replies, "I'm out of my jurisdiction when I tender advice about political processes and institutions. With that caveat, I'd recommend one institution and one process. Institutionally—I assume a successful constitutional text quickly becomes a nest of institutions—any basic constitutional document should contain normative language that unequivocally states a commitment to infusing public policy with certain values." Sensing a reaction from Strega, Whaide bows to her and adds, "Begging the Minister's indulgence." He continues: "As part of the process of civic education—which should include debate about and adoption of specific public policies—people can learn that these are not empty words but concepts around which civil society is organized."

"Lots of luck," Ion Zingaro says. "We can't persuade most citizens that Gypsies are their political and moral equals. According to the *Economist*, we're 'at the bottom of every socio-economic indicator: the poorest, the most unemployed, the least educated, the shortest-lived, the most welfare-dependent, the most imprisoned, and yes, the most segregated.'"[70]

"All the more reason to etch normative language into a constitutional text," Whaide replies.

"I'm concerned about education, the old-fashioned three R's," Strega says. "I fear that religion would become the fourth R in public schools. Your suggestions require the state to inject religion into curricula."

"Morality, yes; religion, no. There's no defensible reason why children should be taught that murder, rape, and theft are matters of taste."

"You take easy cases," Strega notes. "And even they may not be easy, as Mr. Pyknites showed with inquisitors and Comanches. But what about divisive issues such as sex between consenting gay adults? How do we teach about that in public schools? If we do it in a nonjudgmental way, we raise moral and religious issues no less than if we teach that it is good or bad. What about a right of the terminally ill to end their suffering? These sorts of questions raise moral issues about which religious leaders bitterly disagree. What about religion itself? Is it better than atheism or agnosticism? Or

70. "Europe's Spectral Nation," May 12. 2001, p. 29.

should we teach that some kinds of religion are better or that one is the very best?"[71]

"Teaching morality without teaching religion is difficult," Whaide admits, "but not impossible. At varying ages and grades, one could teach basic moral principles. As students mature, one could present the alternatives and the arguments for each. The greatest difficulty is to prevent such instruction from descending either to the lowest common denominator, to the typical liberal 'you have your preference, I have mine, and we can't judge between them' or the frequent fundamentalist response, 'The Bible (or the Qur'an) gives the right answer, so we don't have to think about the problem.' Instead, we can teach general moral principles and, while letting the children draw their own specific conclusions, expect them to be logical in their reasoning and insist that they know they are making choices that have serious consequences for themselves and others."

"Where will you find," Strega asks, "pedagogic paragons who won't use such instruction for indoctrination of their own sectarian beliefs or disbelief in religion? And when educators talk about consequences, they must include the next world. Someone earlier cited Hobbes's saying that the sovereign must be the head of the church, for the power to threaten a man with death pales beside the power to condemn him to hell for all eternity. Do you want a national church?"

"You know the answer to that."

"I know you'll deny you do and believe your denial is true; but your ideas would set us down that road. Let me shift a bit. What about religious schools?"

"What about them?" Whaide asks.

"Would you allow them no matter what they teach?"

"Of course. Only a totalitarian would not."

"Two things," Strega muses. "First, after a dozen years of religious indoctrination, would children really have a free choice about whether to choose religion over atheism? Second, aren't you logically bound to outlaw religious schools, or even religions, whose teachings contradicted your fundamental principles?"[72]

"The family is usually in a much better position than a bureaucracy to know what's in a child's interests. Although some families are dysfunctional, they typically provide a warmer, healthier setting for children than do public institutions. Basically, I reject the idea that the state, on such an all-

71. For an effort to cope with these sorts of issues and maintain strict doctrinal purity, see Joseph Cardinal Ratzinger (later Pope Benedict XVI), *Truth and Tolerance: Christian Belief and World Religions*, trans. Henry Taylor (San Francisco: Ignatius, 2004).

72. Strega's argument parallels that of James G. Dwyer, *Religious Schools v. Children's Rights* (Ithaca, NY: Cornell University Press, 1998). See also the review by Stephen G. Giles, "Christians, Leave Your Kids Alone!" 16 *Con'l Comm.* 149 (1999).

important matter as the relationship of people to their Creator, can legitimately impose a 'curriculum.' You're suggesting that the state force children to be free of God."

"Indeed! But you would coerce adults as well as children into accepting your version of morality by having the state incorporate those moral concepts into its ordinary laws. You would force citizens to be free of all practices you think enslave them, differently from but no less totally than addiction to narcotics?"

"It's not the same. First, religion isn't slavery. Second, religious commitments do not always last a lifetime. Every day, adults modify or even reject their parents' religious views. I agree that groups like the Amish pose special problems; and I share the misgivings of Justice William O. Douglas about allowing parents to deny their children further free public education after eight years.[73] But for the state to impose a uniform curriculum for religion—or morals—seems to me a giant step toward totalitarianism. My suggestions regarding moral education would by no means exclude a parental right to put children in other academically qualified classes or even schools to obtain alternative forms of moral education."

"The short answer," Strega snaps, "is that your ideas can work only in a confessional state."

"That's not true," Pastor Glückmann says.

"Good people," Colonel Martin intervenes, "we have explored this issue about as much as we fruitfully can. Once again, these debates have educated, and humbled, me. I had always thought of 'politics' as combining petty jobbery and gossip to help friends and punish enemies. Until now, I had not realized how thoroughly politics is enmeshed with morality. I now have a glimpse of its grander designs, which makes me recall that I once read that Aristotle referred to politics as the 'master art.'[74] Finally I understand what he meant. I also realize that, in many ways, I favor a perfectionist state. Perhaps all military men who take their profession seriously do. We live under a code of honor that sharply distinguishes between right and wrong. On the other hand, I wonder how many civilians share our clear notions. I also wonder how unclouded my own notions would be if the soldier's roles were not so narrowly defined. As did all of my brother officers, I had great difficulty in opposing the junta. The word *mutiny* stirs like fiery bile in a professional soldier's belly; obeying orders comes easily. We confronted a moral dilemma: obeying orders meant killing unarmed women; we would have behaved as despicably as did Chinese officers in Tiananmen Square. But heeding our consciences meant mutinying. Some chose to obey, others to disobey, still others to avoid choice. All of us had heavy hearts."

73. Discussed, in part, in Wisconsin v. Yoder, 406 U.S. 205 (1972).
74. *Nicomachean Ethics*, bk. 1, ch. 2, 1094b.

"What caused you to make the choice you did?" the Jesuit asks.

"We humans are enormously complex beings, with vast talents for self-deception. None of us can ever be absolutely sure why he or she made a particular decision, at least one of serious import; but I remembered Charles De Gaulle's describing his choice in June 1940 as between honor and discipline. I believe—I hope—I chose honor, as he did."

"Is there a point to this reminiscing?" Strega asks.

"Forgive my rambling. I was trying to say that while my own preferences are clear, I am deeply concerned about dividing our people. Would the demands of a perfectionist state shred our society? Should we not confine perfectionist policies to areas in which there is widespread agreement? If not, I fear we will again find ourselves resorting to force on a large scale."

"The chair is saying," Pyknites notes, "that compromises are essential here. When morality is involved, it is usually better that government do less than more, to operate pragmatically rather than in a tightly principled fashion. That way we are likely to increase rather than decrease freedom."[75]

"But," Whaide answers, "all public policy, even a policy of inaction, curtails some people's freedom. I recall a dissenting opinion by Oliver Wendell Holmes dismissing as a 'shibboleth' the notion that a citizen is free to do what he likes as long as he doesn't interfere with the similar right of others. That liberty, Holmes said, 'is interfered with by school laws, by the Post Office, by every state or municipal institution which takes [a citizen's] money for purposes thought desirable, whether he likes it or not.'[76] We enjoy a large amount of freedom because our neighbors do *not* have unlimited freedom—which is to say, everyone's freedom must be limited if we are to live together. Laws setting minimum wages and maximum hours, regulating sale of alcoholic beverages, banning slavery, and criminalizing traffic in addictive drugs as well as child pornography all directly attack moral problems by restricting some people's freedom. Pedophiles look on laws against adults' having sex with children as oppressive, and racists view laws against discrimination as crushing society's values.

'To repeat myself, every important governmental policy at least indirectly involves morality. If you merely want to increase freedom, repeal laws against parents' selling their children or factory owners' buying slaves or hiring goons to break strikers' skulls. You won't do those things, because freedom is not your principal goal. It is a means—a cherished means, but still only a means—to your government's principal goal: helping its people live good lives. Because I doubt we shall ever have unanimous agreement on what constitutes the good life, a perfectionist state should not try willy-nilly to

75. Some of what Martin and Pyknites say here reflects Joseph Raz, *The Morality of Freedom* (Oxford: Clarendon, 1986), esp. p. 429.

76. Lochner v. New York, 198 U.S. 45, dis. op. (1905). *Lochner* was subsequently overruled.

outlaw practices some officials or even a majority of voters deem wrong. Unsupported by reasoned arguments, 'moral offensiveness' is not sufficient cause for governmental regulation. A perfectionist state, true to its principles, must move along the lines Mr. Pyknites claims for deliberative democracy, subject to the sorts of norms that Professor Deukalion includes in constitutional democracy. It rests on the belief that the roots, though not all manifestations, of morality are real and universal, not differentiated artifacts of various societies; it rests on the belief that we can *reason* together on all moral issues and resolve most of them. Government should not be restricted to negotiating *around* moral problems."

"If I may, Mr. Chairman," Wei puts in, "this debate is fascinating, but shouldn't these questions be addressed to whatever legislature and/or judiciary this caucus proposes? We are now discussing prudence, and, although all of us favor that virtue—and many of us are full of it—there is no way we can require others to be wise."

"Maybe not," Deukalion cuts in, "but we can establish processes that will force public officials to think and to give reasons for their decisions."

"This debate has made us all much wiser," Martin says. "Let us move ahead. Do we need further discussion? If not, let us decide on a basic governmental system. We face three choices: guided capitalism, representative democracy, or constitutional democracy. When we map institutions and processes under any one of those, we can insert such increments of consociationism and perfectionism as we wish."

"Question! Question!" several members call out.

"Very well," Colonel Martin says, "let us vote. Let us do so in reverse order of our discussions: first on guided capitalism, next representative democracy, then constitutional democracy."

"I object," Strega says. "We face three choices. In such situations, the first option voted on is very likely to lose, as Condorcet demonstrated in 1793.[77] Instead, we should use written ballots with each of us ranking our choices. If no proposal gains an absolute majority as first choice, we can then count second choices."

"I agree," Pyknites puts in. "But I offer a slightly different suggestion. Let's use the system the Estonian constitutional assembly employed: vote separately on each option, counting only positive votes. After the first ballot, we drop the proposal with the fewest votes, then vote again, this time on the remaining two."[78]

"Very well, the Chair will treat it as an alternative motion. Do we have a second for either proposal?"

---

77. For a discussion, see Walter F. Murphy, *Elements of Judicial Strategy* (Chicago: University of Chicago Press, 1964), pp. 85–87 and literature cited.

78. See Rein Taagepera, "Estonia's Constitutional Assembly, 1991–1992," 25 *JBS* 211, 223 (1994).

"I second Mr. Pyknites's proposal," Gregorian says.

"I second Minister Strega's proposal," Zingaro volunteers.

"Let us have a show of hands on Ms Strega's proposal," the chair asks. He looks around the room. "I count eight for. Those opposed?" He pauses. "I count twelve opposed, with four apparently not voting. The Minister's motion fails. All those in favor of Mr. Pyknites's motion? I count sixteen for, eight opposed. That motion is adopted."

Colonel Martin continues, "If there is no further procedural motion, we shall vote on each of the substantive proposals, counting only affirmative votes."

After the first balloting, the tally is constitutional democracy, 12; representative democracy, 10; guided capitalism, 2. "This count means that we proceed to choose between constitutional and representative democracy," Martin says. That count is 12–11 in favor of constitutional democracy, with one abstention. "For the record," the chair notes, "if we had been tied, I would have voted for constitutional democracy."

"Still, it was a very, very close vote," Pyknites says. "We should keep that fact in mind during further decisions."

"Mr. Chairman," Minxin Wei says, "may I make a practical proposal? In keeping with our earlier decision to look on all decisions as tentative until we have completed our work, I propose that we reaffirm that policy by agreeing that we shall reexamine this decision after we have discussed whether, in fact, constitutional democracy is a viable option for us."

. "Do I hear a second?" the chair asks.

"Second," Pyknites says.

"Very well. This proposal is fully in keeping with the spirit in which we agree to proceed. All in favor? . . . I count twenty-one votes. The motion carries." Martin taps his gavel on the rostrum. "We are in recess until tomorrow morning at 0930."

CHAPTER FOUR

The Possibility
of Constitutional Democracy

We have now to consider what is the best constitution and the best way of life for the majority of states and men. In doing so we shall not employ a standard of excellence above the reach of ordinary men . . . or the standard of a constitution which attains an ideal height. We shall only be concerned with the sort of life which most men are able to share and the sort of constitution which it is possible for most states to enjoy.

ARISTOTLE

The following morning Colonel Martin gavels the caucus back into session. "Last night, we decided that we would try to create a constitutional democracy, *if* such a regime is feasible. We now address that issue. We have on board three scholars who can help us. I have asked them to focus on what they would consider 'internal' preconditions. We, of course, are free to question them about foreign affairs. Our first speaker is Professor Claude Sprachfehler of the University of Toronto."

At the podium, Sprachfehler smiles sheepishly. "I apologize, but I get very nervous before strange audiences; therefore, I want to read my paper rather than summarize it."

Minister Strega starts to speak, but the chair cuts her off. "We understand. The stewards will serve espresso around the room." The members of the caucus brace themselves.

Some Internal Preconditions for Constitutional Democracy

The most obvious constitutional democracy precondition is military and economic strength sufficient, either alone or in alliance with others, to withstand foreign aggression. However, this condition was excluded from discussion. A second obvious candidate would be a political culture receptive to constitutional democracy ideals. Later today, that issue will be focused on by Professor Francesca Vaccarino; it is not addressed directly here, though it will be touched on. A third candidate is a prosperity-producing economy. That, too, was excluded, because it will analyzed by Professor John Maynard. In addition to these three, the following internal conditions are most likely to be constitutional democracy preconditions:

1. Absence of adamant opposition to constitutional democracy from the armed forces.
2. Presence of a sufficient number of citizens with constitutional democracy commitments to form a critical mass possessing the skills (a) to operate such a government and (b) persuade other citizens to accept constitutional democracy principles and its specific rules.
3. Open and reasonable communications efficiency within the general population and between government and the people.
4. A high literacy level.
5. Sufficient economic, ethnic, religious, and cultural homogeneity or a deep and widely felt toleration so that people can cooperate with each other.

The presence of all these candidates, as well as others such as a large, educated, and politically active middle class, would enormously increase chances of constitutional democracy's success. However, if the question refers to *preconditions,* each candidate should be looked at.

Military Neutrality

For any political system, at least passive acceptance by the armed forces is an absolute precondition. If those who virtually monopolize violence instruments are ready to turn their weapons against a regime, that regime will either conform to military demands or become a civil war victim.[1] The roll could be called of constitutional democracy fetuses aborted by military coups in Asia, Africa, and Latin America.

Although positive military support is always useful and sometimes, as in the Portugal constitutional democracy transition[2] as well as in your own, may be essential, that aid need not be necessary. Neutrality could be sufficient. However, one of the most important polity maintenance statecraft tasks is to persuade the armed forces to adopt the ethic of Anglo-American military professionals and abstain from further political intervention.[3] Once in power, civilian leaders must lessen military hostility or continue military support.[4]

1. The shah of Iran, hardly a constitutional monarch, remained in power as long as the military and secret police remained loyal and were willing to shoot down the mullahs' rioters. Once the military's support faded away, the shah was doomed, as was the Old Communists' coup against Mikhail Gorbachev in 1991. See, generally, Said Amir Arjomand, *The Turban for the Crown: The Islamic Revolution in Iran* (New York: Oxford University Press, 1988), esp. chs. 5–8.

2. Factions within the Portuguese military played several rather complex roles in ending the dictatorship. See Nancy G. Bermeo, *The Revolution within the Revolution* (Princeton, NJ: Princeton University Press, 1986).

3. Samuel Huntington, *The Soldier and the State* (Cambridge, MA: Harvard University Press, 1957), saw the Prussian army as representing the paragon of military neutrality in politics. After World War I and during the Weimar Republic, however, the German army was a frequent player in

Civilian Leadership

Constitutional democracy will not appear by magic. As has been said by Philippe Schmitter, it must be chosen by "real live political actors."[5] In short, leaders matter. Although they need not form an aristocracy based on family, wealth, or ethnicity, they must be an elite of considerable talent and probably education as well. A polity is doomed if that elite is so skill- and resource-deficient as not to be able to persuade others of constitutional democracy's desirability and later to move them to internalize needed system values. It is impossible in the abstract to accurately speak about the minimal size of this elite, but they must include leaders with political and economic expertise who can reach other elites as well as broad segments of the public. Below higher-echelon leaders, there must be a trained civil service as well as a judges corps either accustomed to working or ready to learn how to work within constitutional democracy.

India and Ireland were fortunate in these respects: trained civil servant cadres, experienced politicians, and seasoned attorneys were ready to run the new governments. Black Africa was unfortunate. Neither the British nor the French had trained many native civil servants or helped many locals gain experience in leadership positions—except as guerrilla band commanders.[6] The Belgians treated the Congolese even more shabbily. "No colony had ever faced independence so ill-prepared," a UN official said. "No Congolese had ever taken part in the business of government or public administration at any important level. Only seventeen out of a population of 13.5 million had university degrees. There was not one Congolese officer in the Force Publique, which was to become the Armée Nationale Congolaise."[7]

Communications and Literacy

Interstrata political communications are preconditions. Language commonality and widespread literacy seem essential. If only Urdu is spoken by one group and only Chinese by another, the two have little hope of communicating complex ideas and cooperating politically. Nevertheless, it is shown by India and Italy that constitutional democracy can function

---

politics. And during the final stages of World War II, professional soldiers, not civilians, attempted to assassinate Hitler and the military negotiated surrender to the Allies.

4. See the discussion in Chapter Eleven.

5. "Interest Systems and the Consolidation of Democracies," in Gary Marks and Larry Diamond, eds., *Reexamining Democracy* (Los Angeles: Sage, 1992), 158–59. See also Nancy Bermeo, "Democracy in Europe," 123 *Daedalus* 159 (1994).

6. See H. W. O. Okoth-Ogendo, "Constitutions With Constitutionalism: Reflections on an African Political Paradox," in Douglas Greenberg, Stanley N. Katz, Melanie Beth Oliviero, and Steven C. Wheatley, eds., *Constitutionalism and Democracy: Transformations in the Contemporary World* (New York: Oxford University Press, 1993).

7. Brian Urquhart, "The Tragedy of Lumumba," *N.Y. Rev. of Bks.*, Oct. 4, 2001, p. 4

in a nation beset by a babel of tongues. India has about seventy different languages. And as is often true, language is linked to ethnic identity and pride,[8] while hostility is provoked by certain "foreign" tongues. A complicated and not very happy compromise was worked out by the constitutional text framers under which Hindi became the official language, with English allowed for fifteen years (later extended). In addition, either Hindi or one of ten (later fourteen) regional languages could be established as official by state legislatures.[9]

A similar though less serious problem was suffered by Italy. In 1870, the Tuscany dialect, a modern version of Dante's language, was christened by the national government as "Italian." It was the mother tongue of those who lived around Florence and Siena and was spoken and read as a first or second language in the North as well as among the better educated throughout the peninsula. However, it was unintelligible to most people in the South and many in the North. Each region had its own language; some, like Romanesco,[10] have a revered literature. Despite government efforts, "Italian" remained a foreign tongue to many millions of citizens until almost three decades after World War II. People from different areas, such as the Abruzzi, Bologna, Naples, Sicily, and Venice, were unable to understand each other, much less Alto Adige German or Val D'Aosta French. A high degree of language unification was finally, though still incompletely, brought about by television.

Yet India and Italy became constitutional democracies in spite of language diversity[11] and widespread illiteracy. Thus we should be careful not to overweight either factor. Even so-called developed countries fall short of "functional" universal adult literacy. About 21 percent of American adults cannot read English; in Britain, with a far smaller immigrant population, the rate is slightly higher.[12] Illiteracy can be partially compensated for by television and radio. If we can generalize from studies of

8. See, for example, Sumathi Ramaswamy, *Passions of the Tongue: Language and Devotion in Tamil India, 1891–1970* (Berkeley: University of California Press, 1997).

9. See the Indian constitutional text, Articles 343–51 and the Eighth Schedule; and the discussion in H. M. Seervai, *Constitutional Law of India*, 3rd ed. (Bombay: Tripathi, 1984), 2:23. Article 6 of South Africa's constitutional charter recognizes eleven official languages and instructs the government to "elevate the status and advance the use of" other indigenous languages as well as to "promote and ensure respect for languages," including German, Greek, Gujarati, Hindi, Portuguese, Tamil, Telugu, Urdu, Arabic, Hebrew, Sanskrit, and other languages "used for religious purposes."

10. Many northern Italians refer to the Roman dialect as Romanaccio; -*accio* is a suffix denoting grossness. More correctly, though not according to common usage, Romanaccio refers only to the vulgar slang used in Rome.

11. Another example is offered by Canada. Despite latter-day government efforts to respect Quebec's language and traditions, Canadians for generations maintained constitutional democracy while using English as the dominant language and letting the Quebeçois fend as best they could.

12. See "Does Class Size Matter?" *Economist*, July 31, 1999, p. 48.

the U.S. electorate, it is probable that citizens glean more politically relevant information from these two media than from newspapers and magazines. Even in a nation where such appliances are rare, literacy low, and communication between center and periphery poor, sufficient communications may be operative for constitutional democracy's purposes. Care must be taken here, as is warned by Robert A. Dahl,[13] not to think exclusively in terms of Western models. It should be remembered that well into the twentieth century in the United Kingdom and the United States most political debates were carried on through public speeches. A great deal of communication can be sustained by less developed societies *within* face-to-face communities. And literate delegates can be chosen by each community as representatives to other political arenas. Thus an attenuated democracy form could immediately function even with small literacy and poor communications. Under such circumstances, constitutionalism would probably be damaged more than democracy, for basic rights would be unlikely to be understood by illiterates, and the likelihood would be that many rights violations would go undetected. Nevertheless, a form of constitutionalism, if not a robust form, might function passably well.

Peaceful Pluralism

"Nonviolent factionalism" is essential. Respect for human rights is required by constitutionalism. Negotiating and compromising—promise making and keeping—are required by democracy. Thus an essential question for constitutional democracy is how much factionalism can be tolerated. The question might be turned around: Can a free people exist without a high degree of factionalism? "Turbulence and contention," it was observed by Madison in *The Federalist* No. 10, have been the heritage of republics: "Liberty is to faction, what air is to fire." No matter how fully citizens agree about basic principles, they will inevitably divide along politically relevant lines.

Neither is the significance of economic differences denied,[14] but another problem is the focus here. The world over, Samuel P. Huntington

13. *Democracy and Its Critics* (New Haven, CT: Yale University Press, 1989).

14. For studies of property as a continuing raw sore in American politics, see esp. John Brigham, *Property and the Politics of Entitlement* (Philadelphia: Temple University Press, 1990); Richard Epstein, *Takings: Private Property and the Power of Eminent Domain* (Cambridge, MA: Harvard University Press, 1985), and *Forbidden Grounds: The Case against Employment Discrimination Laws* (Cambridge, MA: Harvard University Press, 1992); Richard K. Matthews, *If Men Were Angels: James Madison and the Heartless Empire of Reason* (Lawrence: University Press of Kansas, 1995), esp. chs. 4–5; Stephen R. Munzer, *A Theory of Property* (New York: Cambridge University Press, 1990); Jennifer Nedelsky, *Private Property and the Limits of American Constitutionalism* (Chicago: University of Chicago Press, 1990); and Bernard Siegan, *Economic Liberties and the Constitution* (Chicago: University of Chicago Press, 1980).

claims, the most volatile problems of domestic politics are now being generated by tribal hostility.[15] A generation ago, it was thought by Karl Deutsch that as the world was shrunk by technology and social and economic mobility increased, differences between groups would decrease.[16] He was only partially correct. Many of us have become more acutely aware that humanity shares a common fate, but many people have become more pugnaciously aware of membership in a particular tribe. Such membership is often a, if not *the*, principal source of identity and pride, with some neighbors perceived as both threatening and morally inferior. Tribes distinguish themselves by culture, religion, language, race, national origin, or all of these. The word *ethnic* is used here as shorthand for these markers of social and political difference.

Americans boast that their nation has been enriched by diversity. Nevertheless, discrimination against immigrants from "alien" cultures, whether Catholic, Jewish, Asian, African, or Hispanic, has not been stopped by repeated self-congratulations.[17] Still, American difficulties are paled by those of many other countries. Not only have Burundi, Israel, Lebanon, Northern Ireland, Pakistan, Rwanda, South Africa, Sri Lanka, the Sudan, and the crumbs of Yugoslavia been ravaged by ethnic violence but also places as disparate in history and culture as Bulgaria, India, Iran, Iraq, Kenya, Nigeria, and Romania. Nor have these problems yet been resolved by Australia, Canada, China, Germany, Indonesia, Japan, Malaysia, the Philippines, Spain, Turkey, or the United Kingdom.

It is tautological to say that as long as groups war with each other they cannot live together in peace. It is impossible for constitutional democracy to survive among peoples whose mutual hatred boils into genocidal rage. But it is not implied that everybody must love everyone else. On the contrary, constitutional democracy might be begun where ethnic tensions are rife and even occasional marauder bands assault other group

15. See esp. Samuel P. Huntington, *The Clash of Civilizations and the Remaking of World Order* (New York: Simon and Schuster, 1996); Donald L. Horowitz, *Ethnic Groups in Conflict* (Berkeley: University of California Press, 1985); Robert A. Goldwin, Art Kaufman, and William A. Schamba, eds., *Forging Unity Out of Diversity: The Approaches of Eight Nations* (Washington, DC: American Enterprise Institute, 1989); Milton J. Esman, *Ethnic Conflict in the Western World* (Ithaca, NY: Cornell University Press, 1977); Michael Ignatieff, *The Warrior's Honor: Ethnic War and Modern Conscience* (New York: Henry Holt, 1998); Dennis L. Thompson and Dov Ronen, eds., *Ethnicity, Politics, and Development* (Boulder: Lynne Rienner, 1986); Barry R. Chiswick, ed., *Immigration, Language, and Ethnicity: Canada and the United States* (Washington, DC: American Enterprise Institute Press, 1992); and Laura Silber and Allan Little, *Yugoslavia: Death of a Nation*, rev. ed. (New York: Penguin, 1997).

16. *Nationalism and Its Alternatives* (New York: Alfred A. Knopf, 1969).

17. See Rogers M. Smith, *Civic Ideals: Conflicting Visions of Citizenship in U.S. History* (New Haven, CT: Yale University Press, 1998).

members.[18] That conflict can be reduced by the new government's prosecuting "hate crime" perpetrators. A sense of security and limits on permissible behavior can be built.

At times, martial rule may be necessary for order preservation and rights protection. For centuries, this tactic has been used by the British for control over Ireland. Because of violence among India's ethnically fractured population, "a stunning array of legislation"[19] gives the military control over large areas of unruly provinces. Between 1951 and 1970, the army was called on more than 450 times to quell domestic violence, and in the eighteen months between June 1979 and December 1980, another 64 times.[20] During the last several decades, I have lost count.

Consociationism can be congruent with constitutional democracy. Federalism can provide additional ethnic autonomy and can mix with consociationism and constitutionalism. Examples abound. Swiss federal arrangements were made easier by the then rather clean ethnic-group geographic distribution. Similarly, in Canada federalism was attractive because of the concentration of one of the two conflicting European cultures in a single province. India's initial choice was also driven by the country's myriad divisions. More or less along language lines,[21] the states of Andhra, Masarashtra, Gujarat, Harvana, and Punjab were later carved out. In 1978, analogous problems were faced by Spain's constitutional text framers in confronting Basque and Catalan separatism, but the Spanish opted for "autonomous communities" rather than formal federalism.[22] According to Article 2 of the constitutional text:

18. See, for instance, Saul Newman, *Ethnoregional Conflict in Democracies: Mostly Ballots, Rarely Bullets* (Westport, CT: Greenwood, 1996).

19. Stephen P. Cohen, "The Military and Indian Democracy," in Atul Kholi, gen. ed., *India's Democracy* (Princeton, NJ: Princeton University Press, 1988), p. 128.

20. Ibid., p. 124.

21. Due to invasions, migrations, and shifting boundaries, no Indian state is linguistically homogenous. In Assam, for example, only about 60 percent of the population speak Assamese as their first language.

22. Articles 143–58 laid out the specific powers and duties of such communities. For analyses, see Andrea Bonime-Blanc, *Spain's Transition to Democracy* (Boulder: Westview, 1987); Michael W. Giles and Thomas D. Lancaster, "Political Transition, Social Development, and Legal Mobilization in Spain," 83 *Am. Pol. Sci. Rev.* 817 (1989); José Maria Maravall and Julián Santamaria, "Political Change in Spain and Prospects for Democracy," in Guillermo O'Donnell, Philippe C. Schmitter, and Laurence Whitehead, eds., *Transitions from Authoritarian Rule: Southern Europe* (Baltimore: Johns Hopkins University Press, 1986); and Peter McDonough, Samuel H. Barnes, and Antonio Lopez Pina, "The Growth of Democratic Legitimacy in Spain," 80 *Am. Pol. Sci. Rev.* 735 (1986).

Alec Stone Sweet believes that constitutional usage has changed Spain pretty much into a federal state: *Governing with Judges: Constitutional Politics in Europe* (New York: Oxford University Press, 2000), p. 64; here Stone Sweet follows Robert Agranoff, "Federal Evolution in Spain," 17 *Int'l Pol. Sci. Rev.* 385 (1996).

The Constitution is based on the indissoluble unity of the Spanish nation, the common and indivisible homeland of all Spaniards, and recognizes and guarantees the right to autonomy of the nationalities and regions which make it up and the solidarity among them.

A more radical solution is offered by secession.[23] Splitting a country into several independent nations, each with its own ethnic identity, is likely to be effective where antagonistic ethnic groups live in separate areas, as in the old Czech and Slovak Republic. Ethnic divisions may not follow geographic lines, and even when they do, a majority may be willing to pay heavily in blood for national unity, as was learned by Basques, Ibo, Kurds, and Sikhs and perhaps will be learned by Quebeçois. In the United States, unity was eventually bought at a gory cost; the price and degree of unity for the other countries remain to be seen.

The least evil outcome might be for minorities to be pacified with guarantees of rights protection. However, if that guarantee could be trusted and kept, secession would not be needed. We see a tragic American example, though it concerned regional rather than ethnic groups. On the eve of the Civil War, Congress, by the required two-thirds vote of both houses, proposed an amendment to the constitutional text that would have formally and forever transferred all power over slavery within the states to the states themselves.[24] Although the Supreme Court had ruled that a presidential signature on a proposed constitutional amendment was unnecessary,[25] James Buchanan signed the resolution. Later, in his inaugural address Abraham Lincoln said he supported the amendment's purpose that "the federal government, shall never interfere with the domestic institutions of the states, including that of persons held to service,"[26] a policy he believed was already constitutional law. Nevertheless, the amendment, which ironically would have become the Thirteenth, failed to convince Southern leaders that their interests were still safe within the Union.

---

23. For most Americans, the word *secession* causes an involuntary reflex of revulsion, linked as it is in their history not only to harsh civil war but also to desperate efforts to maintain slavery. But as the breakup of the Soviet Union demonstrated, secession may be a move toward peace and freedom. For a dispassionate study of the problem of constitutional failure and the breakdown of the constitutional order, see esp. Mark E. Brandon, *Free in the World: American Slavery and Constitutional Failure* (Princeton, NJ: Princeton University Press, 1998).

24. Section 1 of the proposed amendment read:

No amendment shall be made to the Constitution which will authorize or give to Congress the power to abolish or interfere, within any State, with the domestic institutions thereof, including that of persons held to labor or service by the laws of the said State.

25. Hollingsworth v. Virginia, 3 Dall. 378 (1798).

26. *The Collected Works of Abraham Lincoln*, ed. Roy P. Basler (New Brunswick, NJ: Rutgers University Press, 1953), 4:262. The best discussion of the Corwin amendment and, in the American context, the general problems of cohesion versus secession is Brandon, *Free in the World*.

Where ethnic groups are mingled together and not apt to respect each other's rights, population exchanges might be possible. Attendant hardships might make this policy unattractive, though far less so than the Christian-Muslim slaughter in Yugoslavia. And if exchanges were negotiated so that no one became stateless, some harm could be averted. Other solutions include persuading smaller groups to accept a large degree of culture assimilation. However, because persuasion often involves coercion, it may pose serious normative problems. Forced culture homogenization, such as English attempts to eradicate Catholicism from Ireland or more recent Bulgarian efforts to Slavicize ethnic Turks and make them renounce Islam,[27] violate constitutional democracy principles.

More tangled normative problems are posed by less intrusive assimilation methods, such as the "melting pot": immigrant groups are pushed to adopt dominant values, customs, and language—to become ingredients in a cultural stew. Leaving aside the question of the extent to which this model fits U.S. experience,[28] the degree to which this strategy would result in minority coercion is problematic, for informal government pressures are often powerful. In the nineteenth century, for example, it was perceived by American Catholic bishops that "neutral" public schools were educating students not merely to become good citizens but good *Protestant* citizens.[29] To protect against this religion indoctrination, parochial schools were established by the bishops. A century later, similar charges of imperialism were voiced by blacks, women, and gays. In response, many universities adopted Afro-American, Women's, and Queer studies programs to explain and advance values different from those of the dominant culture.

The adjective *tangled* was carefully chosen for the problems culture poses for constitutional democracy. Three vectors intersect: First, eth-

27. Article 11 (4) of the Bulgarian constitutional text that came into force after the revolution bans political parties founded on ethnic or religious lines, and Article 44 (2) prohibits organizations that call into question the nation's territorial integrity or foment ethnic or religious hatred. In April 1992, six judges of the Constitutional Court held that these provisions outlawed the Movement for Rights and Freedom, a party with 99 percent Turkish membership—and incidentally had the third largest number of deputies in Parliament. The constitutional text, however, requires that seven of the twelve judges must agree on such a decision. Five of the twelve disagreed with the majority; the twelfth judge was ill and did not participate. For details, see "Turkish Party in Bulgaria Allowed to Continue," 1 *East. Eur'n Con'l Rev.* 11 (Summer 1992).

28. See the challenge by Nathan Glazer and Daniel Patrick Moynihan, *Beyond the Melting Pot: The Negroes, Puerto Ricans, Jews, Italians, and Irish of New York City* (Cambridge: MIT Press, 1963), discussed below.

29. For a fascinating study showing that the bishops' perception was essentially accurate, though incomplete, see Richard D. Mosier, *Making the American Mind: Social and Moral Ideas in McGuffey Readers* (New York: Columbia University Press, 1947); and John T. McGreevy *Catholicism and American Freedom: A History* (New York: W. W. Norton, 2003), esp. introduction and ch. 1. See, more generally, Jay P. Dolan, *The American Catholic Experience: A History from Colonial Times to the Present* (New York: Doubleday, 1985), ch. 10.

nic groups are apt to view their own heritage as the best and therefore to proselytize, perhaps without being aware of it. Second, a dominant group is likely to exert strong, if informal, conformity pressures on other citizens. This interference may be subconscious through insistence on specific customs and linguistic forms as "correct" or more directly through job control and university admission. Third—and here's the rub: denying dominant group members the right to proselytize or influence public policy is no less a violation of constitutional democracy than denying those rights to smaller ethnic groups.

Where ethnic loathing is present, solutions are likely to be found, if at all, only in government-brokered armistices, and political institution design would be of great significance in securing peace. Consociational-ism could help. The objective would be political pluralism organized along the lines of what Nathan Glazer and Daniel Patrick Moynihan call a "smorgasbord,"[30] which, rather than trying to blend citizens into a single culture stew, recognizes a variety of culture options, all sharing a commitment to constitutional democracy.

Further, mutual consent to secede, federalize, regionalize, assimilate, or coexist might come *after* rather than *before* establishment of constitu-tional democracy. Securing such a settlement—and then creating condi-tions it would benefit most factions to continue—would be the primary statecraft task.[31] In that process, simultaneously missionary and pastoral, allowing citizen participation would promote interest clarification to each other and, hopefully, peaceful negotiations.

It is directly argued by many pluralism theorists that chances for stability greatly increase when economic and ethnic lines crosscut rather than parallel.[32] If ethnic group members are scattered across all economic classes, economic policies are less likely to impact different ethnic groups unequally. Moreover, mutual trust might be helped by goal clarification and interest bargaining, as well as by promise making and keeping. If so, education of current and future generations in constitutional democracy principles would be easier. If, however, hostility remained high and trust low, secession might be the only peaceful alternative.

A summary: It is argued that successful constitutional democracy establishment is dependent on only three of the five candidates exam-ined: military neutrality; an energetic, determined, and skilled pro–constitutional democracy leadership cadre; and a peaceful pluralism

---

30. *Beyond the Melting Pot.*

31. Giuseppe Di Palma, *To Craft Democracies* (Berkeley: University of California Press, 1990), wrote about the importance of transitional political agreements between authoritarian leaders and dissident groups. His reasoning applies equally well to disputes among ethnic groups.

32. David B. Truman offered the classic argument: *The Governmental Process* (New York: Alfred A. Knopf, 1951).

commitment or peaceful separation acceptance among the population. It is not contended that constitutional democracy success chances would not be enhanced by the presence of many other candidates.

Demos Pyknites gains recognition. "I ask the Chair's indulgence, but Professor Sprachfehler's first 'condition' or 'precondition' identifies the eight-hundred-pound gorilla that has been sitting among us: the intentions of the Chair and the Chair's military colleagues."

"I thought," the chair interrupts, "that we had been clear about our intention to step aside as soon as this body and the people can constitute and operationalize a new political system."

"We have heard that, yes. But—no disrespect intended—we can't help wondering what, if any, strings are attached. Will you, for instance, insist on an amnesty or issue such a proclamation yourselves? Will you demand guarantees of the military's autonomy from regular political processes, say, in control over your budget and promotion of officers?"

"I can speak for myself and I hope for my brother officers as well. Emphatically no to all of your questions. I understand your concern, but remember that the atrocities that sickened us all were committed by the so-called Special Guards and the secret police—euphemisms for thugs with licenses from the government. All of us who rebelled against the junta are colonels. None of us was ever in a policy-making position within the government, and thus none of us needs amnesty. As I've said, the decision to disobey the junta was difficult for all of us, because we were and still are professional soldiers. But that decision was basically a moral one; we could no longer stomach a regime that had become so perverted and corrupt. The past few weeks are as close as any of us have ever come to exercising political power; and as reasonably intelligent and devoutly patriotic men, we want our country to be governed under a fair and efficient political system, not to govern. I cannot promise that if this new government becomes oppressive and corrupt like the old regime, we shall only sit in our barracks and drink; but I can promise that we are not seeking special benefits for ourselves or our profession.

"Let me speak more generally about the officer corps as a whole. We colonels will soon die or retire, and others will take our places. Therefore, this caucus must think hard about how to address the military as a whole. It is essential that you or the new government establish relationships between the regime and the military like those existing in Britain and the United States. You must devise institutions that make military officers believe that constitutional democracy or whatever other regime you bring into being respects them and is worthy of their respect."

"I hope you understand," Pyknites says, "that it was necessary to get this matter out in the open. I thank you, as I believe we all do, for your response." At that point, the caucus gives a standing ovation.

The chair taps his gavel. "Thank you. Now, Ion Zingaro has a question."
"It is for Professor Sprachfehler. Are you familiar with our ethnic diversity?"

"In general, yes."

"Then you know we are a conglomeration of Protestants, Jews, Catholics, Muslims, each uneasy in the company of the others as well as of the approximately one-sixth of us who say they are agnostic or atheist. In addition, we have a black community, about sixty thousand Gypsies, almost twice as many people of Chinese origin, and a large number of Catholic immigrants from Asia and Latin America. There is long-standing friction between Catholics and Protestants as well as among Protestant sects. Catholics whose families have been here for generations don't trust their immigrant coreligionists. Many Jews are Sephardic refugees from Iran, Iraq, and North Africa. Their culture does not sit well with Jews who come from families that have been here for a couple of centuries. And hostility exists between all Jews and Muslims. And, of course, everybody hates Gypsies."

"What's your question?"

"That's background for my question. You speak of democratic processes as generating trust among hostile groups, but I'm certain that most of our people, Christians, Jews, or Muslims, would vote out of office any party whose leaders sat down and negotiated with Gypsies. And I suspect that Christians and Jews would be very leery of parties that contained large numbers of Muslims, as Muslims would be of parties that advanced the interest of Jews."

"Perhaps you're right," Sprachfehler says. "Majority hostility can create smaller group unity; if mixed with ethnic hatred, civil war may be produced. If that's the case, either country division or a regional autonomy form should be seriously considered. One of your first leadership tasks is public policy creation that discourages violence. Your people need not love one another, only be willing to live together in peace. You must convince group leaders of their long-term interest in living together in harmony, then help them convince their own people. Separation is the only peaceful alternative."

"Radically decentralized federalism and secession," Jessica Jacobsohn breaks in, "create problems for minorities within minorities, as I've mentioned. Muslims are not apt to treat Christians, Jews, or Gypsies any better than those groups have treated Muslims.[33] And if Muslims install Shari'a rules, I, for one, won't tolerate 'local autonomy.'"

"I agree. If local autonomy is adopted, it must have a universal rights floor under it."

---

33. For an account of the mutual hatreds existing on the cusp of World War II among the various peoples of Yugoslavia, including those generated by Muslims' rule over Christians and Jews in Bosnia, see Rebecca West, *Black Lamb and Grey Falcon: A Journey through Yugoslavia* (New York: Penguin, 1940), esp. pp. 293–413.

Anita Baca intervenes: "Professor, I must share my horror at forcibly moving populations. It, like, totally shocks me. I've read about what the Bulgarians did to Turks after World War I and again in the 1980s and what the Czechs did to the Sudeten Germans after World War II.[34] And the Serbs' ethnic cleansing in Bosnia and Kosovo sickened all civilized people. So did the Kosovars' revenge. Human beings aren't trees that can be transplanted, right?"

"Right; but, please, forced population transfer was called a 'lesser evil'—lesser than leaving people to be murdered in a Bosnia- or Kosovo- or Rwanda-style civil war. My message is simple: if national unity is to be kept, a minimum of mutual trust must be felt. If that trust isn't felt at the beginning, it must be created, the nation dismembered, dissidents jailed, or a civil war fought."

Pastor Glückman speaks up: "To hold a country together, martial law may sometimes be necessary, and that raises additional difficulties. You cite British policy in Ireland, which brought terror and civil war. India's experience doesn't encourage me. Martial law undercuts respect for constitutional democracy and also encourages military officers both to ignore equality before the law and to think they can govern more wisely than civilians."

"Agreed," Sprachfehler responds. "Martial law is at best a short-term palliative. Other less radical means exist. In the American South after the School Segregation Cases, martial law was not invoked by Dwight Eisenhower and John F. Kennedy, but troops were sent into Alabama, Arkansas, and Mississippi to protect blacks' rights. Eventually, racial equality was accepted by most white Southerners, though it is still bitterly resented by some of them. Constitutional democracy was helped by military force. It's prudent to be worried. There is no short-run cure for ethnic hostility. Life hasn't been easy in any multiethnic society; it will be especially difficult for you, because almost none of your people have lived together as *citizens* with members of other groups. But the situation is not hopeless."

Václav Pilsudski, the minister of justice, speaks: "I'd like to shift the topic. What's your assessment of our chances of our having a critical mass of civil servants, including judges, to make constitutional democracy work?"

"Well," Professor Sprachfehler says, "you face an Eastern Europe situation more than an Africa situation. You have a trained administrative cadre and educated judges, though it is not clear how many of them have a constitutional democracy commitment. However, most administrators and judges have experiential learning capabilities as well as future anticipation abilities. Self-interest may tell them their careers are dependent on becoming good constitutional democrats. Moreover, though the special knowledge required

34. See Alfred-Maurice de Zayas, *A Terrible Revenge: The Ethnic Cleansing of the East European Germans, 1944–1950* (New York: St. Martin's, 1986).

for governing was vastly underestimated by Lenin in *State and Revolution,* it is possible to carry on many government operations with noncareer officials. Eamon DeValera was a high school teacher, Václav Havel a playwright, and Ronald Reagan an actor in B-movies before becoming effective government leaders. The U.K. and U.S. practice of choosing amateurs as judges, legislators, and administrator chiefs may not be ideal for a modern political system, but government efficiency and citizen freedom are often in tension. In sum, your road will be rocky, but your chances seem good to me."

As Professor Sprachfehler finishes, Professor John Milton Maynard, an economist from the Harvard Business School, enters the room. He is wearing tennis clothes and carrying a Durbin racket. Without waiting for an introduction, he places his racket on the podium and begins.

Economic Preconditions

I had the pleasure of sitting in on your debates the last few days. That made my assignment easier. You've covered much of the ground I had planned to go over, so my message can be short, though not simple.

A change in political systems does not depend on the efficiency of the existing economy; indeed, the relationship may be inverse. It is the economically dissatisfied who are apt to demand political change; the prosperous seldom do. Thus, one cannot say that a certain level of income is a precondition, in a strict sense of that term, at the beginning of any kind of political regime. But one can say that a marked—I like that word; it seems definite but in fact is vague—improvement in general economic conditions is critical to a regime's survival. I also like the word *critical.* Many patients in critical condition die, while many others live. Thus the word coveys a sobering message while leaving open a handy exit if things improve.

"Cute, but what's the point?" Strega asks.

Thank you. My point is that some new regimes have survived over the long haul despite failing to make dramatic economic improvements. Yesterday, someone cited two constitutional democracies, India[35] and Ireland. Ireland has made sizable economic strides only in the past fifteen years, and India, though it still suffers from widespread poverty, has made great progress only in the past decade. If you want to include other kinds of regimes, you might look at Spain during most of Franco's reign,

---

35. For studies of India's political economy, see esp. Lloyd I. Rudolph and Susanne Hoebler Rudolph, *In Pursuit of Lakshmi: The Political Economy of the Indian State* (Chicago: University of Chicago Press, 1987), and Pranab Bardhan, *The Political Economy of Development of India* (New York: Oxford University Press, 1999).

China under Mao, or Kenya under Daniel Arap Moi. All endured decades of poverty. A constitutional democracy could remain consistent with its own ethic, fail to create more prosperity, and still be viable when economic causes were not among the basic forces behind the change or the level of income was such that people were willing to endure some financial privation for the sake of political goods.

Since World War II, it is clear that the chances of some form of democratic regime's surviving are heavily reinforced by that government's producing a real measure of prosperity. Although others have reached similar conclusions,[36] Adam Przeworski and Fernando Limongi have given the most succinct statement of the complex relations here: "The emergence of democracy is not a by-product of economic development. Democracy is or is not established by political actors pursuing their goals, and it can be initiated at any level of development. Only once it is established do economic restraints play a role: the chances for the survival of democracy are greater when the country is richer."[37] They go on to say that current wealth is far less important than whether income is rising or falling. Thus democracy has a better chance of surviving in poorer countries where economic conditions are improving than in richer countries where income is falling.

Yesterday, you debated whether economic conditions were at the root of the junta's overthrow. If the majority is correct, you can have a wide degree of constitutional freedom and democratic control over public policy. But that correctness would not mean that improving the economic status of your citizens will not affect the lifespan of your new polity.

My message, I said, is not simple, but it should be clear: although economic change is not a precondition for the birth of a constitutional democracy, it is very likely to be a *post*quisite for its long-term survival. Some authoritarian regimes have been quite adept at promoting economic development—Lee's Singapore and Pinochet's Chile come quickly to mind—but most others have not. And, most decidedly, the argument that economic development yields political freedom is false. Still, if I disagree with Minister Strega on the necessity of economic reform's preceding political reform, I agree with her that you will need

36. See, for example, the essays by William Glade, "On Markets and Democracy"; Cal Clark, "Modernization, Democracy, and the Developmental State in East Asia: A Virtuous Cycle or Unraveling Strands?" Steve Chan, "Democratic Inauguration and Transition in East Asia"; Joseph S. Berliner, "'The Longest' Transition"; Jeffrey Herbst, "Understanding Ambiguity during Democratization in Africa"; and Peter M. Lewis, "A Virtuous Circle? Democratization and Economic Reform in Africa"—all in James F. Hollifield and Calvin Jillson, eds., *Pathways to Democracy: The Political Economy of Democratic Transitions* (New York: Routledge, 2000).

37. Adam Przeworski and Fernando Limongi, "Modernization: Theories and Facts," 49 *World Pols.* 155, 177 (1997).

162 Creating a Constitutional Democracy

much—and intelligent—governmental regulation of the economy both to advance and protect your economy.

I stress the last point. Foreign investors will be swarming around you like buzzards, ready to pick your bones. Bankers, yours and foreign, will be anxious to make speculative loans, hoping the World Bank or the International Monetary Fund will bail them out if projects fail. Many of my colleagues have preached the virtues of classical economic theory and its public-policy child, laissez-faire. They disregard the generations of suffering that combination has caused. Entrepreneurs are out to make money; it's what they do. If in the process they wreck lives, they soothe their consciences by claiming they have also created wealth for yet other people. Foreign entrepreneurs have no reason to care what carnage they leave behind in somebody else's country. If you let robber barons roam freely about your house, they will pillage.

I've said enough. When I advised governments in Russia and Eastern Europe, I always stressed the necessity of privatization—a painful process, but like taking adhesive tape off a hairy part of the body, it is least painfully done when done swiftly. Because your economy was and remains mostly private, you do not face such problems. Let's move to discussion.

"Professor," Minister Strega asks, "if, in fact, economic anger had brought about the junta's downfall, how would your conclusion change?"

"Then I would think that some economic reform, though still not a condition for the beginning of constitutional democracy, would be more urgently needed. Because most economic reforms cause a great deal of short-term suffering, constitutional democracy, like representative democracy, has huge difficulty carrying out radical reform. Policies whose pain is sharp can bring harsh punishment at the polls. According to Jon Elster's theory, for democracy, (1) basic economic reform—he was concerned mainly with privatization but his reasoning applies more generally—presupposes reform of prices, for labor as well as goods; (2) reform of prices must reflect the market, again for labor as well as goods; (3) democratically responsive government cannot survive price reforms that either keep the worst-off poor or the best-off rich; but (4) a basic economic reform to a true market economy will produce enormous disparities in wealth and cause high unemployment or inflation or both.[38] Hence this sort of economic reform cannot occur simul-

38. Jon Elster, "The Necessity and Impossibility of Simultaneous Economic and Political Reform," in Douglas Greenberg, Stanley N. Katz, Melanie Beth Oliviero, and Steven C. Wheatley, eds., *Constitutionalism and Democracy: Transformations in the Contemporary World* (New York: Oxford University Press, 1993); see also J. C. Sharman and Roger E. Kanet, "International Influences on Democratization in Postcommunist Europe," in James F. Hollifield and Calvin Jillson, eds., *Pathways to Democracy: The Political Economy of Democratic Transitions* (New York: Routledge, 2000).

taneously with or soon after establishment of democracy. Constitutionalism erects additional barriers by morphing property rights into constitutional rights, thus preventing, as in India, some important phases of reform."

"Pardon me," Jacobsohn interrupts, "but didn't Elster qualify his claims? Was he as dogmatic as you make him out to be?"

"Of course. That's why I can cite him and still argue as I do. Authoritarian regimes may seem to have an easier time generating economic development than hybrid democracies, but their record is poor, and they carry a risk of high—and permanent—damage to this caucus's goals."

The chair turns to Maynard. "Professor, we thank you for your time and comments. We shall certainly give them due weight . . . Let us take a fifteen-minute recess, fifteen minutes not sixteen, and take up the issue of political culture."

The next speaker, Professor Francesca Vaccarino of the University of Rome, appears fourteen minutes late, meticulously dressed in a dove gray silk suit. She ignores Colonel Martin's displeased glare, puts on a pair of black horn-rimmed glasses, picks up a sheaf of handwritten notes, and begins.

Political Culture

I constructed my paper without the opportunity to read the words of my colleagues, so there is—how does one say?—overlap. I shall attempt not to repeat them. I must also apologize that my English is awkward. Alas, my message is also complex. Political culture is very important to any regime. In facts, there must be what Harry H. Eckstein referred to as "congruence" between a political culture and any viable political system.[39] *Dunque,* we can say that a political culture congruent with constitutional democracy is a *condition* for the survival of such a regime.

But the problem is not simple. I stress you two causes. First, no particular political culture is uniquely necessary. Every constitutional democracy that has endured across several decades is multicultural. Even the United Kingdom has historically included Scots, Welsh, and Irish alongside Anglo-Saxons; more recently, of course, Pakistani, Indians, Arabs, and West Indian blacks form sizable minorities. Nevertheless, some political cultures are incompatible with constitutional democracy. There may be, as in Israel among Jewish groups, "resentment, and even loathing and lasting hatreds,"[40] but those people must be willing to live

39. Harry H. Eckstein, "A Theory of Stable Democracy," in his *Regarding Politics* (Berkeley: University of California Press, 1992); "Russia and the Conditions of Democracy," in Harry H. Eckstein, Frederic J. Fleron Jr., Erik P. Hoffmann, and William M. Reisinger, *Can Democracy Take Root in Post-Soviet Russia?* (Lanham, MD: Rowman and Littlefield, 1998); and Harry H. Eckstein and Ted Robert Gurr, *Patterns of Authority* (New York: Wiley, 1975).

40. Avishai Margalit, "Israel: Why Barak Won," *N.Y. Rev. of Bks.*, Aug. 12, 1999, p. 47; and

together in peace. There must be *fiducia*—you say "trust"?—not trust that others will want wise or just policies but that they will behave as decent citizens. Democracy, Taylor Branch has told, requires "having faith in strangers."[41]

My ultimate words predict the second cause: it is possible that government and parts of civic society can, if not create such a culture, at least plant and nourish seeds. Professor Maynard's word *postquisite* is pleasing to me. At the initiation, there need not be a plenum of trust, only a willingness to see if other groups can keep their word and, meanwhile, a commitment that one's own group will behave honorably toward others. If that plant takes root, then the needed culture can grow.

Allora, I step back and explain you what I mean by political culture. Like a nation's physical setting and resources, customs and ideals influence its political character and operations. Social scientists have invented the expression *political culture* to encompass these politically relevant ideas and habits. That term announces that norms of conduct, patterns of action, symbols of good and evil, and even fundamental notions about the nature of human beings and God help shape people's *vista* of politics, what sorts of political systems they judge legitimate, what sorts of institutions and policies they accept as valid, and how they treat and want government to treat fellow citizens. Three sets of beliefs are especially important: about a deity, about authority, and about humanity. If most modern nations and all constitutional democracies are multicultural, it must follow, I say of new, that every constitutional democracy, perhaps every nation, possesses several political cultures.

Religion, the state, and citizenship interact at the abstract and concrete levels. Indeed, each is merely an ingredient; their interactions create the cultures themselves, and those different cultures interact—sometimes they clash—with each other. Today I speak you mostly about interactions.

People who believe in capricious deities are apt to view life and politics differently from people who believe in a just deity who loves humanity.[42] Those who deny a deity may also differ from these others about political fundaments. Faith or disbelief in divinely ordained principles can have gross impacts on how people view political legitimacy. Religions usually codify principles and stabilize organizations to teach them, make them more specific, and enforce them. When a people have piety,

Charles S. Liebman, "Jewish Fundamentalism and the Israeli Polity," in Martin E. Marty and R. Scott Appleby, eds., *Fundamentalism and the State: Remaking Polities, Economies, and Militance* (Chicago: University of Chicago Press, 1993).

41. Quoted in Stanley N. Katz, "Does Constitutionalism Require a Civil Society?" Jefferson Lecture, University of California, 1999.

42. See Lucian W. Pye, *Politics, Personality, and Nation Building: Burma's Search for Identity* (New Haven, CT: Yale University Press, 1962).

the political system must either conform, at least overtly, to dominant theological principles or battle with religious leaders.

According to me, Professor Sprachfehler is correct to speak against determinism. Politics may gain the people's loyalty even against clerical resistance. But, I pray, note well I say *may*. Ireland provides an example. During the nineteenth century, when the British tried to use the Vatican to repress Irish nationalism, Irish leaders made an answer: "We get our religion from Rome but our politics from home." And many of the parish priests, ardent nationalists, agreed with the politicians and disagreed with their bishops and the Vatican. *Ecco,* the conflict was not clergy versus popular leaders, but some clergy and popular leaders versus other clergy. The story repeats itself during the civil war in the 1920s, when Irish bishops excommunicated members of the Irish Republican Army. Of new, the village priests were often nationalists. Thus, the IRA could be both vehemently anticlerical and devoutly Cattolic.

When religious beliefs are widely and deeply held and political leaders oppose those beliefs, it is likely to take a cataclysmic event for political leaders to win a quick and telling victory. It is improbable, for example, that any Japanese leader in the 1940s could have vanquished Shintoism without a disastrous defeat like that nation suffered in World War II.[43] Even Lenin and Stalin were unable to erase Christianity in Russia or Islam in the Central Asian republics.[44] The Soviets were, as Americans say, ahead in the game, but the Orthodox Church and Islam, all and two, survived Marxism. You are in a situation different from either Douglas MacArthur or Lenin. You have neither conquered a people nor are you willing to use terror to create a new political system. *Dunque,* you cannot impose a constitutional order that violates prevailing religious tenets.

Ecco, the thought races: *Italia* had only three religions—Cattolicism, atheism, and indifference. Because the third predominated, founders of Fascism and constitutional democracy had an easy time. Perhaps. But Mussolini told that his goal was social justice as Pope Leo XIII had preached in *Rerum Novarum* (1891). Later, the founders of the Repub-

---

43. As a counterexample, one might cite the French Revolution's execution of Roman Catholicism. Let me, I pray, say two things. First, in the minds of the revolutionary leaders, the Church had become closely identified with the corruption and oppression of the *ancien regime,* and irreligion had become "an all-prevailing passion, fierce, intolerant, and predatory." I must add that Alexis de Tocqueville thought it had been an error to link the Church so closely with the corruption of the *ancien regime: The Old Regime and the French Revolution,* trans. Stuart Gilbert (New York: Doubleday, 1955), p. 149. Second, the Catholic Church survived the French Revolution in much better condition than the Russian Orthodox Church survived Marxism.

44. For ultimately unsuccessful Soviet efforts to "modernize" Russia's Islamic southern rim by easing traditional restrictions on women, see Gregory Massell, *The Surrogate Proletariat: Moslem Women and Revolutionary Strategies in Soviet Central Asia, 1919–1929* (Princeton, NJ: Princeton University Press, 1974).

lic, mostly Christian Democrats, more plausibly told the same, as they and their American sponsors frightened the Vatican with the specter of communism.

Your country possesses these three religions and Protestants, Muslims, Jews, and Gypsies as well. *Dunque*, you must—how does one say?—keep many balls in the air. You must have concern about what is acceptable to each of these groups, while always fastidious not to offend the majority, if, in fact, a majority exists on religiously tinctured issues. Constitutional democracy, emphasizing human dignity, does not of itself conflict with the basic theology of any of those religions. *Ecco*, the principal problem I vision is constitutional democracy's stress on rights and freedom as the goal of the state. According to me, that will not always ride well with strict adherents to any of these religions. They are apt to view freedom as a means, usually desirable but one that can lead to sin. Fortunately, such problems are likely to complicate governing a constitutional democracy rather than veto its establishment.

Now I speak about authority. But we cannot yet depart religion. Ideas about deities influence our *vista* of authority in general. For a political system to be stable, it must enjoy a great deal of "harmonic convergence"[45] between official concepts of authority and citizens' experiences in their families, schools, posts of labor, and churches. If those institutions are dictatorial, it will be difficult for the values of constitutional democracy to thrive in the public square, as Weimar Germany illustrates. A democratic constitutional order sat on top of an authoritarian social order.[46] As Thomas Mann allegedly said, Weimar was a republic without republicans.

Ecco, most people in Western societies find themselves in the middle, where the sources, nature, and scope of political authority are more complex. Americans and Europeans tend to think of popular election as the sole source of legitimate authority, but that *vista* is limited. We can recall ourselves Ms Baca's word about the historic use of the *lotteria*. And also, for some groups, benediction by religious personages donates legitimacy. For centuries, the central argument of political theory in Europe centered on the "two swords," with the Church insisting on its discretion to bestow the secular sword. And clergy dominated coronation ceremonies of monarchs for even more centuries. In Islam, Allah is the ultimate sovereign, not the people. During much of Muslim history, the khalif was His representative and supposedly ruled with the approbation of the *ulama*,[47] the wise holy men. In fact, the khalif often ruled solo but still claimed delegation from Allah.

45. The phrase is Maureen Dowd's: "Liberties: Truth or Dare," *N.Y. Times*, Aug. 12, 1998.
46. See esp. Eckstein, "Theory of Stable Democracy."
47. The *professoressa* had probably read Muhammad Qasim Zaman, *The Ulama in Contemporary Islam* (Princeton, NJ: Princeton University Press, 2002).

For other peoples, tradition may be critical. An American Central Intelligence Agency official who fought in the Vietnamese highlands arrived at a Montagnard village soon after the Vietcong had made a visitation. They had raped many women and stolen food, then had taken the *capo* into the piazza and, at a blow, expelled his brains into the dirt to encourage the people to provide the VC with food and information. Thus the CIA official had no difficulty to persuade the villagers to accept American weapons to defend themselves against another visitation. Then he made a grand mistake: he told they needed a new *capo* and should make an election. Angry villagers explained that the American had insulted the village's customs. Their *capo* was always the oldest male from a certain family. The American lost the villagers' support.

History may become tradition and together produce conditions that make constitutional democracy more or less possible. I cite you the Mezzogiorno, the south of Italia. For centuries, the people there knew only oppressive rule by foreigners; government became, and to much extent remains, the enemy. Other relationships there paralleled those with government. People of similar economic status did not cooperate for mutual advantage; rather, a *padrone*—you say godfather?—donated favors and exacted obedience in return. Relationships between rulers and ruled in political and private life were hierarchical, often enforced by violence outside the control of the state. For the *mezzogiorni*, constitutional democracy, with its cooperation, bargaining, shared trust, and mutual recognition of inalienable rights, does not resonate with real life. Historically, they had not known the myriad private institutions that in much of the Western world had mediated between state and citizen—or in this case state and denizen. There was only the Church, whose interests, above the level of the parish priest, were seldom those of the people; and then there were the Camora or the Mafia, whose interests were only in power through terror and extortion.

I pray you, let me make an intervention to my own presentation. I am less disturbed about the usual indicia of political culture than I am about the facts that you lack mediating institutions. What labor unions the junta allowed you were farces. Your churches could not have auxiliary associations like they have in free countries; manufacturers have no organizations . . . I could go on but you understand. You may certainly initiate a constitutional democracy, but I doubt if you can long continue it, without secondary associations.[48] They aggregate and present inter-

48. Vaccarino is borrowing from Robert D. Putnam, *Making Democracy Work: Civic Tradition in Modern Italy* (Princeton, NJ: Princeton University Press, 1993), and his *Bowling Alone: The Collapse and Revival of American Community* (New York: Simon and Schuster, 2000). Even though she is Italian, she has not read Filippo Sabetti, *The Search for Good Government: Understanding the Paradox of Italian Democracy* (Montreal: McGill: Queen's University Press, 2000), who takes issue

ests to government and give people a sense of belonging, of cooperation with and trust in one another; they also provide training for democratic leadership.

Limits on power are also important. The West reveres limited government, but it was not always so, nor is it now universally so. Of new, religious norms enter as limits and demands on political authority, all and two. Sometimes natural law, revelation, or ecclesiastical dogmas restrain civil authority; sometimes they require governmental action—for example, to punish sinners. More positively, religion may require divinely ordained social policies. According to me, it is no accident that many Orthodox Jews in Israel are angry at their Supreme Court for ruling that the country has the—you say "rudiments"?—of a secular constitutional text.[49] For the ultra-Orthodox, the Halakhah is *the* constitutional text. And for many Muslims the Qur'an offers the only true constitutional document.

Dunque, it is probable that your people, inexperienced with either constitutionalism or democracy and devoted to their religious precepts, will have difficulties with the regime you propose. Still, I vision this only as an obstacle, not an insurmountable absolute barrier. This complexity underlines—that word is proper?—the necessity of skilled leadership.

My paper also speaks about attitudes regarding humanity. You have already discussed the essence of my message: to the extent people lack a *vista* of humanity as one family, all entitled to equal respect, they will not make perfect citizens of a constitutional democracy. According to me, however, constitutional democracy does not require perfect citizens. It can survive if its people have a certain amount—one cannot say exactly how much—of mutual respect and trust. If groups cannot live together in peace, constitutional democracy is doomed. I am also in accord with Professor Sprachfehler that the political system you stabilize can do much to augment, even create, peace among your citizens. Like Professor Maynard, I accept your judgment that your people can, at the

---

with Putnam's analysis regarding Italy. Ariel C. Armony, *The Dubious Link: Civic Engagement and Democratization* (Stanford, CA: Stanford University Press, 2004), disagrees more fundamentally with Putnam. He points out that citizens' participation in many "civic" organizations, such as the White Citizens Council in the United States and pro-Nazi and procommunist groups in Weimar Germany, can undermine both constitutionalism and democracy.

49. Bergman v. Minister of Finance, 23 (I) P.D. 693, trans. in 4 Israel L. Rev. 559 (1969); United Mizrahi Bank v. Migdal Cooperative Village, [1995] 49 (iv) P.D. 221, trans. and excerpted in 31 *Israel L. Rev.* 764 (1997). For analyses, see esp. Martin Edelman, "The New Israeli Constitution," 36 *Middle Eastern Studies* 1 (2000); Aharon Barak, "The Constitutionalization of the Israeli Legal System as a Result of the Basic Laws and Its Effect on Procedural and Substantive Criminal Law," 31 *Israel L. Rev.* 3 (1997); Gad Barzilai et al., "Supreme Courts and Public Opinion: General Paradigms and the Israeli Case," *Law and Courts,* Winter 1994, p. 3; and Menachem Hofnung, *Democracy, Law, and National Security in Israel* (Dartmouth, UK: Aldershot,1996).

initiation, live together without violence. Officials will possess an opportunity to persuade them that long-lived *fiducia* is in their interests.

Ecco, I am also in accord with Professor Maynard that the economic system does not determine the political system. The fact that your economy is performing poorly can function to your advantage, *if* you can add even small amounts of prosperity to your people. For the long run, the regime's chances of survival increase as prosperity increases.

In sum, my paper tells that although some forms of culture might make constitutional democracy impossible, your culture does not present such impediments. Let me risk offending by reiterating that you still must be carefully attentive to your people's differing cultures. That overused word *multicultural* translates for you as "much difficult labor."

"Professoressa," Ajami comments, "although I have serious reservations about some aspects of constitutional democracy, I care about a civic culture. More than a century ago, Herbert Spencer and William Graham Sumner said that stateways can't change folkways. Were they not correct? The real base of society is its culture; it shapes both politics and economics: 'culture makes all the difference.'[50] Politics reflects, it does not create, a social order. It pains me, but no Islamic country is a democracy of any species. Nor have all peoples of other beliefs made democracy work. The littered trails of failed efforts in Latin America and Africa so attest. In the first, mixtures of authoritarian forms of Roman Catholicism and Spanish heritage stress obedience and honor while denigrating liberty and compromise, thus dooming constitutional democracy. And nothing in the lives of most Sub-Saharan Africans makes constitutional democracy intelligible, much less desirable."

"If an intervention to an intervention is permitted," Vaccarino interrupts, "politics is sometimes the dependent variable, sometimes the independent variable; sometime it acts, sometimes it is acted upon, sometimes it reacts. Regard the mode in which constitutional democracy influenced the Cattolic Church during Vatican II."

"I do not understand," Colonel Martin interrupts.

"Perhaps I can explain," Atilla Gregorian offers. "Until after World War II, papal attitudes toward democratic and constitutionalist theories were negative, despite the affinity between positive constitutionalism and the teachings of encyclicals such as *Rerum Novarum* and *Quadragesimo Anno*. During that period, Rome went so far as to command that the Jesuits silence John Courtney Murray because he was preaching the constitutionalist doctrine of separation of church and state. Moreover, despite Thomistic emphasis on 'subsidiarity,' that is, allowing insofar as possible decisions to be made

50. David S. Landes, *The Wealth and Poverty of Nations: Why Some Are So Rich and Some So Poor* (New York: W. W. Norton, 1998), p. 516.

at the lowest level so as to accommodate local differences, the Vatican was (and is) still trying to run the Church as a monarchy operating through a centralized bureaucracy. Some change came at the Second Vatican Council. There, pastoral bishops who had been living in constitutional democracies and wanted a voice in running the Church phrased their arguments in language parallel to those of theorists of their secular regimes. At home, priests, who knew bishops were often as deaf to them as the Vatican was to bishops, used similar arguments for participating in governing their dioceses. The laity, who found their pastors deaf to their concerns, wanted parish councils so they, too, could share governance. Professional theologians around the world also deployed the language of constitutionalism in their quest for due process when brought up before Rome or local bishops on charges of doctrinal error. Much of the turmoil within the Church during the 1960s pitted arguments for constitutional democracy against those for absolute monarchy.

"Although changes were not as full or as lasting as the majority of bishops, priests, and laity wanted, changes were real. Since 1966, every few years synods of bishops from around the world meet in Rome to advise the pope; most pastoral bishops call diocesan synods in order to consult with their priests; and most parishes have councils of laity to advise pastors. Moreover, ecclesiastical courts as well as the Holy Office itself have refined procedures to bring their practices somewhat more in line with constitutional democracy's norms of due process. And constitutional democracy triumphed when in 1979 Pope John Paul II in New York City publicly preached the doctrine of John Courtney Murray.

"Spillovers from democracy and constitutionalism were not the only causes of these changes, but those forces have significantly increased internal institutional tensions in at least two important respects: (1) by buttressing the reformers' cause with successful secular arguments and (2) by providing a widely understood and respected vocabulary to express normative concepts. To combat most reforms, opponents were forced to rely on ideas and practices that human experience had discredited. In moving toward constitutional democracy, my church has been late rather than unique. Nathan O. Hatch attributes much of the democratization of American Protestantism to the political ideals of the Declaration of Independence."[51]

"Many social theorists," Vaccarino says, "say groups like the church are primary organizations and government is secondary. *Allora*, the story the Padre has told shows that a supposedly secondary association, the state, has changed a primary association."

51. *The Democratization of American Christianity* (New Haven, CT: Yale University Press, 1989), pp. 9–11. I am indebted to Stephen Macedo, *Diversity and Distrust: Civic Education in a Multicultural Democracy* (Cambridge, MA: Harvard University Press, 2000), p. 55, for pointing out this similarity.

Ajami persists: "Your examples are Japan and Germany and to a lesser extent the Catholic Church. But we are not the Allies after World War II; neither are we a collection of bishops. Nor are we thugs who would ram the 'best' political system down the throats of an unwilling—and unprepared— people. It took centuries for constitutional democracy to germinate in Britain and the United States, and it hasn't fully blossomed there yet. And recent popes are undoing the reforms of Vatican II because the Church was not prepared for many of those changes. For our part, we must begin slowly . . . a little democracy . . . a little constitutionalism . . . a little authoritarianism . . . then a little more of the first two and less of the third. For decades we will have to lead, sometimes push, our people, to help build a culture that will enable them to accept constitutional democracy. We must force our people to be free, but force them very slowly and very gently."

"*Va bene*, you make a large thesis. We are in accord about the prudence of gradual change. Even sainted geniuses cannot stabilize constitutional democracy at a blow. The United States has not done so after more than two centuries. You confront long and difficult labor."

"It is good that you retreat."

"Do not mistake clarification for retreat. Your thesis possesses three parts; the first is correct, but the second is wrong and wars with the third. The first is that a specific culture is necessary. I spoke of a range of cultures and a certain level of awareness of the world existing outside of oneself, family, and vicinage, and also a willingness, as Professor Sprachfehler said, to live in peace with people outside one's own tribe. *Allora*, I have no *vista* of a constitutional democracy's stabilizing soon in villages whose people possess no understanding of the outside world, or constitutional democracy's having been possible in societies like those of the nineteenth-century Comanches, where outsiders were things to loot, rape, torture, and kill. Because you do not find yourselves in either kind of situation, this part of your argument has truth but not relevance.

"*Dunque*, the second part of your thesis," Vaccarino continues, "is that stateways cannot change folkways. I grant you the changes in the Cattolic Church have only been partial, but do not the conversions of Germany and Japan refute Sumner?"

Pyknites cuts in: "I'm not sure. In the 1920s, each had experienced a period of democracy if not constitutionalism. And some of those leaders were still alive in the later 1940s to help fashion new constitutional orders."

"Of new, I say Sumner was wrong, though not completely so. According to me, Montesquieu was correct when he said that the state 'cannot change its religion, manners, and customs in an instant.' Those ultimate three words are critical. *Allora*, you told about Germany and Japan. A few leaders, even great ones like Konrad Adenauer, do not of themselves alone constitute a culture, though they may redirect one. By definition, culture's norms must be widespread among a population. So I give to you another example: India. Its traditions included little about either democracy or constitutionalism. Hinduism never possessed a tendency toward equality. Women were little better than property, to be burned after their owners' deaths, and the caste system denied equal dignity. When the concept 'constitutional' made its face in political discourse, it was in the narrow sense of existing colonial processes and institutions—what Professor Deukalion termed *constitutionism*, not *constitutionalism*. I quote you Professor Tapan Raychaudhuri, who has told that it is an error to believe either the broader or truncated concept of constitutionalism 'was *the* or even *a* central theme in the nationalist discourse.'[52] And Mohandas Gandhi's mass politics, with his fervor for village autonomy and fear of industrialization and the state, possessed a political *vista* 'out of tune with constitutional democracy.'[53] Most important, did the hundreds of millions of poor peasants who heard Gandhi's orations hear them as promises to finish their economic misery or to confer the blessings of constitutional democracy? In India, Sunil Khilnani says, 'democracy was constructed against the grain, both of a society founded on the inequality of the caste order, and of an imperial and authoritarian state. If the initial conditions were unlikely, democracy has had to exist in circumstances that conventional political theories identify as being equally unpropitious: amidst poor, illiterate and staggeringly diverse citizenry. Not only has it survived, it has succeeded in energizing Indian society in unprecedented ways.'[54]

"*Senta*, India possessed countervailing assets, including a small but politically active, Westernized middle class, a corps of trained civil servants, and eloquent, determined prophets, Gandhi and Nehru, maestros of the political arts. Not least important, in 1949, the leaders of the Congress Party had the *vista*, patience, and skill to utilize these assets to vanquish opposition, doubt, and indifference.[55] You should take much comfort from that example."

"Perhaps."

"More exists. There was no fit at all between constitutional democracy's notions of individualism and historic Indian ideals. According to Professor T. G. Vaidyanathan, 'India's dominant principle celebrates the abrogation if not the very extinction of personality, whereas the Western concept of romantic love joyfully celebrates the extension of personality and often person-

52. "Constitutionalism: The Indian Experience," in Douglas Greenberg, Stanley N. Katz, Melanie Beth Oliviero, and Steven C. Wheatley, eds., *Constitutionalism and Democracy: Transformations in the Contemporary World* (New York: Oxford University Press, 1993). Throughout this provocative essay, Raychaudhuri uses *constitutionalism* in the narrow sense of "constitutionism."
53. Ibid., p. 208.
54. *The Idea of India* (New York: Farrar, Straus, and Giroux, 1998), pp. 9–10.
55. Granville Austin, *The Indian Constitution: Cornerstone of a Nation* (Oxford: Oxford University Press, 1966), remains among the very best works on the modern Indian founding.

ality itself.'[56] He continues: 'The [traditional] Indian self, by definition, lacks reflexive awareness of itself. . . . The self as a homogenous, independent entity capable of moral choice, discrimination and reflexiveness is a Judeo-Christian conception wholly inapplicable to the Indian psychological reality.' According to me, this 'reality' offered rocky ground in which to plant a theory based on individual dignity and autonomy.

"Yet constitutional democracy has survived for more than fifty years. And increasing numbers of Indians have become more individualistic, even materialistic. Exact allocation of credit is impossible among factors such as constitutional democracy, economic development, moral progress, or moral corruption. But according to me, the political system must take some responsibility. India's leaders have used democracy to build the state, very different from the European model of using the state to build democracy.[57] Constitutional democracy thus preceded two of its supposed *preconditions:* a receptive culture and a state."

"I need to think about it before trying to rebut you."

"*Mó*, I have fear that I appear ungracious in adjoining that the second part of your thesis not only is wrong but also contradicts the third part. The third tells you have need to proceed slowly, as the government changes the culture—exactly what you previously said stateways could not do."

"If a visitor may be permitted," Professor Deukalion interrupts, "we might think in more general terms about state and society. Neither is monolithic. Every society has many divisions. Sex, age, and health push people to value different distributions of goods differently. Madison claimed that property was the greatest cause of faction, but religion certainly ranks at or near the top. Even if everyone is nominally of the same group, the existence of orthodoxies and heresies—and thus of sects, 'little enders' and 'big enders' —is practically universal. We can say much the same about the state. No state is monolithic. Even would-be totalitarian states such as Stalin's Soviet Union, Mao's China, and Hitler's Germany were run by people whose ideas and ambitions conflicted with each other. At times the ability of dictators to dictate was complete, but those periods were short lived. The cracks that soon appeared may have been small, but they were real. And, of course, founders of constitutional democracies try to divide power, to pit ambition against ambition and interest against interest. In a struggle to influence public policy and popular behavior, different portions of the state— really different public officials—try to induce different social groups to sup-

56. "Authority and Identity in India," 118 *Daedalus* 147–48 (1989). See also Ashis Nandy, "The Political Culture of the Indian State," 118 *Daedalus* 1 (1989).

57. Maya Chadda, *Building Democracy in South Asia: India, Nepal, Pakistan* (Boulder: Lynne Rienner, 2000), p. 143. See also Gary Jeffrey Jacobsohn, *The Wheel of Law: India's Secularism in Constitutional Context* (Princeton, NJ: Princeton University Press, 2003).

port their policies. Joel Migdal has said that modern societies are always 'becoming' and states 'continually morph.' The relationship between the two is typically symbiotic.[58] The state may be the most important collection of instruments of social change, but neither is it the only such collection nor is it, itself, impermeable to changing forces from within society.

"Competitions for power among public officials often change the institutional competencies, if not the basic structure, of the state's institutions; and as they struggle, those officials try to enlist various social groups by giving them at least some of what they want, thereby perhaps frustrating other groups. And as social groups compete against each other, they, in turn, try to enlist state institutions on their side. Insofar as they are successful, they may change both the state and the society. In sum, Professor Vaccarino is right: the question is not whether the state can change society or society can change the state; rather it is how much and under what circumstances one can change the other."

"My dear professors," Federika Strega cuts in, "your ideas of political culture are slippery."

"*Forse,*" Vaccarino says. "But you attended the law faculty of the University of Chicago. And according to me, no lawyer should criticize others for slippery concepts."

The members chuckle as Strega says, "Touché, touché. But tell me something about society and political culture that directly bears on our work. You say political culture is not 'determining' but still important; that government can change society but not too fast or too much. What aspects of political culture are preconditions for constitutional democracy? Do we have them?"

"*Giusto,* equitable questions. First, no particular culture can be a precondition, because no constitutional democracy has a single culture. *Pero,* as I have told, some cultural elements are essential: most people must have some sophistication, accept the necessity of government, believe they possess rights that neither government nor other citizens can violate, recognize that fellow citizens possess the same rights, and be willing to utilize only peaceful means to settle disputations. These are important conditions, and the state can cultivate them among its citizens."

"Then we face a great difficulty," Professor Jacobsohn intervenes. "Oppression has made *government* a dirty word. Our people believe *they* have rights, but I doubt they believe that those who disagree with them do. As for peaceful means, they suffered much violence from government and have had their lives saved by violence against government."

"You do face great difficulty, but you are not without hope. Your people

58. *State in Society: Studying How States and Societies Transform and Constitute One Another* (New York: Cambridge University Press, 2001), pp. 23, 50, 59.

abandoned the old regime. Therefore, a large portion of them probably possess what Catholic moral theology calls 'a right disposition' toward constitutional democracy. They have learned much from other nations; they can learn more, and you can instruct them. According to me, a people do not require profound quantities of these cultural 'traits' at the initiation, but they must quickly make roots if constitutional democracy is to survive."

"*We* must instruct them? We *know* those traits, but do we *internalize* them?" Strega asks.

"*Ecco,* the answer lies in your hearts. I mention a related difficulty, a 'dissident culture'—that is, an orientation toward politics that often develops while fighting against an oppressive regime. Paul Wilson has said the *capi* of the Czech and Slovak Republic suffered such a malady. I quote you him: 'These leaders believed in political solidarity; a community could be created in which people of vastly differing political views and backgrounds could bury their differences and work together on a project that had a higher meaning and deep principles than "mere" politics.' But maintaining a constitutional democracy involves much 'mere politics,' because people who are in accord on fundaments may yet disagree about who should obtain what from the political system.

"A 'belief that compromise means surrender' may exist as a natural reaction against the sordid moral compromises that existence under the old regime required. Wilson told that the Czechs' experience had deprived them of the skills—and desire—to practice the give-and-take necessary to building consensus.[59] *Ecco,* times do occur when one cannot compromise; but in constitutional democracy, it is usually obligatory to try negotiation and compromise."

"Do you think a good Muslim can be a good citizen of a constitutional democracy?" Ajami asks.

Vaccarino smiles. "You nicely rephrase Aristotle's famous question. I am not a specialist about things Islamic. Do you still want my opinion?"

"Yes," Strega cuts in. "And it's interesting that the first professor who confesses to not being the world's greatest expert on everything is a woman. Refreshing."

"*Allora,* first, Carl J. Friedrich, the great explainer of constitutionalism, thought that constitutionalism's values were rooted in Christian beliefs,[60] implying that it could flourish only in a society that adhered to the Christian, perhaps Judeo-Christian, tradition. On this point he was wrong—according to me and according to the evidence. I cite you India and Japan: both are constitutional democracies, neither is in the Christian or Jewish tradition.

"Then for Islam: my paper makes bibliographic citations the Mufti will

59. "The End of the Velvet Revolution," *N.Y. Rev. of Bks,* Aug. 13, 1992, pp. 57ff.

60. *Transcendent Justice: The Religious Dimension of Constitutionalism* (Durham, NC: Duke University Press, 1964), esp. p. 17.

not need but his colleagues might find utile.[61] We have need of two distinctions: between the words of the Qur'an and historic practice and among differing interpretations of that text. According to many writers, the Qur'an itself does not preclude constitutional democracy. In facts, L. Carl Brown points out, Islam has been much freer than Christianity in religiously ori-

61. For general discussions, mostly of Arab versions of Islam, see Fouad Ajami, *The Dream Palace of the Arabs: A Generation's Odyssey* (New York: Pantheon, 1998); Raymond William Baker, *Islam without Fear: Egypt and the New Islamists* (Cambridge, MA: Harvard University Press, 2003); James A. Bill and Robert Springborn, *Politics of the Middle East*, 3rd ed. (New York: HarperCollins, 1990); L. Carl Brown, *Religion and the State: The Muslim Approach to Politics* (New York: Columbia University Press, 2000); Dale F. Eickelman and James Piscatori, *Muslim Politics* (Princeton, NJ: Princeton University Press, 1996); Noah Feldman, *After Jihad: America and the Struggle for Islamic Democracy* (New York: Farrar, Straus and Giroux, 2003); Gilles Kepel, *Muslim Extremism in Egypt: The Prophet and the Pharaoh* (Berkeley: University of California Press, 1995), and *The War for Muslim Minds: Islam and the West* (Cambridge, MA: Harvard University Press, 2004); Bruce B. Lawrence, *Shattering the Myth: Islam beyond Violence* (Princeton, NJ: Princeton University Press, 1998); Robert W. Hefner, ed., *Remaking Muslim Politics: Pluralism, Contestation, and Democratization* (Princeton, NJ: Princeton University Press, 2005); Ann Elizabeth Mayer, *Islam and Human Rights: Tradition and Politics* (Boulder: Westview, 1991), esp. chs. 9–10; Daniel E. Price, *Islamic Political Culture, Democracy, and Human Rights* (Westport, CT: Praeger, 1999); Olivier Roy, *The Failure of Political Islam* (Cambridge, MA: Harvard University Press, 1994), and *Globalized Islam: The Search for a New Ummah* (New York: Columbia University Press, 2004); Edward Said's now classic *Orientalism* (London: Routledge and Kegan Paul, 1978); and Anthony Shadid, *The Legacy of the Prophet: Despots, Democrats, and the New Politics of Islam* (Boulder: Westview, 2002). For essays on legal problems internal to Muslim communities, see Robert Gleave, ed., *Islamic Law: Theory and Practice* (New York: Tauis, 1997); and for essays on Islam and war, especially holy war, see Harfiyah Abdel Haleem et al., eds., *The Crescent and the Cross: Muslim Approaches to War and Peace* (New York: St. Martin's, 1998); and Gilles Kepel, *Jihad: The Trail of Political Islam* (Cambridge, MA: Harvard University Press, 2002). For studies of the condition of women in Islamic nations, see Miriam Cooke, *Women Claim Islam: Creating Islamic Feminism through Literature* (New York: Routledge, 2000); Haled Esfandiari, *Reconstructed Lives: Women and Iran's Islamic Revolution* (Baltimore: Johns Hopkins University Press, 1997); Elizabeth Warnock Fernea, *In Search of Islamic Feminism* (New York: Doubleday, 1998); Deniz Kandiyoti, ed., *Women, Islam, and the State* (Philadelphia: Temple University Press, 1991); Fauziya Kassindja and Layli Miller Bashir, *Do They Hear You When You Cry?* (New York: Delacorte, 1998); Saba Mahmood, *Politics of Piety: The Islamic Revival and the Feminist Subject* (Princeton, NJ: Princeton University Press, 2004); and Khalida Messaoudi with Elisabeth Schlema, *Unbowed: An Algerian Woman Confronts Islamic Fundamentalism*, trans. Anne C. Vilna (Philadelphia: University of Pennsylvania Press, 1998).

Abdullahi Ahmed An-Naim, *Toward an Islamic Reformation: Civil Liberties, Human Rights, and Islamic Law* (Syracuse, NY: Syracuse University Press, 1990), argues that the Shari'a utilizes the Prophet's more specific commands, designed to allow the then small sect to survive in a hostile environment, at the expense of the Qur'an's more general principles, which support human rights. Thus, according to him, it is the Shari'a's misinterpretation of Islam that makes it conflict with constitutional democracy, not the Prophet's message itself. Farid Esack, *Qur'an Liberation and Pluralism* (Chichester, UK: Oneworld, 1997), a member of South Africa's Truth Commission and founder of the political-religious movement Call to Islam, attacks much traditional interpretation of the Qur'an as a rationalization for oppressive governments. John L. Esposito and John O. Voll, *Islam and Democracy* (New York: Oxford University Press, 1996), are rather optimistic about the possibility of an Islamic democracy. Quite appropriately, they point out that democracy is a contested concept and analysts should therefore not believe that Western models have exclusive claims to democratic legitimacy. On the other hand, their case studies fail to unearth a single Islamic democ-

ented political theorizing.[62] Nevertheless, as the Mufti has told, no Islamic democracy exists. Moreover, few Muslim countries have made serious efforts to stabilize constitutional democracy, and none has long retained it. *Ecco*, Turkey, a militantly secular state, has made some brave attempts, but its history is pitted by episodes of martial law and frequent violations of human rights under civilian or military rule. Pakistan calls itself an 'Islamic republic' and has proclaimed the perhaps incompatible ideals of constitutional democracy and an Islamic state. It, too, has endured much life under military rule; even under civilian government its connections to democracy or constitutionalism have been tenuous. Malaysia has made feeble democratic efforts and has stabilized a form of authoritarian consociationalism, which manifests some democratic trappings that might cede future fruit. Other Islamic nations range from Jordan and Egypt, which offer some democratic processes, to Syria, which remains a brutal dictatorship. Ergo, practice donates small encouragement."

"You are preaching my message," Ajami says. "Please continue."

"*Giusto*, traditional interpretations of the Qur'an, most importantly in Islamic law, the Shari'a, donate no more. According to me, Abdullah Ahmed An-Naim is correct: the Shari'a, as now comprehended, is incompatible with constitutional democracy. Women cannot be equal to men; nonbelievers cannot be equal to believers; it is a capital offense to persuade a Muslim to convert to another religion, for the converter as well as the converted; and the Shari'a's harsh criminal processes run contrary to Western notions of legal protections. But, I stress you, the Shari'a is an encrustation on Islam, vulnerable to surgery."

"I agree," Ajami notes, "and I apologize for enticing you to say it. But my

racy. Moreover, they focus on what many scholars call representative democracy rather than constitutional democracy. For more general analyses of these problems, see Khaled Abou Fadl, *Islam and the Challenge of Democracy*, ed. Joshua Cohen and Deborah Chasman (Princeton, NJ: Princeton University Press, 2004). Shadid, *Legacy of the Prophet*, analyzes efforts to transform Islamic politics into a more "mature" incarnation that would further both a civil society and a less authoritarian governance.

To the contrary, Elie Kedourie, *Democracy and Arab Political Culture* (Washington, DC: Washington Institute for Near East Policy, 1992), contends that "there is nothing in the political traditions of the Arab world—which are the political traditions of Islam—which might make familiar, or indeed intelligible, the organizing ideas of constitutional and representative government" (p. 5; see also ch. 6). Bernard Lewis, *The Political Language of Islam* (Chicago: University of Chicago Press, 1988), is almost equally pessimistic about the chances of constitutionalism or democracy in an Islamic country. Speaking of Islam in South and Southeast Asia, Lucian W. Pye, *Asian Power and Politics: The Cultural Dimensions of Authority* (Cambridge, MA: Harvard University Press, 1985), p. 278, says, "In a peculiar way Muslim ideals of power and authority find martial law and military rule very attractive." See also ch. 10. For a useful analysis of the literature on Islam and democracy, see Masoud Kazemzadeh, "Teaching the Politics of Islamic Fundamentalism," 31 *PS* 52 (1998). Jane I. Smith, *Islam in America* (New York: Columbia University Press, 1999), examines the growth and peculiarities of Islam in the United States.

62. *Religion and State.*

colleagues, peace be upon them, are more likely to believe you than me. The Shari'a's voices are not the voice of the Prophet, peace be upon him, but mere interpretations of his words. Many people dispute the traditional interpretations of Qur'an and the Shari'a, as your paper's bibliographic footnote demonstrates. These people—'liberals'—argue that 'fundamentalists'—a term as ambiguous as 'liberals'—misread the Prophet's message. Islam itself is compatible with many forms of democracy. You have mentioned An-Na'im, a Sudanese; he is among the more prominent. So also are Farid Esack, a theologian from South Africa, and Reza Aslan,[63] born in Iran but now teaching about Islam in the United States. In Iran itself, prominent writers such former president Seyyed Khatami and Abdol-Karim Soroush[64] contend that Islam, properly understood, encourages democracy and defends human rights. In the United States there is a movement of young Muslim men and women who practice the new interpretations and try to convert others in the Islamic world."[65]

"Aren't you being overly optimistic, Mufti?" Pynites asks.

"Perhaps, but Islam is in turmoil. Osama bin Laden and his hate-filled followers make the headlines, while heavy-handed American operations like the invasion of Iraq and torture of prisoners and brutal Israeli treatment of Palestinians turn suicidal terrorists into Muslim heroes. But these fanatical thugs do not represent the mainstream of Islam. Most of my people are seeking new ways, peaceful ways, and democracy is far more appealing to them than bombs. It is not the West's version of democracy, but our version. Our religion urges us to seek consensus and community, *ummah*. Islamic democracy offers such a possibility not only in a fight against despotic regimes but also as a political structure for a just society. This form of democracy has a good chance of becoming a reality, not today, next year, or in the next five years, but in the foreseeable future. I am less sure about what you call constitutionalism. Human dignity has always been central to Islam, but for the West removal of tyranny means liberty. For devout Muslims the absence of tyranny is not liberty but justice.[66] They equate Western liberty with materialism and sexual promiscuity. And, I say with sorrow, too many of my brothers, peace be upon them, equate justice with revenge. Thus, I am less optimistic about constitutionalism's taking firm roots. I know that Nathan Brown[67] has shown that constitutionalist institutions have begun to grow in the Middle East, but I doubt if they will become more than dwarf

63. *No God but God: The Origins, Evolution, and Future of Islam* (New York: Random House, 2005).

64. Soroush is the pen name of Hossein Dabbagh. For summaries of his and Khatami's political writings, see Shadid, *Legacy of the Prophet*, chs. 6-7.

65. "The New Islamists," *Newsweek*, Mar. 16, 1998, pp. 34ff., and Smith, *Islam in America*.

66. Shadid stresses this point: *Legacy of the Prophet*, p. 67.

67. *Constitutions in a Nonconstitutional World: Arab Basic Laws and the Prospects for Accountable Government* (Albany: State University of New York Press, 2002).

plants until Islamists thoroughly revise the Shari'a. And that revision is one I wholeheartedly support."

Anita Baca interrupts. "I totally admire your views; they're awesome. But aren't you liberals a tiny minority? Isn't it critical that, in Islam, Allah is sovereign, not the people? In Islam, there can be no separation of church and state. There can be no equality among people, no religious freedom if we define it to include the right to criticize or renounce Islam or to convert others to another religion. And the Shari'a makes women chattel, right?"

"You have reason but not in a plenary mode," Vaccarino speaks before Ajami can reply. "I respond you by point. First, in these days, liberal Muslims are a minority in the Islamic world, but so were constitutional democrats in the West a century and a half ago. Slavery existed in the United States until 1865, and severe racial discrimination was approbated by law until only a few decades ago. Second, yes, for Muslims there can be no separation of church and state. But you must comprehend that for Sunni Muslims, more than 90 percent of Muslims in the world, there is no such thing as a church on the Cattolic model. Thus the idea of separation has no relevance for them.

"Of truth, according to traditional teaching, Allah is sovereign for Muslims," Vaccarino continues. "But Islam is here in accord with Judaism, early Liberalism, Cattolicism, and much of Protestantism. For the Israelites, the earth belonged to Yahweh; the chosen people only held it in trust for Him. The great *padron* of liberalism, John Locke, wrote as if God were the ultimate sovereign.[68] For many believing Christians, God alone is sovereign. For them, a law, to be moral, must conform to His law, the which Cattolic moral theologians define as 'right reason.' Historically, that requirement donated much power to clerics. What changed to permit good Cattolics to become good constitutional democrats is interpretation, influenced, according to me, by constitutionalism and democracy. Vatican II acknowledged officially what Cattolic theologians and laity had long believed was the proper interpretation of natural and divine law: government exists to protect human rights, including religious freedom. Some conservative Cattolics, like some conservative Protestants and ultra-Orthodox Jews do not accept that change, and nether do many conservative Muslims. This struggle is not finished and may never be.

"*Allora,* your other point is the most difficult. The Shari'a rejects equality of women; but, I say of new, the Shari'a is not the word of Allah. Like the Torah, the Qur'an ordains genital surgery only on males. Second, we should

---

68. Richard Aschcraft, "The Politics of Locke's Two Treatises of Government," in Edward J. Harpham, ed., *John Locke's Two Treatises of Government: New Interpretations* (Lawrence: University Press of Kansas, 1992). Leo Strauss said in seminars that he believed Locke was an atheist, the real reason that he attacked Filmer rather than Hobbes. I am not aware that this conclusion appears in Strauss's writings.

remember that women were not allowed to vote in much of Europe and America until the twentieth century, and the United States allowed many forms of legal discrimination against women into the second half of that century. Israel has also lagged on women's rights. When Golda Meier was prime minister, she could not give sworn testimony in court because a woman could not be expected to tell the truth. Furthermore, until 2000 women were not allowed to hold religious ceremonies at the Western Wall ceremonies at the Western Wall; they were allowed then because of a decision by the Supreme Court, not based on a statute enacted by the popularly elected Knesset. Third, there are some favorable omens in the Muslim world, and we Romans put much faith in omens: women have served as president of Indonesia and as prime ministers in Bangladesh, Pakistan, Turkey, and even India, which possesses a significant Muslim minority."[69]

"I do not find a few token women as prime ministers encouraging in the context of mutilation and oppression," Strega says.

"I am of accord that women lack their rightful power in either East or West.[70] But if you are asking if any Islamic country will soon adopt constitutional democracy, I agree with the Mufti and say no, though American military power is pushing Iraq in this direction. That failure will, however, not be due only to religion. Muslim leadership tends to be feudal, their tribal customs hostile to modernization. *Allora,* you do not face those problems. According to me, it would be not be prudent for you to assume that your Muslims do not wish to live within a system that protects their rights and the rights of others. Probably, most of them already believe that women are equal to men. I recall you that Professor Ann Elizabeth Mayer tells that she has never found a single Muslim woman aware of international human rights who thought that Islam prevented her claiming those rights."[71]

"Please allow me." Ajami says, "to add a few words. The existence of regimes throughout the Middle East that are both oppressive and Muslim only in name has encouraged reformers to claim that a return to true Islam is

69. For data on women's holding political office in the West, see Rebecca H. Davis, *Women and Power in Parliamentary Democracies: Cabinet Appointments in Western Europe, 1968–1992* (Lincoln: University of Nebraska Press, 1997), and Alan Siaroff, "Women's Representation in Legislatures and Cabinets in Industrial Democracies," 21 *Int'l Pol. Sci. Rev.* 197 (2000). The *Economist* reported (Apr. 23, 2005, p. 100) that Rwanda had the highest proportion of women in Parliament, almost 50 percent, followed by Sweden, Finland, the Netherlands, and Spain. The United States ranked near the bottom, well below even Pakistan.

70. In a footnote to her paper, *la professoressa* cites "Germany: *Kinder. Küche,* CDU?" *Economist,* Mar. 11, 2000, p. 54, showing that although 31 percent of members of Parliament were women, no woman had yet headed a large political party, and only one of the sixteen *Länder* was led by a woman. Moreover, women hold less than 10 percent of the positions in the senior civil service, only 6 percent of higher management jobs in private industry, and 6 percent of the top university professorships. The latter figure is not likely soon to change radically because in 2000 two-thirds of doctoral candidates were male. The footnote adds that in 2005 Angela Merkel became Chancellor of Germany.

71. *Islam and Human Rights,* p. 218n16.

the answer to all of the region's political and economic problems. False! Our religion is not a political ideology; it does not have answers to all problems; rather, it outlines our relationship to Allah and thus to each other, relationships of peace, justice, and love. Where it has been co-opted as the ideology of rulers, as in Iran and the Sudan, it has been corrupted and brought a double failure, strengthening tyranny and weakening religious belief."

"I agree with the Mufti and the Professoressa," Tuncer Kirca adds.

"Thank you," Vaccarino says. "Let me demonstrate you why I am more optimistic than the Mufti about Muslims' being open to constitutional democracy. I quote you from a booklet published by an Islamic educational group in the United States. It warns that we must distinguish between what is Islamic and what is not Islamic in the treatment of women, then tells: 'In Islam women are completely equated with men in the sight of Allah in terms of spiritual rights and responsibilities. . . . Islam views men and women as equal but not identical. Thus rights and status are equal.'[72] "According to me, these are encouraging words."

At this point, the chair intervenes: "Colleagues, we have grilled our speakers at great length. I suggest we debate these issues ourselves, with, of course, our honored guests invited to participate. But first, we should attend to matters physical. Let us adjourn for two hours for dinner."

Two hours and five minutes later, the caucus reconvenes. Jacobsohn opens the debate: "The best strategy to establish constitutional democracy is to begin with small steps."

"And what might those be?" the chair asks.

"Because we must take these steps more or less simultaneously, I do not imply a sequence of events. We must begin by educating our people, teach them about constitutional democracy by encouraging them to participate—through voting, discussing public policies among themselves, and campaigning. We should also promulgate an interim bill of rights to provide guidelines to instruct citizens, judges, administrators, and, not least, ourselves. During this process, we must also decide if we want to have a constitutional text or should proceed by developing customs—and somehow bring citizens in on those sorts of decisions. Whatever our choices, we must create governmental institutions that both fit our needs and fulfill our people's basic expectations."

"And rising expectations about standards of living are among the latter," Minxin Wei says. "I agree with Professor Maynard's first point: although we don't need prosperity to begin constitutional democracy, we'll be in trouble if we don't soon improve the economy—Indian and Irish experiences notwith-

72. Islamic Cultural Center, *Islam: A Brief Guide to the Teachings of Islam* (Tempe, AZ: Islamic Cultural Center, n.d.), p. 27.

standing. Polish discontent with economic performance brought 'reformed' communists back for a time, and economic chaos has made the chances for Russia's continuing toward constitutional democracy very dicey. Maynard's third point is wrong. Elster himself wrote that each of his propositions "might be contested. Fine tuning and incrementalism by the authorities, and willingness in the population to accept temporary hardships and inequalities, might sustain a feasible path to a stable market democracy."[73] It would be more efficient to impose a new economic system than to work reforms out through democratic bargaining subject to constitutional guarantees, but we'd risk a terrible political price. Change is necessary and likely to cause enormous hardships. The new regime must shoulder the burden of persuading the people to suffer in the short run so they can prosper in the long run. We've been preaching about constitutional democracy; we can't ignore its demands when we need to do something important."

"And we may fail," the chair notes.

"We may," Wei agrees. "But that's a risk we must take."

"May I make a question?" Vaccarino asks.

"Be our guest, as the Americans say," the Chair replies.

"I make the Mufti this question: What are his reservations about constitutional democracy?"

"I do not believe," Ajami replies, "that we should try to establish a constitutional democracy like that of the United States. Although economic reform is necessary, I see our principal problems not as economic but as moral. Many people think that moral relativism is the 'default setting' for all peoples and that liberty requires license."

"Now wait, Ibrahim," Pyknites says brusquely, "I don't believe that all morals are equal, but I know that we come from several different moral cultures, none of which can conclusively demonstrate its superiority. If we impose one we alienate others."

"So you, my friend, peace be upon you, would have the state represent the least common denominator?"

"No," Pyknites explains, "I would have the state enforce as much as we can agree on without badly dividing society."

"I confess that I still don't understand the Mufti's argument," Vaccarino says.

"My point," Ajami answers, "is that we will have little difficulty persuading most of my Muslim brothers and sisters in this country of the importance of democratic and limited government and of the legal and moral equality of men and women. But you will not persuade them that all morals are relative, that individual freedom means the right to do whatever makes us feel good including promiscuous sex and then abortion to kill the consequences, that

73. "Necessity and Impossibility," in Greenberg et al., *Constitutionalism and Democracy*, p. 271.

abuse of alcohol or drugs is a 'crime without a victim,' and that 'gay marriages' should be lawful. I shall not repeat arguments about the existence of moral standards that are not relative. Here I speak of the fact that a majority of our people so believe, and we cannot offend that belief and hope to persuade them to accept a political system that contradicts that belief. Just as Westerners tend to wrongly identify the horrors of Iran and the Sudan as inherent in an Islamic state, so Muslims, again wrongly, tend to see licentiousness as inherent in constitutional democracy. Our problem will be to convince them that we can construct a polity in which they can have freedom without authorizing moral license."

"I may sound like Pollyanna," Pilsudski puts in, "but though I think the ethnic-moral issue is serious, it is not insuperable. We are all here discussing these issues, and that 'we' includes men and women of every ethnic group. All of us here realize that Liberalism's moral laissez-faire is itself a moral claim. I hope we can do better. Our people deserve a chance to try."

"Yes, but not to try license, to make our nation an abomination before the face of Allah—or the Most High or God, as Jews and Christians name Him."

After three more hours of discussion, the chair interrupts: "This debate has been enlightening as well as long. With due humility, we have all assumed our country has a skilled and determined political elite, present in this chamber, to make constitutional democracy work. What most of us have been saying about other so-called preconditions, with the possible exception of interethnic harmony, presumes an affirmative answer to our question about the feasibility of constitutional democracy. Most of us are now discussing how to cope with ethnic and moral divisions. Thus the chair will entertain a motion to give an affirmative answer to the question of practicality. Do I hear such a motion?"

"So moved," Pilsudski says.

"Second," Gregorian adds.

"Question," Jacobsohn says.

"Very well," the chair continues, "all in favor, please raise your hands." He pauses, looks around the room, and counts. "The motion carries, seventeen to seven. Let us move to the next set of issues. All the things just mentioned may have to be done simultaneously, but we can only make one decision at a time. The chair proposes that we consider these aspects separately, make tentative decisions on each, and then, when we are done, debate and construct an overall scheme for a new political system. The first item, it seems to me, is whether we should have a constitutional text. If so, our work could be extraordinarily complex either in designing more or less permanent institutions ourselves or in setting up one or more institutions to do that work. We should reflect on these problems. Thus I propose that we take the weekend off to think and discuss matters informally among ourselves. I should add that all of our learned advisers have agreed to stay at least until the end of next week—except for Professor Maynard, that is. He has a pair of tickets to Wimbledon."

Colonel Martin again looks around the room. "Hearing no objection, it is so ordered. We are in recess until Monday at 0900 hours." The gavel slams down, and the colonel leaves the dais.

CHAPTER FIVE

To Draft or Not to Draft
a Constitutional Text

A constitution is not an act of a government, but of a people constituting a government.
                                                    THOMAS PAINE

The force of words . . . [is] too weak to hold men to the performance of their covenants.
                                                    THOMAS HOBBES

At 0858 Colonel Martin walks behind the dais, a double espresso in his left hand, the gavel in his right. Despite the fact that fewer than twenty members of the caucus are present, precisely at 0900 he slams the gavel down. "I call the caucus to order. The first item of business is whether to create a constitutional text. Professor Retlaw Deukalion will give us the benefit of his wisdom." The elderly professor walks to the podium.

To Write or Not to Write a Constitutional Text?

Earlier, I invoked Genesis's theological account of creation, most importantly the chaos that preceded Yahweh's work and, in the form of human passions, continues to wreak havoc in our lives. Law is among the more obvious efforts to channel those passions. Writing constitutional charters and creating theories to justify them are also products of that project. These operations are, however, both more specific and more general: more specific because constitutional texts proclaim themselves part of the genus "law"; more general because they partake of practical politics and its never-ending search for peace, prosperity, and self-fulfillment for all citizens. Moreover, the justification for any constitutional document, indeed any constitutional order, ultimately rests on arguments from political philosophy, moral theology, or both. Every such charter depends on its acceptance as a higher law; each reflects faith in the power of words to spawn loyalties by plucking what Abraham Lincoln called "the mystic chords of memory." Alas, eloquent language has often disappointed. We can cite dozens of failures of "parchment barriers" to stay "the lash of power."[1] Yet we can also cite successes. A political chemistry

---

1. The phrase is Paul Carrington's: "Of Law and the River," 34 *J. of Legal Ed.* 222, 226 (1984).

—or alchemy—can transform sheets of paper into hoops of steel. Language can become, "a god-like code which man seeks to fathom and control."[2] Why are the words of some constitutional documents effective and others unavailing?

I wish I could give you the key, but I cannot. Many factors operate, including some over which we have small control, such as the aggressiveness of other nations. Some are more subject to our influence, such as the power to imagine a constitutional order and the political craftsmanship to construct a text to advance that order by fitting and, at the same time, changing existing cultures. Also important is patient leadership to cope intelligently with the mundane, often dreary problems of everyday public life. Not least, of course, is luck. But Fortuna, as that sixteenth-century male chauvinist Niccolò Machiavelli said, is a woman: "she lets herself be overcome by the bold rather than by those who proceed coldly."[3]

It is in this tangled context, exemplified in the discussions last week about culture and constitutions, that I analyze the principal reasons for and against a charter. There are at least four strong sets of arguments against trying to write a binding constitutional agreement. First, the effort is likely to be futile. Covenants, Thomas Hobbes sneered, "being but words and breath, have no force to oblige, contain, constrain, or protect any man but what it has from the public sword."[4] And that weapon, he believed, could be effectively wielded only by an omnipotent despot. Three and a half centuries later, we still share much of Hobbes's cynicism. Common experience shouts that people often lie when pledging their individual or collective honor and, when they initially mean to keep their word, frequently forsake vows for pleasure or profit. Most Americans of the Revolution began as patriots, but many soon became profiteering poltroons.[5]

A second argument contends that tradition and existing legal and political systems provide norms adequate to achieve as much constitutional democracy as a people want or can currently maintain. New Zealanders could thus follow the British model reflected in their own customs: enough citizens have been content with their parliamentary system and common law that the colonists can politically prosper.[6]

2. Geoffrey Hughes, *Swearing* (Cambridge, MA: Basil Blackwell, 1991), p. 38.
3. *The Prince*, ch. 25, trans. Luigi Ricci and E. R. P. Vincent (New York: Random House, 1940).
4. *Leviathan*, pt. 2, ch. 18.
5. Glenn Tucker, *Poltroons and Patriots: A Popular Account of the War of 1812*, 2 vols. (Indianapolis: Bobbs-Merril, 1954), applied the term to participants in a different war, but it equally fits the colonists from 1777 until 1781. See Joseph J. Ellis, *His Excellency George Washington* (New York: Alfred A. Knopf, 2004), chs. 3–4.
6. Like the United Kingdom, New Zealand still has in place a set of quasi-constitutional texts labeled as constitution acts or amendments to constitution acts. Despite these formal titles, these documents are subject to modification or repeal by a simple act of Parliament. In 1986, Parliament

"Just a moment," Baca interrupts. "Who says the Maoris' customs or even wishes were reflected in that choice?"

"No one whom I know," Deukalion admits. "The Maori might have preferred a more constitutionalist system. You're right, I should say the politically dominant whites preferred to adopt the Westminster model."

Many observant Jews have offered a similar reason for not drafting a constitutional charter for Israel: since the time of Moses the Torah and later the Halakhah have provided the fundamental law, political as well as moral, for a Jewish state.

A third reason against a constitutional text is that there is insufficient agreement to endow such a document with the reverence a founding charter needs. Many less religiously observant Israelis claimed that this condition obtained in their country: Jews of assorted national, cultural, linguistic backgrounds, professing a variety of religious views, including atheism,[7] and holding widely differing opinions about the meaning of a "Jewish state" have emigrated to live with Sabras and Arabs, people who are not only politically and religiously divided from each other but also among themselves. It took some rather vaguely worded enactments by the Knesset and creative interpretations by the Israeli Supreme Court to bring a partial text into being.[8]

A fourth argument concerns any group's limited capacities to understand the future. Leaders often lack sufficient experience to fashion a document suitable even for the present. Only very naive or very vain men and women can believe either in their own political prescience or in their moral authority to impose their visions on later generations. Each generation needs to live within its own wisdom about how to function in a constitutional democracy, or, indeed, whether to continue to live under such a regime. This was Thomas Jefferson's oft-repeated message. He could tolerate a constitutional text, but only if it included a bill of rights and did not survive the founding generation.

---

considered a proposal "to bring together into one enactment certain provisions of constitutional significance," but as of late 2005 it had not entrenched this bill, nor have judges yet exercised judicial review. Like their English relatives, they have, however, honed statutory interpretation into a sharp instrument. See Roger S. Clark, *New Zealand* (Dobbs Ferry, NY: Oceana, 1987), one of the volumes in the series Constitutions of the Countries of the World, ed. Albert P. Blaustein and Gisbert H. Flanz.

7. See esp. Martin Edelman, *Courts, Politics, and Culture in Israel* (Charlottesville: University of Virginia Press, 1994), and "The Utility of a Written Constitution: Free Exercise of Religion in Israel and the United States," 11 *Shofar* 35 (Summer 1993); Thomas L. Friedman, "Whose Country Is It?" *N.Y. Times*, June 27, 1998; and Gary Jeffrey Jacobsohn, *Apple of Gold: Constitutionalism in Israel and the United States* (Princeton, NJ: Princeton University Press, 1993), chs, 2–3.

8. For details, see Martin Edelman, "The New Israeli Constitution," 36 *Middle Eastern Studs.* 1 (2000), and the discussion below in Chapter Fourteen.

Prudence counsels caution. Constructing a new constitutional order is "as dangerous almost as the exploration of unknown seas and continents," Machiavelli claimed.[9] The murkiness of the past, the confusion of the present, the multiple voices with which the future simultaneously promises bonanzas and threatens disasters should make every sensible person anxious. Moreover, intelligent, self-reflective human beings understand that their perceptions of reality, no less than their remedies for its ills, are fogged by personal, possibly idiosyncratic, and perhaps even subconsciously held conscience, urges, and values. "Ambition, avarice, personal animosity, party opposition, and many other motives not more laudable than these," Alexander Hamilton conceded, "are apt to operate as well upon those who support as those who oppose the right side of a [constitutional] question."[10] Awareness of the awful responsibility of creating a charter that purports to organize and direct a constitutional order as well as realization of one's own—and, even more acutely, of one's colleagues'—frailties must inevitably tempt all but the super-arrogant to echo Noah Webster's claim that "the very attempt to make *perpetual* constitutions, is the assumption of a right to controul the opinions of future generations; and to legislate for those over whom we have as little authority as we have over a nation in Asia."[11]

American experience may be misleading. The founders of 1787 stood in a long line of framers of political covenants dating from the Mayflower Compact of 1620 through dozens of colonial charters and state constitutional texts. Colonists had functioned reasonably well under those agreements.[12] In 1787, the bulk of white adult American males were citizens of systems that had tried, with shortcomings as obvious as they were serious, to combine respect for fundamental rights with a significant measure of self-government. And the men at Philadelphia were old hands at politics within such systems. Of the fifty-five delegates slated to attend the convention, twenty had already participated in drafting state constitutional texts, forty-two had served or were then serving in Congress under the Articles of Confederation, thirty were or had been members of state legislatures, and seven were former governors.[13] Equally eager to

9. Niccolò Machiavelli, introduction to *Discourses on the First Ten Books of Titus Livy*, trans. Christian E. Detmold, in *The Prince and the Discourses* (New York: Random House, 1940).

10. *The Federalist*, No. 1. He continued: "My motives must remain in the depository of my own breast. My arguments will be open to all, and may be judged by all."

11. "Bills of Rights," in Noah Webster, *Collection of Essays and Fugitive Writings on Moral, Historical, Political and Literary Subjects* (Boston: Thomas and Andrews, 1790), p. 47 (italics in original).

12. See esp. Daniel J. Elazar, "The Political Theory of Covenant," 10 *Publius* 3 (1980); Donald S. Lutz, "From Covenant to Constitution," 10 *Publius* 101, and *The Origins of American Constitutionalism* (Baton Rouge: Louisiana State University Press, 1988).

13. Two delegates were also college presidents, an office that even then required some political

assume public office were hundreds of other seasoned politicians. That amount of experience in operating the machinery of a budding constitutional democracy is likely to be as rare as it is valuable.

The principal reasons for a constitutional charter mirror those against. First, to claim that such texts are exercises in futility overlooks the many cases in which such documents have helped form and maintain political systems. Neo-Hobbesians can cite the political histories of Sub-Saharan Africa and Latin America, but they would have to skip over evidence from Australia, India, Japan, North America, Western Europe, and now Eastern Europe as well.

Second, existing traditions may be woefully inadequate to sustain constitutional democracy. Indeed, Michael Walzer has said that traditions are sites for argument. It would then be useful, perhaps essential, either to specify in advance most of the basic rules of and limitations on politics or to have the luxury of centuries for such norms to develop. Spoken words quickly evanesce. After the lapse of a few years, practice and history tend to fuse into legend and propaganda, and neither the content nor the meaning of tradition is ever obvious. In apparent contrast, words embossed onto paper convey an impression of permanence. All who run can read, now and in generations to come. When those compacts concern such fundamentals as governmental power and individual rights, the case for writing things down becomes very strong. *Clara pacta, boni ami,* the Romans used to say.

Third, where wide disagreement exists, writing down what most people can agree on and leaving the rest to be settled over time according to specified rules and within set substantive limits, so the argument goes, offers a better chance of success than merely persisting with disagreement. Calculated ambiguity can represent political wisdom.

Fourth, as for needing long practical experience before being able to write viable rules, practical experience itself indicates the contrary proposition can hold. Intelligent men and women can to learn from the experience of others. After World War II, Germans, Japanese, and Italians, albeit with prodding from their conquerors, were able to write constitutional charters to pilot polities that still flourish. When the Velvet Revolution came in 1989, even fewer Eastern Europeans had known life under constitutional democracy. One can make a sound argument that before World War II only Czechoslovakia and Germany had veered toward constitutional democracy; and Germany's experience ended in 1933, Czechoslovakia's in 1939. Thus, when Central and Eastern Europe

---

skill. Thirty members were lawyers, though that biographical datum may have been dysfunctional. For details, see Max Farrand, *The Framing of the Constitution of the United States* (New Haven, CT: Yale University Press, 1913), ch. 2.

took up constitutional reform in 1990, few people had firsthand experience as citizens under nonauthoritarian rule. "In this part of [East] Germany," the prime minister of Saxony remarked, "you have no one of working age who has lived under conditions other than a command society or dictatorship."[14] Nevertheless, Poles, Hungarians, Czechs, and Slovaks drafted new constitutional charters and their nations have functioned as constitutional democracies, though Bulgaria, Romania, Russia, and Uzbekistan have had less success.

Opponents of a constitutional text speak of the dangers of premature decisions and drafters' inevitable arrogance. Yet for all its audacity, the role of framer of a fundamental law may be a part that must be played, at least through an orchestral performance.[15] Time is likely to do little to dim the allure of temporizing. And what begins as a more or less accidental practice may settle into permanency, for good or evil. Much of what Americans naively consider parts of their "constitution" are no more than long usages whose systemic implications may not have been considered until they entered the political system. Founders must address the question Hamilton posed in the opening paper of *The Federalist:* "whether societies of men are really capable or not of establishing good government from reflection and choice, or whether they are forever destined to depend for their political constitutions on accident and force."

A more positive reason for drafting a text is that subsequent debates about adoption may teach citizens as well as officials about constitutional democracy. Self-consciously confronting such critical problems as what it means for the present to try to bind the future can educate participants. Those discussions may also supply worthwhile experience in how to operate such a system.

"Wait, please, Professor," Pastor Glückmann says. "You raise questions and then offer competing solutions. That may generate discussion in seminars, but here it's annoying. We grasp the problems; it's answers that elude us. Should we or shouldn't we opt for a constitutional text?"

"Let me back into an answer. Anthropologists tell a story about the president of a new university who was examining plans for the campus. She noticed there were no paths among the buildings. She asked the planning architecture why and was told, 'Some of us want to lay out the paths we think most efficient; others want to see what routes the students choose before put-

14. John Tagliabue, "Dresden Journal: As the East Hunts for Its Bootstraps, He's Helping," *N.Y. Times,* May 3, 1991.

15. The phrase is Felix Frankfurter's, describing how the United States Supreme Court produces its official opinions. *The Commerce Clause under Marshall, Taney, and Waite* (Chapel Hill: University of North Carolina Press, 1937), p. 43.

ting in pavement. You have to make the decision.' I think—I stress *think*—that were I a member of this caucus, I'd try to draft a constitutional charter."

"Why?" the pastor persists. "Biblical interpretation shows that written words have much less lucidity, exactness, and permanence than we would like. Texts often create new problems as they resolve old ones, and the new may be as serious as the old. For centuries Jews have fought over the meaning of the Torah. Muslims have done a great deal of killing over the true message of Allah the All Merciful. And Christian have shown how enthusiastically they can slaughter each other for the interpretive purity of Jesus' gospel of love."

"I could not have said it better, Pastor. The American framers recognized these difficulties. When congratulated on the excellence of the text of 1787, Gouverneur Morris replied that the document's worth 'depends on how it is construed.'[16] Madison was more prolix: [N]o language is so copious as to supply words and phrases for every complex idea. . . . When the Almighty himself condescends to address mankind in their own language, his meaning, luminous as it must be, is rendered dim and doubtful by the cloudy medium through which it is communicated."[17] The sources of confusion, he explained, were the complexity of political relations, the 'imperfection' of human conceptualization of those problems, and the corruption that people's self-interest brought to the creation of rules. He might have added another pair of sources: (1) the necessity of framers' compromising among competing interests, values, and aspirations and (2) framers' failure to think through political problems and carefully rank the values they seek to promote.

"Haven't you just undercut your own argument?" Jon Kanuri, the black economist, asks.

"No. Because no text offers a panacea does not mean that a carefully crafted charter can't be useful. Jews dispute what the Torah means, Christians the Gospels, and Muslims the Qur'an; but those documents define Judaism, Christianity, and Islam. With apologies to the pious, I do not believe that without these texts those religions would have survived. In the secular realm, it is difficult to deny that the American document, despite near-catastrophic failure in 1861 and lesser but still significant failures since, has helped identify what the United States is all about. Indeed, that charter, Hans Kohn claimed, 'is so intimately welded with the national existence

---

16. Quoted in Edward S. Corwin, *Court over Constitution* (Princeton, NJ: Princeton University Press, 1938), p. 228. Under his breath, Deukalion mutters that he's always found this alleged quotation a bit too good to be authentic.

17. *The Federalist*, No. 37. Justice Hugo L. Black remained unshaken in his faith that the written word, at least of the American constitutional text, conveyed a clear and permanent meaning: "I shall not at any time surrender my belief that the document should be our guide. . . . I prefer to put my faith in the words of the written Constitution itself rather than to rely on the shifting, day-to-day standards of fairness of individual judges." Re *Winship*, 397 U.S. 358, dis. op., 378 (1970).

itself that the two have become inseparable.'[18] With somewhat weaker evidence, Owasi Masako claims the so-called MacArthur Constitution 'has effectively become Japan's identity.'"[19]

"Aren't you trying to transplant American love of a constitutional text here ?" Pyknites asks.

"No," Deukalion replies. "I warned that American experience in drafting constitutional texts was far more extensive than yours. You shouldn't make *your* decisions because of their successes—or failures. Furthermore, I deliberately did not allude to the alleged utility of the American constitutional text in coping with cultural diversity. We shouldn't impose the image of the ethnically and culturally diverse America of the early twenty-first century onto the more homogeneous colonists of the eighteenth. And although debates over ratification showed sharp divisions, those splits centered less on cultural heritages and fundamentals of political theory than on the extent to which the new text would carry out a widely shared, if vaguely defined, ethos. The speed with which Federalists agreed to a bill of rights and Anti-Federalists accommodated themselves to the 'new order for the ages' supports this interpretation. The truly divisive issue, Madison claimed, was slavery,[20] and the convention dodged that problem. Seeing the choice as one nation with slavery or two nations, one with and the other without slavery,

18. *American Nationalism* (New York: Macmillan, 1957), p. 8. Political scientists frequently point to that text as one of the primary reasons that ideologically based political parties have had little attraction for Americans: "the Constitution" seems to settle most basic political issues. For example, Walter F. Murphy and Michael N. Danielson, *American Democracy*, 9th ed. (New York: Holt, Rinehart and Winston, 1979), pp. 187–88. For one of more cogent discussions of the constitutional charter and American political identity, see Samuel P. Huntington, *American Politics: The Promise of Disharmony* (Cambridge, MA: Belknap, Harvard University Press, 1981), esp. ch. 2.

19. Quoted in Lawrence Ward Beer and John Maki, *From Imperial Myth to Democracy: Japan's Two Constitutions* (Boulder: University of Colorado Press, 2002), p. 184.

20. The states, Madison claims to have told his colleagues at Philadelphia, "were divided into different interests not by their difference of size, but by other circumstances; the most material of which resulted partly from climate, but principally from (the effects of) their having or not having slaves." Madison's Notes, in Max Farrand, *The Records of the Federal Convention of 1787* (New Haven, CT: Yale University Press, 1966), 1:486. John Rutledge of South Carolina, Madison says, told the convention about the slave trade: "Religion & humanity had nothing to do with this question—Interest alone is the governing principle with nations—The true question at present is whether the Southn. States shall or shall not be parties to the Union." Ibid., 2:364. Pierce Butler and Charles Cotesworth Pinckney, also from South Carolina, expressed the same sentiments. See Madison's reports of Butler's speech of July 13 (ibid., 1:605) and Pinckney's of Aug. 22 (ibid., 2:371). (Despite being both an undergraduate and graduate alumnus of Princeton, Madison persistently misspelled Pinckney's name as "Pinkney" and Rutledge's as "Rutledge." Of course, orthographic orthodoxy was, at the time, difficult to practice. Noah Webster's *American Spelling Book,* which became popularly known as "the Blue-backed speller," had been published only in 1783. The unabridged version of his *American Dictionary of the English Language,* the first full-scale dictionary on this side of the Atlantic, did not appear until 1828. In the interim, John Breckinridge of Kentucky, one of Jefferson's leaders in the Senate, was unsure of the correct spelling of his own name.) Among the best analyses of the framers' "great silence" on the question of slavery is Joseph J. Ellis, *Founding Brothers: The Revolutionary Generation* (New York: Alfred A. Knopf, 2001), ch. 3.

neither the framers nor the ratifiers allowed human decency to stand in the way of expediency."

"Very well," Kanuri says, "I'm not totally convinced we should draft a text."

"I'm not *totally* convinced either," Deukalion agrees. "Each of the reasons against such a document may hold in your case. Much depends on your skill in crafting a charter and persuading your fellow citizens that it will give them the best political system possible in a flawed world."

"You flatter us to think we have such skills," Federika Strega puts in. "Our people are so divided that Moses would find it more difficult to unite them behind a single constitutional text than he did rallying the Israelites around the Ten Commandments—and as you remember, Yahweh helped out by slaughtering many of the not-so-loyal opposition."

Deukalion smiles. "Contrary to rumor, I wasn't there; but I read about it.[21] You'd be wise not to count on Yahweh's intervening again. And remember, the rest of the Israelites had to wander around in the desert for forty years, the conventional lifetime of a generation, so that a new people, born outside of Egypt, could take up citizenship in the Promised Land. You're not apt to get that kind of divine help either. That biblical story ties in with what, to me, is the most important reason to try a text. Your work only begins when you create political institutions. More important for the long run, you're trying to fulfill Aristotle's definition of a constitution. You're trying to shape a way of life for your people, and to make that 'way' a reality, you must create citizens. The debates, arguments, even turmoil that proposing a constitutional charter breeds will provide superb instruction for your people. They can begin to learn to be citizens of a constitutional democracy by acting like citizens of a constitutional democracy.

"Let me exceed the scope of my mandate," Deukalion adds, "and look ahead to interpretation. I urge you not to call the document you prepare 'a constitution.' You'll only perpetuate the confusion in which Americans, especially American judges, wallow. They can never make up their minds *what* it is they're interpreting: all of the text, most of the text, earlier glosses—whether usage, commentary, or formal constructions—the political theories underlying the text, or an entire political culture. Give your document its own name, perhaps 'The Basic Law' like the Germans', or invent your own, such as 'The Constitutional Charter.' But make it plain that the constitutional text is only one part, albeit it a central part, of 'the constitution.'"

"I'm confused," Minxin Wei interjects. "Weren't you talking about creating a constitution?"

"Sorry, I've been speaking on two levels. In the short run, you'd be trying to draft a constitutional text, which would take you a step—an important

21. As a learned scholar, Deukalion is well aware of the doubts about the historicity of the story of Exodus. See Israel Finkelstein and Neil Asher Silberman, *The Bible Unearthed: Archeology's New Vision of Ancient Israel and the Origins of Its Sacred Texts* (New York: Free Press, 2001).

step, but only one step—toward your longer-range objective, a new constitutional order. You recall Socrates' comment in *The Republic:* 'This discussion is not about any chance question, but about the way one should live.' The 'constitution' itself is a continuing discussion about the political order, about how citizens should live. The charter, if it is authoritative, will always be an important subject of that discussion, but the conversation occurs in the context of demands on and the ideals of the political system, not simply around the document's words. And the participants include elected officials who are initiating, continuing, or terminating what threaten (or promise) to become established practices. You will be interpreting a broader constitutional order. And those others who interpret will include not only judges, legislators, and administrators but also ordinary voters. Even journalists and academic commentators can play a part here. 'If judges make law,' the great American scholar Edward S. Corwin said, 'so do commentators.'[22] The interpretive enterprise requires participants to cope with the work of past interpreters and anticipate the problems and solutions of future interpreters."

"You describe a messy business," Wei muses. "Is our work here really worth a damn?"

"Hannah Arendt said something that may hearten you: '[C]onstitution making is the noblest of all revolutionary deeds.'[23] But you must also keep in mind that even if you yourselves draft a text, you will not be the only creators of what will become your constitution. Neither were the people who met in Philadelphia in 1787 or in Tokyo in 1946 or in Herrenschiemsee and Bonn in 1949 or in the various assemblies in South Africa from 1991 until 1996 the sole creators of a 'constitution' for the United States, Japan, Germany, or South Africa. Those people *began* new constitutional orders. Words cannot control the future, but the right words can help shape the future."

"Are you claiming drafting a constitutional text and maintaining a constitution order run into each other?" Minister of Justice Pilsudski asks.

"I am. Every student of American history can tell you how much John Marshall shaped the constitutional order through interpretations of the constitutional text. In Canada and Germany . . ."

"Let's not elaborate now," the chair interrupts. "We take up constitutional interpretation later.[24] For now, let's focus on whether we should have a constitutional text."

Demos Pyknites speaks next. "I've made it clear that I think we need a representative rather than constitutional democracy. I lost on that issue, though I still hope to persuade some of you to change your minds. My honest conclusion is that a constitutional text is an effort to halt history. What the learned professor calls a constitutional text should be written at the

22. Review of *The Law of the Constitution,* by Charles K. Burdick, 22 *Mich. L. Rev.* 84 (1923).
23. *On Revolution* (New York: Viking, 1965), p. 185.
24. See below, Chapter Fourteen.

end of our revolution, not at the beginning.[25] Jefferson put it best when he wrote that 'the ground of liberty is to be gained by inches. . . . It takes time to persuade men to do even what is for their own good.'[26] Let us begin with an elected parliament, then let our people's experience demonstrate what rights, beyond those to open political participation, they deem fundamental. After a generation or two they can draft a constitutional text, if they want, or, as I would prefer, Parliament could, as does the Israeli Knesset from time to time, enact 'basic laws' by an extraordinary majority and require a similar extraordinary majority to repeal them. Because these 'basic laws' will reflect hard experience as well as hard thought, they will be wiser guides for our constitutional development."

"Mr. Pyknites, peace be upon him," the Mufti says, "has offered us an alternative that we should seriously weigh. If being undecided means being open minded, then I am truly open minded. I find Professor Deukalion's arguments powerful. On the other hand, I remember reading the remark of Gouverneur Morris, who had more to do than any other person with the actual wording of American constitutional text, when he spoke of such a charter that did not fit its people: 'Paper thou art and unto Paper thou shalt return.'"[27]

"May I treat your remarks as a motion, Mr. Pyknites? Thank you. We need a second. Yes. Further discussion? No? Then let us vote. The parliamentarian and I count eight votes for, twelve against, and four abstentions. The motion fails. We shall have a constitutional charter. The next issue before us is who shall do the drafting. We ourselves could do that work, but I don't find that assumption a self-evident truth. Let's discuss alternatives. Ms Baca?"

"I propose that we call for a truly representative assembly to draft a constitutional charter. Let me share with you why. We have three options: Parliament, this caucus, or a popular assembly. It's easy, you know, to eliminate the first. The members of Parliament are almost all sycophants whom the junta selected. And any text even an honestly elected parliament created would be suspect, because MPs have an interest in crafting institutions and electoral rules to, like, totally maximize their own chances to continue in office. This caucus shouldn't do the job either. We were, you know, appointed, and that would take away from the legitimacy of any charter we'd propose. We don't represent the people."

25. Pyknites is paraphrasing a member of the first Knesset, which adjourned without writing a constitutional document for Israel. See Gary Jeffrey Jacobsohn, *The Wheel of Law: India's Secularism in Comparative Constitutional Perspective* (Princeton, NJ: Princeton University Press, 2002), pp. 237–38.

26. Jefferson to Rev. Charles Clay, Jan. 27, 1790, quoted in Stanley Elkins and Eric McKitrick, *The Age of Federalism: The Early American Republic, 1788–1800* (New York: Oxford University Press, 1993), p. 197.

27. Quoted in Elkins and McKitrick, *Age of Federalism*, p. 319.

"Accepting for the sake of argument that your criticisms are correct," Minister Pilsudski intervenes, "how does it follow that a popularly chosen assembly will be any better?"

"I have shared with you how I think delegates should be chosen. But the assembly's link with the people would give its work a legitimacy that neither we nor Parliament have. Right? As a graduate student, I've read a lot of James Madison, and I recall his writing that a constitutional document is of 'no more consequence than the paper on which it is written unless it be stamped with the approbation of those to whom it is addressed.'"[28]

"I second Ms Baca's proposal," Pyknites says. "I agree with her reasons against our or Parliament's writing a charter. A campaign to choose delegates to a convention would provoke debate and so involve the people in the constitution-making process. It would both give them a stake in the new political system and help prepare them for their role as citizens. Moreover, a convention would dissolve as soon as the charter was drafted. Its members, unlike legislators, would operate behind what John Rawls might have called a *thin* veil of ignorance:[29] they might aspire to public office but would lack the linkage between personal ambitions and institutional status that even fair-minded legislators might have."

"I disagree. We should do the drafting ourselves," Jessica Jacobsohn says. "And I so move."

"Let the chair interrupt: do we have a second for that motion? Thank you, Minister Pilsudski. Please go on, Professor."

"Fate, God, or some other force has put us in the position of founders. We are not a cabal conspiring against the public good. Yes, we're an appointed elite, but drafting a constitutional text is necessarily the work of an elite. The only question is, which elite? Who is better equipped to do this work than we ourselves? We operate behind the same thin veil of ignorance as would members of a convention. And who would set up the rules for choosing a convention? Parliament? That option would have flaws much like allowing Parliament to draft the new charter. Could we somehow 'enact' those rules? Even if we could finesse the problem of the legality of that action, we would open the process to the same criticism that Mr. Pyknites levels against this body as drafter."

"Not so," Pyknites replies. "We could urge the Colonels to set up a fair national election, after a full, open debate, for an assembly."

"As a man of theology rather than politics," Atilla Gregorian says, "I speak humbly. But it seems to me that the arguments for our scripting the new charter are more persuasive. Delegating that crucial task to another body might be wise under many circumstances, but the composition of that assem-

28. *The Federalist*, No. 40.
29. *A Theory of Justice* (Cambridge, MA: Harvard University Press, 1971).

bly is a mystery. In making laws, Aquinas said, the people must have a voice superior to that of rulers.[30] But some person or group has to draft positive laws for them; the whole people cannot. Isn't it more prudent to rely on men and women of large and known talent? Let the people play their superior role by approving or rejecting our work though a national referendum."

Toward late afternoon, Colonel Martin says, "We have had full discussion on alternatives. In our wisdom no one proposes a new parliament to do the drafting. Thus we have a clear choice between an elected assembly and our own humble selves. I ask for a show of hands for those favoring an assembly... For those preferring we do the task... The parliamentarian and I count nine votes for an assembly, fifteen for this caucus. Let us stand in recess until eight p.m., when we shall begin long labor."

At 8:02 Colonel Martin again calls on Professor Deukalion to offer some general observations on drafting a constitutional charter.

Constructing a Constitutional Charter

Some of what I have to say merely sums up earlier discussions, but it's important to keep certain points in mind. The first, again, concerns political culture. Because of constitutional democracy's commitment to individual liberty, it can tolerate little coercion and requires the people's positive consent—not merely acquiescence to *force majeure* but agreement that this is the constitutional order they *should* have because, despite its imperfections, it's the best they *can* have.

I concede that some eminent scholars believe that passive popular acquiescence is sufficient.[31] For long-established and successful constitutional orders that may well be so. You, however, are creating a new constitutional order. Your work is very different from simply maintaining a flourishing political system. You need "positive consent," because you will ask your people to stop being mere subjects and become citizens, to participate in ruling themselves under the principles of constitutional democracy. That is a transformation that neither force nor mere acquiescence can accomplish.

Admittedly, no constitutional democracy—or representative democracy—has ever succeeded in inducing many citizens to make their political roles constantly paramount in their lives. Nevertheless, the goal of a constitutional text must be not simply to outline governmental structures and processes but also to help construct a new "way of life." If a polity is to flourish, its public ideals must influence most aspects of its people's public choices and even many of their private choices. You must establish

---

30. *Summa Theologica*, 1–2, qu. 97, art. 3, reply 3.
31. See, for example, Russell Hardin, *Liberalism, Constitutionalism, and Democracy* (New York: Oxford University Press, 1999), esp. ch. 4.

a constitutional order that will produce congruence between your people's personal values and those of the social and economic orders.[32]

Your new constitutional order must change some aspects of society even as it reflects others. The purpose of this change is to breed an independent citizenry attentive to their duties as well as to their rights and, at the same time, sensitive to the rights and duties of others. Few citizens will become perfect constitutional democrats, but most should behave toward each other and public officials very differently from the ways in which they behaved under authoritarian rule. If a civil society is to have a charter, it must not only lay down rules for a government but also articulate many of the basic principles, values, and aspirations[33] that will reconstitute a people from a collection of humans sharing a common geography into citizens sharing a common creed.

Again, my message is controverted. Some learned scholars think a constitutional text should only offer a blueprint for government and not try to effectuate ideals, that it should concern itself with processes and be "content-neutral."[34] Where a polity has long flourished and is not riven by ethnic, economic, or ideological divisions, it may be enough that the constitutional document simply outline the anatomy and physiology of the political system. When, however, a nation has no history of harmonious civil life under free government and groups are set against groups, it is essential that the constitutional charter remind, or even instruct, the people and their officials why it is they have come together to try to form a national community. In the United States, the Anti-Federalists wanted the new constitutional text to include a bill of rights, "to give existence, or at least establish in the minds of the people truths and principles which

32. For an explanation of "congruence" and its importance to political systems, see Harry H. Eckstein, "Toward a Theory of Stable Democracy," Research Monograph 10, Center of International Studies, Princeton University (1961), reprinted in his *Regarding Politics: Essays on Political Theory, Stability, and Change* (Berkeley: University of California Press, 1992), ch. 5; Harry H. Eckstein, "Congruence Theory Explained," and Frederic J. Fleron Jr., "Congruence Theory Applied: Democratization in Russia," both in Harry H. Eckstein, Frederic J. Fleron, Erik P. Hoffmann, and William M. Reisinnger, eds., *Can Democracy Take Root in Post-Soviet Russia?* (Lanham, MD: Rowman AND Littlefield, 1998).

33. For explanations of the aspirational function of a constitutional document, see Sotirios A. Barber, *On What the Constitution Means* (Baltimore: Johns Hopkins University Press, 1984), and Gary Jeffrey Jacobsohn, *The Supreme Court and the Decline of Constitutional Aspiration* (Totowa, NJ: Rowman and Littlefield, 1986). For a bitter but intellectually muddled attack on the idea of constitutional aspirations, see Lino A. Graglia, "Constitutional Mysticism: The Aspirational Defense of Judicial Review," 98 *Harv. L. Rev.* 1131 (1985).

34. See, for instance, Giovanni Sartori, *Comparative Constitutional Engineering* (New York: New York University Press, 1994), p. 202. He would confine a constitutional text's statements of ideals to preambles, which he treats as being of little importance. His principal example of misplaced aspirations is the Soviet document, hardly that of a constitutional democracy. I usually find Sartori among the most astute of students of comparative politics, but here his claim seems a mere *ipse dixit* that would leave a constitutional order free of values, a result I doubt he would endorse.

they may never have otherwise thought of, or soon forgot."[35] Although Madison initially opposed such a statement, he soon saw the wisdom of the Anti-Federalists' argument. Achievement of his prophecy about the American Bill of Rights should be your goal: "The political truths declared in that solemn manner acquire by degrees the character of fundamental maxims of free Government, and as they become incorporated with the national sentiment, counteract the impulses of interest and passion."[36]

My second point relates to legitimacy. You recall King Lear's musings:

Lear: . . . Thou has seen a farmer's dog bark at a beggar?
Glouster: Ay, sir.
Lear: And the creature run from the cur? There thou mightst behold the great image of authority; a dog's obeyed in office. . . . Through tatter'd clothes small vices do appear; Robes & furr'd gowns hide all. Plate sin with gold, and the strong lance of justice hurtless breaks; Arm it in rags, a pigmy's straw does pierce it.

A successful constitutional charter will be both a source and a measure of legitimacy. It will plate political power with the gold of authority. And to confer legitimacy, the legitimator must itself be legitimate. I'll talk about popular approval in a moment. For now, I'll focus on norms. The ideals that confer legitimacy vary from culture to culture, and from time to time within any single culture.[37] Every society has its own values, traditions, and customs. Leaders who try to transform a people operate under conditions of restricted choice. The text's values and aspirations must build on some of the existing culture's norms and will likely have to repudiate others. And there are limits to the number of old beliefs and customs a new order can persuade people to reject.

The wisdom of most important public policies will be controversial, and often so will the authority of government to make that policy. Thus, very early on, a new order must not only establish its own legitimacy but also bestow legitimacy on officials who speak in its name. Earlier I mentioned the role of constitutional interpretation. That enterprise, which also operates within conditions of restricted choice, is critical in this

35. "Letters from the *Federalist Farmer*" (1788), reprinted in Herbert Storing, ed., *The Complete Anti-Federalist* (Chicago: University of Chicago Press, 1981), 2:324.
36. Madison to Jefferson, Oct. 17, 1788 in *A Republic of Letters: The Correspondence between Thomas Jefferson and James Madison, 1776–1826*, ed. James Morton Smith (New York: W. W. Norton, 1995), 1:565.
37. Max Weber's treatment of political legitimacy is still among the most useful: *The Theory of Social and Economic Organization*, trans. A. M. Henderson and Talcott Parsons (New York: Free Press, 1947), pt. 3. See also David Easton, *A Systems Analysis of Political Life* (New York: Wiley, 1965), chs. 1, 10–15, and "A Re-assessment of the Concept of Political Support," 5 *Br. J. Pol. Sci.* 435 (1975).

phase of constitution making, for a charter will probably need to employ principles whose boundaries are indistinct. The history of the Ten Commandments shows that even Yahweh had difficulty writing rules broad enough to apply to all situations and specific enough to settle every important question.

A catastrophic national shock may give founders wider opportunity to reform society. When the old system of values has exploded, a people may be eager for radical political, economic, and social transformation. You have been spared that "blessing." But even in Germany and Japan after 1945, mutations built on as well as broke from the past. Douglas MacArthur and his staff changed much and tried to change even more in Japanese government and society; but, shrewdly, they utilized many existing institutions.[38] The emperor lost his divinity, not his throne. The Great White Shogun breathed new life into the parliament the Mejei had earlier created, making it responsible to a much broader electorate. The administrative and judicial bureaucracies remained largely intact, as did most of the existing legal system, an Asian cousin of the Civil Law. And to staff the higher levels of the restructured governing apparatus, the victors accepted not only Japanese politicians who had opposed military rule but also even many from the old governing apparatus itself.

In the western zones of Germany, the Allies provided an outline but

38. There is a huge literature in English on the making of the Japanese constitution and the influence, often heavy-handed, of the Supreme Commander Allied Powers. See esp. Beer and Maki, *From Imperial Myth to Democracy;* William K. Cummings, *Education and Equality in Japan* (Princeton, NJ: Princeton University Press, 1980); John W. Dower, *Embracing Defeat: Japan in the Wake of World War II* (New York: W. W. Norton, 1999); Kyoko Inoue, *MacArthur's Japanese Constitution: A Linguistic and Cultural Study of Its Making* (Chicago: University of Chicago Press, 1991); Toshio Ishio, *Unconditional Democracy: Education and Politics in Occupied Japan, 1945–1952* (Stanford, CA: Hoover Institution Press, 1982); Kazuo Kawai, *Japan's American Interlude* (Chicago: University of Chicago Press, 1960); Alfred C. Oppler, *Legal Reform in Occupied Japan: A Participant Looks Back* (Princeton, NJ: Princeton University Press, 1976); Koseki Shōichi, *The Birth of Japan's Postwar Constitution,* trans. Ray A. Moore (Boulder: Westview, 1998); Kenzo Takayanagi, "Some Reminiscences of Japan's Commission on the Constitution," in Dan Fenno Henderson, ed., *The Constitution of Japan* (Seattle: University of Washington Press, 1968); Robert E. Ward, "Origins of the Present Japanese Constitution," 50 *Am. Pol. Sci. Rev.* 1007 (1956), and "Reflections on the Allied Occupation and Planned Political Change in Japan," in Robert E. Ward, ed., *Political Development in Modern Japan* (Princeton, NJ: Princeton University Press, 1968); Justin Williams, "Making the Japanese Constitution," 59 *Am. Pol. Sci. Rev.* 665 (1965); and U.S. Department of State, *Report of the United States Education Mission to Japan* (Washington, DC: Government Printing Office, 1946). The most important documentary source is Ray A. Moore and Donald L. Robinson, eds., *The Constitution of Japan: A Documentary History of Its Framing and Adoption, 1945–1947* (Princeton, NJ: Princeton University Press, 1998), a CD-ROM containing eight thousand typescript pages of materials that had been in the possession of Charles Kades, the American officer who supervised the drafting of the constitutional text. Much of this material, imcluding debates within the Diet and Privy Council, had not been previously available even in Japanese. Moore and Robinson have analyzed this massive material in their *Partners for Democracy: Crafting the New Japanese State under MacArthur* (New York: Oxford University Press, 2002).

not a blueprint for a new constitutional text. They were able to put greater distance between themselves and constitution makers than in Japan because many of the German framers had been refugees from Nazism and some of them were much more sophisticated advocates of constitutional democracy than were the Allied high commissioner and his staff. The commission did intervene on occasion, but usually the "suggestions" were of marginal significance.[39] The Basic Law retained much that was old. It drew its ideals from Immanuel Kant, reinstituted a federal arrangement that reached back to the Holy Roman Empire, modified Weimar's proportional representation, and retained variations on the parliament and chancellor that had existed under both Weimar and the kaiser. Most important in building on the past, the preamble looked ahead to when the two Germanys would again be one: "The entire German people are called upon to achieve in free self-determination the unity and freedom of Germany."

Even these two cases indicate that to maximize the constitutive enterprise's chances, founders must take their own past into account. They cannot, at will, erase myths and memories. They must make choices: accept some old myths, rehabilitate others, and destroy yet others and create new myths. To minimize trauma, the language of the new or revised institutions and aspirations must demonstrate respect for much of what the society has historically cherished. I might add, parenthetically, that although the American-backed government in Iraq could co-opt some of Saddam Hussein's officials, it had little in the way of constitutionalist or truly democratic institutions on which to build.

It would also be helpful to make a plausible case that constitutional democracy's ideals are rooted in tradition. In the turmoil immediately following World War II, some Japanese leaders countered claims that the constitutional text read like it had been translated rather awkwardly from English into Japanese (in many places, true) by arguing, with remarkable imagination, that the historical linkage between the emperor and "the people" was an indicium of a democratic tradition: the emperor's embodiment of sovereignty had been an expression of "the general will of the people." Others sought reinforcement in such sources as imperial

---

39. The standard work in English on the making of the Basic Law remains John Ford Golay, *The Founding of the Federal Republic of Germany* (Chicago: University of Chicago Press, 1958). See also Lucius D. Clay, *Decision in Germany* (New York: Doubleday, 1950), and *The Papers of General Lucius D. Clay: Germany, 1945–1949,* ed. Jean Edward Smith, 2 vols. (Bloomington: Indiana University Press, 1974); and Dennis L. Bark and David R. Gress, *A History of West Germany* (Cambridge, MA: Blackwell, 1989), vol. 1, pt. 3. Donald P. Kommers has in progress a book on the founding of the West German constitutional order. For a fascinating account of the background of Germany's "conversion" to constitutional democracy, see Richard L. Merritt, *Democracy Imposed: U.S. Occupation Policy and the German Public, 1945–1949* (New Haven, CT: Yale University Press, 1995).

poetry and the Charter Oath of 1868.[40] During the early 1990s, Hungarian leaders showed similar resourcefulness in building normative bridges between constitutional democracy and such great events as the Golden Bull of 1222. Not to be outdone, many Poles implied that the national charter of 1792 had been continuously operative. With a mix of ignorance, idealism, and cynicism, Australians, Canadians, and Americans often connect their constitutional orders to the barons at Runnymede.

In reconstituting a polity, it may be useful to borrow from other nations. But neither constitutional texts nor specific institutions can be easily transplanted from one state's soil to another's. Founders must first of all naturalize these borrowings into familiar forms by writing them in words that echo happy, if gauzy, memories.

"What you're saying is that we'll have to become spin doctors," Strega interrupts.

I prefer to look on the process as one of converting values.[41] To bond text and culture, you must win the people's hearts, not merely their minds. You'll have to rely on emotional as well as intellectual persuasion. The process is not unlike courtship. The bulk of citizens, Rogers Smith has written, "have found irreplaceable the engaging, reassuring, inspiring, often intoxicating charm provided by colorful civic myths."[42] Look at the way the Japanese clung to their imperial myths up to and through the end of World War II, how many Germans bought into Nazi myths of their being "the master race," and Americans that their civil war was fought to end slavery. Most people do not feast off the kind of cerebral debates you're enjoying. You must give them some of that information and allow them to obtain whatever more they want, just as you must also allow your people to consider diverse evaluations. At the same time, you need to use emotional persuasion. The civic myths you create and redact should connect a people to each other as citizens by telling stories that have a factual basis but are also aspirational. These stories must identify the people as a single political unit. Your ethnic divisions require you to create an "imagined community."[43] At the same time, those myths must also define what it means to be a citizen of a constitutional democracy. You must engage in a politics of memory, persuading your people to recall some events, forget others, and reconstruct yet others.

Process is not always distinguishable from substance. In constitution

40. See Moore and Robinson, *Partners for Democracy*, p. 190 and chs. 12–13 generally.

41. For a discussion, see Thomas R. Rochin, *Culture Moves: Ideas, Activism, and Changing Values* (Princeton, NJ: Princeton University Press,1998), esp. ch. 3.

42. *Civic Ideals* (New Haven, CT: Yale University Press, 1998), p. 33.

43. B. R. O. Anderson, *Imagined Communities* (London: Verso, 1983).

making, ratification is critical to legitimating the legitimator. And in the modern secular world, no process confers legitimacy on a constitutional order like popular consent. For Orthodox Jews, devout Muslims, and pious Christians, authority ultimately comes from God, not human beings. Although few Christians still raise this issue in politically meaningful ways, many Muslims and Orthodox Jews do. Yet the idea of government by consent seems to be gaining ground even among those two groups.

Not all countries have used referenda. Canadians and Australians got their constitutional texts as gifts from the queen. After World War II the Japanese people did not have an opportunity to vote on their new charter. The Germans and the occupying powers at least allowed the legislatures of the *Länder* to approve the Basic Law. Constitution making in Iraq and Ireland may be more relevant to your situation. In a desperate effort to make up for their lack of planning, the United States and its few allies jury-rigged a government and directed the drafting of a provisional constitutional text, which in due course the new government proclaimed to be in force. By standards of the Middle East, drafting was swift and consultation wide, though by Western standards the latter was very limited. There was no referendum. What could have been a firm first step compounded anger and bitter war against both the occupiers and the new Iraqi governors.[44]

Ireland provides a sharp contrast. When the South was still bitterly divided after a bloody civil war, with divisions between political parties repeating divisions in that conflict, legislators looked across the parliamentary pit at men who had killed their brothers. The country was operating under a charter the winners had drafted; its very terms had been one of the causes of war. Worse, the document's authority partially rested on its having been approved by the British Parliament as a part of the treaty of peace of 1921—what Eamon de Valera called "the damned treaty"—that ended Ireland's revolt against Britain and, in part, on recognition of continued British sovereignty over the Free State.[45]

44. See esp. Larry Diamond, *Squandered Victory: The Bungled Effort to Bring Democracy to Iraq* (New York: Times Books, 2005); L. Paul Brenner III with Malcolm McConnell, *My Year in Iraq: The Struggle to Build a Future of Hope* (New York: Simon and Schuster, 2006); and George Packer, "Caught in the Crossfire: Will Moderate Iraqis Embrace Democracy—or Islamist Radicalism?" *New Yorker*, May, 17, 2004 (I have used the online version found at www.newyorker.com/printable/?fact/040517fa_fact). The provisional constitutional text is officially entitled Law of Administration for the State of Iraq. It can be found at www.oefre.unibe.ch/law/icl/iz00000_.html.

45. Parliament's passage of the Statute of Westminster (1931) ceded self-government to the various dominions, and the Free State of Ireland then had dominion status. An interesting paradox followed: the British Privy Council held that because the treaty and the constitutional text depended on British law, the Statute of Westminster permitted the Irish to renounce its terms (Moore et al. v. A.G. et al., [1935] I.R. 472). On the other hand, the Irish Supreme Court ruled that Dáil Eireann,

When de Valera, the leader of the losers in the civil war, became prime minister, he presided over the drafting of a new text and submitted it to a referendum. "We are going back to the sovereign authority, to the Irish people," he said. ". . . It is they who will enact it, and when they enact it . . . any judge or anybody else, who is not prepared to function under it, can resign and get out."[46] Popular approval was close but clear. Opposition leaders could sneer at the new document as "de Valera's constitution," but they had to accept its legitimacy because they knew it was also the people's constitution.

No one would seriously argue that Ireland's acceptance of a new constitutional charter was solely due to a referendum or Iraq's continued civil war to the absence of a popular vote, but I do believe a referendum is necessary for you if you want democracy as well as constitutionalism.

My third point is also familiar. Compromise is an omnipresent necessity in the ordinary politics of constitutional democracy. It is also necessary in the politics of constitution making. Practical considerations force founders to tailor their visions of an ideal polity not only to what the electorate will accept but also to what their colleagues will approve. Politically powerful groups within the people are apt to have their own diverse sets of goals, none of which is likely to be entirely consistent internally and few of which are likely to be fully consistent with each other. Moreover, those goals will often pertain more to the economic than the political sphere. You are apt to envy Rousseau's legislator who could will a constitutional order into existence.

One of your sources of strength arises from the oppression of the old regime. Your people can't help believing life in a constitutional democracy will be better. That was also true for Germans and Italians after World War II, Spanish and Portuguese in the 1970s, and Argentines, Brazilians, Chileans, and Uruguayans[47] in the 1980s. Central and Eastern Europeans experienced much the same reaction in 1989–1990. The far tougher task is to transform rejection of an oppressive system into a positive acceptance of a new political faith.

"Thank you, Professor," Colonel Martin says. "Once again you have given us much to think about; once again the chair is embarrassed by his own

---

sitting as a constituent assembly, had by approving the treaty "entrenched" the charter as fundamental law for the Free State and thus placed it beyond the reach of the Irish legislature (The State (Ryan) v. Lennon et al., [1935] I.R. 170). See John M. Kelly, *Fundamental Rights in the Irish Law and Constitution*, 1st ed. (Dublin: Allen Figgis, 1961), pp. 7–8.

46. Quoted in Kelly, *Fundamental Rights*, p. 7.

47. Most Chilean and Uruguayan adults had lived for many years—and Argentine adults for a few—in nations that had had real claims to being constitutional democracies, giving these people some advantage over their Iberian cousins.

incompetence. After we decided to draft a document ourselves, I should have had us immediately discuss how to have our work ratified. This time I offer a *mea maxima culpa.* Ms Baca and Mr. Pyknites came close to offering motions for ratification through a popular referendum. Would either of you care to offer such a motion?"

"I would," Baca says.

"And I second it," Pyknites adds.

"Discussion?" the chair asks. "I see no one seeking recognition. Any other proposals for ratification? Again no one seeks recognition. Very well, all in favor say aye. Opposed say nay. I heard only one opposing voice. Thank you, Minister Strega. The motion carries.

"It is now nine o'clock. We're not up to any more clear thinking tonight. Let us stand in recess until 0930 tomorrow morning."

CHAPTER SIX

Drafting 1
The Shape of the Constitution

It is the business of the legislature to follow the spirit of of the nation, when it is not contrary to the principles of government; for we do nothing so well as when we act with freedom, and follow the bent of our national genius.　　MONTESQUIEU

At 0929, Martin gavels the caucus back into session. "Professor Jacobsohn has a general proposal about how we should proceed. Professor?"

"Although I strongly favor having a constitutional charter, that choice poses special problems. The ultimate fate of our enterprise will depend heavily on how interpreters read it. And those people will face the 'hermeneutic dilemma': the text must be understood as a whole, yet the whole cannot be understood without understanding its parts. There is no escape from this dilemma, but we, as framers, can ease interpreters' burdens and perhaps make their work more 'authentic.' Toward that end, I suggest we follow a practical four-step procedure: first, lay out the charter's architectural plan; second, discuss but only tentatively approve individual provisions; third, return to the architecture and revise it as well as individual clauses so that the charter fits together as a coherent whole; then, fourth, turn over the document to a committee on style to provide the appropriate language and instruct this group to return the penultimate draft to us for final amendment and approval."

"Wait," Baca interrupts. "Shouldn't we first talk about a preamble that will express the goals we are aiming for?"

"Would not," the chair asks, "a preamble be the first item of business after we decide on an architectural scheme and how best to handle the issues that plan raises?"

"I wonder," Minxin Wei muses out loud, "but how can we adopt an architectural scheme without either begging a mass of critical questions or actually deciding them and so de facto creating the framework after we've made all the important decisions? If, for instance, we decide to open the document with a bill of rights or place it at the end or somewhere in between, we will have opted for a bill of rights—a course we should take only after thoughtful deliberation. One can say much the same thing about federalism versus unitary government or a parliamentary versus a presidential system.

Let's decide those sorts of questions first and then, before we send a draft to a committee on style, devote some time to architectonics."

"Even though I badly want a bill of rights," Ion Zingaro, the Gypsy poet says, "I agree that we should not decide those sorts of questions without searching debates."

"I'm persuaded," Jacobsohn capitulates. "I renumber my first step as the third."

"Do we have a second for the amended proposal?" the chair asks.

Several voices shout, "Second!" The chair then asks for the yeas and nays, and the motion carries handily.

"Now," the colonel continues, "I have a congruent proposal—it should be coming up on your screens—that pertains to the order in which we take matters up.

1. Should we write a preamble? If so, what should it say and what should be its authority?
2. Should we have a unitary or a federal state?
3. A presidential or parliamentary government? Or perhaps something along the French lines?
4. Related: who shall be head of state?
5. What kind of electoral system should we establish?
6. What sort of judicial and legal system should we have—our current Civil Law system or some other?
7. Do we want judicial review? If so, who shall exercise that power—all ordinary courts, some ordinary courts, or a separate constitutional court?
8. That question leads to the broader issue of constitutional interpretation: Do we want to specify by whom and how? If so, what answers do we give to each of these subqueries?
9. Should the charter Include a bill of rights? If so, what form should it take?
10. Do we want to include anything about the duties of citizenship? If so, what?
11. Not least: How should the constitutional charter be ratified and later amended?

Thus my proposal states an order of business. I suggest we adopt it but feel free to modify it either by taking items somewhat out of order or by adding issues as discussion develops. Mr. Pyknites?"

"If we're going to write a constitutional text, the Chair's proposal is eminently sensible. Still, it leaps over a critically important question: What life span do we foresee for this document? Is it to be designed 'to endure for ages to come' or to function as a first effort that will move us down the road to free government? (I use that ancient term to avoid rehashing old arguments.)

I favor a short-lived charter, of course, hoping that when we're 'by season seasoned' we'll turn to representative democracy."

"I don't want a constitutional text either," Strega asserts, "but telling the people they don't have a long-range stake in the regime is tantamount to surrendering."

"Well," Pyknites says, "we shouldn't forget that the current American constitutional text is that nation's second national charter. The first, the Articles of Confederation, lasted for a decade; it provided excellent experience on which to build a more lasting system. Why should we be afraid to admit that we have a great deal to learn about self-government? Thomas Jefferson thought a constitutional order should not last longer than the lifetime of the generation that created it. If we want another example, we can look to Japan. It's unlikely that many sophisticated Japanese believed that 'MacArthur's Constitution' would long survive the American occupation. And in the early 1960s, the Japanese government appointed a commission to look into constitutional 'reform.' In keeping with their history, these people traveled around the world to examine other political systems and talk to foreign scholars.[1] That Japan has kept MacArthur's Charter unamended is largely due to the government's policy of treating the system as more a representative than a constitutional democracy and the Supreme Court's acquiescence in that piece of constitutional interpretation. Let me offer yet a third example. West Germany's Article 146 has a sundown clause: 'This Basic Law shall cease to be in force on the day on which a constitution adopted by a free decision of the German people shall come into force.'"

"I agree," Professor Jacobsohn says, "with Minister Strega, though only partly. First, Madison effectively responded to Jefferson, warning of the dangers to political stability of frequent 'recurrence to the people.'[2] Second, after more than a half-century, the Japanese have not yet so much as amended their constitutional document. Third, when the time came for reunification, the Germans invoked not Article 146 but Article 23, which provides for the accession of other territories into the Federal Republic. The Basic Law remains in force. Moreover, the American Articles of Confederation were supposed to establish 'a perpetual Union.' Had the constitutional convention in 1787 not boldly exceeded its authority, replacement of the Articles would have required the unanimous consent of the thirteen states. Given that our authority is even shakier than that of the men at Phila-

1. At least part of this work has been translated into English: *Comments and Observations by Foreign Scholars on Problems concerning the Constitution of Japan, 1946* (Tokyo: Secretariat of the Commission on the Constitution, 1964).

2. The quotation is from *The Federalist* No. 49, but Madison's discussion spills over into No. 50 as well. For a more general discussion of Madison's views on this and related points, see Richard K. Matthews, *If Men Were Angels: James Madison and the Heartless Empire of Reason* (Lawrence: University Press of Kansas, 1995).

delphia, we must be equally bold and show that we have faith in our work. By crafting an amending clause, we can allow ourselves to change the charter as we develop more experience. Let's not broadcast our insecurities."

"Do you wish to offer a formal motion, Mr. Pyknites?" the chair asks.

"Yes. I move that the text we adopt have a clause that provides for a constitutional convention, elected by the people as provided by the legislature, to meet ten years from adoption of this text, to consider submitting a new charter to the people."

"Second?" Colonel Martin asks. Several moments of silence follow. "Second?" More silence. "Very well, the motion fails for want of a second. The parliamentary situation is a bit muddled. The chair has made an informal proposal. Can I ask for unanimous consent? Hearing no objection, we shall proceed. With a prayer that this morning's efficiency is an omen, let us move to the agenda's first item, the question of a preamble. Mr. Pyknites?"

"If I may speak through my bruises and make another recommendation, it would be that we keep this paragraph simple, perhaps 'We, the people of Nusquam, wishing to obtain the blessings of democratic liberty for ourselves and our posterity, do give ourselves this Constitutional Charter.'"

"Forgive me," the chair interrupts, "but we have not yet decided to have a preamble."

"Not formally," Pyknites replies, "but once we decided on writing a text we decided on a preamble. I ask the caucus's unanimous consent to that proposition."

"I object," Strega cuts in. "Opening the text with a steaming chunk of rhetoric is foolish."

"If," Father Gregorian volunteers, "the Chair will construe Mr. Pyknites's request as a formal motion, I second it."

Aside from a deep sigh from Strega, there is no further discussion and the motion carries handily. The chair then recognizes Václav Pilsudski, the minister of justice.

"I approve of economy of language, and I hate to dispute Mr. Pyknites, but our preamble needs to say something more. The American jurist Oliver Wendell Holmes once wrote that general principles do not decide concrete cases.[3] Nevertheless, general principles can *help* prevent some disputes from arising and can *help* settle others. Wise constitutional writers know that wise constitutional interpretaters must always look to the constitution's general purposes—not to intent, to what the framers meant to say, and not to how framers and ratifiers specifically understood words and concepts, but to what the objectives of a charter must be. Moreover, our spelling out those objectives will constantly remind interpreters that they are construing the fundamental law of a constitutional democracy—not a statute, not a section of a

3. Lochner v. New York, 198 U.S. 45, dis. op., 76 (1905).

code, not an executive decree, but *the* fundamental law, which has certain far-reaching goals. I hope that our preamble will further those ends by declaring our objective of establishing a constitutional democracy, embodying the political values we cherish."

"I follow the Minister of Justice, may his entire household bask in peace," Mufti Ibrahim Ajami says. "Our preamble should affirm not constitutional democracy but our commitment to certain broad values such as the great and equal dignity of all men and women. Doing so would move our government toward truly being 'the shadow of Allah on earth.' I would also prefer that we invoke His blessings, by whatever name we wish to call Him, but that might generate social division and so displease Allah."

"I agree on all counts," Pastor Glückmann adds, "sadly on the last."

"Yes," Father Gregorian says.

"We have," the chair notes, "a clear, simple statement by Mr. Pyknites that we state that a new constitutional convention should meet within ten years to consider a new charter. Do we have other proposals? Professor Deukalion, can you suggest alternatives?"

"I'm not sure you need help. The caucus seems familiar with the American constitutional text. The members might also might consider the language of Article 1 of the German Basic Law:

1. The dignity of man shall be inviolable. To respect and protect it shall be the duty of all state authority.
2. The German people therefore acknowledge inviolable human rights as the basis of peace and justice in the world.

The Irish preamble stands between the German and American models:

We, the people . . . seeking to promote the common good, with due observance of Prudence, Justice and Charity, so that the dignity and freedom of the individual [man and woman] may be assured, true social order attained, the unity of our country restored, and concord established with other nations . . .

You could look at a dozen other scripts, but you'd see only variations. You might consider combining the Mufti's and the Minister's suggestions with some of Mr. Pyknites's language and that of these documents."

"How about," Jacobsohn offers, "something like 'We the people of Nusquam, to protect the great and equal dignity of all men and women and obtain the blessings of liberty, security, and social justice offered by constitutional democracy, do establish this Constitutional Charter for ourselves and our posterity.'"

"Needless to say," Pyknites notes, "I think that is much too much."

"It's offensively pious," Strega says.

"It does not go far enough," Baca objects. "We should add references to 'community,' or we'll seem to be adopting the, you know, frightened male ideal of isolated individualism. And the allusion to 'social justice' is too oblique. Right? Let me share with you Article 45 of the Irish constitutional charter: 'The State shall strive to promote the welfare of the whole people by securing and protecting as effectively as it may a social order in which justice and charity shall inform the institutions of national life.' What follows is a list of general policies promoting equal rights of men and women to maintain decent standards of living, against the amassing property and the control of essential commodities in the hands of a few, providing state assistance where appropriate to private enterprise, directing concern for the 'economic interests of the weaker sections of the community' as well as for the protection of the health of all citizens. Now those are policies we all—or almost all—endorse. If we care about these things, let's, like, put that concern right up front so that we as well as later interpreters can never forget the kind of people we are and the kind of community we aspire to be. The Indians have used Article 45 as a model in their constitutional text, and so have the Italians. Do we want to tell our own people that we don't care about such issues?"

"I want better health care," Strega admits, "but it makes no sense for a poor nation like ours to 'constitutionalize' rights that require government to spend money it doesn't have. If we opt for guided capitalism. it might make sense a decade or two from now to create such constitutional rights. But for the foreseeable future, under constitutional democracy that language would at best be so much hot air, at worst a cruel hoax."

"Well," Gregorian says, "the Irish text announces these policies as guidelines for public policy, not as judicially enforceable constitutional rights. That puts the responsibility—and the pressure—squarely on elected officials. Mr. Pyknites should like that."

"I do like putting full responsibility on elected officials, but I don't like our determining, before we understand various political situations, the content of public policy."

"But," the Mufti says, "Ms Baca's proposal, peace be upon her, requires only that public policy be directed toward social justice. Would it be a bad thing for those who want the people's votes to compete as promoters of social justice?"

"No," Pyknites replies, "the root of my objection is that I'd like our charter to be as simple as possible."

The debate goes on for another fifteen minutes. Then the chair persuades Pyknites and Jacobsohn to put their suggestions as motions. Both are duly seconded, and during later discussion Jacobsohn accepts Baca's addition of a version of Ireland's Article 45 as a friendly amendment. The caucus then approves Jacobsohn's amended alternative, 15–9.

Minister Pilsudski speaks next: "Mr. Chairman, your agenda has a subitem here, the authority of the preamble. The United States has had long disputes about the extent, if any, to which interpreters should be guided by the preamble. For reasons best understood, perhaps, by psychiatrists or artful politicians—I use that latter word in a pejorative sense, not Aristotle's—the U.S. Supreme Court has seldom taken that country's preamble seriously. Our difficulty is more complex. We want interpreters to keep the charter's purposes firmly in mind, though we don't want to make the clauses relating to social policy judicially enforceable. I suggest that rather than try to decide the issue now, we brood on it and return to it when we discuss judicial review and constitutional interpretation."

"That sounds good," the chair says. "Hearing no objection, let us instruct the secretary to remind us of this pending problem at the appropriate times and move to the next item. Now, we have been in session for more than two hours. Let us recess for coffee and return in seventeen and a half minutes."

After the break, the chair begins by asking Professor Deukalion, "Please tell the others about our conversation over coffee."

"Well, during the 1960s, many intellectuals preached that institutions were of small importance; culture and informal processes were what really mattered. Harking back to Tocqueville, some of these scholars expressly included in the concept of culture the number and strength of private, voluntary associations that are independent of the state. These factors are truly significant, as are the personalities and skills of leaders. But your experience under harsh authoritarian rule has taught you that institutions are also of enormous consequence: They shape as well as are shaped by culture and informal processes; they socialize leaders, help weed out some ambitious men and women, and facilitate the careers of others. They 'affect the flow of history' by educating the people as well as leaders in the rules of the game, opening some avenues to power while closing others, and 'endowing some individuals, rather than others, with authority and other types of resources.'[4] Institutional structures greatly affect how political parties operate, how many and what kinds of private associations flourish, how interest groups lobby government, if indeed they can lobby at all, how the people judge leaders and would-be leaders, and what public policies government will pursue. Institutions seldom determine outcomes, for they 'have a degree of elasticity through which political actors work.'[5] Nevertheless, by sculpting

4. James G. March and Johan P. Olsen, *Rediscovering Institutions: The Organizational Basis of Politics* (New York: Free Press, 1989), pp. 159–60.

5. Bert A. Rockman, "The Performance of Presidents and Prime Ministers and of Presidential and Parliamentary Systems," in Kurt von Mettenheim, ed., *Presidential Institutions and Democratic Politics* (Baltimore: Johns Hopkins University Press, 1997), p. 55; see also R. Kent Weaver and Bert A. Rockman, "Assessing the Effects of Institutions," in Weaver and Rockman, eds., *Do Institutions Matter? Government Capabilities in the United States and Abroad* (Washington, DC: Brookings Institution Press, 1993).

political processes, institutions channel substantive policies. They matter, and they matter greatly.[6]

"Obviously, both constitutional and representative democracy can exist under a variety of institutional arrangements, but they cannot long exist under some institutional arrangements, nor at all under yet others. Thus, although your choices during the next few days may seem less dramatic than between constitutional and representative democracy, they are nonetheless crucial to Nusquam's national future.

"The next question on the Chair's agenda is whether to have a unitary or federal state or something in between, such as Italy's regionalism.[7] We are familiar with claims that federalism protects diversity, encourages experimentation, and, not least important, limits power.[8] But you have no history of hostile regionalism or, outside of sports, sharp regional rivalries. Jews and Catholics are mostly urban dwellers, but neither group is concentrated in any particular part of the country. Your other minorities are also rather evenly distributed. Of course, lack of parochial identifications is not fatal to federalism; boundary lines may engender political loyalties. Iraq was conceived in the petri dish of a British mandate after Versailles; nevertheless, dictators have cultured aggressive nationalism among its people. More relevant to your situation, Germany's division after World War II disrupted the lines of old principalities, and the West German founders' choice of federalism—insofar as they had a choice—meant that some *Länder* were instant creations. Despite the absence of historic roots, new loyalties soon flowered.

"Still, lack of local identification does not strengthen the case for federalism, and you seem united around the goal of keeping the political system simple. Some of you have also voiced a fear that federalism might be used, as it was in the American South, to shield discrimination against minorities. In sum, I don't see any serious reason for you to adopt any form of federalism or even regionalism."

"Mr. Chairman," Minxin Wei speaks up, "our learned guest has put the matter neatly if somewhat verbosely. I ask unanimous consent that we opt for a unitary state."

6. See, generally, Jack Knight, *Institutions and Social Conflict* (New York: Cambridge University Press, 1992).

7. Merely reading texts would lead one to believe that Spain, too, has a form of regionalism, but Alec Stone Sweet, following Robert Agranoff, concludes that of the work of the Spanish Constitutional Tribunal has turned Spain into a federal state. Alec Stone Sweet, *Governing with Judges: Constitutional Politics in Europe* (New York: Oxford University Press, 2000), pp. 64–65 and ch. 3 generally. Agranoff, "Inter-governmental Politics and Policy: Building Federal Arrangements in Spain," 3 *Regional Politics and Society* 1 (1993); and "Federal Evolution in Spain," 17 *Int'l Pol. Sci. Rev.* 385 (1996).

8. For an interesting approach to federalism, see Vicki Jackson, "Ambivalent Resistance and Comparative Constitutionalism: Opening Up the Conversation on 'Proportionality,' Rights, and Federalism," 1 *U. Pa. J. Con'l L.* 583 (2005).

"Discussion? A comment? Objection? Hearing only silence, it is so ordered. Let us move to the question of the nature of national political institutions. Minister Pilsudski."

"Although I have heard much talk that the traditional tripartite division of legislative, executive, and judicial offices is unrealistic, I have heard no alternative. Our lack of experience discourages me from trying linguistic innovations. I propose that our text should candidly admit it is creating 'separate institutions *competing* for shared power' rather than pretending to 'separate powers.'"[9]

"Do I hear an objection? A counterproposal? Very well, the motion carries without dissent. Let us move to problems of institutional design. First is the choice among a presidential, parliamentary, and French dual system. For expert advice, we have invited Professor Juanita Ferrer, professor of the philosophy of law of the Universitat Pompeu Fabra in Barcelona."

A tall, slender, blondish woman in her early forties, Ferrer, a Catalan, speaks rapidly but softly in English. Her only trace of an accent is a slight lisp.

Parliamentarianism Versus Presidentialism

When asked which was the best constitution, Solon replied: "Tell me first the people and their time." I can point out advantages and disadvantages of parliamentarianism and presidentialism; you, not I, must judge which would be better for your nation.

"What is it with academics?" Strega interjects. "We've listened for hours to your colleagues tell us on the one hand there's something or other and on the other hand there are five fingers. We realize you're not an expert on our country. Just tell us which system you think is best for us and explain why. We can discount your ignorance by our own."

Ferrer smiles as she replies.

Yes, we academics suffer from a common ailment known in America as the CYA syndrome. But your chair has instructed me to provide background analysis. I shall comply, though I shall also try to honor your request within the limits of my *déformation professionnelle*. First, I put aside a plural executive such as the one John C. Calhoun advocated for the United States. It is impractical, as Uruguay discovered.[10] Neither do I

9. Charles Jones, "The Separated Presidency," in Anthony King, ed., *The New American Political System*, 2nd ed. (Washington, DC: American Enterprise Institute, 1990), p. 3. In the first edition of *Presidential Power* (New York: John Wiley, 1960), p. 33, Richard E. Neustadt had described the American political system as "separated institutions *sharing* power."

10. For analyses of Uruguay's various presidential arrangements, see Luis Eduardo Gonzáles

recommend the Fifth Republic's dual executive. There the president and the National Assembly—the lower house of Parliament—are popularly elected, though not at the same time. The president, who is the chief of state, appoints the prime minister, who is the head of government. The text authorizes only the National Assembly to remove the prime minister, but strong presidents have unblinkingly exercised that power.[11] The president can also dissolve the assembly and call for new elections. That complex system has functioned reasonably well,[12] in part because the constituencies of the president and the assembly have usually coincided. But it does not take much imagination to visualize the impasse that could result when the president is from one side of the political spectrum and the prime minister from the other. When such "cohabitation" has occurred, the president has been little more than a figurehead in domestic politics.

In reality, the French arrangement has alternated between presidential and parliamentary systems.[13] Your inexperienced people would quickly have to learn how to operate both systems. France has many advantages that you lack, not least of which is a superbly trained civil service. That elite corps has provided stability through all the changes France has endured.[14] You should aspire to create such a body of experts, but that achievement lies in the distant future. You now need government that is simple. You do not have a Charles de Gaulle to bless your work and dominate it long enough to calm the sort of crisis that destroyed the Fourth Republic.

Finland and Portugal have also had some success with a dual executive—Poland less.[15] I would match those experiences with a pair of fail-

---

and Charles Guy Gillespie, "Presidentialism and Democratic Stability in Uruguay," in Juan J. Linz and Arturo Valenzuela, eds., *The Failure of Presidential Democracy* (Baltimore: Johns Hopkins University Press, 1994); Matthew Soberg Shugart and John M. Carey, *Presidents and Assemblies: Constitutional Design and Electoral Politics* (Cambridge: Cambridge University Press, 1992), pp. 97–99, 101–2, 127–28.

11. John A. Rohr, *Founding Republics in France and America* (Lawrence: University Press of Kansas, 1995), p. 77: "Cohabitation aside, prime ministers have served de facto at the pleasure of the president."

12. For a perceptive analysis of the French system, see Ezra N. Suleiman, "Presidentialism and Political Stability in France," in Linz and Valenzuela, *Failure of Presidential Democracy.*

13. For example: Maurice Duverger, "A New Political System Model: Semi-presidential Government," 8 *Eur'n J. of Pol. Res.* 165, 186 (1980); Suleiman, "Presidentialism and Political Stability in France," p. 151; and Arend Lijphart, "Presidentialism and Majoritarian Democracy: Theoretical Observations," in Linz and Valenzuela, *Failure of Presidential Democracy,* p. 95.

14. See esp. Ezra N. Suleiman, *Power, Politics, and Bureaucracy: The Administrative Elite in France* (Princeton, NJ: Princeton University Press, 1974); and Rohr, *Founding Republics,* chs. 1–2, 7.

15. Michael Bernhard, "Semipresidentialism, Charisma, and Democratic Institutions in Poland," in Kurt von Mettenheim, ed., *Presidential Institutions and Democratic Politics* (Baltimore: Johns Hopkins University Press, 1997).

ures.[16] Although the French do not like to admit it, Weimar Germany's disastrous mixture provided a model for their system.[17] Then there is the mess that Russian executive arrangements, which to a large extent follow the French, have fomented. The Duma and Boris Yeltsin, even when his own man was prime minister, could not govern together, and neither could govern alone when the opposition controlled the Duma. The French have had enough experience to survive such cohabitation; Russia came close to anarchy. Given Putin's authoritarian ways, omens of an ugly future may have been flashing in Yeltsin's tantrums.

Thus, I recommend either of two straightforward systems: an American-style presidency or a British-style cabinet government. Either can function with proportional representation[18] and judicial review, though PR fits presidentialism less well. The United States has a presidential system and judicial review; Australia, Ireland, and Canada have parliamentary systems and judicial review; Australia and Ireland have multimember districts and PR, while Britain, Canada, and the United States use single-member, winner-take-all districts. The choice is between a prime minister whose tenure depends on Parliament's approval and a president who serves for a set term and is directly responsible to the electorate. Alas, as usual, social science is not much help here. Although thoughtful scholars like Arend Lijphart, Juan J. Linz, Bert A. Rockman, Giovanni Sartori, and Alfred Stepan have worried about that issue, we have few scientific studies that test hypotheses against hard data.[19]

Sensing some restlessness in the audience, Ferrer quickly adds:

Still, I recommend a parliamentary system. But of itself that recommendation says little. There are many kinds of parliamentary systems,

16. I do not mention Lebanon's dual executive. It is improbable that human wisdom could construct a constitutional order that could have peacefully, much less democratically or constitutionally, run a country so bitterly divided internally along religious lines and savagely torn by the larger Arab-Israeli conflict.

17. See Cindy Skach, *Borrowing Constitutional Designs: Constitutional Law in Weimar Germany and the Fifth French Republic* (Princeton, NJ: Princeton University Press, 2006)

18. To save time, Professor Ferrer is speaking as if there were only one form of proportional representation. She knows, of course, that this system can take many forms. For a discussion, see Giovanni Sartori, *Comparative Constitutional Engineering: An Inquiry into Structures, Incentives, and Outcomes* (New York: New York University Press, 1994), chs. 1-3.

19. See esp. Juan J. Linz, "The Perils of Presidentialism," 1 *J. of Democ.* 51 (1990), and his "Presidential or Presidentialism: Does It Make a Difference?" in Linz and Valenzuela, *Failure of Presidential Democracy*. See also Rockman, "Performance of Presidents and Prime Ministers"; Anthony King, "Foundations of Power," in George C. Edwards III, John H. Kessel, and Bert A. Rockman, eds., *Researching the Presidency: Vital Questions, New Approaches* (Pittsburgh: University of Pittsburgh Press, 1993). Alfred Stepan and Cindy Skach, "Presidentialism and Parliamentarianism in Comparative Perspective," in Linz and Valenzuela, *Failure of Presidential Democracy*, analyze some of the few scientific studies as well as report on their own work.

and, like presidentialism, each promises unknown rewards and imposes costs no one can now calculate. I return to this point shortly.[20]

My principal reason for recommending a parliamentary system is that, properly designed, it allows more flexibility—in length of time a government can serve and in facilitating coalitions or consociationalism —than does a presidential system. Every society suffers from some degree of factionalism; even your old regime had cliques within the ruling elite who brutally represented certain interests in society. Because, as Madison said, "[l]iberty is to faction what air is to fire," your problems of division will grow, though I hope oppression will be absent. You have all the causes that Madison diagnosed: differences of religion, ideology, attachments to aspiring leaders, as well as "various and unequal distributions of property."[21]

A president's set term offers a form of stability; everyone knows a president will remain in office for a designated period of time, unless, of course, he or she dies, becomes incapacitated, commits egregious crimes, or is the victim of a coup. If the president is a competent leader, a set term is good; but if he or she is not competent or fails in a major crisis, you are left with a wounded duck until his or her term expires. Think of Bill Clinton in the United States: disgraced in 1998, he remained in office for two years, morally bankrupt, paving the way for a change in dominant parties that would drag the United States into a bloody and stupid war. Parliamentary systems offer stability of a different sort: shorter governmental life spans but longer-lived constitutional orders. A prime minister's tenure is indefinite, though limited. Much modern practice has made the PM more the master than the servant of parliament; but when he or she stumbles or loses public confidence, the servant turns master. Either parliament can directly replace the PM or the voters can do so indirectly through a general election that can occur with only a few weeks' notice.

Your ethnic divisions require a regime that provides not only stability but also accommodation, and it is here that parliaments excel. Accommodation is not impossible under presidential government.[22] Indeed,

20. For a classification of parliamentary systems and a refreshingly skeptical analysis of the virtues of presidentialism, parliamentarianism, and presidential-parliamentary regimes, see Giovanni Sartori, "Neither Presidentialism nor Parliamentarianism," in Linz and Valenzuela, *Failure of Presidential Democracy.*

21. *The Federalist* No. 10.

22. In 1977 Arend Lijphart made a similar statement: *Democracy in Plural Societies: A Comparative Exploration* (New Haven, CT: Yale University Press, 1977), p. 224. Twenty years later he changed his mind: "[P]residentialism is inimical to the kind of consociational compromises and pacts that may be necessary in the process of democratization and during periods of crises, whereas the collegial nature of parliamentary executives makes them conducive to such pacts" ("Presidentialism and Majoritarian Democracy," p. 97).

one might argue that in the United States each of the two major parties is itself a coalition and, further, a de facto grand coalition operates when one party controls the White House and the other Congress. But such flexibility has been rare elsewhere. I repeat Professor Deukalion's warning against copying the particulars of the American model. That country was blessed in 1787–1788 with professional politicians who had long experience operating a nascent constitutional democracy. You, however, start at the beginning.

As for consociationism, in the United States federalism, bargaining between the president and Congress, and decentralized parties allow such conciliatory agreements. Nevertheless, the ruling elites have historically—and callously—disregarded the rights of Asians, blacks, Hispanics, Native Americans, and women. Minorities have had to rely on judges to protect them, risky for any people and especially dangerous for you because your jurists have no experience with—and Nusquam has no tradition of—judicial independence. Your legal profession, controlled by the junta, has rejected the judicial roles that seem proper in established constitutional democracies.

If we look beyond the United States, we see that presidentialism has usually produced weak, divided government. Probably because of those characteristics, presidentialism often yields not merely unstable governments but unstable regimes; presidents have been the victims of coups much more often than prime ministers.[23] A president and legislature independent of each other discourage party discipline. Neither the president nor legislators have to stand for reelection when the latter reject measures on which the president has staked his or her reputation. The likelihood of continuing conflict abets political impasse, as each institution goes its own way to please its peculiar constituencies. Even in the United States, complaints about *immobilismo* are common. For less than half the fifty years between 1950 and 2000 were the president and a majority of both houses of Congress members of the same party—about the same ratio as in most other presidential systems. As a result, changes in American public policy come in sporadic bursts, with deadlock—and boredom—the more common scenario.[24] You cannot afford deadlock; you cannot afford boredom. To establish a new political system, you must first engage, then transform, your people.

23. See the data in Stepan and Skach, "Presidentialism and Parliamentarianism," p. 124, and, later in this chapter, Professor Jacobsohn's critique of this article.

24. "Deadlock" is hardly a recent phenomenon in American politics; see, for example, James M. Burns, *The Deadlock of Democracy*, rev. ed. (Englewood Cliffs, NJ: Prentice-Hall, 1963); Samuel Lubell, *The Future of American Politics* (New York: Harper and Row, 1952); and Elmer E. Schattschneider, *The Semisovereign People: A Realist's View of Democracy in America* (New York: Holt, Rinehart and Winston, 1960).

Presidentialism also poses more subtle difficulties. American, French, and Latin American political history have led Lijphart to conclude that presidential government "spells majoritarianism,"[25] and majoritarianism pushes parties toward the center, toward a two-party system. That system may be healthy for established constitutional democracies. But your inexperience and history of sharp ethnic divisions make political bipolarization dangerous. You need to ease the alienation of smaller groups; you need their commitment to the new constitutional order; and you are unlikely to get that commitment through a party system that focuses on the demands of the political, social, and economic center of your country. You are more likely to secure that commitment by giving your ethnic minorities representatives in Parliament and the possibility of sharing in a governing coalition.

Let me be clear: parliamentarianism does not guarantee success. A prime minister can be removed more easily than a president, but he or she can do serious damage before being fired. Neville Chamberlain lacked both vision and courage; Franz Von Papen lacked integrity; and Bettino Craxi, alas, did not lack venality. Furthermore, multiparty representation can produce stalemate. Constructing favorable circumstances for parliamentarianism requires hard—and constant—labor.

I mention several essential conditions that you must quickly create. First is an electoral system that enhances Parliament's capacity for adjustment and compromise but minimizes its vulnerability to stalemate. Second are parties that, as Sartori puts it, are "parliamentary fit,"[26] that is, responsible when in power *or* in opposition and willing to play these roles fairly under the system's rules. Parties like those of the Nazis and communists under Weimar or even most of those under France's Third Republic will doom any kind of democratic system.

Third, what form of parliamentarianism best fits your needs? Initially, let me mention a version I strongly advise against, that which the Israelis used from 1996 until 2001. They allowed each voter, in effect, to cast one ballot for prime minister and another for a party slate for members of parliament, the Knesset, or one vote for PM when the incumbent resigned without dissolving parliament. This arrangement would supposedly be more democratic and bestow greater prestige on the prime minister. But that prestige, if, indeed there is any, can be erased by the fate of the winner's party in the parliamentary election. In 1999, Prime Minister Ehud Barak's Labor Party had only 25 seats out of 120 in the Knesset; the Likud, Ariel Sharon's party, had only 19 votes when he defeated Barak in 2001. Sharon had to play one-armed paper hanger in

25. "Presidentialism and Majoritarian Democracy," p. 101.
26. "Neither Presidentialism nor Parliamentarianism," p. 112.

forming and operating a fragile eight-party coalition. It is difficult to see any democratic advantage in a loss of party control and therefore responsibility.

Now, with that version aside, I can speak more systematically. Giovanni Sartori categorizes parliaments in relation to the prime minister as those in which that person is (1) *first above unequals*, with the parliamentary party pretty much subordinate to his or her wishes; (2) *first among unequals*, one who leads but with less freedom; and (3) *first among equals*, where the PM is merely the agent of the elements making up the majority. This last invites unstable, ineffective government. I urge you to adopt either the first or the second—or some combination of the two—to allow prime ministers institutional space in which to direct public policies either through their party or through a small coalition. Your best hope lies in parliamentarianism with a head of government with the sort of authority of the German chancellor or the British PM.[27] To prevent clusters of small parties from bringing virtually all governance to an end, you should include something like the Federal Republic's "constructive vote of no confidence": Parliament can remove the prime minister only by electing a successor.[28]

Back to the electoral system. Its two principal functions are not easily reconciled: facilitating control by the majority while ensuring representation of minorities. Proportional representation is designed to cope with this conundrum. Thus some form of PR would better fit your situation, I believe, than the Anglo-American single-member, winner-take-all electoral method or the French two-stage process. An electoral system should also prevent Parliament from turning into a bear pit in which special interests veto each other's policies but cannot either govern

27. Article 64 of the Basic Law provides that the chancellor appoints and dismisses ministers. Article 65 seems to modify this authority: although the chancellor shall set guidelines for the cabinet, each minister "shall conduct the affairs of his department autonomously and on his own responsibility." Ministers' "autonomy" has been much more from each other than from the chancellor, whose authority over the cabinet has been limited largely by the necessity of keeping a coalition together or the Christian Democrats' two wings united.

28. The Basic Law, Article 67, reads:

1.   The Bundestag can express its lack of confidence in the Federal Chancellor only by selecting a successor with the majority of its members and by requesting the Federal President to dismiss the Federal Chancellor. The Federal President must comply with this request and appoint the person elected.

Despite efforts by drafters of the Fifth Republic's constitutional text to increase governmental stability, Article 50 states:

When the National Assembly adopts a motion of censure, or when it disapproves the program or a declaration of general policy of the Government, the Prime Minister must submit the resignation of the Government to the President of the Republic.

From 1958 until 1998, no French government lasted the five years of maximum parliamentary life.

alone or combine into a ruling coalition. To achieve that goal, I suggest you follow another German model and include in the text a statement that no party can obtain seats in Parliament without receiving a minimum percentage of the national vote.

Father Gregorian asks the first question: "If every majority is a cluster of minorities, won't PR and parliamentarianism merely shift the arena for formulation of majorities from the larger political and social processes to the legislature? And if so, it that a good thing?"

Ferrer stares at the ceiling for a moment, twisting a strand of hair in her fingers, then responds: "To both questions: it can be. In a society that lacks webs of nongovernmental organizations such as unions and professional associations, majorities will coalesce more swiftly and efficiently among professional politicians in Parliament. That situation may change over time. If your political system endures for a decade, you can then think about changing institutional structures."

Jessica Jacobsohn speaks next: "During and after World War II, Ferdinand A. Hermans described PR as having led Europe to the brink of anarchy during the interwar years.[29] Forty years later, I was allowed to visit the United States. Political scientists there were still pretty much agreed that coalition governments are unstable; coalition governments, in turn, have usually been caused by proportional representation's rewarding small, single-interest parties; thus stable government requires parties that strive to win a majority of popular votes. To get majoritarian parties, a country needs single-member, winner-take-all districts and a presidential system, because these institutions arouse parties' majoritarianesque lusts. Those libidinous urges require broadly based appeals; although they often dull the edges of policy differences between parties, they also make those organizations function as unifiers of diverse geographical, ethnic, and economic groupings. Now you preach the gospel of a parliamentary system with PR and coalition, perhaps even consociational, government. Have we been so isolated that we're unaware of momentous developments in political science?"

Ferrer begins twisting her hair again, seeming to devote her full attention to that task. After a full thirty seconds, she looks up and speaks very softly. "First, I make no claim about the best form of rule. Professor Sartori summed it up when he said that 'no electoral system is best for all seasons.'[30] I merely explain what I think is best for your country right now. Second, I do not criticize the parochialism of American political scientists. On the whole, their system works well for citizens and groups who can afford large con-

29. Ferdinand A. Hermans, *Democracy or Anarchy: A Study in Proportional Representation* (Notre Dame, IN: University of Notre Dame Press, 1941); and *Europe between Democracy and Anarchy* (Notre Dame, IN: University of Notre Dame Press, 1951).

30. *Comparative Constitutional Engineering*, p. 75.

tributions to politicians' campaign funds. Nevertheless, after studying 150 elections in countries with majoritarian and proportional electoral systems, G. Bingham Powell concluded that PR's record of achieving congruence between voters' wishes and public policies enacted into law was better than that of majoritarian systems."[31]

"These are not parochial judgments," Jacobsohn interrupts. "Hermans was German; Powell is an American; and Michael Debré, the chief architect of the Fifth Republic's constitutional text, wrote that in the Fourth Republic, PR and coalition governments left no one 'responsible for the general interest.' That system produces, he said, 'a coalition of party interests which sets up camp in the state and shares its spoils.'[32] And the persistent deadlock that Italy suffered under PR finally led that country in 1993 to change to a method that chooses 75 percent of MPs through plurality voting and only 25 percent through PR."

Ferrer again hesitates, then replies: "I agree with Hermans's and Debré's specific critiques. On the other hand, no one can blame Italy's problems solely on PR. The change of 1993 did little, if anything, to stabilize parliamentary politics, though it did bring some new players into the game. But there's more positive evidence. PR has also gone hand in hand with stable government and often stable coalition government, for example, in Australia, Belgium, the Federal Republic of Germany, Ireland, the Netherlands, and Sweden."

"Aren't you agreeing with political scientists like Maurice Duverger[33] who say that electoral laws are more important than social cleavages in determining the nature of a party system?"

"No, I think that the relationships among electoral systems, parties, and social divisions—and constitutional structures and political history as well—are, as Gary Cox puts it, 'symbiotic.'[34] Although electoral systems can encourage or discourage or even rough-hew events, alone they don't *determine* much. They certainly affect the number and nature and political parties, but,

---

31. *Elections as Instruments of Democracy* (New Haven, CT: Yale University Press, 2000).

32. "The Constitution of 1958: Its *Raison d'Etre* and How It Evolved," in William G. Andrews and Stanley Hoffmann, eds., *The Fifth Republic at Twenty* (Albany: State University of New York Press, 1981), p. 15.

33. Maurice Duverger, *Political Parties* (New York: Wiley, 1954), and his "Duverger's Law: Thirty Years Later," in Arend Lijphart and Bernard Grofman, eds., *Choosing an Electoral System* (New York: Praeger, 1986). Gary W. Cox, *Making Votes Count* (New York: Cambridge University Press, 1997), ch. 2, discusses Duverger's "law" and the countertheories it provoked. See also the analysis of how social cleavages affect party systems in Harry H. Eckstein, "The Impact of Electoral Systems on Representative Government," in David Apter and Harry H. Eckstein, eds., *Comparative Politics* (New York: Free Press, 1963).

34. *Making Votes Count*, p. 17 and ch. 11 generally. Some people might read Sartori, *Comparative Constitutional Engineering*, ch. 3, esp. pp. 40ff., as denigrating the importance of electoral systems. I interpret him as stressing their importance but understanding that, alone, they do not predestine a particular party system.

I repeat, so do a nation's political history, socioeconomic cleavages, and general constitutional order. Compare the United States and Israel. Federalism and a long history of geographic separation and diversity predisposed the United States to locally oriented parties. Israel, without either federalism or a strong history of localism, could rather easily make the entire country a single electoral district. And that national constituency gives physically scattered groups an opportunity to muster votes behind candidates from splinter parties, which tend to reflect religious divisions among Jews. In that constitutional, historic, and religious setting, PR has encouraged small parties."

"And won't," Jacobsohn persists, "the mixture of PR with ethnic divisions like ours proliferate parties and make it extremely difficult to operate a government?"

"In your situation, pure PR will encourage that result. But I recommended an impure system of PR in the form of a floor under the percentage of votes a party must receive before sending representatives to Parliament. I also recommended a constructive vote of no confidence. Professor Hermans approved those additions. They certainly discourage splinter parties."

"How high should this floor be?" Ion Zingaro asks.

"There is no universally correct answer. When the French used PR in the Fifth Republic, they set 12 percent as the minimum, which strikes me as too high; Israel uses 1.5 percent, which has done little to stop proliferation. The Poles adopted the Germans' formula of 5 percent. I doubt that a constitutional charter should set a specific number. It might, however, be wise to state that Parliament can set a floor to avoid the constitutional doubts that Germany experienced."[35]

Minister Pilsudski speaks next: "Professor, you quoted Sartori, but didn't he argue that the floor for MPs was unimportant in reducing the number of German parliamentary parties? Rather, it was the Federal Constitutional Court's outlawing the Neo-Nazi and Communist parties and so eliminating from electoral contests parties of the extreme right and left."[36]

"He does make that argument, and without doubt the Court's decisions, sparked by complaints lodged by Konrad Adenauer's government, have had a significant impact. But the judges didn't outlaw the Communist Party until the floor had been in effect for some years, and while the government has moved against some other Neo-Nazi organizations, it has pretty much chosen to ignore reformulated if not re-formed communist parties. In fact, parties rather far to the right and the left continue to exist in the Federal

---

35. Eventually the Constitutional Court upheld that authority: Bavarian Party Case, 6 BVerfGE 84 (1957); excerpted and reprinted in Walter F. Murphy and Joseph Tanenhaus, eds., *Comparative Constitutional Law* (New York: St. Martin's, 1977), p. 578.

36. *Comparative Constitutional Engineering*, p. 106. The decisions were in the Socialist Reich Party Case, 2 BVerfGE 1 (1952), and the Communist Party Case, 5 BVerfGE 85 (1956), both reprinted in *Comparative Constitutional Law*.

Republic, but they have never become a force in the Bundestag, even after reunification."

"I'd like to talk about a different matter," Tuncer Kirca says. "Can we create a party system as well as governmental institutions?"

"Two points: First, as Germany's Basic Law recognizes, political parties are themselves governmental institutions. Although they differ in significant ways from courts, legislatures, and administrative agencies, parties are essential to a constitutional democracy and will remain so until someone develops new institutions to aggregate interests, win elections, staff governments, and be held responsible for a government's choices of public policies. Second, you are building the structures within which a system of parties will develop. Thus you are inevitably configuring a party system."

"Professor Ferrer," the chair intervenes, "let me return to an earlier issue. The core of your objection to the French model is that it invites conflict among public officials. But isn't that one of the instruments by which constitutionalism restrains power? I recall an American founder's saying something like 'If public officials are at each other's throats, they will not be at ours.'"

"I am not familiar with that quotation, but certainly Madison tried to pit power against power. Yet even if we concede his genius, too many can be too much. Your constitution must *empower* as well as limit public officials. In 1787 America's needs for positive government were less than yours—or theirs today. Your political system must dismantle old social and economic orders and construct new ones, while at the same time creating new citizens and new rights. It isn't wise to design a government for eighteenth-century America or to utilize complications the French have bred. You are better off with only an independent judiciary, a parliament that controls the executive branch, and a head of state who can use moral force to mediate conflicts. Once again I argue for simplicity. If you facilitate a free society, checks on power will arise that we cannot now even imagine."

"I'm not optimistic about a system's spontaneously developing checks, but I want to open a related issue," the chair continues. "We might consider the French bar against legislators' having cabinet posts. De Gaulle wanted to make that ban prospective as well: a minister could never again become a legislator—impractical in France and probably here. But separating, even temporarily, legislative and executive careers might both strengthen constitutionalist checks and broaden perspectives."

"You might," Ferrer rejoins, "compromise by allowing, as Italy does, nonlegislators to join the cabinet."[37]

"Which would make the existence of the check depend on the prime

37. Articles 92–96, which specify the authority of the cabinet—"the Council of Ministers"—are silent on the qualifications for cabinet posts, other than that ministers must be appointed by the president of the Republic on the advice of the prime minister and that the government must have the confidence of both houses of Parliament.

minister," Jacobsohn notes, "and he or she might not want to be reined in. I'd prefer an outright ban. It's simple and fits with Alexander Hamilton's argument that there should be unity as well as energy in the executive."[38]

"I, too, would prefer an outright ban," the chair agrees. "But I rule myself and Professor Jacobsohn out of order. We can discuss that option later. We should direct questions to Professor Ferrer."

"Is either Professor Ferrer or our Chair advocating," Minister Pilsudski asks, "a French separation of administrative and legislative competence— that is, between topics on which Parliament can legislate and those that can be regulated only by administrative decrees?"

The chair shakes his head, but it is Ferrer who speaks: "I am not. You don't have large numbers of civil servants with the necessary expertise and *esprit*. And you'd also need to build up a complex body of law that was simultaneously administrative and constitutional."

"Agreed," Pilsudski says. "I just wanted the issue clear. I am deeply worried about bureaucrats. Given the way our civil servants have been trained and allowed to operate, we're going to have serious difficulties controlling them. One shortcoming of parliamentarianism is that ministers seldom become experts in the problems their ministries address. And they have even less understanding of the byzantine politics among the administrators they supposedly direct. The American presidential model offers more hope because it encourages Congress and the president to compete for power. Legislators want to control governmental agencies, to exercise what purists insist is executive power. They understand that administrative details can be as important as general guidelines, so they spend their careers on specialized standing committees that oversee, frequently micromanage, executive agencies. A president may initially believe the executive branch is *his*, but the sheer number of bureaucrats inhibits his power. On the other hand, it is very difficult for administrators to escape the long arm of one or another powerful legislator. These elected officials specialize in the issues important to their constituents, and they control agencies' budgets. Let a bureaucrat ignore a representative's interests and that official's agency will soon find its funds in jeopardy.[39] Perversely, the oft-criticized American party system increases legislators' incentives to manage administrators. Lacking a strong national party organization whose endorsement is needed for reelection,[40] members of Congress must curry personal favor with constituents: get bureaucrats off

38. *The Federalist*, No. 70.

39. For one president's efforts to reassert power not only over "his" branch of government but over public policy generally, see Charles Tiefer, *The Semi-sovereign Presidency: The Bush Administration's Strategy for Governing without Congress* (Boulder: Westview, 1994).

40. Near the end of the twentieth century, increased availability of so-called soft money to national parties strengthened the control of those organizations over candidates, especially those in need of monetary support. Still, the situation in the United States is not like that of Britain or Germany.

their backs or cut through red tape to obtain benefits for them. Can we pass up that limitation on government?"

"Is it wise to ignore administrators' power? Absolutely not," Ferrer answers. "The real question is how best to control them while achieving other objectives. What you say about the United States may be correct, but is it correct for other presidential systems? I don't know, but I doubt it. Incidentally, it is not unusual for MPs in Britain, Canada, and Ireland to intervene with administrative agencies for constituents or even put embarrassing questions to the relevant minister at a session of Parliament. And many countries, especially on the Continent, have well-developed systems of administrative law that hedge bureaucratic power and protect individual citizens."

"Yes, but you don't recommend the French administrative system."

"No, I don't. Under any regime, bureaucrats have leeway to execute their own policies and modify, sometimes even sabotage, the policies of their supposed masters. And a constitutional order that respects private property inevitably privileges the more affluent. My point is that the American system is not the only or perhaps the best way to limit bureaucratic power."

"What about our authorizing some sort of legislative veto?" the chair asks.

"Well," Ferrer replies, "I'm not sure how a legislative veto would operate in a parliamentary system. I'd need to see a lot of evidence before I'd recommend it."

"Haven't most new democracies chosen presidential government?" Jacobsohn inquires.

"Yes. But it's not clear that presidentialism has been uniformly good. Alfred Stepan and Cindy Skach followed the fate of regimes in ninety-three countries that became independent between 1945 and 1979. Only fifteen of the ninety-three were continuously functioning as democracies during the period 1980–1989, and each of these fifteen had begun and remained under a parliamentary system. Not one presidential or hybrid regime survived as a democracy."[41]

"But," Jacobsohn interrupts, "most of Stepan and Skach's presidential governments are in Africa and Latin America. They also include as presidential such regimes as those of North Korea, Syria, and North and South Vietnam, none of whose rulers ever took democracy seriously."

Ferrer nods but says nothing.

41. "Presidentialism and Parliamentarianism," p. 124. Stepan and Skach also examined the fifty-three countries other than the industrial nations of the West that tried democracy for one or more years between 1973 and 1979. Of the twenty-five that adopted presidential government, only five remained democratic for ten or more consecutive years. Seventeen of the twenty-eight that chose parliamentarianism reached that age. We encounter methodological difficulties similar to those met in discussions of democracy and peace: the relevant studies do not distinguish between representative democracy and constitutional democracy.

"Let's look at the fifteen 'successful' democracies," Jacobsohn continues. "We get that number by counting as individual nations tiny former British colonies in the Caribbean like Barbados, the Bahamas, Dominica, Jamaica, Trinidad, St. Lucia, and St. Vincent, which together have fewer people than Madrid. Then we add the Solomon Islands, with a large scattering of land but only about 150,000 inhabitants; four former British and Australian protectorates: Nauru, with about 5,000 people and less than ten square miles of dry land; Papua New Guinea, which has lots more territory and people but is still primitive and sparsely inhabited with a population density of about twenty-five people per square mile; Kiribati, a series of islands stretching across a vast area of the South Pacific but including fewer than 90,000 people; and then Tuvalu, a 'country' of 9.4 square miles with a population of 10,000. We also include Fiji, which in 2000 had a coup that overthrew that supposedly successful government. Then we graduate to other former parts of the British Empire: Botswana, among the smaller African states, with a population of only a million and a half; Israel, which had been part of the Mandate of Palestine; and finally India, the only large nation in the fifteen. What we have are shards of the British Empire. The message says little about parliamentarianism but a lot about British influence. Myron Weiner claimed that 'tutelary democracy under British colonialism appears to be a significant determinant of democracy in the Third World.'[42] You seem to support his hypothesis. Maybe we should ask the United Kingdom to annex us for a generation and then free us."

Ferrer smiles. "I doubt if the British would be interested. They've been privatizing their empire for a half-century and will have the job pretty well done whenever they can muster the courage to get out of Ireland and Gibraltar."

"That doesn't answer my question."

"It doesn't. Yes, British influence has been important, but their tutelage has often failed. Some former British holdings that adopted presidentialism had short life spans as democracies: Iraq, for instance. And H. W. O. Okoth-Ogendo points out that the English made few efforts in Africa to help their colonials learn about democratic rule.[43] Something else must also be going on."

"Usually there is. But let's accept Okoth-Ogendo's analysis. Only one of the fifteen 'successful' examples is African. The other fourteen are in Asia, the Caribbean, or Oceania, where the British or Australians did seriously try

42. "Empirical Democratic Theory," in Myron Weiner and Ergun Özbudun, eds., *Competitive Elections in Developing Countries* (Durham, NC: Duke University Press, 1987), p. 19.

43. H. W. O. Okoth-Ogendo, "Constitutions without Constitutionalism: Reflections on an African Political Paradox," in Douglas Greenberg, Stanley N. Katz, Melanie Beth Oliviero, and Steven C. Wheatley, eds., *Constitutionalism and Democracy: Transformations in the Contemporary World* (New York: Oxford University Press, 1993).

to educate locals. We're still left with political tutelage rather than parliamentarianism as the critical variable."

Ferrer hesitates then says, "I'm not sure."

"Well, the evidence is strong. There's also the matter of political culture. Do you really think the Latin American military would not have seized power from parliamentary governments? Hasn't the problem there been culture rather than institutional arrangements? Forgive me for seeming rude, but how many countries with a Spanish heritage—other than Spain itself, and you for only about thirty years—have been stable democracies, let alone stable *constitutional* democracies?"

"Chile, Costa Rica, Uruguay, and Venezuela have decent records, certainly as compared with the rest of Latin America."[44]

"Yes, and all four have had presidential systems," Jacobsohn says.

"I concede your point; but remember my contention was that at this time in your political history, parliamentarianism with PR would give you a better chance of maintaining constitutional democracy than would presidentialism, with or without PR. I did not—and do not—claim that parliamentarianism is an ideal form of government for all people at all times."

"What's your evidence? P. D. James, herself a governmental functionary for many years, is far less sanguine than you. She speaks of the British regime as requiring ministers to run departments, fulfill parliamentary responsibilities, and spend weekends listening to constituents. This system, she says, 'might have been designed to ensure that major decisions were made by men and women tired to the point of exhaustion. It certainly ensured that they were heavily dependent on their permanent officials.'[45] We don't want exhausted ministers, and we don't have a corps of competent bureaucrats skilled in or committed to any version of free government, as you yourself have noted."

"Novelists are not to be taken seriously," Ferrer replies. Before she can respond further, however, other members of the caucus begin answering Jacobsohn's arguments. The ensuing conversation indicates that although all the speakers agree they should not establish a dual executive, they are divided between a presidential and a parliamentary system.

"If you'll forgive another intervention from the chair," Martin says, "our recent history of dictatorship makes a presidential system seem too risky, and because that sentiment is likely to be widely shared in the larger population, it would generate unease for the system before it even began."

"But what about Fiji and its coup in 2000?" Strega asks.

"Professor Jacobsohn disposed of the usefulness of examples from Ocea-

---

44. See Scott Mainwaring, "Presidentialism in Latin America," 25 *Lat. Am. Res. Rev.* 157 (1990); reprinted in an abridged version in Arend Lijphart, ed., *Parliamentary versus Presidential Government* (New York: Oxford University Press, 1992).

45. *A Taste for Death* (New York: Alfred A. Knopf, 1986), pp. 19–20.

nia when she cross-examined Professor Ferrer," the chair responds. "Look, we're closely divided between representative and constitutional democracy. I suggest we accommodate both sides here by opting for a British-style parliament, topped by judicial review. The Australians, Canadians, Indians, Irish, Japanese, and Norwegians—perhaps others as well—have done this."

"That seems to me like a fair compromise," Minxin Wei says.

"I favor a compromise, but only when there are very strong reasons on both sides," Jacobsohn replies. "And I have heard no compelling argument for parliamentarianism."

"True, but then I have heard no compelling argument for presidentialism either," Pastor Glückmann says. "And that double absence, it seems to me, is itself a compelling reason for compromise. I move that we adopt a parliamentary system."

"Second," someone shouts.

"Exactly what kind of parliamentary system?" Jacobsohn asks.

"Let us proceed step by step," the chair says. "First the genus, then the species. Our debate has been long and thorough; let us vote." The tabulation shows fourteen for a parliamentary system and nine for a presidential, with Minister Strega voting "present."

After this decision, the chair notes that still open is the question of which version of parliamentarianism the caucus wants. "I think this issue is integrally connected to the kind of electoral system we want. Let us take up that issue next."

Mufti Ajami, with Zingaro seconding, immediately proposes a system of PR and multimember districts.

"Our minorities need to know that their rights will be protected within Parliament," Pyknites immediately attacks. "I want to accommodate minorities, but this proposal will produce governmental paralysis. It invites an Italianate system of unstable coalitions run by 'a loose assortment of parties which squabble about every decision and fight for every minor appointment.' Any proposal for public policy will become 'the disputed rope in a tug of war.'[46] We will quickly go from democracy into anarchy, as Professor Hermans would have said. We should look to Westminster, not Rome."

Professor Jacobsohn joins Pyknites. Her principal concern is that PR and multimember districts would weaken the case for formal constitutionalist checks. Thus she, too, emphasizes the risk of ineffective government. "We know the obvious examples, and look at Israel today: fragile coalitions that the religious parties can tear apart on the slightest whim."

"Wait," Baca puts in. "PR provides stable government in Belgium, Germany, Ireland, and the Netherlands, right? The countries where PR has failed have had either no threshold or such low ones as to allow zillions of

---

46. "Italy: Same Old Place," *Economist*, Dec. 12, 1998, p. 53.

interest groups to have seats in Parliament. I would, you know, propose a friendly amendment: adding Professor Ferrer's two qualifications and requiring a positive vote of no confidence and a threshold of popular votes that a party receive to obtain seats in Parliament."

"I accept Ms Baca's amendment, peace be upon her," Ajami says.

"We need," Pyknites argues, "an efficient and democratic system. Any decent parliamentary system encourages bargaining in the production of policy, but PR gives a veto to many groups who believe—often wrongly—that a given policy would adversely protect their narrow, parochial interests. The 'common good' would be lost. Our system will resemble Michel Debré's description of France's Fourth Republic: 'a coalition of party interests which sets up camp in the state and shares its spoils.' Our economic situation demands a regime that can enact effective public policies; our political situation demands a government that can act decisively to further economic development and social cohesion."[47]

"Then why don't you support my proposal for guided capitalism?" Strega asks.

"Because it threatens liberty," Pyknites replies. "And as long as I have the floor, let me offer another objection to PR for our political system. It invites ethnic parties, and it invites parties grounded on narrow economic interests. We need parties that cut across these lines, that, as Professor Jacobsohn said, unify rather than divide us. If we had ethnically based parties, we wouldn't need elections; we could take a census every five years and divide parliamentary seats that way. And insofar as parties were ethnically based, their leaders would have no incentive to work for national unity. Their jobs would depend on highlighting the differences between 'them' and 'us'—hardly what this country needs."

"I would ask," Gregorian says, "Professor Deukalion's opinion."

"Again, I'm not sure my opinion is worth much. I've lived in Italy and the United States, one with PR and one without. Surely neither is especially well governed, though Italy is less so. I suspect that for the economic policies you need, a winner-take-all arrangement would be more efficient; but over the long haul, PR would probably better protect the civil rights of minorities and ensure their political support, but only in a negative way. That is, with PR, government would be less likely to oppress than it would under a winner-take-all system. On the other hand, it would be extremely difficult to get positive governmental action to protect the rights of those whom powerful segments of society might be oppressing. Although I agree that it is better that threats to minority rights not survive the legislative process, I would prefer to rely on other, constitutionalist checks so as to leave room for posi-

47. "Constitution of 1958," p. 15. Debré continues: "Under this system, the executive, legislative, and administrative power is shared by the leadership of the parties, no one of which can ever obtain a majority and consequently ever feels responsible for the general interest."

tive governmental action to protect civil liberties. I am also impressed by Mr. Pyknites's last argument. PR can protect, but it often does so by dividing."[48]

"Spoken like a parochial American," Strega mutters. "PR is strange to you, therefore it is bad."

"PR is not strange to me, Ms Minister," Deukalion says tartly. "You may not know it, but up until a few decades ago PR was quite commonly used in American politics at the local level. And my reservations come from Mr. Pyknites's cogent arguments."

"We have a motion, duly seconded, before us," the chair puts in. "Further discussion? Very well, let us vote. The tally is sixteen for the amended motion, seven opposed. Ms Strega is 'present.'"

"Mr. Chairman," Wei interrupts, "did we settle on the kind of prime minister we'll have? I mean 'first among equals' or whatever, according to Sartori's categories?"

"To the extent we can prudently go, yes," Colonel Martin replies. "PR will limit the power of the head of government, but setting a floor for seats in Parliament limits the number of parties, and requiring Parliament to choose a new prime minister rather than merely dismissing the incumbent strengthens the PM, as will allowing him or her to choose cabinet members from outside of Parliament. Beyond this, it will be up to individual PMs to make what they can of the office."

At that point, Jacobsohn moves that the caucus ban legislators' holding cabinet posts. "I have three principal reasons. It will (1) heighten legislative and executive frictions and operate as a constitutionalist check, (2) bring to the cabinet people who are skilled in the work of their ministries, not only giving the government more control over bureaucrats but also sharpening public policy, and (3) if, when government changes, former ministers stand for election and win, bring to Parliament legislators who are more informed about how to execute as well as design public policy."

Pyknites shakes his head. "Alas, I find my erstwhile ally's reasoning confusing if not confused. She claims that this provision—unique, as far as I know, to France—will simultaneously limit government and make it more efficient. One or the other, please."

"But aren't those our objectives?" Jacobsohn asks. "Don't we want government that is both efficient and limited?"

"Yes," Pyknites admits, "but your amendment moves us toward neither objective."

"My concern is different," Gregorian says. "We want Parliament to become, as the American founder Charles Pinckney said, 'a nursery of States-

48. See Donald L. Horowitz's arguments: "Constitutional Design: An Oxymoron?" in Ian Shapiro and Stephen Macedo, eds., *Designing Democratic Institutions,* Nomos 42 (New York: New York University Press, 2000).

men.'[49] Would many ambitious and talented men and women stand for Parliament if they had to resign their office to join the cabinet?"

"After leaving the government they could stand for Parliament again," Jacobsohn answers.

"Perhaps, but if their successors were from their own party, they might claim squatter's rights. The loss of good people could be severe. And taking ministers out of Parliament would leave to nonexperts the task of defending the ministries' policy proposals."

"Well," Jacobsohn says, "the French experience with ministers' returning to Parliament is encouraging. They have often been able to do so. As for your second point, by following the French practice of allowing ministers to speak in Parliament and answer questions, we'd eliminate the problem of nonexpertise."[50]

"Where would ministers who are not legislators come from?" Kirca asks. "Will they be bureaucrats? And if so, can they return to the civil service when government changes?"

"I don't know who they'd be," Jacobsohn answers. "The need for parliamentary support would mean that most ministers would be chosen from among MPs. Others might well be civil servants, with future careers subject to general laws. In France, they can return to the civil service. In Italy, judges and procurators—magistrates—sometimes serve in the ministries, and I vaguely recall that one or two have been in the cabinet; they can return to the bench. As for your second question, a noted attorney or a *retired* judge might become head of the ministry of justice or a professional diplomat head the ministry for foreign affairs. The cabinet might, God help us, even include a professor or two."

"God help us, indeed," Strega mutters.

"I would join your prayer," Ferrer puts in, "but Romano Prodi, certainly among the best prime ministers Italy has had, went into politics directly from the University of Bologna to the cabinet."

"Could a parliamentary majority or coalition lose its control if some of its members had to resign to join the government?"

"Yes," Jacobsohn concedes, "but the prime minister would keep that possibility in mind in choosing his cabinet. Requiring legislators to resign and allowing the prime minister to reach outside of Parliament for his cabinet complement each other."

"I am torn," Zingaro says. "My people are distrusted, even despised. We need constitutionalist checks to protect us against government; but we may also need government to protect us against fellow citizens. My schizo-

49. Madison's notes for Aug. 14, 1787, in Max Farrand, ed., *The Records of the Federal Convention of 1787* (New Haven, CT: Yale University Press, 1966), 2:283.

50. See the discussion in Rohr, *Founding Republics,* p. 111.

phrenia makes me support an Italianate solution: allow the prime minister to pick cabinet members from outside of Parliament, but require that Parliament approve the cabinet."

Further debate shows that the caucus is divided much as is Zingaro. By a close vote, Jacobsohn's proposal loses; but the caucus adopts a substitute motion to permit the prime minister to select cabinet members who are not serving in Parliament and allow any minister to speak and answer questions in Parliament.

On the next item on the agenda, most of the founders agree that if a prime minister is to be chief of the government, they need a head of state, what Walter Bagehot would term the "dignified" part of government to complement the "efficient" prime minister, cabinet, and parliament.[51] This office, the caucus concludes, should be largely ceremonial and its powers ministerial. At the insistence of Pyknites, the founders table a proposal, imitating Article 26 of the Irish constitutional text, to give the president discretionary authority to refer a bill he or she believes unconstitutional to the constitutional court for an opinion on its validity. On the other hand, the caucus approves a motion to incorporate a version of Article 74 of the Italian constitutional text, which gives the president a suspensory veto: he or she can return a bill to Parliament, explaining his or her objections. If Parliament repasses it, he or she must promulgate it as law.[52]

At this point, the chair again intervenes: "It is now seven p.m., and we are all tired after a remarkable day's work. Rather than proceeding after dinner, let us recess until tomorrow at 0900. Hearing no objection, it is so ordered." The gavel goes down.

"Today's initial item of business is the makeup of the legislature," the chair announces to begin the next morning's session.

"We need a two-house parliament," Professor Jacobsohn cuts in. "Many unitary constitutional democracies—France, Ireland, Italy, Japan, Spain, and the United Kingdom, for example—have adopted bicameralism. And . . ."

Pyknites interrupts the interruption: "In the eighteenth century, the Abbé Siéyès argued against a bicameral legislature: 'If the two assemblies agree the second chamber is unnecessary; if they disagree it is obnoxious.'[53]

---

51. Walter Bagehot, *The English Constitution*, 2nd ed. (Garden City, NY: Doubleday, 1872), p. 63.

52. Article 87 of the Italian constitutional document provides that the president shall promulgate duly enacted laws. The argument has been made, however, that by forbidding the president to commit "any affront to the Constitution," Article 90 authorizes, if not requires, him to refuse to promulgate a law he deems unconstitutional. The words of Article 74 regarding a law Parliament has passed after the president has resubmitted it with his objections, "it must be [then] promulgated," would seem to offer both a course of presidential action and a limitation on presidential authority to interpret the constitution.

53. Quoted in Herman Finer, *The Theory and Practice of Modern Government*, rev. ed. (New York: Holt, 1949), p. 403.

That's plain common sense. Moreover, we've been stressing simplicity in constitutional design: one is simpler than two."

"Your citation of Siéyès is apt," Jacobsohn continues. "Like you, he wanted an all-powerful, unicameral legislature to represent the general will; the result for us might well be another totalitarian regime. We would have what Benjamin Franklin said the British Parliament aspired to: 'omnipotence without omniscience.'[54] Furthermore, we should not carry simplicity too far, otherwise we would not try to establish a constitutional democracy at all. It's a very complex political system."

"Indeed," Pyknites notes, "and that means the case for an additionally complicating element such as bicameralism must be strong, very strong."

"Let me make a case." Jacobsohn says. "A half-century ago, the eminent political scientist Herman Finer said that legislatures are bicameral for two reasons: 'as part of federalism, and as the result of a desire to check the popular principle in the constitution.'[55] We can focus on the second reason and add a third, which Finer classified as a motive: to imbue the legislative process with greater deliberation than unicameralism allows.[56] When we opted for a parliamentary rather than a presidential system, we eliminated a classic constitutionalist check, an independent executive. And nothing in recent memory makes it likely that our people can expect judges to protect them from tyranny. Like most Civil Law nations, we have not regarded the judiciary as a coequal branch of government.[57] Lacking popular esteem, judges will inevitably lose in a two-sided struggle against politicians who claim to speak with the voice of the people. One of the great protectors of American constitutionalism has been legislators' realization that weakening judicial power might benefit the president more than Congress. One long-dead political scientist claimed that this understanding was critical in the Senate's rejection of Franklin Roosevelt's Court-packing plan.[58] Without an independent president, our system will badly need intralegislative checks."

"The American Congress is also bicameral," Pyknites notes.

"Yes," Jacobsohn says, "but senators and representatives compete, as legislators, against the executive for power. Without the incentive to join together against a common rival, two houses will compete with each other to be the true legislative voice."

"Perhaps," Pyknites responds. "But members of a unicameral parliament

54. Quoted in Alpheus Thomas Mason, *Free Government in the Making*, 3rd ed. (New York: Oxford University Press, 1965), p. 91.

55. Finer, *The Theory and Practice of Modern Government*, p. 399.

56. Ibid., pp. 399–400.

57. Doris Marie Provine, "Courts in the Political Process in France," in Herbert Jacob et al., eds., *Courts, Law, and Politics in Comparative Perspective* (New Haven, CT: Yale University Press, 1996), p. 177.

58. See Walter F. Murphy, *Congress and the Court* (Chicago: University of Chicago Press, 1962), esp. ch. 11.

must answer directly to the voters and cannot push responsibility off on an-other institution. Given your love of Madison, you'll recall his claim in *The Federalist* No. 51 that 'the primary control on the government' is 'a dependence on the people.' And with a prime minister subject to Parliament, the bureaucracy will constitute an independent base of power. We've heard Minister Pilsudski's concerns about bureaucrats. Rational legislators will see judges as protecting their constituents—and therefore themselves—against such people. Thus, British mythology notwithstanding, power struggles will never be two sided. Bureaucrats will always be contestants, watching jousts between legislators and judges with all the dispassion of hungry jackals circling a pair of battling lions. Whoever wins, they will feed off the carcass of the loser. Rational legislators will beware of 'winning' too much when they attack judges."

"I agree that party leaders should see judges as potential allies as well as potential competitors," Jacobson replies. "The 'outs' should see judges as brakes on the 'ins,' and the 'ins' should realize that they themselves may need judges to protect them when they are the 'outs.' But people in or out of power seldom make choices that would be rational in the long run when passions scream for short-run gains. Constitutionalism's basic function is to reinforce reason against passion; our basic function is to create institutions to facilitate that task. We need more than a single thin strand in our network of checks."

"If," Pyknites persists, "we add bicameralism to PR's proliferation of political parties, we invite stalemate precisely when we need energetic government. But if we construct open political processes and a unicameral parliament, and forbid judicial review or at least limit it to keeping those processes open, we allow governance that's efficient, responsive to the people, and apt to protect individual rights. We keep talking about government's threatening civil rights, but, as Mr. Zingaro has pointed out, minorities sometimes need positive governmental action to protect their rights. Look at the American experience. Where would women, blacks, and ethnic minorities be without civil rights legislation?"

"We've had too much experience with rulers claiming to speak for the people to trust unfettered democracy," Jacobsohn answers. "The temptation for leaders to identify their own interests with the people's is too strong. We need competitors for the role of *vox populi* or at least for *vox republicae.* I'll quote Madison back at you. In the same sentence about dependence on the people, he added that 'experience has taught mankind the necessity of auxiliary precautions.' His idea of pitting power against power is wise. We opted for that strategy when we chose constitutional over representative democracy.

"Before I finish," she continues, "let me stress the importance of deliberation and debate in the legislative processes. A parliament must be of a 'convenient' size lest it become a cabal, and a nation as diverse as ours needs a parliament with a large enough membership to represent a variety of groups, certainly several hundred representatives. That means there will be little time for full discussion on most issues. To remedy that flaw, we can create an upper house with membership of fifty or so; then there can be fuller debate and more mature reflection."

"A third house would provide greater opportunity," Pyknites says, "and a fourth still greater."

The debate continues until the break for lunch. Much of the discussion indicates that the choice for constitutional over representative democracy was closer in some founders' minds than they themselves had realized. Still, a majority of the caucus holds to the earlier decision. Shortly before one p.m, the chair proposes that after lunch and double espressos, the caucus proceed as if it approved a bicameral legislature, decide on the arrangement of powers between the two and the method of choosing members of the upper house, then, with a clearer idea of likely institutional relations, reconsider the choice between uni- and bicameralism. The members agree to address those issues.

That later discussion indicates that, led by Professor Jacobsohn, the founders most in favor of constitutionalism and most wary of democracy support an institution along the lines of the American Senate: a branch equal in power to the lower house and whose members are elected from larger electoral districts that vary in population and serve much longer terms than MPs. Led by Pyknites, the representative democrats propose an elected version of the British House of Lords, Canadian Senate, or Irish Seanad, institutions that allow additional deliberation but can only delay, not defeat, legislation.

After ninety minutes of sharp dispute, Minxin Wei suggests a version of the Japanese House of Councillors, some of whose members are elected from local districts and some from the nation considered as a single district. Although councillors come far closer to the democratic norm of equal representation than do American senators, the power relationship is decidedly tilted toward the lower house. In keeping with Japanese political style, most disputes are resolved by negotiation; but when serious differences arise, the lower house may override the councillors' objections by either a majority or a two-thirds vote, depending on the kind of issue involved.

Pilsudski suggests France's Senate as an alternative model. Its members, about half as numerous as those in the lower house, are elected by local officials for a term of nine years and thus form a potential check on popular democracy. Still, their power depends on the government. If the houses disagree and the government does not intervene, the two are equal: differences must be settled in a joint committee and agreed to by both houses. The government, however, may opt to allow the lower house to pass the bill without further senatorial involvement.

Eventually, the caucus narrowly agrees on a House of Councillors, which could brake legislation yet could not, over the long term, prevent the lower house from governing. Thus, the founders adopt a proviso, subject to later amendment regarding emergencies, that to become law a bill must be approved by both houses. In case of disagreement, each house should appoint half the members of a conference committee, whose work must be submitted to each house. If the committee cannot agree or either house rejects the bill, the lower house could repass the measure and restart the conference process. If disagreement persists, the two houses would meet in joint session and debate under the rules of the lower house. Each member would have a one vote.

The caucus sets the number of councillors at fifty, serving for six-year terms, with a third of the members to be elected every two years.[59] Councillors would be chosen by direct popular election under a variation of PR: the nation would form a single district, but with "set-asides" so that candidates running as Gypsies (or whose parties designate them) will obtain at least two seats and, similarly, candidates running as Jews or Muslims (or whose parties so designate them) at least five seats each, with these numbers to be adjusted after each decennial census. Then the caucus adopts an additional proviso: no matter what the census shows, the number of "set-asides" for each of these groups will never be fewer than two.

Pyknites and his allies secure agreement that the prime minister would be responsible only to the lower house. Councillors would have no formal part in his selection or removal.

"Now that we have sketched the nature and composition of the upper house," the chair says, "we need to reexamine our decision for bicameralism. But first, we should make certain we agree on some aspects of the lower house. Given a parliamentary system, we need only set a maximum term, one that is long enough to further governmental stability but not so long as to allow representatives' mandate from the people to die of old age."

Understanding that no figure will meet both conditions simultaneously, the caucus quickly settles on a five-year maximum as reasonable. Discussion then turns to questions of specific legislative issues. Still led by Jacobsohn, the more committed constitutional democrats secure majority agreement that bills, except the budget, could be introduced in either house. Pyknites's dissent is eloquent. There is also considerable dispute about how to phrase the delegation of legislative powers. Pyknites proposes a single, declarative sentence along the lines of the American constitutional text: "All legislative power shall be vested in Parliament, to consist of two houses." Minister Pilsudski wants to add a nonexhaustive list of clarifying examples.

Professor Jacobsohn speaks again. "Our people are not accustomed to a

59. To eliminate the possibility of fractional seats, the caucus decides that at the councillors' first session two additional members, selected by lot, will also serve the full six-year term.

political system in which powers are shared; therefore, there is much to be said for the educational effects a list of examples might produce. But Canada's history persuades me that such a litany, even coupled with a clear statement that its purpose is to illustrate rather than restrict, is dangerous. Section 91 of the British North America Act of 1867, which was Canada's basic constitutional document until 1982, read:

> It shall be lawful for . . . the Senate, and the House of Commons, to make Laws for the Peace, Order, and good Government of Canada, in relation to all Matters not coming within the Classes of Subjects by this Act assigned exclusively to the Legislatures of the Provinces; and for greater Certainty, but not so as to restrict the Generality of the foregoing Terms of this Section . . . [a string of examples followed].

The British Privy Council, which for many decades functioned as Canada's *supreme* Supreme Court, construed these examples not as illustrating but as limiting Parliament's authority.[60] Canada's situation was complicated by federalism and the British government's compulsion to protect Quebec against the English-speaking majority. The fate of that constitutional language shouts a warning."

"Yes," Pyknites agrees, "a warning against judicial review."

"I would remind my colleagues," the chair intervenes, "that Mr. Pyknites himself properly admonished us this morning, when we were discussing the powers of the president, that we had not yet decided to establish judicial review. Thus his remark is out of order. We have two duly seconded motions before us regarding wording. Let us vote, remembering our earlier agreement that we can later modify specific language." A majority of members agree on Pyknites's simpler version.

"There is another serious set of legislative matters we must address," Baca says. "Alexander Hamilton charged that elected representatives 'sometimes fancy that they are the people themselves.' This was, you know, not a unique observation. 'The people can never wilfully betray their own interests; but they may be possibly be betrayed by the representatives of the people,' James Madison wrote. He also said that 'against the enterprising ambition' of the legislature 'the people ought to indulge all their jealousy and exhaust all their precautions.'[61] The initiative, referendum, and recall provide remedies. A significant minority of the electorate should have authority to propose legislation and even constitutional amendments. If that minority obtains the required number of signatures, their proposal should go on the ballot at the next election and be voted up or down by the people. So I pro-

---

60. Ch. 8 of Murphy and Tanenhaus, *Comparative Constitutional Law*, reprints some of the more important of these rulings. See, generally, G. P. Browne, *The Judicial Committee and the British North America Act* (Toronto: University of Toronto Press, 1967).

61. *The Federalist*, Nos. 63 and 48.

pose that Parliament can submit proposals to the people for their approval—as I believe all proposed constitutional amendments should be submitted. And, of course, the people should have the right to recall at any time their supposed representatives."

"No!" Pyknites shouts. "I have not argued for direct democracy but for *representative* democracy. I'll agree that constitutional amendments be submitted to referenda, because they change the basic rules of politics. But most people are not apt to spend the time to master the complexities of most public policies. Even many learned lawyers have difficulty understanding regulatory codes, and many legislators are often unsure of the reach of the rules they have enacted. And the threat of short-circuiting legislators' or executives' careers if they make immediately unpopular decisions will distract their attention from serious problems and probably warp their judgment."

"You're, like, making my case," Baca says. "If neither legislators nor lawyers can understand the law, we need the common sense of common men and women in law making."

"We have another of those occasions," Jacobsohn says, "when I am in total agreement with Mr. Pyknites because he, for once, is not only right but also in agreement with Madison, who argued vehemently for a *representative* republic, in which elected representatives would temper and refine public opinion.[62] Hamilton concurred. He attacked pure democracy—and Ms Baca is advocating a form of pure democracy—as 'the deceitful dream of a golden age.' He added, 'The ancient democracies . . . never possessed one feature of good government. Their very character was tyranny; their figure deformity.'[63] Experience in the United States, especially in California, shows how right Hamilton and Madison were. Insofar as your proposal pertains to ordinary legislation, it will produce much foolishness. The recall would be especially dangerous in a parliamentary system."

"We must," the chair rules, "focus on Ms Baca's proposal. Do I hear a second? I do. Let us hear the yeas and nays . . . Clearly the nays have it. Representative, not direct, democracy.

"Now," Martin continues, "let me summarize our decisions so far. We have decided to try to construct a constitutional democracy and to have a constitutional text that we ourselves shall draft and submit for ratification by the entire electorate. That text will contain a preamble stating our goals and aspirations. We have decided against federalism and presidentialism, opting instead for a bicameral parliamentary government with a requirement for a constructive vote of no confidence in the lower house. We have added an unusual feature: the prime minister will be able to reach outside of Parlia-

62. Esp. *The Federalist*, No. 10.
63. *The Federalist*, No. 6, and his speech to New York's ratifying convention, June 21, 1788, as, perhaps correctly, reprinted in Jonathan Elliot, ed., *The Debates in the Several State Conventions on the Adoption of the Federal Constitution*, 2nd ed. (Washington, DC: n.p., 1836), 2:250.

ment, subject to its consent, to recruit ministers. The president will be chief of state, not head of the government, but he or she will have authority to ask Parliament to reconsider legislation. We have also chosen a system of proportional representation, with Parliament authorized to require by law that, before being entitled to any legislative seats, a party receive a minimum percentage of popular votes.

"Next, we must move to the structure of the legal and judicial system. And those issues, difficult enough on their own terms, raise even more difficult questions of the scope of judicial power, most especially—and most controversially—the matter of judicial review. Let us adjourn for twenty-four hours to reflect both on our progress—how the text as so far outlined will structure a political system—and on how our ideas about other aspects of the constitutional order will fit in with what we have done."

CHAPTER SEVEN

Drafting 2
The Judiciary

Courts stand as havens against any winds that blow.   HUGO L. BLACK

Courts love liberty most when it is under pressure least.   JOHN P. FRANK

At 0859 the chair opens the caucus. "Today, we address the problems of creating a judicial system. Our first speaker is Professor Takeo Bengoshi of the Law Faculty at Tokyo University. A graduate of that university, he also attended the Legal Training and Research Institute and later earned a Ph.D. in jurisprudence from the University of California at Berkeley."

A trim, short, man in his early forties, Bengoshi moves to the podium. He is dressed in gray slacks, an expensive red cardigan, and an open-necked white shirt. A gleam of sunlight reflects off his spit-shined black loafers. He smiles but does not bow to the audience.

Organizing the Judiciary

One of the maxims of both constitutional and representative democracy is that the judiciary must be impartial between litigants and therefore protected against interference from other governmental officials as well as from private citizens. Such affirmations may sound trite, but they are basic to a civil society. Further, the ways in which the legal system is organized and the judiciary is staffed are essential to an effective legal system. Most developed nations have adopted one of two systems, the Civil Law or the common law,[1] although some Muslim countries, developing nations still, live under modified versions of the Shari'a—a gentle reminder that you and your legislators should always be sensitive to the interests of your Muslim minority.

Because you live under the Civil Law, you know that "the sovereign" meticulously arranges substantive and procedural rules into comprehen-

---

1. Scandinavian countries have their own systems, related to but different from the Civil Law of the rest of Europe, and many Orthodox Jews in Israel would liken to (re?)instate Halakhah, Jewish religious law.

241

sive, logically ordered sets of codes, each a coherent, seamless whole.[2] All people interested in legal careers study law pretty much as an "undergraduate major," attending lectures similar to what American students get in courses in political science, though with much heavier emphasis on normative theory than on the physiology of real-world politics. The number of students may be huge; the University of Naples has more than twenty thousand young men and women enrolled in its law faculty, which boasts only a couple of dozen professors. Graduation is conditioned on passing comprehensive examinations, not on successfully completing individual courses as in the United States.

Few of these young men and women intend to become practicing attorneys, notaries, judges, or procurators. To pursue any of those careers, an applicant must pass additional written and oral examinations and then begin professional training. Germany tries to provide similar preparation for all branches of the legal profession, while France and Italy separate the schooling of magistrates from those who wish to go into private practice. The minimum period of training, including time spent at a university, ranges from five to six years. The minimum, however, may fall far short of the real. It is not uncommon for the actual period to consume ten years.

Whatever the variations on Civil Law, judicial aspirants seek admission to a distinct profession and do so soon after completing their studies in the law faculty. Thus they are usually in their twenties. In Italy, candidates who pass state examinations immediately enter the judicial service as *uditori* (auditors). In France, Germany, and Japan, passing the examinations only qualifies candidates to participate in a training program and, after, to take a second set of exams. The Italian program consists of fifteen months of on-the-job training; the first ten involve interning in various courts and prosecutorial offices, and the last five more specialized training in a judicial or prosecutorial office. France requires twenty-seven months of attendance at the École Nationale de la Magistrature as well as practical work with judges and procurators. Germany provides thirty months of on-the-job training supplemented by seminars,[3] and Japan

2. This is not, however, the only model of the Civil Law. See Robert Paschal, "A Report on the French Civil Code Revision Project," jointly published in 11 *La. L. Rev.* 261 and 25 *Tul. L. Rev.* 205 (1951).

3. For a brief but excellent overview of continental legal education, see Anna Mestitz and Patrizia Pederzoli, "Training the Legal Professions in Italy, France, and Germany," in C. Neal Tate and Torbjörn Vallinder, eds., *The Global Expansion of Judicial Power* (New York: New York University Press, 1995); and Carlo Guarnieri, "Judicial Independence in Latin Countries of Western Europe," in Peter H. Russell and David M. O'Brien, eds., *Judicial Independence in the Age of Democracy: Critical Perspectives from around the World* (Charlottesville: University Press of Virginia, 2001). See also Giuseppe Di Federico, *La preparazione alle professioni legali nella Repubblica Federale Tedesca e in Francia* (Rome: Ministry of Justice, 1987); Erhard Blankenburg, "Changes in Political

requires two years' study at the Legal Training and Research Institute. Those who enter the judiciary begin as junior judges on collegial courts and work their way through what is, in effect, a civil service. Promotion is supposedly based solely on merit, as determined by a review panel's evaluations of junior judges' writings and "fitness reports" submitted by senior judges. Retirement is mandatory, varying between the age of sixty-five and seventy-two.

Professors are the heroes of the Civil Law, while judges tend to be anonymous worker bees. The president of the highest court can go into a chic restaurant in the capital and not be recognized by the maitre d'. On collegial courts, opinions are unsigned and reported as unanimous. Under the Civil Law's culture, the sovereign legislator speaks, not the judge, and because the translation of that voice is the product of logical deduction, dissent could only encourage error or, worse, cast doubt on law's status as an exact science. Traditionally, what earlier judges said was supposedly of scant importance. Some Civil Law systems even forbade judges to cite precedents (though not legal scholars) to justify their decisions. In fact, of course, judges have long been quite aware of earlier interpretations. For example, long before programs like Lexis and West-Law were filling American jurists' computer screens, Italy had a central databank of summaries of the Court of Cassation's interpretations (*massime*) of the codes, furthering a version of stare decisis.[4] In more recent decades, especially because of the work of constitutional courts and the European Court of Justice, it is now common for Civil Law judges to cite previous decisions.[5] Still, the myth, though damaged by reality, persists: "The Law speaks, not the judge."

Under the common law, the organization and even the very concept of law are far less tidy. Alfred, Lord Tennyson called it a "wilderness of single instances." As Oliver Wendell Holmes said, "It is the merit of the common law that it decides the case first and the principle afterwards."[6] Legislatures enact statutes on an ad hoc basis. "Codes" tend to

---

Regimes and Continuity of the Rule of Law in Germany," and Doris Marie Provine, "Courts in the Political Process in France," in Herbert Jacob et al., eds., *Courts, Law, and Politics in Comparative Perspective* (New Haven, CT: Yale University Press, 1996), pp. 266–74 and 201–6; John Henry Merryman, "Legal Education There and Here: A Comparison," 27 *Stan. L. Rev* 859 (1975); and Anna Mestitz, "Education and Training of Magistrates and Lawyers in Italy," report to Ninth World Conference on Procedural Law, Lisbon, 1991. Guarnieri, Mestitz, and Pederzoli are all members of Di Federico's Center for the Study of the Ordinary Judiciary at the University of Bologna.

4. For a brief summary, see Costantino Ciampi, "A Comparative Analysis of the Different Electronic Systems for the Storage and Processing of Legal Information in Italy," in *Italian National Reports to the Ninth International Congress of Comparative Law, Teheran, 1974* (Milan: Giuffrè, 1974).

5. See esp. Alec Stone Sweet, *Governing with Judges: Constitutional Politics in Europe* (New York: Oxford University Press, 2000), p. 146.

6. "Codes and the Arrangement of the Law," in *The Collected Works of Justice Holmes: Complete*

be compilations that cluster statutes, often passed in different eras to cope with different facets of similar problems. These rough collections usually can be understood only through their annotations, that is, the interpretations judges have given them. Nevertheless, the common law echoes the myth that judges are merely mouths of the law. Jurists who repeat this fable usually do so out of fear of scandalizing the citizenry—or themselves. If, however, we generalize from public opinion polls in the United States, most ordinary citizens do not put much faith in denials that judges make both law and policy,[7] and surely few reflective judges or lawyers do. Nor have the human biases of this legal system long been a secret. John Locke described the law as the "Phansies and intricate contrivances of men, following contradictory and hidden interests put into words."[8]

The common law has no equivalent of the Civil Law's professional judges. Jurists go to the bench after careers as private practitioners, professors, prosecutors, or other governmental officers. Selection is by the executive and/or the legislature, or, as in most American states and some Swiss cantons, popular election. The partisanship of the process varies from country to country but is fraught with estimates—and misestimates —of candidates' attitudes toward public policies. Harold Laski's study of English judges showed that an overwhelming majority who served between 1832 and 1906 had been political activists (more than half had been MPs), and the lord chancellor's selections furthered his party's policy objectives.[9] Lord Halsbury, who served for two decades as lord chancel-

---

Public Writings and Selected Judicial Opinions of Oliver Wendell Holmes, ed. Sheldon M. Nowick (Chicago: University of Chicago Press, 1995), 1:212. (The article was originally published in 1870.)

7. See various articles reporting the results of surveys conducted by Walter F. Murphy and Joseph Tanenhaus, cited in their "Publicity, Public Opinion, and the Court," 84 *Nw'n L. Rev.* 983, esp. n17 (1990).

8. *Second Treatise on Government,* ch. 2. Although Jefferson was a lawyer, his hostility toward the common law, at least in the English version, is legendary. But even Madison was far from being an admirer. As he wrote in the Report to Virginia's House of Delegates for the Committee on the Alien and Sedition Acts:

> [T]he common law never was, nor by any fair construction ever can be, deemed a law for the American people as one community. . . . It is, indeed, distressing to reflect that it should ever have been made a question, whether the Constitution . . . could ever intend to introduce in the lump, in an indirect manner, and by a forced construction of a few phrases, the vast and multifarious jurisdiction involved in the common law . . . a law that would sap the foundations of the Constitution as a system of limited and specified powers. A severer reproach could not, in the opinion of the committee, be thrown on those who framed, or those who established it, than such a supposition would throw on them.

Much of this report is reprinted in Marvin Meyers, ed., *The Mind of the Framer: Sources of the Political Thought of James Madison* (Indianapolis: Bobbs-Merrill, 1973), pp. 299–349; the quoted passage is at p. 325.

9. *Studies in Law and Politics* (London: Allen and Unwin, 1932), p. 164.

lor, chose men "of little or no legal learning whose previous career in public life had been largely in the service of the Conservative Party" or else his own relatives.[10]

Later in the twentieth century, things changed somewhat. During the 1960s and early 1970s, Fred L. Morrison found, party membership had "no apparent effect on the selection" of British judges, and few had been political activists.[11] Still, "the most salient fact about the appointment of judges," J. A. G. Griffith noted, "is that it is wholly in the hands of politicians."[12] Griffin was an iconoclast, but his description was accurate. If partisan considerations declined in significance, sociopolitical concerns did not. Judges on important U.K. courts are apt to be upper- or upper-middle-class Oxbridge graduates and staunch supporters of the status quo.[13] Female judges are more numerous now than in the past, but they also fit this social mold.

Most American state judges are popularly elected, frequently running on party tickets and candidly campaigning about the kinds of decisions they will render if elected. Promises may even involve specific cases. In the midst of the struggle for civil rights, a judge in Alabama ran for reelection on a pledge to decide a case before him so as to drive the National Association for the Advancement of Colored People out of the state. And after his reelection he tried to do so.[14] This example may be extreme, but pledges to sentence drug dealers or child molesters to long prison terms, lavishly apply the death penalty, or follow some other decisional course are common.

Federal judges, of course, are appointed by the president with the advice and consent of the Senate. It is a given that the president will try to put ideological allies on the bench and that senators will make similar

10. R. F. V. Heuston, *The Lives of the Lord Chancellors, 1885–1940* (Oxford: Oxford University Press, 1964), p. 36; quoted in Herbert M. Kritzer, "Courts, Justice, and Politics in England," in Herbert Jacob et al., eds., *Courts, Law, and Politics in Comparative Perspective* (New Haven, CT: Yale University Press, 1996), pp. 91–92.
11. *Courts and the Political Process in England* (Los Angeles: Sage, 1973), p. 87 and ch. 3 generally.
12. *The Politics of the Judiciary,* 3rd ed. (London: Fontana, 1988), p. 17.
13. See Kritzer, "Courts, Justice, and Politics in England," and sources cited at pp. 91–92.
14. For details of the judge's behavior, see *Southern School News,* July 1958, p. 11. The state supreme court affirmed the judge. Eventually the case twice reached the U.S. Supreme Court, and both times the justices reversed. NAACP v. Alabama, 357 U.S. 449 (1958), and NAACP v. Patterson, 360 U.S. 240 (1959). Alabama's attack on the NAACP was part of a concerted segregationist effort to halt the march of black civil rights. See Walter F. Murphy, "The South Counterattacks: The Anti NAACP Laws," 12 *West. Pol. Q.* 371 (1959); and Robert H. Birkby and Walter F. Murphy, "Interest Group Conflict in the Judicial Arena," 42 *Tex. L. Rev.* 1018 (1964). I once asked Thurgood Marshall, who had been the NAACP's counsel in the Alabama case, why he had not requested the trial judge to recuse himself for prejudice. Marshall responded that he had suggested it to the judge, who angrily asked Marshall if he thought the court could not render a fair decision. The judge's demeanor, Marshall noted, was such that he believed he would have been held in contempt and jailed had he given a truthful reply.

efforts, treating federal judgeships within their own states, in Senator Everett Dirksen's words, as "grand political plums."[15]

In common law countries, technical craftsmanship is a significant, but seldom the controlling, factor in judicial selection. The wide discretion that judges have in interpreting common law rules, executive orders, statutes, treaties, and constitutional texts and subtexts is too wide and the effects of such interpretations on public policy too important for political actors to put opponents or even neutrals on the bench.

At the end of World War II, it seemed that stable constitutional democracy was a monopoly of cultures cohabiting with the common law. Democracy of several flavors had failed in Germany, Italy, Spain, Poland, Eastern Europe, and Latin America. A constitutionalist critic of the Civil Law might thus have plausibly argued that the Civil Law was a basic cause for these failures. Derived from Justinian's efforts to codify the law of imperial Rome, its modern reincarnation was due to Napoleon's efforts to bring order to his empire. However facilely proponents might transfer the system's concept of "sovereign legislator" from emperor to parliament, the image of an all-powerful ruler who wills law into existence grates against norms of limited government.[16]

Equally damaging, a constitutionalist critic might continue, is the

15. There is a vast literature on the selection of judges in the United States. For discussion and citations, see generally Walter F. Murphy, C. Herman Pritchett, Lee Epstein, and Jack Knight, eds., *Courts, Judges, and Politics: An Introduction to the Judicial Process,* 6th ed. (Boston: McGraw-Hill, 2005), ch. 4. The best works on the selection of federal judges for lower courts are Sheldon Goldman, *Picking Federal Judges* (New Haven, CT: Yale University Press, 1997), and Lee Epstein and Jeffrey Segal, *Advice and Consent: The Politics of Judicial Appointments* (New York: Oxford University Press, 2005).

16. Democratic theorists might look with less concern than would constitutionalists on the concept of the popularly elected parliament as sovereign legislator. Still, democratic theorists might worry that the notion of unity that inheres in the term *legislator* and the civil law's endemic drive for systemic unity and theoretical coherence might impede the necessary untidiness of bargaining and compromising in a pluralistic society. Here, such theorists might fear, the Civil Law would move judges to interpret codes and freestanding statutes as if they were the product of a single mind and thus overlook or even undo the myriad adjustments, not always logically symmetrical, that made governmental action possible. Insofar, however, as one can judge from decades of parliamentary politics in Italy and the Federal Republic of Germany, compromise and bargaining have abounded, even as judges continue to speak of "the legislator." See, for example, the use of that term by the Bundesverfassungsgericht: Joint Income Tax Case, 6 BVerfGE 55 (1957); Bavarian Party Case, 6 BVerfGE 84 (1957); Homosexuality Case, 6 BVerfGE 389 (1957); Party Contribution Tax Cases, 8 BVerfGE 51 (1958); Volkswagen Denationalization Case, 12 BVerfGE 354 (1961); Party Finance Cases, 20 BVerfGE 56 (1966); Privacy of Communications Case, 30 BVerfGE 1 (1970); and Abortion Reform Law Case, 39 BVerfGE 1 (1975). On occasion, the Federal Constitutional Court has also carried over this penchant for the singular in speaking of "the framer" of the Basic Law: Socialist Reich Party Case, 2 BVerfGE 1 (1952). These cases are translated and reprinted in abridged versions in Walter F. Murphy and Joseph Tanenhaus, eds., *Comparative Constitutional Law* (New York: St. Martin's, 1977); for other examples, see Donald P. Kommers, *The Constitutional Jurisprudence of the Federal Republic of Germany,* 2nd ed. (Durham, NC: Duke University Press, 1997).

Civil Law's hubris: tempted, as were Adam and Eve, by pride, it tries to fill every void the deity left, eliminate all chaos, impose perfect form, and bottle up the great wind. When the Civil Law's "obsession for formal rules and procedures"[17] escapes from the courtroom to wider political arenas, the system's supposed cardinal virtues become mortal sins. Orderliness, rationality, and comprehensiveness hone effective intellectual instruments to settle disputes between private citizens as well as matters of criminal law; but difficulties multiply when political leaders with those mental sets address such complex problems of constitutional physiology as the reach of legislative power, the ambit of rights to privacy and religious freedom, or interstitial compromises among competing economic groups. These sorts of issues are far less amenable to tautly principled solutions.

The mentality that the Civil Law fosters, this critic might argue, encourages impossible feats of political engineering, as evidenced in the minutely detailed constitutional documents of Civil Law nations. Political decisions have consequences that their makers cannot foretell; only in the most general and perhaps even aprincipled way can political leaders conquer unanticipated obstacles. The Civil Law's seducing leaders to attack the unknown with tightly reasoned deductions from formal rules is likely to proliferate chaos. In sum, the constitutionalist critic might charge, the Civil Law mentality invites rigidity and inspires principled but impractical policies.

Worse, this critic might add, the Civil Law's commitment to the legislators' will and consequent denigration of judicial authority leave judges no respectable room to maneuver when confronted by governmental oppression. Unable to reconcile defending individual rights with the Civil Law's crabbed conception of proper judicial roles, jurists are apt to pander to power. Many professional German judges prostituted their offices to Nazism.[18] And during the Occupation French judges offered similar services at discount prices.[19]

When Civil Law judges have demonstrated flexibility, they have often done so for self-advancement, rather than for the common weal. For

17. Allan Christelow, *Muslim Law Courts and the French Colonial State in North Africa* (Princeton, NJ: Princeton University Press, 1985), p. 38. Christelow was speaking of the French legal system, but his remarks might apply with equal accuracy to the Austrian, German, Italian, Spanish, and Swiss systems.

18. See esp. Ingo Müller, *Hitler's Justice: The Courts of the Third Reich*, trans. Deborah Lucas Schneider (Cambridge, MA: Harvard University Press, 1991); the German title of this book was *Furschtbare Juristen* (Dreadful Jurists). Donald P. Kommers, "National Socialism and the Rule of Law," 54 *Rev. of Pols.* 493 (1992), argues that Müller overstates the case against German judges, though Kommers concedes that numerous professional jurists obsequiously served the Nazis.

19. Eichard Weisberg, "Legal Rhetoric under Stress: The Example of Vichy," 12 *Cardo. L. Rev.* 1371 (1991).

instance, Italian magistrates have turned judicial independence to great private profit, interpreting statutes and the constitutional text to increase their own salaries, run for elective office, and serve in administrative agencies with the option of returning to the bench with full credit toward seniority and retirement. Even more than most Civil Law countries, Italian judges have substituted seniority for merit. Indeed, Giuseppe Di Federico asserts that seniority is "the *only* criterion" for promotion in Italy.[20] And to protect their reputations, some magistrates harass critics by trumping up criminal charges against them.[21]

In contrast, our critic might contend, the common law matured as an effort to curb the monarch's arbitrary power. The Civil Law looks first to sovereign prerogative, while the common law looks to individual freedom. Its centerpiece is habeas corpus, the great writ of liberty,[22] not the will of a sovereign. The common law avoids the Civil Law's ambition. Its methodology subtly teaches that it is wiser to live with some, rather than attempt to remove all, chaos, to skirt rather than fill in the abyss, to hunker down when the great wind blows rather than attempt to bottle it up. In short, the common law begins from an unspoken but powerful presumption that reason has only limited capacity to control passion. By preferring an inductive, case-by-case approach over deduction from gen-

20. "The Italian Judicial Profession and Its Bureaucratic Setting," 1976 *Juridical Rev.* 40, 54–55.

21. Di Federico and his students have been the most vocal critics of the magistrates' competence and integrity. For example, Giuseppe Di Federico, "The Crisis of the Justice System and the Referendum on the Judiciary," in R. Leonardi and P. Corbetta, eds., *Italian Politics: A Review* (London: Pinter, 1989), 3:25; "The Italian Judicial Profession and Its Bureaucratic Setting," 1976 *Juridical Rev.* 40; introduction to Francesca Zannotti, *Le attività extragiudiziarie dei magistrati ordinari* (Padova: Cedam, 1981); "Le qualificazioni professionali del corpo giudiziario," 1985 *Rivista Trimestrale di Scienza dell'Amministrazione* 21; "Costi e implicazioni istituzionali dei recenti provvedimenti giurisdizionali e legislativi in materia di retribuzioni e penzioni dei magistrati," 1985 *Rivista Trimestrale di Diritto Pubblico* 331; and his edited volume *Preparazione professionale degli avvocati e dei magistrati* (Padova: Cedam, 1987). Also Carlo Guarnieri, *L'indipendenza della magistratura* (Padova: Cedam, 1981), and *Pubblico ministero e sistema politico* (Padova: Cedam, 1984), esp. chs. 4–5; Francesca Zannotti, *Le attività extragiudiziarie dei magistrati ordinari* (Padova: Cedam, 1981), and "The Judicialization of Judicial Salary Policy in Italy and the United States," in C. Neal Tate and Torbjörn Vallinder, eds., *The Global Expansion of Judicial Power* (New York: New York University Press, 1995).

After years of threats failed to silence Di Federico, the magistrates began a series of prosecutions. After additional years of expensive and difficult litigation, appellate courts reversed the convictions. For charges against the Magistratura related less to competence than to integrity, see Stanton H. Burnett and Luca Mantovani, *The Italian Guillotine: Operation Clean Hands and the Overthrow of Italy's First Republic* (Lanham, MD: Rowman and Littlefield, 1998).

22. During the 1990s, the U.S. Supreme Court cast a shadow on the continued efficacy of the Great Writ in that country. In 1996, a Republican-controlled Congress passed the Anti-terrorism and Effective Death Penalty Act, which further restricted the once Great Writ. Despite promises to protect civil liberties, President William J. Clinton meekly signed the bill into law. Laurence H. Tribe summarizes the cases in *American Constitutional Law*, 3rd ed. (New York: Foundation, 2000), 1:501–18. See below, Chapter Fourteen, for various antiterrorist acts.

eral principles and by recruiting judges from the ranks of public officials and seasoned attorneys, it places heavier weight on practical experience than on logic as "the life of the law."[23]

In a common law system, the constitutionalist critic might assert, judicial statesmanship embodies a willingness to rise above principle. This choice of flexibility over consistency—a tolerance for incoherence— spills over into broader political arenas and encourages all public officials to work within the messiness of politics. The American version of common law, with judges acting as constitutional interpreters, heeds its own subliminal instructions by simultaneously lauding judges as creative statesmen and as dispassionate mouths of the law.

It is easy to fault this constitutionalist critic. Her simplistic view simultaneously vilifies the Civil Law and idealizes the common law, performing each task using marvelously selective evidence. The Civil Law is not so principled as she claims, nor the common law as free wheeling. More than fifty years ago, Robert A. Pascal argued that the French model of an all-inclusive code is not the only paradigm that Civil Law need, or even does, emulate.[24] And certainly no one familiar with the behavior of judges in post–World War II Italy, France, Germany, or, more recently, Spain would see them as automatons.

According to Morrison, who studied law at Oxford during the early 1960s, the segment of English legal education conducted at universities is both parochial and a parody of the Civil Law; the prevailing philosophy is positivist in the tradition of John Austin and Hans Kelsen.[25] "[I]t is simpler for an English lecturer to assure the student that there is a single right answer to a particular question. . . . That answer must be found by deductive reasoning, based upon a close reading of earlier cases, not by an inductive process, based upon additional factors." At the Inns of the

23. Oliver Wendell Holmes Jr., *The Common Law* (Boston: Little, Brown, 1881), p. 1.

24. "A Report on the French Civil Code Revision Project," 11 *La. L. Rev.* 261, and 25 *Tul. L. Rev.* 205 (both 1951, joint publication).

25. I would distinguish the more sophisticated positivism of British scholars such as H. L. A. Hart and Joseph Raz, Americans such as Anthony Sebok, and Australians such as Tom Campbell. For Hart, see his *The Concept of Law* (Oxford: Clarendon, 1961) and *Essays in Jurisprudence and Philosophy* (Oxford: Clarendon, 1983); the bibliography collected in P. M. S. Hacker and Joseph Raz, eds., *Law, Morality, and Society: Essays in Honour of H. L. A. Hart* (Oxford: Clarendon, 1077), pp. 309–12; and commentaries on his work, esp. Neil MacCormick, *H. L. A. Hart* (Stanford, CA: Stanford University Press, 1981); B. E. King, "The Basic Concept of Hart's Jurisprudence: The Norm out of the Bottle," 1963 *Cambr. L. J.* 270; and the searing critique by Robert N. Moles, *Definition and Role in Legal Theory: A Reassessment of H. L. A. Hart and the Positivist Tradition* (Oxford: Blackwell, 1987). For Raz, see his *Practical Reason and Norms* (London: Hutchinson, 1975); *The Authority of Law* (Oxford: Clarendon, 1979); *The Morality of Freedom* (Oxford: Clarendon, 1986). For Sebok, see his *Legal Positivism in American Jurisprudence* (New York: Cambridge University Press, 1998); and for Campbell, see his *Prescriptive Legal Positivism: Law, Rights, and Democracy* (London: Cavendish, 2004).

Court, barristers conduct the training and "reinforce the claims of legal certainty."[26] Since Morrison's time, the influence of faculty like Ronald Dworkin at Oxford and other American scholars, including the critical legal studies movement,[27] have broadened British legal education, though positivism probably still dominates the practicing profession.

Legal education in the United States is almost completely in the hands of academic lawyers. Soon after graduation, would-be attorneys must pass bar examinations in their own state and, if they pass, are licensed to practice law there. In fact, most of them know little about the nuts and bolts of practical work. Fortunately for their clients, these fledgling attorneys usually begin as junior members of firms and learn under senior lawyers. Still, American law professors have a much more personal role in their charges' legal training than does the Civil Law professoriate, whose influence, though massive, tends to be through scholarly writing rather than through face-to-face instruction. Many American professors have served, at least briefly, as private or governmental attorneys, and some continue to take occasional cases, but they tend to be teachers rather than practitioners. Furthermore, their students are university graduates, unlike in Civil Law systems,[28] and have already been exposed to diverse ideas about the nature and functions of law. At elite schools, professors are often ambitious to be esteemed as economists or philosophers, and all are supremely confident of their understanding of politics. They push students to view law as a form of social control or as a manifestation of a political philosophy, breeding skepticism about judicial claims of scientific detachment.

Yet at lesser schools and even scattered among the faculty of the very best are professors who use much the same deductive method as their narrowly positivist peers in Britain or the Continent. Furthermore, neither a social-scientific or philosophic approach to law guarantees that it will season principle with prudence. Only a few decades ago, Alexander M. Bickel attacked judicial policy making through constitutional inter-

---

26. *Courts and the Political Process in England,* pp. 79–80.

27. Among many studies of this diversified group in the United Kingdom, see esp. Peter Fitzpatrick and Alan Hunt, eds., *Critical Legal Studies* (London: Basil Blackwell, 1987); Alan Hunt, "The Theory of Critical Legal Studies," 6 *Oxf. J. Legal Stud.* 1 (1986); Martin Krygier, "Critical Legal Studies and Social Theory: A Response to Alan Hunt," 7 *Oxf. J. Legal Stud.* 26 (1987); Neil MacCormick, "Reconstruction After Deconstruction: A Response to CLS," 10 *Oxf. J. Legal Stud.* 539 (1990); Terrence L. Moore, "Critical Legal Studies and Anglo-American Jurisprudence," 1 *J. of Legal Stud.* 1 (1990); David Andrew Price, "Taking Rights Cynically: A Review of Critical Legal Studies," 48 *Cambr. L. J.* 271 (1989); Alan Thomson, "Critical Legal Education in Britain," 14 *J. L. and Soc'y* 183 (1987). An Australian then teaching at Oxford wrote one of the more trenchant critiques of critical legal studies: John M. Finnis, "On 'the Critical Legal Studies Movement,'" 30 *Am. J. of Jurispr.* 21 (1985).

28. Many American law schools do not formally require a bachelor's degree for admission, but as a practical matter it is a necessity.

pretation because such decisions tend to be principled rather than pragmatic and thus ill fit the untidy world of politics[29]—much the objection the constitutionalist critic voiced about the Civil Law.

The historical record is also more mixed than the constitutionalist critic implies. During its finest hours, the common law has checked would-be tyrants, but it began as an obedient instrument of royal power.[30] Although Latin America has been a Dumpster for democracy, that continent's problems run far deeper than its legal system. On the other hand, Switzerland has long been a stable democracy, even, one can reasonably claim, a stable *constitutional* democracy; and, except during the Nazi conquest, so have Austria, Belgium, and Holland. Since World War II, Italy and Germany have also been resolute constitutional democracies. Despite sputtering through three republics since 1871—again except during the Nazi conquest—France has not wavered in its commitment to democracy and in recent decades has moved closer toward constitutional democracy. Spain and Portugal threw off authoritarian regimes more than thirty years ago and have been following the same path as other nations of Western Europe. Thus it is patently false to assert that the Civil Law is incompatible with constitutional democracy.

Moreover, as shameful as was the record of Civil Law judges during the years of Nazism and as shabby as has been the readiness of some contemporary Italian magistrates to milk judicial independence for personal gain, the record of common-law judges has not always been a thing of constitutionalist beauty. An American need not go back to *Dred Scott*.[31] In 1944 Korematsu v. United States[32] validated the arbitrary imprisonment of more than 100,000 citizens merely because of their race and provides a grotesque reminder that even the best of common-law judges are not always courageous. Even Justice William O. Douglas, surely the most independent man ever to sit on the U.S. Supreme Court, squelched a dissent and voted with the majority. Explaining that switch, he later said that he had always "regretted" not dissenting.[33] Canadian judges also

29. *The Morality of Consent* (New Haven, CT: Yale University Press, 1975). See also the attacks on systematic theories of American constitutional interpretation by critics as politically separated as Robert H. Bork, *The Tempting of America* (New York: Free Press, 1990); Harry H. Wellington, *Interpreting the Constitution* (New Haven, CT: Yale University Press, 1990); and Laurence H. Tribe and Michael C. Dorf, *On Reading the Constitution* (Cambridge, MA: Harvard University Press, 1991).

30. Martin Shapiro, "Judicial Independence: The English Experience," 55 *No. Car. L. Rev.* 577, 651 (1977).

31. Dred Scott v. Sandford, 19 How. 393 (1857).

32. 323 U.S. 214 (1944)

33. *The Court Years, 1939–1975: The Autobiography of William O. Douglas* (New York: Random House, 1980), p. 280. See also "Transcription of Conversations between William O. Douglas and Walter F. Murphy, 1961–1963," typescript, Mudd Library of Princeton University (also accessible

turned blind eyes toward the incarceration of Japanese-Canadians,[34] though with less moral blame since their nation had not yet added a bill of rights to its constitutional texts. British judges, of course, could easily rationalize wartime internment[35] or, more recently, imprisoning suspects in Northern Ireland without allowing them to cross-examine witnesses or even to know the exact charges on which they were being tried. These Diplock courts also considered statements defendants made under duress as long the statements were obtained without "torture, inhuman or degrading treatment."[36] For several decades, however, the reports of the European Court of Human Rights in Strasbourg were studded with decisions finding that the British, with their judges slyly winking, had in fact been torturing Irish prisoners to obtain confessions.

In addition, the perception of Civil Law judges as mere technicians working within the tight framework of a code is outdated in most European constitutional democracies. Alec Stone Sweet has shown that in France, Germany, Italy, and Spain, the work of constitutional courts has pushed judges of ordinary courts to "behave as constitutional judges," treating the codes "less as a set of sacred commands issuing from the sovereign, and more as a system of rules that must be coordinated with other systems of rules," most importantly the constitutional law developed by constitutional courts.[37]

Still, even if the Civil Law does not exclude constitutional democracy, prudent founders might be concerned that the system substantially reduces constitutional democracy's chances. If the Civil Law is in fact a hindrance, founders could opt for constitutional democracy and (1) restructure the legal system, eradicating the Civil Law and adopting the common law wholesale, or (2) keep some of the Civil Law intact and invent new or selectively borrow from common law or other systems.[38]

"We appreciate this lecture on comparative law, Professor," Jacobsohn interrupts. "But our time is limited and we need guidance. What legal and judicial systems do you recommend for us?"

---

online), pp. 358–60. I had read in Frank Murphy's papers what Douglas in our conversations called a partial dissent and in his autobiography a concurring opinion. I thought it was a dissent. In any event, after this reported conversation, I tried to probe a bit more deeply into his feelings about *Korematsu.* "I caved in," he said testily. "I am ashamed! Do you want to know anything more?" I was young but not totally stupid, so I meekly replied, "No."

34. Co-operative Committee on Japanese-Canadians v. the Attorney General, [1947] A.C. 87.

35. Liversidge v. Anderson, 1942 A.C. 206 (House of Lords).

36. For a description of the so-called Diplock courts, see John E. Finn, *Constitutions in Crisis: Political Violence and the Rule of Law* (New York: Oxford University Press, 1991), chs. 2–3.

37. *Governing with Judges,* p. 116, and ch. 4 generally.

38. It may be that this third option, mild reform, will become known as "the Romanian solution."

Bengoshi smiles and replies: "I have been expecting that question. The common law is an impractical option for you. Your people are accustomed to the Civil Law; moreover, the common law developed slowly over centuries. Worse, you'd be imposing a strange legal system at the same time you're creating a new constitutional order. You lack judges, prosecutors, and attorneys to operate such a system, and you don't have many professors who could teach the next generation.

"Those are negative reasons. Let me offer a positive justification for retaining the Civil Law. The constitutionalist critic may be flat wrong: what she alleges as the Civil Law's major political flaws—comprehensiveness and reliance on logically interrelated rules to structure an entire system—may be political virtues for a nation trying to reconstitute itself. The incoherent character of American constitutional interpretation, even the inability of interpreters to decide what it is they are interpreting, may be rooted in the common law's toleration of intellectual disorder. Intellectually rigid men and women could transubstantiate the critic's nightmare into flesh, but the 'Civil Law mind' might also push you as founders now and interpreters later to think through the implications of what is being constructed and construed. Clear enunciation and ranking of objectives could facilitate adaptation to changing circumstances. No one in politics can get all he or she wants; knowing one's priorities facilitates efficient compromises."

"A Civil Law system revised in what way?" the chair asks.

Bengoshi resumes his lecture.

One change would be adoption of the common law's habeas corpus to provide judges with an instrument to curb arbitrary power.[39] Another would be a serious "speedy trial" provision. People can languish in your jails forever waiting for trial. A decade or so ago, Italy adopted such a law, but it still allows detention for as long as six years before trial—absurdly long. The Americans have opted for ninety days, perhaps too short.

But I don't want to offer a litany of suggestions; most of them would be for Parliament anyway. The essence of the reforms I have in mind could be sketched in a bill of rights, with details filled in by legislation and judicial interpretation. I'll address only a few items of constitutional design. First, separate the two corps, judges and procurators. Germany and some other Civil Law nations do[40]; like you, France and Italy do

39. In Chile during General Pinochet's dictatorship, Solidarity, the organization for civil rights led by the politically conservative auxiliary bishop of Santiago, filed hundreds of petitions for the analogous writ of *amparo* in the name of people secretly arrested. Those lawsuits did not secure the prisoners' freedom, but they usually forced the government to concede it was holding the prisoners and prevented their winning the general's special prize—a one-way helicopter flight over the Pacific.

40. As in most other realms of German political life, the Federal Parliament legislates, but the *Länder* administer the programs. Thus for the training, recruitment, and retention of legal person-

not.[41] Your distress under that arrangement is not unique. Not only does an Italian procurator sometimes later sit as the judge in a case he himself was prosecuting, but in criminal trials judges hear arguments between procurators and private attorneys. You don't need be a cynic to distrust proceedings in which one of the advocates is the judge's professional colleague. I might add that any criticism of procurators or judges is a criticism of the other. The two corps should check each other rather than form a "juristic sewing circle" of old friends and classmates.[42]

Second, to train judges and procurators to be legal craftsmen as well as constitutional democrats, I urge entrenchment of an institution like France's École Nationale de la Magistrature or Japan's Legal Training and Research Institute. The École holds competitive entrance examinations; winners pursue a twenty-seven-month program of class and practical work. Then they face a second set of examinations. Our institute operates directly under the Supreme Court. Admission is extremely difficult. We accept only about 2 percent of those who take the examinations, while the École accepts from 15 to 25 percent. Japanese students pursue a two-year course of study and on-the-job training; then they, too, take a second examination and can enter private practice or become procurators.[43] Those who wish to pursue a judicial career serve ten more years as assistant judges, when they alternate between additional courses at the institute and practical work. At the end of that period, they may be promoted to full rank. In fact, those who complete this rigorous course can serve until retirement, although officially they receive only a series of ten-year appointments. About half of our judges stay on until retirement; most of the others go into private practice.

Your institute's primary objective would be to ensure that all new judges and procurators—it would be better to have separate schools, but you couldn't staff two faculties—are carefully selected and educated as well as trained. You should be suspicious of any system that your current magistrates controlled. Although the Italian Ministry of Justice administers entrance examinations for the judiciary, thereafter careers of junior

nel, regulations and actual practices vary somewhat from *Land* to *Land.* In Bavaria, for example, it is not unusual for judges and procurators to switch careers, though the two professions are formally separate.

41. German *Länder,* however, train all legal professionals together, while France and Italy train magistrates separately from attorneys going into private practice.

42. This was Edward S. Corwin's description of the American Bar Association in the late nineteenth century: *Liberty against Government* (Baton Rouge: Louisiana State University Press, 1948), p. 138.

43. The procuratorship is not as closed in Japan as in most other Civil Law systems. Some private practitioners and law professors enter that profession, as do a few judges. For a thorough study of procurators in Japan, see David T. Johnson, *The Japanese Way of Justice: Prosecuting Crime in Japan* (New York: Oxford University Press, 2002).

magistrates are in the hands of older judges. The training younger jurists receive there is slipshod. Worse, they can continue in their judicial careers until retirement without subsequent screening or significant professional education. [44] And technical expertise is important but much less so, for you, than a sympathetic understanding of the new constitutional order. Your current judges are apt to be uninformed and, in some cases, hostile.

"You're right about the hostility of some judges," Minister Pilsudski agrees, "but how will our courts operate until a new generation of judges and procurators is produced?"

"Yes. Purging magistrates poses both practical and normative problems. After unification, the West Germans required all East German judges, procurators, and law professors to resign. Jurists from western *Länder* were available as replacements. If you tried mass removal, you'd have no judicial system left, and you'd maul the constitutionalist value Americans sum up as 'due process.' Perhaps you can do more selective weeding; I simply don't know."

"We can easily cull a lot of magistrates," Pilsudski puts in. "In the late 1980s, when the communists were trying to reform their regime in Hungary, Kálmán Kulcsár, the minister of justice, gave the worst of hard-line communist judges two choices: resignation or trial for crimes of political oppression. All of them chose the former. The remaining judges got the message."

"That's one solution. The Germans tried some communist judges, but lustration made a mess there and in Eastern Europe generally.[45] Unless you embed amnesty in your text or create a committee for truth and reconciliation as South Africa did, I think the matter should be left to Parliament, subject, of course, to a bill of rights that bans ex post facto laws."

"We can discuss amnesty and lustration at another time," the chair intervenes. "We should now focus on the judiciary and let Professor Bengoshi finish his paper."

Bengoshi nods toward the chair. "I add only that you can appoint some current judges and procurators who are sympathetic to constitutional democracy to the institute's faculty. Many law professors must also share your objectives—Professor Jacobsohn, for example. Now, it might be more useful for me to respond to questions."

---

44. Di Federico, "Crisis of the Justice System," 3:35.

45. Eventually, Germany's Federal High Court held that, to justify convictions, the evidence had to show clear violations of human rights or gross abuses of power. See Blankenburg, "Changes in Political Regimes," pp. 275–76.

For Eastern Europe more broadly, see esp. A. James McAdams, ed., *Transitional Justice and the Rule of Law in the New Democracies* (Notre Dame, IN: University of Notre Dame Press, 1997), and below, Chapter Thirteen.

"What about educating lawyers?" the chair asks. "We'll need attorneys to translate law for our citizens."

"Yes. I should have included private attorneys among the institute's students. I distrust making judges and procurators classmates, but those dangers will be mitigated if private attorneys are included in the same classes. That arrangement might also facilitate fuller understanding that would enhance the capacity of judges, procurators, and attorneys to check each other."

"What's the practice in other countries?"

"The École trains only magistrates; in Italy, practicing lawyers are trained through apprenticeship to licensed attorneys; our institute prepares all branches of the legal profession. Neither Italy nor Germany uses an institution like ours or the École."

"Would this institute teach some religious law?" asks Mufti Ajami, "the Canon Law of the Catholic Church, the Shari'a, and the Halakhah?"

"I would want such subjects taught at both the institute and university law faculties. All legal professionals should be knowledgeable about and sensitive to various religious rules. But this caucus can't micromanage curricula."

"How do we birth a new generation of legal professionals?" Strega asks.

"Alas, not by cesarean. As I said, the rector must carefully choose a faculty from among current and former judges, procurators, and professors. Bring in as visitors professors, judges, attorneys, and officials from successful constitutional democracies. Retirees form another pool of resources. Parliament should also require judges and procurators who are not graduates of the institute to study there for several months. Most of them would have greater need for education in the new constitutional order than would younger jurists. But I'm only trying to convince you that such an institution is both beneficial and feasible. Your role ends when you etch it into the constitutional text."

"Control worries me," Pilsudski says. "The Ministry of Justice's administering the judiciary could threaten independence. If judges administer themselves, Italian problems may reappear."[46]

"A dilemma, yes. Historically, the Civil Law did not consider the judiciary a coequal branch of government, nor did the English. Common law judges were initially 'faithful servants of a monarchial regime bent on centralizing political authority.'[47] But for many reasons, not least of which were battles between Crown and Parliament and what Martin Shapiro calls 'the marvelously impenetrable lump of lore-ridden'[48] law that judges created, they were able to wrest more independence than were their continental

46. For a set of stimulating essays on problems the concept of judicial independence raises, see Stephen B. Burbank and Barry Friedman, eds., *Judicial Independence at the Crossroads: An Interdisciplinary Approach* (Thousand Oaks, CA: Sage, 2002).

47. Shapiro, "Judicial Independence," p. 651.

48. Ibid.

cousins. Some common-law countries have eased problems by making judicial promotion the exception rather than the rule.[49] Where judging is a career, as in the Civil Law, a jurist who is not promoted is a failure. That fact encourages them to look over their shoulders at those who can bestow promotion—one reason that Civil Law systems have made seniority so important for promotion."

"Fascinating, but what do you recommend?" Pilsudski asks.

"As you say, putting judicial administration under the ministry of justice threatens judges' independence. Our Japanese method places administration under the supervision of the Supreme Court, which, in turn, allows the General Secretariat, run by senior judges, to take care of most matters and so threatens independence in a different way: junior judges are afraid to offend the secretariat or justices of the Supreme Court.[50] In Italy, the Higher Council of the Judiciary pretty much runs the judicial system. Twenty of its thirty-three members are judges elected by their colleagues, ten are elected by Parliament, and three are ex officio members, one of whom, the president of the Republic, almost never sits with the group. I won't repeat the problems this arrangement creates."

"Let me try yet again: what do you suggest?"

"I'd create a revised Italian-style Higher Council of the Judiciary with only nine members. Four would be elected by professional judges, two by each house of Parliament. The president would be the ninth member. He or she would have no personal, political, or professional interest at stake and could chair the group to ensure that elected politicians don't manipulate the judiciary for partisan purposes and judges don't pervert judicial independence for their own gain."

"I like it," Pilsudski says.

"So do I," Jacobsohn adds.

"Professor Bengoshi has offered," the chair says, "a set of recommendations. We should now debate them as well as any other proposals. But first we need a member to propose them."

"I do," Jacobsohn volunteers.

"Second!" someone calls out.

"Let us proceed. Mufti?"

49. Somewhat more than half of American Supreme Court justices first served as lower judges on federal appellate courts or state supreme courts, but the total number of Supreme Court justices in all American history is about 110, making the odds against such "promotion" small indeed. It is, however, not unusual for state judges to work their way up through the ranks. Moreover, Ronald Reagan and George Bush (1981–1993) often used district judgeships as proving grounds for the ideological purity of candidates for the courts of appeals and, similarly, used appellate posts to test potential nominees for the Supreme Court.

50. See Joseph Sanders, "Courts and Law in Japan," in Herbert Jacob et al., eds., *Courts, Law, and Politics in Comparative Perspective* (New Haven, CT: Yale University Press, 1996), p. 326, citing Setsuo Miyazawa, "Administrative Control of Japanese Judges," 25 *Kobe L. Rev.* 46 (1991).

"My question about teaching religious law reflected concern about the reach of the secular legal system. Many groups, mine especially, want certain personal affairs governed by their own laws. Our new legal system should permit citizens to have matters like marriage, education of children, and divorce handled by their own rules."

"I'm sympathetic to special protections for religious groups," Father Gregorian puts in, "but I see problems. What if, in a divorce case, the woman opted for a civil court and the man for a religious tribunal? Suppose one spouse converted to another religion or embraced a different sect within the same religion? And where do we draw the line between public and personal matters?"

"All citizens," Jacobsohn injects, "must be bound by the same set of laws. If not, why call ourselves one country? Why even talk of a bill of rights if its provisions will not apply equally to all of us? Equal protection of the laws means the protection of equal laws. Women will be the victims if religious tribunals handle so-called family matters. Under the Muslim law of divorce, the husband gets custody of the children; and if he returns his wife's dowry, he need not provide any support for her beyond three months. I've talked before about the Shah Bano Case from India. A husband turned out his wife of forty-three years for a younger woman and claimed he owed his first wife nothing after three months. The Supreme Court ruled that secular law took precedence, but Parliament then passed a statute allowing Islamic law to prevail between Muslims."[51]

"You take a formalistic view of our law," Ajami says. "The judges and the husband's friends counsel him to be generous. And in *Shah Bano* the husband had actually already paid his ex-wife 'alimony' for more than two years, besides returning her dowry."

"Yes, sixteen dollars a month. Some generosity! And if the husband isn't so kind, the wife will be left in dire poverty—and without her children."

"Suppose she accepts those consequences when she marries?" Ajami asks.

---

51. In Mohammed Ahmed Khan v. Shah Bano Begum, [1985] 3 S.C.R. 844, the Indian Supreme Court held that, despite Muslim law, a divorced woman was entitled to alimony. The resulting rioting by Indian Muslims frightened the government of Rajiv Gandhi. Eventually Parliament passed a bill ironically labeled the Muslim Women (Protection of Rights on Divorce) Act. Women whose husbands divorced them were authorized to ask local boards for charity. For discussions, see: Saleem Akhtar, *The Shah Bano Judgment in Islamic Perspective* (New Delhi: Kitab Bhavan, 1994); Asghar Ali Engineer, ed., *The Shah Bano Controversy* (Bombay: Orient Longman, 1987); Gary Jeffrey Jacobsohn, *The Wheel of Law: India's Secularism in Comparative Perspective* (Princeton, NJ: Princeton University Press, 2003), pp. 106–7, 116; Raj Janak Jai, ed., *Shah Bano* (New Delhi: Rajiv, 1986); Gerald James Larson, *India's Agony over Religion* (Albany: State University of New York Press, 1995), pp. 256–61; John Mansfield, "Personal Laws or a Uniform Civil Code?" in Robert Baird, ed., *Religion and the Law in Independent India* (Delhi: Maohar, 1993).

"Are such decisions really free in traditional Islamic families where marriages are typically arranged? And then there's the practice of genital mutilation of girls. If raising children were under your law, the state could not ban clitorectomy."

"I've said it before," Ajami responds testily, "clitorectomy is not required by the Qur'an or the Shari'a! It's a horrific practice, done by some Muslims and some non-Muslims as well."

"Islamic law may not require it, but many, possibly most, fundamentalist Muslims maim their daughters, sincerely believing they are obeying the Qur'an, the Shari'a, and Allah Himself. And they do so with the approbation of Islamic judges."

"There may be middle ground," Pilsudski interrupts. "First, include a clause that would read something like 'The same laws shall apply to all persons within the nation.'[52] Then, also allow freely consenting parties to settle certain kinds of disputes in religious courts. This settlement would be legally binding if a civilian court holds that its terms do not violate constitutional standards."

"Much too complicated for a constitutional text," Jacobsohn comments.

"May I say something?" Professor Bengoshi asks. "I agree that women will always lose in religious courts and the Minister's proposal is too complicated for a constitutional text. You face a double tension, first between rights that accrue to individuals as individuals and those that pertain to groups. American constitutional interpretation shows how difficult it is to discern which rights fall into which category and, worse, to decide how to cope with those that partake of both, as so many do.[53] One might look on that conflict as writ large in the intractable dispute between those who think the central right is to participate in making political decisions and, on the other side, those who seek to protect individuals against political decisions even if they participated in those decisions.

"The second tension: Probably most of your citizens will think of rights as theirs, as individuals, and that these trump conflicting rights of groups. On the other hand, you have sizable minorities who are apt to conceive of rights as properties of groups. For them, equal protection means that government must treat groups equally, not that groups must treat their own members equally. *Shah Bano* illustrates the clash between religious and secu-

52. Article 44 of India's constitutional text reads: "The State shall endeavor to secure for the citizens a uniform civil code throughout the territory of India." This article, however, appears in part 4 of the constitutional document, which is exempted from judicial enforcement. Thus, judges could not invalidate the statute throwing divorced women onto the mercy of Islamic courts.

53. See the debate between Owen M. Fiss, "Groups and the Equal Protection Clause," 5 *Phil. and Pub. Affrs.* 107 (1976), and Paul Brest, "In Defense of the Anti-discrimination Principle," 90 *Harv. L. Rev.* 1 (1976).

lar law. Conflicts in Israel tend to be *within* one religion: between the law Orthodox rabbis apply and the secular law that less orthodox Jews want.[54] So, too, in an ethnic rather than religious context, do Canada's difficulties with self-rule for indigenous peoples. Tribal cultures tend to be male-dominated; to prevent discrimination against women, the Supreme Court has ruled that tribal regulations cannot take precedence over equality."[55]

"I now have," the chair says, "a clear understanding of our problem, but no clear idea about how to cope with it. What do you suggest?"

"In many ways, your problem mirrors what we Japanese faced after World War II. The concept of individual rights was not unknown, but it was strange to most of us. Our concept of rights principally pertained to one's station in life. Our change to a more Western orientation influences my response. Being an inscrutable Oriental, I suggest both a clean decision and a murky compromise. Constitutional democracy demands certain individual rights. Therefore, be clear though general in the text. Leave details for political adjustment, but within a constitutional framework that forbids publicly sanctioned discrimination on the basis of race, ethnicity, religion, or sex."

"This solution will not please my people," Ajami says.

"Only two 'solutions' are open," Bengoshi replies. "Either your nation abandons what has become one of constitutional democracy's central tenets or Islamic law accepts what many Muslim scholars—and you yourself—claim is the true message of the Qur'an: men and women are juridical as well as moral equals."

"We have had sufficient debate," the chair intervenes. "Going over this ground again will not produce progress. Let us move on . . . Retaining the Civil Law requires no action by this body; indeed, establishing any legal system may be more properly left to Parliament. Do I hear any other motions? No? Then let us vote."

The caucus approves by voice votes motions to (1) establish the judiciary as an independent branch of government; (2) separate the two professional

54. See Martin Edelman, "The Utility of a Written Constitution: Free Exercise of Religion in Israel and the United States," 11 *Shofar* 35 (1993); Martin Edelman, "'Protecting' the Majority: Religious Freedom for Non-Orthodox Jews in Israel," in Frederick A. Lazin and Gregory S. Mahler, eds., *Israel in the Nineties: Development and Conflict* (Gainesville: University of Florida Press, 1996); Martin Edelman, "A Portion of Animosity: The Politics of the Disestablishment of Religion in Israel," 5 *Isr. Studies* 204 (2000); David Hartman, *Israelis and the Jewish Tradition: An Ancient People Debating Its Future* (New Haven, CT: Yale University Press, 2000); Gary Jeffrey Jacobsohn, "Three Models of Secular Constitutional Development: India, Israel, and the United States," 10 *Studies in Am. Pol. Devl't* 1 (1996); Gary Jeffrey Jacobsohn, *Apple of Gold: Constitutionalism in Israel and the United States* (Princeton, NJ: Princeton University Press, 1993); and Shene Ur Zalmon Abramov, *Perpetual Dilemma: Jewish Religion in the Jewish State* (Rutherford, NJ: Fairleigh Dickinson University Press, 1976).

55. Attorney-General v. Lavell, [1974] S.C.R. 1349, handed down before the Charter of Rights went into effect. For a thorough study of the problems, see Patrick Macklem, *Indigenous Difference and the Constitution of Canada* (Toronto: University of Toronto Press, 2001).

corps of judges and procurators; (3) protect judicial independence by providing that the salaries of judges and procurators must not be reduced during their term of office and that at least every five years the legislature must adjust judicial salaries to increases in the cost of living; (4) authorize the legislature to create an institute to select and train judges, procurators, and attorneys; (5) set mandatory ages for the retirement of judges and procurators; and (6) create a Grand Judicial Council, to be composed of three judges, three procurators, and two members of each house of Parliament, presided over by the president of the republic as a voting member, to oversee assignments, promotions, and discipline, with the proviso that every judge and procurator must attend a specialized course of study at the institute for three months every five years and pass a set of examinations at the end of that program.

"It is now," the chair notes, "1:46 p.m. We have done a remarkable amount of work during the past four hours. We owe Professor Bengoshi thanks for his clarity and learning. Let us adjourn until 1600 hours, or four p.m. Then we must take up the question of establishing judicial review and, if so, in what form. Professor Deukalion will begin with a few general remarks."

At 4:01 Retlaw Deukalion again takes the podium.

Most states that have reconstituted themselves since World War II have embedded judicial review in their constitutional systems. Indeed, it has become the hallmark of constitutionalism; but it's by no means essential to constitutionalism, and it also poses many difficulties. At their best, judges check any possible tyranny of the majority,[56] protect the values of the constitutional order, defuse the frustration of those who lose in the more obviously political processes, and help legitimate controversial decisions regarding public policy. Still, even when judicial review operates at its optimum level, it provides these benefits at a high cost to the right of a majority to effectuate public policies. And it goes without saying, though I shall say it anyway, that judges, like legislators, do not always operate at an optimum level. Judges are vulnerable to all human failings. The most realistic hope is that a wisely designed political system will make it highly probable that the good judges do will far outweigh the damage they do.

Let's look at three basic models. The first is the American: All courts of general jurisdiction can interpret the constitution. Australia, Canada, India, Ireland, Japan and Norway, among others, have arrangements that are similar, although their differences can be significant.[57] Under this

56. Tom Ginsburg argues that judicial review provides insurance for losers in electoral battles: *Judicial Review in New Democracies* (New York: Cambridge University Press, 2003).

57. For instance, the federal and provincial governments can ask the Canadian Supreme Court

model, any litigant, whether public official, private citizen, or corporation, can challenge the constitutionality of a statute, treaty, executive order, or administrative regulation. The most important restriction here is that a litigant may do so only in the context of a *case*—a word of art designating a real, not academic, conflict between parties who have opposing legally protected interests at stake, one of whose is immediately threatened. A few state courts can issue advisory opinions if requested by their own officials, but no federal court can decide constitutional questions outside of actual cases. Moreover, most American courts have developed guidelines to further limit the occasions on which they will decide constitutional issues; judges follow these guidelines when it pleases them and ignore them when that course is more pleasing.[58]

Strictly speaking, an American decision invalidating a governmental action binds only the parties to the case, their agents, their successors in office, and those who cooperate with them while knowing a judicial order is in effect. A statute declared unconstitutional stays on the books until the legislature repeals it.[59] Practically, however, the doctrine of stare decisis and the widespread, however simplistic, belief that judges are the ultimate constitutional interpreters *usually* give such decisions a far wider effect, especially if made by the U.S. Supreme Court. I stress "usually." American belief in judicial supremacy has been a sometime thing. Congress, the president, governors, and state officials, as well as judges of lower courts, have on occasion frustrated the Supreme Court.[60]

At the other extreme is the French model: Constitutional review is exercised by the Conseil Constitutionnel as an active participant in the legislative process. This institution is not a court in the formal sense but a

for advisory opinions, and the Irish president may also so ask the Supreme Court. The Canadian tribunal's standards of "justiciability" are confused, as are those of the U.S. Supreme Court. See Lorne M. Sossin, *Boundaries of Judicial Review: The Law of Justiciability in Canada* (Scarborough, ON: Carswell, 2000). Ireland's rules regarding "standing to sue" are very porous compared to those of the United States. See the Marts Acts Case, [1970] I.R. 317, 339, discussed in Walter F. Murphy and Joseph Tanenhaus, eds., *Comparative Constitutional Law* (New York: St. Martin's, 1977), pp. 93–94.

58. Louis D. Brandeis laid down the most famous of these guidelines in his separate opinion in Ashwander v. TVA, 297 U.S. 288 (1936). For a brief discussions of these and similar judicially created precepts, see Walter F. Murphy, C. Herman Pritchett, Lee Epstein, and Jack Knight, eds., *Courts, Judges, and Politics: An Introduction to the Judicial Process*, 6th ed. (Boston: McGraw-Hill, 2005), ch. 6.

59. Marbury v. Madison, 1 Cr. 137 (1803), perhaps the most famous decision in American constitutional history, held that §13 of the Judiciary Act of 1789 was unconstitutional because it enlarged the Supreme Court's original (trial) jurisdiction, even though that section's words nowhere pretended to enlarge that jurisdiction. In any event, federal courts routinely invoked §13 until 1943, when Congress included it in revised form in the All Writs Act.

60. See Walter F. Murphy, *Congress and the Court* (Chicago: University of Chicago Press, 1962), *Elements of Judicial Strategy* (Chicago: University of Chicago Press, 1964), chs. 2, 4–6, and Murphy et al., *Courts, Judges, and Politics*, ch. 8.

council of former presidents of the republic plus nine other people, three chosen by the current president of the republic, three by the president of the National Assembly, and three by the president of the Senate. Former presidents serve for life, the other members for nine-year terms.[61] In practice, however, former presidents have almost never taken their posts as councillors. The political affiliation of other members, Stone Sweet says, has been "the single most important criterion" for selection. The overwhelming number have been former legislators or cabinet ministers or have served on the staffs of either parties or governmental offices. Only rarely has a professional judge been chosen.[62] The Conseil does not hear "cases" in the common law's sense but offers binding opinions on the constitutionality of bills pending in Parliament. Article 61 of the French constitutional text provides that such questions may be presented only by the president of the republic, the prime minister, the president of the Senate or National Assembly, sixty deputies, or sixty senators. The last two provisions pretty much ensure that all important and controversial legislation will be referred to the Conseil. And Article 62 of the constitutional charter stipulates: "A provision [of a bill] declared unconstitutional may not be promulgated nor may it enter into force. The decisions of the Conseil Constitutionnel may not be appealed."

The third model is that of Germany, a central court exercising constitutional review. Designed by Hans Kelsen for Austria after the collapse of the Hapsburg empire, it was more or less copied after World War II by Germany and Italy and, later, by most countries in Europe. Kelsen was concerned to keep alive the myth that judging and policy making are separate enterprises. He wanted the advantages of judicial review without the disadvantages of openly involving judges in politics, as they inevitably are when exercising judicial review. His solution was to create a single constitutional court that would decide constitutional questions, with "ordinary" judges retaining jurisdiction over "ordinary" matters of the Civil Law.[63]

The German Constitutional Court's jurisdiction is marvelously complex.[64] It sits in two separate senates, but because you're highly unlikely to

---

61. Article 56. That article also provides that three members shall be chosen every three years.

62. *The Birth of Judicial Politics in France: The Constitutional Council in Comparative Perspective* (New York: Oxford University Press, 1992), p. 50, and ch. 2 generally. (Since publishing this book under the name Stone, he has changed his last name to Stone Sweet.)

63. See Kelsen, "Judicial Review of Legislation: A Comparative Study of the Austrian and the American Constitution," 4 *J. of Pols.* 183 (1942); and, more generally, Mauro Cappelletti, *Judicial Review in the Contemporary World* (Indianapolis: Bobbs-Merrill, 1971).

64. Articles 21 and 92–93 of the Basic Law spell out that jurisdiction. For analyses, see Wolfgang Zeidler (late president of the Court), "The Federal Constitutional Court of the Federal Republic of Germany: Decisions on the Constitutionality of Legal Norms," 62 *Notre Dame L. Rev.* 504 (1989); Donald P. Kommers, *The Constitutional Jurisprudence of the Federal Republic of Germany*,

want such a division, I'll treat the Court as a single entity. It hears three kinds of issues. First, it responds to questions referred by ordinary judges who find constitutional issues embedded in cases before them. The Constitutional Court does not decide these cases, only settles the questions. Second, individual litigants may file "constitutional complaints," alleging that some governmental action is violating one of their basic rights. To winnow through these requests, the Court utilizes procedures similar to those the U.S. Supreme Court follows with petitions for certiorari. Third, the government of the Federation or of a *Land* or one-third of the members of the Bundestag may ask the justices to answer a constitutional question about a law or treaty. This kind of review is sometimes called "objective," because its purpose is solely to declare what the constitutional order ordains.[65] This third procedure differs from that of the Conseil Constitutionnel in that it reaches only legislation that has already been enacted or a treaty that has been signed. Thus it does not as directly involve the Constitutional Court in the legislative process, though of course governments of both the Bund and *Länder* anticipate the Court's reactions to their own actions and well as react to its opinions.

The Court's decisions on constitutional issues are final and binding on all governmental agencies, *Land* as well as Bund,[66] and the judges have reiterated this requirement. As they said in their very first opinion, their decision to nullify a federal law is

> to be published in the *Federal Law Gazette*. The declaration together with the main reasons for the decision binds all constitutional organs of the Federation . . . in such a way that no federal law with the same content can again be deliberated and enacted by the legislative bodies and promulgated by the federal president.[67]

"With the permission of the Chair," Deukalion says, "we could now begin debating. Although judicial review is not necessary for all nations that

---

2nd ed. (Durham, NC: Duke University Press, 1997), ch. 1; and Donald P. Kommers, *Judicial Politics in West Germany* (Los Angeles: Sage, 1976).

65. The law governing the Bundesverfassungsgericht's jurisdiction initially allowed the Plenum, the Constitutional Court's two senates sitting together, to issue advisory opinions at the request of either the president of the Bund or, acting together, the government, the Bundestag, and the Bundesrat. In 1956, after the Plenum had expressed reservations about the propriety of this jurisdiction and the government began to fear the Court might interfere with its treaty-making power, Parliament repealed that provision. See Kommers, *Judicial Politics in West Germany*, p. 101.

66. The Federal Constitutional Court Act of 1951 says: "1. The decisions of the Federal Constitutional Court shall be binding upon the constitutional bodies of the Federation and of the *Länder* as well as upon all law courts and public authorities."

67. The Southwest Case, 1BVerfGE 14 (1951), trans. and excerpted in Walter F. Murphy and Joseph Tanenhaus, eds., *Comparative Constitutional Law* (New York: St. Martin's, 1977), pp. 208–11. For an explanation of "the main reasons for the decision," see Zeidler, "Federal Constitutional Court," p. 520.

want constitutional democracy, I think it is for yours. Your people and even most of those who will become legislators do not yet have the political culture that can make any sort of democratic system work without institutional restraints."

"And without a chance to make and correct their own mistakes, these people are unlikely to develop the sort of culture—or cultures—representative democracy needs," Pyknites puts in.

"If that were true," Jacobsohn replies, "then most Western Europeans lack such a culture—a conclusion that flies in the face of all the evidence."

The chair intervenes: "We've already rehearsed arguments for and against judicial review in abstract terms. What kind of review would you suggest we adopt, Professor?"

"First let me eliminate the French model."

"Even if staffed in whole or part by professional judges?" Gregorian asks.

"Yes. Staffing solely by professional judges would make that institution even worse."

"Or even if its members were popularly elected, say for terms that did not coincide with those of members of Parliament, and its judges must include members of minorities, as is the Canadian practice—say at least one Jew, one Gypsy, and one Muslim?" the mufti asks.

"Yes to both questions. First, experience in the American states shows that serious problems with contributions to campaigns inevitably arise where judges are elected. Even if judges are not prejudiced in a case because law firms representing litigants contributed a large sum of money to put them on the bench, it's difficult to appear impartial. Even were a judge to decide against that firm, he or she could appear to have been compromised by bending over backward not to appear compromised. Either way, such decisions generate distrust of the judicial system. Second, American state experience also shows that, as in New York,[68] leaders of the two parties can secretly negotiate about who will run and thus, in effect, appoint judges without any responsibility for their choices. If a judge turns out to be stupid, inefficient, or even corrupt, party leaders can say that he was the people's choice. That perverts democracy. Third, popular election will destroy one of the basic purposes of judicial review: protection against the tyranny of the majority. Judges who must keep looking over their shoulder to the next election for the public's reaction to their decisions, as well as to interest groups, law firms, and fat cats for the money to run for reelection, can hardly act more disinterestedly than legislators."

"But aren't American federal judges influenced by public opinion?" Pyknites asks.

---

68. Wallace Sayre and Herbert Kaufman, *Governing New York City* (New York: Russell Sage, 1960), ch. 14, esp. pp. 538–48.

"The relationship between federal judges and public opinion is complicated. Presidents, senators, and representatives can hide behind what they claim the Supreme Court has done or will do.[69] And courts sometimes follow, just as they sometimes create, public opinion. In each situation, individual judges both hear and try to activate different voices."

"Couldn't we," Pilsudski asks, "have something of both worlds by providing for popular election of judges of the constitutional court for a single lengthy term? I'd have as much faith in the people as in allowing, as the Germans do, Parliament to do the electing."

"The call is closer there," Deukalion agrees. "For me it would depend on how candidates were nominated. The two houses of the German Parliament are run by disciplined political parties that, in turn, are led by seasoned professional politicians who know that they'll be blamed for poor judicial choices. Thus they're under strong pressure to choose honest, capable men and women who treasure the constitutional system. If candidates were to be self-selected, that is, if anyone who met certain minimal qualifications could stand for election, I'd be opposed. There would be no one to hold accountable for a bad judge."

"What do you mean by 'a bad judge'?" Pastor Glückmann asks.

"One who is corrupt, intellectually incompetent, or an ideologue. But let's leave the term general for now. If candidates for the constitutional court were by nominated by parties, I'd object less strenuously, because the voters at the next election could hold those organizations responsible. I would still, however, see real problems in secret negotiations among party leaders, as now in fact take place in Germany and Italy."

"Then how would you choose judges for this constitutional court?" Jacobsohn asks.

Before Deukalion can answer, Colonel Martin interrupts: "We're wandering. I rule, always subject to the caucus's pleasure, that we must immediately address several sets of questions. First, do we really want some form of constitutional review? If the answer is yes, what sort of constitutional review is best for us? Third, what sort of procedures should we have for constitutional review? . . . Mr. Pyknites, I assume that you wish to speak against judicial review?"

"I do. First, let me merely summarize my objections. Except in Japan, in whatever form judicial review operates, it impedes democratic processes. You've heard my arguments and what Robert Dahl has to say. Let me briefly quote from an analysis by a pair of scholars of Canada's experience with judicial review under its Charter of Rights: 'Our primary objection is that it

---

69. Walter F. Murphy, "Congressional Reliance on Judicial Law Making," paper delivered at the 1963 Annual Meetings of the American Political Science Association, New York.

is deeply and fundamentally undemocratic. . . . The growth of courtroom rights talk undermines the fundamental prerequisite of the decent liberal democratic politics: the willingness to engage those with whom one disagrees in the ongoing attempt to combine diverse interests into temporarily viable governing majorities.'[70]

"Now, I'll look at Professor Deukalion's models," Pyknites continues. "First and worst is the French Conseil Constitutionnel. It's a tribunal of 'preview' and has become a third, unelected, unresponsive, and irresponsible house of Parliament. And its powers are not merely negative. In imposing an absolute veto on proposed legislation, its opinions often spell out what regulations it will accept. Facing a brick wall, the French government gives in. The German Constitutional Court provides a middle model. Citizens who are unhappy with the work of their elected representatives' legislation cannot invoke the Court's jurisdiction until a bill has become law; but after, judges have can wreak havoc with their Parliament's choices of public policies. The records of all Western European constitutional courts have caused scholars to refer to the judicialization of politics there as an accomplished fact.[71] Moreover, the German Court can, after holding a statute void, reinstate a regulation the supposedly invalid act replaced. That is legislation, by any definition."

"Is that really true, Professor Deukalion?" Minxin Wei asks.

"Only on several occasions," Deukalion answers. "The most famous came when the Justices invalidated the Abortion Reform Act.[72] In their opinion, they ordered reinstatement of the old law criminalizing abortion. That sort of action might surprise outsiders, but it was hardly as a shock to students of constitutional courts. Hans Kelsen had called attention to the fact that the Austrian constitutional text of 1920 authorized the Constitutional Court so to rule in order to prevent ripping a hole in the legal system.[73] In general, however, the German Court has preferred to risk making a breach to legislating."

70. F. L. Morton and Raines Knopff, *The Charter Revolution and the Court Party* (Toronto: Broadview, 2000), p. 149.

71. See, for example, Stone Sweet, *Governing with Judges;* Tate and Vallinder, *Global Expansion of Judicial Power.*.

72. 39 BVerfGE 1 (1975), trans. and excerpted in Walter F. Murphy and Joseph Tanenhaus, eds., *Comparative Constitutional Law* (New York: St. Martin's, 1977), pp. 422–28; and Kommers, *Constitutional Jurisprudence of the Federal Republic of Germany*, pp. 336–46; for a full trans., see R. E. Jonas and J. G. Gorby 9 *John Marshall J. of Prac. and Proc.* 551 (1976).

73. "Judicial Review of Legislation," p. 199. The relevant section read: "If by a decision of the Constitutional Court a statute or a part of a statute has been annulled on the ground of its unconstitutionality the legal rules derogated by the mentioned statute come [back] into force simultaneously with the decision of the Constitutional Court unless the latter provides other wise." Kelsen called this clause an authorization for a "positive act of [judicial] legislation," something he elsewhere opposed.

"One case is one too many," Pyknites says. "I need add little about the American model. Even while proclaiming pride in their humility, those judges have usually thought themselves more competent to govern than the people's elected representatives. Moreover, in the Dred Scott Case (1857), the court tried to end the divisive controversy over slavery in the territories. The result made a civil war more likely. Almost a century and a half later, five of the justices in *Bush v. Gore* pretended they were preventing a political crisis over the election of a president, even though the constitutional text leaves it to Congress to determine which electoral votes are valid and Congress had, by statute, provided such a means. More generally, it is doubtful how often in the Supreme Court's many battles with Congress and the president the justices interpreted the constitutional order more accurately or wisely than did competing institutions.

"Professors Deukalion and Jacobsohn concede all of this but dismiss it as a price one pays for judicial protection of minority rights. Let's look at that claim. In France the Conseil safeguarded the rights of a monopolist, a minority of one, to control a huge share of the French press and television; and the German Constitutional Court protected the reputation of a political whore who made propaganda movies for the Nazis. In the United States, Dahl has shown that the Supreme Court has typically shared the constitutional views of the ruling coalition.[74] And when the justices have decided to protect minorities, they have done so for people such as slaveholders, robber barons, and gang-bangers who carry guns near public schools. Too often when oppressed minorities have brought their causes to court, as did labor unions, citizens being herded into concentration camps because their ancestors had been born in the wrong country, or public officials speaking for victims of the Holocaust against neo-Nazis, judges have trotted out white canes. When some states punished Native Americans who have traditionally used peyote in their religious ceremonies, the Court sustained the governmental action. When Congress enacted and the president signed legislation protecting Native Americans' free exercise of religion, the Court angrily struck down this protection of supposedly sacred values of the First Amendment. In effect, the justices asserted that their interpretations, even when contrary to the constitutional text's plain words, must be followed.

"If judicial review works poorly in the United States, France, Germany, Italy, and Spain, which have also have long experience with constitutional democracy, why should we think it will work well in our country? Every day that we live under the benign tutelage of judges, we will be denying ourselves and our people the right to self-government. Jefferson said that an informed

74. "Decision Making in a Democracy: The Supreme Court as a National Policy Maker," 6 *J. of Pub. L.* 279 (1957); but see also Jonathan D. Casper, "The Supreme Court and National Policy," 70 *Am. Pol. Sci. Rev.* 50 (1976), and Murphy et al., *Courts, Judges, and Politics*, ch. 2.

and active citizenry is the *safest* protector of their own rights.[75] I would go further and say such a people form the *only* real protection of those rights."

"Mr. Pyknites has used every piece of evidence that supports representative democracy and has skipped over every item that weakens his case," Professor Jacobsohn says. "Of course judges make mistakes. They sometimes defend the rights of people who deserve no defense, just as they sometimes sustain democratically made decisions that deserve no respect. Nevertheless, the rights of women in Italy, of blacks and women in the United States, and of those accused of crime in most nations would be considerably weaker had not judges intervened. Equally important, in most countries with judicial review, judges have had to intervene to keep Mr. Pyknites's beloved political processes open, protecting rights to vote, to speak, and to write about public affairs against laws enacted by popularly elected legislators."

"I have a question," Glückmann says. "I recall from our earlier discussions that Mr. Pyknites was an adamant moral relativist. And . . ."

"To the extent," Pyknites cuts in, "that I do not believe that you or I can by reason alone persuade people who fundamentally reject our scheme of morals. I accept our scheme. But I also understand that it is, as far as much of the world is concerned, peculiar or even flat-out wrong.

"That statement might be called," Gregorian notes, "deterministic relativism mixed with loyalty to culture."

"Whatever," Glückmann continues. "It seems to me that Mr. Pyknites opposes judicial review because he doesn't believe demonstrably right answers to political or moral questions exist. He thinks that the safest way to resolve such issues is through majority rule. In effect, he transplants his moral relativism in the political arena. Am I correct so far?"

"You oversimplify my position, but go on."

"Perhaps in oversimplifying an idea we catch its essence. My point is that you oppose judicial review because it implies that correct answers to many fundamental constitutional problems exist and that a group of intelligent men and women, protected from outside pressures, can reason together to find those answers. Instead, you believe that while a decision reached by a majority of the people may or may not be correct, popularity bestows legitimacy on it."

"You have asked several questions," Pyknites answers. "I assume that 'a group of intelligent men and women' is code for *judges*. Yes, they might find answers to fundamental constitutional questions that you and I would deem correct, but I also believe that they do so less often than do legislators responsible to the people, when both voters and officials act according to the principles of deliberative democracy."

75. Letter to John Taylor, May 28, 1816, in *The Works of Thomas Jefferson*, ed. Paul L. Ford (New York: Putnam's Sons, 1905), 11:527.

"Let me clarify my questions," Glückmann says. "Is there something intrinsically valid in majority rule? Would, for example, the Holocaust have been a legitimate policy had it been approved by a majority of freely elected representatives of the German people rather than a coterie of Nazi thugs? Or is the capacity of majority rule to legitimate policy merely that in many modern cultures people associate it with democracy?"

"First, I do not believe that even after almost a decade of Nazi rule, freely elected representatives in Germany would have endorsed the Holocaust," Pyknites says.[76] "If they followed the principles of deliberative democracy, they certainly would not have. To answer the more general question lurking behind your example: I do not think that any group of men and women, however intelligent, reasonable, and learned, will be able to achieve consensus on important issues of public policy such as a right to die, abortion, the limits of free speech, the reach of religious freedom, the best way to promote education or prosperity. Even in this august body, despite our most earnest efforts, we disagree sharply. And we resolve those disagreements just as do courts, legislatures, and commissions—that is, by voting, with the majority carrying the day. Given my loss on such issues as constitutional versus representative democracy, you could not expect me to contend that the majority is always right. But I know of no rational, peaceful decisional processes other than reasoned argument followed by a vote in which the majority wins."[77]

"Then," Gregorian puts in, "you justify majority rule solely as a decision-making device?"

"Yes, and one that all democratic societies accept—except, of course, when the fundamental rules of the political game are involved; then we ask for an extraordinary majority or a majority across time or several institutions. If that makes me a moral relativist, I have lots of company."

"We're wandering into another mushy debate about morality," Strega warns.

"All politics is ultimately about morality," Gregorian says. "But I ask Pastor Glückmann if his characterization of constitutionalism and judicial

76. Pyknites's claim is not testable, but it is contestable. Daniel Jonah Goldhagen's *Hitler's Willing Executioners: Ordinary Germans and the Holocaust* (New York: Alfred A. Knopf, 1996), incited a firestorm of debate both in the United States and in Germany over how readily "ordinary Germans" participated in the Holocaust. See also Eric A. Johnson, *Nazi Terror: The Gestapo, Jews, and Ordinary Germans* (New York: BasicBooks, 2000), who argues that although ordinary Germans were not guiltless, responsibility was principally located within the Nazi hierarchy and the members of the Gestapo, who were carefully chosen because of their hatred of Jews and ruthless disdain for basic morality.

77. See the debate among Ronald Dworkin, Jeremy Waldron, Amy Gutmann, and Paul W. Kahn, in Harold Hongju Koh and Ronald C. Slye, eds., *Deliberative Democracy and Human Rights* (New Haven, CT: Yale University Press, 1999).

review implies moral realism—that a statement can be objectively true or false or objectively better or worse."

"Yes," the pastor answers. "Acceptance of human dignity as the fundamental value of any legitimate political system implies the existence of a moral 'there' out there. That existence depends on the structure of reality, not on the beliefs of any person or culture. We might disagree about what that value requires in specific situations, but we do not disagree that we can and do know what that it is a good toward which any legitimate political system must strive."

"I disagree," Jacobsohn responds. "Although I accept human dignity as *the* basic goal of constitutionalism, not every constitutionalist does.[78] Further, I don't think constitutionalism even implicitly contradicts relativism. Too many constitutionalists are relativists. I myself am, at least to some extent."

"Yes," Deukalion says, "but I think they suffer from intellectual schizophrenia. How can you endorse human dignity as *the* basic value of a legitimate political system and still believe this judgment is relative?"

"It's *my* basic political value," Jacobsohn replies, "but intelligent, decent men and women might prefer other values and thus other kinds of political systems. Mr. Pyknites, for instance."

Gregorian rejoins the debate: "To acknowledge that others disagree with you for reasons that are neither stupid nor venal does not make you a relativist. Besides, even democratic theory must either accept the human dignity as a basic value—why else 'one person, one vote'?—or defend itself simply as the best promoter of stability. And that claim that won't pass even a moderately strict empirical test. Why do we want to limit government if not to protect that sacredness we ascribe to human life and freedom?"

"Perhaps," Pyknites puts in, "only to protect our own derrières and those of the people we love. We know we can't accumulate enough power to defend ourselves against either a lynch mob or tyrants. We also know that we can't protect ourselves without persuading others that the political system we want will also protect their lives, families, and property. Democratic theory need not rest on the importance of human dignity; plain old-fashioned self-interest is a sufficient basis for representative or, for that matter, constitutional democracy."

"Then," Gregorian asks, "your only justification is self-interest? But if we look at democratic systems over the ages, we see they haven't been very good at preserving public peace; this undermines the foundations of your claim. You're left with no moral or empirical grounds either for your political system or for your own courageous resistance to tyranny."

78. See, for example, William F. Harris II, *The Interpretable Constitution* (Baltimore: Johns Hopkins University Press, 1993), pp. 97–98.

"It isn't fair to look at democracy 'over the ages'; it has only been since the middle of the nineteenth century that we developed institutions that meet democracy's premises. And I see protecting myself and fellow citizens as good morality. Representative democracy does protect human dignity, but that need not be its primary justification. I thought the junta evil; but as I have said, I could never persuade my uncle, nor could all the priests, pastors, rabbis, and ulama in Nusquam. And my uncle, a Yale man, was certainly intelligent and educated."

"Question!" Strega calls out, joined by several others.

"Does anyone else wish to speak?" Martin asks, then pauses and looks around the room. "I neither see hands nor hear requests . . . Alas, the parliamentarian says that we do not have a motion before us. Does anyone move that we adopt some form of judicial review?"

"So moved," Jacobsohn says. "Second!" several others shout.

"Very well, this choice is a simple yea or nay. May I see the hands of those who vote yea? Those who vote nay? . . . By my count and that of the parliamentarian, we have thirteen votes for, ten opposed; Minister Strega abstains. The motion carries. Mr. Pyknites?"

"As a democrat, I accept, albeit sorrowfully, this decision. I propose that we establish the best aspect of that institution—keeping democratic processes truly democratic—and not permit judges to second-guess the substantive policy judgments of the people's representatives."

"Would you state your proposal as a motion?" the chair asks.

"I move that we establish a single tribunal outside the ordinary judiciary. This tribunal would hear disputes involving claims (1) by political parties, interest groups, journalists, or individual citizens, that a statute or administrative regulation restricts freedom of expression or assembly; (2) by political parties, interest groups, journalists, or individual citizens, that legislation or administrative regulations deny the right to cast a vote equal in weight to that of every other citizen in an election for any office of Nusquam; and (3) by a defendant in a criminal case who claims the state is either denying him or her the full procedural protections of the criminal code or is treating him or her differently from other people under similar circumstances."

"Second?" the chair asks. "Very well, discussion? Professor Jacobsohn."

"We've debated this idea several times before. More than twenty-five years ago the American scholar John Hart Ely elegantly argued that the U.S. Supreme Court's proper role was precisely that which Mr. Pyknites has outlined.[79] Professor Ely's logic led him to widen the scope of the Court's proper function to include ensuring equal treatment of minority groups, just as Mr. Pyknites's third jurisdictional heading seems to. This sort of provision lets a constitutional camel into the democratic tent. If we're going to have

---

79. *Democracy and Distrust* (Cambridge, MA: Harvard University Press, 1980).

judicial review, and I urge that we do, let's propose it openly and honestly so our people can accept or reject it. That is a democratic argument."

"I certainly want to cabin judges' hunger for political power," Pyknites responds. "I don't claim that my proposal will automatically bring nirvana. For it to work at all will require much effort. We have an advantage over the United States: we have no history of judicial intervention in the policy choices of legislators and administrators. I agree that the Civil Law's notion that legislating and adjudicating are conceptually and practically distinct is largely fantasy; but it is a fantasy whose mystical powers have restrained judges to a narrower ambit than that of their colleagues in systems with judicial review. I think we can so restrict judges of this special tribunal. If we can't, Professor Jacobsohn should be happy, for we would then have a system of judicial review more like the one she wants."

"But," Jacobsohn comes back, "at a terrible cost to democracy. We should not be asking the people to approve a document that we have good reason, based on much experience, to believe will fail to do what we say it will do."

"I have," Zingaro says, "a different objection. If we cabin judicial review, how do we protect the rights of small minorities? Obviously, I'm worried about Gypsies, but other groups may come under attack. Only a cockeyed optimist would believe our having a seat or two in Parliament would protect us. I agree with Professor Deukalion: we don't yet have the political culture that would restrain our voters and their representatives, and I'm not ready to wait a century or two for that culture to develop. I'd like to make an alternative proposal."

"We're sufficiently flexible to multitask. Go ahead," the chair agrees.

"I propose that we adopt a system of judicial review like that of Japan. While we, as they have, would retain the Civil Law, we would allow every court of major jurisdiction to invalidate any statute, provision of the codes, or administrative regulation challenged in a case before that court."

"Do I hear a second? I do. Very well. Let us add this item to our debate."

"There's nothing more to discuss," Strega says. "We've talked about judicial review until we've bored the tops off our desks."

"There is something important to discuss," Pyknites intervenes. "My third jurisdictional heading, which Professor Jacobsohn dislikes, actually addresses much of Mr. Zingaro's objection. It provides a strong form of legal equality in criminal prosecutions."

"Not, however, in such areas as economic regulation and welfare," Zingaro replies.

"Correct," Pyknites admits. "Those are matters for a popularly elected legislature, where we guarantee small minorities like Gypsies representation."

"Would the Chair permit yet a third alternative?" Jon Kanuri asks. "Impressed by the closeness of our commitment to constitutional democracy and judicial review, I offer a compromise, taking off on the Chair's phrase 'constitutional review' rather than the narrower term 'judicial review.' I know that in Canada, France, Germany, Ireland, Italy, and the United States constitutional questions are often thoroughly debated in the legislative process. This is probably true in many other countries as well. In Italy, when legislators believe a bill raises constitutional questions, the matter is sent to a special committee, and, as I understand it, Parliament has always accepted that committee's judgment. Let us require Parliament to establish a permanent, joint standing committee called something like the Committee for Constitutional Review. It could be composed of, say, fifteen members of the lower house, whose membership would reflect the representation of parties there, plus five members of the upper house, chosen at random. The president would chair this group but have no vote. At the request of one-third of the members of either house, this committee would conduct an inquiry into the constitutionality of any proposed legislation whatsoever. This committee would hold hearings, inviting testimony both from the people and/or their experts who requested the hearing and from the bill's supporters. The committee would then decide the question and issue a formal justification for that decision. Dissenting opinions would be published. If a majority of the committee voted against a bill's validity, it could not become law unless approved by three-quarters of both houses of Parliament."

"I hear a second," the chair says. "Discussion?"

"Is our multitasking sufficiently sophisticated to allow a fourth alternative?" Wei asks.

"If waging war were as difficult as keeping up with you people," Colonel Martin answers, "I would never have taken up the profession of arms. Yes. Please state your motion."

"I propose that we adopt judicial review on the German model, with a central constitutional court whose members would be chosen by Parliament for single terms of twelve years."

"Second!" a member exclaims.

"Discussion?" the chair asks.

"For the love of God, if there is a God," Strega says, "let's vote."

"Further discussion?" Martin repeats. "No? Then we'll vote in our Estonian fashion."

The first ballot shows eight votes for Pyknites's constitutional court of limited jurisdiction, seven for Wei's German model, six for Kanuri's legislative review, and two for Zingaro's Japanese model, with Strega abstaining. The second ballot, with Zingaro's proposal dropped, is 8-8-8.

"The chair," Martin announces, "will break this tie by voting for the German model. That means it will survive until the next ballot. I've consulted with our parliamentarian, and his knowledge of the Estonian system is, like mine, exhausted. The chair therefore rules, subject as always to your correction, that we vote on whether Mr. Pyknites's proposal or Mr. Kanuri's will be on the final ballot. Any objections to this procedure? Very well, a show of hands. All in favor of the constitutional court of limited jurisdiction? All in favor of constitutional review by a legislative committee?

"The parliamentarian and I count nine for Mr. Pyknites's proposal, thirteen for Mr. Kanuri's, with two abstentions. Our final choice, then—unless we later change our minds—is between legislative review and the German model. All in favor of legislative review? All in favor of the German model?

"The vote is 13–11 in favor of the German model. I sense some strategic voting on the previous ballot, but that's irrelevant. Let us recess for the night."

CHAPTER EIGHT

Drafting 3

A Bill of Rights

The great and chief end *therefore, of Mens uniting into Commonwealths, and putting themselves under Government,* is the Preservation of their Property.   JOHN LOCKE

[T]he right, *as well as the* mode, *or* manner, of acquiring property, and of alienating or transferring, inheriting, or transmitting it, is conferred by society . . . and is always subject to the rules prescribed by positive law.   JUSTICE SAMUEL CHASE

After gaveling the caucus into session, Colonel Martin speaks. "Today we begin drafting a bill of rights and have several basic options: to restrict ourselves to a bare-bones listing of fundamental rights, leaving it to experience to flesh out these rights, or to write a detailed account ourselves. Cutting across these two options are a pair of others, not mutually exclusive. One would specify, as does the Irish charter, certain 'rights-like' directives for public policy but exempt them from judicial enforcement. These could supplement or replace judicially enforceable rights."

"What would, like, be the purpose of that?" Anita Baca interrupts.

"To list the republic's basic aims so that all 'who run can read,' giving voters a yardstick to measure officials' policy decisions," Demos Pyknites answers. "The Irish directives have been more or less copied in the constitutional texts of India, Italy, and South Africa."

"Thank you," Colonel Martin says. "The other cross-cutting alternative is interpretive instructions. The Ninth Amendment to the American text provides a good example: 'The enumeration in the Constitution of certain rights shall not be construed to deny or disparage others retained by the people.' When the subject of the verb is a third-person noun or pronoun, *shall* makes the verb imperative in mood and thus commands interpreters to construe rights broadly."

"If we go that route," Jessica Jacobsohn notes, "we'd better invent a super-imperative mood. The American Supreme Court has paid scant attention to that clear command.[1] The Ninth has been called 'the for-

---

1. Although some opinions have mentioned the Ninth Amendment in passing—for example, Roe v. Wade, 410 U.S. 113 (1973)—the case that most firmly rests on that amendment is Griswold v.

gotten amendment.'[2] Justice Robert H. Jackson admitted that he couldn't recall what it said;[3] that great textualist Hugo L. Black pretended those words didn't bind judges;[4] and Judge Robert H. Bork called it 'an ink blot.' "[5]

"Your problem may not be as severe," Retlaw Deukalion puts in. "Most American schools stopped teaching grammar decades ago, and now even scholars and judges are not ashamed of being ignorant of their language's having moods for verbs and parts of speech. But more important, I wouldn't be optimistic about such instructions' having much effect. Aharon Barak, the president of Israel's Supreme Court, claims that no document can interpret itself.[6] I suspect he's right, though I wouldn't oppose an effort to try to guide interpreters."

"Pity," Pyknites adds. "I'd like to horse-tie interpreters. Still, American judges are wise to pretend the Ninth Amendment isn't in the document they swore to uphold; this history provides another example of how unreliable judges are both as constitutional interpreters and as defenders of citizens' rights."

"We should learn from other nations' problems," Atilla Gregorian says, "but our vision shouldn't be restricted by their history. I move that, immediately after the preamble, we insert something like the following: 'Interpreters are directed to construe this document and the larger constitutional order it guides so as best to achieve the basic purposes just listed.' That language is not perfect, but it's clear enough to instruct any honest interpreter."

"Second? Yes. Discussion? Professor Jacobsohn?"

"That language is clear, but American experience does not give me much faith. Still, I can't think of anything better. And it has the advantage of pertaining to the entire constitutional order."

"Totally cool," Baca says.

"I can't support this proposal," Pyknites objects. "It's too open ended; it would authorize judges to discover whatever they wanted in the 'constitutional order.' I propose a friendly amendment. Delete the words 'and the larger constitutional order it guides.' "

Connecticut, 381 U.S. 479 (1965). Even there, the opinion of the Court brought in the First, Third, Fourth, and Fifth amendments as well.

2. Bennett B. Patterson, *The Forgotten Ninth Amendment* (Indianapolis: Bobbs-Merrill, 1955).

3. Robert H. Jackson, *The Supreme Court in the American System of Government* (Cambridge, MA: Harvard University Press, 1955), p. 74.

4. Griswold v. Connecticut, 381 U.S. 479, dis. op. (1965).

5. Quoted in *Wall St. J.*, Oct. 5, 1987, p. 22; for a longer statement of his views, see his *The Tempting of America: The Political Seduction of the Law* (New York: Free Press, 1990), pp. 183–85. See also Sotirios A. Barber, "The Ninth Amendment: Inkblot or Another Hard Nut to Crack?" 64 *Chi.-Kent L. Rev.* 67 (1988).

6. *Purposive Interpretation in Law* (Princeton, NJ: Princeton University Press, 2005), p. 218.

"I can't accept that change," Gregorian replies. "It's destructive, not friendly."

"Very well. A second for the amendment?" the chair asks. "Yes, thank you. Further discussion? No? A show of hands, please . . . The parliamentarian and I count eleven votes for, twelve against, and one abstention. The amendment fails.

"Now, more discussion on Father Gregorian's basic proposal? No? Then let us vote . . . The parliamentarian and I count twelve votes for, ten opposed, and two abstentions. The motion carries—barely. The next item concerns the choice of a format."

"I move we first try to construct a set of rights," Jacobsohn says. "As we go along, we can consider how detailed to make individual clauses. Some can be general, but others will have to be detailed. Our officials are inexperienced in protecting rights and will need as a lot of guidance. Still, I understand that no matter how specific we are, many situations will develop that our words won't seem to cover."

"I second that," Minister Pilsudski agrees. "We have models in the European Convention of Human Rights as well as in various national charters. We'll probably go different ways for different rights."

"Need I say," Pyknites adds, "I'd prefer it to be very general."

"Don't forget," Jacobsohn says, "your own reasoning against Father Gregorian's proposal: general wording empowers judges as well as legislators. The American Supreme Court has done much of its work through vague 'due process' clauses."

"All the more reason not to make rights judicially enforceable," Pyknites mutters.

"Do I hear," the chair asks, "additional proposals? No? Further discussion? Very well, let us vote . . . The parliamentarian and I count nineteen votes for the motion, four opposed, and one abstention. The motion carries. Let us proceed with the rights themselves. Professor Jacobsohn?"

"The opening cluster of rights should be those to dignity, respect, life, and liberty; the last can be taken away only by a conviction on a criminal charge in a duly constituted court of law."

"Second?" Colonel Martin asks. "Yes. Very well. As we debate, I beg you not to rehash arguments for and against inclusion of 'human dignity.' However much we discuss other parts of Professor Jacobsohn's proposal, let's simply vote that part up or down."

"Question!" someone shouts.

"If there is no further discussion, let us proceed . . . The parliamentarian and I count fourteen votes for, seven against, and three abstentions. Carried. I'll enter a note to the committee on revision to harmonize this language with that of the preamble. Professor Jacobsohn?"

"I have a simple motion: 'The death penalty shall not be imposed.'"

"Second?" the chair asks. "Very well. Discussion? Minister Strega?"

"An absolute ban on executions is soft-headed. What about treason? Desertion in time of war? Killing a prison guard while serving a life sentence? Raping and murdering children? People will demand—and somehow exact—revenge. Other prisoners often torture and murder child abusers. In those situations, we'd be abetting lynching."

"What is at stake in capital punishment," Gregorian says, "is the sanctity of human life. If we authorize killing except in self-defense or in defense of an immediately threatened third party, we disrespect human life. Most civilized countries—the United States is the great exception—ban executions, and it is no accident that the murder rate in America is higher than in societies that outlaw capital punishment. And within the United States, states such as Texas that kill prisoners have a higher murder rate than those that do not. If, as we have heard Justice Louis Brandeis quoted, government is the great teacher, capital punishment instructs citizens that human life is expendable."

"Next you'll argue," Strega snaps, "that permitting abortion conveys that same message."

"'Thou hath said it,'" Gregorian replies.

"It's always difficult," the Mufti puts in, "to determine when the Minister, peace be upon her, is stating her own beliefs or inciting us to probe more deeply into issues than we would prefer. I respond to the second possibility. I fully agree with the Reverend Father, peace be upon him as well. The Shari'a's harsh punishments do not conform to the teachings of the Qur'an. Allah is all merciful and commands us to be like Him. If we put the matter in simple secular terms, capital punishment does not have much, if any, deterrent effect. All the studies show that."

"I'm glad," Strega says, "that the Mufti disagrees both with the norms of Islamic religious law and the practice of Islamic countries. But there are additional reasons for capital punishment besides deterrence. One is that by imposing the ultimate punishment for murder, society does in fact positively communicate respect for life and considers disrespect unforgivable. There is also an economic reason. It is very expensive to guard, house, feed, and otherwise care for murderers for twenty-five-plus years. Most people convicted of murder are healthy young males. That money could improve medical care for law-abiding citizens. I'd put murdering garbage back into the food chain and use the money for children's hospitals."

"I have a question for the Chair," Jon Kanuri says. "What is your experience regarding the utility of a firing squad in keeping soldiers from deserting in battle?"

Colonel Martin closes his eyes and thinks for a few moments. "My experience is limited. I am a Marine, and we have never accepted draftees. Moreover, here in Nusquam I commanded troops only in peacetime—except, of course, during our late row with the junta. In combat in Angola and the Balkans, my troops were also professionals. For them, fear of a firing squad is much less important than fear of betraying loyalty to comrades, organization, and, if you'll forgive my sentimentality, the ideals of the profession of arms. For a professional soldier, honor is the great, the central, almost the sole virtue. Thus I do not believe that abolishing capital punishment would affect the efficiency of a professional army. I doubt it would have much effect on draftees either, if the war did not seem foolish or futile."

Martin looks around the room. "Do we need more discussion? No? Very well, let's vote on banning executions. We count fourteen for the ban, ten against. Mr. Zingaro?"

"I have several proposals. First, let's back up a bit. Somewhere, though not necessarily in the bill of rights itself, we need a requirement that every public official will swear that he or she will support the constitutional order as the supreme law of the nation and will defend that order against all enemies whomsoever. I leave the exact wording until later. This provision, though obvious, is extremely important in that it will tie public officers to the constitutional system and push them to internalize its values. Most specifically, it turns them into defenders of the entire constitutional order against all persons, even their colleagues."

"Is there a second? Yes. Discussion?" the chair asks.

"I don't like mixing a requirement of an oath with a claim to the constitution's supremacy in political affairs," Minster Pilsudski says, "but I support the motion."

After a pause of several seconds, the chair asks: "Other discussion? Comments? Very well. All in favor, please raise your hands. All opposed. The parliamentarian and I count twenty-three for, none opposed, and one abstention. Your next proposal, Mr. Zingaro."

"It relates to citizenship and consists of three parts:

1. All persons born or naturalized in Nusquam are citizens of Nusquam. Government may not remove the citizenship of a natural-born citizen. Naturalized citizens may lose their citizenship only if convicted in a court of law, within five years of naturalization, of having committed fraud to attain that citizenship.
2. Nothing in Section (1) shall restrict the rights of individuals to renounce their citizenship or to emigrate to other countries, providing they do not stand accused of a felony when they attempt to exert the right of expatriation or emigration.
3. All citizens shall have a right to travel within Nusquam and to live wherever they choose.

These provisions are self-explanatory. The junta exiled a number of dissidents and, by decree, made them stateless. Many other tyrannical regimes have followed a similar course. Eric Maria Remarque's novel *Arch of Triumph* reveals more poignantly than tons of legal evidence the cruelty of dooming people to wander from country to country.[7] The right to expatriate should be dear to anyone who advocates democracy or constitutionalism. It protects those who believe that the political system has so violated its basic principles that they can no longer give it their allegiance. The final section merely affirms basic rights to travel and reside within the country."

"Second? Discussion? Minister Pilsudski?"

"I hate to carp, but language that recognizes a constitutional right to live where one chooses is troublesome. I'd choose to live in a mansion if I had such a right. I suspect Mr. Zingaro meant only that everyone has a right to live where he or she can afford to."

"I didn't mean to start a land rush for the most desirable houses, only to outlaw segregated residential zones," Zingaro admits. "Should I modify the wording?"

"No," Pilsudski replies, "I support the proposal, with the understanding that our committee of revision will craft more exact language."

"Very well," the chair says. "No one else is seeking recognition. Let us vote . . . The parliamentarian and I again count twenty-three for, none opposed, and one abstention. Your third proposal?"

"Neither Parliament, the courts, nor administrative agencies shall make any law, decision, or regulation that denies any person the equal protection or benefit of the nation's laws."

"I, like, totally agree," Baca says, "but I want us to go further."

"Of course all persons should be equal before the law," Pyknites says, "but this proposal opens our political system to judicial interference. To avoid reopening our debate on judicial review, I propose that we adopt the proposal but without committing ourselves to judicial enforcement."

"Actually, I prefer judicial enforcement, but in the interest of moving ahead, I accept for the time being," Zingaro says. "I do so, however, with the understanding that we shall return to this matter."

"If I may make an observation," Deukalion says, "fatigue may be causing you to miss noticing that you're creating a nest of problems. First, let's go back to the discussions of democratic and constitutionalist theory. There are several kinds of both. Equality before the law is not a simple concept. Do you want to follow the dominant trend of American constitutional jurisprudence and look at the issue from the point of view of the individual or, as do some American scholars[8] and the dominant trend of Israeli constitutional juris-

---

7. Trans. W. Sorrell and D. Lindley (New York: Appleton-Century, 1945). The book was later made into a movie starring Charles Boyer and Ingrid Bergman.

8. See, for instance, Owen Fiss, "Groups and the Equal Protection Clause," 5 *Phil. and Pub. Affrs.* 107 (1976). Paul Brest responded: "In Defense of the Anti-discrimination Principle," 90 *Harv. L. Rev.* 1 (1976).

prudence, as pertaining more to groups? Second, I'm not sure where Mr. Zingaro is going here. There is a vast difference between 'equal protection of the laws' and 'equal benefit from the laws'; and 'equal opportunity under the laws' differs from both, as the drafters of the American Fourteenth mend-ment should have known."

"So what do you suggest?" Zingaro asks.

"That you consider carefully what you write in your charter. Equality is a complicated issue. It's tied to democratic as well as constitutionalist theory. Your choice of PR with some seats reserved for minorities like Gypsies leans toward the Israeli rather than the American model."

"Perhaps," Jacobsohn intervenes, "I should explain the Israeli model." The chair nods assent. "That country has been described as an 'ethnic de-mocracy.'9 Arabs and Jews are citizens, but only Jews have certain civic responsibilities, such as military service, and Arabs have fewer rights. In fact, they're second-class citizens. We don't want that difference. And in some matters Arabs and Jews are bound by different rules. Islamic law, admin-istered by religious tribunals, governs Muslims in questions of marriage and divorce, while Jews, observant or not, are subject to the jurisdiction of rab-binical courts in matrimonial cases."10

"Equality and sameness are different concepts," Deukalion agrees. "And multiethnic societies have serious problems here."

"At first," Zingaro says, "I was thinking, as a Gypsy, that allowing special rules and even special courts for some matters important to minorities like us would be good. I don't see us assimilating—or wanting to assimilate. My fellow Gypsies and I would like to keep our cultural identity, and I'd wager that Muslims would too. I want my children to speak Rom, to understand and practice our customs. I'll take care of those things, either individually or in conjunction with other Gypsies. But yesterday's discussion convinced me that the state's involvement would perpetuate our status as third-class citi-zens. I want my people to be both full-fledged citizens of Nusquam and full-fledged Gypsies."

"Native Americans have faced a similar difficulty," Jacobsohn says. "They're officially citizens and, if they wish, can live on reservations subject to their own laws and customs and can speak their own language. In fact, however, segregated living pretty much condemns them to the edges of poverty."

"I think what Mr. Zingaro wants," the colonel says, "is acceptance as fellow citizens with respect for cultural differences."

9. The phrase is Sammy Smooha's in *Israel: Pluralism and Conflict* (Berkeley: University of California Press, 1978), p. 108, but Jacobsohn read it in Gary Jeffrey Jacobsohn, *The Wheel of Law: India's Comparative Constitutional Context* (Princeton, NJ: Princeton University Press, 2003), p. 78.

10. See Marc Galanter and Jayanth Krishnan, "Personal Law and Human Rights in Compara-tive Perspective," 34 *Israel L. Rev.* 101 (2000); and Jacobsohn, *Wheel of Law*, pp. 81–86.

"Exactly," Zingaro replies.

"I may have misled the caucus," Deukalion puts in, "when I spoke of 'the American model.' I meant using the individual rather than the group as the relevant unit, not discriminating against groups. God knows there has been too much of the latter in the United States. There is a lot of uniformity across diverse ethnic and social groups, but Glazer and Moynihan were accurate when they described America as a smorgasbord rather than a melting pot."[11]

"I like that analogy," Zingaro says, "a smorgasbord with each group keeping its distinctive flavor but being an equally important part of the feast."

"Alas," Deukalion says, "'equal importance' is more difficult to attain than 'distinctive flavor.'"

"I totally agree with Mr. Z's reasoning," Baca says.

"What," Minister Strega asks, "do you have to say about language rights?"

"That's not relevant," Colonel Martin responds. "A century and a half ago, the people who founded this nation had, as Giuseppe Mazzini and and Vittore Emanuele would in Italy, the good sense to legislate a common language. They chose English, Mazzini and Emanuele chose the Tuscan dialect. Now that the junta is history, we're free to teach and speak our separate languages, but we have one common tongue that links us all. We don't need the sorts of arrangements that India, Switzerland, Canada, and Spain have. Does anyone disagree?[12]

"I see no hands. Mr. Zingaro, do you wish to rephrase your motion?"

"I do: 'All persons shall be equal before the law as administered by administrative or judicial institutions.' That is sufficiently general to mandate equal treatment."

Before the chair can ask, several calls of "Second!" sing out. Martin looks around: "Discussion? Again I see no hands. Let us vote . . . The count is 18–5–1. Minister Pilsudski?"

"I have a much simpler proposal: 'Parliament may not pass a bill of attainder or an ex post facto criminal law.' Those of you familiar with the American constitutional text will recognize both prohibitions. I added the word *criminal* because, despite what the U.S. Supreme Court said in 1798,[13]

---

11. Nathan Glazer and Patrick J. Moynihan, *Beyond the Melting Pot: The Negroes, Puerto Ricans, Jews, Italians, and Irish of New York City* (Cambridge, MA: MIT Press, 1963). Deukalion does not mention two older books that are among the more insightful on this point: Michael Novak, *The Rise of the Unmeltable Ethnics* (New York: Macmillan, 1972); and Thomas Sowell, *Ethnic America: A History* (New York: Basic Books, 1981).

12. Among the more relevant items in a very large professional literature on the topic of ethnic political self-determination are Will Kymlicka, *Multicultural Citizenship* (New York: Oxford University Press, 1995); Will Kymlicka and Alan Patten, eds., *Political Theory and Language Rights* (New York: Oxford University Press, 2003); and Stephen Macedo and Allen Buchanan, eds., *Secession and Self-Determination*, Nomos 45 (New York: New York University Press, 2003).

13. Calder v. Bull, 3 Dall. 386.

the historicity of the claim that ex post facto referred only to criminal laws was not then clear, and such a restricted meaning would not be obvious to those of us raised in the Civil Law tradition.[14] To permit regulation of the economy, I would make the distinction crystal clear."

Once more the motion is seconded, and the vote is twenty-three to one. "Mr. Kanuri?"

"We must also include a central provision of any charter of rights. 'Neither slavery nor involuntary servitude shall exist in Nusquam except as punishment for a crime for which an accused shall have been convicted after a fair trial in a court of law.' That wording is closer to the American Thirteenth Amendment than Article 4 of the European Convention on Human Rights; the real point is for us to go on record in favor of the basic message."

"Second?" the chair says. "Yes. Any discussion necessary? Ms Baca?"

"I support the proposal, but I want us to endorse a positive conception of freedom. I propose that we insert as an opening phrase 'Freedom being a fundamental right of all men and women.'"

Kanuri nods his head several times. "I happily accept Ms Baca's amendment."

"A show of hands, please," the chair says. "The parliamentarian and I count twenty-four for, zero against, and no abstentions. Congratulations, Mr. Kanuri and Ms Baca; your arguments for freedom have persuaded Minister Strega to vote."

"Thank you," Kanuri says. "I have a second proposal, if I may: 'All persons accused of a crime shall have the right to the assistance of legal counsel. If the accused cannot afford an attorney, the government shall appoint one at no cost to the defendant.' We all know of many people, mostly poor people—you're an exception. Mr. Pyknites—who were imprisoned because they couldn't afford legal aid. When we get to the final draft, we can modify this clause to exclude petty offenses."

The chair repeats the parliamentary rite, and the proposal carries, 22-0-2. "Pastor Glückmann?"

"I hope to continue our hedonic tone: 'Freedom of religious belief and unbelief shall be inviolable. Actions based on grounds of conscience shall not be regulated except by laws whose direct purpose and effect are to protect the safety or property of other citizens.' I'm not happy with this language, but later we can refine it too."

14. For doubts about the correctness of the Court's limitation in *Calder* of the sweep of ex post facto, see William W. Crosskey, *Politics and the Constitution in the History of the United States* (Chicago: University of Chicago Press, 1953), vol. 1, ch. 11. Section 1 of Article 7 of the European Convention on Human Rights has carefully spelled out its prohibition on what Americans would call ex post facto laws. Section 2, however, goes on to exempt many crimes against humanity from the necessity of a specific statutory ban: "This Article shall not prejudice the trial and punishment of any person for any act or omission which at the time when it was committed was criminal according to the general principles of law recognised by civilised nations."

"This one," Strega says, 'bothers me; but to show my cooperative spirit, I second it."

"Discussion? Vote? The parliamentarian and I tally twenty-four for, none opposed. Mr. Wei?"

"We need firm constitutional protection for rights of private property and investments. First, I move to include clauses requiring the government to pay its debts and forbidding it to take private property without compensation. As Minister Strega has reminded us, we desperately need foreign investment. Second, we must include broad protection of rights to own, use, and dispose of property. I do not, incidentally, oppose authorizing the government to break up monopolies."

"Do I hear a second?" the chair asks. "Thank you, Ms Strega. Discussion on the first of Mr. Wei's proposals? Ms Baca?"

"Do we mean to, like, obligate ourselves to pay off the debts the junta incurred? That makes me want to hurl. What about the bills those scum ran up at whorehouses?"

"Those were probably freebies," Strega interrupts.

Baca ignores the minister. "The luxuries for these people and their wives? What about the wages owed to torturers, the debt to the United States for training special police to root out political opposition? We let these scumbags escape with the Swiss bank accounts intact. That's enough."

"If we renege on our debts," Wei responds, "we tell foreign investors we can't be trusted."

"May I suggest a compromise?" Colonel Martin asks. "Adopt a clause that restricts the obligation to pay debts to the government under this constitutional text and leaves it to Parliament to handle the junta's debts as it seems prudent."

"Excellent," Pyknites calls out.

Hearing an approving murmur, Wei concedes. "It doesn't give us the best opportunity, but it's better than no guarantee at all. I accept the Chair's proposal as a substitute amendment."

"I see no one seeking recognition," the chair says. "Let us have a show of hands . . . The parliamentarian and I count twenty-two votes for the amended motion. Now we move to the more difficult part of Mr. Wei's proposal. Mufti?"

"I deeply respect Mr. Wei, peace be upon him, but property is a complex concept. It is a social construct, a product of social relationships. My professorial research assistant has found a remark of Justice Brandeis: 'All rights are derived from the purposes of the society in which they exist; above all rights rises duty to the community.'[15] As much as we need foreign investments, we cannot permit pirates, foreign or domestic, to pillage our country. Besides, a

---

15. Duplex Printing Co. v. Deering, 354 U.S. 443, dis. op., 488 (1921).

right to property really refers to a web of social relationships. To 'own' property is to have a bundle of entitlements that, in fact, exclude a private citizen's full control over 'things.'[16] Thus a large measure of public regulation of 'property' is legitimate. Other more traditional analyses offer similar justifications. We have read Article 43 of the Irish constitutional text. It acknowledges a natural right to own, transfer, bequeath, or inherit property, then goes on:

> The State recognizes, however, that the exercise of the rights mentioned in the foregoing provisions of the Article ought, in civil society, to be regulated by the principles of social justice. The State, accordingly, may as occasion requires delimit by law the exercise of the said rights with a view to reconciling their exercise with the exigencies of the common good.

Our charter should include words to this effect. For Islam, wealth is a responsibility, not a right. Religious directives aside, social justice demands a limit on the amount of and the ways by which persons, especially corporations, can gain and retain wealth."

"I share," Wei responds, "the Mufti's concern. But we operate in a world in which ambition and greed propel most people most of the time. We should avoid a Hobbesian war of all against all, even in economics, but we must also realize that the creation of wealth—wealth to build schools to educate children and hospitals to care for the aged and infirm, widows and orphans—requires our giving much room, not a free pass but much room, to entrepreneurs. I recall Mexico's efforts to further social justice by making patents common property. The result was that resourceful Mexican inventors moved to other countries and patented their ideas there.[17] A disaster. Without economic development, our people will share poverty, not wealth."

"The nature and reach of rights to property," Deukalion sententiously intervenes, "are among the most heatedly debated topics in moral theology and jurisprudence.[18] If you explore the philosophical implications of alterna-

16. See, for example, Bruce A. Ackerman, *Property and the Constitution* (New Haven, CT: Yale University Press, 1977); and the essays by Charles Geisler, Peter Salsich, and Joseph Singer in Charles Geisler and Gail Daneker, eds., *Property and Values: Alternatives to Public and Private Ownership* (Washington, DC: Island, 2000).

17. See George M. Armstrong Jr., *Law and Market Society in Mexico* (New York: Praeger, 1989).

18. See, for example, Ackerman, *Property and the Constitution;* Bruce A. Ackerman, *Social Justice in the Liberal State* (New Haven, CT: Yale University Press, 1991); Edward S. Corwin, *Liberty against Government* (Baton Rouge: Louisiana State University Press, 1948); Ronald Dworkin, *A Matter of Principle* (Cambridge, MA: Harvard University Press, 1985), esp. ch. 12; Richard A. Epstein, *Takings: Private Property and the Power of Eminent Domain* (Cambridge, MA: Harvard University Press, 1985); George E. Garvey and Gerald J. Garvey, *Economic Law and Economic Growth* (New York: Praeger, 1990); C. B. MacPherson, "Human Rights as Property Rights," *Dissent,* Winter 1977, pp. 72–77; Frank I. Michaelman, "Welfare Rights in a Constitutional Democracy," 1979 *Wash. U. L. Q.* 659; Stephen R. Munzer, *A Theory of Property* (New York: Cambridge University Press, 1990); Jennifer Nedelsky, *Private Property and the Limits of American Constitutionalism* (Chicago: University of Chicago Press, 1990); Robert Nozick, *Anarchy, State, and Utopia*

tives, you'll have weeks of hard debate. On the other hand, relying on common sense and the experience of other modern nations could allow you to quickly agree on some general principles. I suggest you look not only at Ireland's constitutional text but also at those of Germany, Spain, and Italy—the European Convention on Human Rights doesn't provide much help here—and adapt language to reconcile the competing demands of individual acquisitiveness and social justice."

"We should adopt," Jacobsohn says, "Justice Harlan Fiske Stone's solution in 1938 at the end of the U.S. Supreme Court's fight with Franklin Roosevelt: judges protect political participation and the other rights listed in the Bill of Rights and pretty much leave it to legislatures to regulate economic affairs. The only condition for valid economic regulation is reasonableness."[19]

"That sort of near-plenary grant to the legislature would drive foreign investors away quicker than an epidemic of an airborne HIV virus," Wei responds. "Investors have little enough faith in a constitutional democracy, zero if you don't handcuff a popularly elected legislature."

"I agree," Strega says.

"What about something along the Irish or German lines?" Gregorian asks. "Article 14 of the German Basic Law reads:

1. Property and the right of inheritance are guaranteed. Their content and limits shall be determined by law.
2. Property imposes duties. Its use should also serve the public weal.

Section 3 goes on to permit expropriation 'only in the public weal' and with compensation. The Spanish constitutional charter contains quite similar clauses.[20] Would these sorts of provisions serve the needs you foresee?"

(New York: Basic Books, 1974); Roland J. Pennock and John W. Chapman, eds., *Property* (New York: New York University Press, 1980); Margaret Jane Radin, "Property and Personhood," 34 *Stan. L. Rev.* 957 (1982); Margaret Jane Radin, *Reinterpreting Property* (Chicago: University of Chicago Press, 1993); John Rawls, *A Theory of Justice* (Cambridge, MA: Harvard University Press, 1971); Charles A. Reich, "The New Property," 73 *Yale L. J.* 733 (1964); Thomas Schaffer, Carol Mooney, and Amy Boettcher, *The Planning and Drafting of Wills and Estates* (New York: Foundation, 2001), ch. 1; William Van Alstyne, "The Recrudescence of Property Rights as the Foremost Principle of Civil Liberties," 43 *Law and Contemp. Probs.* 66 (1980).

19. United States v. Carolene Products, 304 U.S. 144, note 4 (1938). For the history of this footnote and a basic bibliography, see Walter F. Murphy, James E. Fleming, Sotirios A. Barber, and Stephen Macedo, *American Constitutional Interpretation,* 3rd ed. (Westbury, NY: Foundation, 2003), pp. 687–91; for *Carolene Products'* application to constitutional questions involving property, see ibid., ch. 16.

20. Article 33 provides the following:

1. The right to private property and inheritance is recognized.
2. The social function of these rights shall determine the limits of their content in accordance with the law.
3. No one may be deprived of this property and rights except for a justified cause of public utility or social interest after proper indemnification in accordance with the provisions of law.

"Any of these," Wei says, "might be sufficient if worded to protect investments, by foreigners as well as citizens, as property. Perhaps saying property rights belong to 'persons' would suffice. Actually, I like the Irish wording, with its concern for social justice and reminders about the proper purposes of public actions . . . Very well, I make this part of my motion."

"Second? Yes, thank you. Further discussion? Ms Baca?"

"I'll get to my general criticism in a minute, right? But first a specific point now. You have all totally forgotten that the junta seized lots of property—life savings, homes, businesses, and plain old cash—and gave them to its members and supporters. There was no compensation, only jail for those who protested. What compensation do we offer to these people?"

"What sort of constitutional provision," Wei asks, "would do justice for those people without endangering the rights of innocent third parties who in good faith bought such property?"

"This problem is serious," Pyknites says. "It's better handled by remedial legislation than convoluted constitutional language."

"But," Baca replies, "remedial legislation would, like, violate our banker's ban."

"Other countries must have faced this problem," the chair says. "Professor Deukalion, can you enlighten us?"

"I may only confuse things. There are four general patterns of policy on this issue. The Irish maintained the status quo; they did not even try to take back churches the English had stolen from them. The Irish like to think they were being Christian in forgiving their enemies, but Britain was then a first-rate military and economic power. Ireland feared the one and needed the other. Second, the Germans enacted legislation to cope with Nazi and later communist seizures in the East. Some justice has been done, but so has some injustice. Hungary tried similar legislation but ran into constitutional difficulties. South Africa incorporated complex clauses into its constitutional charter. Sections 1–3 of Article 25 provide the usual protection for property and compensation for what is taken in the public interest. Then come §§6 and 7:

6. A person or community whose tenure of land is legally insecure because of racially discriminatory laws or practices is entitled, to the extent provided by an Act of Parliament, either to tenure which is legally secure or to comparable redress.

7. A person or community dispossessed of property after 19 June 1913 as a result of past racially discriminatory laws or practices is entitled, to the extent provided by an Act of Parliament, either to restitution of that property or to equitable redress.

To carry out those provisions, the South African Parliament established a land commission, but this program has not yet produced anything approaching full restitution.[21]

"Zimbabwe took a fourth course that combined diplomacy, constitutional guarantees, constitutional amendment, and violence to recover land the English settlers had seized. To stop civil war in 1979, whites and blacks agreed to explicit constitutional guarantees protecting property rights and to allocate whites twenty of the one hundred seats in parliament for seven years so they could, at least during that period, prevent repeal of the protective clauses.[22] It was not until 2000 that Robert Mugabe, the dictator, had Parliament amend the constitutional text to allow appropriation of land without compensation. He did so in the context of squatters' attacks, which he probably instigated, against whites. But Zimbabwe's disintegrating economy did not permit simple solutions. Faced, on the one hand, with the probability of massive withdrawals of foreign investments and, on the other, with promises of financial aid from Britain, Mugabe temporarily stopped appropriating land without compensation. The situation has degenerated, and Zimbabwe has left the Commonwealth in disgrace; by mid-2005, it was threatened by civil war, bankruptcy, and mass starvation."[23]

"Those are not attractive options," the chair comments.

"Those clauses are too unwieldy," Baca says. "Let's simply say that, because we respect private property, we reject the junta's expropriations. Then we could have a second clause stating that persons who acquired such property in good faith would, after a judicial proceeding, be allowed to keep it and the government would compensate the original owners or their heirs."

"Where would the government get the money to pay those bills?" Strega ask. "Besides, if we go back far enough, we'll find that all property is based on theft or extortion by thugs."

"Ms Baca and Minister Strega both have a point," Kanuri says. "We can't guarantee a right to keep property that was stolen within the vivid memory of a huge segment of the population and pretend to be setting up rules for a

21. According to the *Economist*, as of April 2000, only 4,000 of the 63,400 claims of blacks for redress for eviction had been settled (Apr. 15, 2000, p. 39). The first order for a forced sale came in March 2001, and that decree provoked not only demonstrations by white farmers but also a lawsuit in the Constitutional Court: "Land Expropriation in South Africa," *N.Y. Times,* Mar. 15, 2001.

22. Article 16 contains ten sections, thirty-nine subsections, and six subsubsections. See, generally, Jeffrey Ira Herbst, *State Politics in Zimbabwe* (Berkeley: University of California Press, 1990); for details on the agreement of 1979, see Jeffrey Davidow, *A Peace in Southern Rhodesia: The Lancaster House Conference on Rhodesia, 1979* (Boulder: Westview, 1984).

23. Rachel L. Swarne, "With Foreign Aid Promised, Zimbabwe Calls Off Squatters," *N.Y. Times,* Apr. 14, 2000.

just society. Nevertheless, we can't simply steal that property back, and we can't afford to rebuy it."

"Would you state your proposal as a resolution, Ms Baca?" the chair asks.

"Yes. I propose that we amend Mr. Wei's motion saying that the title to any property seized by the junta can be challenged in a court of law."

"Thank you. Second? Very well. Discussion?"

"Would you agree," Wei asks, "that our drafting committee should define property to include not merely tangibles like real estate but also copyrights, patents, stocks, bonds, and other securities?"

"Of course."

"Then I can—reluctantly—accept your proposal as an amendment," Wei agrees.

"Further discussion?" the chair asks. "Very well, let us vote . . . The parliamentarian and I count sixteen votes for, eight against. The motion carries. Mr. Kirca?"

"I make a double-barreled proposal, that we guarantee a right to associate, to form and join organizations. I confess an interest here. As a labor leader, I am trying to protect workers' rights to form real unions, not the shams the junta dominated. Unions should be able to engage in collective bargaining and to strike when members think that's in their best interest. The right to strike would carry the right to picket, an important form of free speech. But I also have a broader agenda. We have all heard Professor Deukalion speak of the strong basis for democratic government that civic organizations establish; we have also read about that connection.[24] I propose we establish a positive right to form associations, whether business, religious, literary—whatever. I could make a long speech, but given what we've heard and read, that won't be necessary."

"Bless you for that mercy," Colonel Martin says. "Second? . . . We do. Mr. Pyknites?"

"I would only stress how critical such a right is for any form of democracy."

Wei speaks next: "I agree and would go further. I propose we also recognize a right to 'disassociate,' a right not to join or, once having joined, to resign from any association."

"This is a blatant attempt to legitimize union busting!" Kirca interrupts. "It has nothing to do with a right to associate, only with owners' privilege to break unions."

24. See esp. Robert D. Putnam, *Making Democracy Work: Civic Traditions in Modern Italy* (Princeton, NJ: Princeton University Press, 1993), and *Bowling Alone: The Collapse and Revival of American Community* (New York: Simon and Schuster, 2000). Ariel C. Armony, *The Dubious Link: Civic Engagement and Democratization* (Stanford, CA: Stanford University Press, 2004), disagrees. He points out that citizens' participation in many "civic" organizations, such as the White Citizens Councils in the United States or pro-Nazi and procommunist groups in Weimar Germany, undermine both constitutionalism and democracy.

"One moment, please," the chair says. "Do we have a second? We do. Mr. Wei?"

"My amendment has everything to do with a right to associate. How can a person be free to associate if he *must* join or remain in an organization? A real right is one that the individual invokes for him- or herself. If someone else controls it, it is hardly a right for the individual concerned. I favor a right of workers to organize, to bargain collectively, and even to strike and picket. But I cannot agree that an individual surrenders all meaningful control over this right when he or she joins a group. We have already provided that a person can renounce citizenship."

"Mr. Wei," Minister Pilsudski asks, "what about requiring lawyers to join a bar association? Many American states so require."

"There are special circumstances there," Wei says. "Some American states have, in effect, made bar associations governmental agencies to control admission to law practice and to discipline attorneys. I don't object to government's requiring professionals like doctors or lawyers to meet general standards established by their colleagues."

The chair calls for a vote. Wei's amendment carries 13–11. The final vote on Kirca's amended proposal is 13–4, with seven abstentions, including Kirca himself. The chair then recognizes Anita Baca.

"We're going down the American path, like totally. By listing these negative rights, we perpetuate injustice and social oppression. Government is not the only threat to freedom and happiness, right? If we want a just society, we need positive constitutionalism, too. We didn't merely outlaw slavery, we recognized the right of all people to freedom. Let's recognize other rights as well—for example, to as much free education as a person can use and to a decent standard of living. Let's make it clear that the public welfare means more than national defense and protecting the property of the rich. We've allowed the rich can keep what they have earned (and even stolen) and the poor to remain poor. The rich will keep a stranglehold not only on economic affairs but also on what constitutes merit. They'll still be the gatekeepers to the upper echelons of society. And the members of this elite were the junta's supporters—straight white males. Right?"

"Me, a straight white male who supported the junta?" Wei asks.

"You're an exception." Baca smiles and continues: "I want to protect rights not only against government but also against the dominant class."

"Could you give us some language?" Minister Pilsudski asks gently.

"I want a positive, constitutionally entrenched right of every worker, male, female, gay, or bisexual, to be free from discrimination and to earn a living wage. I want a positive, constitutionally entrenched right of every human being to decent housing, to an adequate diet, to as much education as his or her talents justify, and to freedom from sexual harassment. I want these rights protected not only against government but also against employers, labor unions, and religious organizations. I also want a positive, constitutionally entrenched right to breathe clean air and drink water unpolluted by toxic wastes. I want a positive, constitutionally entrenched right to read newspapers and listen to TV and radio not controlled by huge corporations, a positive, constitutionally entrenched right not to be demeaned by pornography that, like, depicts women as males' sexual toys. I want women to have a positive, constitutionally entrenched right to equality within the family and to have her husband share the burdens of housework and raising children, and a woman's positive, constitutionally entrenched right to financial compensation in case of divorce."

"Why not," Strega cuts in, "a woman's freedom to have an abortion? Shouldn't women have a right to choose how their bodies will be used?"

"No one has a right to take a human life," Baca responds.

"But a fetus is not fully human!"

"What is it, a giraffe with human DNA? If fetuses weren't human, drug companies wouldn't want their stem cells."

"We live in a strange world," Gregorian muses. "It's a crime to kill a sea turtle, but it's legal, indeed socially acceptable, to dismember a human fetus moments before its birth."

"Please," the chair intervenes, "let's leave discussion of abortion until last. Let's first try to settle matters on which we can reach consensus."

"Peace be upon you, Ms Baca," the Mufti says. "Did you not mean to say protection against *religious discrimination,* not protection against religious *organizations?*"

"No, I totally did not. I want protection against the sexual discrimination practiced by religious organizations that make women second-class citizens. Right? I don't merely mean permitting clitorectomy. I also mean imposing dress codes on women, not allowing them to become priests, ministers, or imams, or accepting 'honor rape' as a male right."

"Did I see you raise your hand, Pastor?" the chair asks, almost prayerfully.

"I started to, but out of prudence, I yield to Father Gregorian. Ms Baca is one of his."

"What would you do about—'to' might be better—churches that don't allow women to become ministers?" Gregorian asks."

"First, by listing that as a woman's right, I'd put moral pressure on churches to treat women as truly being entitled to equal respect and dignity with men. Second, Parliament could enforce these provisions by legislation that could include making churches that discriminate ineligible for governmental assistance and disallow as tax deductions contributions to them.[25]

---

25. See Bob Jones University v. United States, 461 U.S. 574 (1983), which upheld the Internal Revenue Service's decision to deny a tax-exempt status to a private school practicing racial discrimination.

Would I close them down? No, but not because that would be unjust, only impossible."

Jacobsohn speaks out: "Ms Baca, as a woman, I'm sympathetic, but also deeply troubled. You speak as if terms like *pornography* are self-defining. Not true. Putting them in a constitutional text could stifle free exchange of ideas rather than protect women. I see similar problems with inserting into a constitutional charter a right to freedom from sexual harassment. I wouldn't want us to end up with the sort of ludicrous codes of political correctness that some American colleges adopted in the 1990s. More important, if we enacted all of your ideas, we'd invite legislators to become totalitarian guardians of propriety and judges to become inquisitors."

"False. Putting this declaration in the constitutional charter delegitimizes the usual excuse that such injustices are private matters and thus outside the scope of public concern. That alone makes my proposal like totally essential to real community. It leaves each one of us free to worship God in our own way but not to create organizations that enjoy privileges granted by the state and then use those privileges to discriminate for reasons that should be odious to a free people."

"But," Jacobsohn persists, "wouldn't we be setting up two categories of religious organizations, those whose beliefs about men and women we disapprove and those whose beliefs we approve? Why stop with women? What about the divinity of Jesus or the authority of the Bible? Whey can't we sanction religious organizations that deny these supposed truths?"

"If you, as a moral relativist, look on discrimination because of sex as merely a matter of personal or cultural choice, yes; but not if you, like, think that moral truth exists, that we can often if not always discover it, and that some acts are evil in themselves. If we reason together, we 'll agree that discrimination because of sex is no less wrong than discrimination because of ethnicity. Both deny the equal dignity and worth of members of the community. Beliefs about Jesus and the Trinity are just that, beliefs. Right? In contrast, invidious discrimination involves acts, acts that harm individuals as well as the social order. Our root problem in such matters is that most of us have been infected by a neurotic male fear of true community. Thus we erect obstacles to community by conflating theological beliefs and morally harmful acts. Professor Rheaux von Whaide shared with us his reasoning that the state's stopping people from acts that are truly harmful, even if only to themselves, does not interfere with real freedom. In fact, what I propose protects people who would discriminate as well those being discriminated against. Professor Whaide, perhaps you can comment."

"In general, I agree," Whaide responds, "but specific questions are not easily settled. Although 'right reason' will surely tell us that discrimination can be wrong, prudential concerns may come into play. Many people adhere to religious beliefs non- or even irrationally, and those beliefs can run deep and generate zeal that only fanatical secular creeds like Nazism can match. Thus, I would treat religious beliefs and even practices with great caution. On more principled grounds, we must recognize that to distinguish is not the same as to discriminate; and to discriminate, which *could* mean only to take difference into account, is not the same as to discriminate invidiously. It is right reason that must convince us that a particular discrimination is invidious. It is not wrong to make decisions based on distinctions that, in fact, relate to a person's capabilities for a given task. To deny all blind people drivers' licenses is not an invidious discrimination, while denying a license to all women or Chinese or Muslims is. In contrast, affirmative action need not constitute invidious discrimination if its purpose is to allow members of a disadvantaged group, accurately identified, a chance to reach a level of true, not merely formal, equality."

"Professor, Pilsudski asks, "could you suggest language that could allow affirmative action for the disadvantaged without denying equal protection to those who have not been disadvantaged?"

"On the plane from Australia, I was perusing South Africa's constitutional text. Let me quote from Article 9 §2:

> Equality includes the full enjoyment of all rights and freedom. To promote the achievement of equality, legislative and other measures designed to protect or advance persons, or categories of persons, disadvantaged by unfair discrimination may be taken."

"Interesting language," Pilsudski says, "broad enough to stretch toward both of our goals. If we don't take it up at this point, I hope our committee on revision will."

"The record will note your desire," the chair agrees. "Pastor Glückmann?"

"Whatever the abstract virtue of Ms Baca's proposal about religious organizations, we have no chance of getting popular approval for a constitutional charter with that clause in it. Most Catholics, Muslims, and Orthodox Jews would be adamantly opposed, as would many Protestants. And even if we did get such a document accepted and tried to implement the clause, we'd face civil war. Jews will cite 1 and 2 Maccabees, even though the Orthodox do not accept those books as part of their canon. Muslims will heap hadiths and verses from the Qur'an proclaiming Allah alone as sovereign. Protestants will rely on the third chapter of Acts of the Apostles, wherein St. Peter asks the priests: 'Is it right in God's eyes for us to obey you rather than God?' Catholics would cite that passage and also note that in 2000 the Vatican reminded all public officials of the absolute priority of God in public affairs."[26]

---

26. Alessandra Stanley, "Just What Politicians Needed: A Patron Saint," *N.Y. Times,* Oct. 29, 2000. The occasion was the announcement that on Oct. 31 the pope would proclaim St. Thomas More the patron saint of politicians.

"But what tears a nation apart more than invidious discrimination because of race, ethnicity, or sex?" Baca retorts.

"I sympathize with Ms Baca's goals," Kirca puts in, "but I also share Professor Jacobsohn and Pastor Glückmann's concerns. And I have an additional worry. A liberal constitutional order *needs,* not merely should tolerate, some dissident individuals and organizations. Which public policy is best is seldom clear, and the answer often changes with changing circumstances. Political prudence requires us to question governmental judgments about the desirability of the basic constitutional order as well as about the wisdom of specific policy choices. In my early days in a Western school, I was required to read John Stuart Mill, and I recall—with the help of my research assistant—his saying: 'Even if received opinion be not only true, but the whole truth; unless it is suffered to be, and actually is, vigorously and earnestly contested, it will, by most of those who receive it, be held in the manner of prejudice, with little comprehension or feeling of its rational grounds. And not only this, but . . . the meaning of the doctrine itself will be in danger of being lost or enfeebled.'[27]

"We want public opinion to internalize the values of constitutional democracy, but not for our people to forget the rational grounds of those principles. If we peacefully brought all religious creeds into line with what the current majority considers public morality, we would cut off an important source of criticism necessary to a free, open political system. We don't want a closed society. My assistant has provided me with another quotation, this one from Sotirios A. Barber: 'Our commitment to self-critical thought and our desire to be recognized as reasoning creatures requires some toleration of illiberal private associations because it is from these associations that some of the premises of self-criticism come and because reasons as such are eventually submitted, not imposed.' "[28]

"Not relevant!" Baca says. "I don't want us to be intolerant of what these people believe or preach. I only want to make it clear, totally, that when they invidiously discriminate, they offend public moral values. I'd stigmatize their *acts,* not their words. Right? Carried to its logical conclusion, an argument that we should allow acts that we think morally wrong because they offer critical evaluations of our values means we should tolerate terrorists because they offer an alternative not only to representative and constitutional democracy but also to reasoned argument."

"Mr. Pyknites?"

"In prison, I read another of Professor Barber's books in which he warned against clinging to 'a closed conception of the good.'[29] He also wrote

27. *On Liberty,* in *On Liberty and Considerations on Representative Government,* ed. R. B. McCallum (Oxford, Blackwell, 1948), ch. 2, p. 46.

28. *On What the Constitution Means* (Baltimore: Johns Hopkins University Press, 1984), p. 143.

29. *The Constitution of Judicial Power* (Baltimore: Johns Hopkins University Press, 1993), p. 220.

that moral realists must be open to the possibility that their judgments are mistaken.[30] But if the constitutional charter states that the antidiscrimination principle trumps what many of our citizens believe is the word of God, we leave little room for reasoned discussion. I'm an agnostic, but I realize that religious beliefs present a very serious and tangled problem, one that Parliament, representing the entire people, would be better suited to resolve than we are. But the problem is here before us, and so we must deal with it. I ask the patience of the Chair and the caucus so I can offer a complicated alternative that may appease, if not satisfy, Ms Baca as well as her critics."

"Please proceed," the chair says.

"We have reached a stage where we must look at our work in a systemic fashion. We are, after all, creating a whole, a thing, we hope, whose parts fit well together."

"What has that got to do with my proposal?" Baca asks.

"Please hear me out. We have agreed to a document that sets up parliamentary government with bicameralism and proportional representation, retains our Civil Law system, establishes judicial review, and embodies a bill of rights as well as a preamble that lays out certain goals for our polity. I have bowed to the will of the majority and accepted all of these. I urge you to look at what we have proposed as a *political system* and then reconsider some aspects of our decisions. What I suggest is not my ideal form of governance, but I think it well fits this caucus's perceptions of Nusquam's needs and aspirations."

"Be specific!" Strega barks.

Pyknites continues. "I now retreat and go along with our adopting a preamble setting out our basic goals and values and announcing our purpose to protect as much individual freedom as is compatible with the public good, while recognizing the equal dignity and respect to which all men and women are naturally entitled. I would include the sort of interpretive instructions that we earlier approved, though more out of hope for, rather than faith in, their efficacy. I would follow those statements with directives of positive policy goals on the Irish model. As for a bill of rights, I suggest that, in addition to the proposals we have adopted, we recognize, as absolutely essential to civil government, freedom of speech, press, and assembly and the right to cast a ballot equal in weight to that of every other citizen. In short, I would adopt, with modifications of language to fit our circumstances, the European Convention on Human Rights. I would, however—and here I retrace old arguments—allow judges to strike down as unconstitutional only two classes of governmental actions: (1) those touching on the rights of the criminally accused and (2) those affecting rights to speak, write, assemble, and vote."

30. Ibid., p. 233.

"Despite your criticisms of the U.S. Supreme Court, you'd still trust judges to protect democratic political processes?" Strega asks.

"No, I trust judges to protect their own authority."

"What about," Baca asks, "my concerns, with which you are supposedly sympathetic?"

"I would include them in a declaration like Article 45 of Ireland's constitutional text."

Kanuri breaks in: "I've forgotten what that article says."

"It's on our hard drives," Pyknites explains. "Because it runs to two pages, I'll read only the first section and summarize the rest: 'The State shall strive to promote the welfare of the whole people by securing and protecting as effectively as it may a social order in which justice and charity shall inform all the institutions of the national life.' More particularly, public policy 'shall'— note again the imperative mood makes what follows obligatory rather than merely hortatory—be directed toward ensuring that all men and women may earn a living wage; protect private economic initiative; institute a system of control over community resources 'as best to subserve the common good'; prevent monopolies and similar exploitations of the public; safeguard 'with especial care the economic interest of the weaker sections of the community, and where necessary, to contribute to the support of the infirm, the widow, the orphan, and the aged'; and, finally, to protect the health and safety of men, women, and children so that 'citizens shall not be forced by economic necessity to enter avocations unsuited to their sex, age, or strength.'"[31]

31. The full text of Article 45:

The principles of social policy set forth in this Article are intended from the general guidance of the Oireachtas [Parliament]. The application of those principles in the making of laws shall be the care of Oireachtas exclusively and not be cognisable by any Court under any of the provisions of this Consitution.

1. The State shall strive to promote the welfare of the whole people by securing and protecting as effectively as it may a social order in which justice and charity shall inform all the institutions of the national life.

2. The State shall, in particular, direct its policy toward securing
   i. That the citizens (all of whom, men and women equally, have the right to an adequate means of livelihood) may through their occupations find the means of making reasonable provision for their domestic needs.
   ii. That the ownership and control of the material resources of the community may be so distributed amongst private individuals and the various classes as best to subserve the common good.
   iii. That, especially, the operation of free competition shall not be allowed so to develop as to result in the concentration of the ownership or control of essential commodities in a few individuals to the common detriment.
   iv. That in what pertains to the control of credit the constant and predominant aim shall be the welfare of the people as a whole.
   v. That there may established on the land in economic security as many families as in the circumstances shall be practicable.

"Wait," Baca says. "That last sounds sexist to me, like, totally. What 'avocations' are unsuited to a person's gender?"

"First," Pyknites replies, "in context, it isn't sexist. The article asserts the equality of men and women. Second, Ms Baca has surely read about sweat-shops where poor young women have been forced to work—and sometimes to die—under miserable physical conditions and the damage that labor imposed on the health of those women.[32] Third, as our colleagues have been, I am talking about a provision we might adapt, not copy. I'm trying to clarify how we might achieve your goals without setting words into constitutional stone that we, or later generations, might regret."

"Under your scheme," Zingaro asks, "who protects Gypsies, Muslims, and Sephardic Jews?"

"I repeat," Pyknites replies, "those groups will have little to fear from a parliament whose members are chosen by proportional representation with some seats set aside for them. More particularly, judges could provide additional protectors if and when any Gypsy or anyone else were accused of crime or if and when any person's political rights were threatened. I'm no fan of judges, but I think they will be quite efficient in protecting individual rights within courtrooms. By defending citizens against government there, they would be defending their own turf.

"But let me speak more positively and paraphrase what others have said here: By acknowledging the dignity of each and every human being and ranking as fundamental such rights as those to equal treatment by government and fellow citizens, our constitutional charter educates both the people and public officials. We set up the public conscience as a bulwark of liberty and also remind public officials that opponents at the next election will use against them any violation of the constitutional charter. I quote Professor Jacobsohn's hero, James Madison: "It may be thought that all paper barriers against the power of the community are too weak to be worthy of atten-

---

3.   1°.   The State shall favor and, where necessary, supplement private initiative in industry and commerce.

 2°.   The State shall endeavor to secure that private enterprise shall be so conducted as to ensure reasonable efficiency in the production and distribution of goods and as to protect the public against exploitation.

4.   1°.   The State pledges itself to safeguard with especial care the economic interests of the weaker sections of the community, and, where necessary, to contribute to the support of the infirm, the widow, the orphan, and the aged.

 2°.   The State shall endeavor to ensure that the strength and health of workers, men and women, and the tender age of children, shall not be abused and that citizens shall not be forced by economic necessity to enter avocations unsuited to their sex, age or strength.

32. See the "Brandeis Brief" submitted in Muller v. Oregon, 208 U.S. 412 (1908); Clement E. Vose, "The National Consumer's League and the Brandeis Brief," 1 *Midw. J. of Pol. Sci.* 267 (1957); and Alpheus Thomas Mason, *Brandeis: A Free Man's Life* (New York: Viking, 1946), pp. 248–52.

tion. . . . [Y]et, as they have a tendency to impress some degree of respect for them, to establish the public opinion in their favour, and rouse the attention of the whole community, it may be one means to controul the majority from those acts to which they might be otherwise inclined.'"[33]

"You are an optimist," Zingaro replies.

"We're covering old ground," Jacobsohn says, "but education in democratic political culture is not likely to be instantaneous. What happens in the meantime, when our people are still nursing old grudges against other groups?"

"A problem," Pyknites admits. "I'd gamble on the good sense of our people. If we make judges guardians who can overrule elected representatives on substantive matters, we suffocate democratic culture in its crib."

"I see not one but several gambles here," Minister Pilsudski speaks out. "First that parties and their candidates will educate voters rather than galvanize their resentments. The second is that most voters will listen and learn."

"It may be," Deukalion says, "that Mr. Pyknites's fears of judicial review are as exaggerated as are Professor Jacobsohn's hopes. Martin Shapiro argues that courts are likely to be most politically influential in governmental systems that have federalism and a form of separation of powers as well as a judicially enforceable bill of rights.[34] You will have the last, but not federalism; and parliamentary government tends to meld legislative and executive powers. Officials in the two layers of government as well as in separate executive and the legislature sometimes need judges to intervene on their behalf. They tolerate occasional judicial bites on their own political legs as the price of protection against rivals. Thus your judges who try to guard putative rights against government will be much more vulnerable than are judges in more complex political systems."

"I'm not sure whether this theory comforts or frightens me," Pilsudski says.

"At least it helps construct a continuum of judges' political importance ranging from the weak Supreme Court of Japan, which functions in a unified parliamentary system with a bill of rights, to Australia's somewhat stronger High Court, which operates as part of a federal parliamentary system without a bill of rights, to Canada's even stronger Supreme Court, placed within a federal parliamentary system with a bill of rights, to the very powerful Supreme Court of the United States, which works with two other sup-

---

33. 1 *Annals of Congress* 440–41.

34. "The European Court of Justice," in Peter H. Russell and David M. O'Brien, eds., *Judicial Independence in the Age of Democracy: Critical Perspectives from around the World* (Charlottesville: University Press of Virginia, 2001). In some ways, Shapiro's argument is an improvement on that of Walter F. Murphy, *Congress and the Court* (Chicago: University of Chicago Press, 1962), pp. 256–62. What follows in the text is a further continuation, albeit one that is still incomplete, of the basic theory.

posedly coordinate branches of the national government in a federal system with a bill of rights. This theory, however, does not explain why Ireland's Supreme Court has exercised greater authority than Italy's Constitutional Court. Both function within parliamentary systems with bills of rights, but Italy has a weak, but apparently budding, form of federalism. Obviously many other factors have been at work. In sum, we have only the germ of a theory to help us understand judicial power."

"An interesting academic exercise," the chair notes, "but our time is limited. We are marching, countermarching, and crisscrossing our own wake, if I can mix naval and military metaphors. Let us focus on a bill of rights. Mr. Pyknites has offered a coherent plan. Do I hear a second? I do. Rather than slavishly follow Robert's Rules, let us again multitask and consider any other proposals before voting. Hearing no objection, I invite further discussion. Father Gregorian?"

"I have several substantive concerns about what Mr. Pyknites and Ms Baca have said. They have linked rights that compete if not conflict, such as free speech and press on the one hand and protection against pornography and hate speech on the other. To some extent we might look on each of these freedoms as good in themselves. The first two allow us to express our thoughts without fear of governmental sanctions, while the third would protect the dignity and equality not only of women but of all members of ethnic and religious minorities. Still, I wonder how these 'goods' fit together. Interpretations of the American First Amendment worry me deeply. Could Professor Deukalion offer some hope or at least some light here?"

"Let me say two things," Deukalion responds. "First, I share your concern about American constitutional interpretation in this area. I note with sadness that most Americans, including critics of interpretations that bother you and me, seem to look on their bill of rights as almost divinely inspired. Certainly the charter as a whole is widely revered as a sacred document. I believe someone has already noted that Madison implied that 'the finger of that Almighty hand' had been at work during all of American history.[35] And American constitutional arguments, even scholarly ones, have often been much like those among theologians of the same religion: critical of the correctness of this or that interpretation but not of the underlying document and the values it proclaims.[36] I must add, of course, that the 'values it pro-

---

35. *The Federalist*, No. 37.

36. For a similar argument, see Robin West, "Constitutional Skepticism," *72 Bost. U. L. Rev.* 765 (1991); I have used the revised version in Susan Brison and Walter Sinnott-Armstrong, eds., *Contemporary Perspectives on Constitutional Interpretation* (Boulder: Westview, 1993). There are, however, significant exceptions to uncritical adulation of the American constitutional text. See, for example, Sanford V. Levinson, *Constitutional Faith* (Princeton, NJ: Princeton University Press, 1988). More basically, Sotirios A. Barber has reiterated his belief that adherence to the constitution— or to any political or moral order—is always subject to critical reevaluation through reasoned argu-

claims' are frequently those that interpreters have read into the charter rather than those the plain words announce."

"Where are you going?" Strega cuts in.

"To my second point," Deukalion answers. "Even if American constitutional scholars have typically been parochial, there is no good reason that you should be. Judges in the United States have sanctified freedom of speech and press partially because they have misread their own text[37] and partially because that charter does not list any countervailing rights, say, to a decent reputation or to be accepted as a human being rather than merely as a sexual object. You, on the other hand, can recognize countervailing rights. There are many other models for a bill of rights, not only those of individual nations but also the multinational European Convention on Human Rights. You can mix and match as well as create your own language."

"That comforts me," Mufti Ajami says. "I favor freedom of speech and press, but I do not think those rights constitute licenses for skinheads to stir up hatred against fellow citizens or pornographers to pander to lust by degrading women or, worse, children."

"Does anyone," the chair intervenes, "propose specific language that would protect freedom of speech and press yet also protect against degrading women or spreading ethnic hatred?"

"I don't think," Pyknites says, "that we can construct such language that would be both general and intelligible. We'd have so many 'but if' clauses that no one could parse the sentences."

"You may be right," Minister Pilsudski agrees. "Judge Learned Hand

---

ment: *On What the Constitution Means* and *The Constitution of Judicial Power.* One could also argue that constitutional amendments evidence dissatisfaction with the constitutional text, if not the constitutional order; but in the United States, amendments have often been aimed at "correcting" misinterpretations of the document or performing "housekeeping chores," rather than repairing fundamental errors in the text or in the constitutional order. The Thirteenth, Fourteenth, Fifteenth, and Nineteenth amendments are significant exceptions to this general tendency.

37. The First Amendment does not read: "Congress shall make no law . . . abridging freedom of speech or of the press." Rather, the actual wording is much more specific: "Congress shall make no law . . . abridging *the* freedom of speech, or of the press . . ." Inclusion of *the* before *freedom* restricts the clause's ban to a particular conception of freedom of speech and press. Few textualists or originalists pay much heed to this wording. Leonard Levy—*Legacy of Suppression* (Cambridge, MA: Belknap Press of Harvard University Press, 1960) and, more important, *The Emergence of a Free Press* (New York: Oxford University Press, 1985), which revises some arguments and conclusions of the earlier work—has shown that the conception of freedom of speech and press was not, at the time the amendment was adopted, nearly as expansive as it has become. Whether American judges have been careless or wise in (mis)reading the text is an entirely different matter. Pretending that *the* is not there or contending that it is meaningless or that it forms a "constitutional mistake" each poses interesting problems of interpretation and adaption. Certainly any of these alternatives to a "plain-words reading" makes the document more consonant with democratic theory and closer to what many Americans believe the framers accomplished. For a similar judicial correction of framers' "poor draftsmanship," see the Supreme Court's editing of the text of the Eleventh Amendment in Hans v. Louisiana, 134 U.S. 1 (1890).

once said that 'words are chameleons, which reflect the color of their environment.'[38] So, let us construct an environment as well as craft words. I suggest separate articles, such as this:

> Article 1. (a) Freedom of speech and press shall be inviolable, but such freedom shall not extend to denigrating others because of their race, religion, sex, ethnicity, or national origin.
> (b) The right of women, as individuals and as a group, to dignity includes the right not to be the subject of any means of commercial communication that depicts them as mere sexual objects.
> (c) Parliament may enforce these provisions through appropriate legislation.

"That article," Jacobsohn says, "establishes Parliament as a censor to determine what speech, words, or pictures are pornographic and what words constitute 'hate speech.' Suppose some women argue that fundamentalist Mormons' or Muslims' advocating polygyny threatens the core value of equality. Would that be hate speech? And pornography: what about *The Birth of Venus*? Suppose *Hustler* put a color photo of that on its cover. Would that constitute pornography? And who can tell which contemporary art will not be considered masterpieces fifty years from now? Moreover, men should be entitled to protection as well. I've watched women stare at Michelangelo's *David* for an hour without realizing the statue also had a face and hands and feet. Suppose *Elle* or a magazine aimed at gays put that on its cover—would that be pornography?"

"You're raising issues that can be settled only on a case-by-case basis," Pyknites replies.

"Agreed," Jacobsohn says, "but these are cases from which you would exclude judges and leave legislators to formulate the rules and then the police, who, whatever their virtues, are neither learned or sensitive art critics, to apply those rules. Judges would be mere spectators."

"No," Pyknites answers. "My proposal would leave the issue of pornography to be settled by deciding if it were a work of art, some other form of communication, or an appeal to lust. Those kinds of questions would fall under the jurisdiction of the courts."

"An appeal to hate can be a form of communication," Jacobsohn persists. "Many decent people say neo-Nazis are moral slime. Is that a hate crime? Appeals to lust can also illuminate political alternatives. 'Make love, not war' was a battle cry in the United States during the Vietnam War. Pornography can also be a virulent, if vulgar, form of social protest. The American Supreme Court may have seemed silly in finding nude dancing a form of expression, but some people think that is precisely what they're doing. Are

---

38. Commissioner of Internal Revenue v. National Carbide Co., 167 F. 2d 304, 306 (1948).

we back to Potter Stewart's 'I don't know what it is but I can recognize it when I see it'?"[39]

"Colleagues," Colonel Martin intervenes, "as Mr. Pyknites has said, we should be looking at our work as creating an integrated constitutional order. We are debating critical issues, but some of them are too specific for this stage of our work. It is now 12:23. Let us recess for lunch and private discussions. We reassemble at four p.m. By then, someone might come up with a comprehensive plan, or we can tinker with Mr. Pyknites's scheme."

At 3:59 the chair gavels the caucus back into session. "Rumor hath it that Professor Jacobsohn and Minister Pilsudski have a proposal for us. Minister?"

"First, we thank Mr. Pyknites for forcing us to think systemically, and we endorse much of his proposal, such as writing into the charter a version of the Irish Article 45, with many of the positive rights Ms Baca stressed. We leave enforcement of those, in the first instance, to Parliament and, ultimately, to the voters. The bill of rights that we recommend follows what we have already approved and includes the additional protections Mr. Pyknites has suggested. Pretty much we follow the European Convention on Human Rights, but we ensure that rights to reputation are also protected. The major difference from Mr. Pyknites's plan is that the Constitutional Court could rule on alleged violations of any or all of these rights. That difference, of course, is consequential."

"Yes," the chair admits, "it certainly is. Because two of you have introduced the measure, it does not need a second. And we have many times been over the case for and against judicial review. We have no need to rehash those arguments. Does anyone wish to raise a point we have not already debated?"

"Like, a parliamentary inquiry, please," Baca says. "What happened to my proposal? I made it this morning, and then we switched to other motions. Do we get to vote on mine?"

"My apologies," the chair says. "I had thought that both Mr. Pyknites's proposal and that of Minister Pilsudski and Professor Jacobsohn incorporated much of what you want. If you would like to make a separate motion that goes beyond these plans, please do so. If it is seconded, we shall discuss it and vote on it with the other items."

"Thank you. I propose that we add to the usual catalog of negative rights a list of positive rights pertaining to the equality of women, a healthy environment, and free competition in communicating political ideas through the mass media. These rights would, like, run against private citizens, corporations, and eleemosynary institutions as well as government. These rights would be enforceable through judicial as well as political processes. I leave exact wording to a later point."

---

39. Jacobellis v. Ohio, 378 U.S. 184, concur. op. (1964).

"Second? Thank you. Discussion? Mr. Wei?"

"I'm sympathetic to Anita's goals, but who could enforce these rights? Take education, for example: judges couldn't appropriate money to provide access to schools that don't exist. Similarly, it's not practical to ask judges, in the absence of legislation specifying procedures and defining torts and criminal acts, to protect the environment or guarantee women equal access to employment. Judges might enjoin specific actions causing pollution or discrimination, but they couldn't create or finance the agencies needed to execute comprehensive policies. The cardinal advantage of directives of positive policy is enabling voters to hold MPs' feet to the fire when government *either* falls short of *or* exceeds what the people want badly enough to pay for."

"My plan would, you know, push Parliament into doing just what you say," Baca answers. "A judicial decision that schools needed to be built or a river needed to be cleaned up would generate huge pressure on Parliament to appropriate money and to enact new laws."

"Perhaps," Jacobsohn says, "but without parliamentary action, these clauses would be dead letters. If responsibility lay with Parliament, then that body could authorize many kinds of judicial proceedings, including criminal prosecutions, specify civil remedies, and appropriate money for positive governmental action."

"But would Parliament act if the matter were solely under its authority?" Baca asks.

"Giving Parliament sole authority," Pyknites put in, "would allow the political opposition to beat up on incumbents at the next election, if—and it's a big if—the people really wanted such rights protected. If they didn't, then nothing we say or do is going to matter much anyway."

"You mean the constitutional text we propose and the people will debate won't affect our political culture?"

"Touché," Pyknites says. "What we say and do will have an effect, an enormous effect—I hope. But, if proponents of the policies you advocate don't work hard and continuously to convince the voters, nothing very significant will happen. Your plan gives responsibility to nonelected judges and lets Parliament off the hook."

"The arguments have been stated fully," the chair says. "Ms Baca's proposal goes on our list of proposals. Let's turn first to judicial enforcement of the bill of rights. We'll follow our version of the Estonian system for the three plans: Ms Baca's, Mr. Pyknites's, and that of Minister Pilsudski and Professor Jacobsohn. On the first ballot each of us can choose any of the three. For the second, we shall drop the proposal that secured the smallest number of votes. Let us proceed. . . . The parliamentarian and I count three votes for Ms Baca's plan, ten for each of the others, and one abstention.

"Let us proceed to the second ballot, choosing between the two remaining options . . . The vote is twelve for Mr. Pyknites's and twelve for Professor Jacobsohn's.

"I'm no Solomon," Martin continues, "but let me suggest we try a third way. Throughout our discussions we have been closely divided on judicial review, so closely that a document announcing a categorical yea or nay would threaten harmony within this body and bode ill for the people's ratifying it. So I propose—and I hope that our rather free parliamentary procedures allow the chair to offer a motion—a third way, something along the lines of the Canadian Charter of Rights. First, we would draft a statement of specific goals of public policy, following the lines of Article 45 of the Irish constitutional text, explicitly mentioning much of what Ms Baca has urged on us. Those goals would not be cognizable by any court. Then we would have a bill of rights along the lines that we had begun to discuss, all of which would be cognizable by the Constitutional Court. In defining the reach of rights to vote, to speak and write about public affairs, to free exercise of religion, to equality of treatment, to retain or renounce citizenship, and to certain procedures when accused of crime, for instance, judicial interpretations would bind all governmental agencies. On other issues, such as regulations pertaining to private property (though not of fair compensation for seizure), conscientious objection from military service, privacy, travel, and judicial procedures in civil suits (including slander and libel), Parliament could override judicial decisions regarding constitutionality, providing it specifically said it was passing the statute despite a previous judicial interpretation and did so by a vote of three-fifths of its membership. Any statute so enacted would automatically expire sixty days after the next general election. Parliament could reenact it, but only by the same supermajority and after explicit acknowledgment of what it was doing."

"So," Jacobsohn comments, "Parliament could suspend most of the bill of rights—in effect drastically amend the constitutional text *and* the constitutional order by a three-fifths vote?"

"Not quite. Parliament would also have to say it was directly contradicting the constitutional court's constitutional interpretation. We'll have a general election at least every five years, and members of Parliament would have to stand for reelection on that record."

"Thus they could oppress only smaller, more unpopular minorities," Zingaro retorts.

"It could come to that, if our people do not internalize the values of constitutional democracy," the chair concedes. "But Parliament could not override judicial interpretations of the document's provisions regarding political participation and equality before the law or those relating to the rights of the accused in criminal trials, all essential to the protection of minorities. Canada's record under Article 33 is quite good, and that article recognizes parliamentary authority in constitutional interpretation that is more extensive than what my plan concedes."

"Canada's national record is good," Jacobsohn says, "but that of the provinces, especially Quebec in abridging the rights of the English-speaking minority, is nothing to be proud of. Besides, Canada has a political culture that we can only envy. That their elected officials have not abused such authority does not offer even a hint that ours will be so respectful of civil rights. Although I appreciate your efforts to compromise, you are trying to reconcile the irreconcilable."

"I, too, appreciate the Chair's efforts," Pyknites speaks up. "And although I prefer my own plan, his is more likely to win this caucus's endorsement. I second it. Out a sense of mercy, I include only by reference all the arguments I've offered earlier about judicial review."

"God bless you," Colonel Martin says. "Might we pray that Professor Jacobsohn show the same compassion upon the multitude?"

"Yes. I bow to the caucus's fatigue," she answers.

"Further discussion?" the chair asks. "Very well, let us vote. We have a duly seconded motion before us. It includes Irish-style directives for general policy goals, a bill of rights with full judicial protection, but with Parliament authorized to override, by a three-fifths majority, judicial interpretations of these rights except those pertaining to freedom of religion, political participation, compensation for seized property, equality before the law, and judicial procedures for criminal trials. That override would have to state its purpose and would expire after the next general election, Does anyone feel it would be fairer to revote on the other proposals? Hearing no such motion, we proceed to a show of hands. . . . The parliamentarian—for obvious reasons, I do not offer an official count of my own—registers seventeen votes for, six against, and one abstention. The motion is carried. We stand in recess until 0945 tomorrow morning. Amen."

CHAPTER NINE

Drafting 4

Special Cases

Men feared witches and burnt women. JUSTICE LOUIS D. BRANDEIS

The dogmas of the quiet past are inadequate for the stormy present.

ABRAHAM LINCOLN

At 0945 the following morning, the members slowly—some unsteadily—
take their places. The mood is subdued. The loudest sounds come from the
bubbling of Alka-Seltzer and the sloshing of aspirin tablets being stirred into
coffee cups. "Colleagues," Colonel Martin begins, "we have reached what
Winston Churchill would have called the end of the beginning. We shall
soon be able to turn our draft document over to a committee on revision, and
all that will remain for the full caucus is to examine their work carefully.
Today, two huge problems demand our attention. First is emergency powers.
Second is the most divisive issue we face, abortion: what, if anything, do we
say about it? In the interests of harmony, let us first turn to emergency
powers. Our speaker is Professor John Ecco of Trinity College, Dublin. He
is one of the world's leading scholars on this topic."

Ecco, a heavy-set man in his early fifties, walks on the stage, holding up a
thick loose-leaf binder.

These documents have all been scanned into your server. You can
access them during my talk and your own discussions.[1]

Machiavelli claimed that "in a well ordered republic, it should never
be necessary to resort to extra-constitutional measures; for, although they
may for a time be beneficial, yet the precedent is pernicious, for if the
practice is once established of disregarding the laws for good objects,
they will in a little while be disregarded under that pretext for evil purposes." No republic, he added, will be perfect unless it has by law pro-

---

1. Learned readers will recognize a marked similarity between Professor Ecco's arguments and
those of John E. Finn, *Constitutions in Crisis: Political Crises and the Rule of Law* (New York: Oxford
University Press, 1991). Those same readers may discern that Ecco has also taken intellectual nour-
ishment from essays in Mark Tushnet, ed., *The Constitution in Wartime: Beyond Alarmism and
Complacency* (Durham, NC: Duke University Press, 2005).

vided a "remedy for every emergency, and fixed rules for applying it."[2] Of course, a constitutional text that includes clear instructions for every kind of emergency is impossible. The framers of the American constitutional document hardly tried. Article I, which pertains to Congress, authorizes that branch to declare war, raise armies and navies, and establish rules, including appropriation of money, for the armed forces. The sole specified limitation, beyond the lengths of military and naval appropriations, is phrased in the passive voice: the "writ of Habeas Corpus shall not be suspended, unless when in Cases of Rebellion or invasion the public Safety require it." Article II, which pertains to the president, designates him as commander in chief of the armed forces and the militia when called into federal service. He takes an oath to support and defend the constitution, as do legislators and judges.

I suspect the sketchy nature of this language was no accident. Both Madison and Hamilton—we can only guess what most of the other framers thought—strongly disagreed with Machiavelli. It is vain, Madison wrote in *The Federalist* No. 41, "to oppose constitutional barriers to the impulse of self-preservation . . . because it plants in the Constitution itself necessary usurpations of power." Hamilton was more blunt. The power to defend the nation, he wrote in *The Federalist* No. 23, "ought to exist without limitation, because *it is impossible to foresee or define the extent and variety of the means which may be necessary to satisfy them.*"

Machiavelli and Hamilton mark two undesirable extremes. No human being can fill the Florentine's prescription, and Hamilton opens the gates to tyranny. Officials who claim to perceive grave threats to national security are often mistaken or mendacious. There are less extreme examples than Hitler's persuading the Reichstag in 1934 to give him full emergency powers. Out of office, Thomas Jefferson opposed the Alien and Sedition acts; yet when he himself was in the White House, he deemed Aaron Burr's swashbuckling expedition into Spanish territory seditious. To justify using the army to arrest his former vice president, Jefferson wrote that the "law of necessity, of self-preservation, of saving our country when in danger, are of higher obligation [than the constitutional text]."[3] In fact, he relied heavily on reports from an American general who was a spy for the Spanish, and they stood to lose if Burr's adventure succeeded.

2. *Discourses on Titus Livy,* trans Christian E. Diamond (New York: Modern Library, 1940), bk. 1, ch. 34, p. 203.

3. To Thomas Colvin, Sept. 30, 1810, in *The Writings of Thomas Jefferson,* ed. Andrew A. Lipscomb (Washington, DC: Thomas Jefferson Memorial Association, 1903), 12:418. Most of the letter is reprinted in Walter F. Murphy, James E. Fleming, Sotirios A. Barber, and Stephen Macedo, *American Constitutional Interpretation,* 3rd ed. (Westbury, NY: Foundation, 2003), pp. 1532–34.

The dangers confronting Abraham Lincoln were very real, but whether they necessitated imprisoning thousands of American citizens on mere suspicion and trying some of them by courts-martial when the ordinary courts were open is another matter.[4] More pernicious than the immediate harm done were the precedents Lincoln set. Less sensitive and intelligent officials have invoked his memory to sanction violations of basic rights. For example, it is difficult to see what threat to national security Eugene Debs posed by speaking against American participation in World War I at a Socialist Party convention or how Jacob Abrams imperiled the country by scattering from a rooftop in New York City leaflets, written in English and Yiddish, that called for a national strike to protest American intervention in the Russian civil war.[5] The Palmer Raids and the Great Red Scare of the 1920s netted far more political dissenters than subversives. During World War II, the mass imprisonment of American citizens whose ancestors had been born in Japan was the product of racial bigotry and economic envy disguised as patriotism. The McCarthy era resumed witch hunts for those whom the senator, through his alcoholic fog, viewed as "Pinkos" or "Comsymps."

Without doubt, occasions arise when the nation's safety is, in fact, threatened. Still, even during international crises, basic constitutional questions cannot be decided by such simplistic formulas as *inter armes silent leges*. It is always prudent for drafters of constitutional texts as well as constitutional interpreters to ask: What doth it profit citizens of a constitutional democracy to preserve national security at the price of becoming denizens of a police state? "[N]ational defense," Earl Warren wrote for the U.S. Supreme Court, "cannot be deemed an end in itself. . . . Implicit in the term . . . is the notion of defending those values and ideas which set this nation apart."[6] The sticking point is that unchecked power is very likely to be abused. Even Lincoln might have become, as many contemporaries charged, a dictator. And had he been a saint—not a claim an informed analyst would make for the leader of any

4. Daniel Farber, *Lincoln's Constitution* (Chicago: University of Chicago Press, 2003), argues that many of Lincoln's policies regarding internal security were constitutional. Still, Farber concedes that the record is mixed. Some uses of military tribunals, if not unconstitutional, "were unnecessary and unjust," and the president's intrusions on free speech were "excessive" (pp. 177–75). For another sympathetic but not uncritical evaluation of Lincoln's policies, see Mark E. Neely Jr., *The Fate of Liberty: Abraham Lincoln and Civil Liberties* (New York: Oxford University Press, 1991). For an account whose title reveals its author's thesis, see Thomas J. DiLorenzo, *The Real Lincoln: A New Look at Abraham Lincoln, His Agenda, and an Unnecessary War* (New York: Three Rivers, 2002).

5. Debs v. United States, 249 U.S. 211 (1919), and Abrams v. United States, 250 U.S. 616 (1919), sustained their convictions under the Espionage Act of 1917. See the discussion of these cases in Chapter Fifteen.

6. United States v. Robel, 389 U.S. 358 (1967).

modern country, with the possible exception of Nelson Mandela—a nation, as Justice David Davis said for the Supreme Court, "has no right to expect that it will always have wise and humane rulers."[7]

Furthermore, the choices are rarely dichotomous: save the nation and destroy the constitutional order or save the constitutional order and lose the nation. Rather, choices usually revolve around a far messier question: how much of the constitutional order can be preserved without harming the nation? Such a judgment requires officials to be devoted not only to their own career and their party's future but much more to their country and its political system.

Instructed by the Weimar Republic's use of the president's emergency powers and understanding that coping with emergencies inevitably increases executive power, Carl J. Friedrich offered a set of principles to control what he called "constitutional dictatorship."[8] First, any increase in executive power should be done according to rules specified by the constitutional text. Second, some agency other than the executive should have authority to declare a state of emergency; third, that agency should set precise time limits for the use of extraordinary powers. And fourth, the objective of the policy must be to defend the constitutional order, not subvert it.[9] I'd add a fifth principle: the constitutional document must set up an agency independent of the executive to monitor the conformity of his or her actions to the conditions the constitutional text prescribes, made specific by the institution declaring the emergency.

No constitutional charter establishes all of these principles, though most go much further than does the American document. Article 16 of the French constitutional text, for instance, authorizes the president of the republic, when he deems an emergency to have arisen, to "take such measures as these circumstances require, having consulted officially with the Prime Minister, the President of the [two legislative] chambers, and also the Conseil Constitutionnel." The president must inform the nation of his or her decision and cannot dissolve Parliament during the emergency. Moreover, whatever measures the president takes "must be prompted by a desire to ensure for public constitutional authorities the means of fulfilling their functions within the shortest possible time. The Conseil Constitutionnel shall be consulted about them."

Articles 115a-i of the Basic Law provide more detailed directives for what it calls "a state of defence." If time allows, Parliament, by at least a

7. Ex parte Milligan, 4 Wall. 2 (1866).

8. *Constitutional Government and Democracy: Theory and Practice in Europe and America,* 4th ed. (Waltham, MA: Blaisdell, 1968), ch. 25. He distinguishes among various kinds of emergency situations such as martial rule and states of siege.

9. János Kis, *Constitutional Democracy,* trans. Zoltán Miklósi (New York: Central European University Press, 2003), p. 569.

two-thirds vote in the Bundestag, invokes emergency powers. The federal government may then assume joint jurisdiction over much of the police powers of the *Länder;* procedures for enacting laws may be shortened; and the chancellor becomes the commander in chief of the armed forces. The government may keep individuals under arrest for as long as four days, if no judge is available for a hearing. If there is insufficient time for Parliament to convene, the joint committee—composed of members of the two houses, none of whom is a cabinet official, with each political party having its proportional number of seats—acts for the legislature. A two-thirds vote is required to approve a declaration of emergency and to determine that Parliament is unable to perform its functions.[10] If the committee so determines, it may exercise all the functions of the full parliament except that it cannot amend the Basic Law or suspend its operation. The terms of the president, members of Parliament, and, by inference, the chancellor are extended until six months after the end of the state of emergency.

Further checking governmental power, Article 115g commands: "The constitutional status and the exercise of the constitutional functions of the Federal Constitutional Court and its judges may not be impaired." Furthermore, the joint committee cannot amend the law relating to the Federal Constitutional Court, unless, by a two-thirds votes, the judges themselves agree that such measures "are necessary to maintain the capability of the Court." In addition, Article 101 forbids creation of special tribunals or removal of a prisoner from the jurisdiction of a lawful federal court.

Chapter 5 of the Spanish charter allows for suspension of many constitutionally guaranteed rights, and Article 116 establishes procedures much like those of the Basic Law. A state of emergency can last for only thirty days, renewable once.[11]

I could detail provisions of other constitutional texts, but you can call these up on your computers. So I'll skip to my recommendations. First, I'd suggest that you include in your constitutional charter the sorts of principles that Professor Friedrich advocated. Then I'd add a pair of other items. First, establish an independent monitor to play the role that Article 115g of the Basic Law and Article 126 of the French document provide for a constitutional court or its equivalent. Because in your debates you've distinguished between a constitutional text and a constitutional order, I suggest adding a clause something like this: "Although an emergency regulation may legitimately violate the specific wording of

10. To deny legitimacy to rump meetings, the Basic Law adds that the required two-thirds must constitute at least a majority of the Joint Committee.

11. The Spanish text distinguishes among states of alarm, emergency, and siege, but procedures for invoking and continuing them are the same.

this charter, no such provision may validly contradict the basic principles of constitutionalism or democracy."

"Thank you, Professor, for a lucid and succinct presentation and also for the useful collection of documents. Now, discussion? Ms Baca?"

"You suggest we follow the German model, right?"

"Adapt, not follow, and with the modification I just suggested."

"How much faith," Pyknites asks, "do you have in judges' standing up against a government that insists that certain measures are needed to cope with an emergency?"

"Not much, but by giving judges loaded weapons, you may force an executive to think twice or even thrice before violating the charter or the underlying constitutional order. In the midst of what she believes is a crisis, a chief executive wouldn't want to provoke a public row with judges. They can't save a country, but they can give the people a better chance to save themselves."

"As a Gypsy," Zingaro puts in, "I don't think giving public officials pause would stop them from oppressing a despised minority for more than a few milliseconds."

"Yes," Strega says. "Madison and Hamilton were right. If we must have a constitutional text, it shouldn't mention emergency powers. Let officials figure it out when the occasion arises."

"I differ," Pyknites says. "A reasonably effective solution exists: revive the sort of arrangement the Canadians once had.[12] Let me explain. When the PM perceived a dire emergency, he could invoke martial law and suspend certain statutes and parts of the constitutional text such as those providing that a prisoner be immediately arraigned before a judge and protecting the right to assemble. The PM was obliged to call Parliament into session within seventy-two hours and put to that body his case for invoking martial law. The motion on the table was 'Parliament approve the PM's action.' If that motion failed to win three-fifths of those voting, who must constitute at least a majority of the full house, the declaration of emergency expired within seventy-two hours. Such a defeat also constituted a vote of no confidence, and the government would fall. If the motion carried, the state of emergency continued for no longer than sixty days. At the end of that period, parliamentary approval, by the same extraordinary majority, was again required. I move we adopt such a policy."

"Would you," Minister Pilsudski asks, "include provision to maintain the integrity and jurisdiction of the constitutional court during this period?"

12. For citations and an account of an application in 1970 of the provisions of the War Measures Act, see Walter F. Murphy and Joseph Tanenhaus, eds., *Comparative Constitutional Law* (New York: St. Martin's, 1977), p. 686. Canadian governmental action to cope with emergencies is now controlled by the Emergencies Act, 1988, C. 22 (assented to July 21, 1989).

"As you know, I don't think judges will help here. From my time at Yale, I recall a dissent by Justice Robert H. Jackson—I have it here. 'I would not lead people to rely on this Court for a review that seems to me totally delusive. . . . If the people ever let the war power fall into irresponsible and unscrupulous hands, the courts wield no power equal to its restraint. The chief restraint upon those who command the physical forces of the country . . . must be their responsibility to the political judgments of their contemporaries and to the moral judgments of history.' "[13]

"I understand," Pilsudski continues, "but I have a different fear: special courts could be mere tools of executive oppression. Therefore, I propose as a friendly amendment: 'Neither Parliament, the executive, nor any judicial body shall authorize special tribunals outside of the courts provided for in this constitutional charter to hear criminal cases. Parliament may authorize establishment of courts-martial, but their jurisdiction shall be limited to members of the armed forces on active duty at the time of the alleged offense for which they are to be tried.' "

"I share your concern and accept your amendment," Pyknites says.

"I think Mr. Pyknites has us on the right track," Wei says. "But I would want to add yet another clause to the effect that no emergency regulation can discriminate among citizens on the basis of their ethnicity, race, or ancestry."

"Or religion?" Ibrahim Ajami asks.

"Most certainly," Wei concurs. "Mr. Pyknites?"

"I would agree to the full proposal, but I doubt that it will do much good. If we're hit by Islamic terrorists, the government will discriminate against Muslims. I say that with sorrow, Mufti."

"You're probably right," Ajami agrees.

"I like Professor Ecco's suggestion that we ban the government's using emergency powers to violate the basic principles of constitutionalism or democracy," Baca says.

"It's silly enough to think that 'parchment barriers' will restrain officials who control the army and the police," Strega responds. "It's sheer idiocy to think that these people would respect abstract principles of constitutionalism or democracy."

"I don't agree," Glückmann says. "We all have reason and, with a little reflection, can deduce the basic principles of constitutionalism and democracy. We don't want even to seem to authorize such measures as torture—and that brings up an important issue. I move we further amend Mr. Pyknites's proposal to forbid torture as well as special courts."

13. Korematsu v. United States, 323 U.S. 214 (1944). For a study that, from an analysis of decisions of the U.S. Supreme Court from 1941 to 2004, concludes that war affects nonwar cases more than cases arising out of the war, see Lee Epstein, Daniel E. Ho, Gary King, and Jeffrey A. Segal, "The Supreme Court during Crisis: How War Affects Only Non-war Cases," 80 *N.Y.U. L. Rev.* 1 (2005).

"Let's not be hasty," Strega cuts in. "I dislike most of the policies of the Bush administration, but he may not be totally wrong in authorizing torture. I recently read an article by Judge Richard A. Posner, my mentor at the University of Chicago. He puts a common hypothetical: A terrorist has aerosol bombs filled with the smallpox virus. We capture a confederate who knows where the bomber is hiding. What methods can we use legitimately to make that confederate talk? As much as it takes is Posner's answer, and it's mine, too.[14] I'd tear out his eyes to save the lives of innocent children and even not-so-innocent adults. And I'd bet every person here would do the same. Posner suggests that it is much more socially responsible to use cost-benefit analysis to evaluate torture: do the costs—and he admits there are many—outweigh the benefits? Asking that question is the only intelligent way to proceed."

"Wrong, like, totally wrong!" Baca says. "This must be the easiest decision we've faced. There are all sorts of international agreements condemning torture, along with decisions of the European Court of Human Rights. Torture denies human dignity."

"What dignity do terrorists' victims have?" Strega responds.

"Winning by becoming as evil as terrorists really means to lose," Baca says.

"I'd rather win and live than die along with hundreds of thousands of others."

Gregorian intervenes, speaking softly. "I find myself in an awkward position. I agree wholeheartedly with Ms Baca, and yet, as horrible as torture is, there are occasions in which it may be necessary—not to say moral, only necessary. What should officials in Judge Posner's scenario do, allow those people to die because they don't want to dirty their hands? I think not."

"For once," Strega says, "I agree with Father Gregorian's sense of *realpolitik*, a sense for which Jesuits are famous. We're better off not mentioning the problem in our charter at all."

Minister Pilsudski speaks next. "We move from one troubling issue to another. Of course we all abhor torture, but—I'm torn, so much so that I'd say we should be silent."

The chair looks around at a room full of troubled faces. "As a professional soldier, I recognize the temptations; as a decent human being, I share the

14. "Torture, Terrorism, and Interrogation," in Sanford V. Levinson, ed., *Torture: A Collection* (New York: Oxford University Press, 2005), p. 293. Since revelations of the methods of interrogation used in Guantánamo Bay and Abu Ghraib prison, a large literature on torture has blossomed. The classic article is Michael Walzer's "Political Action: The Problem of Dirty Hands," originally published in 1971 and reprinted in ibid. See also Mark Danner, *Torture and Truth: America, Abu Ghraib, and the War on Terror* (New York: New York Review of Books, 2004), which contains a fascinating collection of official American documents; and Seymour Hersh, *Chain of Command: The Road from 9/11 to Abu Ghraib* (New York: HarperCollins, 2004).

revulsion. Let me offer an unhappy compromise. We adopt a simple clause: 'Admissions obtained through torture, inhumane treatment, or threats of such actions shall not be admissible in a court of law.' That wording would not allow police to torture people suspected of 'ordinary' crimes."

"I also accept those words as a friendly amendment," Pyknites says.

"Discussion? Professor Jacobsohn?"

"I agree with Ms Baca's earlier point," Jacobsohn says. "I move that we add a sentence protecting basic principles of constitutionalism and democracy even during emergencies."

"Second," Ms Baca says.

"Discussion? I see no hands. Let us vote first on Professor Jacobsohn's amendment ... The secretary and I count ten votes for. The amendment fails.

"Now, on Mr. Pyknites's motion? . . . We count only one vote against. The motion carries. Let us recess for fifteen minutes."

Somewhat surprisingly, all the members are in their seats within twelve minutes. The chair checks his watch, smiles, and says, "It seems we're unanimous on at least one point: each of us wants to get this business settled. I think we also know, however, how divided we shall be on the next item, abortion. It's our 'irrepressible conflict,' almost as divisive as slavery once was for the United States. We can pray the results will not be as disastrous; our being civil would be helpful."

"Yes," Jacobsohn says, "if we can't agree, let us narrow the scope of our disagreement by seeking consensus at the core."

Baca speaks: "If 'at the core' means we agree that human dignity is our central value and human life is sacred, then the issue of abortion is easily settled, constitutionally at least. Only when another human life is at risk could we remain true to that central value and say that a mother has a constitutional right to kill the human fetus she's carrying."

"And what about the dignity of the woman?" Jacobsohn asks. "Doesn't her human dignity require that she control her own body and life? How much dignity does she have if she is required to let a fetus bloat her belly and disrupt her life for nine months, then have the legal responsibility and financial burden of caring for a child she doesn't want? That smacks of involuntary servitude."

"Forgive me," Kirca interrupts, 'but technically isn't the fetus a parasite?"

"No," Baca answers. "A parasite is a member of one species that feeds off a member of another species. Some people, even a few scholars who should know better, try to argue that a fetus is not human.[15] What is it, a kanga-

---

15. See, for instance, Judith A. Baer, *Our Lives before the Law: Constructing a Feminist Jurisprudence* (Princeton, NJ: Princeton University Press, 1999).

roo? A fetus gets half of its genes from each of its parents, not from dogs or other animals. To abort is to kill a human being whose life we should consider sacred."

"I agree," Jacobsohn says, "that at some stage the fetus becomes human, but the concept of 'human' is a difficult one. We can't really call a fetus in its initial stages a human being, certainly not for some months until it develops a brain and a nervous system. Before then, it's only potentially human, and we have to weigh what is potential against what is real. The pregnant woman is, in fact, a human, and too often she's a teenager, a child who is neither emotionally nor financially able to care for herself, much less another child. But even when the mother is a mature adult, surely Ms Baca's notion of human dignity demands that the mother, not the state, determine how her body will be used and her life focused."

"I disagree about when human life begins," Baca replies. "It begins when a new human life is formed. Besides, the mother's burden need not be for long. Many couples are anxious to adopt. In the United States, pregnant women can often sell their babies for tens of thousands of dollars. It's illegal but it happens."

"Not as often as you imply," says Strega. "How many right-to-lifers do you know who have adopted unwanted babies?" The minister continues before Baca can answer. "I accept that genetically the fetus is human, and after a few months, MDs can produce ultrasound images of a baby. These things have arms, legs, fingers, and toes, just as many aborted fetuses do. But genetic origins and physical appearances are not enough to make a thing a human. Not until late in pregnancy do fetuses have operative brains, hearts, and lungs. What is critical is that a fetus is only a prospective member of the human species. It has no consciousness, much less a life plan. It is probably less a human person than someone with late-stage Alzheimer's. We should not use some people's religious values as an excuse to ordain that a woman has a legal obligation to carry a fetus to term. The only way we should make any decision is through utilitarian morality or, if you prefer, economic reasoning. A child is a heavy burden not only on its parents but, especially when the mother is a poor and single, also on society. Our scarce resources will be devoured by the costs of pre- and postnatal medical care, food, clothing, and schooling. The financial and emotional strain of rearing a child in neighborhoods full of drugs, alcohol, and crime will wreck any hope poor families have of decent lives. The odds are high that an unwanted infant born into poverty will be ill-fed, ill-educated, and physically and even sexually abused. If female, she will probably become an unwed teenage mother herself and repeat the cycle. If male, the child is apt to become a criminal, injure others, and spend much of his life in prison, all of which will cost society pain and money. A pair of economists from Stanford and the University of Chicago attribute much of America's recent drop in crime to the large number of abortions that poor single mothers have obtained."[16]

"Don't you mean abortions that poor *black* women have obtained?" Kanuri asks.

"I do not, though some hostile critics have so charged. I link crime only to poverty and lack of love, not to race or ethnicity."

"This danger may be greater than many of you realize," Zingaro adds. "The junta encouraged Gypsies, recent immigrants, and the poor generally to have abortions, along with sterilizations. A lot of people approved those policies, including many of the middle and upper classes who could afford private clinics. I also suspect that 'freedom of choice,' because it removes a cost to males' proclivity to sexual promiscuity, is a very popular policy among young men."

"Yes, I know," Strega says. "But I dissociate myself from sexism just as I do from racism."

"If you would, like, allow abortion because of a child's costs to its parents and society, then would you allow euthanasia for the elderly who need expensive medical care?" Baca inquires.

"Of course," Strega replies. "And I also believe that killing infants with expensive and fatal diseases is justified. We cannot afford medical costs for them or for old people who are demented or suffering from terminal illnesses."

"Humanity is a terminal illness," Gregorian remarks.

Strega ignores him. "The costs of what we give to these people are immediately paid by taxpayers and, over the long run, by those people with curable illnesses who must go without treatment. That's not a rational allocation of resources. If we had opted for guided capitalism, we might have had the means in twenty or thirty years, but not under constitutional democracy. Your pretended humanitarianism is, in fact, cruel. We should put our limited resources where they will do the most good for the most individuals. Generations will come after us. We need to respect what John Rawls called the 'just savings principle.'"[17]

Glückmann stands. His voice is shaky. "Do you set an age limit for killing babies—or the elderly, for that matter?"

"I cannot draw a bright line. For infants, legal euthanasia should come before they gain a sense of consciousness of themselves as persons, before, that is, they can begin to formulate life plans. For the elderly, when they lose

---

16. The minister is referring to John J. Donohue III and Steven D. Lane, "Legalized Abortion and Crime," *Quar. J. of Econ.*, May 2001; available from the Social Science Network Electronic Library: http//ssrn.com/paper.taf?abstract_id-174508.

17. *A Theory of Justice* (Cambridge, MA: Harvard University Press, 1971), pp. 284ff.

their own sense of self, when they can only feel and no longer think, when their life plans are in shambles."

"How do we know these things? Who would make these decisions?" the pastor asks.

"Because we can have only approximate knowledge, I would leave the matter up to the parent or guardian, with some minimum judicial supervision to ensure that euthanasia was not simply a means to collect insurance or an inheritance. The court could seek its own medical advice."

"Again," the Mufti says, "for her provocative clarity, I thank the Minister, may peace be upon her. I recall her, as a vegetarian, arguing during our meals against our eating meat because it is cruel to animals. Is it her argument that cows have consciousness and life plans and therefore their lives are intrinsically more valuable than those of infants and the elderly?"

"Of course not. We kill sick and elderly animals. I don't advocate eating them, or people for that matter."

"Let me be clear," Jacobsohn says. "I do not endorse the Minister's reasoning."

"The Minister," Baca replies, "is only carrying your logic to its, you know, logical conclusion. If it's legitimate to kill a fetus when, in the womb, it is completely dependent, you must agree that it is legitimate to kill it when, outside the womb, it is still completely dependent."

"No," Jacobsohn objects. "When a baby is outside of the womb, people other than the mother may take care of it."

"Other people?" Strega interrupts. "You mean society. You're simply shifting the burden of care from the mother to society. You waste our collective resources."

"I don't think so," Jacobsohn replies. "*My* premises don't lead to *your* conclusions. Besides, intelligent people should also be prudent people and not carry their reasoning to its extreme."

"Not if you reject logic," Baca says, "but I thought that constitutional democrats totally believed in the primacy of reason in formulating public policy. Right?"

Before Jacobsohn can answer, Gregorian remarks: "The Minister's arguments parallel those of Princeton's famous ethicist Peter Singer.[18] He admits that those who believe in a right to life are absolutely correct that the fetus is alive and human, but he uses the same kind of rigorous economic reasoning —he calls it a version of utilitarianism—to make a case for abortion, infanticide, and euthanasia. George Will has described him as 'the abortion-rights movement's worst nightmare.'"[19]

---

18. See esp. his *Practical Ethics,* 2nd ed. (New York: Cambridge University Press, 1993), and *Rethinking Life and Death: The Collapse of Our Traditional Ethics* (New York: St. Martin's Griffin, 1996).

19. "The Last Word," *Newsweek,* Sept. 13, 1999, p. 90.

"Perhaps," Deukalion says, "Will is right for the wrong reason. Singer may be a very clever prolifer who satirizes, à la Dean Swift, the prochoice position by showing the reaches to which its logic propels society. Not only does his rigid application of the logic of freedom of choice justify abortion, infanticide, and senilicide, but he seems to extends it to cover bestiality as well.[20] The Minister may have fallen into a savagely funny trap by taking his writings at face value. We should be familiar with such practices, not only by philosophers such as Spinoza and possibly Machiavelli[21] but also by the Russian samizdat writers and your own Ion Zingaro."

"Whatever," Jacobsohn says. "I reject Singer's conclusions as I do Minister Strega's. I recognize a clash of rights here. I'm repeating myself, I know, but I want to be clear. On one side is the right to life of the fetus, which is not yet fully human in any practical sense—its brain shows no electrical activity before its sixth week, and it is not fully viable on its own until the twenty-third week.[22] The competing right is that of the mother, who is fully human, to bodily integrity and generally to choose how to live her life. Before a fetus can live outside the womb without heroic medical aid and with a reasonable chance of living a normal life—imprecise terms, I admit—I think we should resolve the conflict in favor of the woman. As the fetus's chances of a normal life outside the womb increase, so does its claim to life. The choice is tragic, but we live among tragic choices. Before viability, I would let the woman decide, not a bureaucrat. Once the fetus has a reasonable chance of living outside the womb, I would give more weight to its right to life, a right that would become stronger as its chances of living increased."

"Life is a continuous process, not a set of isolated leaps," Gregorian says. "Imagine our Colonel. He was once a zygote in utero. But was he not becoming the person he is today? So, too, he was once a fetus, six weeks old, then fourteen, then twenty-three, then a newborn. At each stage he was becoming the man he is today. We can continue that process: He was a boy, a teenager, a young adult. In all these aspects he was in essence, though not in full development, our chair. Next year he may become an even greater hero. To have ended his life at any stage—zygote, fetus, infant, boy, young man, or colonel—would have killed our leader."

"This debate," Pyknites complains, "could go on forever. And this is not

---

20. For his nonjudgmental view of humans' having sex with animals, see his review article "Heavy Petting," www.nerve.com/opinions/singer/heavypetting/main.asp. Singer, however, frowns on humans' having sex with chickens, because such activity is fatal to the fowl.

21. See Leo Strauss, *Persecution and the Art of Writing* (Glencoe, IL: Free Press, 1952), and his *Thoughts on Machiavelli* (Glencoe, IL: Free Press, 1958). In his graduate seminar on Machiavelli, Strauss put forth an elaborate, almost kabbalistic theory of Machiavelli's writing in code. For a satire depicting a leading white supremacist during the 1950s as a heroic practitioner of secretly subversive writing, see my review of *The Sovereign States: Notes of a Citizen of Virginia* by James Jackson Kilpatrick, 67 *Yale L. J.* 1505 (1958).

22. See Michael S. Gazzaniga, *The Ethical Brain* (New York: Dana, 2005), ch. 1, esp. pp. 4ff.

the proper forum to try to resolve irresolvable conflicts—which is why I favor allowing an elected parliament to work out a compromise, perhaps changing as conditions change, that most people could live with."

"Except aborted fetuses," Gregorian adds.

"Colleagues," Colonel Martin says, "most of us agree that human life is sacred and that a fetus is human. The question that divides us is whether it is fully human That issue, in turn, involves deeper questions of what it means to be fully human. Moreover, because the mother is also human, she is entitled to great respect and a wide range of autonomy. The bedeviling issue is how far that range extends. We agree that autonomy does not include the right to kill a human person who does not threaten similar harm to another person. These questions interlock and, alas, they do not do so in a 'gender-neutral' way. Women, not men, bear children, and women typically carry the heavier burden of raising children. And those burdens continue through life. Justice William J. Brennan Jr. once remarked that nothing changes a person's life so much as having a child.[23] Those of us who are parents know that the burdens of having children, like the joys, cease only with death."

"May I ask Professor Deukalion's opinion on this conundrum?" Minister Pilsudski asks.

"Were the decision mine alone, I would include in the charter recognition of the fetus as human with a right to life. I would, however, also state that abortions were permissible when continuing the pregnancy threatened the mother's life or a grievous injury to her health. I'm also deeply troubled by requiring a woman who is pregnant because of rape to carry the child to term. Including that condition as an exception would require very careful language, as well as moral reasoning. I'm not certain I can square that circle."

"What practical advice would you give us?" the chair asks.

"I offer small advice: Temporize. Instruct your committee on revision to prepare several versions of a clause expressing commitment to the sanctity of life and to the great and equal dignity of all human beings. Choose whichever phrasing you think best and leave the specific policies to Parliament and the Constitutional Court. That's a prudent solution, not a clean moral choice."

"I find it, like, cowardly," Baca says. "It's exactly what Mr. Pyknites wants."

"I may be cowardly," Deukalion agrees. "I am against abortion under most circumstances. It privileges death over life. But I do not believe that this caucus, even if it were unanimous, could convince our opponents that we were right. We can't convince them, and both sides have to live together in peace. Therefore, I would compromise. A closet philosopher might say *Fiat*

23. Eisenstadt v. Baird, 402 U.S. 438 (1972).

iustitia, ruat coelum, but a practical human being, knowing he could not save all of the unborn, would try to save more rather than fewer of them. I suggest a clear statement in a constitutional charter that human life is sacred and, with the Constitutional Court part of the decision-making processes, allow the political processes to make the initial choice."

"Every soldier," Colonel Martin says, "knows that the line between cowardice and prudence is exceeding fine. In all candor, Anita, what the Professor suggests is not what he wants, what you want, what Father Gregorian wants, or—and I speak more candidly than I usually do—what I want. But we're in the minority in this caucus and in the country as a whole. The best we're likely to get is a compromise like that of Germany. In a straight-out fight, we'd lose, as you say, like totally."

"May I," the Mufti asks, "propose Professor Deukalion's suggestion as a motion?"

"Of course. Is there a second? Thank you. Discussion? Minister Strega?"

"I make a third proposal: the constitutional document should unequivocally recognize a woman's right to terminate her pregnancy. As a gesture of goodwill, I'd include a limitation 'through the end of the seventh month of pregnancy except where the mother's life was in grave danger.'"

"Second? Thank you. Jessica?"

"I might support the Minister's proposal if she would add that the state had a duty to take all reasonable measures to preserve the life of an aborted fetus."

"No!" Strega snaps. "We can't afford to take care of thousands of premies every year."

"Very well," Jacobsohn says, "I move that the charter recognize a woman's right to terminate a pregnancy until the fetus is viable, and if an abortion takes place after that date, the state has a duty to take reasonable measures to preserve the infant's life."

"Second? Thank you. We now have the main alternatives before us and have said, several times over, what needs to be said. Let us proceed to vote in our usual Estonian method. . . . The parliamentarian and I count three votes for Minister Strega's motion, five for that of Ms Baca and Father Gregorian, and eight each for Professor Jacobsohn's and the Mufti's. We now drop the motion with the least support, Minister Strega's, and vote for the strongest three.

"We count twelve votes for Professor Jacobsohn's proposal, two for that of Father Gregorian and Ms Baca, and ten for the Mufti's.

"Now the final choice, the motions of the Mufti and the Professor. We count twelve for each. The Chair will break the tie in favor of the Mufti's proposal.

"It is now 1900 hours. None of us is completely happy with the result, but we could never agree on a simple solution. We have to be content with a small victory and recess until 0930 tomorrow morning. In the meantime, let's enjoy our meal and then a good night's sleep."

The next morning, the members arrive on time and seem cheerful. It is the colonel who is late. He arrives at 9:45, and he appears distracted as he tucks his cell phone in his pocket and opens the session. "Professor Deukalion has asked to make a few comments before we begin. Professor."

"Thank you, Colonel. First I'd like to thank you for allowing me to be an informal participant. It's been an education as well as an honor. You have accomplished a set of almost superhuman tasks. But as an adviser, I must say that there is still some very important unfinished business that, in my judgment, you should attend to: the whole matter of constitutional change. I don't mean amending the text but the flip side of that process, limits on amendments. Some constitutional texts, such as Germany's, contain what have been called 'eternity clauses' that explicitly forbid certain kinds of amendments. Even where there is no express prohibition, courts in some countries—India, Bangladesh, and California, for example—have invalidated amendments on substantive grounds. The issue spreads out. If some kinds of amendments are invalid, can the government ban political parties that advocate them, as have Germany and Russia? If government can ban 'unconstitutional political parties,' can it also punish citizens who advocate the polices the banned parties endorse? These are not easy questions, but neither are they trivial for a new constitutional democracy."

"I agree," the chair says, "and though I hear some groans of fatigue from some members, I had thought that these issues should be on our agenda . . . Excuse me, may we take a ten-minute recess? My assistant says I have some urgent messages." The colonel leaves the dais and goes into an adjoining room, where he is joined by two armed Marine officers.

Not ten but fifteen minutes later, he returns; his expression is somewhere between dour and grave. His cell phone's microphone is still in his ear. "Ladies and gentlemen, I have received some very disturbing news. A group of middle-ranking members of the special police and the army have been meeting with some bankers and executives of oil companies. These people are plotting a counter-coup to restore a tyrannical political system."

"How credible is this information?" Minister Pilsudski asks.

"Always difficult to tell with such intelligence, but experts whom I trust say their sources are reliable and substantiate rumors that have been oozing around for several days."

"This morning," Minister Strega says, "I, too, had phone calls from my staff. They've heard similar rumors and say that serious money is coming into the hands of the special police. I've dissented from most of our decisions, but I do not want another junta in place. Although I still think you people are misguided, at least you're concerned about Nusquam. Those pigs in the special police and the oil cartel are selfish and corrupt. What do you advise us to do, Colonel?"

Before Martin can reply, Minister Pilsudski asks: "How about your people, Colonel? Can they do anything?"

"I cannot say much at this point, other than that those of us in the military who helped bring down the junta are weighing our options. I think this caucus can help by immediately producing a constitutional text. I hope that in the next few minutes we can appoint a committee on revision and have them prepare a full draft for us within the next forty-eight hours so we can present it to the country as a positive alternative to more pseudo-fascism. Each of us should put ourselves and our research assistants at the committee's disposal."

"That means, like, we can't address the problems Professor Deukalion has just brought up, right?" Ms Baca asks.

"I'm afraid not," the colonel says, "but the committee might move part of the way and include some language about certain document parts' being unamendable. I'm not suggesting that the committee should, only pointing out that it could. What the committee doesn't address we'll have to leave to future amendments. As I recall, the Americans didn't have a bill of rights until several years after their constitutional charter was operative."

"I move," the Mufti says, "that we appoint as a committee of revision our chair, Minister Pilsudski, Father Gregorian, Mr. Pyknites, Mr. Wei, and Professor Jacobsohn. We also authorize them to co-opt any other members of this caucus they wish, to use our research assistants, and to consult with any of our visiting experts."

"Second!" Minister Strega shouts.

"Discussion?" the colonel asks. "I see no hands. Let us vote. I do believe the motion carries unanimously. I hope now you understand why two companies of Marines, along with a platoon of tanks, have reinforced our guards. We cannot permit anyone to enter or leave the grounds until our work is completely done.

"Now, I would ask the members of the committee, their research assistants, and Professor Deukalion to come with me to the conference room on the second floor so we can begin our work."

Epilogue

[The constitutional document] is now a Child of fortune, to be fostered by some and buffeted by others.   GEORGE WASHINGTON

The chapters in this part have demonstrated some but hardly all of the imponderables that complicate crafting a skeletal constitutional order through "reflection and choice." Indeed, one might argue that members of the caucus did not have to confront many of the more difficult problems of transition. The old regime was overthrown by what in effect was a coup by a group of military officers who wanted a political transformation that would minimize the possibility of a return to tyrannical rule. The caucus did not have to negotiate pacts with outgoing officials[1] as in Poland, Hungary, Spain, and Brazil or compromise with angry armed forces as in Argentina, Chile, and Uruguay; nor did it have to bargain, as did some Africans, with victorious guerrilla leaders whose long struggle against colonialism had made them popular heroes, eager to enjoy the spoils they believed their labors had captured. Neither did the caucus have to rummage through the rubble left by a sultanistic regime whose power had been taken over by men and women of the same ilk. Furthermore, the founders of Nusquam's new political system did not confront many other problems common to new states: no great power threatened to veto their choices; their people were located within recognized national bounds, with no significant minority crying out for redemption by a neighboring country; and although some ethnic groups were hostile toward others, none of these was united by a common geography or history that would engender dreams of separate nationhood.

Nevertheless, as must all political architects, members of the caucus had to deal with severe problems, not least of which were the unknowns, domestic and foreign. Typically, founders must play a multiperson, three-dimensional form of ghostly chess extended through an indeterminate period of time. The rules change periodically and are never fully clear; some players come and go without their exits and entrances or even their identity

---

1. It is true, however, that, in order to prevent further violence, the colonels have allowed the junta to leave the country with Swiss bank accounts intact. For pacts generally, see Giuseppe Di Palma, *To Craft Democracies* (Berkeley: University of California Press, 1990).

being announced; many moves will be concealed for years; and individual squares on the board randomly spring up to toss pieces (and perhaps players) out of the game. This enterprise, sensitive founders must often believe, involves what Learned Hand called "shoveling smoke." It is not a game for the fainthearted nor for those who suffer from insomnia. Long, wakeful nights worrying about how the future will treat one's handiwork invite suicidal depression.

The caucus's professorial research assistants and the learning, if not always the wisdom, of its consultants enabled these founders to utilize the literature of the social sciences. And despite occasional grammatical and syntactical howlers, the caucus's members were articulate, if seldom eloquent. With that much said, it is unlikely that either learned scholars or experienced statesmen would look on this group as exemplary models for constitutional engineers. But then widely accepted, realistic standards for constitutional architects are nonexistent. Ideal founders would have fluid eloquence, razor-sharp analytical skills, enormous academic learning, and total and instant recall, as well as practical wisdom in distinguishing the desirable from the attainable, long and clear vision, immense integrity, great courage, and greater luck—in sum, they would be righteous philosopher-kings who had accumulated much political experience. Alas, fate-blessed, politically active, brilliant saints have been rare or else have suffered from such an overload of modesty as to closet themselves from public view.

How to discover or train people who approximate such paragons to muster and maximize talents for architectural politics are not tasks in which Western scholars, who often boast of loving constitutional (and less often constitutionalist) government, have invested many resources. Lack of popular interest in the problem is understandable, for few citizens have ever had much of a voice in choosing the original designers of their constitutional order. Yet the absence of concern among political scientists and academic lawyers does not speak well for our collective judgment.[2] The dearth of professional literature on the problem indicates that the vast majority of scholars treat political systems, as Max Lerner would have put it, as "having been brought by constitutional storks"[3] rather than birthed in pain by reasoning, fallible, idealistic yet selfish human beings.

It may be that, unless we find a way to delve into prehistory, we cannot identify the *original* founders of any political system. Constitution making involves creativity, but, inevitably, it also involves adaptation of the past both to the present and to visions of the future, adjustment of one's own and others'

2. Harry H. Eckstein has made a more general complaint about a paucity of literature on constitution making as well as constitutional drafters: "Notes on the Designs of Constitutions," paper presented at the Conference on the Design of Constitutions, Program on Democratization, University of California at Irvine, June 10–12, 1993.

3. *Ideas for the Ice Age* (New York: Viking, 1941), p. 259.

interests, personal and political histories, cultures, and institutional preferences. In that sort of process, the people who later operate the system continue the work of founding, though not always work of which the founders
would approve. What Bruce Ackerman calls "constitutional moments" do
occur, times when efforts to create a new regime or adapt an older one produce dramatically changed political structures, processes, and even values.[4] It
makes a difference for public officials and private citizens alike whether they
are adjusting the constitutional order of Josef Stalin, Mao Tse-tung, James
Madison, or Douglas MacArthur.

How to choose members of a convention such as Nusquam's poses a
closely related problem. There is much to be said for having candidates
selected by free and open popular elections, although in a country that already has operative democratic processes such a method gives a great advantage to those already in politics: the experienced and too often cynically self-
seeking professionals. In countries just emerging from authoritarian or totalitarian rule, the old rulers are likely either to skew selection of delegates to
their own benefit or to bargain with reformers to do much of that work for
them as part of the price of peaceful transition.

Nusquam's colonels did not follow democratic processes in choosing
members of this caucus, but neither did the selection of the people who, with
Allied "assistance," drafted the German and Japanese constitutional texts.
One could make similar though much more qualified evaluations of the
methods used to select those who wrote the British North America Act of
1867 or the French, Indian, Irish, and Italian documents. Of course, members of the Philadelphia Convention were selected by state legislatures. On
the other hand, delegates to the American ratifying conventions in 1787–1788
were chosen by elections that were among the most democratic since the fall
of Athens in 322 B.C., even though all women, almost all blacks and Indians,
and some poor white males were denied the franchise.

Part I ends with much work for the caucus to complete. Many matters,
such as the processes of and limits on amendments to the constitutional
charter as well as more specific issues such as regulating campaign finance,
which in the United States has become a fertile garden of bribery, have not
yet even been discussed, much less decided. Moreover, there is no report of
the committee on revision for the members to debate, amend, and finally
approve before submitting the document to the people. And the demons of
constitutional-maintenance-through-constitutional-interpretation skulk in
the shadowy interstices of textual language, ready, like surly trolls, to bite
unwary public officials.

The purpose of these chapters, however, was not to produce a detailed

---

4. "Constitutional Politics / Constitutional Law," 99 *Yale L. J.* 453 (1989); and *We the People:
Foundations* (Cambridge, MA: Harvard University Press, 1991).

constitutional text for a mythical nation but to explore some of the more significant problems that founders face in trying to create a basic charter to guide a newly established polity. In a more conventional analytic fashion, the chapters in Part II take up some of the problems associated with maintaining and changing a constitutional democracy.

I would note two additional points. The first is personal. The caucus's decisions are not necessarily those I would have made had I been Rousseau's legislator. Professor Deukalion, who comes closest to making my arguments, frequently fails to persuade his hosts, and those failures sometimes involve issues that matter deeply to me. But one price of composing fiction is that the characters whom authors like to believe they have begotten can take on lives and, more important, minds of their own. To be sure, authors can force fictive persons to do or say whatever they want, but *force* is the operative word. *Persuading* these characters is sometimes impossible without destroying their integrity—and credibility. This restriction on creativity cannot help but make reflective writers sympathize with the difficulties the Deity generated when She granted men and women free will.

A second point relates directly to future difficulties of constitutional interpretation. An originalist would be hard put to speak accurately about framers' "intent" or "understanding." First, no member spoke on every issue; many members did not speak at all; and those who spoke often disagreed with one another, revealing different goals, different intentions, and different understandings. As Felix Frankfurter once noted about the adoption of the American Fourteenth Amendment, in the end the framers voted on the proposals, not on the speeches.[5] None of these sorts of omissions and contradictions is likely to be absent from the birthing of any constitutional document through the midwifery of an assembly; certainly they were present in Philadelphia during the summer of 1787.[6] Problems of discovering what the millions of ratifiers—those people in whose collective name the charter would claim to speak—intended or understood make the difficulties of psychoanalyzing the caucus seem trivially easy.

In a general sense, however, it is possible to use, accurately and intelligently, original understanding of constitutional purpose. A preamble can speak of the polity's general aims and underlying principles, as does the structure of the governmental system the document tries to beget. Yet although the text purports to aid in establishing and maintaining a constitutional democracy, it remains difficult to discern which particular variant of either normative theory or which combination thereof the caucus *as a whole* took as its lodestar. In any case, I would classify such analyses as employing a

5. Adamson v. California, 332 U.S. 46, concur. op. (1947).
6. See esp. the article by James H. Hutson, editor of Max Farrand's *The Records of the Federal Convention of 1787:* "The Creation of the Constitution: The Integrity of the Documentary Record," 65 *Tex. L. Rev.* 1 (1986).

philosophical much more than an historical approach,[7] for the objective is not to discover what conceptions the authors had in mind but to explore the norms the text has endorsed, the premises on which these must logically be based, and the implications of these concepts for the polity's future. This shift in hermeneutic methodology from static re-creation of a single set of events and minds to philosophical exploration will facilitate a task that is simultaneously daunting, dangerous, and necessary: constitutional maintenance through constitutional interpretation.

7. One might rightfully contend that any dispute over meaning here, even if philosophical, rests in part on historical analysis. This claim is obviously true. Carried further, it would also turn astrophysics into a historical science, given that the phenomena observed and analyzed happened thousands, millions, or perhaps even billions of years earlier. Most of my friends who are historians eschew such imperial ambitions. Were the mathematical expertise needed for astrophysics less awesome, we might observe a less humble reaction.

II

Maintaining a Constitutional Democracy

Introduction

[S]eeing that everything which at has a beginning has also an end, even a constitution such as yours will not last for ever, but will in time be dissolved.

SOCRATES

Maintaining a constitutional order is a subtask of maintaining national stability, for a country can peacefully make some sorts of change in its regime without altering its international status and obligations or, in the domestic sphere, fundamentally altering its rules regarding individual rights. A shift, for example, from representative to constitutional democracy is not likely to destabilize the nation. Neither is a change from one form of constitutional or representative democracy to another form of either. Even a move from either constitutional or representative democracy to guided capitalism need not, though it certainly might, generate a violent reaction—which is not to deny that such a shift's import for citizens could be enormous.

The chapters in this part follow a more standard format than did those in Part I. These take up the problems of constitutional democracy at the point at which part I ended and focus on how leaders of such an embryonic regime can maintain their political system and guide it into maturity. The general and accurate, if not especially helpful, answer is, by pursuing policies that gain and retain the loyalty and affection of their people while protecting them from foreign aggression. Although these chapters concentrate on governmental action, if a new political system is to enable its citizens to live together in peace while pursuing the varying material and spiritual goals they believe necessary for the good life, individuals and nongovernmental organizations must also carry out complex and complementary collections of policies. For this reason, the initial chapter in this part deals with the creation of citizens for a constitutional democracy.

If political problems ever occur in a vacuum, it is the vacuum of a tornado's vortex rather than that of a test tube. Although we who suffer from the effects of original and not-so-original sins can think and even speak about several problems at once, few of us can coherently write about more than one thing at a time. Thus I invoke academic license and address interrelated issues seriatim, a luxury public officials never enjoy. Moreover, the sequence of chapters in this part reflects a convenient analytical scheme rather than the "correct" temporal or lexical order of public choices.

The initial goal of constitutional maintenance is to create what Tocqueville called "habits of the heart," to instill in citizens and public officials alike the conviction that their constitutional order is the most efficient of feasible alternatives in actualizing their country's ideals and in carrying out the more specific functions that most charters list: (1) guarding the people from foreign predators (providing for the common defense); (2) securing order within the country and protecting peaceable citizens from rapacious neighbors (ensuring domestic tranquillity); (3) enacting public policies that allow citizens to maximize their economic advancement (promoting the general welfare); and (4) achieving these ends with due regard for fundamental fairness as well as the rights and integrity of all citizens (establishing justice and securing the blessings of liberty).

The first chapter focuses on the metamorphosis of former denizens of a tyrannical regime into self- and other-regarding citizens of a free political order, to alternate, like a radar's transponder, between being rulers and ruled, demanding respect for their own rights while simultaneously respecting the rights of others and fulfilling their own duties to society and its governmental order. It may be an exaggeration, even a contradiction, to argue that, in a constitutional democracy, government can "create" citizens; but surely public policies can facilitate or impede a people's manumission from passive denizens into informed, active, and responsible citizens.

A second set of problems concerns the (re)establishment of a competent professional public service whose members are committed to the success of constitutional democracy and whose basic loyalty is to that constitutional order rather than to a different regime or to a particular party, faction, ethnic group, or person. These officials include not only the usual bureaucrats who collect taxes, pay pensions and subsidies, and regulate business and labor but also the police, the military, and internal security services. All of these people, especially professional soldiers, could pose grave dangers to the new polity. No matter how civil a society, it is still vulnerable to brute physical force; and the military can amass firepower that can overwhelm not only individual citizens but also the police.[1] Thus converting the military as well as the police into loyal citizens is no less important than attaching civilians to the values of the constitutional order.

A third set of specific problems revolves around the fact that in a complex society any important public policy is likely to create disagreement. Inevitably, such a policy will advance some interests and values while threatening

---

1. Thus the Nazis created their private army in the form of the SS, and in the Soviet Union the KGB had its own military arm. Both organizations placed loyalty to a party leader above the standard military chain of command and, more importantly, above what had become the military concept of honor based on serving the state rather than a particular ruler.

others. Not only will some people doubt the wisdom of almost all far-reaching governmental actions, but questions about the legitimacy of such public choices often divide society. Thus a stable polity needs institutional mechanisms, set up before disputes arise, that can efficiently settle controversies not only between individuals and between groups but also between public officials as well as between officials and private citizens—settle, that is, constitutional questions and do so according to procedures that most officials as well as most politically active and aware citizens will, most of the time, consider legitimate and therefore binding. The most obvious (and, again, interlocking) issues to be resolved here are these: (1) *What* it is that interpreters are to interpret: the text, the broad constitutional order, some thing(s) between, and/or implicit in one or both? (2) *Who*—which persons or institutions—interpret which parts of the constitutional *What*? What person or institution, if any, has ultimate interpretive authority? (3) *How* should authoritative interpreters interpret *Whatever* it is they interpret?

Finally, constitutional maintenance necessarily involves change, for, as Benjamin Disraeli said, finality is not in the language of politics. A constitution that cannot change cannot endure. All modern constitutional texts establish means of amendment; but as important as formal emendations can be, they may be much less significant than informal changes brought about by practice, custom, morality, and interpretation. Like the law itself, constitutions must be stable, yet they cannot stand still. Reconciling stability and change is difficult as both a practical and an intellectual matter. Sooner or later, a critical question is likely to arise: What, if any, are the limits on systemic change for a constitutional democracy? What if some changes subvert the very nature of the constitutional order? Can such changes—as well as efforts to effect them—be invalid?[2] No less important, can invalid changes themselves be invalidated? If the answer to the last two questions is yes, then one must face additional questions: By whom and how? Revolution, Locke's "appeal to heaven," is always a possibility, though typically a dangerous one. Another alternative is appeal to heaven's putative representative on earth, for example, the pope during the Middle Ages or a religious council as in Iran after the shah. On a secular level, options include parliamentary back-benchers who can force new elections, executive officials who can refuse to carry out policy, and judges who can declare a constitutional change unconstitutional.

There are at least two serious omissions in this listing of purposes: peaceful relations with other nations and domestic prosperity. For reasons of space as well as competence, I place analysis of a successful foreign policy beyond the scope of this book and leave to scholars who specialize in international

---

2. A further question arises: by what standards can we judge such changes to threaten the basic constitutional order? Chapters Fourteen and Fifteen address that problem.

relations the work of solving age-old difficulties of war and peace. This delegation, more prudent than generous, does not, however, eliminate all discussion of such constitutional problems as emergency powers that international crises often exacerbate. Conversely, a nation's constitutional structures and processes help shape the formation of foreign policy.

Due humility requires similar self-restraint in discussing the second set of problems, how leaders of a new political system can help citizens increase their prosperity. Earlier and later chapters, however, do sketch some broad parameters. The gospel of communism, as variously preached by Lenin, Stalin, and Mao, with aspirations for an eventually disappearing but in the interim omnipotent state, is no more compatible with constitutional democracy than is fascism. Furthermore, Chapters Two and Three demonstrated that the short-run fit of constitutional democracy with coercive (or guided) capitalism is exceeding poor. This sort of regimen offers promise for constitutional democracy only in the sense of providing a quick fix for economic woes. In the real world, guided capitalism has facilitated prosperity much more than political freedom. It would not be unreasonable to describe the People's Republic of China since the mid-1990s as having adapted a form of (very) coercive capitalism. A mainland Chinese version of constitutional democracy, if it ever comes, is unlikely to arrive before the end of the twenty-first century. Governmental practices in most other coercive capitalist states are less oppressive, but prospects for a change to constitutional democracy are small. Ruling elites in Singapore and Malaysia cling to power; Thailand retains its mix of mildly authoritarian government and democratic forms, seasoned by occasional military coups. Efforts to uninstall the old rulers of Indonesia have brought more civil strife than fundamental political reform. As President Abdurrahman Wahid explained in mid-2001: "[T]hose who insult the president will be arrested. . . . If you say the right things, OK. But if you utter slander, you will be detained. For me, this is democracy."[3] In South Korea, the political system has taken on many of the indicia of constitutional democracy, but that result has come about through a series of coups as well as through peaceful transfers of power. Only in Taiwan has a guided capitalistic system peacefully made significant steps toward such a transition; and, even so, the island may find itself, as Hong Kong did, absorbed by mainland China before its transformation is complete.

The remaining basic economic options open to leaders of a constitutional democracy are laissez-faire capitalism, moderate socialism, and some sort of hybrid, perhaps a form of welfare capitalism in which government regulates and redistributes but does not command. American as well as Western and now Eastern European experience demonstrates the terrible price in human suffering that laissez faire imposes. Even when "the market" functions well—

3. Interview by Lally Weymouth, *Newsweek*, May 21, 2001, p. 42.

and it often malfunctions[4]—it is a cruel tyrant that has no respect for the poor, weak, or downtrodden. It is unlikely that constitutional restraints could long stem the tide of popular anger at such costs,[5] even assuming leaders could persuade a majority of citizens that the tenets of unrestrained capitalism do not flatly deny constitutionalism's basic principle of human dignity.

Normative as well as practical factors are at work. Citizens of a nascent constitutional democracy in the Western world are likely to have inherited many of the basic Judeo-Christian moral norms; both stress social justice and duties to the poor. As chapter 15 of Deuteronomy puts it: "Is there a poor man among you, one of your brothers in any town of yours in the land that Yahweh your God is giving you? Do not harden your heart or close your hand against that poor brother of yours, but be open-handed with him and lend him enough for his needs. . . . Always be open-handed with your brother, and with anyone else in your country who is in need and poor." Indeed, the claim that "owners" hold the land in trust for the poor would not be an inaccurate summary of the social message of the Old Testament. Cain asked his famous question, "Am I my brother's keeper?" Yahweh's "yes" was unspoken, but no less resounding for that silence. The sayings of Jesus reiterate and amplify the traditional Jewish theme: the road to perfection begins with selling one's goods and giving the proceeds to the poor. And modern Jewish and and Christian social doctrines echo those precepts. Despite Michael Novak's heroic efforts of to canonize capitalism, Catholic social teachings have frequently condemned laissez faire and have been wary, at best, of capitalism itself as breeding materialism.[6] Especially eloquent are such papal encyclicals as *Rerum Novarum* (1891), *Quadregesimo Anno* (1932),

4. Some economists would contend that *malfunctions* is the wrong word here. The market can be measured only in terms of its efficiency in producing economic gain; human suffering is not a relevant factor, except to those people unfortunate enough to be living in a country whose market functions inefficiently.

5. See, for instance, Anthony Downs, *An Economic Theory of Democracy* (New York: Harper and Brothers, 1957), and Jon Elster, "The Necessity and Impossibility of Simultaneous Economic and Political Reform," in Douglas Greenberg, Stanley N. Katz, Melanie Beth Oliviero, and Steven C. Wheatley, eds., *Constitutionalism and Democracy: Transformations in the Contemporary World* (New York: Oxford University Press, 1993). Both examples often cited here of nations that for decades remained poor and yet remained stable constitutional democracies, India and Ireland, rejected laissez faire, with India's public polices having been much more socialist than Ireland's.

6. See, for instance, Michael Novak's *The American Vision: An Essay on the Future of Democratic Capitalism* (Washington, DC: American Enterprise Institute, 1978); *Freedom and Justice: Catholic Social Thought and Liberal Institutions* (San Francisco: Harper and Row, 1984); *The Spirit of Democratic Capitalism* (Lanham, MD: Madison Books, 1991); *The Catholic Ethic and the Spirit of Capitalism* (New York: Free Press, 1993); *On Corporate Governance: The Corporation as It Ought to Be* (Washington, DC: American Enterprise Institute, 1997); and *Three in One: Essays on Democratic Capitalism*, ed. Edward W. Younkins (Lanham, MD: Rowman and Littlefield, 2001). Catholic condemnations of laissez faire can be gleaned at least from Leo XIII's *Rerum Novarum* (1891), if not from his *Humanum Genus* (1884) or Pius IX's *Quanta Cura* with attached Syllabus of Errors (1864).

Pacem in Terris (1963), *Populorum Progressio* (1967), and *Centesimus Annus* (1991).[7] These sorts of social teaching alienated nineteenth-century Liberals, whose gospel of Social Darwinism stressed individual economic freedom and the social benefits of greed. Especially after 1929, however, Catholic teachings attracted latter-day liberals, who came to realize that unbridled economic freedom leads to misery and chaos. (In the United States, the issue of contraception would strain this alliance, and the later issue of abortion would shatter that economic alliance.)[8]

Communitarian motifs also run through Muslim teachings. The obligation of charity (*zakat*) is one of the five pillars of Islam. Even charging interest on loans is forbidden.[9] Hamas and Hezbollah, famous in the West for carrying out suicide bombings against unarmed civilians, are better known in Lebanon, Gaza, and the West Bank for operating schools, orphanages, hospitals, and clinics, providing food and potable water for devastated villages, and helping find jobs for the unemployed and housing for the homeless. These activities are, of course, closely tied to the organizations' political objectives—which do not include establishing constitutional democracy—but they also represent a means of carrying out religious obligations.[10] In Turkey, the Justice and Development Party, ideological successor to the two banned Islamist parties Refah and Virtue, has pursued similar welfare operations. It is less pietistic than Hamas and Hezbollah, rejects the violence that characterizes many of their overt political activities, and so far has not been unsympathetic toward constitutional democracy. In Parliament, its leaders push for government to support a free market while still regulating the economy to ensure honesty in economic affairs and to eliminate ethnic discrimination, thus fostering fairer distribution of material goods and lessening bias against Kurds, who are, after all, still Muslims.[11]

7. Especially useful, though somewhat dated, are Michael Walsh and Brian Davies, eds., *Proclaiming Justice and Peace: Papal Documents from "Rerum Novarum" through "Centesimus Annus"* (Mystic, CT: Twenty-third, 1991); and David M. Byers, ed., *Justice in the Marketplace: Collected Statements of the U.S. Catholic Bishops on Economic Policy, 1891–1984* (Washington, DC: United States Catholic Conference, 1985). The most important pronouncement of American Catholic bishops was *Economic Justice for All: Pastoral Letter on Catholic Social Teaching and the U.S. Economy* (Washington, DC: U.S. Catholic Conference, 1985).

8. John T. McGreevy, *Catholicism and American Freedom: A History* (New York: W. W. Norton, 2003), chs. 5, 8–9.

9. Muslims, like Jews and Christians before them, have demonstrated considerable ingenuity in avoiding this prohibition, allowing bankers to charge fees and commissions rather than calling these costs "interest."

10. See Anthony Shadid, *Legacy of the Prophet: Despots, Democrats, and the New Politics of Islam* (Boulder: Westview, 2002), esp. ch. 4. Shadid is quite, perhaps overly so, optimistic about these two groups' desire to become "normal" participants in a civil political order. For a more general study of politics and good works in the Muslim world, see Janine A. Clark, *Islam, Charity, and Activism* (Bloomington: Indiana University Press, 2004).

11. In addition to Shadid, *Legacy of the Prophet*, ch. 4, see Zita Öniş and E. Fuat Keyman,

These normative considerations tie in with more practical concerns. A successful constitutional democracy needs a sense of community among its citizens, a feeling that however they are separated by religious, racial, geographic, or economic factors, they are all united as a people who share the same nationality and political ideals. The "most common and durable source of factions," Madison claimed in *The Federalist* 10, "has been the various and unequal distribution of property." Had he been more sensitive to the plight of the slaves who worked his plantation or had the imagination to envision the problems that a melange of religions would spawn, he might have been less dogmatic in his analysis.

Even so, although a constitutional democracy cannot change the color of its citizens' skins, convert them from one religion to another, or even erase geographical peculiarities, it can ease economic differences. Rich Romans understood this point and offered bread and circuses to the poor. Later, as the empire became more Christian, motivations changed from duty to the state to duty toward fellow men.[12] But attachment to the polity and Judeo-Christian-Islamic virtue both further attachment to the nation as a community. Modern leaders would be wise to imitate Romans as "lovers of the city" and consider aid to the disadvantaged one aspect of maintaining constitutional stability. Without doubt, such aid may soothe public and private consciences by striving to meet religious standards of charity, but a state also has strongly compelling secular reasons to assist the poor: not only to reduce disaffection but also to bring economically disadvantaged people into the ranks of informed, active citizens—to give them and their children a fair chance to become productive members of society, people who can bear their own burdens of civic responsibility as well as claim constitutional rights.[13] Mary Ann Glendon sums up the practical situation: "Despite our attachment to the ideal of the free, self-determining individual, we humans are dependent social beings. . . . Almost all of us spend much of our lives either as dependents, or caring for dependents, or financially responsible for dependents. To devise constructive approaches to the dependency-welfare crisis will require acceptance of this profound and unchangeable fact of life."[14]

If old-fashioned capitalism is eliminated, a constitutional democracy has a choice between only moderate socialism and some sort of hybrid capital-

---

"Turkey at the Polls: A New Path Emerges," in Larry Diamond, Marc Plattner, and Daniel Brumberg, eds., *Islam and Democracy in the Middle East* (Baltimore: Johns Hopkins University Press, 2003). They use the term *postdevelopmental* to characterize moderate Islamic groups such as Justice and Development.

12. See Peter Brown, *Poverty and Leadership in the Later Roman Empire* (Boston: University Press of New England, 2002).

13. The focus of John Rawls's most famous book was, of course, on a just political economy: *A Theory of Justice* (Cambridge, MA: Harvard University Press, 1971).

14. "Discovering Our Dependence," *First Things*, no. 146 (Oct. 2004), pp. 11, 13.

ism, either of which allows a great deal of free enterprise while permitting government some leeway both to regulate businesses and to redistribute assets to those whom Lyndon Johnson's father described as "caught in the tentacles of circumstances." Whatever specific policies government chooses, it would be conducive, if not absolutely necessary, to the maintenance of constitutional democracy for the government to help—and seem to help—increase prosperity while respecting constitutional rights to private property and demands for social justice and sustaining (or increasing) a widespread sense of personal responsibility for one's own life and for others' lives as well—a set of ambitions that only the most courageous or foolish could simultaneously pursue.[15]

Initially, it is likely that a new constitutional democracy will confront a massive task of economic reform.[16] It pleases Americans and Western Europeans to believe that the demise of communism during the closing years of the twentieth century was primarily the product of an epidemic of demands for human rights, but the abject economic failures of governments in Eastern Europe probably played a more significant role. On the positive side, as Barbara Geddes has shown, constitutional democracies are more likely than authoritarian regimes both to try basic economic reform and to succeed when they do try.[17] In the recent past, reform has often involved dismantling much of the economic apparatus—privatizing, in the current jargon—that the old regime had erected in the form of state-owned and state-subsidized enterprises. Not only has this need been vital in China, Eastern Europe, and the erstwhile wannabe socialist nations of Egypt, Syria, Tunisia, and Algeria but also in Fascist Spain and authoritarian states in Latin America. That governmental bureaucrats ran (and sometimes still run) these firms or depend on administering them for their rice bowls accentuates the importance of reforming, perhaps re-creating, the state's bureaucracy.

The complexity of this snarl of issues varies between byzantine and labyrinthine. Even Classical Liberals wanted active government, first to establish a market economy and second to police it. After all, the Night Watchman

15. Benjamin I. Page and James R. Simmons, *What Government Can Do* (Chicago: University of Chicago Press, 2001), provide an excellent analysis of constitutional democracy's potential (and obligation) to further a just society. I must note, however, that I do not endorse their uncritical acceptance of a woman's right to choose to kill her unborn child, and I would place greater stress on a governmental goal of helping citizens to exercise primary responsibility for their own and their family's welfare.

16. Making an argument much more common among political scientists than among economists, Douglass C. North, Nobel laureate in economics, has contended that political institutions and processes can make a huge difference in economic change and performance: *Institutions, Institutional Change, and Economic Performance* (New York: Cambridge University Press, 1990).

17. "Challenging the Conventional Wisdom," in Larry Diamond and Marc F. Plattner, eds., *Economic Reform and Democracy* (Baltimore: Johns Hopkins University Press, 1995). (Pinochet's Chile would not fit the pattern Geddes describes.) She speaks of democracies, but in context I think she means constitutional democracies.

State was supposed to protect private property against theft and fraud; safe-guard against private incursions into putative rights to contract freely; enforce the obligations of past and future contracts; maintain a postal service, a system of patents and copyrights, and a means of peacefully adjudicating disputes; establish a sound currency; punish labor unions as conspiracies; set up consulates abroad to facilitate foreign trade and investment; and, of course, defend national assets against foreign depredations. All these and similar actions necessary to a capitalist economic system require government to pursue many positive public policies and to collect taxes to pay for those policies. The objective of the negative constitutionalism of Classical Liberalism and its allies laissez faire and Social Darwinism was never to prevent government from regulating the activities and interests of *all* groups but to minimize governmental regulation of the activities and interests of owners and managers of businesses. The real questions about governmental actions that touch on economic affairs have never been answerable with a mere yes or no, but rather, of what sort and for whose benefit?

The values of constitutional democracy also require much governmental regulation of individuals, groups, and corporations; and that web must stretch beyond restrictions on labor and management to include, perhaps, establishing price supports for those, such as farmers, whose work is necessary to the nation's economic independence; obliging all economic actors to respect principles of nondiscrimination in employment; securing minimum standards of food, shelter, and medical care for all children regardless of parents' income; and subsidizing people who are un- or underemployed and/or disabled. Only in an ideal world would these sorts of policies further social justice while spreading prosperity without diminishing the drive of the less fortunate to become economically self-sufficient. That price may be necessary for social stability.

Such regulations should spur technological advancements in defense, health care, communications, and industrial and agricultural production and so enlarge opportunities to compete in foreign markets. For its part, a central bank—now a necessary governmental institution—must control inflation and fire up or dampen the economy, while stabilizing the national currency. Further tangling this knot of competing demands, public spending for such governmental projects as flood control, defense contracts, and military bases must take into account not only allocating resources efficiently in a purely economic sense but also the extent to which certain regions need such projects to create or restore decent standards of living. And, of course, insofar as the political system operates democratically, such decisions must take into account the political power of local officials, whose vision is apt to be parochial—not a cheering prospect.

The story is far from done. Economic considerations aside, a healthy constitutional democracy cannot allow monopolies to flourish lest the usual discount from economic to political power shrink. Communications pose special difficulties. Because representative democracy requires freedom of the press (which includes radio television, and the World Wide Web as well as the so-called print media), most governmental regulation is threatening. But that same necessary linkage also requires positive governmental action to ensure that private interests do not control the flow of information and block the people's capacity to learn about varying points of view.

"Justice," Madison wrote in *The Federalist* 51, "is the end of government. It is the end of civil society. It ever has been and ever will be pursued until it be obtained or until liberty be lost in the pursuit." Not only does the American constitutional charter specify justice as one of the new polity's purposes, but the body of the document provides ample means to work toward that end.[18] More recent constitutional texts offer more detailed and explicit directions to guide a polity toward social justice. Most such charters lavishly authorize governmental intervention in economic relations, speaking of governmental *obligations* to facilitate social justice. Thus the problems of economic legislation that arise mostly concern the wisdom, not the legitimacy, of particular policies. The Basic Law, for instance, proclaims Germany to be "a democratic and social federal state," and Article 15 allows nationalization of property, providing that compensation, in an amount reviewable by courts, is paid. South Africa's document designates "social justice" as one of the nation's objectives and says each citizen has rights to "adequate housing," medical care, "sufficient food and water; and social security, including, if they are unable to support themselves and their dependents, appropriate social assistance." Further, the "state must take reasonable legislative and other measures, within its available resources, to achieve the progressive realisation of each of these rights."[19] The oft-quoted Article 45, §2 of the Irish text is imperative in mood:

The State shall, in particular, direct its policy towards securing

I.   That the citizens (all of whom, men and women equally, have the right to an adequate means of livelihood) may through their occupations find the means of making reasonable provision for their domestic needs.
II. That the ownership and control of the material resources of the community may be so distributed amongst private individuals and the various classes as best to subserve the common good.

Chapter 3 of Spain's charter recognizes rights, inter alia, to "health protection," "an environment suitable for the development of the person," and "decent and adequate housing." That chapter also commands the state to

---

18. See esp. Sotirios A. Barber, *Welfare and the Constitution* (Princeton, NJ: Princeton University Press, 2003).

19. Preamble and Chapter 2, esp. Articles 26–27.

"assure the social, the economic, and juridical protection of the family," provide for "the complete protection of children," enact policies that "insure work safety and hygiene, and personal income within the framework of a policy of economic stability, and guarantee necessary rest through limitations on the length of the work day, [and] paid periodic vacations," "promote favorable conditions for social and economic progress and for a more equitable distribution of regional and personal income," and create a publicly funded system of social security and unemployment insurance.

This partial listing of factors that influence economic policies necessary to maintain a polity justifies this book's prudence in offering much, though not total, deference to those political economists and moral philosophers who have the technical knowledge, analytical skills, and concern for competing considerations of efficiency and justice demanded by constitutional democracy's commitment to respect for the great and equal dignity of all human beings. The single, and huge, qualification to the lengthy preceding sentence is that such formulators of public policy operate democratically within the scope of positive as well as negative constitutionalism, raising serious question about potential clashes between individual rights and public obligations—a daunting task.

CHAPTER TEN

Creating Citizens

Now that we have made Italy, we must make Italians.

MASSIMO D'AZEGLIO (1860)

Even a small group of men and women can, if they control enough physical and fiscal power, create a constitutional democracy. But to preserve such a system, they must convince the mass of the population to become constitutional democrats.

Here, founders confront a perennial political problem: articulating the values of the new constitutional order with those of putative citizens. As Aristotle pointed out, the "excellence of the citizen must be an excellence relative to the constitution."[1] People who in one kind of state would be law-abiding patriots could be subversives in another. The issues go beyond simple acceptance or rejection. Governmental regulation is most effective when it forbids carefully designated kinds of actions. But for a modern society to operate with more than a modicum of efficiency, its people must be willing to do more than meekly bow to public policies. They must also be ready to act positively in ways that cannot be precisely specified in advance, to support, with their time, money, sweat, and perhaps blood, campaigns against foreign enemies or domestic disorders. They must be willing to initiate actions for the common weal before governmental officials can construct a viable policy. Citizens must also pass on to their children fidelity to the constitutional order's fundamental values. In sum, for any kind of political system to endure and prosper, large numbers of its people must, most of the time, internalize enough of the regime's norms to act willingly and, on occasion, even selflessly to promote and perpetuate the most important of these values.

Like most forms of governance, constitutional democracy is a human artifact and thus unnatural. No such regime has—or could have—come into existence without much concerted effort, including clever manipulation of ideas and symbols. Constitutional democracy's unnaturalness makes especially acute the difficulties of creating a supportive political culture. Post-

1. *The Politics*, bk. 3, ch. 4, §3 (1276b), trans. Ernest Barker (London: Oxford University Press, 1946), p. 101.

modernists are correct in accusing this sort of regime of demanding "intimacy, giving, self-sacrifice, and mutual service,"[2] and despite millennia of evangelism by missionaries of Judeo-Christian ethics, these virtues remain scarce. Australia, Canada, the United Kingdom, and the United States were graced by long periods in which social and political norms could gradually adjust to each other; most other nations have been less fortunate.

The years after 1990 exposed Eastern and Central Europeans to political norms and institutions alien to their national histories. Furthermore, the very concept of political freedom may resonate differently across groups within the same country. Some ethnic minorities, having once themselves formed independent political entities, see freedom more as group self-determination than as individual liberty.[3] The sense of significant difference that keeps ethnic identity vibrant has on occasion also produced friction, as between Muslims and Orthodox Christians in Bulgaria or between Magyars and Romanians in Transylvania; secession, as between Ukrainians and Russians; and bloody violence, as attested by thousands of coffins among the shards of what was once Yugoslavia[4] and hundreds of thousands of Hutu and Tutsi graves in Rwanda.

Leaders of a fledgling constitutional democracy must rapidly persuade their people to accept the norms of this peculiar regime and also help various groups see each other and their neighbors as fellow citizens, a task that multiculturalism complicates.[5] For constitutional democracy to work. potential citizens must accept a set of basic norms and also believe that their political commonality is more important than their cultural differences. Moreover, for a constitutional democracy to move toward its goals, public officials cannot have a monopoly of concern for rights and obligations. Al-

2. Pauline Marie Rosenau, *Post-modernism and the Social Sciences* (Princeton, NJ: Princeton University Press, 1992), p. 54.

3. Curiously, the notion of a Black Nation with sovereignty over its own territory within some portion of what is the United States—a plan the Communist Party touted in the 1920s and 1930s—never caught on among African-Americans, though the concept of a black nation within a nation has had a real, though limited, appeal. See Wilson Record, *The Negro and the Communist Party* (Chapel Hill: University of North Carolina Press, 1951); and E. E. Essien-Udom, *Black Nationalism* (Chicago: University of Chicago Press, 1962). A push for "black power" within the American political system has been more typical of African-American goals. See also William L. Van DeBurg, *New Day in Babylon: The Black Power Movement and American Culture, 1965–1975* (Chicago: University of Chicago Press, 1993); and John T. McCartney, *Black Power Ideologies: An Essay in Afro-American Political Thought* (Philadelphia: Temple University Press, 1992).

4. See Susan L. Woodward, *Balkan Tragedy: Chaos and Dissolution After the Cold War* (Washington, DC: Brookings Institution, 1995).

5. The best cross-cultural work in English on ethnicity and politics is still Donald L. Horowitz, *Ethnic Groups in Conflict* (Berkeley: University of California Press, 1985). I use *multicultural* and *multiculturalism* as descriptive terms denoting a "demographic fact," not as means for normative analysis. Stanley Fish has demonstrated the quagmires into which the latter usage leads: *The Trouble with Principle* (Cambridge, MA: Harvard University Press, 1999), ch. 4.

though both constitutionalist and democratic theory stress individual rights, each also depends heavily on citizens' being driven by a strong sense of civic duty.[6] It is, therefore, crucial that many private citizens believe—or act as if they believed—that others are entitled to the same rights as they themselves and that such mutual respect is in the public interest as well as for their private profit.

Depending on social and political circumstances, the mutation in individual attitudes required to transform denizens into citizens may be slow or abrupt. Neither change will be easy, as Yahweh realized when He left the tribes of Israel to wander about the desert for forty years, the traditional life span of a generation, so that those who entered the Promised Land would be uncorrupted by habits that Pharaoh's rule had instilled. Leaders who would establish a constitutional democracy face tasks more difficult than transferring obedience from one tyrannical system to another. Constitutional democracy not only pursues certain substantive goals but also outlaws a wide range of means. Intellectual persuasion should be the principal, though not the sole, instrument of conversion. As with all conversions, appeals must include emotional elements. A republic, Noah Webster said, is "an empire of reason." It is, however, also a human empire built for men and women whose brains are bicameral, who respond to music, poetry, romance, myth, love, and hate as well as to logic.

This chapter focuses on two problems. The first is how to "create" citizens for a constitutional democracy, an assignment that could involve reshaping a country's culture(s). Here we return to a matter that earlier chapters addressed: can leaders change a nation's dominant culture(s) to make constitutional democracy possible? The second problem is like unto the first: how to augment what citizens, as parents, do to pass those values on to the next generation, to socialize their children into constitutional democracy.[7] One cannot, however, make prudent decisions here without having a clear idea both about what one wishes to achieve and what the practical options are. Thus we turn first to the sort of person an ideal citizen of a constitutional democracy would be, next to the character of those men and women who would not meet the highest standards but would still adequately perform the tasks of citizenship, then to those people who would be, if not hostile to, at least disaffected from constitutional democracy. After those sketches, we return to the core problem of bonding citizens to their polity.

6. For a sharp critique of emphases on rights, see esp. Mary Ann Glendon, *Rights Talk: The Impoverishment of Civic Discourse* (New York: Free Press, 1991). It is precisely because of the human penchant to identify one's own good with that of the public that democratic theorists insist on "one person, one vote" and constitutional theorists insist on institutional checks on a majority, even when it is formed through "one person, one vote."

7. For a very different approach, see Richard Dagger, *Civic Virtues: Rights, Citizenship, and Republican Liberalism* (New York: Oxford University Press, 1997).

Types of Citizens

There are three general ways to solve problems of fit between citizens and the political system. First, mold the system to the population's culture. Second, mold the citizenry to the demands of what is to become "their" system. Third is some sort of mix of the first two. Each has its own difficulties. To a degree, every stable system has adapted to "the genius" of its people. But the problem we address is how to stabilize not *any* political system but a particular and somewhat strange kind of regime. Thus this general solution offers only hints about how to deal with a misfit that arises when a people have had little or no experience with the demands constitutional democracy imposes on its subjects and rulers. Those hints become even more vague when, as is likely, the population reflects not one but several not easily compatible cultures.

The second method, molding citizens, poses a difficult task for any political system. Whatever the effectiveness of draconian solutions, such as controlled breeding and free distribution of mind-altering drugs as in Aldous Huxley's *Brave New World,* they are anathema to constitutional democracy.[8] Equally abhorrent are the coercive apparatuses used by Nazis, fascists, Stalinists, and Maoists. Yet without some kind of state-directed reorientation of citizens, transition to constitutional democracy may be impossible; at very least, its chances of success severely diminish.

The third option opens a middle way, and many moral philosophers assure us that virtue stands in the middle. There are practical steps here that might seem attractive: for instance, lengthening the transition to constitutional democracy while trying gradually to educate the people, both formally through instruction and informally through participation in the political processes. The philosopher's middle, however, may be mushy. Delay may mean no transition at all. There are "constitutional moments," which may not soon or ever recur.

Ideal Citizens

As earlier chapters have repeatedly pointed out, constitutional democracy is a political hybrid, resting on a pair of normative political theories that are usually compatible but coexist in a state of tension and occasionally in open conflict. At root, they share a basic value: respect for the dignity of all human beings. Constitutionalist and democratic theorists differ on many points, but they agree that government, society, and individual citizens are obliged to

---

8. In *The Republic,* Plato reports that Socrates was willing to consider controlled breeding, but he was not arguing for constitutional democracy. Regarding *Brave New World,* one might also note that even these methods do not rid the utopia of all dissidents; after all, the novel's central character is a refusenik. George Orwell's Big Brother is more successful. In the end, *1984*'s sometime dissenting hero "loved Big Brother."

treat all citizens with great and equal respect.[9] More specifically, both see each person as a carrier of rights and responsibilities. Nevertheless, each allows important distinctions among the rights to which sane adult citizens and, on the other hand, those to which minors, prisoners, the mentally incompetent, and aliens are entitled. Only the former have valid claims to full political participation.

According to Aristotle, a person "who enjoys the right of sharing in deliberative or judicial office attains thereby the status of a citizen of his state."[10] Similarly, democratic theory requires that citizens, as subjects of the law, must also be makers of the law.[11] At minimum, each citizen has a right to a voice and a vote in who shall hold public office as well as a right to stand for office. Many democratic theorists insist that citizens not only have a right to participate by speaking out on issues and by voting but also have a civic duty to engage in these sorts of activities.[12] From these participational rights many others flow, such as to associate and assemble with fellow citizens, with sufficient privacy to be able to reflect on and consult with others about electoral choices free from harassment before and retaliation after voting.[13] For its part, constitutionalist theory demands that all persons have certain additional rights. Some are more procedural, such as those associated with concepts such as due process; others are more substantive, such as claims to privacy and freedom of conscience.

Ideally, citizens would understand their entitlements and possess the resources necessary to utilize protective processes. No less important would be recognition and acceptance of duties to fellow citizens and the polity. Ideal citizens would be politically aware, active in trying to persuade fellow citizens about desirable public policies, knowledgeable about how to communicate opinions to officials, how to hold them accountable through electoral, administrative, and/or judicial processes, and also ready to fulfill their own political obligations. In the economic sphere, ideal citizens would strive to become self-sufficient, forgoing immediate gratifications to achieve inde-

---

9. I put aside the important question whether the norms of constitutional democracy extend beyond national boundaries and require such respectful, evenhanded treatment of all human beings of whatever race or nationality. I would contend that the logic of constitutional democracy's ethos— "We hold these truths to be self-evident, that *all men* are created equal," the Declaration of Independence says, not merely "all American colonists"—does so require; but I shall not make that argument here.

10. *The Politics*, bk. 3, ch. 1, §12 (1275b), p. 95.

11. Michael Walzer, "Philosophy and Democracy," 9 *Pol. Th.* 379, 383 (1981).

12. Will Kymlicka and Wayne Norman, "Citizenship in Culturally Diverse Societies: Issues, Contexts, Concepts," in Kymlicka and Norman, eds., *Citizenship in Diverse Societies* (New York: Oxford University Press, 2000), pp. 8–10, summarize much of this literature. Brandeis had made the same point in his concur. op. in Whitney v. California, 247 U.S. 357 (1927).

13. Only the last, a right to political privacy, may seem an unusual claim. For a fuller discussion, see my "The Right to Privacy and Legitimate Constitutional Change," in Shlomo Slonim, ed., *The Constitutional Bases of Political and Social Change in the United States* (New York: Praeger, 1990).

pendence.[14] Aristotle's description of the "good citizen" conforms to many of constitutional democracy's needs: a person who "possess[es] the knowledge and the capacity for ruling as well as for being ruled, and the excellence of the citizen may be defined as consisting in a 'knowledge of rule over free men from both points of view.' "[15]

Adequate Citizens

Reality, alas, seldom mirrors the ideal. Oft-repeated surveys of public opinion make it crystal clear that only a minority of citizens meet these standards. Most citizens would fail high school tests about governmental structures, tend to distrust politicians, do not put politics near the top of their personal priorities, and seldom discuss public policies with fellow citizens who are apt to disagree with them. In fact, when the directors of the first systematic survey of American voters' reactions to a presidential campaign began to analyze their findings, they put them aside for a year because the results were sharply at odds with what they as consumers of democratic theory had expected to find.[16] Subsequent researchers have constructed more nuanced gauges of voters' political awareness, knowledge, and interests; still, for most citizens, those levels remain well below the ideal.[17]

For constitutional rights we have even fewer survey data, but available information is not encouraging. If we use incidence of litigation as a measure, the evidence for concern about rights hardly overwhelming. For some people, legal processes offer attractive means to protect rights against hostile governmental action, but routes to courts are toll roads that impose high fees. Without organizational assistance, such as is provided in the United

14. This listing is quite similar to that of William Galston, *Liberal Purposes: Goods, Virtues, and Duties in the Liberal State* (New York: Cambridge University Press, 1991). Because I formulated my list before reading Galston and do not believe that a constitutional democracy need be the same as a liberal state, I stick to my own. See my "Creating Citizens for a Constitutional Democracy," in Michael Dunne and Tiziano Bonazzi, eds., *Citizenship and Rights in Multicultural Societies* (Keele, UK: Keele University Press, 1995).

15. *The Politics,* bk. 3, ch. 4, §15 (1277b), p. 105. In this discussion, Aristotle moves back and forth between citizens in general and citizens of a democracy.

16. Paul F. Lazarsfeld, Bernard B. Berelson, and Hazel Gaudet, *The People's Choice: How the Voter Makes Up His Mind in a Presidential Campaign* (Des Moines: Duell, Sloan, and Pearce, 1944); see the discussion in Peter H. Rossi, "Four Landmarks in Voting Research," in Eugene Burdick and Arthur J. Brodbeck, eds., *American Voting Behavior* (New York: Free Press, 1959).

17. The classic study is Gabriel A. Almond and Sidney Verba, *The Civic Culture: Political Attitudes and Democracy in Five Nations* (Princeton, NJ: Princeton University Press, 1963). For more recent analyses, see, inter alia, Sidney Verba, Norman H. Nie, and Jae-On Kim, *The Modes of Democratic Participation* (Los Angeles: Sage, 1971), *Participation and Political Equality: A Seven Nation Comparison* (New York: Cambridge University Press, 1978), and *Elites and the Idea of Equality* (Cambridge, MA: Harvard University Press, 1987); Gabriel A. Almond and Sidney Verba, eds., *The Civic Culture Revisited* (Los Angeles: Sage, 1989); and Sidney Verba, Kay Lehman Schlozman, and Henry E. Brady, *Civic Voluntarism in American Politics* (Cambridge, MA: Harvard University Press, 1995).

States by the American Civil Liberties Union and the National Association for the Advancement of Colored People or in Germany by political parties and governments of *Länder*, most private citizens could not afford to challenge public policy in the courts unless they themselves were the targets of criminal prosecutions.

Measuring acceptance of civic duties is even more difficult. Positive expressions of patriotism are often self-serving, and most negative indicia, such as tax evasion, draft dodging,[18] and criminal activity, are indirect and affected by the probability of being caught and the harshness of penalties. Furthermore, a citizenry may score low on one measure and high on another. In Italy, for example, evading taxes is a matter of personal pride, but turnout at elections is usually high. In the United States, less than half of eligible citizens go to the polls even for presidential elections, but most people promptly and honestly pay their taxes even though they realize that their system of taxation is unfair and many officials of the Internal Revenue Service are corrupt.

Adequate citizens are occasionally if not constantly attentive to politics; they have access to and occasionally process large chunks of political information. They may not cooly analyze what they obtain, but their political preferences are not necessarily irrational. Party labels allow voters to predict reasonably accurately the policy choices that candidates are apt to make. Citizens regularly hold elected officials accountable for "errors" in formulating policies and/or estimating constituents' preferences. The rotation of parties in power is sometimes traumatic but still common in stable constitutional democracies. Even Japan, where the Liberal Democratic Party has ruled most of the time since the end of World War II, has had several intraparty transfers of power.

Equally important is the set of attitudes that Adequates are likely to have toward themselves, society, and the political system. To a large extent, they are or want to become self-reliant, to control their own lives. On the other hand, although they are not likely to frequently debate public policy with people who are not friends, neither are they the isolated individuals whom many postmodernists admire, people who abjure community, shy "away from collective affiliation and communal responsibility in modern terms, [and consider] them a hindrance to personal development and a threat to privacy."[19]

---

18. Margaret Levi, *Consent, Dissent, and Patriotism* (New York: Cambridge University Press, 1997), offers an interesting study of draft evasion as a means of understanding the costs of political consent.

19. This description is that of Rosenau, *Post-modernism and the Social Sciences*, p. 54; see generally ch. 3, "Subverting the Subject." Some postmodernists want a different kind of individual. "Fred Dallmayr," Rosenau points out at p. 58, "seeks to go beyond the domineering individual (subject) who looks to mastery and submission. He substitutes a vision of an 'open-ended, non-possessive

Although Adequates tend to be wary of government, they also realize they sometimes need government and are willing to make sacrifices for the public order. Committed not only to the nation but also to most of the political system's norms, they tend to be patriots who view the state as neither master nor milk cow. Furthermore, although they may bitterly resent certain public policies, want structural reforms, and even be less than fully attached to some aspects of constitutional democracy itself, they are content to use elections and judicial processes rather than violence and believe that if governmental authority over them must be limited, so must legitimate governmental power over their neighbors.

Americans tend to be Adequates, but after Watergate they held Richard Nixon responsible for his conduct. In the late 1980s and early 1990s, Italians reacted even more decisively against *tangentopoli*, the corruption festering within the Christian Democratic Party and its allies, and wiped out several of these organizations. Even India, where grinding poverty has helped perpetuate ignorance and ethnic and religious violence often explodes, provides evidence of public attentiveness to and protection of constitutional democracy. In the mid-1970s, Indira Gandhi invoked emergency rule. She tried to stifle democracy by imprisoning leaders of the opposition and to eliminate constitutionalist checks by crippling the judiciary. India's voters responded by turning her out of office at the next election.

The Disaffected

A constitutional democracy must tolerate citizens who oppose the officials in power and the policies they are pursuing; more important, constitutional democracy needs some such people to keep the system true to its values. But a wide chasm separates opposition to particular officials or public policies from opposition to the political system. The term for the former, *loyal opposition*, expresses a concept that tyrannical regimes cannot accommodate. For them all opposition is apostasy. With that much said, like every political system, constitutional democracy will have citizens who categorically reject the political order. Sometimes that rejection will be grounded in rational self-interest: no governmental system can always fair to all of its members. At other times, antipathy will be a product of personality: some people resent *all* forms of authority. Rejection may also stem from deeply held beliefs. Many religious people—whom, for lack of a better term, we call fundamentalists—categorically reject equality between members of different castes or sexes or between true believers and infidels. Indeed, some reject almost every idea associated with modern Western civilization. In addition,

individuality' capable of communalism, association, community, anticipative-emancipatory practice. At the same time his new subject is not the reasoning humanistic citizen of the Enlightenment" (citing Dallmayr, "Political Inquiry: Beyond Empiricism and Hermeneutics," in Terence Ball, ed., *Idioms of Inquiry* [Albany: State University of New York Press, 1987]).

neofascist racists are alive and well not only in Germany, Italy, and Spain but also in France, the United Kingdom, the United States, and assorted Muslim states. Even people who were once committed to constitutional democracy may become disaffected. Gross disparities between aspiration and reality may convince some people that constitutional democracy itself is a pious fraud.

Expressions of disaffection vary from political apathy, to support for radical parties such as Italy's now defunct neofascist MSI (Movimento Sociale Italiano), to religiously grounded terrorism[20] such as that of Al Qaeda. The magnitude of the threat to the political order depends on several factors, not least of which is the capacity of ambitious leaders to mobilize large groups of people whom the society has left behind—people who lack hope as well as faith in the political system. Within the United States, young, poor Afro-American and Hispanic men in decaying city centers provide an appalling example. Born into poverty, hounded by prejudice, profiled by police, and lacking incentives to stay in school, they see small chance of earning a decent living. Drugs and crime seem to mark their options, further increasing prejudice, not only against them but also against the much larger number of their ethnic kin who struggle to achieve success within the system. In Israel, legal, economic, and social discrimination against Arab citizens within Israel proper and Palestinians in the Occupied Territories has created an even more volatile threat to political stability.

The disaffected are true aliens. If they understand the political system, they neither respect nor follow its principles. To the extent any society leaves such people psychologically outside, it breeds trouble for itself. If they are numerous and concentrated—especially if they are ready to take up arms—that society courts disaster. To survive, an established constitutional democracy can rely on its minority of "ideal" private citizens, providing that (a) the percentage of disaffected is small, (b) most public officials themselves come close to fitting the model of ideal citizen, and (c) the bulk of other citizens are at least "Adequates" who support the constitutional order and can be aroused against officials who violate its norms.

Although new leaders may believe that their most immediate mission is to replace or retrain officials who remain in place, creating a large number of both ideal and adequate citizens must also have high priority. It is from these private citizens that future public officials will have to come, and if many officials remain hostile to constitutional democracy, the future may be quite short.

20. Jessica Stern argues that terrorists' motivations are always multidimensional but alienation is among the more important elements. *Terror in the Name of God: Why Religious Militants Kill* (New York: HarperCollins, 2003). Similarly, Olivier Roy sees jihadists as having taken up the cause of terror because it links them to something. *Globalized Islam: The Search for a New Ummah* (New York: Columbia University Press, 2004).

The Tasks of Creation: Forging a National Identity

Creating cadres of Ideals and Adequates is a frightening task, but there is a necessary and equally frightening prestep. Before a people can build a political system, they must have a collective consciousness as a nation. Without a sense of belonging to a country, citizenship can have little practical meaning. The people's common consciousness must refer both to those who are included and to others who are excluded. Connections to family, clan, religious, and ethnic group are typically tight, but stretching those lines beyond immediate kinship and friendship strains the links, as the histories of Eastern Europe and Sub-Saharan Africa cruelly illustrate. In less extreme forms, the problem has been common. The Declaration of the Rights of Man, busy guillotines, and Napoleon's legions could not instantly persuade peasants that they were French citizens. That conversion was slow and painful, consuming more than a century.[21] It may take even longer to convince Britons (and Swedes, and Danes, and . . .) that they are citizens of a federalized continent.

North Americans have faced similar issues, and their records attest to the difficulties involved. The Declaration of Independence spoke of "*these* United States" or "*these* United Colonies," signifying an alliance rather than a unity. And the first constitutional text claimed to establish a "Confederacy," a "firm League of Friendship"among sovereign states. The second constitutional charter, that of 1787, also refers to "the United States" in the plural.[22] Seventy-five years later, large numbers of Americans, including graduates of West Point such as Robert E. Lee and Jefferson Davis, still thought of themselves as citizens of their states first, of the South second, and of "the United States" last. Sebastian de Grazia's description of America before the Civil War as "a country with no name" is apt.[23] Canada continues to suffer from similar problems, with Quebeçois still mulling over secession. "I know that Quebec is my country," René Levesque said when he was a provincial minister. "I'm not quite convinced that Canada is."[24]

Creating a sense of national identification is a continuous process. What Robert Hughes said about the United States is to some extent true of every nation: "America is a collective work of the imagination whose making never

---

21. Eugen Weber, *Peasants into Frenchmen: The Modernization of Rural France, 1870–1914* (Stanford, CA: Stanford University Press, 1976).

22. Article 3, §3 reads: "Treason against the United States, shall consist only in levying War against *them* . . ." (italics added). For a study of the gradual development of the notion of the "United States" as a singular noun and thus a nation, see Sebastian de Grazia, *A Country with No Name: Tales from the Constitution* (New York: Pantheon Books, 1997).

23. De Grazia, *Country with No Name.*

24. Quoted in Edward M. Corbett, *Quebec Confronts Canada* (Baltimore: Johns Hopkins University Press, 1967), p. 34. See, generally, Peter H. Russell, *Constitutional Odyssey: Can Canadians Be a Sovereign People?* (Toronto: University of Toronto Press, 1992),

ends, and once that sense of collectivity and mutual respect is broken the possibility of Americanness begins to unravel."[25]

Nation builders can look to a conceptual quadrangle enclosing possible alternatives. At one corner is an option supposedly not open to constitutional democracies: completely subjugate the minority group(s), as the United States tried with Indians in the nineteenth century, Serbia and Croatia with Muslims, Turkey with Kurds, and czarist Russia with Jews. This policy may be coupled with expulsion, as several Central and Eastern European nations tried after both world wars, or even with ethnic cleansing. The other three corners offer models compatible with constitutional democracy. One of these prescribes amalgamation of all citizens into a single culture. This is the so-called American way: assimilation is the goal, *e pluribus unum* the mantra. A third corner contains an arrangement that accepts difference and affirms separate but equal status of ethnic groups, as in Israel, allowing each jurisdiction over some matters, such as marriage and divorce, as they pertain to members. The fourth corner offers a version of federalism, with boundaries set so that each of the major groups governs its own subdivision, as in Belgium, Canada, Spain,[26] India, and the United Kingdom. One could also look on the Netherlands' consociational democracy as a functional analogue.

Most nations mix and match these models. In the United States, assimilation has often meant not a cultural blend but adherence to the mores of the white upper-middle class. Moreover, public policy has sometimes excluded groups such African Americans and Asians. Glazer and Moynihan claim that, in fact, "smorgasbord" more accurately describes America than does "melting pot."[27] Native Americans are the most obviously unassimilated group. Many members of other groups have also maintained their own language and culture. Indeed, in Miami and throughout the Southwest, more Spanish may be spoken than English. In some New York neighborhoods, Yiddish is the language of choice and the dress is Hasidic. Most large cities have Chinatowns as well as Korean and Vietnamese enclaves where English is a foreign tongue and the customs are Asian.[28] Amazingly, despite

25. *The Culture of Complaint* (New York: Oxford University Press, 1993), p. 13.

26. Spain's constitutional text prescribes regionalism, not federalism, but the drift of Spanish constitutional development has been toward federalism. See Robert Agranoff, "Federal Evolution in Spain," 17 *Int'l Pol. Sci. Rev.* 385 (1996).

27. Nathan Glazer and Patrick J. Moynihan, *Beyond the Melting Pot: The Negroes, Puerto Ricans, Jews, Italians, and Irish of New York City* (Cambridge, MA: MIT Press, 1963). Two older books are among the most insightful on this point: Michael Novak, *The Rise of the Unmeltable Ethnics* (New York: Macmillan, 1972), and Thomas Sowell, *Ethnic America: A History* (New York: Basic Books, 1981).

28. Much the same phenomena occurred in the late nineteenth and early twentieth centuries for German, Italians, and Polish immigrants. They, however, have largely, though not completely, been absorbed into the mainstream of America.

glaring defects, the American approach has worked well for that country in generating fidelity to the constitutional order.

Italy also has a heterogeneous population. Even though most citizens are nominally Catholic, North and South differ in political history, economic development, language, and culture. Since unification, Rome has officially endorsed assimilation, but television and superb soccer teams have been more effective in bringing Italians together than has public policy. Family and neighborhood probably still outrank the nation in loyalty, and a Sicilian is not likely to feel a common citizenship with a Tuscan. Italy, however, manages to stagger along, even though the popularity of the Northern League in Italian elections during the late 1980s and early 1990s revealed deep-seated resentment of subsidies to the South and prejudice against southerners, strongly hinting that, fourteen decades after unification, the country has not yet solved its problems of national identification.

In Israel, Jewish and Muslim communities are culturally and often physically separate.[29] Despite bitter differences among Jews, Israel has remained, as its Declaration of Independence proclaimed, a Jewish state. The system produces, Benjamin Akzin writes, "unequal pluralism."[30] Although granted some measure of autonomy, Arabs are second-class citizens. Few Jews and Arabs trust each other, much less view each other as fellow citizens. Equally few Arabs feel loyalty toward the Israeli state.

A blend of political and ethnic federalism has done quite well in Belgium. Canada survives as a nation but, as already noted, with deep cracks in its people's sense of common citizenship. Spain has had only partial success with that arrangement. The Catalans seem reasonably content with their quasi-federal status, but Basque terrorists continue bombings. In India, state lines do not always coincide with those of various ethnic groups, but the central government has respected local languages and also allowed Muslims to set their own rules for marriage and divorce. This policy has not been uniformly successful, as indicated by a long series of ethnic riots that have sometimes verged on uprisings. The Hindu Nationalist Party's popularity threatens to destroy the fragile structure of India's secular state.[31] Recurrent crises with Pakistan may bring many Indian groups closer together but at the same time are likely to further distance Muslims from Hindi.

The English have had real success in smoothing over divisions between

29. During Israel's early years, Arabs included a large Christian minority. Emigration both from Israel proper and the Occupied Territories has been greatly reduced their number.

30. *State and Nation* (London: Hutchinson University Library, 1964), p. 44; quoted in Gary Jeffrey Jacobsohn, *Apple of Gold: Constitutionalism in Israel and the United States* (Princeton, NJ: Princeton University Press, 1993), p. 62. In ch. 3, Jacobsohn offers a superb analysis of the ways in which the concept of citizenship plays out in Israeli politics.

31. See Gary Jeffrey Jacobsohn, *The Wheel of Law: India's Secularism in Comparative Context* (Princeton, NJ: Princeton University Press, 2003), esp. ch. 6.

Celts and Anglo-Saxons by allowing Scots and Welsh a measure of auton-omy. In contrast, England has supported the Protestants it transplanted to Ireland and for centuries tried to subjugate Catholics, finally giving the South dominion status within the empire in 1922 and then ignoring its later secession.

At the very outset of the founding of a constitutional democracy, ethnic and religious cleavages present leaders with a critical decision. Where these differences have bred such hatred that chances of achieving broad political identity and restrained political action are tiny, leaders must seriously con-sider dividing their country.[32] Whether or not the decision of Czechs and Slovaks to break up their federation was wise under the specific circum-stances of 1992–1993, maintaining Yugoslavia as a single, centrally ruled state would probably have shed more blood than did later civil wars.

More generally, these sorts of problems underline the necessity of state-craft in creating institutions and processes. Just as Giuseppe Di Palma has argued that during transitions to constitutional democracy[33] it is possible to construct institutions and processes to protect the interests of economic and ideological groups, so too it should be equally possible (and difficult) to construct institutions and processes both to safeguard the interests of diverse groups and to convince them that the new political system will protect those interests. Indeed, lowering the stakes of political conflict by dividing power, fracturing majorities, setting procedural and substantive limits on govern-mental authority, and establishing institutions to oversee those restrictions are prototypical constitutionalist moves.

Where leaders seek to preserve national unity, they must emphasize mutual economic advantages. English-speaking Canada's refusal to commit to a free-trade agreement with an independent Quebec or to continue subsi-dizing that province has sapped some of the strength of separatist sen-timents. At the same time, leaders must accommodate—and be seen to accommodate—differences that divide their people. A constitutional text that included guarantees of certain contested rights, such as linguistic equal-ity as in Canada and India, would not be sufficient unless it was coupled with institutions and public policies to make those rights effective. Rhetoric would also be essential. "We live by symbols," Oliver Wendell Holmes said, echoing Edward Gibbon's claim that "mankind is governed by names."[34] In

32. For insightful analyses of constitutional decay, see Mark E. Brandon, *Free in the World: American Slavery and Constitutional Failure* (Princeton, NJ: Princeton University Press, 1998); and Abdullahi An-Na'im, "The National Question, Secession, and Constitutionalism," in Douglas Greenberg, Stanley N. Katz, Melanie Beth Oliviero, and Steven C. Wheatley, eds., *Constitutional-ism and Democracy: Transformations in the Contemporary World* (New York: Oxford University Press, 1993).

33. *To Craft Democracies: An Essay on Democratic Transitions* (Berkeley: University of California Press, 1990).

34. Quoted in de Grazia, *A Country with No Name*, p. 402.

multicultural nations, the cross, the crescent, and the menorah may both divide and unite, but other words and symbols—a flag, anthem, myth, or epic poem—may bring groups together. Shared memories of heroes such as Joan of Arc, George Washington, Horatio Nelson, or Giuseppe Garibaldi might also be effective. Even battles may perform that function, and defeats may serve as well as victories: Thermopylae, Masada, Bunker Hill, the Alamo, the Marne, the Easter Rebellion,[35] Pearl Harbor, Stalingrad, the Warsaw Revolt, Iwo Jima, or the World Trade Center, for instance.

In 1776, Thomas Jefferson drafted a declaration that not only detailed American grievances but, more importantly, announced a creed around which revolutionaries could unite: "We hold these truths to be self-evident, that all men are created equal and endowed by their Creator with certain unalienable rights." That document laid out ideals—as long as "all men" did not include women, Indians, or blacks—that resonated in colonial political culture and whose rhetoric wove emotional ropes to bind scattered colonists together. "There was not an idea in it," John Adams wrote to a friend, "but what had been hackneyed in Congress for two years before."[36] Although miffed by Adams's comment, Jefferson admitted that his purpose had not been "to invent new ideas" but to provide "an expression of the American mind"—precisely what was needed.[37]

Eleven years later, in the midst of another crisis of national unity, James Madison proudly (and cleverly) played on the sacrifices and triumphs of the revolution:

> Hearken not to the unnatural voice which tells you that the people of Amer-
> ica, knit together as they are by so many chords of affection, can no longer
> live together as members of the same family; can no longer continue the
> mutual guardians of their mutual happiness; can no longer be fellow citizens
> of one great respectable empire. . . . [T]he kindred blood which flows in the
> veins of American citizens, the mingled blood which they have shed in
> defence of their sacred rights, consecrate their union, and excite horror at the
> idea of their becoming rivals, aliens, enemies.[38]

Such eloquent invocations do not guarantee success. In 1861 Abraham Lincoln's appeal to "the mystic chords of memory" and "the better angels of

---

35. The usual term in Ireland is "the Rising."

36. To Thomas Pickering; quoted in Carl L. Becker, *The Declaration of Independence* (1924; reprint New York: Vintage, 1958), p. 24.

37. The first phrase was addressed to James Madison, Aug. 30, 1823; reprinted in Robert Ginsburg, ed., *A Casebook on the Declaration of Independence* (New York: Crowell, 1967), pp. 30–32. Jefferson's original draft had also attacked the king for promoting the "execrable commerce" of slave trade, but Congress cut that part because it might have been divisive. The second phrase was addressed to Henry Lee, May 8, 1825; reprinted in Ginsburg, *Casebook*, pp. 32–33.

38. *The Federalist*, No. 14.

our nature" failed to stem secession.[39] Still, political leaders can maximize chances of success through skillful use of mass media of communications to deploy both reason and rhetoric along with appeals to self-interest.[40] In culturally and/or geographically isolated regions, it would be critical for national leaders to establish (or thicken) bonds with local leaders—in essence to build a national alliance of political parties.

Leaders might also follow the nineteenth-century French example by using universal military service as "the school of the nation" to foster a sense of national identification.[41] By moving young men (and possibly women) to other parts of the country and compelling them to associate with people of other geographic, ethnic, and religious origins, the government could reduce provincialism. A sometime corporal, later Führer, fully understood the educational utility of military service. As he wrote in *Mein Kampf,* the army should be "a school for the mutual understanding and adjustment of all Germans. . . . It should furthermore raise the individual youth above the narrow horizon of his little countryside and place him in the German nation."[42] Moreover, since Homer's day leaders have recognized that "wagging the dog" can be an effective, if expensive, means of welding citizens together. Few incitements are as forceful as xenophobic images of foreigners desecrating the homeland. The mullahs in Iran and the Taliban in Afghanistan invoked the specter of the "Great Satan" of America to rally otherwise divided Muslims to their cause. George W. Bush showed that he, too, could play that game by falsely claiming that Iraq was supporting Al Qaeda and had weapons of mass destruction.

Creating Citizens

The work of creating a collective national consciousness may occur in the context of converting or confirming a people to constitutional democracy's complex of values. Each task is difficult, and their simultaneous accomplishment may be impossible.

Perhaps the clearest lessons on how to fail comes from the United States. Late in 1861 the Sea Islands of South Carolina offered a tempting target to the Union. After a series of embarrassing military defeats, Lincoln desperately needed a victory. A blow against South Carolina, especially one that menaced Charleston, the cradle of rebellion, would be sweet. Other military

39. First Inaugural Address, Mar. 4, 1861; in *The Collected Works of Abraham Lincoln,* ed. Roy P. Basler (New Brunswick, NJ: Rutgers University Press, 1953), 4:271.

40. The dangers here are obvious. See the West German Television Case, 12 BVerfGE 205 (1961); translated and reprinted in part in Walter F. Murphy and Joseph Tanenhaus, eds., *Comparative Constitutional Law* (New York: St. Martin's, 1977), pp. 212–15.

41. Rogers Brubaker, *Citizenship and Nationhood in France and Germany* (Cambridge, MA: Harvard University Press, 1992), p. 15. Also see Weber, *Peasants into Frenchmen,* ch. 17.

42. Quoted in Winston Churchill, *The Second World War: The Gathering Storm* (Boston: Houghton Mifflin, 1948), p. 143.

and economic factors entered in: the Union navy needed a refueling station for its blockaders off the Southern coast, and Port Royal offered a pair of deep-water harbors; Northern textile mills needed cotton to stay open, and the Sea Islands then produced the world's finest fiber. Thus, in November, Commodore S. F. Du Pont sailed into Port Royal Sound, disembarked a small army to begin island-hopping amphibious landings toward Charleston, fifty miles north.[43] The plantation owners fled inland with their families, overseers, a few slaves, and what valuables they could load on barges, leaving behind mansions, cotton fields, and more than ten thousand slaves.

Several omens were favorable for transforming these abandoned slaves into citizens. First, despite occasionally strong personal affection (some blacks risked their lives defending the massahs' abandoned homes from looting Union soldiers), almost all these people judged their enslavement as morally wrong. Second, they now *wanted* to become true citizens. Third, the exodus of owners and overseers had stripped the islands of representatives of the old regime and subjected their property to confiscation, eliminating need to negotiate with the powers that had been. But serious problems also existed. The blacks were almost all illiterate,[44] and many spoke Gullah—a mixture of West African dialects salted with Elizabethan English—as their first or even only language. Furthermore, few of these people had ever been off the islands, so they lacked any knowledge of life outside the plantations. Their world was bounded by the Atlantic on the east, swift, treacherous tidal rivers to the north and south, and swamps and slave patrols to the west. They were field hands, carpenters, cotton gin mechanics, cooks, babysitters, midwives, and house servants. Most critically, the army had no plan to cope with, much less make citizens out of, this windfall of human contraband. Their only obvious use was as laborers, a role blacks were loath to continue.

The president, doubtful of the possibility of a biracial society of equals and wary of alienating slaveholding border states, had forbidden the army to free slaves. Moreover, as Willie Lee Rose later noted, there were not many more abolitionists among Abe Lincoln's troops than among Jeff Davis's.[45] The army's concerns were to establish a base for the blockading fleet and then move north to attack Charleston. Feeding and caring for a mass of humanity were onerous and unforeseen burdens. (Only much later would the War Department realize that blacks could flesh out the decimated Union ranks and so authorize local officers to recruit ex-slaves.)

43. These campaigns, meticulously detailed in *The Records of the War of the Rebellion*, provided a model for the operations of the U.S. Marine Corps' amphibious operations during World War II.

44. South Carolina law forbade teaching slaves to read and write, a law that was typically though not universally followed. As anyone who reads the "Rent-A-Slave" ads in pre–Civil War Southern newspapers quickly realizes, a slave who could read and write and had some arithmetic was a valuable moneymaker for the slaveholder.

45. *Rehearsal for Reconstruction: Port Royal Experiment* (Indianapolis: Bobbs-Merrill, 1964), p. 61. These paragraphs depend heavily on Lee's splendid account.

Complicating the army's difficulties, Secretary of the Treasury Salmon P. Chase sent agents to restart the plantations' cotton production. But the blacks wanted to live on "their land" free from all masters. Their speaking Gullah gave them some protection by bewildering whites who could discern enough English words to think they were hearing, if not understanding, their own language. Soon Chase's men were almost as frustrated as the Union commanders. Adding yet another dimension of trouble was the arrival of two groups of missionaries from Boston and New York. Some were intellectual Unitarians, others evangelical Methodists, but all were devout abolitionists. They wanted first to save black people's souls, then to prepare them for full citizenship. Soon, however, they began angrily disputing among themselves about over how to bring salvation to their new flock. As good Southern Baptists, the blacks were confused by both sects, though less so by the Methodists, who could appreciate foot-stomping hymns and fire-and-brimstone preaching at "the shout."

The army was constantly perplexed by the blacks' refusal to provide heavy manual labor, by the treasury men's demands, and by the missionaries' bickering. Commanders often found keeping peace on the islands more difficult than waging war against the Rebels. The sad saga was a snarl of hard work, courage, devotion, contradictory policies, and personality clashes among military, treasury agents, and missionaries, along with bitter sectarian squabbles between Unitarians and Methodists. The situation was worsened by financial scandals, as missionaries and bureaucrats scrambled to buy up confiscated plantation lands. This last angered the former slaves, who believed the land had reverted to them, not to Yankees.

What never emerged was a coherent governmental policy that put the issue of black citizenship even near center stage. When, in 1863, the slaves formally got their freedom, they had no land to maintain themselves or education to understand what "freedom" meant in a white world. At best the Port Royal Experiment provided, as Willie Rose Lee said, "a rehearsal for Reconstruction." Although many of the Sea Island men would die in futile frontal assaults on Fort Wagner, the final Confederate defense south of Charleston Harbor, a century would pass before their descendants would become full American citizens. The most important lesson from the Port Royal Experiment is that to create new citizens there must be unity of command and unity of purpose. Two more successful experiments, those of post–World War II Japan and Germany, provide additional insights.

Japan surrendered on September 2, 1945, and within a few weeks the White House released "The United States Initial Post-surrender Policy toward Japan."[46] This white paper laid down the guidelines for General

46. The official policy maker was the State, War, Navy Coordinating Committee, known as SWNCC. This section of this chapter relies heavily on a research paper done by Judith Lynn Failer

Douglas MacArthur and his staff in Tokyo, collectively known as SCAP. America's primary goal was to ensure that Japan would never again menace the world. To attain this end, the United States sought two subsidiary objectives: (1) limiting Japan's sovereignty to its main islands and demilitarizing the nation and (2) establishing democratic (in fact constitutionalist as well) government. In prescribing the second task, the document's authors showed considerable political sophistication. They wanted not merely to restructure governmental institutions but also to remold Japanese culture: "The Japanese people shall be encouraged to develop a desire for individual liberties and respect for fundamental human rights, particularly freedoms of religion, assembly, speech, and the press. They shall also be encouraged to form democratic and representative organizations." Japanese rehabilitation, MacArthur said, was theological, involving "a spiritual recrudescence and improvement of human character."[47]

The means to tame Japan included removing militarists and their sympathizers from important posts in both the public and private sectors. In all, about 200,000 people, including almost a quarter of public school teachers, were purged, and additional thousands resigned. More positively, the white paper directed SCAP to teach the Japanese about American political institutions, processes, and culture; stimulate political parties; reform the police and judicial systems so as to protect individual rights; release political prisoners; and "democratize" the economic system. Implementing the last policy entailed midwifery and pediatric care for labor unions, land reform, and dissolving the *zaibatsu,* the corporate conglomerates, usually family owned, that formed the backbone of Japan's industries.

Shortly after the occupation began, Prime Minister Shigeru Yoshida asked Colonel Charles Kades, one of the chief architects of the new political system: "You think you can make Japan a democratic country? I don't think so." Most scholars would probably have judged Yoshida's response as realistic. Neither the Mejei constitutional text nor its ensuing constitutional order had demonstrated affection for either democracy or constitutionalism. And certainly the militaristic government of the 1930s and 1940s was inimical to both. Kades, however, replied, "We can try."[48] He and the rest of SCAP did try with a "messianic fervor" that was contagious.[49] Although Japanese

---

of Indiana University when she was a graduate student at Princeton; John W. Dower, *Embracing Defeat: Japan in the Wake of World War II* (New York: W. W. Norton, 2000); Ray A. Moore and Donald L. Robinson, *Partners for Democracy: Crafting the New Japanese State under MacArthur* (New York: Oxford University Press, 2002); and Lawrence Ward Beer and John Maki, *From Imperial Myth to Democracy: Japan's Two Constitutions* (Boulder: University Press of Colorado, 2002). Other sources are cited in the footnotes.

47. Quoted in Moore and Robinson, *Partners for Democracy,* p. 43.

48. Quoted in Dower, *Embracing Defeat,* p. 70.

49. Dower, *Embracing Defeat,* p. 79.

conservatives who initially controlled the government wanted only cosmetic changes, some men who had served in the civilian government during the 1920s were eager to exploit SCAP's "gifts from heaven." Kades would later refer to these people and the converts they (and the devastation of World War II) made among younger Japanese as willing "partners for democracy." Together they sometimes pushed reforms even further than the Americans had hoped. For instance, SCAP wanted equal rights for women and insisted on inserting Article 14 in the constitutional text: "[A]ll of the people are equal under the law."[50] The Japanese then went even further and recognized women's right to equal education, a concession hitherto unthinkable.

The most consequential change came in the structure of the governmental system outlined by the document that became known as MacArthur's constitution.[51] The most famous section of that text, Article 9, renounced war and forbade the organization of armed forces. As drafting began, the emperor publicly admitted (more or less) that he was not divine[52]; SCAP outlawed State Shintoism (though the religious cult of Shintoism remained legal); and freedom of religion became a reality. On their own initiative, the Japanese made three changes important for a society with democratic aspirations. First, they abolished the system of peerage; second, they published the constitutional charter—and translated the civil and criminal codes—in colloquial Japanese rather than *bungotai,* the archaic linguistic form, unintelligible to most ordinary citizens but traditional for governmental documents; and, third, they inserted in the constitutional text a provision that all citizens had a right "to receive an equal education correspondent to their ability."

MacArthur's demand for new elections conducted under rules recognizing freedom of speech, press, and assembly and requiring universal adult suffrage shocked conservative officials. They had planned to continue historic limitations on the right to criticize the government and to restrict the franchise to certain classes of males. The Great White Emperor's order gave the mass of Japanese people an immediate lesson in democracy, and similar teachings from SCAP soon abounded. Through Article 89 of the constitu-

50. The Japanese word, translated into English as "people," is not all inclusive. Although encompassing males and females, it is restricted to Japanese persons; thus its literal terms do not provide for equal treatment of foreigners or resident aliens. Use of this more restrictive word was deliberate, allowing the Japanese to continue to discriminate against Korean residents. See the discussion in Moore and Robinson, *Partners for Democracy,* pp. 393–94.

51. Moore and Robinson, *Partners for Democracy,* offer the best analysis of the drafting of this text and the negotiations between Americans and Japanese; also Koseki Shōichi, *The Birth of Japan's Postwar Constitution.* trans. and ed. Ray A. Moore (Boulder: Westview, 1998).

52. The exact words of his public address to Japan were as follows: "The ties between us and our people have always stood upon mutual trust and affection. They do not depend upon mere legends and myths. They are not predicated on the false conception that the Emperor is divine, and that the Japanese people are superior to other races and dated to rule the world." Quoted in Moore and Robinson, *Partners for Democracy,* p. 46.

tional charter[53] and pressure on the bureaucracy, the Americans tried to limit governmental control of ostensibly private organizations. SCAP also encouraged formation of new nongovernmental organizations, such as credit unions, parent-teacher associations, and the equivalent of 4-H clubs. In an effort to undercut prevailing notions of social hierarchy, other documents stressed the equal dignity of all forms of labor. By controlling all radio stations, SCAP ensured that Japanese officials could not slant the news, and, by having Americans write or at least edit the scripts, SCAP ensured that the people would receive only information they "needed" and commentary that was politically correct, a paradoxical kind of democratic acculturation.

MacArthur and his staff were acutely aware of the importance of educating succeeding generations and quickly established the Civil Information and Education Section, dubbed "the American Ministry for Japanese Education." Underlining this section's importance, SCAP put it almost entirely under the control of Marines. They saw their task as completely revamping the system. Six months later, the Generalissimo invited a committee of twenty-six American educators to visit and advise on how to teach the Japanese about their new political system. Acting on this group's advice,[54] SCAP drafted what would become Japan's Fundamental Law of Education. Its purpose was nothing less than development of the ideal citizen of a constitutional democracy (and perhaps also of Thomas Aquinas's "Perfect Christian Commonwealth"):

> Education shall aim at the full development of personality, striving for the rearing of the people, sound in mind and body, who shall love truth and justice, esteem individual value, respect labour, and have a deep sense of responsibility, and be imbued with an independent spirit, as builders of a peaceful state and society.[55]

SCAP did not repeat the major mistake of the Sea Islands. There was unity of purpose and command; the Great White Father and his staff were fully dedicated to the white paper's goals. Moreover, the occupation was an American operation. Despite efforts by the Far Eastern Commission that the Allies had jointly established, the United States was in sole control. With Japanese leaders as coconspirators, MacArthur managed to outmaneuver the Allies as well as his opponents in Washington. Soon, however, as in Germany, the cold war changed the occupation's basic goal from making

53. "No public money or other property shall be expended or appropriated for the use, benefit or maintenance of any religious institution or association, or for any charitable, educational or benevolent enterprises not under the control of public authority."

54. U.S. Department of State, *Report of the United States Education Mission to Japan*, Far Eastern Series 11 (Washington, DC: Government Printing Office, 1946).

55. Quoted in William K. Cummings, *Education and Equality in Japan* (Princeton, NJ: Princeton University Press, 1980), p. 26.

Japan a neutral, demilitarized state to transforming it into an armed ally.[56] In June 1950, MacArthur himself wrote: "[D]espite Japan's constitutional renunciation of war, its right to self-defense in case of a predatory attack is implicit and inalienable."[57] To facilitate this change, many "purged" leaders were instantly rehabilitated, and the United States encouraged the Japanese to build a small but efficient military establishment operating under the euphemism of a "Self-Defense Force"[58] and returned the Bonin and Ryukyu islands (including Okinawa).

These retreats notwithstanding, the American experiment in remaking Japanese citizens had remarkable success. As do all constitutional orders, Japan's varies from its charter, but MacArthur's document remains in force and, after six decades, formally unamended. Despite "naturalization" of this text, fair and open democratic elections periodically take place, and losers peacefully, if bitterly, leave office. Legislators, administrators, and judges protect constitutional rights, although judges prefer litigants to negotiate their differences according to hallowed Japanese custom. Freedoms of press and speech are real, though inhibited by cultural norms as well as, early on, by SCAP's own penchant for secrecy. Decentralizing control of police and weakening the once nefarious Home Ministry have increased citizens' freedom.

Japanese belief in their racial superiority has by no means vanished, but the mass of citizens have moved light-years away from their rigid, racist, male chauvinistic prewar culture. Although in private corporations women live under glass ceilings familiar to their American sisters, they speak and publish comments on political issues, teach at universities, vote, run for office, are sometimes elected, and hold appointive offices as well. In addition, many leaders of NGOs are women. They were, for example, very active in

56. In November 1946, only months after the new constitutional text went into effect, Ashida Hitoshi, the chairman of the Diet's committee on constitutional revision and later prime minister, wrote a small book—*Interpretation of the Constitution*—arguing that Article 9 forbade only "aggressive war" and not war for national defense. See Beer and Maki. *From Imperial Myth to Democracy,* p. 89. Ashida told his colleagues that whether Japan rearmed for self-defense would be decided "not by way the constitution is written, but by the extent of Japan's democratization and the international situation." Quoted in Moore and Robinson, *Partners for Democracy,* p. 270. Moore and Robinson also point out that the Japanese deleted these remarks from the minutes of the meetings they gave to SCAP. Decades later, the United States pressured the Japanese to join in the Gulf War of 1991 and the war against the Taliban and Osama bin Laden in 2001, interpreting the constitution in much the same way as Ashida had. The Japanese did allocate some money to help the alliance against Sadam Hussein—after all, Japan desperately needs oil from the Middle East—but the most the government would do was provide "logistical support" for the United States in emergencies in its war against Iraq.

57. Quoted in Moore and Robinson, *Partners for Democracy,* p. 321.

58. See James H. Buck, ed., *The Modern Japanese Military System* (Beverly Hills, CA: Sage, 1975).

campaigns to encourage savings and, by 1992, made up almost half of the country's volunteer welfare commissioners.[59]

Japan has partially rearmed, and since 2001 its government has been publicly discussing repealing Article 9. Most officials still avoid responsibility for soldiers' systematic rapes, murders, tortures, and lootings in China and the Western Pacific during World War II, and public schools use textbooks that ignore or whitewash the viciousness of Japan's aggression. Nevertheless, as of early 2006 Article 9 remained in place, and it is probable that the people of no major nation are as committed to pacifism as the Japanese.

In the economic sphere, SCAP's land reform was eminently successful. Less happy was the fate of efforts to build up unions as counterweights to big business. Fear of communist infiltration frightened SCAP into moderating its early supportive (at times creative) policies. In the industrial sector, the *zaibatsu* were broken up. After a few years, however, zeal for trust busting diminished, and *keiretsu*, also huge conglomerates, began to flourish. The latter, however, are not family owned and compete with each other. In contrast, SCAP failed to decentralize banks and found it convenient to work through the existing governmental bureaucracy. During the occupation as during the war, Japan's economic development was run—and continues to be run—less through open markets and more through the central government's ministries, the big banks, and economists working for both. Indeed, the system displays many aspects of guided, though not coercive, capitalism. Japan, Sheldon Garon says, "is a polity whose democratic institutions and firm guarantees of civil liberties coexist with a broad based commitment to [government's] managing society."[60]

In many ways, junctions between Japanese culture and constitutional democracy are jagged, but nowhere in the world is the fit perfect. SCAP's legacy was neither free enterprise nor atomistic individualism, but a form of constitutional democracy different from, yet allied to, that of the West. Most Japanese became at least adequate citizens. Singapore's Lee Kuan Yew would find less cause for joy than would Douglas MacArthur.

Germany presented a challenge similar to Japan's, but the differences were marked. Knowing that the Russians were trying to mold East Germany into a Stalinist political system, the Western Allies merged their zones, the more effectively to change "their" Germans' attitudes. Given greater assets and less rancor, the American Military Government (AMG) was better

---

59. Sheldon Garon, *Molding Japanese Minds: The State in Everyday Life* (Princeton, NJ: Princeton University Press, 1997), p. 179.

60. Ibid., p. 235. My bracketing "government" may misstate Japanese attitudes. Perhaps it would be more accurate to use a phrase something like "governmental management that reflects popular wishes." In either case, here we see evidence of the resilience of traditional Japanese cultural norms regarding proper community action.

positioned than the French or British to make systematic efforts to reform German culture. Rehabilitating these people into constitutional democrats was in many aspects easier than converting Japanese. Language, for instance, presented a less formidable barrier. In 1945–1949 Germany had a history of a *Rechsstaat,* and many middle-aged people were familiar with constitutional democracy's basic values, despite having sold them cheaply during the 1930s. Then, too, a substantial number of Americans spoke German (or quickly learned to do so), with a fluency that very few foreigners would acquire in Japanese. Unlike in Japan, where the emperor and thus the old constitutional order retained legitimacy, Nazism was thoroughly discredited in Germany. Furthermore, an efficient system of public education was ready, if not always willing, to teach constitutional democracy's principles.[61]

In addition, Germany had a larger pool of politicians who were experienced in running a liberal regime.[62] Indeed, many of these Germans were famous for having been publicly and vehemently anti-Nazi. Some, such as Konrad Adenauer, had been living in exile, while others, such as Kurt Schumacker, the leader of the Social Democrats, had been imprisoned in concentration camps. These people were often thorns in the sides of the occupation's commanders, for, having their own ideas of what a *German* constitutional democracy should look like, they resented what they often saw as arrogant, heavy-handed American interference. However annoying their stubbornness (and their own arrogance), most of these people were determined to found a civic constitutional order similar to, but more stable than, the Weimar Republic's.

The overall history of American efforts in Germany to build a new culture and create new citizens paralleled that in Japan,[63] although the basic policy was not as clear and General Lucius Clay lacked MacArthur's charisma. The Japanese were more overtly docile but also more cunning in their

---

61. Richard L. Merritt, *Democracy Imposed: U.S. Occupation Policy and the German Public, 1945–1949* (New Haven, CT: Yale University Press, 1995), ch. 10. Wade Jacoby, *Imitation and Politics: Redesigning Modern Germany* (Ithaca, NY: Cornell University Press, 2000), ch. 6, centers on East Germany but also sheds light on the West. See also Ira Strauber, *Neglected Policies: Constitutional and Legal Commentary as Civic Education* (Durham, NC: Duke University Press, 2002).

62. Which is not to say that Japan was without such people. Especially important were Yoshida Shigeru and Kanamori Tokujirō. Yoshida, who soon became prime minister, had been an anti-militarist diplomat and ambassador to Britain but had been removed by the military faction. Kanamori, a former bureaucrat who also had been ousted by the militarists, was a leading scholar of the Meiji constitutional text; he would work closely with SCAP's staff in drafting the new constitutional document.

63. This section depends heavily on Merritt, *Democracy Imposed.* See also John Ford Golay, *The Founding of the Federal Republic of Germany* (Chicago: University of Chicago Press, 1958); Lucius D. Clay, *Decision in Germany* (New York: Doubleday, 1950), and *The Papers of General Lucius D. Clay: Germany, 1945–1949,* ed. Jean Edward Smith (Bloomington: Indiana University Press, 1974), 2 vols; and Dennis L. Bark and David R. Gress, *A History of West Germany* (Cambridge: Blackwell, 1989), vol. 1, pt. 3.

reactions. Still, the basic tactics of both occupation high commands were more alike than different. In Germany, the Americans tried to purge former Nazis from positions of influence in governmental and private affairs, redirect public education, and control the press and radio. To spread the doctrines of constitutional democracy and the virtues of American civilization, the AMG established America Houses and instituted cultural exchanges. An important part of rehabilitation involved encouraging Germans to join in such civic activities as town-hall meetings and assisting them in reforming private associations, including democratically structured groups for young people to replace the Hitler Youth.[64]

As in Japan, the cold war shifted Americans' emphasis to building an armed ally. Again, as in Japan, despite shortcomings, the campaign produced some stupendous successes. The record of West and later East Germany's allegiance to the norms of constitutional democracy has been unswerving. The contrast in political orientation and allegiance between these citizens and those people who, with tremendous self-sacrifice, fought doggedly for the Third Reich could hardly be more stark.

Thrusting constitutional democracy on an unwilling people raises yet another troublesome issue: can this regime be imposed by force? Empirically, the answer is easy. Edward S. Corwin liked to quote a Vermont farmer's reply to a pollster's question if he believed in baptism by immersion: "Yep, I've seen it done." We can add that lesson to those of the Sea Islands experiment. Normatively, the question is, of course, much more complicated, and it bothered many officials in both SCAP and AMG. The latter took frequent polls of public opinion not only to discover what would be effective in converting Germans but also to understand their reaction to policies. For their part, MacArthur's staff insisted that they were not coercing the Japanese, merely educating them. Japanese references to themselves as "MacArthur's children" undoubtedly made it easier for SCAP to blur distinctions between education and indoctrination.

Earlier I said that the principal instrument in enlisting and maintaining popular support for constitutional democracy must be persuasion that includes emotional appeals as well as rational appeals. One might make a further qualification that devastating defeat in a total war itself makes a powerful case that the loser's political system is dysfunctional. One could also plausibly argue that a people who had enthusiastically supported an aggressive and brutally tyrannical system have at least restricted their moral right to choose their new constitutional order. Even John Stuart Mill admitted there are limits to freedom of choice. Those limits do not, of course, authorize occupying authorities to ignore standards of decency and due

---

64. Although hard comparative data are lacking, it is probable that Weimar (and perhaps also Wilhelmine) Germans were the people in the world most likely to belong to private organizations and associations.

process in their programs of resocialization. Education, propaganda, and subsidies (even as a euphemism for bribes) differ fundamentally from torture and terror.[65]

Founders of a constitutional democracy must talk directly to their people to explain and justify the new political system's goals and structures. As in cementing national unity, reason and rhetoric must join to fuse appeals to tradition with those to logic. A regime also teaches less directly through its decision-making processes. Government, to quote Louis Brandeis yet again, "is the potent, the omnipresent teacher. For good or ill, it teaches the whole people by its example."[66] In this sense, SCAP's penchant for secrecy set the wrong tone, especially for a society unaccustomed to officials' having to account for their actions.

From the outset, the new regime must publicly demonstrate respect for constitutional democracy's basic values. If the regime decides to punish its old rulers, it must move with patient regard for due process that goes beyond technical legal rules and accords with notions of fundamental fairness. In 1990, the Romanian transitional regime's murder of Nicolae Ceauçescu and his wife was of one piece with its later inviting miners armed with clubs to smash the heads of students demonstrating for political and economic reform. Neither action instructed Romanians about what a constitutional democracy expects from public officials and offers to citizens. Nor, one might add, did the reign of terror that followed France's Declaration of the Rights of Man two centuries earlier.

What to do about private citizens who cooperated with oppressive rulers poses similar problems. As Czech, Slovak, German, and Polish experiences with *lustration* show, a regime with totalitarian ambitions and secret police anxious to impress superiors may contaminate a large portion of its denizens and leave evidence in its archives of having contaminated a far larger number. Just as a thorough purge of official ranks could leave few bureaucrats to govern, so an equally thorough *lustration* could leave few citizens to be governed—outside of prisons. Even the lesser punishment of disfranchisement is not likely to be effective, as Yankee efforts during Reconstruction to politically castrate white southern males showed. Section 3 of the Fourteenth Amendment stands only as evidence of righteous indignation.

Temptations for the new government to rule by decree will be powerful, as Boris Yeltsin's and Lech Walesa's tenures demonstrated. For a time such governance may be necessary, but the duration of rule by decree must be brief, and leaders must quickly widen the circle of decision makers to include representatives (elected or not) of varied interests. Most important, the new leaders must understand that constitutional democracy needs to encourage,

---

65. See John E. Finn, *Constitutions in Crisis: Political Violence and the Rule of Law* (New York: Oxford University Press, 1991), pp. 219–21.

66. Olmstead v. United States, 277 U.S. 438, dis. op., 485 (1928).

not merely tolerate, dissent and that dissenters may themselves be ideal citizens.

The way political structures are crafted is critical to the long-run education of a people. Whatever processes the transitional regime uses or inherits, it must swiftly give citizens a psychological stake in the new system and make government responsive to them. The deeper the pool of citizens who learn by participating in politics and who can themselves become public officials, the more democracy is likely to spread. Elections need not come immediately, but they must come soon. Extended delays are likely to breed suspicion and also keep narrow the share of inhabitants who feel a direct link to the new system. The most weighty, perhaps the only weighty, reasons for delay are constructing fair electoral laws and allowing previously fettered groups time to organize and campaign. The most important purpose of early elections is to teach the people about democracy by encouraging them to participate in democratic processes.[67] Robert A. Dahl's claim is on point: "[L]ife in the polis is an education."[68] Here the two strongest arguments for popular ratification of a constitutional text combine (1) the debate's educative effect and (2) popular assent's binding the people to the document. Through ratification the people accept the charter's norms of limited but positive government. By saturating all aspects of political life with constitutionalist and democratic values, the new regime can help make patterns of authority within the entire social-political system, in Harry Eckstein's term, "congruent."[69] Those who participate in politics may also insist on a voice in decision making within the family, school, and workplace.

Political Education for Succeeding Generations

While converting adults to constitutional democracy, the polity must also begin the political education of future generations. "I think," Thomas Jefferson wrote to a friend, "by far the most important bill in our whole code is that for the diffusion of knowledge among the people. No other sure foundation can be devised for the preservation of freedom. . . . Preach, my dear Sir, a crusade against ignorance; establish and improve the law for educating the

67. In this respect, the founding generation of United States offers a poor model. "Power to the people" through widespread political participation ranked low on the priorities of the Federalists, those who got the American constitutional text of 1787 adopted. Those men preferred to protect property rather than encourage participation. See Jennifer Nedelsky, *Private Property and the Limits of American Constitutionalism: The Madisonian Framework and Its Legacy* (Chicago: University of Chicago Press, 1990); and Suzette Marie Hemberger, "Creatures of the Constitution: The Federalist Constitution and the Shaping of American Politics," Ph.D. diss., Princeton University, 1994.

68. *Democracy and Its Critics* (New Haven, CT: Yale University Press, 1989), p. 15.

69. See his "A Theory of Stable Democracy," originally published as a monograph by the Center of International Studies, Princeton University (1961), reprinted as appendix B to Eckstein's *Division and Cohesion in Democracy* (Princeton, NJ: Princeton University Press, 1966), and as ch. 5 of his *Regarding Politics* (Berkeley: University of California Press, 1992). See, more generally, Harry H. Eckstein and Ted Robert Gurr, *Patterns of Authority* (New York: Wiley, 1975).

common people."[70] Because constitutional democracy combines popular government and limited government, adequate as well as ideal citizens must understand their political system and be aware of the choices open to them. As Horace M. Kallen put it, "In a democracy [education for citizenship] is fundamental, for a democracy dares to endow each citizen with the task that Plato . . . left to a hardily trained and expert few."[71] Kallen's claim is equally strong for a constitutionalist state.

But constitutional democracy needs more than a citizenry who are educated. Intelligent, educated men and women can sabotage any civil constitutional order. After all, Josef Goebbels and Albert Speer were highly educated and extraordinarily intelligent. Constitutional democracy needs educated citizens who are, as Aristotle put it, "of a certain character, viz., good and capable of noble acts,"[72] with goodness and nobility defined according to that system's values. Philosophers from Plato to Rousseau to John Dewey to Yale's son George W. Bush have been fascinated by the problems of civic education. Political scientists have developed a thick literature dealing with what they call "political socialization."[73] The AMG in Germany and to an even greater extent SCAP in Japan consciously utilized many of these writings.[74]

The state's inculcating public principles is likely to encroach on parents' freedom to teach their children that commands of their culture are superior to those of constitutional democracy. Religion forms the most obvious—and persistent—source of conflict, though ethnic divisions run a close second. However consonant constitutional democracy's basic principles are with the moral teachings of most of Judaism, Catholicism (at least since Vatican II), and mainline Protestantism,[75] the very notion of requiring knowledge about and participation in politics is unacceptable to some religious groups. Al-

70. To George Wythe, Aug. 13, 1786, in *The Papers of Thomas Jefferson*, ed. Julian Boyd (Princeton, NJ: Princeton University Press, 1954), 10:245.

71. *Culture and Democracy in the United States: Studies in the Group Psychology of the American People* (New York: Boni and Liveright, 1924), p. 65. Robert M. Hutchins repeated Kallen's claim that if the people are going to rule, they need the political education that was once accorded only to rulers: *The Conflict in Education* (Westport, CT: Greenwood, 1953), p. 84.

72. *Nicomachean Ethics*, bk. 1, ch. 9, 1099b.

73. See, for example, Eva T. H. Brann, *Paradoxes of Education in a Republic* (Chicago: University of Chicago Press, 1979); Stephen Macedo, *Diversity and Distrust: Civic Education in a Multicultural Democracy* (Cambridge, MA: Harvard University Press, 2000); Stephen Macedo and Iris Marion Young, eds., *Child, Family, and State*, Nomos 44 (New York: New York University Press, 2003); Charles E. Merriam, *The Making of Citizens* (Chicago: University of Chicago Press, 1931); and Weber, *Peasants into Frenchmen*. See also the reference to Horace M. Kallen, cited below. David O. Sears reviewed much of the early literature in "Political Socialization," in Fred I. Greenstein and Nelson Polsby, eds., *Handbook of Political Science*, vol. 2 (Reading, MA: Addison-Wesley, 1975).

74. See esp. Toshio Nishi, *Unconditional Democracy: Education and Politics in Japan, 1945–52* (Stanford, CA: Stanford University Press, 1982). The works by Merriam and Kallen, cited above, were especially important.

75. The compatibility of Islam and constitutional democracy remains controversial. See the literature cited above in Chapters Two through Five.

though most battles are fought over specific secular policies, the basic notion of loyal citizenship in a secular state may be anathema, as it is to many fundamentalist Christian, Muslims, and Jews. Even state authority to teach, in dispassionate way, about other religions may be abhorrent.[76] Indeed, some groups view diversity of moral ideas as an evil against which impressionable children must be shielded. The knotted nature of these problems readily explains why both Hobbes and Rousseau advocated a state religion.

If government decides to prefer equality over free exercise of religious beliefs, as has been the case in the United States but not in Israel and India, problems for civic instruction are likely to multiply.[77] Can all children be taught in public schools that they are citizens, duty bound to participate intelligently in their government, and that, under their political system, all people of whatever race, religion, sex, or sexual preference are equal? The School Segregation Cases (1954) bitterly divided Protestant fundamentalists in the American South, some of whom believed that the Bible made blacks "drawers of water and hewers of wood" rather than equal to whites. Ironically, biblical references would have made another despised group, Jews, superior to all *goyim*. Then, too, St. Paul's supposed admonition to wives to be subject to their husbands ("supposed" because some scholars of the New Testament believe that those words were added by a redactor) has caused fundamentalists additional trouble. Their usual preaching has been that women should take these words literally. And the Shari'a, if not the Qur'an, teaches that Muslim men are superior not only to Muslim women but to all infidels. Where such groups are numerically small and forgo violence, they do not imperil constitutional democracy, but they may pose a danger to individuals.

There is, of course, a quick response: public schools can teach children that the political system requires government to treat all people *as if* they were equal, but not that people *are* equal. The first difficulty here is that this distinction is probably too subtle for most young children. Furthermore, few teachers have the sensitivity and pedagogical skills clearly to explain such a fine difference. Worse, whatever the teacher tells students often car-

76. See esp. Mozert v. Hawkins County Bd. of Ed., 382 F. Supp. 201 (1984); reversed 827 F. 2nd 1058 (1987); cert. den., 484 U.S. 1066 (1987); and Wisconsin v. Yoder, 406 U.S. 205 (1972). Especially helpful are the discussions in Stanley Fish, *The Trouble with Principle* (Cambridge, MA: Harvard University Press, 1997), ch. 8 generally and pp. 202–3, 210. 220, 291; Macedo, *Diversity and Distrust*, chs. 6–8; and Grant Wacker, *Heaven Below: Early Pentecostals and American Culture* (Cambridge, MA: Harvard University Press, 2001). Although she focuses on violent groups, Stern's *Terror in the Name of God*, esp. ch. 1, offers many insights useful for understanding more "normal" groups.

77. In Bob Jones University v. United States, 461 U.S. 574 (1983), for instance, the Supreme Court held that Congress could deny to a school that practiced racial segregation the tax exempt status accorded to religious and educational institutions. The Court so ruled without denying that the university's directors were sincerely following their religious beliefs. For Israel, see Jacobsohn, *Apple of Gold*, chs. 2 and 4; for India, see Shah Bano's Case, [1985] 3 S.C.R. 844, and the discussions above in Chapter Seven and in Jacobsohn, *Wheel of Law*, pp. 106–7.

ries heavy moral weight, and what the teacher does not impart may also transmit an important message. So, too, if instructors allow discussion, children are likely to hear the system's values defended as well as explained. Indeed, sitting in a classroom with children of different sexes, races, and religions sends a message of equality. It could also be, however, that winning such debates would strengthen a child's faith, just as seeing members of a particular religious or ethnic group perform badly in academic tasks could reinforce beliefs in inequality.

There is no easy solution to such difficulties; in fact, there may be no solution on which all disputants can agree. Although constitutionalists need not be hostile to religion, they do need to defuse religious conflicts. Constitutional democracy cannot allow one sect to maim, kill, or dominate members of other sects. Thus the polity may be obliged to split the fine hair that separates freedom of religious belief from freedom of religious practice. As often noted here, politics and religion cannot be separated. In teaching about citizens' rights and obligations, all systems of government overlap with—poach on—religion. Political leaders can try to ease these tensions by being ready to compromise, but at some important level reconciliation may be possible only by prostituting constitutional democracy or denigrating religious tenets.[78]

If religious dissidents lose on matters vital to their faith, their conscience

78. In the United States, the possibility of the federal government's giving money to colleges and universities founded and operated by religious groups has generated a wholesale secularization of such institutions. The large number of Catholic colleges and universities (more than 140), the determination of many Catholic lay and clerical leaders to emulate the academic standards of the better institutions, and the Vatican's efforts to curb American exceptionalism have created a controversy that is both deep and wide. Many concerned Catholics, not merely conservatives, have charged that these institutions have been selling their religious identity; governors (usually clergy) of these institutions have responded that they are trying to reach a broader audience, stay financially alive, and at the same time protect academic freedom from bureaucrats in local chanceries as well as in the Vatican. The papal encyclical *Ex Corde Ecclesiae* (*From the Heart of the Church*) attempted to bring Catholic colleges and universities around the world under tighter control of the Curia and local bishops. In the United States, where memories of the Church's silencing John Courtney Murray, S.J., for his support of separation of church and state have been kept alive specifically by the treatment of Charles Curran and more generally by the Vatican's indifference to constitutionalist standards of procedural justice, many religious organizations and even some bishops have been trying to modify *Ex Corde* through interpretation. Ironically, the Holy Cross Order, which runs nine universities including Notre Dame, has specifically forbidden one of its own priests to publish defenses of *Ex Corde*, thus offering the strange spectacle of a supposedly Catholic religious order's silencing a priest for supporting the pope. The literature here is vast. See, for example, James Tunstead Burtchaell, *The Dying of the Light: The Disengagement of Colleges and Universities from Their Christian Churches* (Grand Rapids, MI: Eerdmans, 1998), and "Out of the Heartburn of the Church," 25 *J. of Coll. and Uni. L.* 653 (1999); Edward Malloy, "Keepers of the Faith," *Notre Dame Mag.*, Autumn 1999, pp. 31ff.; Paul Saunders, "A Cautionary Tale: Academic Freedom, 'Ex Corde,' and the Curran Case," *Commonweal*, Apr. 21, 2000, pp. 12ff.; Peter Steinfels, "Satisfying Rome and the Academy at Catholic Colleges," *N.Y. Times*, Mar. 6, 1999; and "Everything You Need to Know about *Ex Corde Ecclesiae*," *Crisis*, July/Aug. 1999, pp. 10ff.

may compel them to resort to violence, civil disobedience, or emigration—one reason that the right to expatriation is fundamental to constitutional democracy. No regime can permit violent opposition to its policies, while civil disobedience presents quite different but also difficult problems. Expatriation may seem a cruel option, but individuals should be free to choose it as less morally objectionable than compromising their consciences. Furthermore, expatriation is likely to be less damaging than violence to the equal rights of others and may also be less harsh than internal exile as fanatics, a status to which many liberal theorists cast religious people who reject Liberalism's atheology. Constitutional democracy's denial of totalitarian ambitions imposes a further complication. Its profession of a distinction, fuzzy but critical, between public and private spheres of responsibility allows families, churches, and private schools freedom to teach that constitutional democracy's norms and demands are unjust and to utilize legal and electoral processes to reverse them.

In modernized nations, school attendance for children is compulsory, a requirement that need not be inflexible. Some adjustments within curricula are educationally possible.[79] For example, teaching evolution versus creation is one of the more common battlegrounds, but there is no need to present the two as either-or propositions. Many modern scientists, especially molecular biologists, are highly critical of Darwin, though conceding that given the state of nineteenth-century science his guesses were often brilliant. At most, these critics say, he offered theories about the *development* of life, not its origins. Using critiques by respected scientists would soothe some religious controversy as well as enhance students' education.[80]

More basically, the sometimes impenetrable, sometimes porous, and always sinuous wall of separation that Americans pretend to have erected between church and state need not form a model for other countries, except perhaps for those that revel in conceptual confusion. Without such constitutional constraints, public education could include religious instruction for those students whose parents agreed, conducted by ministers of their own faiths.

Further, compulsory education is not the same as compulsory attendance at *public* schools. Dissident groups can establish their own institutions to supplement or substitute for public schools—a common practice often rec-

79. For a discussion of some possibilities for accommodating religious beliefs in a secular curriculum, see Jeff Spinner-Haley, "Extending Diversity: Religion in Public and Private Education," in Will Kymlicka and Wayne Norman, eds., *Citizenship in Diverse Societies* (New York: Oxford University Press, 2000) Again, *Yoder v. Wisconsin* is relevant.

80. See in particular, Michael J. Behe, *Darwin's Black Box: A Biochemical Challenge to Evolution* (New York: Touchstone, 1998). Frederick Crews has critically reviewed some of this work from the perspective of a true believer in Darwinism who tends to see literal biblical interpretation in analyses that dare to point out Darwin's primitive (for our time) understanding of biology: "Saving Us from Darwin," *N.Y. Rev. of Bks.*, Oct. 4, 2001, pp. 24ff.

ognized by some constitutional charters. For instance, Article 6 of the Basic Law of the Federal Republic of Germany and Articles 41 and 42 of the Irish constitutional text recognize "a natural right" of parents to raise their children, and Article 7 of the Basic Law unequivocally guarantees "the right to establish private schools," though it allows *Länder* to set minimal instructional standards. Article 42 of the Irish charter gives similar authority to Parliament. Article 93 of the British North America Act of 1867, which in this respect continues in force, also guarantees a right to operate religious schools. The American constitutional document does not mention education, but the Supreme Court has held that the charter's general clauses protecting "liberty" safeguard parents' rights to send their children to private schools.[81]

Some groups, of course, may be too small or too poor to establish their own educational institutions, but they may still be able to keep their children out of public schools. The Irish Supreme Court has interpreted Articles 41 and 42 to include parents' right to educate their children at home, providing they meet minimal standards.[82] State courts in the United States have also upheld such a parental right. Alternatively, parents and religious ministers can try to teach their children to reject the moral and/or political teachings they hear in the classroom. These dispensations may diminish society's capacity to maintain constitutional democracy. Private schools and, even more, home schooling reduce children's opportunities to identify themselves as sharing with other children a common citizenship and perhaps to learn about mutual rights and duties in the context of interaction with other children.[83] In addition, if the techniques of instruction encourage, as American public schools once did, memorization over understanding, they may discourage the informed, active questioning and political participation that mark ideal citizens.

On the other hand, a governmental monopoly on education can also threaten the norms of constitutional democracy.[84] The American Flag Salute Cases provided a minidrama, presenting what Felix Frankfurter believed to be the essence of Greek tragedy, "the clash of rights, not the clash of wrongs."[85] The constitutional question revolved around the validity of a

---

81. Or perhaps the economic right of those who operate private schools to run a business: Pierce v. Society of Sisters, 286 U.S. 510 (1925).

82. In Re Article 26 and the School Attendance Bill, 1942, [1943] I.R. 334.

83. Kymlicka and Norman, "Citizenship in Culturally Diverse Societies," p. 38.

84. The justices of the German Constitutional Court were well aware of this danger when, in 1957, they interpreted the Basic Law as excluding education from the control of the Bund, leaving this matter to individual *Länder*. Concordat Case, 6 BVerfGE 309; reprinted in Walter F. Murphy and Joseph Tanenhaus, eds., *Comparative Constitutional Law* (New York: St. Martin's, 1977), pp. 225ff.

85. Memo to Harlan Fiske Stone, May 27, 1940, Stone Papers, Library of Congress; reprinted in Walter F. Murphy, James E. Fleming, Sotirios A. Barber, and Stephen Macedo, *American Constitutional Interpretation*, 3rd ed. (Westbury, NY: Foundation, 2003), pp. 1267–69.

state's requiring children of Jehovah's Witnesses who were attending public schools to salute the flag and recite the pledge of allegiance despite their reading the First Commandment's reference to a "graven image" as including a flag.[86] In the first decision, handed down as Nazi armies were sweeping across France, Frankfurter, for the Court, stressed the central public interest at stake: "The ultimate foundation of a free society is the binding tie of cohesive sentiment."[87] He saw "the precise issue" as being whether public officials were "barred from determining the appropriateness of various means to evoke that unifying sentiment without which there can ultimately be no liberties, civil or religious." Put this way, the question answered itself. Only Harlan Fiske Stone dissented.

Three years and two new justices later, the issue reappeared. Now, six members of the Court held for the Witnesses.[88] "Symbolism," Justice Robert H. Jackson wrote for the majority, "is a primitive but effective way of communicating ideas." Reciting the pledge required children not merely to stand silent but to participate. Thus: "To sustain the compulsory flag salute we are required to say that a Bill of Rights which guards the individual's right to speak his own mind, left it open to public authorities to compel him to utter what is not in his mind."

The specific issues in much of civic education differ from those of the compulsory flag salute, but the underlying conflicts between the demands of individual conscience and those of common citizenship are constant. The problem is likely to be acute in multicultural societies.[89] Civic unity carries with it the possibility of democratic despotism, as Tocqueville warned. The inescapable fact is that constitutional democracy must pursue two sometimes diverging but always compelling national interests: first, to teach future citizens about its political values in order to impart a sense of political community transcending religious and ethnic differences[90]; second, to respect its citizens' wide range of freedom. Public policies that come even close to meeting these two goals are likely to be unsystematic, perhaps disordered. The cause lies, as Frankfurter indicated, in a clash of distinct principles

---

86. When Pontius Pilate became procurator of Judea, he caused near riots by allowing his troops to bring their emblems into Jerusalem. Pilate's action violated an agreement between Rome and the Jews to keep such graven images out of the holy city. Because of this and even more egregious violations of Jewish religious sensibilities, Pilate was recalled to Rome to stand trial. The death of Emperor Tiberius ended the judicial proceedings.

87. Minersville School District v. Gobitis, 310 U.S. 586 (1940).

88. West Virginia v. Barnette, 319 U.S. 624 (1943).

89. Within the narrow ambit of American constitutional interpretation, even *Gobitis* may have survived its specific overruling by *Barnette*. Writing for the Court in Employment Division v. Smith, 494 U.S. 872 (1990), Justice Antonin Scalia quoted at length from Frankfurter's opinion in *Gobitis* to the effect that religious belief "does not relieve the citizen from the discharge of political responsibilities."

90. For a thorough discussion of the problems here, especially the competing values of national unity, parental control of children, and religious liberty, see Macedo, *Diversity and Distrust*.

privileging distinct goods.[91] What is needed, in Charles Taylor's phrase, is "inspired adhoccery,"[92] policies that can keep disorder from turning into incoherence.

Civic education may pose yet other problems for constitutional democracy. Insofar as political socialization involves teaching children about their country's past, it typically depicts national history in a favorable light. Some flavoring of reason with reverence is not necessarily bad. That a people believe their country has historically stood for certain values can help shape future behavior to accord with these values. When, however, the past has been dark, serious difficulties arise. Critics frequently charge that German children are not taught much about the horrors endemic to Nazism; Japanese children learn little about their emperor's troops' systematic rapes, pillages, and murderous treatment of prisoners of war; English schools tend to ignore their country's inhumane treatment of the Irish and exploitation of colonials around the globe; and American schools downplay whites' savage treatment of Indians, fire bombings of Japanese cities, and assorted atrocities in Vietnam and in Iraq. On the other hand, absolutely honest histories could scrape scabs off wounds already burned by multiculturalism's frictions.

Even when no fundamental religious issues are involved, instruction, including that of Liberalism, inevitably transmits values and in contexts that are to some extent authoritarian. To what degree is such transmission to children, obligated to attend school and obey their teachers, but not yet emotionally or intellectually mature, consonant with the values of constitutional democracy even when the values transmitted are those of constitutional democracy itself?[93] When it tries to preserve itself by indoctrinating future generations, is constitutional democracy no different from other forms of governance?

Asking this question is painful for constitutional democrats. Having disingenuously accepted the myth that the Liberal state can be neutral among values, denied that Liberalism itself advocates certain values, and affirmed that teaching there is no rational way of choosing among values is itself "value neutral," many people happily, if unintelligently, go about the business of political education in public and many private schools, celebrating their country's past, praising "the democratic way," and revering, though

91. For a spirited defense of the claim that resolution of such clashes must be, at root, unprincipled, see Fish, *Trouble with Principle*, chs. 9–13. One shortcoming of Fish's brilliantly provocative analysis is that he thinks constitutional theorists have tried to construct theories and principles that are neutral. That task is, by definition, self-contradictory, for a principle or normative theory tries to distinguish what is right or true or good from what is wrong or false or bad—tasks that are inherently unneutral. Fish is certainly correct, however, that many normative theorists who call themselves liberals continue to try to square this circle, and his critique of their work is searing.

92. Quoted by Fish, *Trouble with Principle*, p. 63.

93. Brann lists this questions as one of the paradoxes of education: *Paradoxes of Education in a Republic.*

seldom understanding, their constitution. Schools also teach such values as patriotism, honesty, self-reliance, and individual autonomy, along with respect for public authority and private property, while the mass media often teach that freedom of choice in sexual matters and decisions to terminate a pregnancy (a euphemism for abortion) are facets of autonomy. The problem of political indoctrination in the guise of education is hardly new. Richard D. Mosier's classic study of the "McGuffey readers" showed how these textbooks, widely used in nineteenth-century America, transmitted to generations of schoolchildren a creed quite different from that of the late twentieth and early twenty-first centuries but no less partisan. McGuffey's books accepted the sanctity of private property, linked Protestantism with Americanism, and extolled the political conservatism of Alexander Hamilton and Daniel Webster.[94]

While Americans tend to avoid many of the normative problems of public education through an ostrichlike pretense that liberal instruction is really not political instruction at all, people who have experienced life under tyrannical regimes are apt to be nervous. When debating the problem of "creating citizens," some East Europeans have been inclined to deny the necessity of political instruction, even as they lament their fellow citizens' failures to understand their newly created rights and duties. Still aching from decades of governmental propaganda parading as education, these deniers glimpse ghosts of the Hitler Youth or the Komsomol and hear echoes of efforts to indoctrinate "a new man" for a communist society.[95]

Without doubt, early political socialization, whether within families, on playgrounds, in schools, on television,[96] or in churches, involves elements of coercion. Each of these educative experiences may endanger all sorts of values. As far as schools are concerned, the form as well as substance of instruction communicates political messages. Those messages may conflict with each other and may be received differently by different youngsters. As every parent and teacher can attest, children tune out much normative instruction. The fact remains, however, that every society sends out an immense number of messages about politically relevant values and tries to compel children to conform to them.

It would be suicidal for a young—perhaps even an adult—constitutional democracy to act only as neutral observer in these educational processes. Children who are taught that it is wrong to try to reason or compromise with those with whom they disagree or that it is their civic duty to do whatever

94. *Making the American Mind* (New York: Columbia University Press, 1947).

95. See, for example, Raymond A. Bauer, *The New Man in Soviet Psychology* (Cambridge, MA: Harvard University Press, 1952).

96. Television's enormous capacity to shape (warp?) young minds poses a problem of the utmost seriousness for every advanced society, a potential that makes the Bundesverfassungsgericht's analysis in the Television Case, cited above, all the more cogent.

national leaders tell them would likely become dysfunctional denizens and, if sufficiently numerous, would soon destroy constitutional democracy. If constitutional democrats believe their system should survive because of its intrinsic value and not merely because it is their own, they must try to preserve it across generations. Constitutional democracy is not a "natural" state; its norms are not innate in humans. Indeed, as G. K. Chesterton reminds us, "civilization itself is the most sensational of departures and most romantic of rebellions. . . . [M]orality is the most daring and dark of conspiracies."[97] So, too, the values of constitutional democracy must be learned, and to be learned they must be taught. The values of Jack Merridew and his gang in William Golding's *Lord of the Flies* can be a real option for un- or misguided children.[98]

Still the question remains: what kinds of political education are compatible with constitutional democracy's values? If a polity does no more than soften the indoctrination of totalitarian regimes, does it not surrender its claim to rule by reason rather than force? Any intelligent response must be carefully nuanced. Most importantly, political education compatible with constitutional democracy differs fundamentally in style, substance, and purpose from political indoctrination. Its goal should be to move citizens to think in informed and critically analytical ways about politics. Thus it requires an endless application of critical reasoning. It follows that constitutional democracy's instruction could, in a triple sense, be subversive to any given constitutional democracy and perhaps to the very idea itself. First, its educational methodology may threaten the rice bowls of specific public officials. By teaching citizens to think clearly, carefully, and critically about politics, it should help create a large "loyal opposition." A successful educational system congruent with constitutional democracy is also potentially subversive in a second and deeper sense: it may threaten any particular constitutional democracy, for every political system in the real world is likely to fall far short of its ideals and may need to be repaired, perhaps replaced.

Third, and more deeply yet, such an educational system should encourage people to ask whether constitutional democracy itself is truly the best possible political system to achieve the best possible mix of freedom and responsibility consonant with human dignity.[99] Constitutional democracy is neither ancient nor natural, and it is not necessarily eternal. Future generations may be able to do better. But they can also do much worse, and self-

97. "A Defence of Detective Stories," in Howard Haycraft, ed., *The Art of the Mystery Story* (New York: Simon and Schuster. 1946), p. 6.

98. London: Faber and Faber, 1954.

99. *Pace* Francis Fukuyama, who in *The End of History and the Last Man* (New York: Avon Books, 1992), contends that, in a Hegelian sense, we have reached the end of history. See also the earlier symposium in which Fukuyama stated his argument and critics replied: "The End of History?" *National Interest*, Summer 1989, and Fukuyama, "A Reply to My Critics," *National Interest*, Winter 1989–90.

questioning political education in the values of constitutional democracy is likely to lessen the chances that the future will make more grievous mistakes.

In this deepest sense, civic education consonant with constitutional democracy invites, as Sotirios Barber would say, a peaceful revolution, providing only that the case for that revolution is itself better grounded in reason—and reasons—than is the case for constitutional democracy.[100] It is very useful for any political system to have the public's underlying mix of political norms function as a psychologically tinted prescription lens, coloring and shaping their views of political and social reality to accord with the system's values.[101] Nevertheless, constitutional democracy also needs a core of citizens who respect its basic values because they can offer reasons that lead to and flow from principles, far from neutral, regarding the great and equal dignity of all men and women. With that dignity their central value, constitutional democrats must categorize some courses of private and public action as legitimate, others as illegitimate; some as wise, others as stupid; some as good, others as bad. If this sort of education does not force a people to be free, at least it should predispose them to be free. Rousseau, though hardly a constitutional democrat, would chuckle.

100. *The Constitution of Judicial Power* (Baltimore: Johns Hopkins University Press, 1993), pp. 64–65, 219. One could make a broader point, with which Barber would agree: insofar as constitutional democracy itself is based on reason, it offers those who advocate revolution a chance to prove their case in the realm of reason.

101. See Perry Miller, *The New England Mind* (New York: Macmillan, 1939), p. 5.

CHAPTER ELEVEN

Military and Security Forces

It is always dangerous for soldiers, sailors, or airmen to play at politics. They enter a sphere in which the values are quite different.   WINSTON CHURCHILL

Leaders of a new constitutional democracy must continue most of what that society has come to accept as normal governmental operations. Armed forces must be prepared to deter foreign enemies and security agencies (more civilized than the KGB and Stasi but more efficient than the FBI) to guard against espionage and terrorism. Police must be ready to prevent "ordinary" crimes; there must be courts to try the accused and prisons to incarcerate the convicted. Taxes have to be extracted, pensions distributed, welfare provided, public health facilities maintained, children educated, water supplies kept pure and flowing, food products inspected, garbage collected, streets swept, and sewage plants operated.

The men and women who initially lead their people into constitutional democracy are not apt to have trained enough replacements for the dozens of thousands of personnel who have been conducting these affairs. Lenin's predictions in 1917 about the simplicity of public needs after a communist revolution were naive, even simpleminded. After abolishing social classes, he wrote, "a new generation will be able completely to throw out all of the state rubbish," and any necessary functions the modern state performs could done in a manner similar to that of the postal system.[1] Two points are painfully obvious: First, Lenin had never mailed a letter in Italy. Second, as Soviet experiences no less than those of capitalist and developing nations have demonstrated, a modern or even modernizing country needs marvelously intricate interactions among hundreds of pieces of complex machinery run by skilled technicians and managers organized in the ways that we, perhaps arbitrarily, call a state.

This bank of three chapters will discuss, in general terms, some of the problems this labyrinth of institutions poses for a budding constitutional

---

1. *State and Revolution* (1917; reprint New York: International, 1932). p. 66. Although on p. 69 he concedes that the state's withering away "must obviously be a lengthy process," he thought that "all need for force, for the subjection of one man to another, and of one part of the population to another" would vanish (p. 68).

378

democracy. This chapter focuses on the military establishment and internal security offices, both of which are likely to be large bureaucracies. The next chapter takes up similar issues both for more "ordinary" bureaucrats within executive's civilian agencies and for the people who operate the judicial branch of government. The third discusses the morally and practically difficult questions of punishing officials who had badly abused the inhabitants of the country.

Founders of modern constitutional democracies might envy the good fortune of their eighteenth-century American cousins. Aside from the French forces who sailed away after the victory at Yorktown in 1781, the army that won the war was largely composed of soldiers eager to go back to their farms, not to install a military government or conquer Canada. The colonists' greatest stroke of luck, of course, was having a commander in chief who emulated Cincinnatus. Anxious to take up his plow (or at least to direct his slaves to do so),[2] Washington had mellowed to become at heart a plantation owner and whiskey distiller rather than a commanding general. And, although he was devoid of neither ambition nor *amour de soi* (as general he wanted to be addressed as "Your Excellency," as president as "Your High Mightiness"), he did not aspire to become a dictator or even an elected president for life. The first he might have seized, the latter was certainly his for the asking; but when confronted with these choices, he opted for peaceful transfers of power. Indeed, Joseph J. Ellis remarks, Washington made yielding power an art form,[3] a talent few generals who have liberated nations have cared to cultivate.

During the twentieth century, the military toppled wavering governments across Europe, including Poland, Spain, Portugal, Greece, and Turkey. Much of Sub-Saharan Africa, Latin America, and the Near East passed from colonial or semicolonial status to full independence under military domination, as did Burma, Pakistan, and Taiwan. Generally, the generals' goals were to accumulate power and, especially in Africa, to plunder whatever wealth could be squeezed out of an impoverished people. Only in Portugal did the military's objectives include anything like establishing con-

2. Washington ran Mount Vernon through his own and his wife's slaves. Before the Revolution, he was not, by planters' standards, unusually cruel, although he raffled off slaves of other slave owners who owed him money and whipped his own slaves. After the war, however, he came to see slavery as morally wrong and expressed hopes for gradual emancipation. Against his family's wishes, Washington's will directed that his slaves be freed after his wife's death and Mount Vernon sold with the proceeds going to his freed slaves and their families. Henry Wiencek, *An Imperfect God: George Washington, His Slaves, and the Creation of America* (New York: Farrar, Straus and Giroux, 2003); and James J. Ellis, *His Excellency George Washington* (New York: Alfred A. Knopf, 2004), pp. 160–67, 244, 256–60. Despite eloquent verbal opposition to slavery, Jefferson made no provision to free his slaves during or after his lifetime. In his heart he opposed slavery, in his purse he supported it—or perhaps it supported his purse.

3. *Founding Brothers: The Revolutionary Generation* (New York: Vintage Books, 2002), ch. 4.

stitutional democracy; the young leaders of the Portuguese coup wanted to reform their governmental system.[4] As models, almost all of these soldiers-turned-rulers rejected George Washington, Giuseppe Garibaldi, and Charles De Gaulle, preferring Oliver Cromwell, Napoleon Bonaparte, and Kemal Ataturk, men who merged personal ambitions with grand designs for their country. The Africans and, to a lesser extent, the Asians and Latin Americans also tended to emulate the popular image of Vandals.

The Problem

To peacefully establish a constitutional democracy, would-be leaders must secure the consent, tacit at least, of the nation's military commanders as well as of the directors of the old internal security forces. It is possible, as came close to happening in some communist countries in 1989-1990, that a spontaneous implosion will end the old order, leaving the military who remain loyal to that regime with little to protect. Then, new leaders need only to tiptoe through the tulips of power to assume office. Nevertheless, even in the old Soviet bloc there had been a decade or more of signs, usually missed or misinterpreted, that the governmental and economic systems were disintegrating.

Whatever the final judgment of history on the causes of that collapse, it is improbable that a peaceful change in regime from authoritarian to constitutional democratic will take place (or would have taken place in Eastern Europe during 1989–1991) against a determined decision by the military or security services to preserve the status quo.[5] Depending on the part that senior military officers[6] and secret police played in running the old order, new leaders may have to engage in negotiations somewhat akin to wrestling with rattlesnakes. As long as the troops and agents remain loyal to their chieftains—a critically important condition that does not always obtain—senior officers control a vast array of instruments of physical power. Only a few months before the Berlin Wall came down, the Chinese Army brutally crushed the students' revolt in Tiananmen Square. Party officials in Beijing had been sharply divided over how to cope with the students' demands for

---

4. For analyses of the origins and fate of the first coup, see Nancy G. Bermeo, *The Revolution within the Revolution: Workers' Control in Rural Portugal* (Princeton, NJ: Princeton University Press, 1986); and Kenneth Maxwell, "Regime Overthrow and the Prospects for Democratic Transition in Portugal," in Guillermo O'Donnell, Philippe C. Schmitter, and Laurence Whitehead, *Transitions from Authoritarian Rule: Southern Europe* (Baltimore: Johns Hopkins University Press, 1986).

5. See the discussion in Chapter Four of preconditions for the establishment of constitutional democracy.

6. I say "senior officers" because coups are often led by colonels as well as generals. In fact, Portugal's coup of 1974 that deposed Caetano was led by a group of captains and majors. In any successful coup, lieutenant colonels and colonels are apt to be crucial actors: as commanders of battalions and regiments, they are more likely than generals to command the personal loyalty of their troops.

easing harshly authoritarian rule. Had the generals possessed the courage to side with the minority, China would have become a country (or set of countries) radically different from what it was and has been since.

For the purposes of this chapter, let us assume that through negotiations, internal collapse, widespread mutiny, or foreign conquest, the military and security forces have accepted, at least for the time being, the establishment of constitutional democracy. The new civilian leaders must therefore think in long-range terms about how to keep the military and security forces in check, how to transform these people from masters into servants of—passive or, better yet, committed believers in—constitutional democracy.

The Military

Samuel Huntington has written of civilian control over the military as cut from one of two templates. First is an "objective" form. This includes acceptance by the military that its competence is limited to the profession of arms and that officials of the civilian government should determine domestic and foreign policies, including defense policy. For their part, civilian officials accept a special area of military competence in which officers' judgments should prevail.[7] In direct contrast is a "subjective" form of control, in which civilians officials achieve their supremacy "by civilianizing the military, making them the tool of the state."[8] The latter form, Huntington contends, leads directly into military participation in formulating the nation's public policies.[9]

As cogent as Huntington's analysis may be, it is often impossible to unknot issues of strategic foreign policy from those of strategic military policy. For instance, questions whether a nation would be better served by and can afford offensive missiles or an antiballistic missile system or both involves not only military efficiency but also likely reaction from nearby states that might be threatening or feel threatened. In a constitutional democracy, civilians must have the final word in such decisions.

Moreover, in another sense of the term *subjective*, leaders of a constitu-

7. "Reforming Civil-Military Relations," in Larry Diamond and Marc F. Plattner, eds., *Civil-Military Relations and Democracy* (Baltimore: Johns Hopkins University Press, 1996), pp. 3–4. This definition is clearer than the one he had offered four decades earlier: "that distribution of political power between military and civilian groups which is most conducive to the emergence of professional attitudes and behavior among members of the officer corps," with "professional attitudes and behavior" defined as abstention from governance of the country. *The Soldier and the State* (Cambridge, MA: Harvard University Press, 1959), p. 83.

8. *Soldier and the State*, p. 83. A few lines later on the same page, Huntington subtly shifts his definitions of both objective and subjective control: "The essence of objective civilian control is the recognition of autonomous military professionalism; the essence of subjective civilian control is the denial of an independent military sphere."

9. Michael C. Desch strongly agrees. "Threat Environments and Military Missions," in Larry Diamond and Marc F. Plattner, eds., *Civil-Military Relations and Democracy* (Baltimore: Johns Hopkins University Press, 1996), p. 26.

tional democracy should wish to "civilianize" professional officers, that is, to persuade them not simply to accept civilian control as a dominant element in their code of ethics but also to internalize the values of constitutional democracy, which include civilian control. Under many circumstances, the leaders of a constitutional democracy may have to settle for an officer corps without political commitment beyond that to civilian supremacy, willing to serve a brutally authoritarian regime with the same zeal as a constitutional order committed to individual liberty and the rule of a particular kind of law. Nevertheless, civilian leaders who wish long-run stability for constitutional democracy must seek a positive commitment from the military, decidedly not to Maggie Thatcher or Tony Blair, nor to Bill Clinton or George W. Bush, nor to management or unions, Conservatives or Labour, Socialists or Christian Democrats, Democrats or Republicans—not, in short to a particular leader, faction, interest, or party but to constitutional democracy itself and the norms it embodies.

Turning begrudging military acceptance into wholehearted approval could bear many fruits beyond the two most obvious, enthusiastic defense of the country against foreigners and removal of a looming threat to political stability. For example, in a developing country, the military, with its emphasis on discipline, rationality, and long-range planning, can provide a powerful modernizing force,[10] spreading such habits into the larger society not only via cultural osmosis but also by direct infection through training young men and women and convincing civilian officials of a need to improve public education. A modern army depends on sophisticated weapons, on complex methods of supply, on communications that almost always must be encrypted and then encoded and typically transmitted through electronic means, all of which entail use of computers and satellites. Much of this equipment cannot be operated and maintained by illiterate or even sparsely

---

10. In 1963, Manfred Halpern, a former officer on the State Department's Near Eastern Desk who had become a professor at Princeton, was optimistic about the military's capacity to accelerate modernization in the Near East, where, he believed, it was an instrument of the emerging middle class. *The Politics of Social Change in the Middle East and North Africa* (Princeton, NJ: Princeton University Press, 1963), ch. 13. Morroe Berger shared this optimism: *The Military Elite and Social Change: Egypt Since Napoleon,* Center of International Studies Research Monograph 6 (Princeton, NJ: Princeton University Press, 1960). Alas, "[t]hese expectations were frustrated in less than two decades of military rule. The militaries' political failures were both ideological and organizational. Military officers were committed to secular nationalisms and various interpretations of socialism. They sought to impose these Western-derived systems of political beliefs on populations that did not understand them." James A. Bill and Robert Springborg, *Politics in the Middle East,* 3rd ed. (New York: HarperCollins, 1990), pp. 254–55. For fuller discussions, see Henry Samuel Bienen, *The Military and Modernization* (Chicago: Aldine, 1973), and "Armed Forces and National Modernization: Continuing the Debate," *Comp. Pols.,* Oct. 1983, p. 1; and William Maley, Charles Sampford, and Ramesh Thakur, eds., *From Civil Strife to Civil Society: Civil and Military Responsibilities in Disrupted States* (New York: United Nations Publications, 2003).

educated peasants.[11] Officers, especially, must be technologically skilled, able to supervise the operation of computer-driven devices that locate targets and aim weapons. In sum, the modern profession of arms demands a large cadre of highly trained (though not necessarily broadly educated) personnel. Moreover, a modern army must have behind it, if not factories to manufacture these immensely complicated weapons, at least facilities to maintain and repair them.

Even in so-called developed nations, the military can raise the educational level of citizens. The most obvious means lie in the various schools that each branch of the service must run to train troops in trades useful in all phases of life—for instance, to repair motor vehicles and aircraft; operate radios, radars, and computers; take, develop, and evaluate photographs; and build roads and bridges. Even more basically, a strong civilian government can enlist the military to improve the literacy of the population. Several Latin American regimes have deployed troops as teachers in public schools, and, during his tenure as U.S. secretary of defense during the 1960s, Robert McNamara required each branch of the services to accept a certain percentage of men who were illiterate and teach them how to read and write. Most commanding officers found Operation Bootstrap, as it was called, distracting from their basic mission, but all complied and helped reduce the number of illiterates.

Stable civilian control over the military must involve implanting in the minds of both soldiers and civilians norms that outlaw military intervention in politics—and, again, eventually imbue in them acceptance of other values of constitutional democracy such as respect for human dignity and the necessity of limited government. Any policy, whether directed toward mere military neutrality or a stronger bond to the constitutional order, must translate these beliefs into actual behavior or else function only as prayerful hope. The standard mechanisms of civilian supremacy over the military, such having a civilian head the ministry of defense and making the military's budget depend on short-run appropriations by the national legislature, are of little significance in the absence of a political culture shared at least by the officer corps that legitimizes civilian control. Colonels and generals who believe that they have a moral duty to govern their country when things go sour are apt to seize power and use it as they judge best. This harsh fact may silhouette a vicious political circle: belief that the military is not subservient to civilian officials begets belief in the legitimacy of military governance, which begets coups, which begets beliefs among senior officers that military governance is legitimate, which begets. . . . That circle, however, need not be

11. It is quite possible, of course, to train illiterates how to march, drive trucks and tanks, shoot, use demolitions, and kill in hand-to-hand fighting. In Laos, for example, the CIA successfully trained uneducated Laotians to use radios, although these people could send only simple messages.

unbreakable. Changes in systems of beliefs, brought on by dynamic civilian leaders or military failures to govern efficiently, can weaken and eventually shatter the entrapping arcs.

Although direct efforts to contain military influence may seldom, if ever, be sufficient, they are not necessarily unimportant. We might categorize as positive or negative strategies to achieve the goals, first, of neutralizing the military's opposition and then of converting neutrality into active support. Neither objective will be easy to achieve, and as already noted, during the short run, leaders of a newborn constitutional democracy may have to be content with military neutrality.

Positive Strategies

For the long haul, creating among officers a culture that accepts the values of constitutional democracy will be critical. More specifically in this context, those values will include deep respect for democratic processes and constitutionalist rights, thus excluding as politically immoral not only military government but also criminal procedures that deny the accused due process of law, even when defendants are accused of torturing and murdering to preserve the old regime. Civic education in grade and high schools will be an important element in the insinuation of such a culture. For military and security forces, formal and informal instruction in their professional academies will be especially important. To fulfill their missions, these academies must select (and supervise) instructors who will teach by example as well as precept. Basic training of enlisted personnel could include, subject to the same requirements as for officers, emphasis on the military's duty to obey the nation's duly elected leaders.

As with civilians, the wording of the constitutional text can play an educational role. Provisions that stress civilian supremacy can impress young officers with their duty of obedience to elected leaders. It would help if that document explicitly stated that the head of government is the commander in chief of the armed forces and that he or she must always be a civilian. Article 62 of the Spanish constitutional text designates the king as commander in chief of the armed forces, as does Article II of the American text. A statute also requires the president to resign any military commission he holds before taking office.[12] A statutorily prescribed oath of office can help. In the United

12. Also by statute, a federal judge must resign his or her commission in the reserves, a requirement that has compelled judges who had been in the military to lose retirement benefits for themselves and their spouses that they have accumulated for their service, often a not inconsiderable sacrifice given the niggardly retirement provisions for spouses of deceased judges. Logically, senators and representatives should have to submit their resignations as well. The constitutional text is quite specific on the point. Article 1, §6, 2, says, "[N]o Person holding any Office under the United States, shall be a member of either House during his Continuation in Office." Congress, however, has never taken this clause so seriously as to forbid senators and representatives to retain commissions in the

States, for instance, that oath seems straightforward. Its text makes it clear that an officer's primary obligation is to the constitution rather than to superior officers.

> I, _____, having been appointed an officer in the Army of the United States, as indicated above in the grade of _____, *do solemnly swear* (or affirm) that I will support and defend the Constitution of the United States against all enemies, foreign and domestic, that I will bear true faith and allegiance to the same; that I take this obligation freely, without any mental reservation or purpose of evasion, and that I will well and faithfully discharge the duties of the office upon which I am about to enter, SO HELP ME GOD.

Civilian leaders, however, must keep in mind that the military's relationship to the constitution, text or larger order, can be delicate. As Chapter Fourteen will discuss, supporting and defending a constitution often requires interpretation, and interpreters may reasonably disagree about constitutional meaning. When these disagreements touch on, as they sometimes do, the polity's basic values, disputes may produce national crises. When matters of constitutional interpretation have arisen in such countries as Canada, the Federal Republic of Germany, Ireland, Italy, and the United States, the military have deferred to the civilian branches, most particularly to courts. In Turkey and many Latin American countries, however, professional officers have frequently preferred their own constitutional understandings and have intervened to protect those interpretations against what they deem to be the errors of civilian regimes.

In Latin America, framers have sometimes drafted their constitutional text to legitimize such interventions.[13] These documents, Juan Rial notes, have been "notoriously ambiguous in their definitions of the military's social and political roles," and civilian officials have often construed these terms to invite the military to assert itself "as a power broker in internal confrontations."[14] Examples of civilian and military use of such ambiguities abound. In Argentina, colonels and generals, rationalizing their actions as necessary to save constitution and country, overthrew more or less democratic governments in 1930, 1945, 1955, 1961, 1966, and 1976. In Chile in 1973, Pinochet and his gang honestly feared that President Salvador Allende would destroy the constitutional order and establish a Marxist government. In the latter third

---

military reserves. Legislators can accumulate (or draw) retirement pay. As a result, the American armed services can always count on a core of congressional support for their budgetary hopes, as presidents have often learned to their sorrow.

13. See Alfred Stepan, *The Military in Politics: Changing Patterns in Brazil* (Princeton, NJ: Princeton University Press, 1971), pp. 99–115.

14. "Latin American Constitutions and Their Armed Forces," in Douglas Greenberg, Stanley N. Katz, Melanie Beth Oliviero, and Steven C. Wheatley, eds., *Constitutionalism and Democracy: Transformations in the Contemporary World* (New York: Oxford University Press, 1993), p. 247.

of the twentieth century, Turkish generals several times intervened not only to restore what they believed to be economic order but also to prevent religious fundamentalists from establishing an Islamic state. Only in the last instance did the military have even the faintest purpose of facilitating constitutionalism or democracy.

Persuading the military to accept the processes and substantive decisions of constitutional democracy presents its own special problems. At root is a clash between the ethos of Athens and that of Sparta. Many of the military's particular values are not likely to be shared or fully appreciated by the rest of society. In a nation that has adopted even a modified form of capitalism, achievement of wealth will be highly regarded. On the other hand, professional officers—at least those in Western Europe, North America, India, Japan, Australia, and New Zealand—often share the feudal nobility's professed attitude toward money: seeking wealth is venal, beneath their elevated social status. (In contrast, too many officers in Africa, the Near and Middle East, East Asia, and sometimes Latin America have viewed the profession of arms as a means to make themselves and their families rich.) Pay in the armed services is typically lower for both enlisted men and officers than for civilian jobs requiring comparable skills and imposing comparable responsibility, and the gap usually widens at senior levels. A four-star general who commands perhaps a quarter of a million troops and is responsible for hundreds of millions of dollars of equipment will probably be compensated at a rate less than one-third of that of a CEO of a medium-sized corporation.

Differing attitudes toward money are probably not as important as differing attitudes toward, and conceptions of, honor. (The geographic qualifications noted above still apply.) Although most civilians want and will defend a good reputation as law-abiding, decent, honest people,[15] no corporate executive can expect to be obeyed if he or she orders an employee to lay down his or her life for the good of the firm. Nor in business would a person who refused to obey such an order be branded dishonorable. In this respect, military standards radically diverge from those of the corporate world. Honor as the military defines it includes not only trustworthiness, honesty, and law abidingness but also a readiness to risk, even to give up, one's life to protect country, branch of service, or comrades, especially troops under one's command.

At the highest levels, efficient administrators may replace heroic soldiers as commanders,[16] but valor remains the lodestar of the military ethic. And along with reverence for self-sacrificing courage comes acceptance of tight

15. Without a doubt the concept of personal honor is both stronger and more capacious in Spanish-speaking countries and probably has inhibited even civilians from engaging in the sorts of bargaining and compromise that are elsewhere integral parts of democratic political processes.

16. Morris Janowitz, *The Professional Solider: A Social and Political Portrait* (Glencoe, IL: Free Press, 1960).

discipline that, to civilian minds, often seems to surrender individuality even more than does the military's uniformity of dress. There is a tendency among civilians, especially academics, to look on officers as less than intelligent.[17] For professional soldiers, on the other hand, many civilian demands for individual freedoms, along with what often seem garish tastes in dress and hair, appear as self-indulgence, camouflage for instant gratification that displays weakness of character, just as Western societies' increasing tolerance of homosexuality seems to mean acceptance of "unmanly" behavior as morally acceptable.

Along with a concept of honor, the military tries from the first day of service to imbue into each officer and enlisted man or woman a sense of unity, of a common mission that might include, but usually transcends, personal advantage. Ideally, the members of a platoon, company, battalion, ship, or squadron form, as on St. Crispin's Day, a band of brothers whose overriding task is to live, fight, and perhaps die together in the defense of the nation and *its* honor. Such organizations have little equality but much fraternity. The individualistic pursuit of personal financial advancement at the expense of neighbors, colleagues, supervisors, or stockholders that characterizes corporate capitalism's competitive struggle resonates sourly in organizations such as the U.S. Marine Corps, whose operative credo is "We bury our dead; we carry our wounded; we never desert a comrade."

To be sure, few professional military men and women are saints. Officers and enlisted personnel sometimes offend against their own standards. Professional soldiers also share many of civilians' moral failings. Nevertheless, not without the same halo of self-righteousness that typifies clergy of all religions, military officers tend to view their own standards as higher, more deserving of respect, than those of the civilian world.

Bridging gaps between military and civilian cultures is difficult. War or the threat of war—"When the drums begin to roll"—can briefly turn civilian condescension to admiration, which, in turn, can ease soldiers' antagonism toward their fellow citizens. Like civilian resentment of higher taxes, however, the military's scornful attitude toward civilians may soon return. Kipling's "Tommy" put it well:

> You talk o' better food for us, an' schools, an' fires, an' all;
> We'll wait for extry rations if you treat us rational.
> Don't mess around the cook-room slops, but prove it to our face
> The Widow's uniform is not the soldier-man's disgrace.
> For it's Tommy this, an' Tommy that, an' "Chuck him out, the brute!"

---

17. For what it is worth, I found the very brightest academics at Princeton to be brighter than the brightest Marine officers and even the average academic to be somewhat more intelligent than the average Marine officer (if there are such persons). On the other hand, I judged many Marines to be much more intelligent than all but the very brightest of academics.

But it's "Saviour of 'is country" when the guns begin to shoot;
An' it's Tommy this, an' Tommy that, an' anything you please;
An' Tommy ain't a bloomin' fool—you bet your Tommy sees!

Discovering or even creating foreign enemies can ease tensions between the military and civilian worlds while keeping the military centered on its primary mission and encouraging civilians to forget their disagreements about domestic policies. On his deathbed, Shakespeare's Henry IV advised his son and heir "to busy giddy minds / With foreign quarrels."[18] In 2003, George W. Bush's administration was suspected of employing a wider version of this strategy (also called "wag the dog") in singling out Iraq as somehow posing an ominous threat to American security because of possession of "weapons of mass destruction," aid to Al Qaeda, and efforts to purchase fissionable materials in Africa. Bush's doctoring intelligence to demonstrate these supposed facts, critics said, was designed to distract voters' attention from failures to kill or capture Osama bin Laden, rejuvenate an ailing economy, and to distance the president and vice president from the financial scandals in which their corporate friends were involved.

There is an additional temptation to invoke, or invent, foreign threats. Many, if not most leaders in the Free World deemed great have been leaders in war. Abraham Lincoln, Winston Churchill, and Franklin D. Roosevelt leap into mind. But war can also torpedo political careers, as such shipwrecks as Neville Chamberlain, Édouard Daladier, Paul Reynaud, and General Leopoldo Galtieri of Argentina testify. And the price of war is high in civilian as well as military lives. Homer's "butcher god of war" has an insatiable appetite for money as well as blood. Even peacetime maintenance of an effective force powerful enough to deter an enemy devours taxes, with costs aggravated by necessary redundancy in equipment and personnel. Sooner, if not later, taxpayers are apt to resent the heavy financial burdens.

Public celebrations of victories and heroic deeds—Veterans' Day, for example—can remind the nation of its debts to the military and make professionals feel appreciated. More tangible and probably more effective in binding the military to the constitutional order would be government's providing modern armaments in addition to decent salaries, livable housing, and adequate medical care for military personnel and their families. Generous pensions and continued medical benefits for veterans would also help strengthen the military's affection for the political system. Again, however, these emoluments are costly and likely to be less than popular among taxpayers. Such policies may be wise but are not likely to persuade the military to love civilians—which is quite different from loving their country. Indeed, generating military affection for civilians may be impossible, but then it may not be necessary. Stimulating in military professionals a watchdog's sense of duty

18. *Henry IV,* pt. 2, act 4, scene 5.

toward the people who feed it and minimizing disaffection from the existing constitutional order may be sufficient for political stability, *if* officers have been inculcated with a belief that politics is a field their professional code of ethics forbids them to enter.

Especially important here would be four other policies, one very broad in scope and, on its face, connected only indirectly to the armed services, the other three internal to the military. The broad policy concerns domestic tranquillity. Disciplined military life tends to acculturate officers to regard public disorder as rappelling the nation down toward anarchy. Thus widespread restlessness and, worse yet, riots are likely to rouse a basic conservatism and tempt officers to intervene to restore their vision of public peace. Especially in Latin America, where the unprofessional professional officers' contempt for money has been as weak as their yearning for political power has been strong, commanders have often been hostile to workers and peasants and sympathetic to managers, owners, and the wealthy.[19] Therefore, business leaders have at times invited the army to put down unrest. But persuading senior officers to order their troops back to the barracks has often proved difficult. As General George Washington warned Colonel Alexander Hamilton in 1783, when the colonel suggested utilizing soldiers' anger at not being paid to pressure the Continental Congress into adopting a sound fiscal system: an army is "a dangerous instrument to play with."[20] During the second half of the twentieth century, the government of India was extraordinarily lucky. More than twenty times it called out the army to put down outbreaks of ethnic and religious violence, and yet it did not suffer from even an attempted coup.[21]

Problems of public disorder are typically and closely wrapped up with those of the economy. Poverty, Huntington has pointed out, is connected to the frequency and effectiveness of military coups. Writing in the mid-1990s, he spoke of a "coup-attempt ceiling" and a "coup-success ceiling": "Countries with per-capita GNPs of $1,000 or more do not have successful coups; countries with per-capita GNPs of $3,000 or more do not have coup attempts."[22] The moral is clear: by keeping the economy strong—not always

---

19. Colonel Lucio Gutiérrez of Ecuador is a striking exception. In 2000, he refused to put down a popular rising by Indians and the poor and joined forces with them. The movement failed, and Gutiérrez was arrested and imprisoned. Popular pressure on the government brought about his release after six months. The colonel then resigned from the army and formed a populist political party, the January 21 Patriotic Society, which won the general election of 2002. In January 2003, Gutiérrez, as a civilian, became president.

20. Quoted in Stanley Elkins and Eric McKitrick, *The Age of Federalism: The Early American Republic, 1788–1800* (New York: Oxford University Press, 1993), p. 102.

21. See the discussion in Stephen P. Cohen, "The Military and Indian Democracy," in Atul Kohli, ed., *India's Democracy: An Analysis of Changing State-Society Relations* (Princeton, NJ: Princeton University Press, 1988).

22. "Reforming Civil-Military Relations," p. 9.

the easiest of tasks—civilian officials remove much of the temptation for military efforts to take over government.[23]

The first of the three means internal to the armed forces involves assigning clear and limited missions to the armed forces so as to minimize the military's involvement in national policy making. The primary mission of the armed forces should be national defense, which raises its own fair share of contentious issues of public policy, not least of which may be whether, and if so how much, to rely on troops to combat guerrillas. As military missions expand, officers' temptations to further extend their control may also increase. At the same time, the military's capacity to perform its primary task is likely to contract. Civilian leaders must recognize both tendencies and convince senior officers of the linkage between organizational efficiency and limited roles.

On the other hand, it is unlikely that any country can restrict its armed forces only to national defense.[24] Their discipline and organization allow troops to move quickly to help cope with natural disasters such as earthquakes and floods.[25] Nations with severe problems with trade in narcotics, such as Colombia and the United States, suffer temptations to use the military to attack drug dealers. A navy's technological equipment can foster progress in oceanography, especially surveys of currents and depths of water offshore and within harbors, just as an army's cartographers can help plot a country's topography and the meteorological services of all the branches can assist national weather forecasting. In the United States, the coast guard routinely performs rescue missions and tries to stamp out smuggling by sea.[26] In some Asian and African countries, the army has built roads, while in many Latin American nations the military have special assignments to protect the environment and even teach in schools. In Argentina, Brazil, Chile, Ecuador, and Guatemala, the military have run factories to provide themselves with arms and ammunition and other kinds of supplies and equipment.

These sorts of operations along with the lures they set to lessen civilian

23. Amos Perlmutter put the matter more abstractly and more sweepingly: "[P]raetorianism is characterized by the absence of social mobilization, lack of political institutionalization, and deficiency in executive institutionalization and effectiveness." *The Military and Politics in Modern Times: On Professionals, Praetorians, and Revolutionary Soldiers* (New Haven, CT: Yale University Press, 1977), p. 152.

24. This restriction affects foreign as well as domestic policy. The temptation for civilian leaders to consult the military and accede to its judgment about the former is likely to be greater than the latter. But the dangers can be no less real. For an analysis of recent American problems in this regard, see Dana Priest, *The Mission: Waging War and Keeping Peace with America's Military* (New York: W. W. Norton, 2003).

25. In the United States, it is common for governors to call out the National Guard to help cope with natural disasters.

26. The latter mission explains why the U.S. Coast Guard has since 2003 been under the operational control of the Department of Homeland Security.

control can easily ripple outward. In Argentina, for example, the factories that the military have operated have manufactured goods to sell in domestic as well as foreign markets—an adroit way of avoiding budgetary restraints imposed by civilian governments. In the United States, professional soldiers realize, as do other bureaucrats and legislators, that politically and economically powerful interests are not indifferent to military matters. Manufacturers of weaponry have dozens of billions of dollars at stake in decisions regarding procurement, and labor unions may have their survival and the employment of their members at risk. Individually or together, such groups can exert heavy pressure on both the White House and Congress. Military officers also realize that any president's lease on the White House is much shorter than many senators and representatives' careers on Capitol Hill. During the long tenure of L. Mendell Rivers (D-S.C.) as chairman of the Armed Forces Committee of the House of Representatives, his wish to have as many naval and military facilities in his district as there was real estate available ("Rivers delivers" was his electoral slogan) usually took precedence over the efforts of presidents from Truman to Johnson to disperse bases.

Given that under many circumstances civilian governments will need to rely on the military for operations not directly related to national defense, Louis W. Goodman has suggested a trio of questions civilian officials should ask before approving such undertakings:

1. Does the military's involvement shut out other parties . . . from that activity, thus preventing them from developing critical skills and expanding their activities?
2. Do the armed forces by their involvement gain added privilege and become a special-interest group promoting their own institutional interests at the expense of public and private entities?
3. Does the military begin to neglect its core defense mission . . . ?[27]

A second internal means of enhancing civilian control concerns modes of recruiting and promoting officers. The highly technical nature of war makes it desirable to establish for each branch of the armed services an academy to educate and train junior officers and persuade them to make the military a career. This policy, however functional for military efficiency, has costs beyond the large financial outlays needed to maintain such institutions. It is almost inevitable that these environments will tend to isolate young men and women from the civilian world and do so at a formative period of their lives, probably causing them to drift further away from the larger society and its peculiar political values. Lucian K. Truscott IV, scion of an old army family

27. "Military Roles Past and Present," in Larry Diamond and Marc F. Plattner, eds., *Civil-Military Relations and Democracy* (Baltimore: Johns Hopkins University Press, 1996), p. 38.

and himself a graduate of West Point, uses a pair of fictional characters to describe the special orientation toward the army and away from civilian life the academy tries to create:

> "...West Point is a way of life. That's the way the academy describes itself, literally. A way of life. Quit thinking about West Point as a place, and think of it as being alive, like an animal or a human being. West Point propagates its own species. They're called graduates. West Pointers. They're different from you and me. They're special. They're *better*...."
>
> "Sounds like fascism to me."
>
> "Fascism, smashism. Who gives a damn? You wanted to know what it was like. I told you."[28]

Admirals and generals may be disappointed, and civilian leaders comforted, by the fact that the academies often fail to produce the sort of martial paragons Truscott portrays. Young men and women in their late teens and early twenties may be impressionable, but they have also been known to be rebellious. Furthermore, infusion of more "normally" educated officers into the professional ranks could strengthen attachment to constitutional democracy. If the government limited the size of classes at the academies, the armed services would be compelled to recruit young officers from civilian universities. Even though these people are not apt to be missionaries for constitutional democracy, it is likely they would be more assimilated into the larger society. Such a mix of young officers could be quite useful. Graduates of the academies could help colleagues from universities improve their technical skills and further their understanding of the military's peculiar values, while the latter could help academy graduates better understand the society for which they are ready to lay down their lives.[29]

Second, and closely related, is the matter of promotion. It must be based

28. *Dress Gray* (New York: Doubleday, 1978), pp. 306–7. Calder Willingham's novel *End as Man* (New York: Vanguard, 1947) has become a classic study of the young military officer. For a fascinating nonfictional account of life at the U.S. Military Academy and the values it tries to inculcate in fledgling officers, see David Lipsky, *Absolutely American: Four Years at West Point* (New York: Houghton Mifflin, 2003). For one of the more recent studies of Reserve Office Training Corps (ROTC) programs, see Michael S. Neiberg, *Making Citizen-Soldiers: ROTC and the Ideology of American Military Service* (Cambridge, MA: Harvard University Press, 2000).

29. I base this observation on personal experience of more than five years as a regular officer in the Marine Corps and an additional nineteen years as a reserve officer, service that included teaching at the Naval Academy and the USMC's Command and Staff College at Quantico, Virginia. As a fresh graduate of Notre Dame and a product of the NROTC, I found colleagues from the Naval Academy, Virginia Military Institute, and the Citadel to be far ahead in military knowledge, discipline, and lore. On the other hand, my fellow "civilians" helped remedy deficiencies in the liberal educations of our brother officers. The most intellectually gifted member of my class of more than 350 young lieutenants (about 270 of them graduates of "civilian" universities) was an alumnus of the Naval Academy, the most intellectually challenged a graduate of a private university. In combat, I saw no difference in performance between the two groups. Almost everyone demonstrated considerable competence combined with courage that was little short of astounding.

on demonstrated professional competence, not on the institutional door through which an officer entered the service, and most emphatically not on the influence of family, friends, or public officials. This procedure would not only encourage development of professional competence but also help isolate (and insulate) officers from government's other kinds of business.

A third policy that can ally professional military to the civilian world and its values involves incentives to retire in early middle age. Two different but related subpolicies interact here. First, allowing, as the United States does, officers and noncommissioned officers to retire with generous pensions and medical benefits after twenty years of service is likely to encourage military men and women, while they are still young, to look to the civilian world for a second career. Many officers become colonels or captains, but few rise to the rank of general or admiral, and most people who will not win stars realize what their future holds after fifteen or so years of service. These officers are likely to try to reorient themselves into the way civilians think and act and, in so doing, to ease whatever earlier disdain they may have felt. In the United States, the Retired Officers Association and often the armed services themselves sponsor seminars to help officers and senior NCOs smooth their transitions to civilian life. Indeed, American counselors have built up a cottage industry for such changes in careers.

A correlative policy of "up or out" that requires officers to retire if passed over twice for promotion not only weeds out less competent personnel[30] but also further encourages many able officers not to risk crushed egos. They can, again while still relatively young and drawing a comfortable pension, build a second and rewarding career in the civilian economy.

Each of these polices is expensive, but by encouraging most senior officers and NCOs to plan for life outside the military, they narrow the psychological gap between the two cultures. More important, such policies will help eliminate from the ranks large groups of men and women who, while still able to command much physical force, might become disappointed, even frustrated, with their professional life and blame the civilian world and its governmental system for their unhappiness. Removing potentially disaffected officers and NCOs from the armed service and scattering them about the civilian world is a prudent financial investment.

Negative Strategies

One obvious strategy not open to any civil society is to institute bloody purges such as those the Soviet Union unleashed on the army commander Marshall Mikhail Tukhachevsky and his colleagues in 1937–1938: Stalin executed approximately thirty-five thousand officers, including 90 percent of

---

30. Sometimes these officers are very competent but have specialized skills that are no longer needed.

the Red Army's generals and 80 percent of its colonels.[31] This loss of leaders helps explain the dismal performance of the Soviet army during its campaign against Finland in 1939–1940 and then during the early stages of the war against the Nazis.[32] Stalin's paranoia might partly account for this slaughter, but Robert C. Tucker also sees careful planning behind the murders.[33] Tukhachevsky and some of his fellow generals were veterans of the civil war and had fought under the command of Leon Trotsky, who had since become Stalin's chief ideological enemy. Furthermore, the bulk of these officers were anti-Nazi and would certainly have been offended by the pact that Stalin was planning to make with Hitler. More fundamentally, many of these officers, especially Tukhachevsky, were independent-minded men who might have stood in the way of Stalin's march to total control of the Soviet Union. However grievously these purges harmed the efficiency of the Red Army, they also removed any possibility of effective resistance to Stalin from within the armed forces.[34]

A second and historically related strategy to ensure civilian control over officers involves use of kommisars, party officials, as cocommanders. During the civil war, the Red Army required that all tactical orders, even at the company level, be approved by both the military commanding officer and the kommisar. This system was gradually weakened and virtually abandoned. In 1937, however, Stalin reinstated it, further controlling officers, even in the junior ranks, but also weakening the military's capacity to wage war.[35] It is difficult to see how a constitutional order that preaches separation of the military from the political could require officers to tailor tactical decisions to ideology. In some senses, of course, constitutional democracies do try to require all military personnel to adhere to the regime's standards when such matters as due process for the criminally accused as well as racial and sexual treatment are involved.

31. Leonard Shapiro, "The Great Purge," in B. H. Liddell Hart, ed., *The Red Army* (New York: Harcourt, Brace, 1956), p. 69.

32. During the mid-1930s, Tukhachevsky had been urging Stalin to reorganize and reequip the Soviet army along the lines that Charles de Gaulle was urging France to follow, that is, to rely on the equivalent of the Panzer divisions that the Germans would so successfully use against France and, during the early stages of the war, against Russia.

33. *Stalin in Power: The Revolution from Above, 1928–1941* (New York: W. W. Norton, 1990), pp. 379–84.

34. We shall never know, of course, whether Tukhachevsky and any of his colleagues would have opposed Stalin. He, however, took no chances. Historically, the Russian army had seldom intervened in domestic politics. See Brian D. Taylor, *Politics and the Russian Army: Civil-Military Relations, 1689–2000* (New York: Cambridge University Press, 2003). Even the mutinies that began the October Revolution were not led by colonels and generals but from the outside by Bolsheviks and from the inside by enlisted men and NCOs.

35. Shapiro, "Great Purge," p. 68. Among the most thorough historical works on the Soviet Army are Raymond L. Garthoff's two books *Soviet Military Doctrine* (Glencoe, IL: Free Press, 1953), and *Soviet Military Policy: A Historical Analysis* (New York: Praeger, 1966).

In contrast to purges and kommisars, a policy as old as the Roman Empire raises no normative difficulties for constitutional democracy: ancient Rome forbade victorious commanders to march their legions through the Sacred City. How much this policy protected against military coups and how much it transferred to the Praetorian Guards the power to choose (and kill) emperors is not clear. What is clear is that keeping troops away from the center of political power lowers the chances of successful coups. In this regard, navies, especially those whose ships spend a great time at sea, pose a smaller threat to political stability. The British applied this lesson to their army by scattering troops in the colonies, far from home. Dispersal has the additional "benefit" of allowing a nation to export some of its less savory young men so that they will prey, if prey they must, not on their own citizens but on "less civilized" peoples, as, again, the British did with their garrisons in such distant places as Egypt, India, Ireland, Palestine, and Sub-Saharan Africa.

A frontier may serve the same purposes, as did the American West. Placing installations at such sites as the Dust Bowl of Oklahoma, the deserts of New Mexico, the boondocks of Alabama, Georgia, and Texas, and the swamps of North and South Carolina while turning bases near Washington such as Quantico, Fort Belvoir, Fort McNair, and Fort Meade into centers of education, research, and storage may have been the direct product of congressional pork barreling, but it has also kept tactical units far from the capital, indeed from civilization.

A demand for a small standing army has long been a shibboleth of devotees of republican government. But such a cadre, composed entirely of men and women who volunteered because they want to spend their lives as soldiers and sailors, may pose a greater threat to the constitutional order than would a larger, less dedicated, and more variegated force. Universal military service, with alternatives for conscientious objectors, could inject a stabilizing element. Obedience to senior officers' orders to move against the government is less likely to come from men and women whose connections to the military will, they hope, soon be severed than from military professionals. Furthermore, draftees are likely to fight effectively only in popular wars, internal or external, as France discovered in World War II, the United States in Vietnam, Portugal in Angola, and the Soviet Union in Afghanistan.

Unification of the various branches of the armed services is attractive, especially financially. Many of the same military functions are performed by two or more branches. Uniforms and much equipment could be standardized and money saved on common research and development as well as on larger-scale purchases of such mundane items as shoes, socks, belts, shirts, and caps. There may also be a gain in efficiency as old jealousies and rivalries fade. Officers planning operations would be much less enamored by strategies and tactics that would make their branch of the service look better than others.

Complete unification, however, is impossible. Other than James Bond and Rambo, few people can be commandos, jet pilots, and submarine commanders. As in the civilian world, a high degree of specialization is inevitable, and new rivalries and jealousies are likely develop within a single service, as, indeed, they historically did within the American Navy's conflicts between advocates of battleships and aircraft carriers, within the U.S. Air Force between pilots and missilemen, and within the U.S. Army between advocates of lightly armed, highly mobile ground units and those who favor reliance on more conventional infantry supported by heavy tanks and artillery. Defense contractors have been involved in all of these struggles, their choice of sides depending on what weapons they sell.

Other costs and benefits cannot be measured in financial terms. If one believes arguments for capitalism, competition promotes rather than impedes efficiency. Furthermore, interservice rivalry may yield dividends for political stability. Madison's strategy of limiting government by pitting power against power and ambition against ambition may apply to the military, as does the alleged remark of one of the framers at Philadelphia regarding civilian officials, "If they are at each other's throats, they will not be at ours."[36] It would not be altogether dysfunctional for constitutional democracy were the heads of the various military branches suspicious of each other, willing to cooperate wholeheartedly with each other only under the careful direction of civilian leaders.

Although failed Latin American efforts to divide and pacify the military shout out that interservice rivalries do not offer a panacea, on occasion these rivalries have helped limit tyranny. As the ballots were being counted during the night of the Chilean election of 1989 and it was becoming clear that General Augusto Pinochet would lose his bid for a popular mandate to continue in office, he sent troops into the streets of Santiago. Some diplomats and CIA agents in the American embassy believed that the general was about to declare the election tainted by fraud and thus void. If he had had such plans, they were disrupted when reporters interviewed the commanding general of the air force as he was about to enter the presidential palace. His comment went something like, "Well, we've been beaten." It was hardly mere coincidence that he, along with the navy's chief, had felt Pinochet's budgetary allocations were slighting his branch of the service to benefit the army.

---

36. I have never found a primary source for this remark. It is probably too good to have actually been spoken. Nevertheless, it pretty well sums up the notion of separate institutions competing for shared powers. See Charles Jones, "The Separated Presidency," in Anthony King, ed., *The New American Political System,* 2nd ed. (Washington, DC: American Enterprise Institute, 1990), p. 3.

Security Forces

For an infant constitutional democracy, the reaction of internal security forces to political transformation will also be critical. Where these agencies are extremely powerful, especially if, as in the Soviet Union, they command their own efficient army, the directors of those agencies will have to be included in any negotiations for a peaceful transition. If these people have the heart to struggle—it is possible, as happened in Eastern Europe, that they will not—their secret police and armed forces will constitute a formidable barrier against change. Under such circumstances, these officials will be much less vulnerable to violent overthrow from inside the country than to disaffection, desertion, and/or bribery in the form of bargains that exchange their rapid and peaceful exits for their lives, sweetened perhaps by being allowed to retain their Swiss bank accounts.

The power of security forces has varied from system to system. At least from the time of Stalin's purges in the mid-1930s through Gorbachev's reign in the mid-1980s, the KGB and its predecessors had more actual power inside the Soviet Union than did the Red Army. So, too, under the Nazi regime did the SS, and more particularly the Gestapo. In both cases, each security agency had officers within the armed forces as well as its own elite military units. On the other hand, in many authoritarian systems the secret police have operated, as did the Stasi in the People's Republic of Germany, under the direct control of a civilian government or, as in Argentina, Chile, and other parts of Latin America, as subordinate to a military junta.

There is, however, a critically important difference between the roles of military and the roles of security forces in a constitutional democracy, one that internal security chiefs will quickly perceive. It is improbable that the new regime will want to abolish its armed forces—certainly control them, but not eliminate them. On the other hand, although human nature's inclination toward sin makes some sort of internal security necessary, a constitutional democracy cannot tolerate organizations modeled on the KGB, the Stasi, or the shah's SAVAK. The very existence of a free-wheeling secret police organization would blatantly contradict the regime's norms.

Thus, the new polity must drastically reduce the ranks and power of internal security forces, actions that leaders of security agencies are likely to view (probably incorrectly) as endangering national safety and (correctly) as threatening their personal and institutional futures. That realization increases pressures on the new leaders either to increase the bribes it offers or (perhaps, and) to use force against the secret police. The latter course would be possible only if a substantial portion of the regular military transferred their loyalty to the new constitutional order or if the leaders of the new constitutional democracy had at their disposal a substantial body of armed irregular troops.

CHAPTER TWELVE

Rebuilding the Machinery of the State

The Bureaucracies

Just as the nation-state is the dominant form of territorial organization, no state operates without the instrument of a bureaucracy.   EZRA SULEIMAN

Neither Nature nor Nature's God provides software to translate decisions made by political leaders into operating public policy. Glorious words about government as the promoter of justice, the protector of rights, the keeper of peace, or the guardian of the nation's independence remain merely words until they are consubstantiated into a coherent and more or less consistent series of actions. Government is an artificial creation, and the hopes and aspirations it reflects need to be carried into deeds by similarly artificial creations. For the modern state, these creatures of Leviathan are bureaucracies: public institutions staffed by public officials who have public duties.

These agencies and the people who staff them often frustrate legislators, leaders of the executive branch, and, not least, private citizens. The term *bureaucrat* is seldom applied as a compliment. In the governmental and corporate worlds, "paper shufflers" and "bean counters" frequently seem to be, and sometimes are, small-minded anal erotics who delight in multiplying forms that must be filled out in intricate detail weeks before an organization will even begin to consider making a decision. As Hannah Arendt put it, collectively these people can, if not closely supervised, create a system in which no person, "neither one nor the best nor even the many, can be held responsible" for any action or inaction.[1] Nevertheless, by insisting on "proper" standards, amassing and organizing information, and creating institutional memories, bureaucracies and bureaucrats provide the means to make rational choices among competing policy options and to allocate costs and benefits intelligently. As cumbersome as these organizations are and as annoying as the men and women who run them may seem to be, their work is absolutely essential to the complex operations of all governmental systems and even to those of moderate-sized universities and businesses.

The previous chapter examined problems for maintaining constitutional democracy posed by military and internal security apparatuses. This chapter

---

1. *Crises of the Republic* (New York: Harcourt Brace and Jovanovich, 1973), p. 172.

focuses on less obviously powerful sets of public officials: the administrators who operate the various departments of the executive branch as well as those who supposedly only assist but also sometimes guide legislative as well as judicial officials. If these people were, as Woodrow Wilson claimed they should be, removed "from the strife of politics,"[2] that is, political eunuchs without either policy preferences or discretion, they would be interchangeable agents of governmental action, posing no problems for a new constitutional democracy. The hard fact is quite different. Many bureaucrats do have policy preferences, as Wilson himself would later learn when he was unseated as president of Princeton University by a dean and trustees who had their own ideas about proper policy.

Furthermore, even middle-level administrators often have discretion in carrying out their duties, and discretion confers freedom to act. And freedom to act can not only affect what (and how) policies are being implemented but also reinforce or undermine constitutional democracy—or any other political system. "All public administration," Gerald Caiden points out, "is political; it is an instrument of politics and political values dominate. . . . [P]ublic management cannot be divorced from politics and political culture."[3] Thus leaders of a new government must be concerned not only with the efficiency and honesty of administrative officials but also with their political attitudes. As with the military, their being Democrats or Republicans, Labourites or Conservatives, Christian Democrats or Socialists may be irrelevant, but it would be very relevant if they were fascists, communists, or militant Islamic fundamentalists, because as these dogmas endorse values and attitudes hostile to constitutional democracy's norms.

Bureaucrats in the Executive and Legislative Branches

When deciding how to (re)staff public institutions for the new political order, founders of a constitutional democracy will again envy their eighteenth-century American cousins. The Laocoön-like apparatus of the modern state was far outside the ken of the colonials. After a dozen years under the new constitutional order, governing remained so modest that when President John Adams and his wife Abigail supervised moving the federal capital from Philadelphia to Washington, the entire archives of the executive branch filled only seven packing boxes.[4] Public administration on the Continent was more complex but still rudimentary when compared to the twentieth or twenty-first century. Furthermore, the French Revolution demonstrated that officials of a prior regime could readily be converted, exiled, or recycled back into the food chain.

2. "The Study of Public Administration," 2 *Pol. Sci. Q.* 197, at 209-10 (1887).
3. "Administrative Reform—American Style," 54 *Pub. Admin. Rev.* 123, at 126 (1994).
4. Joseph J. Ellis, *Founding Brothers: The Revolutionary Generation* (New York: Vintage, 2003), p. 205.

Today, of course, a new constitutional democracy would face a far more difficult situation. Not only are leaders apt to be of a moral genre quite different from George Washington, but every political system in developed nations now also has—and needs—thick webs of institutions that regulate, manage, and/or subsidize many aspects of life that, as late as the first third of the twentieth century, were considered private if they were considered at all.[5] The modern administrative state is epitomized not by the flamboyant, creative, charismatic soldier-statesman, such as Giuseppe Garibaldi, Kemal Atatürk, or Simón Bolívar, but rather by the bureaucrat, stereotypically an expert who is competent rather than brilliant, calmly rational, staid, even a bit plodding, and always armed with reams of forms for citizens to fill in.[6] And the numbers of such officials are legion. In the United States, the federal government alone has more than three million civilians on its payroll. Among thousands of duties, these officials follow labyrinthine paths sketched by legislation produced by bargains about bargains that modify compromises. Bureaucrats must collect taxes; regulate banks; operate enormous enterprises; amass, analyze, and distribute statistics about myriad economic and social developments; monitor trading in stocks, bonds, and commodities; set basic interest rates; approve or ban prescription medications; track and curb the spread of communicable diseases; approve financing of medical research; operate a network of hospitals for veterans; oversee the safety of traffic in the air, highways, shipping channels, and railways; dredge harbors; build airports; ensure that labor-management relations follow sometimes baffling legislative standards; protect the environment, including assorted fish and animals whose species may be endangered; underwrite home mortgages; subsidize small businesses as well as farmers; and administer systems of social security, Medicare, and Medicaid in addition to pensions for retired military and civil servants.

Then, too, government is supposed to guard life and property against predators. As crime has gone first national, then global, policing now requires battalions of highly trained personnel, including pathologists and

---

5. Privatization has been returning to favor, sometimes in the guise of "contracting out" public functions, such as torture, to private corporations. One of the goals of this movement has been to transform citizens into clients. For a critical analysis, see Ezra N. Suleiman, *Power, Politics, and Bureaucracy: The Administrative Elite in France* (Princeton, NJ: Princeton University Press, 1974), esp. chs. 1–3.

6. Many bureaucrats, of course, are imaginative and creative. For example, in 1958, T. Kenneth Whitaker, secretary of Ireland's Department of Finance, laid out a comprehensive plan for Ireland's economic development, a plan that involved generous tax rebates and public subsidies to foreign corporations willing to establish facilities in Ireland and employ Irish workers. Results were slow in coming, but within a few decades the Whitaker Plan, as it was called, provided the blueprint for an economic miracle that lifted the Irish economy from among the very poorest in Europe to the fastest developing, bringing a level of prosperity far beyond anything the country had ever experienced. See esp. John F. McCarthy III, ed., *Planning Ireland's Future: The Legacy of T. K. Whitaker* (Dublin: Glendale, 1990).

other forensic scientists, hackers, accountants, and psychiatrists as well as old-fashioned street cops and detectives. Meanwhile, penology has taken on layers of scientific patina. In a development that would have delighted Jeremy Bentham, even the architectural design of prisons has become a specialized function that incorporates electronics to further the supposed psychology of punishment along with the safety of inmates, guards, and the general public.

Before 1989 in the Soviet Union, Eastern Europe, and those parts of the Middle East, such as Tunisia, Egypt, and Syria, that had adopted socialist systems, the situation was even more complicated. In those places, the state owned almost all industries, banks, large commercial ventures, and, in the old Soviet empire, farms. Public officials not only operated these enterprises but also set quotas, prices, lending policies, tariff barriers, and rates of monetary exchange, and they determined how many people would be employed in each sector, with full employment usually taking priority over economic efficiency and benefits for officials' family, friends, and co-conspirators taking priority over all else. What they were unable to regulate with any success was quality. In Eastern Europe after 1989, giving administrators shares in newly privatized businesses and allowing them to buy (and sell) more eased their transition from public servants to private entrepreneurs—and sometimes criminals. Governments in some Arab countries have also tried to privatize state enterprises, but the old bureaucrats have tended to remain in place. Facing loss of jobs and status, these officials have dragged their heels against economic reform.[7]

A shift to constitutional democracy from a tightly authoritarian regime would sharply curtail bureaucrats' arbitrary power not only over economic affairs but over public policy as well. On the other hand, it is doubtful how much such a transformation would reduce their collective importance. As Max Weber commented, neither parliamentary speeches not executive decrees effect public policy. Rather, in modern states "the actual ruler is necessarily and unavoidably the bureaucracy."[8] Many lower officials, such as street cleaners and garbage collectors, are not likely to mold public policies unless they act in concert and go on strike. Then the importance of such humble jobs to modern urban life becomes painfully clear.

Other mid- or low-level officials, such as those who administer health and pension plans, can make a larger, if not huge, impact by rewarding ideological friends and punishing enemies by expediting, delaying, or deny-

7. Although this problem has been acute in Arab countries across North Africa—see, for instance, Michael Field, *Inside the Arab World* (Cambridge, MA: Harvard University Press, 1995), chs. 10–11—the difficulty is more general. See Barbara Geddes, "Challenging the Conventional Wisdom," in Larry Diamond and Marc F. Plattner, eds., *Economic Reform and Democracy* (Baltimore: Johns Hopkins University Press, 1995).

8. Quoted by Suleiman, *Power, Politics, and Bureaucracy,* p. 22.

ing delivery of services or money. Especially where issues of due process are involved, police, prosecutors, and judges—all three are civil servants in Civil Law countries—are apt to exert much more substantial influence. Street cops who regularly "tune up" suspects can undermine formal constitutionalist guarantees, as can procurators who utilize perjured or coerced testimony or conceal vital evidence from defendants and judges who bend the law to punish actual and potential enemies of the regime.

At higher administrative levels, the potential to shape public policy widens. The reality of constitutional democracy seldom reflects the institutionalized analogy of elected legislators (or presidents or cabinet ministers) as principals and professional bureaucrats as agents. The phenomenon of bureaucratic resistance is a favorite topic of colorful anecdote as well as careful study, and it affects (infects?) all organizations, private as well as public, including courts,[9] legislatures, and administrative bodies. Even ecclesiastical organizations are not immune. When asked how many people worked for him in the Vatican, Pope John XXIII allegedly responded, "About half."[10]

That "bureaucrats in Brussels" run the European Union is a frequent charge and almost as frequently is true. In the United States, every senator and representative has a large staff—fifty assistants would be a small number for a senator from a populous state.[11] These assistants are needed, legislators believe, to oversee the work of the huge federal bureaucracy and, more specifically, to encourage or coerce bureaucrats to respond favorably to requests from legislators' constituents. These "legislative bureaucrats" typically specialize in policy areas and often develop close personal relations with bureau chiefs along with considerable technical knowledge. In addition, legislative staff members gather and analyze information, screen communications, brief the senator or representative, draft or edit proposed legislation, and advise on (sometimes, in fact, make) decisions to vote for or against bills.

9. See my "Lower Court Checks on Supreme Court Power," 53 *Am. Pol. Sci. Rev.* 1017 (1959), and *Elements of Judicial Strategy* (Chicago: University of Chicago Press, 1964), ch. 4.

10. I vividly recall having lunch in the Vatican in the private apartment of the *bête noire* of Catholic liberals during Vatican II, Cardinal Alfredo Ottaviani, former prefect of the Sacred Congregation for the Doctrine of the Faith (the old Holy Office that had once been in charge of the Inquisition). I explained that my scholarly interest was understanding how the pope coped with the familiar problem of bureaucratic resistance. He smiled and said, "Ah yes, we in the Vatican say the pope is infallible and almost omnipotent, then we make sure he can do nothing either very good or very bad." My research indicated that His Eminence was close to being correct, though Pope Paul VI was often able to counter his subordinates' power by installing his own (hyperactive) man, Archbishop Giovanni Benelli, as substitute secretary of state, the official in charge of coordinating the Vatican's bureaucracy.

11. Patrick J. Moynihan called this phenomenon an example of "the Iron Law of Emulation." As bureaucracies have grown and perhaps increased presidential power, legislators have sought to increase their influence over the administration of the laws they enact. Moynihan claimed he got this "iron law" from James Q. Wilson, but Wilson believes its father was Moynihan himself. Wilson, *Bureaucracy: What Government Agencies Do and Why They Do It* (New York: BasicBooks, 1989), pp. 259–60.

Judges on many courts also have assistants, not only clerks who certify and file moving papers in the course of litigation but also people who research legal matters, prepare memoranda for pending cases, and draft opinions. Each justice on Germany's Constitutional Court can choose three research assistants, usually professional judges, university professors, or civil servants. These people already have had successful careers and usually serve for two or three years.[12] In the United States, the justices of the Supreme Court can also select several "clerks,"[13] but these are usually young men and women, only a year or two out of law school. They normally serve for only one year, seldom for more than two. Their collective influence in screening cases for the justices to hear and in writing opinions varies from year to year and justice to justice, but occasionally their influence is significant. For instance, the famous footnote in the Carolene Products Case was drafted by Harlan Fiske Stone's clerk, Louis Lusky. For more than two generations, that note (as revised by Stone and Chief Justice Charles Evans Hughes) set the tone for the Court's jurisprudence regarding both economic regulation and civil liberties.[14] In Germany, the influence of the Court's staff lacks, so far as scholars have been able to determine, such a dramatic impact, but the day-to-day influence of these officials is probably greater, if for no other reasons than that they are themselves well established professionals and stay on the job for longer terms than their young American counterparts.

Citizens are more apt to deal directly with administrators and legislative staff members than with elected officials themselves, and these bureaucrats' decisions are, for the individual citizen, likely to be final and immediately consequential. Legislatures frequently anoint with the force of law future administrative regulations that will supposedly carry out a statute's general policy. And even when these regulations lack that much tonnage, they still demand obedience from private citizens, groups, or entire industries. The alternative is to resort to a set of expensive and time-consuming appeals within an administrative chain of command and perhaps beyond to the courts.

The vast number of bureaucrats and the technical expertise they bring to their work make it difficult for prime ministers, presidents, and cabinet officers to function as careful monitors, much less as micromanagers. For men and women in senior governmental posts, time is usually the scarcest resource. They are typically far too busy to meticulously supervise many of

12. Donald P. Kommers, *Constitutional Jurisprudence of the the Federal Republic of Germany,* 2nd ed. (Durham, NC: Duke University Press, 1997), p. 23.

13. As now do all federal judges and most state appellate judges, as well as judges of trial courts of general jurisdiction.

14. For a summary of the origins and history of that footnote, see Walter F. Murphy, James E. Fleming, Sotirios A. Barber, and Stephen Macedo, *American Constitutional Interpretation,* 3rd ed. (Westbury, NY: Foundation, 2003), pp. 679–91.

their supposed subordinates or to acquire the knowledge necessary to do so effectively. Although elected officials might draft, edit, and approve the documents that will become statutes and executive orders, they can direct enforcement in only a very general fashion. Thus it is quite possible in constitutional democracies for supposed public policies to undergo significant changes as administrators decode general principles into specific rules and practical decisions.

Sometimes these mutations in public policy are the result of willful bureaucratic action, but sometimes they are inevitable—and foreseen as inevitable—consequences of legislative choices. Shifting social and physical conditions, rapidly changing technologies, and the exquisitely complex nature of many problems may doom intricately detailed statutes to impotence.[15] In the United States, even the elephantine body of federal tax laws requires more than forty-five thousand pages of IRS regulations to make them explicit. The typical question legislators face is not whether to delegate discretion but how much, to whom, and subject to what kinds of oversight.[16] And when statutes are not narrowly worded, procedures not precisely outlined, and critical terms not exactingly defined, bureaucrats must, as must judges under similar circumstances, weigh intangibles as well as practicalities to make decisions that will often be influenced by idiosyncratic factors, including their own judgments about what is practical, expedient, wise, or just.

The flow of political influences within constitutional democracies may augment bureaucratic freedom. Realizing the importance of how polices are (or are not) carried out, organized groups try to weld tight connections to those administrators whose work materially affects their interests. These links, which are probably more complex in presidential than in parliamentary systems, may establish an iron triangle among pressure groups, legislators, and bureaucrats,[17] opening opportunities for strategic maneuverings

15. In 1890, when pressed during debates on antitrust legislation to provide a specific definition of "a combination in restraint of trade," Senator John Sherman gave a reply that blended candor and optimism: "I admit it is difficult to define in legal language the precise line between lawful and unlawful combinations. This must be left for the for the courts to decide in each particular case. All that we, as lawmakers, can do is to declare general principles, and we can rest assured that the courts will apply them so as to carry out the meaning of the law." 21 *Cong. Rec.* 2400. Institutional jealousy at the wide discretion that legislatures were then beginning to delegate to bureaucrats explains in part early judicial hostility to administrative regulations.

16. For a strategic analysis of when and to what extent it makes sense for legislators to delegate powers to bureaucrats, see John D. Huber and Charles R. Shipan, *Deliberate Discretion: The Institutional Foundations of Bureaucratic Autonomy* (New York: Cambridge University Press, 2002); and R. Douglas Arnold, *Congress and the Bureaucracy: A Theory of Influence* (New Haven, CT: Yale University Press, 1979). For an impassioned critique of the results of legislative delegation in the United States, see Theodore J. Lowi, *The End of Liberalism: The Second Republic of the United States*, 2nd ed. (New York: W. W. Norton, 1979).

17. For American politics, the classic study of this triangular relationship is Arthur Maas, *Muddy Waters: The Army Engineers and the Nation's Rivers* (Cambridge, MA: Harvard University

that enable clever administrators to play elected officials and pressure groups off against one another and so shift the impact of policies toward the direction that they themselves deem best for themselves, their agency, or the nation.

Because of these factors, bureaucrats who are opposed to constitutional democracy, especially if they are encouraged by private organizations with political resources and maintain some support within the legislature and higher levels of the executive branch, will have opportunities to impede, perhaps sabotage, public policies needed to maintain the new political order. Federalism multiplies opportunities to play off the state's periphery against its center.[18] To be sure, administrators who heed the siren calls of local leaders risk sanctions, but in a constitutional democracy, the worst result would be a place in an unemployment line, not in a cemetery.

In sharp contrast, during the early stages of harsh authoritarian regimes, bureaucratic discretion will probably be tightly constrained. In the Soviet Union under Stalin, Germany under Hitler, and, through the 1950s, China under Mao, administrators seemed to act more often as automatons than as officials who had some range of choice.[19] Soon, however, even under would-be totalitarian systems, many supposed drones began behaving in slyly independent ways. As Nazi fortunes declined, officers of the SS, which never tried to recruit men of virtue, became more and more open to bribes, and Luftwaffe and Wehrmacht generals learned how to lie to *der Führer.* When revolutionary fervor faded in China, local and regional party officials resurrected the traditional *kumshaw* as the key to "the back door." Even under

---

Press, 1951). For a more recent account of the ability of a wily congressman to work with agents of the CIA to change American policy in Afghanistan during the 1980s, see George Crile, *Charlie Wilson's War: The Extraordinary Story of the Largest Covert Operation in History* (New York: Atlantic Monthly Press, 2003). For an interesting analysis of "issue networks," see Hugh Heclo, "Loose Jointed Play of Influence," in Anthony King, ed., *The Political System* (Washington, DC: American Enterprise Institute, 1978), pp. 87ff.

18. Joel S. Migdal, *The State in Society: Studying How States and Societies Transform and Constitute One Another* (New York: Cambridge University Press, 2001), p. 54, offers a more abstract description: "To avoid the damage local [nongovernmental] authorities might inflict upon their chances for advancement or even their political survival, many strategically placed state employees accommodate those local figures."

19. The politicos to whom these administrators responded were always executive officers. The ruling elites never shared power with independent legislators or judges. Thus discipline could be harsh as well as rapid. Because no close study of such regimes has been possible, evidence for this apparent robotic behavior is anecdotal, though its existence is supported by the probability that exercising discretion could have resulted in sudden or, worse, slow death. On the other hand, Klaus Kinkel, the West German minister of justice at the time of reunification, argued against excusing East German officials for their crimes, because "[e]ven in dictatorship, the individual's room to maneuver is not just as small as the perpetrators would like us to believe." Quoted in A. James McAdams, "Communism on Trial: The East German Past and the German Future," in McAdams, ed., *Transitional Justice and the Rule of Law in the New Democracies* (Notre Dame, IN: University of Notre Dame Press, 1997), p. 245.

Stalin, factory managers and departmental officials devised mutually advantageous ways to create deceptive reports of fulfilled quotas. And by the time of Nikita Khrushchëv, corruption had become thoroughly institutionalized throughout the Soviet system.

Understanding these facts of political life, almost all founders of a new regime intend to execute a thorough purging of administrative personnel. Occasionally, as when Mao's forces took over China in 1949, they are successful. But as Suleiman points out, "radical change rarely occurs and the pace of change is almost always slow."[20] This historical pattern makes it imperative that leaders of the new constitutional order carefully plan strategic moves that will maximize their ability to reorient the state's administrative apparatus. Limiting analysis to officials whose judgment can make a real difference in the shape of public policies—a restriction that limited time and resources would also impose on the new regime—we might see transitions to constitutional democracy as falling under six general categories, each requiring different means to re-create a loyal and efficient bureaucracy.

First would be the easiest sort, in which the state, though not necessarily the country or the population, is small and rather simple, the new regime is similar to the old in many important respects, and a relatively large coterie of citizens loyal to the new order have had some experience in public administration. The not-quite-yet-united colonies in America found themselves in this situation during the closing decades of the eighteenth century. Enough colonials had served in the bare-bones government of the time that it was simpler to replace most bureaucrats than to retain and reeducate potentially hostile officials. Most British personnel had left (or been run out of) the colonies with their Tory friends to settle in Ontario, the West Indies, or the United Kingdom itself. In addition, the new political system was in many respects quite similar to the old. After all, the rights the Rebels claimed to have been defending were those of Englishmen. Even though public rhetoric substituted "the people" for the king as the apparent ruler and state legislatures (and later Congress) replaced Parliament, much stayed constant. What was loosely thought of as "the rule of law" remained a public ideal. The historic system of criminal justice was still creakily operational. In civil disputes, the common law continued in force—and continued to gradually deviate from its English ancestor. In spite of some state legislatures' making it easier to pay off debts in inflated currency and, more serious in the short run, confiscating Loyalists' assets,[21] the right to own, use, and dispose

20. *Dismantling Democratic States* (Princeton, NJ: Princeton University Press, 2003), p. 280.

21. Despite colonists' promise in the Treaty of Paris, which formally ended the Revolution, to return seized property or to indemnify previous owners, an obligation repeated in the treaty of commerce that John Jay negotiated with the British in 1794 (ratified in 1795), it took several decades of litigation to resolve the issues. The most famous ruling concerning Loyalists' land was Martin v. Hunter's Lessee, 1 Wh. 304 (1816). Because John Marshall and his brother James were among the

of private property remained central to American society. Strengthening those rights and fostering commerce were among the principal reasons for calling the Constitutional Convention of 1787.

Ireland provides a second genre of transition. It differed from the American case in that, by the 1920s, the state had become a much more complex beast. Even so, the Irish had a relatively easy switch. The local population was largely literate, with a substantial, well educated elite. Furthermore, although the formal political change was rather quick—less than seven years elapsed between the Rising on Easter Monday, 1916, and the treaty of peace—the personnel for a transition had long been mustering. By the end of the nineteenth century, the harshness of Britain's colonial rule had been eased by an infusion of Irish Catholics as freely elected Irish members of Parliament and even as bureaucrats. When the IRA's urban guerrilla warfare forced the British in 1922 to cede dominion status to the southern counties,[22] the Irish had a well stocked stable of politically experienced citizens able to operate the state's administrative machinery and institute full representative democracy.

A third and much more difficult transitional scenario occurs when there is a sea change in regimes within a state that has become quite complex and has in place a large and organized bureaucracy. After World War II, the Allies faced that kind of situation with Japan and the western zones of Germany, as did Spain during the mid-1970s. In 2003, Iraq presented Britain and the United States with a far more vexing set of problems in that the bureaucracy, almost all Sunnis in a country whose majority were Shia, was riddled with corruption and, except on matters of internal security, could not be compared in efficiency to the civil service of Germany or Japan.

In most respects, the Spanish had the least difficult tasks. The country had been enduring a prolonged economic crisis. Francisco Franco had stipulated that his successor as chief of state should be the young king Juan Carlos, and he, in turn, had insisted as a condition of his accepting the offer that the state become more democratic. It was clear enough to the remaining

---

speculators who had bought up land that Virginia had seized from Tories, the chief justice did not participate in the decision. For an account of the convoluted financial speculations behind this and similar cases, see Albert J. Beveridge, *The Life of John Marshall* (Boston: Houghton Mifflin, 1919), 4:145-67.

22. The constitutional text of 1923 was issued in the name of the Free State of Ireland. In contrast, the constitutional document of 1937 purports to speak for "Ireland," not merely the southern part of the island. Thus the correct name of the country is "Ireland," not "the Republic of Ireland." It is also technically incorrect to refer to the North as Ulster or the South as the twenty-six counties. The border between the two jurisdictions cuts across Ulster's historic provincial boundaries as well as those of several individual counties. The British desire to include as many Protestants in the North as possible took precedence over preserving old (and not always socially or economically relevant) borders. With that much said, it is common in Ireland to hear references to the Republic and to Ulster (or the Six Counties) for the area that remains under British domination.

Fascists, who had been increasing repression without lessening opposition, that to retain the old order would provoke another civil war. They therefore began negotiating a series of pacts with opposing groups and arranged for the peaceful transfer of power and their own safety and that of their families.[23] On the whole, Spanish bureaucrats understood what the future held for them and pretty much accepted the changed constitutional order. Basically, the new leaders found it necessary only to replace the political appointees in the administrative agencies and left the career officials in place.

The Japanese situation was also relatively simple, although it was hardly easy.[24] There was no cadre of exiles to return to power, as there was in Germany and, to a much lesser extent, in Iraq. On the other hand, for about forty years before the military effectively took over the government, Japan had been creeping toward parliamentary democracy. And during military rule, many of those elected politicians had continued to dance warily around the edges of power. After the war, they were anxious to return the country to its former system of limited representative democracy. Most important, they wanted the emperor to remain as de jure sovereign. MacArthur, however, would not allow, and knew that the Allied governments would not allow, the instauration of the old system. Furthermore, convinced that he understood "the oriental mind," he was anxious to act as the Great White Emperor who would preside over Japan's second great transformation. In so doing, he would teach his "children" to become good constitutional democrats. Many Japanese shared the general's opinion both of himself and of themselves and were ready to do much of his bidding. After all, the population, though basically literate, had been mostly passive receptors of a form of emperor (and state) worship. Individual autonomy had not been part of their culture.

The Japanese bureaucracy, built on the German model, had survived the war intact. It was professional and efficient and, although it had supported the military leaders, had always been careful to protect its own power and had generally been nonpartisan among political parties. Understanding what the victors expected, the Japanese themselves began weeding out ultranationalists from their administrative ranks, and SCAP speedily joined in these efforts. Two organizations received special attention. First, the Americans abolished the Home Ministry, which had been primarily responsible for internal security, and fired most of its senior officials. SCAP, of course, was deeply concerned about the political education that the rising generation would receive and therefore carefully vetted officials of the Ministry of Education as well as individual teachers.[25]

23. See Giuseppe Di Palma, *To Craft Democracies* (Berkeley: University of California Press, 1990).
24. See the literature cited in Chapter Five.
25. Later, when the cold war began, SCAP would again try to purge schoolteachers, this time to remove communists. See Ray A. Moore and Donald L. Robinson, *Partners for Democracy: Crafting*

As in the western zones of Germany, this sort of political cleansing produced some injustices and anomalies. Nevertheless, Japanese leaders and the Americans were careful not to impair basic bureaucratic efficiency. As a result, law and order prevailed; food, though in short supply, was more or less fairly distributed, and MacArthur's directives along with those of the new quasi-government of Japan were carried out expeditiously, usually by the Japanese themselves. Totally absent was the chaos that would beset Afghanistan and Iraq more than fifty-five years later—an absence that allowed Japan's transition to be completed rather smoothly. Equally important, when the occupation ended, the Japanese parliament could count on the civil service to use its wide-ranging discretion to help maintain constitutional democracy.[26]

The German situation threatened to be more complicated. Not only had the people lived under a brutal political system, but the dominant ideology of Aryan superiority had intoxicated masses of the population. The problems, however, turned out to be more practical than ideological. Their crushing military defeat disabused most Germans (as it would most Japanese a few months later) of illusions of the superiority of their tyrannical political system or their own supposed racial purity. Nevertheless, Germany's practical problems were immense. Although the country had had a disciplined bureaucracy, many, perhaps most, of these people were politically tainted, and the need for governance was urgent. Lower-level Nazis were necessary, as Victor Brombert has pointed out, "to ensure the streets were cleaned, to restore public utilities, and to maintain order."[27] Saturation bombings and invasions from both east and west had destroyed much of the country's infrastructure. Burned-out cities were full of bewildered, homeless, and hungry refugees as well as bewildered, homeless, and hungry soldiers returning to the ruins of their former lives.

Removing ex-Nazi officials from power was a logical first step toward constitutional democracy, and the Allies were quite successful in imprison-

---

the New Japanese State under MacArthur (New York: Oxford University Press, 2002), pp. 319–20; and Richard B. Finn, *Winners in Peace: MacArthur, Yoshida, and Postwar Japan* (Berkeley: University of California Press, 1992), pp. 232–34.

26. Both before and after World War II, the Japanese government has delegated broad discretionary powers to bureaucrats. But, J. Mark Ramseyer and Francis McCall Rosenbluth—*Japan's Political Marketplace* (Cambridge, MA: Harvard University Press, 1993)—argue that, at least since 1948, these administrators have by and large carried out policies that the prime minister and the cabinet choose, in part because elected officials have known how to use administrators' ambition as a means of control. Many senior bureaucrats aspire to become members of the Diet. (Sometimes about 25 percent of the Liberal Democrats in the House of Representatives have been retired civil servants. Robert Ward, *Japan's Political System,* 2nd ed. [Englewood Cliffs, NJ: Prentice-Hall, 1978], p. 166.) And it is the leaders of the LDP who determine who enters electoral politics from within their party, giving them a useful weapon to ensure bureaucratic fidelity.

27. *Trains of Thought: Memories of a Stateless Youth* (New York: W. W. Norton, 2002), p. 314.

ing and/or executing the Reich's chief leaders. At lower levels, however, almost all officials had been contaminated by loyal service to Hitler's regime, as had many of their potential replacements, and there were not enough exiles with the skills needed to restaff the bureaucracy. To cope with this double difficulty of great demand and small supply, the Allied High Command began a policy of denazification: punishing some officials, firing others, and trying to reeducate the rest. Rooting out minor Nazis, however, raised its own difficulties. A thorough purging not only would have embarrassed efforts to create a myth that "good" Germans had never supported Hitler but would also have made governance impossible without an infusion of many thousands of American, French, and British personnel, something that was not going to happen at the end of a long and expensive war.

In the short run, denazification in the Western Zones fell far short of complete success. Although Victor Brombert was overly harsh in dismissing the program as "a joke," it was sorely beset by uneven enforcement and spackled with grants of amnesty whose logic often escaped the forgiven and unforgiven alike. Once the Allies delegated the cleansing to the emerging Federal Republic, Konrad Adenauer quietly backed away, preferring a policy of reconciliation to retribution. One's Nazi past, as Richard Merritt put it, was no longer "a topic for conversation." Yet few high-level Nazis returned to office. The overall result was that the men who came to the upper levels of power "were by and large the traditional national conservatives of the Wilhelmine Reich and the Weimar Republic. Denazification, then, rather than bringing about a thorough reevaluation and something new, merely contributed to the restoration of the pre-1933 condition."[28] Nevertheless, these new German leaders, Adenauer most famously, were often exiles or members of the resistance. They had come of political age under the kaiser or Weimar, but they had learned from Weimar's mistakes. In both the constitutional text they drafted and the political system they operated, this old guard tried to profit from their country's horrific experience.

Death, retirement, and prudence completed the massive change the Allies had wanted. Bureaucracy may be immortal, but individual bureaucrats are not. Eventually, ex-Nazi officials found it necessary to die or retire. Either choice created vacancies for a younger, differently oriented generation. And during the time when former Nazis and their collaborators remained in lower administrative offices, most either came to believe in constitutional democracy or were slick enough to conceal their disagreements.

28. Richard L. Merritt, *Democracy Imposed: U.S. Occupation Policy and the German Public, 1945–1949* (New Haven, CT: Yale University Press, 1995), p. 202; see also ch. 7 generally. As he does with other topics throughout the book, Merritt layers his analysis of denazification with the results of public opinion polls that the American military government financed in order to monitor its progress in converting the Germans to constitutional democracy.

Soon, the Federal Republic's bureaucratic system was operating as an instrument of constitutional democracy. Every administrator may not have always advanced that cause, but as a group these officials furthered the goals of the new constitutional order.

The Allies' preference for law and order over more efficient punishment of Nazis looks less unwise in the aftermath of the campaign against Saddam Hussein in 2003. By Arab standards, the Iraqi bureaucracy had been quite efficient. But when American forces invaded, those officials, like the soldiers, disappeared or were later fired. Many weeks after the capture of Baghdad, only seven thousand of the usual complement of forty thousand police were on duty. As garbage piled up in the streets and food supplies ran low, riots erupted in every major city. Looters, joined by professional criminals, plundered banks, private businesses, hospitals, libraries, museums, and archaeological sites, stripped power plants of equipment, raided arsenals and ammunition depots, and even stole radioactive materials from atomic plants. Soon heavily armed bands of guerrillas, some loyal followers of Saddam Hussein and others terrorists from other nations who slipped across porous borders to continue their jihad, began to appear, killing and wounding British and American troops, Iraqi civilians, and officials who cooperated with the coalition.

Despite warnings from the U.S. Department of State, scholars, and journalists that peace in Iraq would be at least as difficult to wage as war, the Department of Defense had seemed blithely unaware that anarchy would flourish in the rubble of a viciously tyrannical regime. Rejecting aid from the United Nations and its professionals as well as its own military experts in civil government, the Bush administration relied for many months on political amateurs and combat troops to govern Iraq, a clumsy combination that surrendered the opportunity to quickly lay solid foundations for a benign political system. Eventually, the coalition rehired Baathists from the ranks of senior and middle-level bureaucrats to run day-to-day governmental operations.

After 1989, the situation in most countries in the former Soviet bloc was more like that of post–World War II Germany than Iraq. A large and experienced bureaucracy, though of doubtful efficiency and wee integrity, was in place. Brombert's comment about needing incumbents was echoed by a former Polish communist official as the old regime began to crumble: "They will need us to run the government. We're the only people who know how."[29] The new Polish regime accepted this fact of life and, by and large, left the old officials in place. For a time, the Czech Republic, Hungary, and the

29. Then Professor, later Senator, Jerzy Wiatr during a seminar at Princeton sponsored by the Bouton Fund, 1990.

newly united Germany used variations of lustration to try to purge not only the bureaucracy but also elected officials.[30] As the next chapter will point out, however, this weapon fired buckshot more often than bullets.

Both before and after the collapse of the Soviet empire, one of the greater complications was corruption. Especially in Russia, managers of state firms —part of the *nomenklatura* in the socialist systems—quickly demonstrated an exuberant spirit of capitalistic entrepreneurship by cheaply buying shares in their old firms, selling them dearly, and making themselves rich off surplus value. As governmental assets evaporated, performing honest civil service became the functional equivalent of taking a vow of poverty—hardly an incentive for ambitious people of talent and integrity to follow careers in public administration. Seventeen years after the collapse of the Soviet empire, creating an honest and efficient civil service remained a work very much in progress, with problems of corruption probably even greater than those of efficiency. A survey of Polish public opinion in 2003 showed that 70 percent of respondents believed that corruption was a huge problem—a percentage that had been steadily increasing over the years.[31] According to Transparency International's ratings for 2005, Russia ranked 126th in the world in honest government, Hungary fortieth, the Czech Republic forty-seventh, Poland seventieth, and Belarus and Ukraine 137th.[32] This propensity to carry out public policies only when bribed has impeded a transition to constitutional democracy as well as maintenance of the still developing system.

A fourth situation, a variation on the third, involves a dramatic change of regimes where a large and competent body of administrators outside the country is ready to restaff at least the upper bureaucratic ranks. The reunification of Germany presented such a scene in 1990. Although few West German leaders were old enough to have had firsthand experience with denazification, they knew it had been less than fully successful and were determined to be more thorough in cleansing the East German bureaucracy of committed communists. Regardless of whether decommunization was as ruthless as many East Germans thought,[33] it was certainly more swift and effective than denazification had been in the West. The outline of the two strategies was similar, however: some officials were tried on criminal charges;

---

30. Hungary made public "lustrable" offenders only if the person involved wished to gain or retain a governmental post. See Gábor Halmai and Kim Lane Scheppele, "Living Well Is the Best Revenge," in A. James McAdams, ed., *Transitional Justice and the Rule of Law in the New Democracies* (Notre Dame, IN: University of Notre Dame Press, 1997), p. 172.

31. "Enough! Corruption in Poland," *Economist*, Apr. 19, 2003, pp. 44-45.

32. www.transparency.org/policy_research/surveys_indices/cpi/2005.

33. The two best studies in English of the East's transition are McAdams, "Communism on Trial," and Jennifer A. Yoder, *From East Germans to Germans? The New Postcommunist Elites* (Durham, NC: Duke University Press, 1999). Wolfgang Seibel has collected an excellent bibliography: "Administrative Science as Reform: German Public Administration," 56 *Pub. Admin. Rev.* 74, 79-81 (1996).

more were fired; others chose to quit to preserve a modicum of respect or their pension; the rest were "reeducated." Other than West German efficiency, the most visible difference between the two policies was heavy use of outside administrators who were native speakers of German and experienced in operating a constitutional democracy. The Federal Republic transferred about twenty-five thousand of its own civil servants to supervisory posts in the East.[34]

A fifth situation may occur where the change in regimes is drastic, most old civil servants exit or are imprisoned, and few trained replacements are available. Such was the general condition of Sub-Saharan Africa at independence. Constitutional democracy was alien to the region before, during, and after colonial rule. Until Namibia became independent in 1990 and South Africa rid itself of apartheid shortly after, no indigenous leader had any experience in or desire to foster constitutional democracy. Many of these new rulers were sergeants who had become instant generals. Furthermore, few trained personnel were available to administer any kind of regime other than a plunderocracy. Most European officials either chose to go home or were forced to leave their posts; and seldom had the French, and even less often the British, trained locals to run a government. The Belgians' record in this regard was the worst. When they left the Congo, only seventeen blacks were graduates of universities. Under all versions of colonial rule, it had been rare for an African to rise above the status of janitor, chauffeur, or NCO. *Uhuru* and transitions to local rule produced many constitutional texts that promised constitutionalism along with democracy, but the new leaders had no interest in such arrangements, and no administrators were available to make such a state a reality, even had these rulers taken their constitutional documents seriously.[35]

As bad as was the situation in Sub-Saharan Africa, that in Afghanistan after the Russians withdrew in 1989 was worse, so much so that it fits into a sixth category for situations in which the initial task is to create a state and government of whatever variety. Afghanistan was one of those countries ("nation" may imply more than is warranted) in which "governments simply do not govern."[36] Historically, the state had been anemic. What passed for governance was as much feral as feudal. Jealous, suspicious to the point of paranoia, and heavily armed warlords dominated separate fiefdoms, with

34. Many, perhaps most, of these officials volunteered for duty in the East.

35. See H. W. O. Okoth-Ogendo, "Constitutions without Constitutionalism: Reflections on an African Political Paradox," in Douglas Greenberg, Stanley N. Katz, Melanie Beth Oliviero, and Steven C. Wheatley, eds., *Constitutionalism and Democracy: Transformations in the Contemporary World* (New York: Oxford University Press, 1993).

36. Samuel P. Huntington, *Political Order in Changing Societies* (New Haven, CT: Yale University Press, 1968), p. 2. See also Joel S. Migdal, "Studying the Politics of Development and Change: The State of the Art," in Ada W. Finifter, ed., *Political Science: The State of the Discipline* (Washington, DC: American Political Science Association, 1983).

little more than pious nods toward a supposed central government in Kabul. There had been small reason to do more: tribal leaders sometimes had bigger and better equipped armies than the central government. Even the Russian-supported communists had not been able to create a state apparatus whose efficiency approached that of the Soviet republics—not a high standard. After the Russians left, a civil war—with feuds among *qwans* (tribes) exacerbated by various brands of religious fanaticism—ravaged the country.

Eventually, the Taliban won out, although they never succeeded in subjugating all the rival warlords. (*Talib* or *taleb* means "student of religious matters.") In politics, the Taliban viewed the state as a set of godless institutions to be destroyed, not transformed. In religious affairs, they demanded strict, literal applications of the Qur'an and the Shari'a, with *literal* defined as conforming to the teachings of the Deobandi movement, a Sunni group in whose schools many Taliban leaders had studied in Pakistan.[37] Gangs of vicious juvenile delinquents, dubbed the Vice/Virtue Police, were encouraged to enforce the Shari'a by beatings in the streets, relieving the Taliban of much of the work of maintaining its version of law and order. Social services were largely relegated to individuals' acts of charity, while commerce was pretty much left free, regulated mainly by levies on trade, especially on shipments of heroin destined for Western nations. With television, radio, and alcohol forbidden, the ruling circle provided popular entertainment through public punishments in soccer stadiums: amputations for thieves, stonings for women caught in adultery, and executions for murderers, carried out by members of the victims' families. There was little need for a foreign ministry. What passed as government maintained conventional diplomatic relations with only Pakistan and the United Arab Emirates, the first being the Taliban's religious and economic benefactor, the second its principal trading partner.[38]

In politicoreligious affairs, the Taliban practiced violence not only against infidels and apostates but also against heretics. As Gilles Kepel has put it,

---

37. Variously described as a movement, a sect, a brotherhood, a school, or all four, the Deobandi began in nineteenth-century India. When the British carved the subcontinent into two countries, the sect took firm root in Pakistan, where the government tried to woo members into an alliance with the regime. In addition to the Islamic faith, they shared hostility toward Hinduism, especially Hindu nationalism, and, as Sunnis, bitter, often violent enmity toward Shi'ite Muslims. For analyses, see Gilles Kepel, *Jihad: The Trail of Political Islam* (Cambridge, MA: Harvard University Press, 2002), pp. 223–24; Ahmed Rashid, *Taliban: Militant Islam, Oil, and Fundamentalism* (New Haven, CT: Yale University Press, 2001); and Muhammad Qasim Zaman, *The Ulama in Contemporary Islam: Custodians of Change* (Princeton, NJ: Princeton University Press, 2003). For a description of the Deobandi madrassah (religious school) in Pakistan that trained many Taliban, see Jessica Stern, *Terror in the Name of God* (New York: HarperCollins, 2003), pp. 222–36.

38. For a clear discussion, at least as clear as a muddled situation allows, of the relationships among the Taliban, various other Afghani factions, the Deobandi, the Wahhabites, Osama bin Laden, and the Saudi royal family, see Kepel, *Jihad*, pp. 217–36.

they "devoutly massacred the ungodly,"[39] a category heavily populated in-country by Shi'ite Muslims. Given the close theological relationship be-tween the Taliban's Deobandite beliefs and those of the Wahhabi sect of Saudi Arabia, many of whose members had fought against the Russians and then remained in Afghanistan, there was an easy fit between the Taliban's leaders and Osama bin Laden's Wahhabite Al Qaeda. The target merely shifted from heretical Muslims to Western infidels, an ironic change in that, as had the mujahedeen generally, the Taliban had greatly benefited during the war against Russia from material and financial aid from the CIA.[40]

Thus, after the American invasion in 2003, those people who wished to establish civil governance in Afghanistan faced massive obstacles. Constitu-tional democracy lay far down the road, decades beyond the range of any mortal's political radar. The initial—and mind-numbing—task was to forge, not merely reform, a state with authority that could, if not control its terri-tory, at least bring the various warlords into some sort of peaceful coopera-tion.[41] There were, however, few locals trained to serve as organizers or even assistants in this creative undertaking and even fewer warlords who were willing to trust their rivals to share in governance. Moreover, the East-West German option was not open. With the possible exception of Pakistan, which was having its own difficulties with violent fundamentalist sects, no Muslim country had a cohort of trained, Pashto-speaking administrative officials who might be loaned to Afghanistan. More than four years after American and tribal forces dispersed the Taliban, governing Afghanistan remained a shaky affair.

In contrast to the miserable administrative legacy Europeans bequeathed black Africa and the confused situations in Afghanistan and Iraq, the British left India a useful bureaucratic inheritance. Long before independence, they had operated a Western-style state, transplanting European institutions and transforming some traditional Indian ways. Then, too, British higher educa-tion was open to an occasional young Indian male who was extraordinarily well qualified. (Nehru graduated from Cambridge, Gandhi from University College, London.) And however niggardly and discriminatory the local educational system was, it did produce a literate elite among hundreds of millions of illiterates and semiliterates. In addition, the British trained and employed thousands of literate locals as civil servants. Although these men

39. Ibid., p. 229.

40. For an interesting account of the machinations of Representative Charles Wilson (D-TX) and maverick CIA agent Gust Avrakotos in pushing the agency to intervene, see Crile, *Charlie Wilson's War*.

41. See, for example, Barnett R. Rubin, *The Fragmentation of Afghanistan*, 2nd ed. (New Haven, CT: Yale University Press, 2002), and "Crafting a Constitution for Afghanistan," 15 *J. of Democ.* 3 (2004); and Seymour M. Hersh, "The Other War: Why Bush's Afghanistan Problems Won't Go Away," *New Yorker*, Apr. 12, 2004. (I used the online version, www.newyorker.com/printable/?fact/040412fa_fact.)

typically held lower-level jobs, some rose to responsible positions and understood the complexities of managing a modern state. Thus, when independence came, a sizable number of Indians were professionally equipped to administer government. They often overmanaged, but at least they knew something of the tasks they were supposed to be performing. This difference in availability of a trained public service between India, on the one hand, and Sub-Saharan Africa and Afghanistan, on the other, does not account for all of the variance in the fate of constitutional democracy among those nations, but it does explain a great deal.

Although the German option was not open to leaders who wished to transform the Afghani and Iraqi political systems, it could become a possibility in other settings. Most obvious would be South Korean assistance to North Korea, if its Dear Leader, Kim Jong Il, ever decided to end totalitarian rule. Although no Arab government has yet adopted constitutional democracy or has a system of public administration that West Europeans would deem very efficient or honest,[42] several countries have a civil service that, by standards of the Arab world, is sophisticated. Under some circumstances, the Saudi or Moroccan government might be willing to loan some administrators to other Arabic-speaking countries to help organize what in the developed world have become basic state functions.

Another pair of possibilities is open to leaders of nations in the fifth and sixth categories. One is to engage not-for-profit NGOs and/or individual freelancers to assist during the transition in establishing a civil service to maintain constitutional democracy. (The back pages of the *Economist* are usually studded with advertisements by such organizations, private and public.) Alternatively or additionally, officials could request the United Nations to send in teams of experts to help run (or even create) the state's administrative apparatus and train local citizens to operate governmental offices.[43]

Although the United Nations employs specialists in fields as varied as banking, fiscal policy, health, agriculture, care of refugees, and control of narcotics, it does not have a permanent corps of generalists. Still, it can summon a large number of experts to the equivalent of active duty. Some of these people may have retired from public service. For instance, Hans Blix, who led the UN inspection teams in Iraq, had been Sweden's foreign minis-

---

42. For a discussion of the Egyptian bureaucracy, see Michael Field, *Inside the Arab World* (Cambridge, MA: Harvard University Press, 1995), esp. ch. 11. Because civil servants make up a large portion of the country's middle class, which the government cannot afford to alienate, leaders must tolerate a large degree of both inefficiency and corruption.

43. This section owes much to the knowledge and insights of my fellow emeritus from Princeton University, Leon Gordenker. Not only has he written and taught extensively about international organization in general and the United Nations in particular, he has also served as an official of and adviser to several UN agencies. See esp. Leon Gordenker, *International Aid and National Decisions: Development Programs in Malawi, Tanzania, and Zambia* (Princeton, NJ: Princeton University Press, 1976).

ter. Others may have run more specific programs of technical assistance. Still other such people may be employed by national governments, NGOs, private businesses, or universities. Indeed, there is a steady circulation of scholars from universities to national governments to NGOs to the United Nations and back again to universities. Many of these people combine scientific expertise with academic accomplishments and practical experience.

Furthermore, the United Nations has used its own personnel to provide general as well as specific forms of assistance. The United Nations' Expanded Program of Technical Assistance has helped nations train their own administrators. During the early 1960s, for example, Secretary General U Thant sent a mission to the Congo that actually ran what passed for a civil service so that local citizens could learn how to perform elementary state functions. Perhaps more successful over the long term will be the United Nations intervention in Kosovo following NATO's expelling the Serbian army. In 1999, the Security Council directed the UN mission there to assume responsibility for all executive, judicial, and legislative functions, with special instructions to build up the country's governmental institutions. The scope of that mandate "was mind boggling," including health, education, energy and public utilities, post and telecommunications. judicial, legal, public finance, trade, science, agriculture, environment, and democratization.[44]

None of these alternatives promises a panacea. Using loaners from friendly governments, the United Nations, or private firms is at best a stopgap measure. Soon a new constitutional democracy must pursue a mutually reinforcing set of policies: at the same time that it tries to remove those bureaucrats who enthusiastically carried out the old regime's policies, it must reeducate those who merely carried out orders. For the long run, it will be necessary to recruit, train, and politically socialize fresh generations of administrators. Initially, the essential element would be a national system of secondary education that graduates literate young men and women who understand basic science, mathematics, and civics. Given the educational standards of many developing countries, creating such a system could itself be a major undertaking, one requiring considerable outside assistance and thus further delaying complete patriation of the public service. Graduates of these institutions would have to be encouraged to continue their education either in universities within the country (if any exist) or abroad. If the latter is the only or wiser choice, the state would have to subsidize and certainly monitor these courses of study.

A new constitutional democracy may have to seek foreign aid to pay for educating its people abroad or even at home. The United Nations offers one

44. See, generally, Simon Chesterman, *You, the People: Transitional Administration and State Building* (New York: Oxford University Press, 2004); and, more specifically, David P. Forsythe, Roger A. Coate, and Thomas G. Weiss, *The United Nations and Changing World Politics,* 3rd ed. (Boulder: Westview, 2001), p. 99.

obvious source of support, as might friendly nations. At one time the Albert Parvin Foundation ran a small program for potential leaders of developing nations, and from time to time the Ford Foundation sponsors such study. Other foundations might offer similar help. Individual universities in more affluent nations might also be persuaded to participate, at least to the extent of providing scholarships. To be successful, such programs must meet at least two conditions. First, the people sent abroad must agree to return home after completing their studies, and the host nation must agree to enforce that commitment, lest the new constitutional democracy suffer the sort of brain drain that afflicted less prosperous countries during the 1950s and 1960s when they sent students to American universities, who then decided to remain abroad. Second, the number of people involved has to be large. How large depends on the size of the bureaucracy needed to run the state and the extent to which incumbents must be removed or reeducated. A trickle of a few new recruits will be almost useless. They might rock the old system initially but are likely soon to be absorbed into it. Enough personnel must return together so that they can have a collective impact on the existing administrative system and do so within a very few years. They must change the system, create a new "organizational culture,"[45] reshape its values and goals, not merely improve its efficiency. To accomplish this sort of transformation, they will need the regime's leaders to intervene frequently and intelligently in the bureaucracy's internal affairs.

If the new political system were to enjoy the political leisure of developing slowly and gradually taking on the functions of most modern states, it might be able to begin by relying, as the British historically have,[46] on broadly educated officials rather than technically trained experts to staff and direct agencies. Even so, broadly educated administrators would need masses of technical information—and, more important, understanding—in one or more such specialized fields as education, engineering, electronics, energy, health care, public finance, and management. Because the complexities of modern science make it impossible for anyone to become expert in more than one or two of such fields, government would have to borrow, rent, or co-opt private experts who would work either outside the chain of command as consultants or within that chain as employees.

Soon the new regime must reorganize and deepen the professionalization of the civil service and, either alone or in conjunction with private universities, establish national institutions of higher learning to train personnel to manage administrative agencies. The former Soviet satellites of Eastern Europe were slow to make either move and paid a severe price in governmen-

---

45. The term is James Q. Wilson's: *Bureaucracy*, pp. 91–93.

46. Development of the British public service was neither smooth nor always easy. See, for example, Henry Parris, *Constitutional Bureaucracy: The Development of British Central Administration Since the Eighteenth Century* (London: Allen and Unwin, 1969).

tal efficiency as well as in loss of public trust. France's École Nationale d'Administration provides a model for a public institution that is elitist and rigorous, dedicated to training higher-level civil servants, while American universities provide equally elitist education that is less rigorous but broader: Princeton's Woodrow Wilson School, Syracuse's Maxwell School, Harvard's Kennedy School, and Georgetown's Foreign Service Institute are among the better known. Business schools, although their graduates' targets are almost always in private profit-making enterprises, can also provide training useful in the public sphere. Graduates of all of these programs are more apt to know a little bit about several specialized technical fields and to realize their complex connections to public policy than to be experts. Nevertheless, sophisticated understanding of the interconnections among public policy, private profits, and various scientific fields is necessary for an effective senior bureaucrat in a private or public organization.

The elitist nature of selection and education for efficient bureaucratic operations can cause problems with democratic notions of equality. On the one hand, as Max Weber pointed out, screening public administrators through examinations replaces older rule by economically or socially advantaged persons with rule by the most qualified. On the other hand, "democracy fears that examinations and patents of education will create a privileged 'caste,' and for that reason opposes such a system."[47] This fear is not groundless. Performance on academic tests often reflects parents' socioeconomic status and the opportunities such a background provides as well as intellectual power and thus, while identifying persons with high ability, may perpetuate a traditional form of inequality.

Not far down the road in a diverse society's life under constitutional democracy, leaders are likely to encounter a more particular and emotionally charged version of this conundrum in the issue of representation—in the sense of both "standing for" and "chosen from," though not in the sense of "chosen by"—within the bureaucracy, judicial as well as executive, of various social and ethnic groups.[48] This problem also occurs in legislatures, but there it can be partially addressed by an electoral system based on proportional

47. *Economy and Society: An Outline of Interpretive Sociology* (New York: Bedminster, 1969), 3:999. Joseph Schumpeter, himself an elitist, claims that "bureaucracy is not an obstacle to democracy but an inevitable complement to it." *Capitalism, Socialism, and Democracy*, 3rd ed. (New York: Harper and Brothers, 1950), p. 206.

48. For a superb study of this problem within the French bureaucracy, see Suleiman, *Politics, Power, and Bureaucracy*, esp. chs. 2–5. For analysis of representation on courts, see Walter F. Murphy and Joseph Tanenhaus, *The Study of Public Law* (New York: Random House, 1971), pp. 37–38. In the United States, it is now accepted that there will be at least one Jew, one Catholic (as of February 2006, there were five Catholic justices), one African-American, and one woman on the Supreme Court. There is also a tradition that presidents will consider geography in nominating justices. In Ireland, part of the unspoken, but often spoken about, agreement between Catholics and Protestants is that at least one of the members of both the Supreme Court and the High Court will be Protestant. Canada has legislated that three of the nine justices of the Supreme Court will be from Quebec.

representation with set-asides for small minorities. Within a bureaucracy the difficulties are less tractable, making it quite possible that the regime will have to institute some form of preferential hiring and promotion. And by whatever name affirmative action is called, it poses serious questions of both fairness and efficiency.

Although no one has a legal right to an administrative post or training for an administrative career, government's denying education, employment, or promotion to people solely on grounds of ethnicity offends constitutional democracy's ideal of equality before the law. Furthermore, government's educating, hiring, or promoting the less qualified over the more qualified is not likely to advance efficiency. On the other hand, a plausible argument that the state is being run by and for certain groups would weaken trust and possibly even threaten stability. Resolving competing claims of talent, equal treatment, and fair representation requires a degree of political acumen and imagination that has so far been beyond the reach of most American officials. They continue, however, to grope awkwardly, and sometimes bravely, with the problem.[49]

Three points stand out in this analysis. First, creating a bureaucracy staffed by people who are reasonably efficient and, at very least, not hostile to constitutional democracy is likely to be extremely difficult, requiring skill and patience.[50] Second, however slow, even tedious, may be the labor of restaffing the state's administrative agencies, it is absolutely necessary. No less than other regimes, to survive a constitutional democracy must be able to have most of its public policies transformed into public realities. Third, whether or not "a professionally trained, rationally structured, and achievement-oriented" bureaucracy is a "functional prerequisite" to constitutional democracy,[51] it is certainly necessary to its maintenance. Whatever transitional expedients new leaders utilize to operate governmental agencies, they must quickly enlist and train a fresh cadre of local citizens or at least instill in incumbent agents a willingness to abide by the new constitutional order's basic principles. Either course must entail instilling in administrators professional standards of competence and integrity. These latter center on the belief

49. The U.S. Supreme Court has done little better than elected officials in rationalizing specific policies of affirmative action as fitting under the Constitution—or, as critics might insist, rationalizing the Constitution to legitimate affirmative action. Compare Grutter v. Bollinger, 539 U.S. 306 (2003), with Gratz v. Bollinger, 539 U.S. 244 (2003).

50. Opposition and hostility differ. In 1966, when working in the basement of the Four Courts in Dublin, the building that houses the Supreme Court—a cold, damp set of rooms in which the unpublished opinions (about 90 percent of the Court's total output) were stored—I befriended the Court's clerk. After a week or so, he confessed that he was opposed to judicial review and much preferred judicially unfettered parliamentary democracy. As far as I could tell from what I saw and from frequent conversations in the homes of several of the justices, the clerk's personal opinions did not influence his professional work.

51. Robert Ward claimed that such an administrative apparatus is a prerequisite: *Japan's Political System*, p. 207.

that a public office is a public trust created for the public purpose of carrying out public policies in a fair, even-handed fashion. Not only should it not be exploited for personal gain, neither should it be used to help family and friends.

It is improbable that, until decades had elapsed, a new constitutional democracy could sculpt an administrative system that could compare in efficiency with that of France or Germany, but the new public service must soon be able to cope with basic problems of law and order, public finance, regulation of economic affairs, and fair distribution of public goods and services. Individually each of these tasks is enormous; together they are truly daunting. Making matters even more difficult is the likelihood of rising expectations: as the system settles in, citizens are apt to expect more from officials and raise their standards for judging adequate performance.

Judicial Personnel

In countries that have lived under various versions of the Civil Law, judges as well as procurators—the latter, as Chapter Seven pointed out, function somewhat differently from prosecutors under the common law—typically follow clearly marked professional careers much like those of civil servants. They must undergo a fixed curriculum during and after education at a university, pass examinations to prove their competence, receive specified salaries for each rank to which they rise, and submit to frequent evaluations to determine promotion. Once they gain tenure, if they do not become grossly incompetent or commit crimes, they can remain in service until they reach the retirement age established by law.

These officials, like other bureaucrats, are supposedly experts who impartially administer the legal system. Among the putative fundamental principles of the Civil Law have been the scientific nature of legal reasoning and the political neutrality of judges, which, coming together, constitute judges as artisans rather than innovators in the common-law tradition. The Legislator, a noun that is always singular and masculine, is sovereign. "He" makes the law, judges merely interpret it. Legal interpretation is supposedly scientific: "the law" is contained in the more or less complete, logically ordered codes the Legislator has enacted. When carefully analyzed, this corpus, which contain a hierarchy of norms, yields one, and only one, correct answer to any legal question. Where a code has lacunae, judges should use its general principles to deduce the applicable rule from the specific provisions.[52]

52. This image of the law and the consequent restricted roles of judges and procurators help explains what led Hans Kelsen to conceive the idea of a constitutional court. He could, with real hope of success, help keep alive the myth that judges were the mere mouths of the law insofar as "normal" cases involving criminal and civil law were involved. But to speak of judges as no more than skilled mechanics when interpreting a constitution strained credulity. And he saw great advantages in having a tribunal that could curb possible excesses of democratically elected governments. Thus,

The fate of these supposedly neutral, scientific judges could pose serious problems for a neonatal constitutional democracy. They may have been happy servants of the old regime, rigorously prosecuting and enforcing its oppressive laws and decrees. To keep them in office may well both enrage their victims and allow these officials to sabotage the norms of constitutional democracy. On the other hand, according to the principles under which they were trained, selected, and promoted, the function of judges and prosecutors is to enforce the letter of the law, not to attempt to ameliorate its terms. Indeed, to have tried to do would have violated the principles of the Civil Law, for "the law" is a logically coherent pyramid. Its general principles are stated, along with the more specific precepts that follow. For a judge to attempt to soften the law's provisions would disrupt its logical coherence, create injustices, and usurp the Legislator's authority. Thus to hold judges and procurators criminally accountable for having followed the positivistic norms of the Civil Law hardly seems just. For leaders who are trying to educate their people in the norms of fairness that constitutional democracy proclaims, the dilemma may be damnably real.

Turning judges and prosecutors out of office may be less unjust, but that option may seem unfair as well as unwise. A purge might convey the message that shrewd judicial bureaucrats should anticipate who will eventually win political struggles and tailor their decisions to please the winners—not a message that is in keeping with the principles of the Civil Law (or the common law or the Shari'a, for that matter). An alternative message is almost as violative of the Civil Law's norms: either do not act in a politically neutral way or resign rather than enforce the law of an authoritarian regime. This policy, of course, also suffers from the defects of toadying to actual or prospective political winners and is retrospective, raising questions about the constitutional legitimacy of ex post facto regulations. Besides, for judges and procurators serving under a tyrannical regime resignation may not be a viable option. "He who is not with me is against me" has been the policy of many brutal governments. Furthermore, resignations might have meant replacement with officials who were true believers in the despots' ideology and were ready to enforce harsh laws so as to discriminate against people who believed in a more civil society.

As a practical matter, mass firings could leave a vacuum in a new constitutional democracy: the judicial branch of government would be unable to function without judges and procurators. The obvious alternatives—military tribunals, courts operated by untrained personnel, or allowing individuals to

---

alongside the "ordinary" courts, he proposed that the Austrian constitutional text include a special court with exclusive jurisdiction over constitutional interpretation. Its members would be chosen, for specified terms, by the legislature and/or executive, not through the usual entrance requirements established for the judicial branch of government. These people would be more analogous to judges in common law systems.

impose whatever remedies they think fitting—are all unattractive. A common law system might have an easier time, because judges and prosecutors have seldom had any professional training other than as practicing lawyers. So, too, a country applying the Shari'a would probably have a large pool of religious scholars to staff the courts. It is difficult, however, to imagine a regime that had constitutionalist aspirations applying the Shari'a.

Kálmán Kulcsár, when he was Hungary's minister of justice during the final stages of the ancien régime, the era of "goulash communism," and the early days of the new system, devised a commonsense policy. The old regime had mellowed during its final two decades. Most of the judges and procurators had been interpreting the laws about as fairly as one can enforce unfair rules. But some older judicial personnel had been closely associated with the repressions of the late 1950s and early 1960s and had gone beyond the letter of the law to punish dissidents. Kulcsár's policy was simple: leave alone those jurists who had been impartially applying the old laws. To the others he gave a choice: immediate retirement or criminal prosecution for abusing their authority. Not surprisingly, they all retired.

In the long run, which may have to be quite short, a new constitutional democracy must train a new generation of judges and procurators. To help in that process, the government may—once more—have to seek assistance from other nations and perhaps the United Nations as well. At very least, it is probable that a fledgling constitutional democracy would have to borrow some faculty and public officials from more mature regimes to help with professional training in what would be expected of judicial personnel in a civil society.

So far we have been assuming that the old political system had operated within a nation-state and had coherently, if unhappily, organized legal institutions staffed with more or less competent officials. That assumption may not hold in Afghanistan, in Iraq, and perhaps in Sub-Saharan Africa. The problem there would be less how to reorganize and restaff administrative and judicial institutions and, more fundamentally, how to create a nation whose inhabitants have a sense of belonging to that larger entity rather than being members of a tribe or extended family. That sense could allow growth of common bonds, of citizenship and fellowship beyond kinship. Only then would it be possible to think about creating a political culture conducive to constitutional democracy and to consider how to construct institutions to make and carry out public policy.

One might reasonably contend, of course, that absence of a sense of belonging to a nation-state in Afghanistan and Africa[53] is necessarily dysfunctional for the flowering of a civil society. Along with the good nation-

---

53. Even though Iraq has survived more than seven decade as a nation, American blunders, exacerbated by ancient ethnic and sectarian conflicts, converted many inhabitants to act more as Shiites, Sunnis, or Kurds than as Iraqis.

states have done there has been much evil, including wars and organized oppression. Perhaps skipping that stage of political development and moving directly to a form of regionalism among Muslims in western Asia and Sub-Saharan Africa would further many of the values that constitutional democracy proclaims. But such regional communities would confront all the same problems of creating and maintaining a polity that nation-states face. First would be the necessity of having a group of energetic, politically astute, and dedicated leaders who would devote their lives to achieving a just political order.[54] Second would be relationships between Islam and secular government. The Qur'an might not pose a serious obstacle, but the Shari'a, as currently interpreted, erects an insuperable barrier.

54. See the discussion in Chapters Two and Three.

CHAPTER THIRTEEN

Dealing with Deposed Despots

An extreme justice is extreme injustice.   CICERO

Reconciliation means we have to meet halfway. I was wronged and almost my entire family was killed. I care about justice and truth.
                    HARIS SILAJDZE, FOREIGN MINISTER OF BOSNIA

The old regime's legacy to constitutional democracy is likely to include the problem of dealing with former officials. The happiest solution for the new political order is for all the former chief officials and whoever among their minions abused their subjects to escape into exile. That event, of course, is improbable. Even if the hegemon and his immediate entourage escape, the hundreds, perhaps thousands, of people who operated within the upper echelons of the government are not likely to get away. Stay-behinds pose a serious and difficult problem for leaders who are committed to constitutionalist norms, especially if they face widespread, impassioned, demands for retribution. Several options, some of which can be used in combination, are obvious: (1) through formal decree or inaction, let the ghosts (and the criminals) of the recent past to fade into history; (2) expose the old oppressors to the community's scorn; (3) offer amnesty on condition of full and public confessions; (4) initiate criminal prosecutions.[1]

The Principal Options
Blanket Amnesty and Social Shame

Ex-officials may have may bargained with the new leaders for amnesty in exchange for a peaceful surrender of power. This kind of agreement may be explicit or implicit. In Spain and later in Hungary, it was "understood" that there would be no reprisals against the survivors of the Fascist and communist regimes, though the Hungarians were somewhat more willing than the

---

1. For a massive collection of documents, see the multivolume work edited by Neil J. Kritz, *Transitional Justice: New Emerging Nations Reckon with Former Regimes* (Washington, DC: U.S. Institute of Peace, 1995).

Spaniards to make exceptions to this general policy.[2] It could also happen, as it did to a great extent in the Russian Federation and to a lesser extent in Poland, that the budding constitutional democracy decides pretty much on its own to ignore former oppressors. The chief security personnel can be fired (although few KGB were immediately discharged)[3] and other offenders left to social sanctions. The rationale would be that it is more important to build unity than to wallow in divisive hatred.

Lustration, used as a form of political vetting and social shaming, offers a second alternative. Originally the term referred to the ritual purification that ancient Romans underwent after each census. Christians later applied it to any sacramental cleansing from sin, as, for instance, baptism.[4] Popular for a time in Eastern and Central Europe after 1989, the policy involved opening the archives of the secret police and allowing information about who had been doing what to whom to become public knowledge. The objective was not merely to shame people who had helped the secret police but, more broadly, to facilitate ousting communist functionaries from administrative posts and to allow voters to reject electoral candidates who had collaborated with the old regime.[5]

In Poland, the former East Germany, and the Czech and Slovak Republic, lustration's results were mixed, exposing many invidious actors but also producing much social and political chaos. Husbands and wives, for instance, discovered that their mates had spied on them, as patients learned about their doctors.[6] And leaders of the resistance, even Václav Havel and Lech Walesa, were accused of having collaborated with the secret police.[7] Part of the confusion was due to the fact that the former regimes had no respect for marriage or the doctor-patient relationship. Another cause was simpler: much of the information in the government's files was bogus. Secret agents must constantly prove they are diligent; reporting contacts with and rumors from fictional informants shows diligence, and security officials have seldom been troubled by qualms of conscience in falsifying records.

2. See Gábor Halmai and Kim Lane Scheppele, "Living Well Is the Best Revenge: The Hungarian Approach to Judging the Past," in A. James McAdams, ed., *Transitional Justice and the Rule of Law in New Democracies* (Notre Dame, IN: University of Notre Dame Press, 1997), pp. 160ff.

3. Indeed, the *Economist* has reported—"Putin Power," Oct. 11, 2003, p. 15—that under President Vladimir Putin, "the security forces have swelled and their alumni are now filling government posts at all levels." The writer added, "Russian democracy is a cynical joke."

4. Before the 1990s, lustration had probably become more common in discussions of witchcraft than in moral theology or politics, a usage not too far removed from what would be experienced in Central and Eastern Europe.

5. See, generally, Herman Schwartz, "Lustration in Eastern Europe," in Kritz, *Transitional Justice*, 1:461, and Andrzej Rzeplinski, "A Lesser Evil?" 1 *East Eur'n Con'l Rev.* 33 (Fall 1992).

6. This kind of informing on relatives, clients, and even parishioners was hardly a communist creation. In Czarist Russia the secret police "turned" some Orthodox priests, persuading them to report any politically dangerous acts they heard under the seal of the confessional.

7. See Wiktor Osiatynski, "Agent Walesa?" 1 *East Eur'n Con'l Rev.* 28 (Summer 1992).

Making matters worse, some people striving for power during the transitional period were quite ready to use falsified data to ruin competitors. As a result, lustration soon lost its luster. Rather quickly the German government restricted access to the Stasi's files. Besides, after the first election post reunification, most East Germans who had had meaningful ties with the old regime dropped out of politics, either voluntarily or because of imprisonment, defeat at the polls, or having been fired. The Czechs allowed their lustration law to lapse, and in 1992 the Polish constitutional court declared theirs unconstitutional as a violation of the basic concepts of "a democratic state ruled by law" and "human dignity" as well as the International Covenant of Civil and Political Rights.[8]

Conditional Amnesty

Conditional amnesty provides a third alternative, one that can partake of both amnesty's remission of physical punishment and lustration's public shaming. At least seventeen countries, including Argentina and Chile, have set up committees to document exactly what happened during their periods of tyrannical rule. Most of these have been feeble fact-finding bodies. South Africa provides the best example of a vigorous truth and reconciliation commission. It invited victims and their relatives to tell their stories and, if they could, identify their tormentors. The TRC was authorized to offer amnesty to people implicated either by this testimony or by its own staff's independent investigations. Suspects included both officials accused of having used heinous methods to maintain apartheid and private citizens, mostly members of the African National Congress, believed to have committed crimes against competing black groups. If not satisfied with the testimony of supplicants for amnesty, the commission could recommend criminal prosecution and did so in more than a hundred instances.[9] Essentially, the TRC required those seeking absolution to meet three basic conditions: confess their offenses fully, honestly, and publicly; demonstrate that they had committed these crimes for political rather than personal reasons; and submit to cross-examination by prosecutors, members of the commission, and victims or their relatives. The commission then judged each petition on its individual merits, if any.

---

8. After this decision, the Polish parliament watered down the statute. For broader discussions of Poland's painful years after the change in regimes, see Andrzej S. Walicki, "Transitional Justice and the Political Struggles of Post-communist Poland," in A. James McAdams, ed., *Transitional Justice and the Rule of Law in New Democracies* (Notre Dame, IN: University of Notre Dame Press, 1997); and Jiri Priban and James Young, eds., *The Rule of Law in Central Europe: The Reconstruction of Legality, Constitutionalism, and Civil Society in the Post-communist Countries* (Brookfield, VT: Ashgate, 1999).

9. Among the more famous instances were the TRC's refusal to absolve Eugene de Kock, one of the most sadistic leaders of a security force that was not noted for tender regard for due process, and the five policemen implicated in the murder of Steve Biko. Although de Kock was convicted, prosecutors dropped the charges against the five police because of insufficient evidence.

Both the immunity from prosecution that leaders of outgoing authoritarian regimes negotiate for themselves and the immunity that truth and reconciliation commissions offer raise grave moral problems: do such agreements and procedures violate fundamental norms of justice? The implications of such issues are also practical for an infant constitutional democracy, generating serious questions about the depth of the new polity's commitment to the values it claims to further. The following sections of this chapter grope with these civic and moral difficulties.

Several other issues carry moral implications but are essentially practical in nature. In the short run, to what extent can such a commission produce truth or what can be accepted as truth? It is unlikely that a report published, as it must be if it is to serve as a catalyst for change, soon after the collapse of the old regime, can constitute a definitive historical analysis. Hiding in the shadows is a more basic question: will knowing the truth lead to reconciliation? "You shall know the truth," the author of John's Gospel asserts, "and the truth will set you free."[10] The Indo-European root of the word *free* is the same as "to love."[11] If we understand *free* in this broader sense, it would include release from hate, from a desire for vengeance, loading the words John reported with heavy political as well as theological cargo. Indeed, a modest version of this broader conception must underlie such commissions. Empirical evidence for such effects is, however, less than virile.

To have a politically meaningful effect, a truth and reconciliation commission's report cannot merely convince dispassionate scholars. Rather, that message must persuade two audiences, who are apt to be hearing-impaired. First would be those people, possibly a large number, who during the period of authoritarian rule had enjoyed moderately happy lives, having chosen, in exchange for the government's leaving them alone, to accept their own loss of liberty and to ignore the suffering of others. A TRC would have to convince these quietists to peep outside their private shells, recognize the old regime's evils, and support fundamental political change. An additional audience would be more difficult to persuade: those people who had been imprisoned, tortured, or murdered, and/or their families.[12] They would need no convincing about the old system's evils or the need for

10. 8:32.

11. Eric Patridge, *Origins: A Short Etymological Dictionary of Modern English,* 4th ed. (New York: Macmillan, 1966), p. 235. C. T. Onions, ed., *The Oxford Dictionary of English Etymology* (New York: Oxford University Press, 1966), p. 375, says the primary sense of *free* in old German is "dear."

12. Ideally, that message should also reach at least some of the people who profited from the old constitutional order. Complete acceptance, however, would be beyond reasonable hope. Officials and families of officials of authoritarian regimes have not been noted, at least for very long, for living in monastic simplicity, and it is improbable that they could be persuaded by reason alone not only to surrender the power, money, and prestige of their official positions but also to accept guilt for assorted felonies.

change, but they might doubt the necessity of following the norms of constitutional democracy in dealing with offenders and/or in recrafting the political order.

Embedded here is the problem of how much truth, with or without love, people really want. Each of us has a self-image that only partly corresponds to reality. The "gie the giftie" might "gie" us is not one that most of us crave, nor are we likely to allow others the full truth about ourselves—precisely why Justice Brandeis called privacy "the right most cherished by civilized men."[13] So, too, every ethnic group and nation has its self-serving myths, founding and continuing, stories that may be true or false, or may synthesize fact with fiction. Only if the past can be accepted as a medley of themes, some cause for pride, others for shame, can "the truth" facilitate political reconciliation. The truth that matters, Michael Ignatieff says, is "interpretive truth," the past as refracted through one's personal and group myths, a truth that only insiders can grasp—not the factual truth that an investigatory commission might, if its members are dispassionate and skilled, produce.[14]

It is little short of remarkable that a murderous orgy did not occur after the end of apartheid in South Africa. Much of the peaceful nature of the exchange of power is due to Nelson Mandela and Archbishop Desmond Tutu's persuading their followers to work for the future rather than avenge the past. The Truth and Reconciliation Commission played an active role during the later stages of this peaceful transition, but its impact is disputed. After conducting a large survey in 2000–2001 regarding public reactions to the TRC's work, James L. Gibson concluded that the process did contribute to acceptance among whites, coloureds, and Asians of the ugly truth about apartheid. Even though three times as many blacks as white said they placed confidence in the TRC's findings, Gibson found "no clear evidence" that the TRC had shaped blacks' views about apartheid. Most likely, they had no need for further instruction in the evils of the old order. More important, however, interracial trust remained low. A Nielsen survey taken in 1998, while the commission's work was still in progress, indicated that two-thirds of South Africans thought that race relations in South Africa had deteriorated since the TRC's hearings began.[15] After publication of the final report, Gibson found that a majority of whites still believed that blacks were likely to commit crimes and 41 percent of blacks believed that whites were likely to do so; one-third of whites thought blacks were untrustworthy, and only

13. Olmstead v. United States, 277 U.S. 438, dis. op. at p. 478 (1928).

14. *The Warrior's Honor: Ethnic War and the Modern Conscience* (New York: Henry Holt, 1998), p. 175.

15. Reported in Robert I. Rotberg, "Truth Commissions and the Provision of Truth, Justice, and Reconciliation," in Robert I. Rotberg and Dennis F. Thompson, eds., *Truth v. Justice: The Morality of Truth Commissions* (Princeton, NJ: Princeton University Press, 2000), p. 19.

about one-fifth of blacks deemed whites deserving of trust.[16] Standing alone, these data do not indicate that the TRC furthered reconciliation, at least in the short run[17]—a result that should not have come as a shock. In the United States, bitter memories among Southern whites about Reconstruction lingered well into the twentieth century, and African Americans' folk memory of slavery and Jim Crow remains sharply alive in the twenty-first century.

The question of whether to establish a TRC cannot be intelligently decided by looking only at these commissions. It is crucial to judge their likely effectiveness in comparison with that of alternative institutions and processes. Martha Minow has argued that a truth commission's exposure of atrocities can be more effective than criminal prosecutions in bringing a people together, but she offers no hard evidence to support her argument.[18] After analyzing respondents' answers to his survey, Gibson concluded that the commission had made important contributions toward creating a civil society in South Africa. Even though his data do not offer muscular support for this conclusion, Gibson's insights, gained from much time and research in South Africa, point toward this effect, as do the observations of other perceptive witnesses such as Alex Boraine.[19]

As in much analysis of political causation, reasoning post hoc, ergo propter hoc is a present, if not always clear, danger, as is the difficulty of unsnarling the many threads that have tangled together to create a multicausal effect. The problem is one of multicollinearity: South Africa's most respected leaders urged forgiveness; the chief revolutionary party, the African National Congress, was tainted with the blood of rival black organizations; people were tired of a long, seemingly escalating guerrilla war; and the new government did not rely exclusively on the commission but also prosecuted some of the worst offenders.

The most positive assessment one can confidently make is that, as the white supremacist regime was collapsing, it had not been clear that the new republic would avoid civil war and the sort of brutal dictatorship that had taken over most sub-Saharan countries. In this precarious context, the TRC carried out its mandate fairly and spread what its members deemed to be the

16. James L. Gibson, *Overcoming Apartheid: Can Truth Reconcile a Divided Nation?* (Los Angeles: Russell Sage, 2004), ch. 3, reports the data. See also James L. Gibson and Amanda Gouws, *Overcoming Intolerance in South Africa: Experiments in Democratic Persuasion* (New York: Cambridge University Press, 2003).

17. The South African government's decision to pay $3,900 to the family of each victim of apartheid who testified or whose family testified before the TRC may or may not have furthered reconciliation. Although the average income of a black family there was only $3,000, many critics attacked the amount as paltry and insulting to the victims. Ginger Thompson, "South Africa Will Pay $3,900 to Apartheid Victims' Families," *N.Y. Times,* Apr. 16, 2003.

18. "The Hope for Healing: What Can Truth Commissions Do?" in Rotberg and Thompson, eds., *Truth v. Justice;* see also her *Between Vengeance and Forgiveness* (Boston: Beacon, 1998).

19. *A Country Unmasked: Inside South Africa's Truth and Reconciliation Commission* (New York: Oxford University Press, 2000).

truth about an ugly past, excoriating some leaders of the African National Congress (which probably angered many blacks) along with white rulers and their minions (which probably angered many whites). The commission tried to lay the base for a political culture that values human rights and recognizes the necessity of due process of law to protect those rights. This double mission is critically important: that a government dominated by black survivors of apartheid chose magnanimity over revenge taught whites, blacks, coloureds, and Asians something about the prudence of forgiveness. That decision certainly enhanced South Africa's status as a responsible nation with powerful ambitions to become a constitutional democracy.

Despite Gibson's excellent empirical work, we still have only a series of shrewd but conflicting guesses about this or any other TRC's effectiveness. Against Minow's claim that full and open confessions are more healing that punishment inflicted by the criminal law we have Hannah Arendt's assertion that human beings cannot forgive what they cannot punish.[20] Supporting data for either claim are sparse. But if forgiveness or amnesia were necessary for reconciliation. healing would be impossible. Great Christians like Archbishop Tutu may be able to forgive and urge others to join them, but some Christian moral theologians understand that *forgetting* wrongs is impossible.[21] What is necessary for reconciliation is a willingness to put aside hatred for particular ethnic groups. That is, black South Africans can continue to despise Afrikaner leaders such as Daniel Malan, John Vorster, Frederick W. de Klerk, and Eugene de Kock; Ulster Catholics can revile Ian Paisley (and, having notoriously long memories, Oliver Cromwell); Jews who returned to Germany can detest Adolf Hitler and Heinrich Himmler; Palestinians can hate Ariel Sharon, Benjamin Netanyahu, and all Mossad agents; and Israeli can revile Yasir Arafat and members of Hamas and Hizbollah. Yet if these people were not willing to try to accept whites, Protestants, Germans, Jews, and Arabs as fellow citizens, civil governance would be impossible.

Criminal Prosecutions

The extent to which the success of South Africa's TRC, if it really was a success, could be duplicated elsewhere is problematic. Leaders with the political skill, charisma, and righteous forbearance of Mandela are not common. Furthermore, it may be that new leaders do not, as a practical matter,

20. *The Human Condition* (Chicago: University of Chicago Press), p. 241. This book was originally published in 1958. I have used the 2nd ed., with an introduction by Margaret Canovan.

21. See, for example, Stanley Hauerwas, *A Better Hope: Resources for a Church Confronting Capitalism, Democracy, and Postmodernity* (Grand Rapids, MI: Brazos, 2000), ch. 9. I should note a distinction here: morality is concerned with the duties that human beings owe to each other; moral theology focuses on these mutual obligations as derivative from the duties that humans owe to the Deity.

have the option of pretending to absolve offenders after they suffer only the humiliation of public confessions.[22] Demands for retributive justice, often difficult to differentiate from revenge, may echo so loudly as to force government to take punitive action, which means choosing a fourth option: criminal prosecution. That course, however, does not necessarily offer a series of surgical strikes. Even under "normal" criminal prosecutions, distinctions between felonies and misdemeanors are sometimes arbitrary.

Where we deal with mass crimes committed by public officials, emotions are likely to bubble over, and the number of both victims and tormentors may be huge. In East Germany, for example, the Stasi directly employed almost 100,000 men and women and indirectly as many as a quarter of a million more.[23] But even those numbers seem tiny when we recall that the Hutus in Rwanda hacked to death about 800,000 Tutsis and the government later arrested more than 120,000 alleged *genocidaires*. Exempting clerks and secretaries from legal sanctions may be easy, but deciding whom to punish at command and operational levels is far more difficult. Should Rwanda, for instance, have limited prosecution to the chiefs who incited their people to mayhem, or was it proper to include those who chopped off body parts?[24] In Latin America and the former Soviet satellites, should the new governments have prosecuted only the senior officials who ordered murder and torture, or included those who shot prisoners, tore out fingernails, crushed testicles, or participated in gang rapes? Should the new leaders also have tried police who did the arresting and jailers who kept the victims imprisoned? And what about paid informers?

Serious questions of ex post facto laws may also arise. Some of the most brutal acts of security officials were probably not criminal under the old regime's laws or are shielded by statutes of limitations. Hungary's new government addressed this situation by criminalizing the more oppressive acts

22. Of course, offenders may experience no remorse for their crimes on behalf of the old constitutional order and thus suffer no humiliation; indeed, their admissions may gain them a certain *éclat* within their reference group.

23. Jennifer A. Yoder puts the figure of "official" Stasi employees at 97,000 with an additional 150,000 "unofficial collaborators." *From East Germans to Germans? The New Postcommunist Elites* (Durham, NC: Duke University Press, 1999), p. 97.

24. See generally, Alan J. Kuperman, *The Limits of Humanitarian Intervention: Genocide in Rwanda* (Washington, DC: Brookings Institution Press, 2001); and Mahmood Mamdani, *When Victims Become Killers: Colonialism, Nativism, and Genocide in Rwanda* (Princeton, NJ: Princeton University Press, 2002). Faced with an enormous burden of investigating and trying so many accused, the Rwandan government established a series of very informal tribunals called Gacca courts, which sat in the open near a village (*gacca* means piece of grass) so that all people in the area could attend and, if they wished, give evidence. These proceedings, Samantha Power said, partook of "the atmosphere of both the witch trials and a Mississippi Christian revival" ("Rwanda: The Two Faces of Justice," *N.Y. Rev. of Bks.*, Jan. 16, 2003, pp. 47–48). The proceedings also bore some resemblance to the grand jury in late medieval England in that they officially accused many of the defendants. The Hutus complained that they were getting victors' justice. Eventually the government freed about eighty thousand of the accused before trial.

and extending statutes of limitations for acts that had been criminal. In 1992, however, the Hungarian Constitutional Court invalidated these efforts. Undeterred, parliament passed a new law, this one based on international agreements regarding crimes against humanity. The Court then sustained almost all provisions of the new statute.[25]

It may also be difficult to find prosecutors and judges with clean hands. Many of these officials may have been intimately linked to oppression. Fresh judicial personnel might soon be in place, but if they are victims or relatives of victims of the authoritarian regime, they may not appear to be disinterested—not a trivial matter where the new government is trying to teach its citizens the norms of constitutional democracy. Thus, if leaders choose criminal prosecution, they may have to ask for the help of the United Nations or request some other international arrangement for a tribunal to try such offenses.[26] In 1993, the UN Security Council established the Inter-

25. On Retroactive Criminal Legislation, Decision 11/1992; trans. in László Sólyom and Georg Brunner, *The Constitutional Judiciary in a New Democracy: The Hungarian Constitutional Court* (Ann Arbor: University of Michigan Press, 2000), pp. 2142D26; and On War Crimes and on Crimes against Humanity, Decision 53/1993; trans. in ibid. pp. 2732D83. For a brief analysis, of the first decision, see "Retroactivity Law Overturned in Hungary," 1 *East Eur'n Con'l Rev.* 7 (Spring 1992); for a longer analysis, see Halmai and Scheppele, "Living Well Is the Best Revenge," pp. 160ff. The second Hungarian decision is discussed in Krisztina Morvai, "Retroactive Justice Based on International Law: A Recent Decision by the Hungarian Constitutional Court," 2 *East Eur'n Con'l Rev.* 32 (Fall 1993 / Winter 1994).

It remains a legal possibility, though a politically remote one, that some officials both of the old South African government and of the African National Congress could be prosecuted outside of South Africa. The new constitutional text forbids punishment for "an act or omission that was not an offense under either national or international law at the time it was committed or omitted" (Article 35, §3, l). John Dugard suggests, however, that many of the acts to which people confessed before the TRC were, at the time of commission, offenses against international law. "Retrospective Justice: International Law and the South African Model," in McAdams, *Transitional Justice and the Rule of Law in New Democracies.* For a more complete analysis of the international law relevant here, see Diane F. Orentlicher, "Settling Accounts: The Duty to Prosecute Human Rights Violations of a Prior Regime," 100 *Yale L. J.* 2537 (1991), and the discussion below under "Fairness, Vengeance, and Prudence."

The U.S. Supreme Court, though only by a 5–4 vote, has held that extending a statute of limitations to punish an alleged sex offender against whom the original limitations had already run violated the constitutional prohibition against ex post facto laws. For the majority, Justice Stephen Breyer wrote: "[T]o resurrect a prosecution after the relevant statute of limitations has expired is to eliminate a currently existing conclusive presumption forbidding prosecution, and thereby to permit conviction on a quantum of evidence where that quantum, at the time the new law is enacted, would have been legally insufficient." Stogner v. California, 539 U.S. 607 (2003). Justices Kennedy, Scalia, and Thomas and Chief Justice Rehnquist dissented.

26. Belgian law allows prosecution of crimes against humanity in Belgian courts, no matter in what venue the acts were committed. Early in 2003, Belgium narrowed its code to allow such prosecutions by non-Belgians only where they themselves were directly injured. Later in 2003, the prime minister announced that his government would amend the law to allow only Belgians to file suit. The law now permits prosecutors to transfer cases to the International Criminal Court in the Hague. See "Too Embarrassing: Why Belgium Is Changing Its Law against Genocide," *Economist,* Apr. 10, 2003, p. 43. During the summer of 2003, Belgian courts threw out private suits against

national Criminal Tribunal for the Former Yugoslavia and so provided a forum in which to try leaders of all sides for atrocities committed before and during the civil wars in Bosnia and Kosovo.[27] Slobodan Milosevic, sometime president of Serbia, was the most famous defendant to grace that court's dock. A similar resolution created a tribunal to try people accused of genocide in Rwanda; to maintain an aura of objectivity, the judges sat in Tanzania. The International Criminal Court, located at the Hague and associated with but not part of the United Nations, offers a forum to prosecute former officials accused of violating human rights and to do so without the aroma of victors' justice and with less danger of exacerbating ethnic hatreds.[28]

Fairness, Vengeance, and Prudence

Any compromise that includes amnesty for the military, secret police, and/or civilian autocrats of the old regime will sit bitterly in the mouths of victims and their families. These people are apt to believe it is dreadfully wrong that their oppressors do not stand trial. But before public officials can bring a criminal action, they must have the will, the power, and the authority to do so. In Poland and Hungary, for example, the new governments had the two latter but chose to be carefully selective in their prosecutions, relying more heavily on what C. Eric Lincoln has called "no-fault reconciliation."[29]

In other situations, new leaders may have the will and authority but lack the power to impose punishment. It is probable, for instance, that the Uruguayan army would have resumed military rule had the civilians tried to repeal the amnesty the junta had conferred on itself and its subordinates

Israeli Prime Minister Ariel Sharon and General Amos Yaron as well as against George W. Bush and General Tommy Franks (Reuters Dispatch, Sept. 24, 2003). American courts have civil jurisdiction over offenses under international law, though, even if successful, litigants are not likely to collect from defendants. Spanish law authorizes Spanish courts to institute criminal trials for offenses against human rights that were committed anywhere in the world, providing those actions had effects in Spain.

27. The official title is the International Tribunal for the Prosecution of Persons Responsible for Serious Violations of International Humanitarian Law Committed in the Territory of the Former Yugoslavia since 1991. For an analysis of the UN Security Council's efforts to establish such courts under Article 41 of the UN Charter, see Fatza Patel King, "Sensible Scrutiny: The Yugoslavia Tribunal's Development of Limits on the Security Council's Powers under Chapter VII of the Charter," 10 *Emory Int'l L. Rev.* 509 (1996); and Rachel Kerr, *The International Criminal Tribunal for the Former Yugoslavia: An Exercise in Law, Politics, and Diplomacy* (Oxford: Oxford University Press, 2004). For a more general study of UN efforts to provide a forum for criminal trials, see Dominic McGoldrick, Peter Rowe, and Eric Donnelly, eds., *The Permanent International Criminal Court: Legal and Policy Issues* (Portland, OR: Hart, 2004).

28. I deliberately say "less danger" rather than no danger. Tim Judah, who covered much of the Balkan wars during the 1990s, claims that in late 2003 many Serbians saw the International Criminal Tribunal at the Hague as being biased against Serbs while Croats viewed that court as biased against Croats. "The Fog of Justice," *N.Y. Rev. of Bks.,* Jan. 15, 2004, pp. 23ff.

29. *Coming through the Fire: Surviving Race and Place in America* (Durham, NC: Duke University Press, 1996), p. 157.

before yielding power.[30] It was not until 2005 that a civilian government felt sufficiently secure to evade the grants of amnesty and begin prosecuting the former president and his foreign minister for kidnapping and murdering people who had opposed the junta.

In 1984, Argentina's civilian government under President Raúl Alfonsín repealed the earlier grant of general amnesty and began to bring army officers as well as commanders of leftist guerrillas to trial for assorted violations of human rights. Several legal obstacles immediately arose. One was an existing statutory requirement that trials of military personnel begin in military tribunals, whose officers were not anxious to try their brothers. The other was the doctrine of "due obedience": the obligation of junior officers to presume the legitimacy of orders from senior officers.

Eventually, the government convicted some of the principals in the "Dirty War," including Leopoldo Galtieri, though for malfeasance in leading the Malvinas War against Britain rather than for kidnapping, torture, and murder. But several mutinies soon showed that the civilian government's control of the military was shaky, and prosecutions halted. In 1989, President Carlos Menem, Alfonsín's successor and a member of the Peronista Party, an organization that had launched a goodly share of Argentina's military coups, pardoned all those who had been convicted.[31] Fourteen years later, more prosecutions became possible when the legislature again repealed previous grants of amnesty. Yet it was Spanish rather than local prosecutors who moved first, and Argentina's President Nestor Kirchner, who had himself briefly been one of the junta's guests, nullified an earlier decree that had forbidden extradition of military personnel.

In Chile, the new civilian government was initially unable to bring Pinochet's pack to trial. The general's retaining both his military rank and the loyalty of a large portion of his troops gave him de facto immunity. During the early stages of the common law, no writ could run against the king because he supposedly controlled the physical force of the realm. For the same reason, no writ can run against a modern general who commands an army ready to protect him. In 2001, when Spain tried to extradite Pinochet from Britain, where he was seeking medical treatment, to try him for murdering Spanish citizens, the Chilean government claimed that its own tribunals should mete out whatever punishment was due. But after winning in

30. This grant was later confirmed by a public referendum in 1989. The Uruguayans understood the price to be paid for return to civilian rule. But in 2005 a leftist coalition government announced that the agreement covered only crimes committed *within* Uruguay and began criminal investigations of murders the junta had committed abroad.

31. This synopsis follows the account of Carlos S. Nino, "The Duty to Punish Past Abuses of Human Rights Put in Context: The Case of Argentina," 100 *Yale L. J.* 2619 (1991). Because of the pardon, Galtieri served only five of the twelve years of his sentence. Some years later, police placed him under house arrest while the courts adjudicated a claim that his grant of amnesty was unconstitutional. He died in 2003, before the legal issues were settled.

British courts, Chilean officials decided to continue to let sleeping generals lie.[32] In 2003, the civilian government announced plans to try several dozen of the junta's security officials. Even then, prosecutors were apparently planning to leave the top echelon of the old regime alone, partly out of fear of the army's reaction and partly out of a desire not to pick at the scabs of healing wounds. Later, after several national elections confirmed the country's recommitment to constitutional democracy, the government changed its mind and awoke the former dictator. Although in September 2005 the Chilean Supreme Court ruled that he could not be charged with some of the murders his regime committed, prosecutors pressed ahead with other accusations. Their task was made less unpopular by revelations of financial corruption and drug dealing within the general's family while he was in office. In the spring of 2006, Pinochet was again under house arrest; but both sides seemed to be hoping that the old man, then almost ninety and in bad health, would for once do the right thing and die before his next trial. He did.

The moral issues surrounding decisions to prosecute or grant amnesty are even more tangled than the practical problems. These decisions raise grave questions about relationships among punishment,[33] justice, and constitutionalist values. Beyond stirring deep anger, immunity raises issues of equality before the law and the polity's commitment of to this ideal. It would not be unreasonable for a people new to constitutional democracy to harbor suspicions of hypocrisy were the government to imprison a man who, while drunk, assaulted another patron in a barroom brawl and yet refuse to prosecute men who had ordered the murder of hundreds of dissidents.

It is certain, however, that if the ghouls who dominate the old regime believe surrendering power will lead them straight to the gibbet, they will have a huge incentive to fight with all their resources. And an internal war is likely to cause heavy casualties among civilians. Such a conflict may not be the greatest evil that can befall a people; in fact, it may effect much good, as, for instance, freeing slaves or releasing an entire people from political bondage. Yet whatever their positive results, civil wars are always savagely bloody and divisive. They may begin as binary battles over principle, but they often

32. In 2000, Chile's highest court had removed the general's immunity and ordered him to stand trial for murder. A year later, the case was dismissed on grounds that Pinochet was mentally incompetent to stand trial. In addition to having diabetes, he had suffered several strokes and was experiencing difficulty walking. Nevertheless, in 2003 he gave a talk at a meeting of retired generals, and various human rights groups went to court arguing that the general was now mentally competent to stand trial on other charges of murder and should be stripped of the immunity. The Court of Appeals dismissed the case. In 2004, prosecutors brought fresh charges, pointing out that he and close family members had kept hidden bank accounts in the United States. As of early 2006, the general was still a free, if now despised, man who still might face criminal prosecution.

33. Some legal and moral theorists have claimed that punishment is dysfunctional for affected individuals as well as for society. For a recent argument to this effect, see Deidre Golash, *The Case against Punishment: Redistribution, Prevention, and the Law* (New York: New York University Press, 2005).

mutate into conflicts among tribes or even neighborhoods, involving jealousy, greed, and alleged personal insults, fueling hatreds that can endure for generations.[34] In short, a civil war can do to a nation what cross-cut shredders did to Enron's ledgers. Thus leaders who recall the free falls into near-anarchy and oppression that occurred in Algeria, Angola, Burundi, Chechnya, Laos, Lebanon, Liberia, Nigeria, Rwanda, Sri Lanka, Yugoslavia, and Zaire must discount the enormity of these evils by their probability—a matter of practical judgment.

In addition, there may be serious doubt as to who would win a civil war. Authoritarian governments may teeter without falling, as illustrated by failed revolts in Hungary in 1956 and Czechoslovakia in 1968 and the tragic fate of China's Democracy Movement in 1989. Each produced its share of corpses without yielding either democracy or constitutionalism.[35] For all the frustration amnesty generates, following Samuel Huntington's advice may be the price of avoiding butchery: "Do not prosecute, do not punish, do not forgive, and, above all, do not forget."[36]

Whether frightened tyrants will begin a civil war is also a matter for practical judgment—for them as well as for the leaders of a movement for constitutional democracy. The old elite may choose to run instead, a possibility that fogs decisions. As Justice Brandeis once wrote, the "great difficulty of any group action . . . is when and what concession to make."[37] Seldom is the choice between a clear good and a clear evil. Typically it is between evils, when doing nothing will itself produce evil. "Every decision of consequence," Hilaire Belloc said, "has grave evils attached to it—or grave risk of evil."[38] Multiplying that difficulty is the fact that leaders frequently must make critically important judgments under conditions of uncertainty, sometimes extreme uncertainty. They cannot be sure of the effects of their choices or the reactions of opponents or even allies. Neither can they be certain that what they perceive as the range of possibilities is not skewed by their own political myopia. Thus they may be obliged to select among partially informed guesses about the probability that a particular course rather

34. For a study that argues that "civil wars are not binary conflicts but complex and ambiguous processes that foster an apparently massive, though variable, mix of identities and actions," see Stathis N. Kalyvas, "The Ontology of 'Political Wars': Action and Identity in Civil Wars," 1 *Perspectives on Pols.* 475 (2003).

35. On the other hand, one might contend that although the Hungarian and Czechoslovak uprisings immediately produced only bloody repression, the anger they revealed soon moved officials, especially in Hungary, to modify the harshness of their rule. The results of these efforts did little if anything to modify the regime's ruthlessness. What effect, if any, China's Democracy Movement had still remains to be seen a decade and a half later.

36. *The Third Wave: Democratization in the Late Twentieth Century* (Norman: University of Oklahoma Press, 1991), p. 231.

37. Quoted in Alexander M. Bickel, *The Unpublished Opinions of Mr. Justice Brandeis* (Cambridge, MA: Harvard University Press, 1957), p. 18.

38. *Letters from Hilaire Belloc,* ed. Robert Speaight (London: Hollis and Carter, 1968), p. 214.

than any of several others will guide their country to what is good. Being forced to tolerate what *seems* to be a smaller evil to avoid what *seems* to be a much larger evil—and to hope, but not be certain, that their decision will yield the least evil—is itself one of the costs leaders must pay for having fallible judgment and blurred visions of the future.

In such situations, hurling moral blame may itself be morally reckless. It would take large globs of information about evil motives and ignored information—in short, convincing evidence of criminal purposes or criminal negligence—to confidently brand as morally wrong a decision to exchange amnesty for a peaceful exit. Philosophers in the safety of their proverbial armchairs may deem a civil war's cost in human lives to be irrelevant to questions of abstract justice, but that price cannot be irrelevant to public officials who are responsible for those lives or to the citizens whose lives are at risk. Leaders of the new constitutional order could shout, "Fiat justitia, ruat coelum!" That cry, however, is more likely to send souls to hell ahead of schedule than to bring justice on earth or cause the heavens to fall. If the leaders judge the options to be civil war or amnesty, the pleasure of inflicting on tyrants the punishment they have earned should take second place to saving lives. No matter what course they select, leaders will have a massive task convincing the new citizens that their choice among public policies was the best possible under the circumstances.[39]

The situation the new constitutional order faces when it considers establishing a commission of truth and reconciliation may be quite different from that which existed before the old regime surrendered power.[40] Although civil war might well remain a possibility, when the government's authority, if not all of its power, has moved into the hands of the new leaders, open warfare is not as likely to occur and, if it does, is less likely to cause the slaughter civil war could have wreaked when the old officials controlled the state's instruments.

---

39. One palliative on which new leaders can insist is the restriction of amnesty to past acts. These pacts should not extend any immunity beyond the date of the agreement, lest the old leaders, as they exit from power, continue to commit criminal acts. Clemncy for past felonies should not become license for future crimes.

40. There are also tricky procedural issues. Dugard argues that the decisions to set up such a commission and the rules under which it will operate should proceed not from political compromises but from legal principles and historic experience ("Retrospective Justice"). Dugard makes a strong but ultimately unconvincing argument—unconvincing because the problem of what do about past public crimes is eminently political in Aristotle's sense of the word. The real questions center on the issues of what compromises should be accepted. For a more complete analysis of the international law relevant here, see Orentlichter, "Settling Accounts," and the discussion below under "Positive International Law." As a practical matter, the issue is moot in South Africa. Not only do the plain words of the statute establishing the Truth and Reconciliation Commission permit amnesty, but South Africa's Constitutional Court has upheld the finality of the commission's decisions: Azanian Peoples' Organization et al. v. President of the Republic of South Africa, 1996 (8) BGLR 1015, 1996 SACLR LEXIS 20.

A dogging practical question that leaders of a fledgling constitutional democracy must face is whether criminal prosecutions will accelerate or slow reconciliation, bringing the new citizens of a new constitutional democracy together into a more just society. To what extent would establishment of a truth and reconciliation commission facilitate or impede that process? Forgoing the sweetness of retaliation against predators may be a cost worth paying.

On the other hand, the quality of mercy has often been strained, pace Portia. The case for amnesty, conditional or absolute, may not be convincing. The new government might be able to follow a punitive policy, assuming its officials—again operating under conditions of imperfect knowledge—correctly judge such a course prudent. Important here will be considerations of whom the old regime, if only virtually, represented. If the rulers constituted a rather small group, say a clique of officers who came to power by controlling the military and security forces, then imprisoning or executing them and their principal henchmen might not produce enduring social disruptions. If, however, as in the remnants of old Yugoslavia, South Africa, or Rwanda, those responsible for criminal atrocities were representative of a large social or ethnic group, the result might rip the nation apart, beyond the power of the current or even the next generation to stitch back together. If such leaders were to be punished, any hope for restored social unity would allow punishment only by outside force, as actually happened to many leaders who organized massacres in the Balkan wars of the 1980s and 1990s.

The new government might find it perilous to offer amnesty if the popular demand for revenge were so strong that the alternative to criminal trials was widespread private vengeance. Mob rule is more likely to provoke anarchy (and perhaps make another coup welcome) than to further any system of civil governance. There are no assurances that the new government could control its people, punish the oppressors, or even remain in power. After World War II, older Europeans had vivid memories of mobs battling in the streets of Weimar Germany and the political system that resulted from public yearning for order. A dismal drama may well play out: lynchings followed by preventive indictments, which incite mobs and then mutinies, which lead to a coup and a return to tyrannical government. Fearing these kinds of effects, the new leaders might refuse to agree to blanket amnesty or, having so agreed, renege on their promise. A clever casuist (or an ordinary attorney) could construct a plausible argument either that murderers and torturers have no right to the truth or that the promise of amnesty was made under duress. In either situation, so a wily casuist could contend, breaking a promise made to criminals does not really constitute lying.

Whatever the outcome, a cry for revenge—often called justice by victims and their families—is a typical human reaction to cruel rule. It may well be, as Paul Seabright has speculated, that humans are genetically predisposed to return evil for evil as well as good for good.[41] This suggestion receives some support from modern psychology, at least in response to evil that is perceived as deliberately inflicted.[42] One moral theologian has compared the driving force of righteous indignation to that of sex.[43] Many men and women may believe that keeping faith with relatives and friends requires retaliation, and most legal systems incorporate an understanding both of this felt individual need to strike back and of a social need for the state to control vengeance. The Shari'a clearly approves revenge, allowing, for instance, relatives of a murdered man to serve as executioners for the government. (More civilized American states permit relatives only to witness the prisoner's final writhing.) More subtly, the Civil Law and common law also acknowledge a legitimate role for revenge in the operations of criminal processes. Indeed, Oliver Wendell Holmes Jr., the Archangel of Legal Realism, claimed "not only that the law does, but that it ought to, make the gratification of revenge an object." He then went on to quote Sir James Stephen: "The criminal law stands to the passion of revenge in much the same relation as marriage to the sexual appetite."[44] Three-quarters of a century later, a former lord chief justice of the United Kingdom told the House of Lords that it was "praiseworthy that the country should be willing to avenge crime."[45]

Justice and Prudence: A Clash of Virtues?

In the years immediately before and after a constitutional democracy replaces a tyrannical regime, justice and prudence may seem to make competing, even conflicting, demands. Let us begin by eliminating two relatively easy problems. First is the justice of punishing. It could hardly be unjust were the new regime to prosecute the predators who had been operating an oppressive political system. They seized or accepted power and claimed to act for the good of that nation and its subjects. By reaping the rewards of power, they assumed an obligation to govern for the benefit of their people. It is hardly unfair that they pay for felonious abuses of power.

A second easy problem concerns a decision not to punish tyrants who are willing to surrender the governmental apparatus *only* on the condition of

---

41. *The Company of Strangers* (Princeton, NJ: Princeton University Press, 2004).

42. See, for example, Dominique J.-F. De Quervain et al., "The Neural Basis of Altruistic Punishment," 305 *Science* 1254 (Aug. 27, 2004). For a philosopher's reassessment of forgiveness and revenge, see Jeffrie G. Murphy, *Getting Even: Forgiveness and Its Limits* (New York: Oxford University Press, 2003).

43. James Tunstead Burtchaell, *Philemon's Problem: A Theology of Grace*, 2nd ed. (Grand Rapids, MI: Eerdmans, 1998), p. 200.

44. *The Common Law* (Boston: Little, Brown, 1881), p. 41. Holmes was a bachelor when he quoted Stephen.

45. Lord Goddard, quoted in H. L. A. Hart, *Law, Liberty, and Morality* (Stanford, CA: Stanford University Press, 1963), p. 61. His Lordship was discussing capital punishment. He approved.

being excused from punishment.[46] The previous section dealt with the issues here. I need only add that the new leaders would exchange what they do not yet have, the power to punish, for what they also do not yet have, the power to help build decent lives for their fellow citizens. Far from Faustian, this bargain would promote justice by facilitating the creation of a civil society. Even Diane F. Orentlicher, who crafts a very careful argument that an assortment of international agreements imposes a duty on successor governments to prosecute tyrants, concedes that "international law does not require governments to commit political suicide."[47]

The truly difficult moral question is whether justice imposes on a constitutional democracy a legal or moral *obligation* to try to punish the criminals who ran the old regime. At the heart of most arguments for the necessity of punishment lies a belief that punishing criminals is essential to victims' receiving justice. The final report of South Africa's Truth and Reconciliation Commission expressed that concern, noting that apartheid's victims voiced "a common refrain": "We've heard the truth. There is even talk of reconciliation. But where's the justice?"[48] And Amy Gutmann and Dennis Thompson warn that the "stability of a political regime itself is not a good or a sufficient reason to sacrifice justice for individuals," because a stable regime can be oppressive.[49]

There are three bases for imputing to constitutional democracy a duty to try to punish deposed despots: victims have a right grounded in (1) the positive law of the state, (2) international law, or (3) justice itself.

Positive Domestic Law

An argument from positive law would have to be that statutes command prosecutors to bring criminal action against former tyrants and their underlings. In most countries still living under tyrannical or even authoritarian regimes, no such obligations exist in fact, although they may be listed in codes. Individuals have only three remedies against abusive officials: (1) in-

46. Spain during the 1970s offers the paradigmatic case. See Giuseppe Di Palma, *To Craft Democracies* (Berkeley: University of California Press, 1990). The round-table discussions that preceded the transfer of power in much of Eastern Europe after the fall of the Berlin Wall followed the Spanish model. Thus, to a large extent in the former communist countries, there was an understanding that the new governments would limit, if not forgo, punishing old officials.

47. "Settling Accounts." Quotation is from "A Reply to Professor Nino," 100 *Yale L. J.* 2641 (1991).

48. *South Africa Truth and Reconciliation Commission: Report* (Cape Town: Truth and Reconciliation Commission, 1998), 1.5.3. For an excellent discussion, see Elizabeth Kiss, "Moral Ambition within and beyond Political Constraints: Reflections on Restorative Justice," in Robert I. Rotberg and Dennis F. Thompson, eds., *Truth v. Justice: The Morality of Truth Commissions* (Princeton, NJ: Princeton University Press, 2000), p. 68.

49. Amy Gutmann and Dennis F. Thompson, "The Moral Foundations of Truth Commissions," in Rotberg and Thompson, *Truth v. Justice,* p. 23.

formal political pressure exerted through an influential patron, (2) assassination, or (3) joining a terrorist or revolutionary organization.[50] On the other hand, representative and constitutional democracies allow aggrieved citizens significant political remedies and often civil, but not necessarily criminal, remedies against abusive public officials. All legal systems recognize an inclination toward retaliation and afford victims a positive legal remedy against harm inflicted by other private citizens. In countries that apply the Shari'a, as we have seen, members of a victim's family have a right to participate in executing a murderer. But with the exception of offenses involving family honor in Muslim nations, governmental systems at least formally forbid private citizens to exact personal vengeance and, instead, offer state action in the form of criminal prosecutions or civil suits. This recognition is essential to maintain public peace.

Nevertheless, the rationale for state-imposed punishment, Carlos S. Nino argued, is not based on "recognition that victims or their relatives have a right to that punishment. It is the consequence of a collective goal imposed by the policy of protecting human rights for the future."[51] And a decision to prosecute for a high crime against the state is eminently a political matter. It is political not in the journalistic usage of the term as referring to things petty, partisan, or expedient but in the Aristotelian sense of politics as being concerned "with virtue above all things," an effort to make "citizens good."[52] Politics thus understood looks to the long- as well as short-range benefit of citizens, which often lies beyond satisfying immediate desires even of the vast majority of the population. Enhancing the chances of citizens to live free and decent lives should take precedence over punishing criminals, however gratifying such punishment may be. Distinguishing between what is merely expedient and what is necessary is, once again, a matter of practical judgment.

Positive International Law

In many countries, international law may provide another remedy. Citing numerous international agreements, judicial opinions, and memoranda by international commissions, Orentlichter makes an eloquent argument that international agreements obligate successor governments to punish the peo-

---

50. Pakistan has occasionally had a form of judicial review, and several Arab countries, most notably Egypt, have the beginnings of such an institutional arrangement. So far, however, no constitutional court has intervened to try to block official policies that employ such methods as arbitrary imprisonment or torture. For an analysis of the real, but fragile, growth of constitutionalism in the Arab world, see Nathan J. Brown, *Constitutions in a Nonconstitutional World: Arab Basic Laws and the Prospects for Accountable Government* (Albany: State University of New York Press, 2002).

51. "Duty to Punish Past Abuses." In distinguishing between "rights established by principles and collective goals imposed by policies," Nino is following Ronald Dworkin, *Taking Rights Seriously* (Cambridge, MA: Harvard University Press, 1977), pp. 90–100.

52. *Nicomachean Ethics*, bk. 1, ch. 2, 1094b; bk. 1, ch. 13, 1102a.

ple who organized and ordered systematic atrocities.[53] Two points detract from her conclusion. First, these agreements have loopholes that allow signatories some discretion. Second, and more important, is the eminently political nature of decisions to prosecute, discussed in the previous paragraph.

The Basic Concept of Justice

If neither positive domestic nor international law imposes on constitutional democracy what Nino called "mandatory retribution,"[54] justice itself may require prosecutions. Defining justice is a prerequisite to discovering its demands, and that task is not easy. Even Socrates was better at exploding false understandings of the concept than at exposing its true essence.[55] For public officials and political theorists who are pure pragmatists or consequentialists,[56] the question of justice is much less important than whether policies of amnesty or criminal prosecution would produce the desired goal(s)—in this context, furthering the peaceful transition to and the political stability of a constitutional democracy. In fact, the question of justice is one that a consistent pragmatist or consequentialist would consider trivial unless he or she believed that other significant political actors would use it to stir up public opposition. The solution would then be to give enough lip service to the prevalent conception of justice, whatever it might be, to weaken opponents. It is, however, difficult to find a pure pragmatist or consequentialist in the real world. Even Judge Richard A. Posner is not always doctrinally orthodox, although he comes close to being what Max Weber termed an ideal type.[57] It

---

53. "Settling Accounts."

54. "Duty to Punish Past Abuses."

55. Socrates' claim that only the just man is happy does not, I believe, entitle one to conclude, as Hans Kelsen did, that Socrates equated justice and happiness. See Kelsen, "What Is Justice?" in his collection of essays, *What Is Justice?* (Berkeley: University of California Press, 1971), p. 2.

56. The philosophy (or philosophies) of pragmatism, as formulated somewhat differently by William James (a psychologist of sorts) and Charles Peirce (a mathematician of sorts), is complex, based on a metaphysics and epistemology that challenged traditional thought of the late nineteenth century. Its overriding concern for consequences originated, so Peirce believed, in Kant's assertion in *Critique of Pure Reason* that once "an end is accepted, the conditions of its attainment are hypothetically necessary." For good introductory essays, see Louis Menand, *The Metaphysical Club: A Story of Ideas in America* (New York: Farrar, Straus, and Giroux, 2001), esp. chs. 9 and 13; and Henry Steele Commager, *The American Mind: An Interpretation of American Thought and Character Since the 1880's* (New Haven, CT: Yale University Press, 1950), ch. 5. In its extreme form, consequentialism, a close ally of pragmatism, also looks primarily to results: the end justifies, if not any means, certainly almost any. Judge Richard A. Posner tries to distinguish pragmatism and consequentialism, at least in the context of adjudication: *Law, Pragmatism, and Democracy* (Cambridge, MA: Harvard University Press, 2003), p. x, and ch. 2 generally, esp. pp. 59–71. He says: "I do not know of any pragmatists who have considered themselves consequentialists, but two notable precursors, Bentham and John Stuart Mill did, and there is no doubt that pragmatism is closer to consequentialism than it is to deontology (duty-based as distinct from consequence-based ethics)" (p. 65).

57. Indeed, it is doubtful that anyone can be a consistent pragmatist or consequentialist, at least insofar as these "philosophies" would not use moral considerations in decision making. The essential

is more difficult to find someone who is totally indifferent to the effects of decisions. Indeed, it is almost impossible to conceive of a serious moral theorist who did not factor likely effects into his or her reasoning. Thus almost every decision maker is pragmatic in the limited sense of being seriously concerned about consequences.

For intellectually consistent moral relativists (moral conventionalists), the task of defining justice should not pose moral or philosophical problems much more difficult than those pragmatists would face. Moral relativism denies that universal standards of morality or justice exist, or argues that if they do exist, they are not demonstrable. (An offshoot of this belief is that all values are equal—itself a value judgment—and therefore clashes among them are not resolvable through intellectual analysis.) Because, so says the relativist, judgments about justice and morality are either idiosyncratic or culture bound, the most that government need do to settle the legitimacy of an agreement with exiting officials is to discover what constitutes "a moral good" or "justice" according to the particular standards (conventions) dominant within a particular community at a particular time. For example, if an overwhelming majority of the people in an Islamic society accept the Shari'a and deem it a grievous moral wrong for an infidel to convert a Muslim to another religion, an intellectually consistent relativist would have to concede that an agreement giving amnesty to rulers who had rigidly enforced the Shari'a's prescription of death for such deeds is not unjust *for that society*.[58] Quite the contrary, punishing these rulers would be unjust. For moral relativism, freedom of religion as well as other "rights" such as the equality of men and women can only be conventions. And the reach, content, and authority of mere conventions vary from society to society.

To be sure, determining what data are relevant, then gathering and analyzing them, can present enormous difficulties. These, however, are largely problems for experts in such fields as political sociology, public opinion polling, and quantitative analysis. Except insofar as the methodology of the social sciences raises epistemological issues, moral relativism can have little to say that is interesting or fundamentally important about justice as a concept. In effect, moral relativism transforms issues of morality into empirical questions about the customs, attitudes, and opinions that prevail in a given

---

difficulty in using results as *the* criterion of choice is that one must still evaluate results by some standard. Posner, for example, wants to maximize economic efficiency. But why? There are competing values. One has to give convincing reasons that an individual or a society should prefer economic efficiency over other values or would be better off by opting for economic efficiency—or any of its competitors. Offering economic efficiency itself as the reason would be circular. It remains unclear how a pragmatist can, with intellectual consistency, justify any particular goal. For a somewhat similar critique, see Stanley Fish, "Almost Pragmatism: Richard Posner's Jurisprudence," 37 *U. Chi. L. Rev.* 1447 (1990).

58. Deuteronomy 14:9–10 commanded a person who was tempted by another Israelite to worship false gods to identify the tempter, even if a brother or son, and have him stoned to death.

society at a given time. In this analytical context, if the moral opinion dominant in any given new constitutional democracy holds that it would be unjust to give amnesty to former officials, then a government's so doing would, by definition, be unjust. If not, then not.

For certain kinds of analytical jurisprudence, the problem is even easier than for its kissing cousin, moral relativism: justice, according to modern legal positivism's prophet, Hans Kelsen, "is not ascertainable by rational knowledge at all. . . . Justice is an irrational ideal."[59] By "irrational" he meant that justice is one society's idiosyncratic choice among values, not a conclusion that can be justified by tightly logical deductions from lexically prior principles or induced from empirical evidence according to the commands and procedures specified by what he calls "the basic norm."[60] For a consistent positivist, there can be only particular justice for a particular legal system. Whatever the law says is to be treated as just, at least within that jurisdiction at that time. *Res ipsa loquitur:* the "thing," the nation's law, speaks for itself, and its word is final. If the explicit terms of relevant statutes do not provide a determinate answer, careful analysis should do so.

Of course, doctrinal chastity no more stops legal positivists from having a deep concern for justice *within* any given legal system than moral relativism prevents conventionalists from being concerned about how their own society practices its values.[61] Analytical jurisprudes such as H. L. A. Hart have been very sensitive about justice within common law systems, especially about what they call "formal justice," the rules that judges should apply and how they should find those rules.[62] In fact, one respected scholar claims that

---

59. Hans Kelsen, "The Pure Theory of Law: Its Method and Fundamental Concepts," trans. Charles H. Wilson, 50 *Law Q. Rev.* 474, 482 (1934).

60. See, inter alia, *General Theory of Law and State* (New York: Russell and Russell, 1945), p. 10. For heroic efforts to restate (and rescue) legal positivism, see Tom Campbell, *Prescriptive Legal Positivism: Law, Rights, and Democracy* (London: Cavendish, 2004); and Anthony J. Sebok, *Legal Positivism in American Jurisprudence* (New York: Cambridge University Press, 1998). Sebok, however, discusses justice only indirectly, and the word does not appear in the index.

61. Applying Kelsen's methodology, a moral relativist might try to arrange a society's values in hierarchical order and argue that endorsement of a basic value—for example, human equality—logically requires that society to accept derivative values, such as sexual and racial equality. To the extent that the mass of the society also accepts logical consistency as a value, such an argument could both fit within moral relativism's boundaries and even convince others. It is however, also possible that most members of a society are perfectly willing to accept exceptions to their general principles or to interpret those principles in particularistic ways. For instance, a society may construe "all men are created equal" to mean "All white males are created equal." If, however, the society accepts the exceptions or particularistic interpretations, a consistent moral relativist must also accept the exceptions and/or interpretations, because relativists deny the existence of universal moral principles that could trump a society's conventions.

62. See, inter alia, his "Positivism and the Separation of Law and Morals," 71 *Harv. L. Rev.* 593 (1958); *The Concept of Law* (Oxford: Clarendon, 1961); and *Law, Liberty, and Morality.* See also B. E. King, "The Basic Concept of Hart's Jurisprudence: The Norm out of the Bottle," 1963 *Cambr. L. J.* 279; and Neil MacCormick, *H. L. A. Hart* (Stanford, CA: Stanford University Press, 1991).

Hart's brand of legal positivism is not incompatible with the universalism of natural law: Hart and his colleagues merely ask questions different from those that moral realists or natural law theorists would pose.[63]

Yet other people manage to proclaim universal moral truths on issues dear to them while asserting moral relativism on lesser matters. On the one hand, moral straddlers reject the possibility of universalistic moral judgments; on the other, they pay tribute to certain rights they baptize as "human."[64] The most famous effort of the twentieth century to make sense of such a bifurcation was John Rawls's restatement of the theory of social contract.[65] As he used the term, justice equals fairness, a usage that comes close to Aristotle's equating "the just" with "the lawful and the fair."[66] Despite this venerable provenance, fairness carries its own ambiguity.[67] And Rawls's description of the original position carefully, perhaps wisely, and surely deliberately excluded from discussion of the background of his fictional social covenant one of the most basic moral issues: do "normal" humans possess an innate capacity to reason about the nature of good and evil, a capacity that precedes, makes possible, and shapes the content of an original covenant?[68] In any event, Rawls used as a model "the original position" in which people operating under a "veil of ignorance" manage to agree on a set of basic (constitutional) rules for a "well-ordered society." Not knowing who they will be in the new society, rich or poor, male or female, white, brown, or

---

63. Robert N. Moles, *Definition and Rule in Legal Theory: An Assessment of H. L. A. Hart and the Positivist Tradition* (Oxford: Blackwell, 1987). Moles believes that Hart and Ronald Dworkin were unaware of the absence of conflict because they did not understand the history of legal theorizing.

64. See, for instance, Ronald Dworkin, *A Matter of Principle* (Cambridge, MA: Harvard University Press, 1985), and *Law's Empire* (Cambridge, MA: Harvard University Press, 1986), esp. pp. 65–70, 82–63.

65. See esp. *A Theory of Justice* (Cambridge, MA: Harvard University Press, 1971), *Political Liberalism* (New York: Columbia University Press, 1993), and *Justice as Fairness: A Restatement*, ed. Erin Kelly (Cambridge, MA: Harvard University Press, 2001).

66. *Nicomachean Ethics*, bk. 5, ch. 1, 1129a.

67. Posner complains, "The problem with words like 'fairness' and 'equality' is that they have no definite meaning." *Law, Pragmatism, and Democracy*, p. 66.

68. Although often read as a universalist (*cosmopolitan* is a term sometimes used), Rawls at places used arguments that bespoke moral relativism. For example, in *The Law of Peoples* (Cambridge, MA: Harvard University Press, 1999), he focused on consent and seemed ("seemed" because, as the next sentence indicates, Rawls confused me about exactly where he stood) to contend that people from different cultures might make different basic choices when operating in the original position behind the veil of ignorance. He saw those choices, including perhaps the denial of sexual equality, as not necessarily morally bad. Many readers, including me, had read *Justice as Fairness* as offering a universalistic explanation of a just society. For a brave effort to rescue Rawls from charges that he sacrificed liberty and equality to moral relativism, see Stephen Macedo, "What Self-Governing Peoples Owe to One Another: Universalism, Diversity, and *The Law of Peoples*," 72 *Fordham L. Rev.* 1721 (2004).

yellow, they seek rules that are just in the sense of being fair to all members of society.[69]

Rawls makes much of justice's requiring reciprocity. And justice as reciprocal fairness does carry more intuitive meaning than justice simply as fairness. Aristotle's notion of justice as proportionality fits that intuition: justice, he says, differs from other virtues in that it is concerned with the good of other people. Thomists agree.[70] John Finnis understands Aquinas's conception of justice as requiring a person to give to others what is theirs. The difficult questions center on what belongs to whom, as Socrates, Aristotle, Aquinas, and Rawls, among others, recognized.[71]

Public officials and political theorists who are not pragmatists, moral relativists, or pragmatists who differentiate themselves from Rawls confront very complex sets of philosophical issues that defy easy solutions. Their analyses move beyond cultural, geographic, and temporal boundaries in order to (try to) determine whether a putative moral good is such under universally applicable standards. Thomists are the usual suspects here, although hardly the only culprits.[72] They speak of certain actions that are bad

69. Although when discussing economic justice Rawls specifies that his "founders" do not know if they will be rich or poor in the society to come, when discussing abortion he does not lift the veil of ignorance. He analyzes the issue as arising among people who are already born (*Political Liberalism*, p. 243n). It would seem that (1) questions about the value of human life and when it begins are more politically (and morally) significant than allocations of property, and therefore (2) the veil of ignorance should obscure the vision of decision makers so that, when constructing their basic constitutional order, none of them would know whether he or she would be among the born or the aborted. It is possible, however, that leaving that veil down would have given an answer different from the one that Rawls preferred. Here he was more a partisan of a specific policy than a detached political philosopher offering a general method of constructing a just society.

70. E.g., John Finnis, *Natural Law and Natural Rights* (Oxford: Clarendon, 1980), ch. 5, esp. p. 133.

71. Kelsen claimed this definition "is an empty formula, because the decisive question is what is that which is everybody's own, is not answered" ("What Is Justice?" p. 13). On this point, Kelsen's reading was either less than careful or less than honest. Some two millennia earlier, Socrates had addressed this very difficulty. When Polemarchus quoted Siminodes's definition as "to pay everyone what is owed to him," Socrates replied: "Simonides is a wise and inspired man. . . . But what on earth does he mean by that?" (*The Republic*, 1.331e; trans. Tom Griffith, ed. G. R. F. Ferrari [New York: Cambridge University Press, 2000]). Aristotle, Aquinas, and modern Thomists have spent a great deal of time and effort trying to demonstrate how a broad concept of justice applies to specific situations in real life. In fact, it would be just to characterize these writers as treating justice less as a general concept and more as a carefully developed attitude reflected in habit. For all of his brilliance, Kelsen was not above creating and then attacking straw men. See Robert P. George, "Kelsen and Aquinas on 'the Natural-Law Doctrine,'" 75 *Notre Dame L. Rev.* 1625 (2000), in which George juxtaposes what Kelsen claimed Aquinas said and what Aquinas actually said. The result does not flatter Kelsen's scholarly integrity. See also note 55, above, for a discussion of Kelsen's spurious argument that Socrates' (Plato's) claim that only the just man can be happy meant that Socrates equated justice and happiness. For a more favorable, though not entirely uncritical, evaluation of Kelsen's general theory, see Posner, *Law, Pragmatism, and Democracy*, ch. 7.

72. Leo Strauss was a bitter enemy of moral relativism and legal positivism, which explains why

in themselves, regardless of actors' motives or the specific circumstances surrounding the choice.[73] Thus, contradicting consequentialists and pragmatists but following Saul of Tarsus, they deny that a good end, even if pursued for the noblest motives, can justify any means, only those that are themselves either good or morally indifferent. Although carefully derived predictions about the results of an action are important elements in moral choice, good results cannot justify acts, such as the deliberate taking of innocent life, that are evil in themselves.

Thomists also differentiate between things that are good in themselves and those that are good instrumentally.[74] As means to other ends, these latter take their moral stamp from the character of their ends.[75] The first argument, that good ends do not justify evil means, has obvious relevance to political morality and resonates well with constitutional democracy, for much of constitutionalism is concerned with regulating, even prohibiting, certain means such as bills of attainder and ex post facto laws, even when directed toward laudable goals. The second argument about the distinction between things good in themselves and merely instrumental goods is somewhat less valuable for analyses of the justice of granting amnesty to vicious felons,

---

he counted Hans Kelsen, a fellow refugee from Hitler, among his chief intellectual enemies. Strauss, however, disclaimed belief in Thomistic natural law. See his *Natural Right and History* (Chicago: University of Chicago Press, 1953). In his seminars, he repeatedly asserted that the first step toward philosophy was to distinguish between one's own benefit and the good. See also the writings of the so-called moral realists, especially Michael S. Moore and Sotirios A. Barber. Moore: "A Natural Law Theory of Interpretation," 58 *So. Cal. L. Rev.* 277 (1985); "Metaphysics, Interpretation, and Legal Theory," 60 *So. Cal. L. Rev.* 453 (1987); and "Moral Theory Revisited," 90 *Mich. L. Rev.* 2424 (1992). Barber: "Judge Bork's Constitution," in Walter F. Murphy, C. Herman Pritchett, Lee Epstein, and Jack Knight, eds., *Courts, Judges, and Politics: An Introduction to the Judicial Process,* 4th ed. (Boston: McGraw-Hill, 1986); "The New Right Assault on Moral Inquiry in Constitutional Law," 54 *Geo. Wash. L. Rev.* 253 (1986); and "Epistemological Skepticism, Hobbesian Natural Right, and Judicial Self-Restraint," 48 *Rev. of Pols.* 374 (1986). For a critical but not hostile analysis of Barber's thesis, see Stanley C. Brubaker's review article at 2 *Con. Comm.* 261 (1985). Hadley Arkes, especially in *First Things* (Princeton, NJ: Princeton University Press, 1986), takes a position quite similar to that of the moral realists.

73. Nevertheless, for Thomists specific circumstances are important. One example of an act they would consider evil under all circumstances is the wanton taking of human life. But they would also agree that one must know the context of the act to decide whether the killing was wanton, in self-defense, or in defense of another (innocent) human being.

74. See, for example, Finnis, *Natural Law and Natural Rights,* pp. 86–90; Robert P. George: *Making Men Moral* (Oxford: Clarendon, 1993), pp. 8–18; and George, *In Defense of Natural Law* (New York: Oxford University Press, 1999), ch. 2. Aristotle made a similar distinction, though as he was not a moral theologian, he did not make as much of the point as did Aquinas and his followers. See *Nicomachean Ethics,* bk. 1, ch. 2, 1094a.

75. I deliberately exclude discussion of motives. Like the road to hell, the path to vicious tyranny is paved with good intentions. Archbishop Desmond Tutu, for example, said that despite the evils of apartheid, some of the Afrikaner officials "genuinely believed" that this policy offered "the best solution to the complexities of a multiracial land." Similarly, no one doubts that Adolf Hitler sincerely thought the world would be a better place if every Jew were dead.

because the question centers on instrumental goods: policies made by governmental institutions and processes. These are designed to accomplish certain ends and so are morally colorable according to the goals sought and the means employed. In the latter choices, the notion of actions evil in themselves becomes relevant.

Even constitutional democracy itself is only an instrumental good. As with any political system, its goodness depends, as Aristotle would have put it, on the extent to which the goals it pursues and the means it employs maximize the chances for its citizens to live decent lives.[76] Obviously, a political system that tries to respect the great and equal dignity of every human being, as constitutional democracy claims to, is not evil in itself. Insofar as the regime's policies conform to its preachments, it is a positive good. Alas, no constitutional democracy always lives up to its own standards. Thus political stability would enhance such a regime's capacity to do good, but in a flawed world, it might also enhance the political system's capacity to do evil.

Justice and Punishment

I have danced around rather than answered, except for pragmatism, moral relativism, and Kelsen's classic legal positivism, the question whether justice, or more broadly basic morality, mandates punishment for tyrants. An affirmation of that demand threatens to legitimate state-imposed vengeance, and most, though hardly all, modern moralists argue against the "pathetic logic of revenge."[77] As a practical political matter, the consequences of revenge will differ, as we have seen, between situations in which the old officials form a relatively small coterie of thugs and those in which, while still thugs, they seem to represent a large ethnic group or social class.

In the second situation, vengeance is less likely to heal social wounds than to breed hatred and incite counterrevenge, starting a society, as Martin Luther King said, on a downward spiral toward darkness. Giving back harm for harm certainly establishes a reciprocal relationship, but whether tit for tat heals is doubtful, as Romeo and Juliet attested.[78] Nothing in the history of

---

76. Compare James Madison: "It is too early for politicians to presume on our forgetting that the public good, the real welfare of the great body of the people, is the supreme object to be pursued; and that no form of government whatever has any other value than as it may be fitted to the attainment of this policy." *The Federalist*, No. 45, ed. Benjamin F. Wright (Cambridge, MA: Harvard University Press, 1961), p. 325.

77. Scott Turow, *Reversible Errors* (New York: Warner Books, 2003), p. 538.

78. Among the best of relevant works by rational-choice theorists is Robert M. Axelrod, *The Evolution of Cooperation* (New York: Basic Books, 1984). He concedes that reciprocal retaliation may engender long lasting feuds and that "is not a good basis for a morality of aspiration." But he also suggests that retaliation that is strong enough to hurt but not quite equal in harm to the original blow can facilitate peace (pp. 137–38). Basically, he contends, a strategy of retaliation pushes both sides toward cooperation. "TIT FOR TAT does well by promoting the mutual interest rather than by

violence and counterviolence between Catholics and Protestants in Ulster, between Israelis and Palestinians, between Shia and Sunni in Iraq, or among various ethnic groups in the Balkans indicates a therapeutic effect. Nevertheless, strong themes in Jewish, Christian, and Islamic theology—which still provide the foundations of much of morality, even among nonbelievers — make precisely the argument that God does and human beings should punish all wrongdoing.[79] Leviticus and Deuteronomy command Israel to put to death kidnappers, murderers, and perjurers as well as those who commit adultery, sodomy, incest, homicide, or have sex with animals, gather wood on the Sabbath, or curse one of their parents. These capital crimes include both sins against Yahweh and violations of the persons or property of other humans. The basic principle of the law of ancient Israel was simple and direct:

> When one man strikes and disfigures his fellow-countryman, it shall be done to him as he has done; fracture for fracture, eye for eye, tooth for tooth. . . . Whoever strikes a beast and kills him shall make restitution; but whoever strikes a man and kills him shall be put to death.[80]

The same sort of retaliatory theme was echoed in the oft-repeated five-stage biblical refrain of national survival. This chorus varied only in detail: Israel sins, suffers, does penance, is forgiven, and is liberated, with its redemption confirmed by a new covenant. All is well for a short time, but sin soon reignites the cycle.

---

exploiting the other's weaknesses. A moral person couldn't do much better" (p. 137). There are two general difficulties, though less so with Axelrod's book than with most studies based on models of rational choice. The first is the simple fact that people do not always behave rationally or even intelligently, a difficulty especially large when, as immediately after liberation from brutal rule, emotions are likely to run high. The second difficulty is that to understand what political actors deem rational, one has to know their hierarchy of values. During the 1960s, U.S. Secretary of Defense Robert McNamara began bombing Ho Chi Minh's small factories in an effort to persuade him to stop his campaign against South Vietnam. A former peasant, Ho Chi Minh did not value factories the way McNamara, a former president of the Ford Motor Company, did. As a result, the North's incentive to compromise was far weaker than McNamara supposed. For the sorts of situations discussed in this chapter, the complicating factor is that avenging a wrong done to one's ethnic or social group may involve a moral duty to keep a sometimes mysterious faith with one's ancestors or comrades.

79. In Africa, where European imperialists were generally replaced by native despots, the religious situation is much more diverse and complex. See Stephen Ellis and Gerrie Ter Haar, *Worlds of Power: Religious Thought and Political Practice in Africa* (New York: Oxford University Press, 2004). Buddhism and Hinduism have themes that stress passive acceptance of evil rather than revenge, but adherents of each have often displayed angry outbursts of retaliatory violence that would do any vengeful Christian, Jew, or Muslim proud. For the difficulties of discerning Hindu "doctrine," see the various opinions by justices of the Indian Supreme Court in S. R. Bommai v. Union of India, 3 SC 1 (1994), and the discussion in Gary Jeffrey Jacobsohn, *The Wheel of Law: India's Secularism in Comparative Constitutional Context* (Princeton, NJ: Princeton University Press, 2003), ch. 5.

For God, at least, the data are weak. In this world, punishment that we can ascribe, albeit with small confidence, to the Deity seems random.

80. Leviticus 24:20–21.

Most ominously, on occasion Yahweh might act capriciously. According to 2 Samuel, for instance, after David confessed to the prophet Nathan that he had had Uriah the Hittite slain so he could add Bathsheba, Uriah's wife, to his own stable, Nathan replied: "Yahweh, for His part, forgives your sin; you are not to die. Yet because you have outraged Yahweh by doing this, the [first] child that will be born to you [and Bathsheba] is to die."[81] The author of 2 Samuel does not speak of any sin committed by the child Bathsheba was carrying.[82] "Fearing" the rage of this "great and terrible" God was prudent indeed.

One of the more common Christian stories of salvation conveys a message of justice as retribution: God demands that humanity expiate sin through suffering. Sinners are not forgiven through contrition alone. Only the agony of a sacrificial Lamb's slow, asphyxiating death on a cross could satisfy divine justice after Adam and Eve's disobedience. The purpose of Jesus' death was to change God, not human beings.[83] Operating within this paradigm, Augustine saw punishment and justice as reciprocal and God as a heavenly Rottweiler, ever waiting to pounce on those who violate His laws. To support his speculations, the holy bishop quoted the sixth chapter of Luke's Gospel: "[W]hatever measure you deal out to others will be dealt to you in return."[84] Indeed, Augustine went so far as to say: "As a rule, just wars are defined as those which avenge injuries . . . or to reclaim something that was wrongfully taken."[85] Across a dozen centuries, Jonathan Edwards, the great Protestant divine, echoed Augustine's message: "Justice calls aloud for an infinite punishment. . . . The wrath of God burns against [sinners]; their damnation does not slumber; the pit is prepared; the fire is made ready; the flames do rage and glow."[86]

The Shari'a's endorsement of retaliation is directly based, so Islamic jurists aver, on the Qur'an. That collection of Muhammad's words sends complex messages: Allah is the "all-merciful," both "benign and forgiving."[87] Still, He accepts repentance "only of those who are guilty of an evil out of ignorance yet quickly repent."[88] Islamic jurisprudence has resolved such ambiguities in favor of vengeance.

To the extent that the Bible, the standard Christian story of salvation,

---

81. 2 Samuel 2:13–14.

82. An atheist might construct an alternative hypothesis that is kinder to Yahweh: Bathsheba had an abortion, and the author of 2 Samuel provided a cover story.

83. Burtchaell argues that this account has the story backwards: the real point of Jesus' death was to change humanity, not God. *Philemon's Problem*, pp. 79–88, and ch. 4 generally.

84. See, generally, *The City of God*, trans. Marcus Dods (New York: Modern Library, 1950), 21.11–14.

85. *Questions on the Heptateuch*, 6:10; quoted in Burtchaell, *Philemon's Problem*, p. 191.

86. Quoted in ibid., p. 81

87. Ch. 4, verse 43.

88. Ch. 4, verse 17.

and the Shari'a express the traditional religious thinking of Jews, Christians, and Muslims, the weight of these moral theologies has clearly been on the side of mandatory punishment. Outside the world of Islam, the force of these orthodoxies may have weakened over the centuries, but they still exert power over many minds. The move from a divine retribution that imposes eternal damnation as payback for sin to a necessity that human authorities punish wrongdoing has been a smooth skate, helping to cloud distinctions between vengeance and rehabilitation, deterrence, restoration of individuals' losses, and repair of damage to the public order. Even assuming what takes a blind leap of mindless faith in shoddy reasoning to accept—that commentators on these texts have accurately described their infinitely loving God as a vindictive double-entry bookkeeper[89]—extrapolating from the supernatural to the mundane is a dangerous conceit. The commands of human justice are murky, and the relationships between sinful humans, punishment, and justice are not linear.

Examination of the purposes of punishment might clarify its relation to justice. Three justifications are generally accepted for inflicting punishment: rehabilitation, deterrence, and restoration. Socrates emphasized the rehabilitative function, though he was impressed by Protagoras's emphasis on deterrence. Using an analogy that both Aristotle and Aquinas would adopt, Socrates compared punishing a person who had committed a crime to giving medicine to a sick person.[90] It is needed "so the wrong-doer may suffer and [be] made whole."[91] From a different perspective, the eminent moral theologian James Tunstead Burtchaell speaks of the necessity of penance as the repentant sinner's "celebration of what God has been forgiving."[92] In actual practice, however, the medicinal value of punishment for the moral sclerotics who have commanded the machinery of tyrannical governments is doubtful. None of those who ordered or operated the German concentration camps or Russian gulags, incited the slaughter of the Tutus in Rwanda, or organized murders for the Argentine or Chilean generals has publicly offered to do penance.

Furthermore, only rarely have any of these people demonstrated even a hint of remorse for having committed murder and torture on a mass scale.

---

89. Jewish commentators might respond that much of the work of Talmudists has been directed toward softening the Torah's harsh strictures. And not all Islamic jurisprudes accept the dominant interpretations of the Shari'a.

90. Aristotle, *Nicomachean Ethics*, bk. 2, ch. 3, 1104b; Aquinas, *Summa Theologica*, 1–2, quest. 87, art. 7. Hereafter all *Summa* references are to this first part of the second part (1–2). For a listing of citations to other places in which Aquinas used this analogy, see John Finnis, *Aquinas: Moral, Political, and Legal Theory* (New York: Oxford University Press, 1998), p. 212n141.

91. *Gorgias*. 480. I have used B. Jowett's translation: *The Dialogues of Plato* (New York: Random House, 1892), 1:541.

92. *Philemon's Problem*, p. 333.

According to Alexander Mitscherlich and Fred Mielke's analysis of the trials of the doctors who conducted the Nazis' experiments on live human beings, most of whom pleaded guilty as charged, not one of them said "I am sorry."[93] Even Albert Speer, who is sometimes cited as the one leading Nazi who admitted evildoing, accepted only responsibility for his actions; he waffled about his guilt. "It is not only specific faults that burden my conscience, great as these may have been," he wrote after twenty years in Spandau Prison. "My moral failure is not a matter of this item and that; it resides in my active association with the whole course of events." The expectant reader waits for a *mea maxima culpa.* Instead, a sadly inadequate explanation oozes out: technology made me do it. "Dazzled by the possibilities of technology, I devoted crucial years of my life to serving it. But in the end my feelings about it are highly skeptical."[94] Skeptical but not remorseful, he could not ask for forgiveness or even say "I am sorry." Questioned near the end of his life about whether he would have acted differently had he as a young man known what he then knew about Hitler and the Nazi regime, he responded, "I don't think so."[95]

Josef Stalin and Adolf Hitler died without expressing remorse; Idi Amin and Leopoldo Galtieri departed equally silent. "Who am I supposed to ask for forgiveness?" Augusto Pinochet inquired of a journalist in 2004. "They are the ones who have to ask me for forgiveness, the Marxists."[96] In testimony before the Truth and Reconciliation Commission, some of South Africa's former officials did appear contrite, even though the commission's rules did not require them to do so. But one does not have to be a cynic to doubt the sincerity of white supremacists who hoped that evidencing sorrow would keep them out of prisons run by blacks. Although Christians believe that repentance, conversion, and redemption are always possible, the moral

93. *Doctors of Infamy: The Story of the Nazi Medical Crimes* (New York, Schuman, 1949) p. 18; quoted in Tzvetan Todorov, *Facing the Extreme: Moral Life in the Concentration Camps* (New York: Holt, 1996), p. 234. For a general analysis of Nazi doctors, see Robert Jay Lifton, *Nazi Doctors: Medical Killing and the Theory of Genocide* (New York: Basic Books, 1986); for a broad analysis of Nazi efforts to pervert German moral sensibilities, see Claudia Koontz, *The Nazi Conscience* (Cambridge, MA: Harvard University Press, 2003).

94. Albert Speer, *Inside the Third Reich: Memoirs* (New York: Macmillan, 1970), pp. 523–24. I once shared an editor with Albert Speer. I had remarked that at least Speer had acknowledged his guilt. Our editor corrected me: in their conversations, Speer had conceded that the charges against him were true, but when our editor made the same comment as I, Speer interrupted to say that he accepted responsibility, not guilt.

95. Quoted by Gordon A. Craig, "Hitler's Pal" (a review of Joachim Fest, *Speer: The Final Verdict* [New York: Harcourt, 2203]), *N.Y. Rev. of Bks.*, Oct. 24, 2003, p. 33. Craig, one of the leading historians of modern Germany, believes that Speer was "haunted by a sense of guilt that he could neither articulate nor escape."

96. Larry Rother, "Chilean Court Revokes Pinochet's Immunity from Prosecution," *N.Y. Times*, May 29, 2004.

rehabilitation of deposed despots is not an outcome on which Las Vegas bookmakers would give odds. Thus, rehabilitative justice for officials of the old regime remains only a remotely possible outcome of punishment.

Threats of punishment may deter decent people who are disinclined to commit serious crimes anyway—not a small accomplishment, of course.[97] But the capacity of such threats to restrain, either psychologically or morally, career criminals or the sort of men who operate brutally oppressive governments is doubtful. The much publicized trials of war criminals at Nuremberg and Tokyo, followed by the execution of most of the defendants, did not slow, much less stop, Stalin, Chiang Kai-shek, Mao Tse-tung, Idi Amin, Kim Il Sung, Kim Jong Il, Slobodan Milosevic, Saddam Hussein, or any of several dozen Latin American generals and African dictators from terrorizing their own people. As Reinhold Niebuhr said, "The whip of the law cannot change the heart."[98] Like Mafia dons, gangsters who are in power do not believe they will be caught. Often they are right.

Yet there is always an "on the other hand" in matters such as deterrence. Whatever the values of studies of threats of and actual punishment on "ordinary" criminals, the number of coprophagers who have done tyrants' dirty work remains small when compared to mass populations in prisons. That fact may speak well for human nature, but it does prevent statistical analysis on which scholars can rely. And here Aryeh Neier, when he was executive director of Human Rights Watch, spoke for "the other hand": "Who's to say that clemency won't simply embolden the torturers, thereby inviting rather than preventing further abuses?"[99]

Punishment's capacity to effect restorative (corrective) justice is also problematic.[100] Heavy fines, if the new government could force ousted offi-

---

97. The Federalist Society, citing a study by the U.S. Department of Justice, says that in state prisons recidivists incarcerated for a violent offense with only nonviolent priors exceed the number of recidivists with a history of a violent prior offense. "The notion that criminality is neatly segmented into violent and nonviolent is fundamentally wrong." "White Paper on the USA Patriot Act of 2001," (2001), pp. 16–17. The study cited is U.S. Bureau of Justice Statistics, *Correctional Population in the United States, 1997* (Washington, DC: Government Printing Office, 2000), p. 57.

98. "The Montgomery Savagery," *Christianity and Crisis*, June 12, 1961, p. 103; quoted in Burtchaell, *Philemon's Problem*, p. 213.

99. Quoted in Lawrence Wechsler, "A Miracle, a Universe: Settling Accounts with Torturers," in Neil J. Kritz, ed., *Transitional Justice: New Emerging Nations Reckon with Former Regimes* (Washington, DC: U.S. Institute of Peace, 1995), 1:497.

100. Of course, that relationship should be problematic. Restorative justice focuses not on hurting wrongdoers but on repairing the damage they have done. For "restorative justice" Aristotle employs a term that Richard McKeon, using the Oxford translation, renders as "rectificatory justice" (*Nicomachean Ethics*, bk. 5, ch. 4, 1132a, in *The Basic Works of Aristotle* [New York: Random House, 1941], p. 1008n). For analyses of restorative justice under modern conditions, see Annalise Acorn, *Compulsory Compassion: A Critique of Restorative Justice* (Vancouver: University of British Columbia Press, 2004), esp. ch. 2; and Mark S. Umbreit, Betty Vos, Robert Coates, and Katherine Brown, *Facing Violence: The Path of Restorative Justice and Dialogue* (New York: Criminal Justice, 2003).

cials to pay, might compensate for damages to property.[101] But no punishment can restore the murdered to life, not even subjecting deposed despots to the Mongols' slow death; nor can permanently locking a tyrant in a cage make whole the numbed minds or crippled bodies of people who have been tortured or give back to those wrongly incarcerated the lost years of their lives. Time swaps occur only in science fiction.

Allowing criminal trials may, of course, serve a commemorative function. Stalin allegedly said that the death of one man is a tragedy, the slaughter of hundreds of thousands is a mere statistic. By allowing victims and their relatives to testify, trials could memorialize those who suffered. No longer would victims be merely anonymous numbers. They and their families could confront their tormentors in public and tell their stories, a process that transforms faceless victims into flesh-and-blood human beings with personal histories of courageous opposition to oppression. Even if that testimony does not penetrate the thick armor of their tormentors' moral autism, it could comfort victims as well as reinforce the revulsion the outside world feels, serving as a reminder, as the perpetrators stand humiliated in the dock, that the face of evil, although always hideous, is also often ordinary.[102] That scene may also be morally educate the educable, if not deter the incorrigible.

On the other hand, testimony before a truth and reconciliation commission—again, modeled on that of South Africa—may achieve that commemorative goal more effectively than criminal trials. This process can provide the stage for what Elizabeth Kiss calls "a national morality play."[103] Victims or their families can tell their stories and present their evidence as coherent packages rather than in the piecemeal fashion required by the rigid rules of a court. "Retrospectively," Lawrence Wechsler concludes, "the broadcasting of truth to a certain degree redeems the suffering of the former victims."[104] And more than postconviction pleadings for a reduced sentence, the prospect of amnesty could pressure even conscienceless pirates to confess their crimes and express remorse. If these former officials craved absolution—if they did not, they would not be before the commission—they would be compelled to testify and then submit to cross-examination. And they would know that perjury could result in double punishment—for the crimes about which they lied and for their perjury. Although these people, often being psychopaths, would probably not feel shame, their publicly expressing contrition would further tar the political order their crimes helped maintain. Moreover, if, as did not happen in Argentina and Chile, those seeking am-

101. For a thorough analysis, see Lawrence Wechsler, *A Miracle, a Universe: Settling Accounts with Torturers* (New York: Pantheon, 1990).

102. See Hannah Arendt, *Eichmann in Jerusalem: A Report on the Banality of Evil* (New York: Viking, 1964).

103. "Moral Ambition within and beyond Political Constraints," p. 70.

104. "A Miracle, a Universe," 1:472.

nesty were questioned about the fates of the thousands of people whom the regime made disappear, the victims' families could have whatever thin consolation harsh truth brings.

Possibly the most important result of putting political predators in prison is to prevent them from doing further harm.[105] As Niebuhr completed his thought about "the whip of the law": "But thank God [government] can restrain the heartless" until they grow new hearts—which, in this context, probably translates "until death do us part." Removal from office usually prevents tyrants from continuing their oppression, although nothing less than a swift execution, as Nicolae Ceauşescu and his wife suffered, can guarantee an end to their career. Tyrants have been known to rise from political graves. Executions, however, may actually help a totalitarian movement by creating martyrs who might be, as Rosa Luxemburg was, more useful to lost causes than are live heroes. New leaders might also recall a stanza from William Blake's "The Grey Monk":

> The hand of Vengeance found the Bed
> To which the Purple Tyrant fled;
> The iron hand crush'd the Tyrant's head
> And became a Tyrant in his stead.

Punishment's protecting citizens against future harm leads to another function, which Thomists classify as retributive but might be more accurately characterized as rehabilitative for the community. Sin, Aquinas argued, disrupts the divine order of things, which only punishment can restore.[106] By analogy, he reasoned that offenses committed by public officials disrupt society's order. This "inequality of justice" can be rectified only by imposing "bads those officials are unwilling to undergo."[107] The purpose of government's inflicting punishment goes beyond paying a debt to injured individuals; more important, it tries to restore (or generate) harmony for the community. Punishment "is requisite" not only that the criminal's soul be

105. So, too, the most socially efficacious result of imprisoning felons is probably that it prevents them from harming others, except guards and fellow inmates.

106. As a Thomist of sorts, I find this argument utterly unconvincing, as I do all arguments that, while proclaiming God's omnipotence, try to impose limits on Her unlimitable power.

107. Finnis, *Aquinas*, pp. 211–15, esp. n153, has an excellent analysis of Thomas's short disquisition on punishment and justice. Throughout this brief discussion Aquinas's focus is on sin, and the punishment to which he usually refers is that which God (supposedly: Thomas offers no data) imposes on sinners. The argument is thus theological, not political. Occasionally, however, Aquinas does include a reference (an aside?) to unjust and criminal acts done to fellow human beings and to punishment imposed by rulers. For instance: "This restoration of the equality of justice by penal consequences is also to be observed in injuries done to one's fellow men" (*Summa*, art. 6). Aquinas's views on tyrannicide, even punishing tyrants, are less than clear, in part because he died before completing *De Regimine Principum*, the work in which he most thoroughly examined those problems. His student Ptolemy of Lucca finished the essay, and it is impossible to say what in that analysis was written by whom.

healed but also "that the disorder [in society] may be remedied by the contrary of that which caused it. Moreover, punishment is requisite in order to restore the equality of justice, and to remove the scandal given to others, so that those who were scandalized . . . may be edified by the punishment."[108]

Seven centuries later, Lord Denning offered a variation on these themes. "It is a mistake," he wrote to the Royal Commission on Capital Punishment, "to consider the object of punishment as being deterrent or reformant or preventive and nothing else." Rather, punishment's "ultimate justification lies in its affirming the community's "emphatic denunciation" of a crime.[109] In a broader sense, of course, Aquinas and His Lordship were talking about an educative function, the state's publicly reaffirming its values by imposing severe physical harm on people who violated those norms. And as an educational device, punishment can play an important role for constitutional democracy, instructing its people about the polity's basic values. But then so can the hearings and final report of a truth and justice commission, as earlier paragraphs contended.

Politics and Justice

Questions of justice and punishment would be of minimal interest to pragmatists, consequentialists, moral relativists, or legal positivists. The former would be concerned with practical effects, and the latter would defer either to local conventions or to the rules of local legal systems. For ardent retributionists, such as Augustine and Jonathan Edwards, these issues would also be of small concern. They would insist on scourging, imprisoning, or executing deposed tyrants. Aquinas, encumbered by a felt obligation to import into politics a theology built around a vindictive God, would tend to agree, though with less vehemence or joy. Socrates and Aristotle would prefer, but probably not require, punishment. Still, these two, and Aquinas as well, tinctured their public morality with splashes of political realism and might have been quite willing to compromise. Rawls's theory of justice, with its heavy infusion of reciprocity, would allow punishment, but his conception of justice as fairness would not demand retribution.

And there is always the haunting question: how much justice even as fairness, much less retribution, do we as individuals really want? When Hamlet asks Polonius to take care of the actors who will put on the play that he has written to "catch the conscience of the King," the chamberlain prom-

---

108. *Summa,* quest. 87, art. 6, reply to obj. 3. See also quest. 87, art. 2, reply to obj. 1: "Sometimes indeed [punishment] is for the good of those who are punished. . . . But it is always for the amendment of others, who, seeing some men fall from sin to sin, are the more fearful of sinning." And quest. 87, art. 3, reply to obj. 1: "Even the punishment that is inflicted according to human laws is not always intended as a remedy for the one who is punished, but sometimes only for others. Thus when a thief is hanged, this is not for his own amendment, but for the sake of others, who at least may be deterred through fear of punishment."

109. Quoted in Hart, *Law, Liberty, and Morality,* p. 65. See also Murphy, *Getting Even.*

ises, "My Lord, I shall use them according to their desert." Hamlet then responds: "God's bodykins, man, much better! Use every man according to his deserts, and who shall scape whipping?"[110] Dante hammers home a similar point: the most frightening aspect of his *Inferno* is that each person agonizing in one of the circles of a horrible Hell is getting exactly what he or she has earned—not a cheering thought for self-reflective people who are not blindly self-righteous. Indeed, as Hamlet confessed to Ophelia, "I myself am indifferent honest, but yet I could accuse myself of such things that it were better that my mother had not borne me."[111] Few of us have committed crimes of rape, torture, or murder, yet by acts of omission as well as commission, most of us, "errant knaves all," have injured or risked injury to our fellow humans—driven an automobile too fast or after one or two drinks too many, spoken racial or ethnic slurs, padded an expense account, or failed to report cash income on tax returns. To insist on exacting exact retribution is hazardous. For others, we may demand a strict accounting of wrongdoing, insist on punishment, and call that process justice; for ourselves we prefer justice to be tempered by mercy.

For those people think both that *justice* is not an empty word and that it differs from revenge, the moral problems surrounding whether, how, and how much to punish deposed despots are shrouded in mist. Some of that mist may lift with a realization that justice looks forward as well as backward. Politics and political justice are concerned not merely with punishing the crimes of the past but also with creating goods for the future, with how to help a people find opportunities to live decent lives, as free in a warped world as lives can be from oppressive government, from fear, from want, and from hate and violence from and toward fellow citizens. Thus, the objective of leaders of a new constitutional democracy should go beyond placating desires for revenge, no matter how understandable, and facilitate the sort of society that maximizes what Jefferson would have called the chances of its citizens to pursue happiness.[112] It is according to this standard, heavily infused with considerations of justice as fair distribution not merely of penalties but also of opportunities to achieve positive goods, that those leaders should make decisions about amnesty or punishment. And those choices must be based on fallible judgments about what courses of public action will

110. *Hamlet,* act 2, scene 2.
111. Ibid., act 3, scene 1.
112. Gutmann and Thompson agree that amnesty is not necessarily unjust. "To the extent that a truth commission guides itself by reciprocal reasons, it fulfills the requirements for moral justification. First, reciprocity—'making a proportionate return for a good received'—is not only a moral principle but also an important aspect of justice. . . . The 'good received' is that others make their claims on terms that each can accept in principle. Because this kind of exchange it itself a form of justice, a truth commission that strives for reciprocity directly addresses the challenge posed by the sacrifice of other kinds of justice" ("Moral Foundations of Truth Commissions," pp. 36–37).

best reconcile the segments of a community that has suffered and continues to experience pain.

Decisions to prosecute, to compromise and offer conditional amnesty, or even grant full pardon and attempt "no-fault reconciliation" are thus eminently political, again in Aristotle's sense. They are concerned with authoritatively establishing goals for society and determining the means that are both most efficiently directed toward those ends and most consonant with the principles of constitutional democracy. A nation fragmented by hate and anger is unlikely to be able to honor those norms or even remain at peace with itself. The ideal society for the survival of constitutional democracy is one in which citizens trust and respect one another; the minimum condition is a society in which citizens do not hate and fear one another. In that context, to attempt reconciliation evidences political, if not moral, virtue.[113]

113. I borrowed the term "political virtue" from Emanuel Sivan, "Illusions of Change," in Larry Diamond, Marc F. Plattner, and Daniel Brumberg, eds., *Islam and Democracy in the Middle East* (Baltimore: Johns Hopkins University Press, 2003), p. 21.

CHAPTER FOURTEEN

Constitutional Interpretation
as Constitutional Maintenance

If the people ever let command of the war power fall into irresponsible and unscrupulous hands, the courts wield no power equal to its restraint.

JUSTICE ROBERT H. JACKSON

If this Nation is to remain true to the ideals symbolized by its flag, it must not wield the tools of tyrants even to resist the forces of tyranny.

JUSTICE JOHN PAUL STEVENS

In every polity, proposed solutions to political problems are likely to be disputed because the efficacy of most public policies is uncertain. What is also likely is that the citizens who will pay most of the costs of a particular policy will not be the same citizens who will reap most of the benefits. More fundamentally, the general nature of the norms expressed or latent in the constitutional text and order makes the legitimacy of various proposals controversial, often for losers but sometimes for winners as well.[1] Thus constitutional interpretation is an integral part of constitutional maintenance.

Designers of a constitutional democracy might deem it expedient to assign assessment of a policy's efficacy to one institution and reserve questions of its constitutional validity to another. This solution, exemplified by creating constitutional courts alongside of parliaments, seems neat; but prudence and legitimacy are often entwined. Authoritatively specifying substantive goals and procedural rules affects immediate allocations of costs and benefits as well as shapes the country's future. Even a dispute that appears

---

1. Probably the most famous instance of a winner's doubts was Jefferson's fear that his acquisition of Louisiana was unconstitutional. After signing the treaty with France, he urged his supporters in the Senate to consent to it "with as little debate as possible, & particularly so far as respects the constitutional difficulty." He then explained: "Our peculiar security is in possession of a written Constitution. Let us not make it a blank paper by construction. I say the same as to the opinion of those who consider the grant of the treaty making power as boundless. If it is, we have no Constitution. . . . Let us go on then perfecting it, by adding, by way of amendment to the Constitution, those powers which time & trial show are still wanting." To Senator Wilson Cary Nicholas, Sept. 7, 1803, in *The Works of Thomas Jefferson*, ed. Paul L. Ford (New York: Putnam's, 1905), 10:10–11n. Jefferson wrote out several drafts of a constitutional amendment, but we have no record of his ever asking his supporters in Congress to propose any such a change.

trivial, such as a city's authority to display a crèche or menorah, may reveal a clash between values widely—and deeply—held within society. Reconciling or ranking them according to the polity's basic norms is seldom a simple task. Occasionally, a choice among competing policies may even risk (or be thought to risk) the survival of the nation itself.

This chapter first presents an overview of the enterprise of constitutional interpretation and next explains the principal peculiarities of constitutional interpretation as a form of constitutional maintenance.

The Enterprise of Constitutional Interpretation

Although interpreters frequently pretend otherwise, they confront five elementary interrogatives: *Why* should anyone interpret the constitution? *When* should interpreters interpret? *What* is it that interpreters are supposed to interpret? *Who* are the legitimate interpreters? *How* should they, whoever they are, interpret?

A response to *why interpret* is straightforward. Most generally, we cannot understand a text, a social or political order, or a philosophy without interpreting it. Gathering data may be a prerequisite to understanding, but the two are separate intellectual operations. To understand, we must decide what those data mean. As Aharon Barak, the president of Israel's Supreme Court, put it, "All understanding comes from interpretation. Pre-interpretive understanding does not exist."[2] More specifically, when we speak of a constitution, we must decide that the word itself comports, as the discussion in the introductory chapter indicated. But even if we accept one of conventional definitions or infer some other, we face additional and more specific difficulties. First, what are its general objectives and the more specific ones that the text and/or the constitutional order specify? But because neither drafters of constitutional texts nor builders of constitutional orders are apt to foresee, much less offer solutions for, all future problems the polity will encounter in pursuing those goals, doubts about the legitimacy of many public policies will become inescapable. Thus arises the necessity of interpretation, that is, milking meaning from the words of text, the norms of political theories, and the teaching of history and tradition.[3]

One answer to the interrogative *when to interpret* is whenever constitu-

---

2. *Purposive Interpretation in Law*, trans. Sari Bashi (Princeton, NJ: Princeton University Press, 2005), p. xv.

3. Keith E. Whittington differentiates constitutional interpretation (by which he means parsing of a legal text) from constitutional construction (essentially political and creative). I admire much of his work but do not find this distinction useful because I think (1) all constitutional interpretation is political in Aristotle's sense of the term and also often creative, and (2) law is itself a product of politics, and thus "legal" interpretation is a subset of political interpretation. I suspect one basic cause of Whittington's insistence is that he believes originalism is *the* proper interpretive mode. *Constitutional Interpretation: Textual Meaning, Original Intent, and Judicial Review* (Lawrence: University Press of Kansas, 1999), ch. 1.

tional issues of constitutional meaning arise, which is likely to be frequently if not constantly.[4] Nevertheless, some public officials and private citizens are unaware that they are, at least indirectly, so acting, while other public officials, quite conscious of what they are doing, believe it is not prudent to advertise this aspect of their work. I have attacked in detail the remaining three queries elsewhere[5] and here only summarize the beginnings of proper answers.

What Is the Constitution That Must Be Interpreted?

INCLUSION. *What* the "constitution" includes is a problem, not a datum. Sanford Levinson has offered a religious analogy to categorize responses. "Protestant" interpreters, such as Hugo L. Black, claim to restrict themselves to the plain words of holy writ, the constitutional charter itself. In contrast, "Catholic" interpreters also target some or all of such other "texts" as original understanding, underlying political theories, previous interpretations, settled practices, traditions, and aspirations—in sum, the broader constitutional order.[6] This division is, however, seldom clear-cut.

Yet no Protestant interpreter, not even Black, has long resisted adding to or subtracting from the constitutional script.[7] And for "Cafeteria Catholics" as well as "Backslud Baptists," a series of daunting questions erupt: What other "texts" besides the charter itself are in the constitutional canon? Assuming interpreters include original understanding, how can they read the minds of men (seldom women) who have been dead for decades or even centuries? Should all previous interpretations or only those that were "cor-

4. For an answer to this question that differs from this chapter's analysis, see Mark A. Graber, "Why Interpret? Political Justification and American Constitutionalism," 55 *Rev. of Pols.* 417 (1994).

5. For the United States, see, for example, my "The Nature of the American Constitution," James Lecture (Urbana: Department of Political Science, University of Illinois, 1989); Walter F. Murphy, James E. Fleming, and Sotirios A. Barber, *American Constitutional Interpretation*, 2nd ed. (Westbury, NY: Foundation, 1995), pts. 2–4. Parts 2–4 of the 3rd ed. (2003) contain a similar analysis, but I took almost no part in those revisions. For other nations: "Constitutions, Constitutionalism, and Democracy," in Douglas Greenberg, Stanley N. Katz, Melanie Beth Oliviero, and Steven C. Wheatley, eds., *Constitutionalism and Democracy: Transformations in the Contemporary World* (New York: Oxford University Press, 1993).

6. American interpreters and scholars who study their work typically restrict the term *constitution* to refer to the text, or occasionally they speak of the unwritten constitution. The distinction is hardly new. John Marshall, after all, spoke of "the spirit" of the Constitution. See, for example. Cohens v. Virginia, 19 U.S. 264, 384 (1821). See also Christopher G. Tiedeman, *The Unwritten Constitution of the United States: A Philosophical Inquiry into the Fundamentals of American Constitutional Law* (New York: Putnam's, 1890). Supposedly, Thomas Reed Powell began his course on constitutional law at Harvard by instructing students not to read the constitutional text. It would only confuse them. Constitutional law was contained in opinions of the Supreme Court, not in the document of 1787 as amended.

7. Black often added what he thought was "original intent," for instance, in Adamson v. California, 332 U.S. 46 (1947), and democratic theory, as for example, in Wesberry v. Sanders, 376 U.S. 1 (1964). He also subtracted, at least as far as judges were concerned, the Ninth Amendment, dissenting in Griswold v. Connecticut, 381 U.S. 479 (1965).

rect" bind current interpreters? What criteria determine an earlier reading's correctness? How do interpreters conclude that particular values are part of the nation's tradition or aspirations? Which practices are truly settled and which only becoming settled (or unsettled)? How do interpreters distinguish between practices and traditions? When the two disagree, which should prevail? Why? Through which of the competing versions of democratic and constitutional theory should interpreters read the nation's foundational norms? How do interpreters discern "evolving standards of decency"?

PURPOSES. Both the constitutional order and the constitutional charter have several objectives,[8] but few texts spell these out in detail. Paralleling Aristotle's expanding the definition of a constitution,[9] we can see three prominent points along a spectrum of goals. The simplest would be to provide a framework for government by spelling out processes and allocations of authority. More complicated would be the idea of a constitution as also memorializing some of society's more basic values. Most complicated would be Aristotle's notion of a constitution as a way of life, not only specifying governmental processes and enshrining certain values as fundamental but also advancing aspirations for a good society. Whatever purposes interpreters discern (and carefully explain and justify) affects what they deem to be included in the constitution. Viewing the constitution as merely detailing governmental processes would be compatible with a view of the constitution as the text and nothing but the text. As interpreters move toward the other end of the spectrum, their vision of the constitution widens.

Who Are the Authoritative Interpreters?

"Just about everybody" is a roughly accurate response to the question *who interprets*. Judges are highly visible interpreters; but every public official sometimes, explicitly or implicitly, interprets the constitution. When legislators vote for a bill, they decide or assume its validity; chief executives do so when they propose or approve legislation. Indeed, the most important piece of American constitutional interpretation was made by a president: "I hold," Abraham Lincoln said in his first inaugural address, "that in contemplation of universal law, and of the Constitution, the Union of these States is perpetual."[10] Less dramatically but still significantly, the West German chancellor decided in 1973 that West Germany could recognize East Germany as an independent nation despite the Basic Law's assertion that the Federal Re-

---

8. One might make a strong case for substituting the closely related concept of function, but at least in this regard I agree with Barak's argument that purpose more accurately reflects what is at issue. *Purposive Interpretation in Law*, chs. 3, 5, and 11.

9. See General Introduction, p. 13.

10. Mar. 4, 1861; in *The Collected Works of Abraham Lincoln*, ed. Roy P. Basler (New Brunswick, NJ: Rutgers University Press, 1953), 4:262–71.

public *was* Germany.[11] Seventeen years later, another chancellor held that East Germany could be admitted into the Federal Republic as individual *Länder* under Article 23 of the Basic Law.[12] The clearer alternative, because the People's Republic was a unitary state, was to invoke Article 146—"This Basic Law shall cease to be in force on the day on which a constitution adopted by a free decision of the [entire] German people comes into force"— and convene a new constitutional convention.

Even a decision by legislative or executive officials that constitutional interpretation is a judicial monopoly is itself a (usually mistaken) constitutional interpretation. Attorneys interpret when they advise clients or argue before judges or other officials. And it is not unknown for journalists and academics to publish articles and books that purport to reveal true constitutional meaning. For their part, voters, again wittingly or no, often construe the constitution when they choose one set of public officials over another, when they try to get a policy enacted into law, or when they defend themselves against criminal charges. Opportunity for popular interpretation is essential to constitutional democracy.[13] If a constitution is to serve as "the vehicle of a nation's life, it cannot be, as Woodrow Wilson said, "a mere lawyers' document."[14]

Legislators and chief executives have tall pulpits from which to expound constitutional doctrines; and the plain words of the charter, by requiring both public officials to swear to defend it, require them to interpret it. The First American Congress provided a model of debate about constitutional meaning, with James Madison directly and Alexander Hamilton by proxy contesting such issues as congressional authority to fund a national debt and establish a national bank. Other questions argued in that congress included the Supreme Court's authority to review state courts' constitutional interpretations and the president's authority to remove executive officials without senatorial consent.[15] Probably not even the famed Webster-Hayne debates

11. The chancellor acted despite the fact that Bavaria had filed suit in the Constitutional Court, challenging the government's authority to sign the treaty. Presented with a fait accompli, the Court upheld the chancellor's decision, though the justices tried to save face by claiming that the "final power to uphold this constitutional order resides in the Federal Constitutional Court." See the Basic East-West Treaty Case, 36 BVerfGE 1 (1973), in Walter F. Murphy and Joseph Tanenhaus, eds., *Comparative Constitutional Law* (New York: St. Martin's, 1977), pp. 232ff.

12. Originally that article read: "For the time being, this Basic Law shall apply in the territory of [the existing *Länder*]." Then in 1956, when the Saarland joined the Federal Republic, a second sentence was added: "In other parts of Germany [this Basic Law] shall be put into force on their succession."

13. For an argument for popular interpretation, see esp. Larry Kramer, *The People Themselves: Popular Constitutionalism and Judicial Review* (New York: Oxford University Press, 2004).

14. *The Papers of Woodrow Wilson*, ed. Arthur S. Link et al. (Princeton, NJ: Princeton University Press, 1975), 18:172.

15. For a masterful analysis of the debates in the First Congress, see Stanley Elkins and Eric McKitrick, *The Age of Federalism: The Early American Republic, 1788–1800* (New York: Oxford Univer-

of 1830 on the nature of the union have matched the quality of those initial discussions, but speeches in later congresses have sometimes exceeded in learning and depth of analysis the spate of opinions the Supreme Court produces to justify decisions.[16]

Other constitutional democracies display similar patterns. It is common for MPs in Australia, Canada, Ireland, and the United Kingdom to heatedly debate constitutional issues. More formally, each house of the Italian Parliament has a standing committee to judge the constitutionality of proposed legislation. Both committees carefully scrutinize all important bills, exercising what is an almost absolute veto. When a member of the French Senate or National Assembly introduces "a motion of unconstitutionality," Parliament's rules require a full debate and vote on the validity of the proposed legislation.[17]

The question *who interprets* essentially asks for an empirical response, but hidden within lie two deeper inquiries: First, when interpreters disagree, whose reading is authoritative? Second, and more fundamental, need there be a final interpreter at all?

To answer the first question first, there are obvious candidates for that post: the executive, the legislature, the courts, and the electorate.[18] Furthermore, a polity may establish departmentalism, that is, divide final interpretive authority among several institutions. Long struggles against kings and more recent experience with dictators have discouraged constitutional democracies from anointing the chief executive as supreme interpreter. Still, the charter of the French Fifth Republic says that the president "shall supervise respect for the Constitution," an ambiguous function. The president of Italy may invoke Article 74 and refuse to promulgate a bill if he deems it either unconstitutional or merely unwise. Parliament may then reconsider its action, and if it repasses the measure, the text says the bill "must be promulgated." Article 90, however, stipulates that the president is responsible for

---

sity Press, 1993); for a useful but less detailed account, see David P. Currie, *The Constitution in Congress: The Federalist Period, 1789–1791* (Chicago: University of Chicago Press, 1997), pt. 1. Currie has continued his analysis of legislative interpretation in a pair of succeeding volumes: *The Constitution in Congress: The Jeffersonians, 1801–1829* (Chicago: University of Chicago Press, 2001), and *The Constitution in Congress: Democrats and Whigs, 1829–1861* (Chicago: University of Chicago Press, 2005).

16. See, for example, the debates in 1957 on proposals to curb the Supreme Court's appellate jurisdiction, discussed in Walter F. Murphy. *Congress and the Court* (Chicago: University of Chicago Press, 1962), chs. 7-10; see also J. Mitchell Pickerill, *Constitutional Deliberation in Congress* (Durham, NC: Duke University Press, 2004); and Jeb Barnes, *Overruled? Legislative Overrides, Pluralism, and Contemporary Court-Congress Relations* (Stanford, CA: Stanford University Press, 2004).

17. Alec Stone Sweet, "Judging Socialist Reform: The Politics of Coordinate Construction in France and Germany," 26 *Comp. Pol. St.* 443 (1994).

18. In the absence of institutional provisions for frequent referenda, the electorate can only (at least peacefully) interpret indirectly through choosing public officials, pressuring them when they are in office, and helping create and maintain a certain kind of constitutional culture. For a defense of interpretation by the electorate, indeed, by "crowd action," see Kramer, *The People Themselves.*

"any affront against the Constitution" he may commit. Thus some commentators believe that if the objection rests on constitutional grounds, the president may still refuse to promulgate the bill.[19] In Turkey and Latin America, military officers have frequently assumed the role of the constitution's special guardians—a role some texts have expressly prescribed—and have overturned civilian governance. During emergencies in the United States, the president has occasionally exercised what has been close to plenary interpretive power, at least until after the emergency has passed.[20] Although both Jefferson and Madison disagreed,[21] legislators have seemed less dangerous. Historically, Parliament has been the definitive interpreter of Britain's constitution, as, until the Fifth Republic was thirteen years old, was the French Parliament.[22] The Dutch and Swiss legislatures still are, though the latter only on questions regarding allocations of national power.

Most constitutional democracies have installed judicial review, and some, most notably Germany and the United States, have apparently ordained judicial supremacy. The German Basic Law, reinforced by jurisdictional statutes, seems to designate the constitutional court as final interpreter.[23] In the United States, at least in *City of Boerne* (1997), the Supreme Court claimed supremacy, although the justices backed down somewhat in Gonzales v. O Centro Espíritu Beneficente União do Vegetal in 2006.[24] Whether

19. Mauro Cappelletti, *Judicial Review in the Contemporary World* (Indianapolis: Bobbs-Merrill, 1971), pp. 6–7.

20. Clinton L. Rossiter argues that the United States has two constitutions, one for peace and one for war. *The Supreme Court and the Commander in Chief*, exp. ed. (Ithaca, NY: Cornell University Press, 1976). For a different view, see Lee Epstein, Daniel E. Ho, Gary King, and Jeffrey A. Segal, "The Supreme Court during Crisis: How War Affects Only Non-war Cases," 80 *N.Y.U. L. Rev.* 1 (2005).

21. As Jefferson wrote Madison on Mar. 15, 1789: "The tyranny of the legislatures is the most formidable dread at present, and will be for long years. That of the executive will come, but it will be at a remote period." *The Republic of Letters: The Correspondence between Thomas Jefferson and James Madison, 1776–1826*, ed. James Morton Smith (New York: W. W. Norton, 1995), 1:588. Madison did not need convincing on this point. More than a year earlier, he had warned in *The Federalist* 49 that "the tendency of republican governments is to an aggrandizement of the legislative at the expense of other departments."

22. See Alec Stone [Sweet], *The Birth of Judicial Politics in France: The Constitutional Council in Comparative Perspective* (New York: Oxford University Press, 1992).

23. Sec. 31 of the Federal Constitutional Court Act of 1951 provides that a decision of that tribunal "shall be binding upon the constitutional bodies of the Federation and of the Laender as well as upon all law courts and public authorities." Much of the text of the statute is reprinted in James K. Pollock and John C. Lane, eds., *Source Materials on the Government and Politics of Germany* (Ann Arbor, MI: Wahrs, 1964), pp. 94–110. For analysis and later amendments, see Donald P. Kommers, *The Constitutional Jurisprudence of the Federal Republic of Germany*, 2nd ed. (Durham, NC: Duke University Press, 1997), ch. 1.

24. City of Boerne v. Flores, 521 U.S. 507. See also Dickerson v. United States, 530 U.S. 428 (2000), in which Chief Justice Rehnquist, a critic of Miranda v. Arizona, 384 U.S. 436 (1966), wrote the Court's opinion striking down a congressional effort to modify that ruling. The chief justice made it clear that constitutional interpretation was the Court's private preserve: "Congress may not

Centro represents a minor aberration or portends a major shift, both presidents and congresses have frequently asserted equal interpretive authority—and made good on those assertions.[25] Echoing Jefferson and adumbrating Lincoln and Franklin Roosevelt, Andrew Jackson said in 1832: "Each public officer who takes an oath to support the Constitution swears that he will support it as he understands it, and not as it is understood by others. . . . The opinion of the judges has no more authority over Congress than the opinion of Congress has over the judges, and on that point the President is independent of both."[26]

Legislators and chief executives who disagree with judges have arsenals of weapons to persuade courts to change their constitutional minds.[27] In some constitutional democracies, even the jurisdiction of courts is subject to legislative adjustment. Although judges seldom die or voluntarily retire, in most countries—the United States is the most important exception—they must retire at a specified age or after serving a set term, thus creating vacancies that dominant parties can try to fill with "right thinking" jurists. Even in the United States, a vacancy on the Supreme Court has occurred approximately every two and a half years, providing, on average, a two-term president three nominations. In Canada, judicial review rested on a statute until 1982, and federal courts remain creatures of statutes, not the constitutional text. What Parliament can enact, Parliament can repeal.[28]

---

legislatively supersede our decisions interpreting and applying the Constitution." (Ironically, Chief Justice Warren's opinion of the Court in *Miranda* had denied setting a rigid constitutional requirement and had invited legislative intervention to formulate new rules for custodial interrogation.) *Boerne* and *Dickerson* did not come without warning. In Cooper v. Aaron, 358 U.S. 1 (1958), in the context of state defiance of the Supreme Court's decision in the School Segregation Cases, the justices unanimously said "the federal judiciary is supreme in the exposition of the law of the Constitution." Later, a majority of the justices had several times made noises about their putative interpretive supremacy over all problems. See Powell v. McCormack, 385 U.S. 486 (1969); United States v. Nixon, 418 U.S. 683 (1974); and INS v. Chadha, 462 U.S. 919 (1983).

25. Occasionally some states have also claimed equal interpretive authority, though the Civil War rendered this assertion moot. See Walter F. Murphy, James E. Fleming, Sotirios A. Barber, and Stephen Macedo, *American Constitutional Interpretation*, 3rd ed. (Westbury, NY: Foundation, 2003), ch. 8, for a brief account and bibliography. See my "Who Shall Interpret the Constitution?" 48 *Rev. of Pols.* 401 (1986); *Congress and the Court*; and *American Constitutional Interpretation*, chs. 7–8. See also Pickerill, *Constitutional Deliberation in Congress*; Barnes, *Overruled*; Mark Tushnet, *Taking the Constitution Away from the Courts* (Princeton, NJ: Princeton University Press, 1999); and Christopher Wolfe, ed., *That Eminent Tribunal: Judicial Supremacy and the Constitution* (Princeton, NJ: Princeton University Press, 2004), esp. the essays by Hadley Arkes, Michael McConnell, and Jeremy Waldron.

26. Veto Message of July 10, 1832, in James D. Richardson, ed., *A Compilation of the Messages and Papers of the Presidents* (Washington, DC: n.p., 1908), 2:581–82.

27. For a brief discussion of these checks in the United States, see Walter F. Murphy, C. Herman Pritchett, Lee Epstein, and Jack Knight, eds., *Courts, Judges, and Politics: An Introduction to the Judicial Process*, 6th ed. (Boston: McGraw-Hill, 2005), ch. 8.

28. For an interesting discussion of the independence of judges in Canada, see Beauregard v. the Queen, [1986] 2 S.C.R. 56.

Departmentalism allows one institution to be supreme for its branch of government or for specific constitutional questions such as federalism.[29] That limited claim is both practically and normatively different from proclaiming universal interpretive finality. The American and Japanese supreme courts have narrowed their assertion of supremacy through the doctrine of political questions, that some constitutional problems lie beyond judges' ken.[30] Canadian justices claim authority to interpret only the constitutional text, although in so doing they have explained the meaning of the broader constitutional order.[31]

Some constitutional texts have made such divisions explicit by specifying areas of constitutional interpretation in which decisions by one or another branch would be supreme. The Irish document, for example, establishes judicial review but also attempts to limit its reach. Article 45 lists principles of social policy to guide Parliament but adds that these "shall not be cognizable by any Court under any of the provisions of this Constitution," seemingly leaving it to the electorate to judge the validity of parliament's judgment.[32] Similarly, Article 28, §3.3° makes Parliament the final judge about what is necessary for "securing the public safety and the preservation of the State in time or war or armed rebellion."[33] This charter also injects a limitation on Parliament's interpretive authority by empowering the president, whose powers are mostly ceremonial, to refer a bill about which he has

---

29. For the supremacy of an institution within its branch, see, for instance, the Irish Supreme Court's rulings in Maher v. A.G., [1973] I.R. 140, invalidating a parliamentary effort to legislate what a court must find as "conclusive evidence"; In Re Solicitors Act, 1954, [1960] I.R. 239, striking down an as invasion of judicial power Parliament's establishment of a special tribunal to discipline attorneys; and Murphy v. Dublin, [1972] I.R. 215, requiring a municipal official to produce documents relevant to a civil suit. In United States v. Nixon, 418 U.S. 683 (1974), the Court's overriding a presidential claim to executive privilege where documents were relevant to a criminal prosecution significantly differed from the Court's claim to general interpretive supremacy there and in *City of Boerne,* just as a more specific claim to supervision over federal courts would have been more limited as well as more defensible in *Dickerson* than Rehnquist's broad assertion.

Regarding specific constitutional questions: limited to the facts of the case, a dispute between state and federal governments, the Supreme Court's assertion of interpretive supremacy in Cooper v. Aaron (1958) does little more than repeat what Chief Justice Roger Brooke Taney had said in Ableman v. Booth, 21 How. 506 (1859). *City of Boerne* and *Dickerson,* however, go much further and assert the general superiority of the Court's interpretive authority over that of Congress.

30. The most heroic American effort to explain the doctrine was Brennan's opinion for the Court in Baker v. Carr, 369 U.S. 186 (11962); for the Japanese Court, see esp. the Sunakawa Case (1959), trans. and reprinted in part in Walter F. Murphy and Joseph Tanenhaus, eds., *Comparative Constitutional Law* (New York: St. Martin's, 1977), pp. 239ff.

31. In the Matter of §6 of the Judicature Act, [1981] S.C.R. 753.

32. Japanese judges have read into their constitution a similar legislative monopoly. See, for example, the Minimum Standard of Wholesome and Cultured Living Case (1948), translated and reprinted in part in Murphy and Tanenhaus, *Comparative Constitutional Law,* pp. 283ff.

33. The Supreme Court has, however, narrowly construed this article: In Re Art. 26 and the Emergency Powers Bill, 1976, [1977] I.R. 159.

constitutional doubts to the Supreme Court for a binding opinion.[34] And in one of the more important references, the president referred a bill pertaining to national security to the Court. The justices recognized Parliament's sweeping powers over matters of national security but said that, despite the text, these were not unlimited.[35]

Canada's Constitution Act makes an uneasy allocation of interpretive authority. Although entrenching a bill of rights and lodging jurisdiction under ordinary circumstances with the judiciary,[36] Article 33 allows the federal or a provincial parliament to block judicial review by announcing that a statute "shall operate notwithstanding a provision" regarding fundamental freedoms, outlined in Article 2, or any of the more specific rights listed in Articles 7–15. Furthermore, the charter's words do not bar a legislature from enacting a statute to undo a judicial invalidation of an earlier law.[37]

Whatever the words or silences of the constitutional document or the claims of the constitutional order, the actual operation of all these arrangements, in fact, produces some form of departmentalism. Although differently prescribed delegations of authority can significantly affect the substantive results of constitutional interpretation, in no constitutional democracy does any single institution have either a monopoly on constitutional interpretation or a guarantee of interpretive supremacy. As Chapter Three showed, when matters of great public import are at stake, constitutional interpretation has been less the result of a proclamation from on high than the product of a protracted dialogue among public officials in different departments, with voters collectively serving as an absent-minded director of an opera.[38] In this process, as Madison would have put it, the interests of the

---

34. Article 26, §1.1⁰.

35. In Re Art. 26 and the Emergency Powers Bill, 1976.

36. The British North America Act of 1867 did protect the right to use French or English in the parliament and courts of the federation or Quebec (Art. 133) and rights regarding establishment of religious schools (Arts. 93.1 and 93.2). In 1960, the Canadian Parliament enacted a *statutory* bill of rights. Article 24 (1) gives ordinary jurisdiction to the judiciary.

37. The Canadian compromise gives representatives chosen by and responsible to the people a powerful voice in constitutional interpretation. But there are at least two checks on infringements of individual liberty. First, the legislature must "expressly declare" that it means to violate a constitutionally protected right, at least as it has been or may be judicially defined. Second, although this exemption may be renewed as many times as the legislature wishes, each exception runs for a maximum of five years. At the national level, such a declaration would be a government's death warrant unless the prime minister could persuade the electorate that a grave emergency existed or the judiciary had egregiously misconstrued the bill of rights. On the other hand, Quebecois' reaction to their government's invocation of Article 33 to shield almost all provincial legislation from judicial review has shown that local majorities may support such action as an assertion of independence from Ottawa, if not necessarily to deprive a minority of putative rights. For a comprehensive study, see Tsvi Kahana, "The Notwithstanding Mechanism and Public Discussion: Lessons from the Ignored Practice of Section 33 of the Charter," 44 *Can. Pub. Admin.* 255 (2001).

38. For the United States, see Murphy et al., *American Constitutional Interpretation*, chs. 7–8;

man are intimately connected to the interests of the place as well as to the various and usually conflicting interests of groups within society.

Second is the question of the necessity of a final interpreter. Some scholars claim that departmentalism threatens the constitutional order.[39] Madison thought otherwise. He denied that the American system set up a final interpreter or that one was necessary.[40] Comparative constitutional history supports his opinion. That such countries as Canada, Ireland, Germany, and the United States follow departmentalism and are well functioning constitutional democracies provides strong evidence that a viable polity can prosper with continual debate about constitutional meaning.[41] Indeed, departmentalism is healthier for a constitutional democracy than having an ultimate interpreter. If a single institution could not only determine the scope of its own authority, that of the other branches of government, and the legitimacy of all public policies but also definitively define the very essence of constitutional democracy, the polity would be in danger. Vesting responsibility for constitutional interpretation among several institutions competing for

Neal Devins and Louis Fisher, *The Democratic Constitution* (New York: Oxford University Press, 2004); Louis Fisher, *Constitutional Dialogues: Interpretation as Political Process* (Princeton, NJ: Princeton University Press, 1988); Pickerill, *Constitutional Deliberation in Congress;* Barnes, *Overruled;* and Tushnet, *Taking the Constitution Away from the Courts.* For Europe, see Alec Stone Sweet, "Constitutional Dialogues: Protecting Rights in France, Germany, and Spain," in Sally J. Kenney, William Reisinger, and John C. Reitz, eds., *Constitutional Dialogues in Comparative Perspective* (New York: St. Martin's, 1999).

39. See Larry Alexander and Frederick Schauer, "On Extrajudicial Constitutional Interpretation," 110 *Harv. L. Rev.* 1359 (1997), and "Defending Judicial Supremacy: A Reply," 17 *Con'l Comm.* 455 (2000); Larry Alexander, "Constitutional Rules, Constitutional Standards, and Constitutional Settlement: Marbury v. Madison and the Case for Judicial Supremacy," 20 *Con'l Comm.* 369 (2003); and generally the symposium in the summer issue of vol. 20 of *Con'l Comm.* (2003).

40. See his speech in the House of Representatives, 1 *Annals of Congress* 519–21 (1789), and his letter to John Brown, Oct. 12, 1788. Both are reprinted in Murphy et al., *American Constitutional Interpretation,* pp. 293–95.

41. Meir Shamgar, past president of the Israeli Supreme Court, asserted that Israel does (or at least should) have a final constitutional interpreter. "Of these two doctrines—the doctrine of unlimited sovereignty of the Knesset and the doctrine of the constituent assembly—I definitely prefer the first, namely the doctrine regarding the unlimited sovereignty of the Knesset." But he was making this claim in order to argue that, unlike the British Parliament, the Knesset could legitimately impose constitutional limitations on future Knessets. Moreover, the context leaves me unsure that Shamgar had given much reflection to the broader issues of constitutionalism per se. Concurring in United Mizrahi Bank PLC v. Migdal Cooperative Village (1995) 49 (iv) P. D. 221, trans. and excerpted in 31 *Israel L. Rev.* 764–802 (1997). Of course, before the passage of the two Basic Laws in 1992, Israel's claim to be a constitutionalist state was badly flawed, and its discriminatory treatment of its Arab citizens continues, at least through early 2006, to mar such claims. For more nuanced evaluations of Israel's constitutional order, see Martin Edelman, *Courts, Politics, and Culture in Israel* (Charlottesville: University Press of Virginia, 1994); Gary Jeffrey Jacobsohn, *Apple of Gold: Constitutionalism in Israel and the United States* (Princeton, NJ: Princeton University Press, 1993); and Gary Jeffrey Jacobsohn, *The Wheel of Law: India's Secularism in Comparative Constitutional Perspective* (Princeton, NJ: Princeton University Press, 2003), esp. chs. 2–3.

power substantially lowers dangers of rule by a special interpretive elite, although it increases the messiness of politics.

In his democratic incarnation, Jefferson claimed that it is safest to vest supreme interpretive authority in the electorate. So, too, one might contend that in a true constitutional democracy final power rests with the voters. Not only do they choose the top layer of legislative and executive officials, but their loyalty keeps the political system alive. It may be true that in a constitutionalist state that is also democratic the people will triumph, but perhaps only in the very long run, when, as John Maynard Keynes said, we are all dead.[42] Citizens' tolerance of misgovernment is usually huge, and that tolerance may not bleach out until effective means of resistance—and skilled resisters—have died. Russians who tired of the czar and Germans who had enough of Weimar soon lost the capacity to resist totalitarian rule. As Jefferson said in his constitutionalist incarnation, "An elective despotism was not the government we fought for."[43] It may, however, be the government a people end up with.

How Should Interpreters Interpret?

Even if the constitutional text itself could answer the interrogative *how*, its response would be suspect, for as Aharon Barak has said, "[t]he text cannot establish what the best system of interpretation is for understanding it, because we understand the text only through its interpretation."[44] In any event, explicit textual instructions are rare,[45] leaving interpreters to formulate their own approaches, that is, to decide what is the most intellectually defensible and practical combination of *what* the constitution includes and *what* are its specific as well as general purposes. The simplest approach would be one that accepted the constitution's purpose as simply to provide a blueprint for governmental organization and the constitution itself as including only the

42. John Maynard Keynes, *Monetary Reform* (New York: Harcourt, Brace, 1924), p. 80. See Chapter Fifteen for the differences on this question between Oliver Wendell Holmes and Karl Lowenstein, a refugee from Nazism.

43. "Notes on Virginia" (1784); in *The Writings of Thomas Jefferson*, ed. Andrew A. Lipscomb (Washington, DC: Thomas Jefferson Memorial Association, 1903), 2:163.

44. *Purposive Interpretation in Law*, p. 218.

45. The American Ninth and Tenth amendments do give specific instructions, albeit negatively. More positively, Article 27 of the amended Canadian constitutional documents says, "This Charter shall be interpreted in a manner consistent with the preservation and enhancement of the multicultural heritage of Canada." Ch. 8 of Walter F. Murphy, James E. Fleming, and William F. Harris II, *American Constitutional Interpretation*, 1st ed. (Westbury, NY: Foundation, 1986), devised a three-tiered scheme of interpretation: Approaches, Modes, and Analytical Techniques. Although I still think this classification makes a great deal of sense, I did not repeat it because both colleagues and students have found it too complex. For a different but not unrelated ordering of schemes of constitutional interpretation, see William F. Harris II, *The Interpretable Constitution* (Baltimore: Johns Hopkins University Press, 1993), esp. ch. 3.

text.[46] This approach would dictate close textual analysis as the chief, perhaps the sole, means of interpretation.

Soon, however, even this bare-bones approach faces difficult questions. For instance, should interpreters restrict themselves to analyzing the document clause by clause, that is, rely on "clause bound interpretivism," or should they look at the charter as a whole, using "textual structuralism," sometimes also called systemic interpretation, seeking what William O. Douglas called the charter's "architectural scheme"?[47] Again, a choice here would require a reasoned justification. In *The Federalist* 40, Madison made a case for structuralism: "There are two rules of construction. . . . The one is that every part of the expression ought, if possible, be made to conspire to some common end. The other is that, when the several parts cannot be made to coincide, the less important should give way to the more important." Almost two centuries later the German Constitutional Court provided similar reasoning: "A constitution[al text] has an inner unity, and the meaning of any one part is linked to that of other provisions. Taken as a unit, a constitution[al text] reflects certain overarching principles and fundamental decisions to which individual provisions are subordinate."[48]

On its face, structuralism—or as Donald Kommers calls it, "holistic interpretation"[49]—offers the more intelligent alternative. Construing each clause in isolation makes it impossible to reconcile apparently contradictory or even merely different language in separate parts of the charter or to rank the various values to which these clauses refer. This interpretive mode treats founders as having done no more than compose a shopping list, a view that forces interpreters to impose a ranking, unspecified by the text, among various powers and rights. Thus, unless interpreters move outside the document —a move that is illegitimate under strict textualists' conception of the constitution—it becomes virtually impossible to formulate a notion of a coherent political system.

Yet structuralism presents its own difficulties. The first involves a constitution's "inner unity." It is usually possible to discern the goals of a constitutional text, but these are typically expressed in lofty, abstract terms. The problem lies less in noting objectives than in persuading other interpreters what specifically those ends require. It is hardly self-evident for

46. As time went by, interpreters might broaden inclusion to include earlier interpretations.

47. "Stare Decisis," 4 *Rec. of the Bar of the State of N.Y.* 152, 157 (1949).

48. The Southwest Case, 1 BVerfGE 14 (1951); reprinted in Walter F. Murphy and Joseph Tanenhaus, eds., *Comparative Constitutional Law* (New York: St. Martin's, 1977), p. 208. In context, the Constitutional Court was referring to the document, the Basic Law, but its methodology could also apply to the constitutional order and might be called systemic structuralism. See Harris, *Interpretable Constitution*, esp. ch. 3.

49. Donald P. Kommers, "Constitutional Interpretation in Germany: Visions of Unity and Dignity," in Jeffrey Goldsworthy, ed., *Interpreting Constitutions: A Comparative Study* (New York: Oxford University Press, 2006), p. 203.

instance, how to secure "domestic Tranquility" while reaping "the Blessings of Liberty." Second, constitutionalism and democracy, in whatever form each takes in a particular constitutional order, proclaim principles that sometimes compete, further shrouding inner unity. And because any answer will be freighted with costs and benefits, it will also be heatedly contested. Adding to the controversy will be the probability that not always logically consistent compromises were needed to secure agreement on the document. Worse, these two interpretive modes form the horns of the "hermeneutic dilemma": to understand the whole document, one must understand its parts; to understand the parts of a document, one must understand the whole.

At the same time, grave problems of language skulk within the text. First, clarity is often not a goal. Many public officials appreciate the utility of "constructive ambiguity"[50] to compromise—and to reelection. Second, even when clarity is a goal, major difficulties remain. As Madison wrote in *The Federalist* 37: "[N]o language is so copious as to supply words and phrases for every complex idea, or so correct as not to include many equivocally denoting different ideas. . . . When the Almighty himself condescends to address mankind in their own language, his meaning, luminous as it must be, is rendered dim and doubtful by the cloudy medium through which it is communicated." John Marshall, no more a postmodernist than Madison, agreed: "Such is the character of human language that no word conveys to the mind, in all situations, one single definite idea; and nothing is more common than to use words in a figurative sense."[51] Although some concepts and even conceptions stay constant, words may change their meanings, and rules of syntax and punctuation shift. As Samuel Johnson noted in the preface to his great dictionary (1755), "Tongues, like governments, have a natural tendency to degeneration."[52] A modern expert in linguistics put it less pejoratively: "The only languages that don't change are the ones that are well and truly dead."[53]

50. The term is Robert Malley's: "Israel and the Arafat Question," *N.Y. Rev. of Bks.*, 19–20 (Oct. 7, 2004).

51. McCulloch v. Maryland, 17 U.S. 316, 414 (1819).

52. Johnson was not always quite so critical of linguistic change. "Language," he also said, "is the work of man, of a being from whom permanence and stability cannot be derived." In *Johnson: Poetry and Prose*, ed. Mona Wilson, p. 130; quoted in David Simpson, *The Politics of American English, 1776–1850* (New York: Oxford University Press, 1986), p. 21.

53. See Kate Burridge, *Blooming English: Observations on the Roots, Cultivation, and Hybrids of the English Language* (New York: Cambridge University Press, 2004), p. 113. For change, see, in addition to Burridge, Jean Aitchison, *Language Change: Progress or Decay?* (New York: Cambridge University Press, 1991); Laurie Bauer, *Watching English Change* (New York: Longmans, 1994); and Otto Jespersen, *Growth and Structure of the English Language,* 10th ed. (Chicago: University of Chicago Press, 1982). Especially relevant to American constitutional interpretation are Simpson, *Politics of American English,* chs. 1–2; and James Boyd White, *When Words Lose Their Meaning: Constitutions and Reconstitutions of Language, Character, and Community* (Chicago: University of Chicago Press, 1984). For the breakdown in communication between North and South prior to the

The squishy language of constitutional scripts further disrupts inter-preters' repose. Such ringing phrases in the American document as "due process of law," "just compensation," and "the equal protection of the laws" have parallels in other charters. Article 1 of Germany's Basic Law declares, "The dignity of man shall be inviolable." Furthermore, these sweeping terms are often linked to qualifications that are no less commodious. For example, Article 2 of the Basic Law states that "[e]veryone shall have the right to life and to inviolability of his person," then adds a qualifier: "These rights may only be encroached upon pursuant to a law." Article 1 of the Declaration of the Rights of Man of 1789, incorporated into the constitutional text of France's Fifth Republic, proclaims, "Men are born and remain free, and possess equal rights. Social distinctions may be established only for the public good." Article 19, clause 1 of the Indian charter states that "[a]ll citizens shall have the right—(a) to freedom of speech and expression"; but clause 2 adds an open-ended qualification:

> Nothing in sub-clause (a) of clause (1) shall affect the operation of any existing law, or prevent the State from making any law, in so far as such law imposes reasonable restrictions on the exercise of the right conferred[54] by the said sub-clause in the interests of the sovereignty and integrity of India, the security of the State, friendly relations with foreign States, public order, decency or morality, or in relation to contempt of court, defamation or incitement to offence.

Not to be outdone, the Hungarians included Article 54 in their charter: "Every person . . . has an innate right to life and human dignity, of which no one may be arbitrarily deprived." It seems that, like the "inalienable rights" to life and liberty sanctified in the American Declaration of Independence, the state may deprive persons of these and perhaps other innate rights as long as it does not do so "arbitrarily," an abstraction that screams out for specification.

Civil War, see Mark E. Brandon, *Free in the World: American Slavery and Constitutional Failure* (Princeton, NJ: Princeton University Press, 1998), esp. ch. 6.

54. The notion that the state, through a constitutional text or otherwise, "confers" rights is alien to most versions of constitutionalist theory. Cf. Edward S. Corwin's claim that rights are not "funda-mental because they find mention in the written instrument; they find mention there because [they are] fundamental." "The Basic Doctrine of American Constitutional Law," 12 *Mich. L. Rev.* 247–48 (1914). Along the same lines, Justice William O. Douglas wrote: "Men do not acquire rights from the government; one man does not give another rights. Man gets his rights from the Creator. They come to him because of the divine spark in every human being." *The Anatomy of Liberty* (New York: Trident, 1963), p. 2. See also Václav Havel's similar comments, "Kosovo and the End of the Nation-State," *N.Y. Rev. of Bks.*, June 10, 1999, p. 4. On the other hand, in their opinions in the Mizrahi Bank Case, cited above, several justices of the Israeli Supreme Court spoke of the Knesset's "granting" Israel a constitutional text. I detect here a residue of British imperial rule—the queen's "most excellent Majesty" "gave" the Canadians the British North America Act of 1867 and the Australians the Commonwealth of Australia Constitution Act of 1900. I detect similar ashes stirring around among the justices' discussions about whether today's Knesset could bind tomorrow's Knesset.

Because fidelity to the document is a moral as well as a legal duty, textual analysis is an indispensable instrument of constitutional interpretation. Whether clause bound or structuralist, however, it cannot successfully cope with the terminological inexactitudes that abound in these scripts. Textualism alone might be an adequate interpretive tool for a nation that has a constitutional text but does not embrace either constitutionalist or democratic theory—that is, a nation that endorses mere constitutionism,[55] with the constitutional charter playing the role of supreme law. Even in such a case, however, it is probable that another political theory would underpin the text.

Interpretation requires additional analytical tools such as those of philosophy, history, and the social sciences to give specific form to such words as "the essence of a basic right" or "social distinctions" that are "for the public good." The need for philosophical analysis is compelling, for neither the document's individual clauses nor the charter as a whole will make much sense without an understanding of the moral and social norms the text attempts to translate into political reality. Attempting to read a constitutional charter without understanding the demands of constitutionalism and democracy is like trying to sing a song without knowing its music. And of one thing we can be absolutely sure, philosophers will disagree among themselves about what are the particular commands of any normative political theory.

For interpreters, historical analyses offer the possibility of gaining perspective, seeing a problem not as a discrete event but as something that, in somewhat different shapes and under somewhat different circumstances, has long been dogging humanity.[56] As Machiavelli put it, "[S]ince men almost always walk on paths beaten by others . . . a prudent man should always . . . imitate those who have been most excellent."[57] Blind imitation may be foolish, but knowing how wise statesmen have dealt with a problem can help others understand the underlying difficulty. History can also, as the eminent scholar John Lewis Gaddis pointed out, imbue an interpreter with a much needed sense of humility.[58]

---

55. See Chapter One, pp. 15–16, for a definition.

56. Stare decisis can be viewed as one form of historical analysis. Yet it cannot, of itself, solve all problems, for it requires some explicit (and convincing) defense of past interpretations as correct. The mere statement "we've read it this way before" might be empirically true but offers no good reason for ever having so read the constitution, much less for continuing to follow that reading. One might construct an excellent prudential argument for stare decisis, but this justification would not demonstrate the interpretation's truth or error.

57. *The Prince*, ch. 6, in *The Prince and the Discourses*, trans. Luigi Ricci and revised by E. R. P. Vernon (New York: Modern Library, 1940), p. 19.

58. *The Landscape of History: How Historians View the Past* (New York: Oxford University Press, 2002), p. 6. Alas, originalists such as Robert A. Bork and Antonin Scalia do not cause the word *humble* to leap into mind.

Historical analyses run the gamut from using history as a snapshot to treating it as a moving picture. Interpreters focusing on a snapshot would try to return to the founding—in the parlance of nineteenth-century German jurisprudence, to think the thoughts founders were thinking. This sort of methodology is pretty much restricted to the United States, and even there, except perhaps for recent amendments, it encounters insuperable difficulties insofar as it seeks certainty. I have detailed these shortcomings elsewhere[59] and only summarize them here.

First of all, the American charter does not begin with "I, James Madison, and a group of friends do ordain this Constitution," nor does it say "We the Lawyers." Rather, that document draws its legitimacy from "the People of the united States."[60] For originalists who preach fidelity to the text, what should be critical is either what the ratifiers thought they were approving or what voters thought the ratifying conventions would approve. In any event,

59. "The Constitution: Interpretation and Intent," 45 A.B.A. J. 592 (1958); "Constitutional Interpretation: The Art of the Historian, Magician, or Statesman?" 87 Yale L. J. 1752 (1978); and "Originalism: The Deceptive Evil," in Robert P. George, ed., Great Cases in Constitutional Law (Princeton, NJ: Princeton University Press, 2000). For an analysis showing the sorry state of documentary evidence about the understanding and/or intentions of the American founders, see James H. Hutson, the editor of Max Farrand's, The Records of the Federal Convention of 1787: "The Creation of the Constitution: The Integrity of the Documentary Record," 65 Tex. L. Rev. 1 (1986); and the articles on the Second Amendment by Saul Cornell, Michael A. Bellesiles, Don Higginbotham, and Robert E. Shalhope in the summer issue of 16 Con'l Comm. (1999). The distinguished historian Herman Belz disagrees in large part with my arguments: "That [original intent] can be ascertained would seem to admit of little doubt if history, as a method of knowing, a discipline, and a profession, is to be accepted as having a legitimate place in scientific investigation." "The Civil War Amendments to the Constitution: The Relevance of Original Intent," 5 Con'l Comm. 115, 137 (1988). But accepting "history as having a legitimate place in scientific investigation," as I do, does not imply that history can answer all questions regarding constitutional interpretation, even all of history's own questions. For example, history cannot justify the use of history to solve current problems, and where historical evidence for one or another alternative account of original understanding and intent conflicts, the most history can do determine on which side the evidence is stronger. History cannot dictate the choice. When founders disagree among themselves, as they almost always have, interpreters must make (and justify) their own judgments. Moreover, Belz does not demonstrate that such a diverse group of drafters, ratifiers of constitutional texts, and other founders of the constitutional order had any single intent or understanding; nor does he or anyone else demonstrate how an interpreter would undertake such a voyage of discovery, if we take seriously the usual claim of constitutional charters that "the people"—that is, ratifiers as well as drafters—gave their nation a constitutional text. For other critiques, see esp. Dennis J. Goldford, The American Constitution and the Debate over Originalism (New York: Cambridge University Press, 2005); Alfred H. Kelly, "Clio and the Court," 1965 Sup. Ct. Rev. 119; Leonard W. Levy, Original Intent and the Framers' Constitution (New York: Macmillan, 1988), ch. 1; Charles A. Miller, The Supreme Court and the Uses of History (Cambridge, MA: Harvard University Press, 1969); Paul L. Murphy, "A Time to Reclaim: The Current Challenge of American Constitutional History," 69 Am. Hist. Rev. 64 (1963).

60. "The People" may be a fiction, but it is a fiction with which interpreters, whether originalists or not, who preach fidelity to the text are stuck. In Australia and Canada, an originalist who was enamored of legalistic argument s might contend that because it was the queen (or the cabinet whose words she spoke) who gave the constitutional text to these former colonies, what she (or that group) had in mind should control interpretation. I know of no one silly enough to make such a claim.

the minutes of the debates in Philadelphia are a mess, and what we can garner of what was said comes from notes taken by men who did not know shorthand. Madison's are the most complete, yet for each six-hour session, his notes can be read out loud as a play in about an hour.

For the campaign to choose ratifiers, millions of documents (dozens of thousands of which reproduce each other) exist, but these show multiple "understandings."[61] For debates in the various ratifying conventions we have only garbled "records" by the official reporters who did not know shorthand either and were sometimes partisans of one side or the other. We also have accounts by journalists, but these are even more tangled. It is impossible to discover collective intentions or understandings held by thirteen separate groups of men who have been dead for almost two centuries and most of whom did not know each other, hear each other's speeches, or read each other's writings. We can be reasonably certain that even the winners did not share a common understanding of concepts such as Union, Justice, Tranquillity, or executive, legislative, and judicial power. Even definitions of such concrete terms as *ex post facto* were not crystalline.

Equally telling, when the Originals themselves began to govern, their understandings of of the new constitutional text and the larger constitutional order differed sharply. Even Publius revealed his two minds, with Madison and Hamilton at bitter odds with each other. If the Originals themselves could not agree on a single understanding, it is unlikely that partisans or even scholars can make that determination from a distance of two centuries. Interpreters can and should seek guidance from the debates before, during, and after adoption; but, while they can draw much practical wisdom, they cannot, at least reasonably, deduce specific solutions to specific problems. From the text's plain words, at least those we think remain plain across the centuries, we can recapture the founders' general purposes—for example, to establish a more perfect union and to provide the blessings of liberty. And from the governmental system outlined, we can, with some confidence, infer they wanted to establish a form of constitutionalist government that was also moderately democratic.

---

61. More than forty years after ratification, Jonathan Elliot published the first of several editions of a four-volume collection of what purported to be records of the ratifying conventions: *The Debates in the Several State Conventions on the Adoption of the Federal Constitution . . .* (Washington, DC: n.p., 1836–1845). These were incomplete and inaccurate. In 1976, Merrill Jensen began publication of efforts to construct a more reliable record. He and his associates put together different accounts of what was said in the conventions and assembled many of the writings circulated during the campaigns to choose delegates. Later John P. Kaminski and Gaspare J. Saldino took over as editors. As of late 2005, twenty volumes had appeared: *The Documentary History of the Ratification of the Constitution* (Madison: University of Wisconsin Press, 1976-). For useful collections of documents for the Bill of Rights, see Helen E. Veit and Kenneth E. Bowling, eds., *Creating the Bill of Rights: The Documentary Record from the First Federal Congress* (Baltimore: Johns Hopkins University Press, 1981); and Bernard Schwartz, ed., *The Bill of Rights* (New York: Chelsea House, 1971), 2 vols.

Originalists also encounter linguistic problems whose difficulties have been magnified by the passage of time. Samuel Johnson's dictionary was published more than thirty years before the Philadelphia convention, but he said that his work was not of great use in America, whose people spoke quite differently from the British. The first comprehensive dictionary of American English was not published until 1828, and its compiler, Noah Webster, was a staunch Federalist who saw his job as being as much political as linguistic. Thus the absolutely essential initial step any serious originalist must take is to construct an accurate dictionary, grammar, and manual of punctuation for late-eighteenth-century America so that we could be quite sure of what the words meant to citizens of 1787–1788.[62] As of early 2006, only William Winslow Crosskey had attempted this forbidding task, and according to critics, he was only partially successful.[63] Merely assuming that twentieth- or twenty-first-century definitions of terms were accepted in 1787–1788 does not meet minimal standards of scholarship. For instance, the phrase "interstate commerce," commonly taken as implied by "commerce among the several states," is not a usage of the founding period. It first occurs in an opinion of the Supreme Court in 1871, more than eighty years after ratification.[64]

Originalists' claim that "James Madison made me do it" fails on three grounds: (1) Even assuming Madison's view should trump those of other framers and ratifiers, we do not know what he would have done in a modern situation. After all, he changed his mind about what the constitution meant

62. Randy Barnett has authored a fascinating and imaginative libertarian (or negative constitutionalist) study of the American constitution, using a form of originalism that seeks "the objective meaning that a reasonable listener would place on the words used in the constitutional provision at the time of its enactment": *Restoring the Lost Constitution: The Presumption of Liberty* (Princeton, NJ: Princeton University Press, 2004), p. 92. Oliver Wendell Holmes Jr., who thought the test of legal meaning was what the words would have meant in the mouth of an ordinary man, should have approved Barnett's technique. Nevertheless, without a comprehensive and authoritative dictionary of American English of the time, we cannot be certain what the plain words plainly implied to a reasonable person of the time. Moreover, the burden of proof rests on Barnett and his allies to show that one and only meaning would have been reasonable to reasonable people of 1787–1788.

63. William W. Crosskey, *Politics and the Constitution*, 2 vols. (Chicago: University of Chicago Press, 1953). In 1980, after Crosskey's death, Chicago published a third volume, coauthored by William Jeffrey Jr. The first two volumes created a seismic tremor in academic circles. For citations to many of these reactions, see David Fellman, "Constitutional Law in 1952–1953," 48 *Am. Pol. Sci. Rev.* 63 (1954), and "Constitutional Law in 1953–1954," 49 *Am. Pol. Sci. Rev.* 63 (1955). Among the reviewers who engaged Crosskey on the accuracy of his definitions was Henry M. Hart Jr., "Professor Crosskey and Judicial Review," 67 *Harv. L. Rev.* 1456 (1954).

64. Although attorneys sometimes referred to "interstate commerce," the Supreme Court did not employ the term until *after* the Civil War: *The Daniel Ball*, 10 Wall. 557, 564 (1871). Crosskey, *Politics and the Constitution*, vol. 1, ch. 3, has a long discussion of the meaning(s) of the word *among* in the eighteenth century, concluding that it often meant "within," as it sometimes still does, rather than "between more than two." To find the term's first appearance in an opinion of the Supreme Court, I used a word search through the CD, published by the old Lawyers Cooperative Publishing Company, that contains all opinions written by justices from 1789 through 1945.

for such important matters as the utility of a bill of rights, the meaning of the "necessary and proper clause," national supremacy, and the reach of judicial review.[65] (2) Therefore, claiming the choice was Madison's, not the interpreters', shirks responsibility and, by concealing the interpreters' choice, offends democratic norms. (3) Pace Machiavelli, blindly following even great statesmen when confronting new problems is grossly imprudent.

Interpreters who prefer to use history as a moving picture rather than as a snapshot are apt to look at changes over time, to regard a constitution as a developing rather than a static entity. Carrying this form of analysis to its logical conclusion are interpreters who call for "contemporary ratification." A constitutional text may be designed not merely to describe governmental processes and list certain rights but also to transform a society. According to Justice William J. Brennan Jr., the fundamental question for constitutional interpreters must be this:

> [W]hat do the words of the text mean in our time? For the genius of the Constitution[al document] rests not in any static meaning it might have had in a world that is dead and gone, but in the adaptability of its great principles to cope with current problems and current needs. What the constitutional fundamentals meant to the wisdom of other times cannot be their measure to the vision of our time. Similarly, what those fundamentals mean for us, our descendants will learn, cannot be the measure to the vision of their time. . . . Interpretation must account for the transformative purpose of the text.[66]

In 1932, Benjamin N. Cardozo suggested an historical method that lies somewhere between originalism and contemporary ratification: translating founders' concepts without being bound by their conceptions. In the style of nineteenth-century German jurisprudence, interpreters must think the thought that founders would have thought were they still alive. The men of 1787, Cardozo noted,

> did not see the changes in the relation between states and nation or in the play of social forces that lay hidden in the womb of time. [This statute restricting the obligation of contracts] may be inconsistent with things that they believed or took for granted. Their beliefs to be significant must be adjusted to the world they knew. It is not in my judgment inconsistent with what they would say today nor with what today they would believe, if they

---

65. For summaries, see Richard K. Matthews, *If Men Were Angels: James Madison and the Heartless Empire of Reason* (Lawrence: University Press of Kansas, 1995), pp. 16–18; and Marvin Myers, ed., *The Mind of the Framer: Sources of the Political Thought of James Madison* (Indianapolis: Bobbs-Merrill, 1973), pp. xxxviii–xlviii.

66. "The Constitution of the United States: Contemporary Ratification," reprinted in Murphy et al., *American Constitutional Interpretation*, pp. 249–54, quotation at p. 252.

were called upon to interpret "in the light of our whole experience" the constitution that they framed for the needs of an expanding future.[67]

Judge Robert Bork, one of the twentieth century's leading originalists, played a variation on Cardozo's theme. In discussing the School Segregation Cases, Bork acknowledged that the same Congress that proposed the Fourteenth Amendment also established racially segregated schools for the District of Columbia. He argued, however, that the objective of the framers of the Fourteenth Amendment was to end legalized racial discrimination. What they did not understand, but we do, is that segregated public schools perpetuate discrimination. Thus we can legitimately invalidate state-imposed segregation.[68] This form of originalism is practically indistinguishable from "purposive interpretation," that is, trying to discover, by means of what John Marshall called "a fair construction of the whole instrument,"[69] the polity's objectives and to construe the constitutional text and/or the constitutional order to achieve those goals. The problem purposivism poses is that it allows interpreters, as Bork did for segregation and Cardozo for state authority over contracts, to move beyond, even against, founders' conceptions.

If the principal danger of non-Borkian originalism lies in interpreters' falsely imputing their own creative choices to the dead, the principal danger in the methods of Bork, Brennan, and Cardozo lies in interpreters' justifying their choices according to their own judgments about current needs, restrained only by the general purposes of the constitutional text and the indistinct borders of the constitutional order. Quite properly, Frank Michelman called William Brennan a "framer."[70] This method could commit the

67. Unpub'd op. in the Minnesota Moratorium Case, 290 U.S. 398 (1932); reprinted in Murphy et al., *American Constitutional Interpretation*, pp. 224–25.

68. *The Tempting of America: The Political Seduction of the Law* (New York: Free Press, 1990), pp. 76–83.

69. Marshall's statement is from McCulloch v. Maryland, 4 Wh. 316, 406 (1819). It is important to distinguish among motivation, intent, and purpose. *Motivation,* pertaining to the reasons behind particular words, thoughts, or deeds, lies within the jurisdiction of psychiatry. It is doubtful that any of us can be absolutely sure of the forces that impel us to pursue certain course of action. In *The Federalist* No. 11, Hamilton offered excellent advice for constitutional interpretation: "My motives must remain in the depository of my own breast. My arguments are open to all, and may be judged by all." *Intent* also refers to a psychological state but is more accessible to empirical research. Most generally it refers to what a person has in mind when he or she uses certain words. It may be possible to discover intent when analyzing documents that were authored by a single person. When we confront text produced by several dozen people, however, the difficulties are usually insuperable. *Purpose* refers to the objective a speaker or actor is trying to accomplish. If confined to the plain words of a simple document, a search for purpose would be rather similar to that for intent; but when the document is very broad in scope and can be read in the context of actions, the two efforts at discovery differ widely.

70. "Superliberal: Romance, Community, and Tradition in William J. Brennan's Constitutional Thought," 77 *Va. L. Rev.* 1261, 1332 (1991).

polity to governance solely under the general principles of constitutionalism and democracy and convert the constitutional text into a hortatory document. In fact, Learned Hand came very close to adopting such a position. Constitutional interpretation, he said, "presupposes an imaginative projection of the purposes of the authors of any document. . . . This is not an impossible or fantastic attempt as to most of the Constitution; but it is utterly impossible practically as to those parts of the Bill of Rights that are now so frequently invoked. These are *only admonitions* to the sense of fair play—that is, that the lawmaker shall not favor himself or his group merely because they are his."[71]

Furthermore, both history as snapshot and history as moving picture fail to provide a remedy for a fundamental political dilemma: constitutional interpretation often demands discretion and choice. The harsh fact is that a constitutional order is always in a state of becoming, the product of development that may revise or even re-create the constitutional order.[72] Because, as Gaddis has noted, historical analysis inevitably involves selecting—excluding as well as including—information, all historical methods produce only partial pictures of a slice of the past. In so doing, interpreters may mistake the part for the whole and so conceal from themselves as well as from others the creativity involved in their work, posing serious risks to constitutionalism, to democracy, and to any union of the two. While hardly free of serious problems, purposivism at least honestly acknowledges that interpreters are choosing, revising, and perhaps even creating. Still, recognizing the enormity of the dangers does little to lessen the necessity of that choosing, revising, and creating. Any solution can be only partial and will involve issues of both *who interprets* and *how to interpret.*

Mitigating the dangers requires sharing interpretive authority so that no one person or institution can monopolize the processes of constitutional reformation. Mitigation also requires candid acknowledgment of interpretive choice. Only after addressing the questions of *what, who,* and *how* and formulating intellectually defensible answers can interpreters, whoever they are, faithfully engage in the enterprise. The difficulty of such a process goes far to account for the fact that public officials, private citizens, and academic commentators usually prefer to silently assume rather than justify answers to these fundamental questions. Those failures raise further problems for constitutional democracy, critical among which is that the lack of such public arguments narrows opportunities for later interpreters, commentators, and voters to choose intelligently among alternatives that affect both immediate public policies and the polity's long-range development.

71. To Felix Frankfurter, Apr. 24, 1957; in Papers of Felix Frankfurter, Library of Congress. My italics.

72. Compare the "theology of emergence": Philip Clayton, *The Emergence of Spirit: From Quantum to Culture* (New York: Oxford University Press, 2004).

Constitutional Interpretation without a Constitutional Text

We can now sketch several plausible scenarios and use them as heuristic devices. First, let us assume the existence of a young constitutional democracy whose founders decided against drafting a constitutional text. Instead, they created a parliamentary system modeled on that of Westminster. These people have bet that their dominant national political culture(s) will respect the values of both constitutionalism and democracy better than will an entrenched bill of rights and judicial review. The first parliament enacts an electoral law: a general election must be held at least every five years; every adult eighteen and older can vote; freedom to discuss political issues is protected, as are rights to assemble and petition government. Parliament also stipulates that political parties are quasi-governmental organizations and specifies only minimal qualifications for citizens' standing as candidates for public office.

Despite conforming to democratic values, these arrangements will not automatically lay to rest serious questions about all public policies' wisdom or legitimacy. Thus, even without a charter, constitutional interpretation will be necessary, because leaders of interest groups and opposition parties are apt to try to advance their interests and visions of the good society. Take, for instance, the extent to which parliament may regulate campaign financing. On the one hand, many voters, incumbents, and candidates can be bought, murdering democratic processes. On the other hand, money is necessary to publicize the virtues of parties, candidates, and their platforms as well as to expose opponents' vices. Therefore, citizens' rights to contribute money and candidates' rights to collect and spend money are important aspects of political participation, raising huge difficulties in construing the norms of this (or any other) version of democracy.

Many intelligent public policies can also create complex difficulties for constitutionalism. For example, a statute that allowed police to arrest people on suspicion of being or aiding terrorists and detain them for long periods without trials would further domestic tranquillity by protecting most law-abiding citizens' rights to life and property. Such a regulation would also, however, threaten to maim the liberty of other innocent, law-abiding citizens who happen to incur the suspicion or ill will of public officials.

Interpreting the demands of democratic or constitutional theory can never be easy, for, as often noted, several variations of each compete for acceptance. Although they all share basic principles—along with imprecisions in statements of those principles—each variant tells a somewhat different story about processes, institutions, and rights as well as about priorities among them. And within each incarnation, major and minor principles, instrumental and ultimate values, as well as processes and goals, can be spun together into a variety of patterns. Interpreting either of these political theories requires, as an initial step, choosing which form of each theory to construe. And always present is the question of what mix of the two theories a particular polity has adopted. As is the case for humans, any given constitutional democracy represents only one of many possible combinations of parents' genes, and development will be affected by the physical and social environments in which they mature.

Thus, even in this simple form of constitutional democracy, MPs—and voters when they go to the polls—confront two of the fundamental questions of constitutional interpretation: *What* is it to be interpreted? *How* must that *what* be interpreted? Because no version of either constitutionalism or democracy is likely to be fully articulated, interpreters must often deduce specific conclusions from vague or unspoken major premises—a euphemism for exercising creative, though not unbounded, imagination. Indeed, on occasion interpreters must retroduce major premises from specific conclusions. When interpreters consider the nature of the union of the two theories, the number of possibilities increases. During crises or even after years of dealing with mundane issues, what emerges may be a revised version of constitutionalist or democratic theory and/or a new account of their blend in this polity.

There is no escape from interpreting the "constitution" with or without a text. If individual officials or citizens refuse to do so, they permit other officials or other citizens to perform that work. A public official or private citizen can abdicate his or her own share of interpretive power, but neither singly nor collectively can they remove the necessity for its exercise. And there is no formula that can turn the interpretive enterprise into an exact—or simple—science.

Constitutional Interpretation with a Partial Constitutional Text

The founders' decisions not to draft a constitutional document may be short lived. Israel provides an example of tag-team writing of a constitutional document. Soon after independence, the Provisional Council of State called for a popularly elected Constituent Assembly to draft a constitutional text. The country, however, was sharply divided. Some Orthodox groups claimed that the Halakhah, Jewish law, was the only proper instrument to govern the Land of Israel. David Ben-Gurion and his then dominant party, the Mapai, thought they would benefit from parliamentary supremacy free from the restraints a constitutional script might impose. In the face of these obstacles, efforts to draft a charter failed.[73] The most the Constituent Assem-

---

73. Martin Edelman adds that, early on, some of the secular parties were unwilling to risk dividing the nation by offending the religious views of the ultra-Orthodox. "The New Israeli Constitution," 36 *Middle Eastern Studies* 1 (2000), and, more generally, his *Courts, Politics, and Culture in Israel.*

bly, reborn as the Knesset, accomplished was passage of the Harari Resolution of 1950:

> The first Knesset charges the Constitutional Legislative and Judicial Committee with the duty to prepare a draft Constitution[al text] for the State. The Constitution[al text] shall be composed of individual chapters in such manner that each of them shall constitute a basic law in itself. The chapters shall be brought before the Knesset . . . and the chapters together will form the State Constitution[al text].[74]

It was widely assumed, although the resolution does not so say, that it would take a two-thirds vote to constitutionally entrench such legislation.

Between 1958 and 1992, the Knesset enacted nine statutes labeled Basic Laws. The constitutional rank of some of them, however, was unclear: not all proclaimed themselves constitutionally entrenched,[75] and some were adopted by simple majority vote. In 1992, the Knesset enacted "The Basic Law: Human Dignity and Liberty." Sections 2 through 7 protected rights to life, liberty, bodily integrity, privacy, and property, though only prospectively. The act did not explicitly mention judicial review—§11 said only: "All governmental authorities are bound to respect the rights under this Basic Law"—but in *Bergman v. Minister of Finance* (1969)[76] the Supreme Court had held that a similar clause in "The Basic Law: The Knesset" subjected later statutes and regulations to judicial review. Then, in 1995, the Supreme Court decided the Mizrahi Bank Case, which raised the question whether a bankruptcy act violated the Basic Law of 1992. The specific issue paralleled that in the Minnesota Moratorium Case (1934): did an earlier statute protecting cooperatives from bankruptcy by extending the time for repaying loans take the lending institution's property and so contravene §3 of this Basic Law, "There shall be no violation of the property of a person"?[77]

The justices upheld the moratorium; and had they not labeled the Knesset's action in 1992 "a constitutional revolution," the case itself would have been unexceptional.[78] For the majority, however, President Aharon Barak

---

74. Quoted in Jacobsohn, *Apple of Gold*, p. 106.

75. Some Basic Laws, such as that enacted in 1992, "Human Dignity and Liberty," operate only prospectively. Still, in the Ganimat v. Israel, (1995) 49 iv) P.D. 589, trans. in 31 *Israel L. Rev.* 754 (1995), President Aharon Barak said the Supreme Court would give great weight to the purpose of this Basic Law in interpreting earlier statutes.

76. 23 (i) P.D. 693; trans. in 4 *Israel L. Rev.* 559 (1969).

77. Section 8 of the Basic Law of 1992 (discussed below) qualified the protected rights and liberties, easing the justices' problems in deciding the case.

78. Not only did Barak use the phrase "a constitutional revolution" in his opinion, but he also employed it in his scholarly analysis of the two Basic Laws enacted in 1992: "The Constitutionalization of the Israeli Legal System as a Result of the Basic Laws and Its Effect on Procedural and Substantive Criminal Law," 31 *Israel L. Rev.* 3 (1997). For scholarly discussions, see Edelman, *Courts, Politics, and Culture in Israel,* and his "The Status of The Israel Constitution at the Present Time," 21

held that not only the first Knesset but also all subsequent Knessets continued to wear "two hats." They were both legislatures empowered to enact ordinary laws and constituent assemblies empowered to create a constitutional text.[79] Next, the Court held that the Basic Law of 1992 was one chapter in a budding constitutional charter, even though the Knesset had not included an entrenching clause, appended any admonition about the act's constitutional status beyond the title "Basic Law," or made the law retrospective. Moreover, it had been adopted by a vote of only 32–21.

Concluding that these Basic Laws formed parts of an embryonic constitutional text required creative interpretation, and one cannot fault the justices, especially President Barak, for lacking imagination An equally, if not more, plausible interpretation of the Harari Resolution was that it allowed future Knessets to experiment with various Basic Laws and later consolidate and codify them into a single coherent document, which a Knesset then could, presumably by an extraordinary majority, proclaim to be the official charter. Democratic governance would seem to require that establishing or amending a constitutional text be done openly, not by stealth. Article 79 (1) of the German charter, for instance, says that it "can be amended only by laws that expressly amend or supplement the text thereof."

Barak's majority opinion built a wide arena for judicial as well as legislative choice. Section 8 of this Basic Law qualified its protection of fundamental rights: "There shall be no violation of rights under this Basic Law, except by a Law fitting the values of the State of Israel, designed for a proper purpose, and to an extent no greater than required."[80] These limitations might be prudent, even necessary, but they also confer vast discretion. Defining a worthy purpose or the degree to which such a purpose limits infringement of a constitutional right opens an ambit of choice as wide as has the more famous American Supreme Court's "levels of scrutiny" test, as Barak conceded.[81] Applying such open-ended criteria demands, not merely invites, interpretive discretion and perhaps creativity as well.

Determining "the values of the State of Israel" presents even more far-

---

Shofar 1 (2003); Jacobsohn, *Apple of Gold;* Gary Jeffrey Jacobsohn, "After the Revolution," 34 *Israel L. Rev.* 139 (2000); and Menachem Hofnung, "The Unintended Consequences of Unplanned Constitutional Reform: Constitutional Politics in Israel," 44 *Am J. Comp. L.* 601 (1996).

On the narrow issue of the validity of the moratorium, the opinions of the Israeli justices were more like the unpublished opinion of Justice Cardozo in *Minnesota Moratorium* than that of Chief Justice Charles Evans Hughes for the majority.

79. Justice Mishael Cheshin, at p. 800, protested that this perpetuation of the constituent power treated that authority as if it were a "personal" attribute to be delegated at will.

80. Unofficial translation by the deputy attorney general and Carmel Shalev, quoted in Claude Klein, "Basic Laws, Constituent Power, and Judicial Review of Statutes in Israel," 2 *Eur'n Pub. L.* 225–26 (1996).

81. Murphy et al., *American Constitutional Interpretation,* chs. 14-18, reprints of many of the opinions of the justices and discusses the leading cases. Barak's concession is at p. 788.

reaching opportunities. The Declaration of Independence called the coun-try a democratic and Jewish state. The range of options and the possibilities of creating new concepts are immense when anointing certain values as democratic, but this ambit is puny when compared to that open in determin-ing *Jewish* values.[82] The history of Israel—of Judaism itself—demonstrates sharp disagreement about who is a Jew[83] and the values *Jewish* connotes. Even the Talmud presents conflicting interpretations of the Torah. Section 8 of the Basic Law of 1992 ventures into the problem of the meaning(s) of the Bible and the political implications thereof.

Just as *Mizrahi Bank* authorizes theologically inspired constitutional en-gineering,[84] so it also declared that the Knesset possesses authority to enact, piecemeal, a constitutional document that embodies the numinous values of a Jewish and democratic state. A coalition led by Labor might entrench constitutional provisions radically different, politically as well as theologi-cally, from those that a coalition of Likud and religious parties would. In-deed, were the religious parties to control a coalition, Israel might face the fascinating problem of the legitimacy under constitutionalism of a provision of the constitutional text. And either coalition might repeal one or more existing basic laws by enacting new legislation.[85] The possibilities of consti-tutional creation and re-creation here may not be infinite, but they stagger the imagination.

Constitutional Interpretation with a (More or Less) Complete Constitutional Text

Let us again change the scenario. Foreseeing the difficulties of testing a public policy's legitimacy solely against the abstract principles of two not always congruent political theories, each of which can take somewhat dif-ferent forms, the founders decide to draft a constitutional document. Many models are at hand. One would be the American text of 1787-1788, which speaks in magnificent generalities rather than with "the prolixity of a legal

---

82. It would be interesting to know how much constitutionalism the word *Jewish* includes. Because the Declaration of Independence says Israel is to be a Jewish *and* democratic state, the problem for democracy is easier. Nevertheless, difficulties could arise were interpreters to decide that the two terms were not in complete harmony and the values of Judaism took precedence over those of democracy.

83. For the Supreme Court's wrestling with this question in the context of the Law of Return, see Jacobsohn, *Wheel of Law*, pp. 72–88.

84. Compare the Indian Supreme Court's mixture of theology and constitutional interpretation as discussed by Jacobsohn: "Three Models of Secular Constitutional Development: India, Israel, and the United States," 10 *Stud. in Am. Pol. Devel't* 1 (1996), and *Wheel of Law*, chs. 4–7.

85. Although Israeli constitutional development has been influenced by Britain's, Israeli juris-prudence has rejected the British rule that one parliament cannot irrevocably bind its successors. See Klein, "Basic Laws, Constituent Power," pp. 228–29; and past president Shamgar's opinion in *Mizrahi Bank*. Klein also raises the question, unanswered by *Mizrahi Bank*, of how or even whether the Knesset might amend a Basic Law.

code."[86] This terse style reflects a belief that a constitutional charter requires "that only its great outlines should be marked, its important objects designated, and the minor ingredients which compose those objects be deduced from the nature of the objects themselves."[87] Although there is much to be said for such a text's being intelligible to a wide popular audience, this model's capacious language demands much (and frequent) interpretation.

Near the other extreme lies the Indian constitutional script, whose style aims at clarity through specificity. In the same-sized font that places the American text within fifteen pages, the Indian charter's 395 major articles, many subarticles, and ten special schedules consume more than two hundred pages. Nevertheless, that document is replete with broadly phrased commands and prohibitions, and its interpretation has been more complicated than the American's. Furthermore, while the U.S. document has been amended only twenty-seven times in more than twenty-two decades (only seventeen times if the first ten are counted as part of the original agreement), with two of those canceling each other out, that of India was amended forty-eight times in its first half-century.[88]

Founders might resort to a more inclusive version of Napoleon's injunction against interpretation of his great Civil Code, but that prohibition would probably have just as little effect as it did for the emperor. The necessity of interpretation is part of the human condition. Trying to establish a new constitutional order and writing a fresh text may solve some problems but at the same time will create—or reveal—others. Anyone familiar with disputes among Jews about the Torah, among Christians about the Gospels, and among Muslims about the Qur'an knows that the text that unites also divides.

Moreover, even the most brilliant authors of constitutional texts can divine only some of the future's problems. They may see other difficulties but choose not to try to solve them. It was not ignorance but prudence that

---

86. Christopher W. Hammons, "Was James Madison Wrong? Rethinking the American Preference for Short, Framework-Oriented Constitutions," 93 *Am. Pol. Sci. Rev.* 837 (1999), examines 104 American state constitutional texts and concludes that "longer and more particularistic" constitutional texts are more durable. The argument is interesting, but despite the Supreme Court's acceptance since the 1990s of much of the Anti-Federalists' hostility toward strong central government, state constitutional documents, long or short, are simply not as important as that of the United States. The triumph of the national government in 1861–65 and the subsequent success of the national constitutional order have given the states the luxury of constitutional tinkering, secure in the knowledge that the national government will protect them from foreign invasion, domestic insurrection, and (usually) economic disaster.

87. M'Culloch v. Maryland, 4 Wh. 316, 407 (1819).

88. Germany's Basic Law, though shorter than the Indian charter, still resembles a code and has also been frequently amended. Between 1994 and 2004, Parliament, by the prescribed two-thirds vote of both houses, amended or deleted twenty-five separate articles. Kommers claims that amendment, rather than interpretation, has been the principal way of effecting constitutional change. "Constitutional Interpretation in Germany," p. 16.

caused the men at Philadelphia to dance around the issue of slavery. To cope with these kinds of difficulties, writers of constitutional documents often resort to abstract language. Later officials who can no longer dodge postponed problems will sometimes seek a formal amendment to the text. But the divisive nature of the problem may preclude obtaining the extraordinary majority most polities require for a formal amendment. At other times, officials may believe they lack time to pursue that process and, instead, move beyond the script's plain words to construe its "spirit." In short, interpreters may find it necessary to look beyond the charter to the constitutional order, thus opening up the problems of creative construction that a text was supposed to remove. It is also likely that, along with normative political theories, the broader constitution will encompass traditions as well as many social and governmental practices. These last, however, may cause constitutional conflicts, with racial segregation in the United States being the most infamous example.[89]

There is also the matter of earlier interpretations. What Michael Walzer said of Judaism is largely true for constitutional charters: their essence "is not found in the text [of the Torah] as [much as] in the interpretations of the text."[90] An intelligent but uninitiated reader of opinions of the U.S. Supreme Court will be fascinated by the lengthy discussions of earlier interpretations and such doctrines as "wall of separation," "one person, one vote," and "strict scrutiny" not found in the text. That reader will also be struck by the paucity of references to the document itself. The question *what* interpreters interpret constantly arises, but the justices seem blithely indifferent to (or unaware of) the fact that they usually construe previous interpretations, not the actual constitutional charter. Only occasionally does the Court take Felix Frankfurter's admonition seriously: "[T]he ultimate touchstone of constitutionality is the Constitution[al text] itself and not what we have said about it."[91]

The German Constitutional Court has never officially said it is bound by earlier interpretations, but the judges are aware of them, cite them, and often explain why they are or are not following them. The judges have also elevated some concepts—*Bundestreue*, loyalty to the federation,[92] for example—into constitutional principles. French tribunals, even the Conseil Constitu-

89. For fuller discussions of the authority of a constitutional text, see my "Constitutions, Constitutionalism, and Democracy," in Douglas Greenberg, Stanley N. Katz, Melanie Beth Oliviero, and Steven C. Wheatley, eds., *Constitutionalism and Democracy: Transformations in the Contemporary World* (New York: Oxford University Press, 1993), pp. 7–12.

90. *Exodus and Revolution* (New York: Basic Books, 1985), p. 144.

91. Graves v. New York ex rel. O'Keefe, 306 U.S. 466, concur. op., 491–92 (1939).

92. See esp. the Concordat Case, 6 BVerfGE 309 (1957); the Atomic Weapons Referenda, 8 BVerfGE 105 (1958); and the Television Case, 12 BVerge 205 (1961), all trans. and reprinted in part in Walter F. Murphy and Joseph Tanenhaus, eds., *Comparative Constitutional Law* (New York: St. Martin's, 1977).

tionnel, rarely cite previous decisions, which does not mean they pay no attention to them. Italian judicial opinions may also be bare of citations to earlier interpretations, but since the 1960s, Italian judges have been using electronic databases that allow them to recover within seconds all previous rulings on any particular issue. Typically legislative and executive officials are also acutely aware of what judges have said about the constitution as well as about many, perhaps varied, interpretations by their own institutions. As with judges, current interpretations tend to reflect, if not repeat, past readings of the document and the constitutional order.

Constitutional Maintenance

On the surface, constitutional interpretation as constitutional maintenance may not differ very much from "ordinary" constitutional interpretation. And, as with interpretation generally, interpreters may not always be conscious of engaging in the enterprise or do so without extensive reflection. In any event, the basic questions that interpreters confront will be the same. The answers, however, may be somewhat different. A response to that part of the interrogative *what is included?* would *necessarily* encompass the text, the polity's aspirations, traditions, social norms, and both constitutionalist and democratic theories. It is not an exaggeration to say that the *what* interpreters construe is the nation's culture (or cultures).

Answers to *how to interpret* stamp the most obvious differentiating marks onto constitutional interpretation as constitutional maintenance. Although interpreters have open all the usual approaches, modes, and techniques, ranging from textual parsing to philosophical reflection, two modes take prominence: purposive and prudential analyses. A combination of these two is essential. If it is unclear how to preserve either the nation or its constitutional order, saving both is truly murky business, demanding what Aristotle called practical wisdom and, as always in matters political, luck. Prudence requires not only good judgment but also philosophical inquiry into the ordering of the polity's values. Careful assessments of current facts, predictions of future events, and estimates of risks mean little without equally careful assessments of the relative worth of competing public goods.

As its name implies, purposive interpretation requires interpreting a document, tradition, legal system, or political order to achieve that entity's goals. A constitutional democracy has two overriding objectives. It shares the first with most political systems: preserving the people's independence so that they and not foreigners determine their future. The second, equally important goal is to allow a people to live under a political system that advances the norms that the two underlying theories endorse. It follows that the ultimate objective of purposive constitutional interpretation is to maintain both the nation and the values of constitutional democracy. In a sense, all rational approaches to constitutional interpretation—perhaps of all interpretation[93]—must be designed to further the system's goals, not merely or not even particular institutional or social arrangements and certainly not the careers of particular officials. The advantage of designating an approach as purposive and then openly adopting it is to force interpreters to keep these twin objectives before them and to read the text, previous interpretations, and the entire constitutional order in this light.

It may seem unnecessary to specify using a prudential interpretive mode, because no intelligent person would deliberately interpret unwisely. But frankly acknowledging the necessity of prudence reminds interpreters that their crucial task is not merely to discover and apply what others have thought to be constitutional meaning. Rather, that task also involves using past as well as current understandings to solve the constitutional problems *now* facing the nation and to do so in ways that respect the as yet unseen needs of a mysteriously unfolding future—in short, not merely to accumulate and organize knowledge but also to couple that knowledge with practical judgment. Interpreters using this combination of analytical modes will be pushed to view the constitutional order *sub specie aeternitatis.*

If the goal of the enterprise of constitutional interpretation is to preserve *both* the nation and constitutional democracy, interpreters must be concerned with the entire field of statecraft. Departmentalism permits—here demands—overlapping allocations of interpretative authority. Because the general welfare includes but reaches beyond issues of citizens' rights, governmental authority, and allotments of power among institutions, interpretation as maintenance might also embrace policies regarding the economy, ecology, and foreign policy. (Under such a sweeping view, the most grievous flaws in the American Supreme Court's work during the period 1890-1937 were a myopic economic vision and an inflated institutional ego.) This wide scope also requires interpreters frequently to ask themselves to what extent they are equipped to speak about particular facets of problems before them. The simultaneous ubiquity of issues of practical politics, textual meaning, normative political theories, and past practices and interpretations makes it necessary that interpretive competences be shared rather than sharply divided. There is no compelling reason for legislators always to abdicate interpretive authority to judges where a principal concern is citizens' constitutional rights or for judges always to cede plenary interpretive authority to the executive when national security touches on civil rights or the authority of other branches of government. Thus it was proper for Congress to decide, contrary to the judgment of the Supreme Court, that free exercise of reli-

---

93. Aharon Barak so argues; he begins with wills and contracts and works his way up through statutes and constitutional texts (*Purposive Interpretation in Law*).

gion includes a right to engage in rituals that Judeo-Christian standards would brand unorthodox.[94] It was also proper for the German Constitutional Court to address the constitutional implications of the Federal Republic's signing a treaty with the People's Republic.[95]

In this context, constitutional interpretation, by whomever conducted, will be untidy. Without doubt, it is dangerous to bestow such an open-ended brief on any person or institution—perhaps the most powerful justification for departmentalism. Preserving democracy presents its own mare's nest of constitutional difficulties. Earlier we saw that one facet of this general difficulty, regulating campaign financing, raises clotted questions. It is possible, of course, that the (not very) plain words of a charter might provide an obvious solution. In fact, however, no charter directly and unequivocally addresses this issue. Instead, interpreters who wish to be faithful to the text must approach the problem by reading meaning out of or into clauses that speak to such concepts as (meaningful) elections, equality of citizenship, and freedoms of speech, petition, and assembly.

Conversations about electoral financing between the German Parliament and Constitutional Court show that a reasonable solution is not impossible. In the United States, dialogues between Congress and the Supreme Court have been less fruitful, in part because Congress reversed the German strategy and depended more heavily on regulating private contributions than on offering public subsidies. Complicating American discourses has been judges' equating political donations and expenditures with free speech. The Supreme Court has fudged by conceding that it is legitimate for Congress to restrict the amount of money a person may give to a candidate or party but not the amount a candidate may spend.[96]

Resort by legislators and judges to more abstract analyses, such as the implications of constitutionalist and democratic theory, would not necessarily solve the problems, but raising the level of abstraction could provide a firmer basis for agreement (and more effective regulation) than does restricting debate to the text's (not very) plain words. Largely absent from the

---

94. Religious Freedom Restoration Act of 1993, 42 U.S.C. 2000bb-2000bb4. Congress passed this act to undo the damage the Supreme Court had done to the First Amendment in Employment Division of Oregon v. Smith, 494 U.S. 872 (1990). In *City of Boerne* (1997), the Court, in a fit of pique at the temerity of legislators' belief that the plain words of the Fourteenth Amendment allowed them to take an expansive view of the First and Fourteenth amendments, invalidated the statute. Gonzales v. O Centro Espíritu Beneficente União do Vegetal, 546 U.S. (2006), barely mentioned City of Boerne and broadly interpreted the protections that Congress had tried to extend to freedom of religion. The Court was unanimous; Justice Samuel Alito took no part in the decision.

95. Basic East-West Treaty Case, 38 BVerfGE 1 (1973); trans. and reprinted in part in Murphy and Tanenhaus, *Comparative Constitutional Law,* pp. 232ff.

96. See esp. Buckley v. Valeo, 424 U.S. 1 (1976); First Nat'l Bank v. Bellotti, 435 U.S. 765 (1978); and Austin v. Michigan Chamber of Commerce, 494 U.S. 652 (1990).

American discussions have been questions of constitutionalism's requirement of equal treatment.[97] Allowing the rich and poor alike to give money to candidates parodies Anatole France's snide comment that the law in its majestic impartially forbids both rich and poor to sleep on park benches.[98]

Achieving and sustaining widely enjoyed prosperity is another important aspect of maintaining constitutional democracy. A polity must be based on a free citizenry, and as Franklin Roosevelt said, "necessitous men are not free men."[99] Freedom from fear, hunger, and want have become integral parts of the aspirations of every constitutional democracy. Although India and Ireland demonstrate that constitutional democracy can endure severe, widespread poverty, continuous economic deprivation invites a change of political systems, as has often happened in Latin America. As the introduction to part II indicated, generating prosperity presents myriad problems for economic as well as political theory. Where government presides over a command economy, freedom will soon become moribund. Even Alexander Hamilton, a friend of "energy in government," recognized that "*a power over a man's subsistence amounts to a power over his will.*"[100] Two centuries later, Charles Reich added that "in a society that chiefly values material wellbeing, the [citizen's] power to control a particular portion of that well-being is the very foundation of [his or her] individuality."[101] On the other hand, positive constitutionalists note that unfettered rights to own, use, and dispose of property allow some private citizens to control other citizens' subsistence and will. Too much regulation stifles individual initiative and responsibility, too little transforms a polity into an oligarchy.

It is hardly surprising, then, that coping with the necessity of and dangers from governmental regulation of the economy has triggered severe problems

97. This issue, which, one could reasonably argue, concerns democratic theory as much as constitutionalist, was central to the German Constitutional Court's rulings, but not in the reasoning reported in American opinions. The most notable exception was Rehnquist's separate opinion in Buckley v. Valeo, 424 U.S. 1 (1976).

98. Bruce A. Ackerman and Ian Ayres have made an imaginative pair of suggestions to resolve this problem: Congress could (1) give to each citizen fifty dollars that can be spent only as one (or more) campaign contributions and (2) remove limits on how much individuals can contribute to parties or candidates but require that the names of all donors be kept secret. The money would be put into a blind trust to be distributed as donors wished. *Voting with Dollars: A New Paradigm for Campaign Financing* (New Haven, CT: Yale University Press, 2002). If contributions are more likely to come to elected officials because of what they have done rather than what opponents promise to do, challengers will have a much more difficult time raising money than will incumbents. Further, Representative Barney Frank of New York doubts that the source of donations would remain secret, and that revelation would defeat the purpose of bringing about equality of citizens in the political processes. Officials, he says, could accurately guess the sources of contributions. "Response to Bruce Ackerman," 57 *Bulletin of the Am. Acad. of Arts and Scs.* 19 (Summer 2004).

99. Message to Congress on the State of the Union, Jan. 11, 1944; in *The Public Papers of Franklin D. Roosevelt*, ed. Samuel I. Rosenman (New York: Harper and Brothers, 1950), 13:41.

100. *The Federalist*, No. 79 (italics in original).

101. "The New Property," 73 *Yale L. J.* 733, 764 (1964).

for both democracy and constitutionalism, especially negative constitutionalism. Historically, one of the principal constitutional questions in Australia, Canada, and the United States concerned the extent to which judicially imposed restrictions on governmental authority violated democratic theory and the extent to which allowing popularly elected officials to closely regulate private property would cripple constitutionalism. In the famous footnote 4 to his opinion for a truncated Court in *Carolene Products* (1938),[102] Harlan Fiske Stone offered a solution: judges should (a) presume the validity of economic regulations, but (b) ensure that the political processes are open so that various interests can freely compete, and also (c) carefully scrutinize legislation that singles out particular minorities. Because American officials have pretty much accepted Stone's solution, questions of the validity of economic regulations now arise much less often there. For Canada, the Privy Council, faced with amendments to the British North America Act and the reduction of its jurisdiction, retreated and left decisions mainly to legislatures, a strategy the Supreme Court and the Charter have endorsed and the Australian High Court has by and large adopted.

As we have seen, newer constitutional texts speak in positive constitutionalist terms about governmental *obligations* to facilitate social justice. They do not merely authorize but direct government to intervene in economic affairs. Applying these commands to concrete cases would give judges nightmares. They would be happy, as was Japan's Supreme Court, to pass those bad dreams on to elected officials.[103] In fact, many newer constitutional texts explicitly delegate primary interpretive authority directly to legislators and indirectly to voters, and, one could reasonably argue, the rest implicitly do so. That allocation, however, does not make constitutional interpretation less important; it merely makes clearer how deeply that enterprise is embedded in practical wisdom. Furthermore, this allocation does not completely relieve judges of interpretive responsibility. Heavily weighting positive constitutionalism does not transform private property into plums to be handed out at will by a dominant party or coalition. Although departmentalism may make elected officials the principal interpreters of the validity of economic policies, judges can still play important roles, sometimes attempting to set limits but more often acting as educators, warning of the dangers certain policies pose.

102. United States v. Carolene Products Co., 304 U.S, 144 (1938).

103. The Court held that Article 25, 1 of Japan's charter—"All people shall have the right to maintain the minimum standards of wholesome and cultured living"—did not create a judicially enforceable individual right, only instructed government to do its best to create a healthy economy. · Minimum Standards of Wholesome and Cultured Living Case (1948), trans. and reprinted in part in Murphy and Tanenhaus, *Comparative Constitutional Law*, pp. 383ff. Stanley N. Katz has argued that such positive rights cannot be effectively enforced by judges. "Constitutionalism and Human Rights: The Dilemma of the United States," Second Walter F. Murphy Lecture, James Madison Program in American Ideals and Institutions, Princeton University, 2002.

Preservation of pluralism in multicultural states is among the more en-snarled of areas in which constitutional interpretation must operate as a form of constitutional maintenance. The Indian text lists conserving the nation's cultural diversity as among the state's main objectives, and Parliament and the Supreme Court have tried to accommodate the varied religious practices of Hindus, Sikhs, and Muslims.[104] Despite Israel's difficulties with its Arab minority, the Supreme Court has permitted Muslims to follow their own religious rules regarding divorce.[105] So, too, the best way to chop one's way through the jungle of American judicial decisions regarding "separation of church and state" is to realize that judges have been far less concerned with spinning coherent legal doctrines than with seeking ways to permit agnostics, atheists, and assorted religious believers to live together in peace.

The most dramatic crises for constitutional interpretation as constitutional maintenance arise when leaders perceive or imagine grave threats to national security. Chapter Nine quoted Machiavelli, Madison, Hamilton, and Jefferson on emergency powers, discussed some of the problems raised by Lincoln's policies during the Civil War, and listed a few of the difficulties his precedents fertilized. Frequent abuses of emergency powers cannot obscure the fact that occasions do sometimes arise when a nation's life is imperiled. Lincoln's question cut to the heart of the matter: is "it possible to lose the nation, and yet preserve the constitution?"[106] But it is equally appropriate to ask: What doth it profit citizens of a constitutional democracy to preserve national security at the cost of becoming denizens of a police state? Even during emergencies, constitutional issues should not be decided on the basis of such simplistic formulas as *Inter armes silent leges.*[107] National defense, as Earl Warren said, is not an end in itself but a means to protect basic values and ideals.[108] Furthermore, interpreters rarely face a dichotomous choice: save the nation and destroy the constitution or affirm the constitution and lose the nation. The question is usually more complex: how much of the constitutional order can be preserved without seriously endangering the nation?

Although constitutional documents typically speak in terms that allow several plausible readings, interpretation as maintenance does not confer blanket permission to violate the terms of the charter. Purposive interpreters, however, must accept that it may, on rare occasions and in the face of dire emergencies, be permissible to ignore the text or even to violate its explicit

104. See Jacobsohn, *Wheel of Law*, esp. chs. 5–7.

105. See ibid., esp. ch. 3, and *Apple of Gold;* and Edelman, *Courts, Politics, and Culture in Israel,* esp. chs. 3–5.

106. To A. G. Hodges, Apr. 4, 1864; in *The Collected Works of Abraham Lincoln,* ed. Roy P. Basler (New Brunswick, NJ: Rutgers University Press, 1953), 7:281.

107. What Cicero actually wrote in his *Pro Milone* was "Silent enim leges inter arma." Lawyers and public officials, however, seem to prefer the snappier version.

108. United States v. Robel, 389 U.S. 258 (1967).

provisions. Framers of constitutional texts cannot accurately foretell the future. Thus their work could prove to be dangerously inadequate as a means of coping with a particular crisis. Constitutional texts may well fail; but, sophisticated interpreters realize, the document forms only one part, albeit a very important part, of the larger constitution, that is, the constitutional order. During such emergencies, John E. Finn has argued, public policies must, at minimum, conform to constitutionalism's basic principles.[109] His advice inheres in constitutional interpretation as constitutional maintenance. Indeed, Lincoln's justification for policies even he deemed extraconstitutional would have been more convincing had he rephrased his question to ask: Are specific commands of the constitutional text to be followed at the cost of destroying both the nation and the larger constitutional order?

The greatest peril, Robert H. Jackson said, does not lie in rationalizing emergency measures to conform to the constitutional charter but in rationalizing that document to conform to emergency policies.[110] Although such rationalizations can destroy a polity, they do not inevitably and permanently ratchet power over liberty.[111] Lincoln's constitutional violations did not persist beyond Reconstruction. On the other hand, suspensions of rights in Argentina, Brazil, Chile, Uruguay, much of Sub-Saharan Africa,[112] and, of course, Weimar Germany endured for many years. Reliance on constitutional democracy's values over the specific terms of the text is dangerous, but it is less dangerous, more intellectually honest, and more practically efficient than twisting the words of that text.

Whatever their long-range effects, emergencies facilitate centralization of power. "It is of the nature of war to increase the executive at the expense of the legislative authority," Hamilton noted in *The Federalist* 8; and it would be reasonable to expand "war" to include all crises involving national security and to add "at the expense of judicial" authority as well as legislative, a double aggrandizement amply illustrated by George W. Bush's actions following the terrorist attacks of 9/11. He refused to be bound by the Foreign Intelligence Suveillance Act, enacted to explicitly outlaw Richad Nixon's warrantless spying on American citizens. Bush refused to follow the law even though the statute makes it easy for the government to obtain a warrant from a special (and secret) court either before or within seventy-two hours after eavesdropping begins.

109. *Constitutions in Crisis: Political Violence and the Rule of Law* (New York: Oxford University Press, 1991).

110. Korematsu v. United States, 323 U.S. 214, dis. op., 246 (1944).

111. Eric A. Posner and Adrian Vermeule make this point: "Accommodating Emergencies," in Mark Tushnet, ed., *The Constitution in Wartime: Beyond Alarmism and Complacency* (Durham, NC: Duke University Press, 2005). For an effort to assess systematically for the United States the effect of emergencies on civil liberties, see Epstein et al., "Supreme Court during Crisis."

112. For Africa, see H. W. O. Okoth-Ogendo, "Constitutions without Constitutionalism: Reflections on an African Political Paradox," in Greenberg et al., *Constitutionalism and Democracy.*

Without doubt, centralized, unchecked power threatens constitutional democracy's very existence. The American Congress's hasty passage of the so-called Patriot Act in 2001 and only marginally more reasoned repassage in 2006 raise grave doubts about legislators' having the courage to oppose a determined executive who claims that national safety is threatened, just as the Nisei cases had raised such doubts about judges. Still, legislators and judges who are less than bold may be coaxed to fight guerrilla campaigns on the fringes of policy. Legislators can insert "sundown clauses" in emergency enactments, requiring, after a specified time when emotions may be calmer, executive officials again to justify grants of extraordinary power. Alternatively or additionally, legislators can give limited appropriations, forcing discussion to be resumed later. For their part, judges can insist that officials scrupulously observe procedural rules, a tactic evident in the American Supreme Court's handling of the cold war cases during the McCarthy era, when the justices encased narrow rulings within sermons about the sacredness of constitutional rights.[113] Despite the plain words of the Irish constitutional text's placing beyond judicial review parliament's authority to cope with crises, the Supreme Court insisted that judges should narrowly construe any such legislation. It would not be construed, the justices stated, as abnegating the arrested person's constitutional rights to an attorney, to communicate with others, or to have access to the courts.[114]

Whatever else they do, worried public officials, journalists, academic commentators, and, most of all, voters must try to persuade government to apply Finn's precept if constitutional democracy is to survive a perpetual war against terrorism. If nothing else—and it is quite possible that there will be nothing else—such departmentalist constitutional interpretations could force a national debate and so deter executive officials who are overly zealous, overly fearful, or overly anxious to hide their grabs for power under the mantle of patriotism. Constitutional democrats should not be Cassandras wailing in the streets about endangered liberties, but they should neither forget nor allow others to forget that assorted Asian and Latin American dictators as well as an Austrian-turned-German used claims of emergency to justify destruction of both constitutional government and civil society. For all her poor public relations, Cassandra was right about the dangers Troy faced. Emergency powers may sometimes be necessary to national survival, but they can sometimes be a Trojan horse. Constitutional democracy requires that officials who seek extraordinary powers bear an extraordinary burden of proof of the absolute necessity of their being loaned such privileges.

---

113. See Murphy, *Congress and the Court*, pp. 109–12; and John Hart Ely, *Democracy and Distrust: A Theory of Judicial Review* (Cambridge, MA: Harvard University Press, 1980), pp. 73–75.

114. In Article 26 and the Emergency Powers Bill, [1977] I.R. 159.

CHAPTER FIFTEEN

Constitutional Change
and Its Limits

[A] nation without the means of its own reform is without the means of its own preservation.

EDMUND BURKE

There are constitutional principles that are so fundamental . . . that they also bind the framer of the constitution.

FEDERAL CONSTITUTIONAL COURT OF GERMANY

Every viable political system must provide some means for innovation. As a nation's physical, technological, and cultural environments mutate, unforeseen problems will arise and require fresh solutions. Furthermore, as economic costs and benefits shift, people who suffer from these changes may try to alter the implications of constitutional principles, or even the principles themselves. Alternatively or additionally, citizens may believe they have learned how to cope more efficiently with old problems and attempt to put these plans into action. So, too, development of a finer or grosser sense of justice may make what once seemed proper appear unacceptable.[1] In an important sense, political systems resemble the Red Queen in *Through the Looking Glass:* they must keep moving in order to stay in place.

The fairness of constitutional changes deeply troubled Jefferson. His solution was to allow each generation to write a new basic charter.[2] During the debates on ratification, Noah Webster put the point bluntly. "[T]he very attempt to make *perpetual* constitutions is the assumption of a right to controul the opinions of future generations; and to legislate for those over whom we have as little authority as we have over a nation in Asia."[3] Madison

---

1. As Antonin Scalia has pointed out—"Originalism: The Lesser Evil," 57 *U. Cinn. L. Rev.* 849 (1989)—moral change is a two-way street. A shared sense of justice may become less as well as more sensitive.

2. This theme ran through much of Jefferson's writings. See, for example, his letter to Madison, Sept. 6, 1789; in *The Papers of James Madison,* ed. William T. Hutchinson and William M. E. Rachal (Chicago: University of Chicago Press, 1979), 12:382ff.

3. "Bills of Rights" (1788), reprinted in Noah Webster, *Collection of Essays and Fugitive Writings on Moral, Historical, Political, and Literary Subjects* (Boston: Thomas and Andrews, 1790), p. 47. Italics in original.

disagreed, arguing in *The Federalist* No. 49 that frequent recurrence to the people to resolve constitutional issues would destabilize a political system.

One solution is to incorporate into the constitutional text itself procedures for amendment. As obvious as this option seems, its inclusion in the American charter of 1787 was "a totally new contribution to politics."[4] Today the novel is the conventional. Since adoption in 1982 of Canada's Constitution Act, the basic document of every constitutional democracy includes such a clause. Some, such as those of Germany and India, provide a straight road, while others, such as that of the United States, offer a twisted path through a political jungle.

Some constitutional commentators, including such eminent jurists as Joseph Story, Thomas Cooley, George Sutherland, and Hugo Black, have contended that formal amendments open the only rightful path to constitutional change because a constitution's meaning should "have a fixed, uniform, and permanent construction."[5] Reality, however, indicates that uniformity across time is not necessary and also that there are many routes to legitimate constitutional change. Formal amendments have been frequent in India and fairly so in Germany, but there was none in Japan or Italy during the first fifty years after World War II nor during the first four decades of France's Fifth Republic. During a much longer time span, the United States has seldom resorted to the amending process. In every constitutional democracy, interpretation and practice have been far more common means to effect constitutional change.

Black's mocking the notion of "a living Constitution" would have been more persuasive if he himself had treated "the constitution" as being restricted to the document. Earl Warren came closer to constitutional wisdom when he wrote that it would be "foolhardy and likewise impossible to declare a moratorium on emerging jurisprudence as it struggles to meet the challenges of our time."[6] When confronting constitutional questions, legislators

---

4. Gordon Wood, *The Creation of the American Republic, 1776–1787* (New York: W. W. Norton, 1972), p. 613. He also asserts that the amending clause "institutionalized and legitimized revolution" (p. 614). This more extended claim conflates three concepts that are important to constitutional interpretation: (1) "amendment," a change within an existing political framework; (2) "revision," a change that may even reshape, without necessarily destroying, an existing political framework; and (3) "revolution," a change that substitutes a radically new political framework for the old. In Raven v. Deukemejian, 801 P. 2d 1077 (1990), California's Supreme Court invalidated a supposed amendment to the state constitutional text on the grounds that it was, in fact, a revision of that document, not an amendment.

5. Story, *Commentaries on the Constitution of the United States,* (Boston: Hilliard, Gray, 1833), vol. 1, §426. For Cooley, see his *A Treatise on Constitutional Limitations* (Boston: Little, Brown, 1868), p. 55: "The meaning of the Constitution is fixed when adopted, and it is not different at any subsequent time when a court has occasion to pass upon it." For Sutherland, see his dis. op. in West Coast Hotel v. Parrish, 300 U.S. 379 (1937), and for Black, his dis. op. in Harper v. Virginia, 383 U.S. 663 (1966).

6. "Science and the Law: Change and the Constitution," 12 *J. of Pub. L.* 3, 7 (1963).

and executive officials often dispose of them as if they presented only practical issues of policy rather than of fundamental principles—in effect, they engage in constitutional interpretation without making much fuss about it, perhaps without even being very aware of the implications of their actions.

The constitution Lincoln bequeathed to his successors was far different from that which he inherited from James Buchanan. One could make similar statements about the legacies of the two Roosevelts. And how much the constitution after John Marshall accorded with the varied views of his fellow founders is a question that can never be definitively answered.[7] In Japan, executive, legislative, and judicial officials have all been adept at adjusting the words of the constitutional text to fit current needs, whether to create a standing army despite the plain words of Article 9 or to relax a clearly specified governmental obligation to provide a decent standard of living. Italian officials have ignored neofascist parties, in effect repealing a clause in their constitutional charter forbidding the formation of such organizations.

The previous chapter argued that constitutional maintenance, including constitutional interpretation, inevitably involves constitutional change. On the other hand, Madison argued that change run amok would destabilize a polity. If the text and the larger order are to command continuing respect, they cannot become like "an excursion ticket, good for this day and trip only."[8] Heraclitus's claim that we never bathe in the same river twice applies to constitutional politics only if the polity endures long intervals between showers. Whether changes will be too frequent or unwise depends heavily on a future that can be only dimly perceived.

Procedural Problems

The frequency and content of constitutional changes are matters for judgment, whose correctness depends, as military strategists would put it, on the terrain and situation. A proposed constitutional change may also raise questions other than those of prudence. The two most fundamental are, oddly enough, procedural and substantive. The procedural inquiry involves at least two steps. First, through what institution is the change being effected? Second, even if the change is evolving through the proper agency, did it do so according to the rules the text itself lays down?

Procedural difficulties are not always simple even if change is proposed

---

7. Having been a member of Virginia's ratifying convention, Marshall considered himself to be a founder—a claim solidly grounded in democratic theory as well as in the text's preamble.

8. This was Owen J. Roberts's protest, dissenting in Smith v. Allwright, 321 U.S. 649 (1944), against the Court's, and, more particularly Harlan Stone's, trickery in undermining, in United States v. Classic, 313 U.S. 299 (1941), Roberts's opinion for the Court in Grovey v. Townsend, 295 U.S. 45 (1935), sustaining the constitutionality of the white primary. In *Allwright*, Stone joined in reversing *Grovey*. Alpheus Thomas Mason tells much of the story in *Harlan Fiske Stone: Pillar of the Law* (New York: Viking, 1956), pp. 586–89, 614–17, 637–39. In *Classic*, Stone needed Roberts's vote, so he carefully omitted mentioning *Grovey*.

through a formal amendment. When, as was the case in Canada before 1982, tradition rather than constitutional text designates the proper process, the problem may be very difficult indeed.[9] Even when the charter prescribes steps for formal amendment, issues may remain. It may not be enough for public officials and private citizens to parse the document. Obscure wording or definitional changes over time may require creative analysis. Although linguistic difficulties seem to have generated few practical problems,[10] questions of procedural legitimacy have sprung up on several occasions. For example, in 1975 when Prime Minister Indira Nehru Gandhi was attempting to change India's constitutional structure to make herself a virtual dictator, she pushed through the Thirty-ninth Amendment while keeping some opposition members of Parliament under what amounted to arrest. It was unlikely that she could have secured the necessary two-thirds vote in both houses[11] had these MPs been free to vote. In any event, the procedural issue became moot after the Supreme Court declared the Thirty-ninth unconstitutional on substantive grounds, and at the next election the people of India voted Gandhi into early retirement.[12]

The labyrinthine amending processes of the United States have provided frequent doubts about procedural regularity. The constitutional text says that a proposed amendment must be born in Congress as a resolution and all reso-

9. Because the British North America Act was an act of the Parliament at Westminster, it could only be amended by that body. Over the decades, however, as the British Empire evolved into the Commonwealth of Nations, Parliament amended the BNA whenever so requested by the Canadian government. The Constitution Act, agreed to by the Parliament at Westminster and by the Canadian Parliament in 1982, acknowledged Canada's authority to amend its own constitutional text. For a complex discussion of the content of Canada's complex amending tradition along with an excellent analysis of the difference between a constitutional text and a constitution, see In the Matter of §6 of *The Judicature Act*, [1981] S.C.R. 753.

10. For an exception, see United States v. Sprague, 282 U.S. 716 (1931). There the Supreme Court rejected an argument that the Prohibition amendment was unconstitutional. The claim was that because the Tenth Amendment distinguishes between rights retained by the states and rights retained by the people, only amendments affecting the authority of states per se could be ratified by state legislatures. Those affecting individual rights had to be ratified by popularly elected conventions.

11. Article 368, which prescribes the procedures for amending the constitutional text, also requires approval by at least one-half of the states for certain kinds of amendments.

12. In Sankari Prasad Singh Deo v. Union, (1952) S.C.R. 69 (decided in 1951), the Supreme Court rejected a challenge that the first amendment was invalid on both substantive and (more or less) procedural grounds. The (more or less) procedural claim had been that the amendment, allowing takings of property, was not for a public purpose. Later Golak Nath v. Punjab, (1967) 2 S.C.R. 762, reversed the substantive holding of *Sankari Prasad Singh Deo*. The U.S. Supreme Court has often wrestled with the problem of "takings" of private property for public use. Hawaii Housing Authority v. Midkiff, 467 U.S. 229 (1984), indicated that it would accept what the legislature said was a public use unless patently unreasonable. Later decisions have taken a much more restrictive view of governmental authority. See esp. Nollan v. California Coastal Comm'n, 483 U.S. 825 (1987); Lucas v. South Carolina Coastal Council, 505 U.S. 1003 (1992); Dolan v. Tigard, 512 U.S. 374 (1994); Tahoe-Sierra Preservation Council v. Tahoe-Sierra Regional Planning Agency, 535 U.S. 302 (2002); then Kelo v. New London, 545 U.S. (2005), returned to *Midkiff*.

lutions must be presented to the president for approval or veto. Despite this seemingly clear language, only one such proposal, the ignominious Corwin amendment that would have forever relegated control over slavery to individual states, was signed by a president.[13] Are, then, all putative amendments to the constitutional document invalid? Wisely, the Supreme Court said no, though its reasoning, that a veto would have been overridden anyway because amendments had passed each house by a two-thirds vote, would have earned the justices a fat F in a freshman course in American government.[14] And other questions have arisen: Having once ratified an amendment, may a state legislature later, but before the proposed amendment has been declared adopted, rescind its ratification? And how long does a proposed amendment that does not contain a sundown clause stay alive after Congress proposes it? The Supreme Court has artfully dodged these latter problems, leaving questions of valid ratifications to the executive department.[15]

More complicated, but never officially treated as serious, has been the legitimacy of the Fourteenth Amendment.[16] This issue is integrally tied to the lawfulness of the Civil War and Reconstruction. As a condition of "readmission" to the Union, Congress required the former Confederate states to ratify the proposed amendment; without their assent, it would have failed to secure the approval of three-quarters of the states.[17] But secession, Lincoln had categorically asserted, was unlawful, and he had justified the war on that piece of constitutional interpretation. If the Union had been indissoluble, the so-called Confederate states had never, in a constitutional sense, been outside the United States. Rather, they had merely been in rebellion, an assertion frequently voiced at the time, as the sobriquet "Johnny Reb" attests. If Lincoln had been correct, Congress could not *require* formerly rebellious,

13. James Buchanan affixed his signature to the resolution on his last day in office, and in his first inaugural address, Abraham Lincoln urged states to ratify it speedily and so head off a civil war. Happily for the long run of American history, only Illinois, Maryland, and Ohio had ratified it before secession and before the good folk of Charleston opened fire on Fort Sumter.

14. Hollingsworth v. Virginia, 3 U.S. 378 (1798).

15. Esp. Coleman v. Miller, 307 U.S. 433 (1939). The Court also held that it could not enjoin the secretary of state from proclaiming that a constitutional amendment had been duly ratified and was part of the canonical text. Fairchild v. Hughes, 258 U.S. 126 (1922). See, generally, John R. Vile, *The Constitutional Amending Process in American Political Thought* (New York: Praeger, 1992).

16. See, for example, Joseph James, "Is the Fourteenth Amendment Unconstitutional?" 50 *Soc. Sc.* 3 (1975); Walter Southon, "The Dubious Origin of the Fourteenth Amendment," 28 *Tul. L. Rev.* 22 (1953); and Ferdinand F. Fernandez, "The Constitutionality of the Fourteenth Amendment," 39 *So. Cal. L. Rev.* 378 (1966). On the fascinating question of ratification outside of Article V, see Akhil Reed Amar, "Philadelphia Revisited: Amending the Constitution outside Article V," 55 *U. Chi. L. Rev.* 1043 (1988). In 1866, the *Democratic Almanac* charged that the Thirteenth Amendment was unconstitutional because it invaded "vested rights." Edward S. Corwin, *Liberty against Government* (Baton Rouge: Louisiana State University Press, 1948), p. 6.

17. At least until the twentieth century, when, if the fate of the Twenty-seventh Amendment is a guide, it might have eventually secured the requisite number of ratifications.

now pacified states to ratify a proposed amendment to the constitutional text in order to "rejoin" a Union they had never constitutionally left.

If, on the other hand, Lincoln's constitutional interpretation had been wrong and the Union had been dissolved in a constitutional sense, then the Civil War had been a war to *change* a weak federal union. It would have been a war to crush dissenters, or, as it is still called in South Carolina, the War of Yankee Aggression. Congress's requiring these errant states to ratify the Fourteenth Amendment *before* allowing them to be "readmitted" to the Union violated the terms of Article V. If those states were outside the Union when they ratified, those ratifications could carry no more constitutional weight than would Samoa's ratification in 2006 of an amendment to authorize prayers in public schools.[18]

Substantive Problems

Even more complex issues arise when, as often occurs, constitutional change is effected by practice or interpretation rather than by formal amendment. In such cases, opponents might reasonably question the validity of a given development. Eleven states violently rejected Lincoln's constitutional interpretation that the Union was indissoluble. A century later, white southerners complained that in Brown v. Board (1954) the Supreme Court had revised the constitutional text. To some extent, they were correct, but they had not complained earlier when the Supreme Court had twisted the charter and, along with Congress, effectively nullified much of the (possibly invalid) Fourteenth and Fifteenth amendments.[19] Germans who rejected departmentalism in constitutional interpretation had a firm base from which to challenge the legitimacy of the chancellor's interpretation that allowed the new Anschluss of 1990: (1) the text seems to say that reunification demanded

18. For a long, awkward, and unconvincing effort to resolve these contradictions, see Texas v. White, 74 U.S. 700 (1868). What is needed to validate the Fourteenth Amendment is some version of prescription perhaps joined to a doctrine of federal guardianship for temporarily insane states, though a Catholic theologian might prefer an analogy to Limbo. Another path, substantive, would lead to the conclusion that slavery itself violated the constitutional order and thus the Thirteenth Amendment had made the text more closely congruent with constitutional and democratic theories. Under such an argument, the Fourteenth and Fifteenth amendments would have been necessary to make the constitutional text conform to the constitutional order. This contention about slavery itself is not a recent invention. See, for example, William Hosmer, *The Higher Law, in Its Relation to Civil Government with Particular Reference to Slavery, and the Fugitive Slave Law* (1852; reprint New York: Negro Universities Press, 1969); and Joel Tiffany, *A Treatise on the Unconstitutionality of American Slavery: Together with Powers and Duties of the Federal Government in Relation to that Subject* (1849; reprint Miami: Mnemsyne, 1969).

19. Plessy v. Ferguson, 163 U.S. 537 (1896), and its progeny. Twenty-three years earlier, Railroad v. Brown, 17 Wall. 445 (1873), had held that a railroad that segregated passengers by race violated a congressional requirement that passengers be treated equally. The majority opinion in *Plessy* did not mention *Brown*.

a new charter, and in any event (2) the Constitutional Court should have decided this issue.

Civil war and passive acquiescence mark the extreme means of settling controversies about constitutional change, with acceptance being more probable as the substantive issue involved declines in significance. But that relationship is hardly invariable. German reunification demonstrated that losers may quickly, if reluctantly, accede on matters of critical import. Mutual adjustment is usually the more rational—and likely—means. Chapter Eight showed the intricate dance steps the Germans and Irish followed to resolve both constitutional questions regarding abortion. In the United States, most white southerners accepted, albeit slowly and begrudgingly, Brown v. Board after Congress and the president concurred in the Supreme Court's interpretation of the Fourteenth Amendment—and put the full weight of federal physical and fiscal power behind that decision. Elsewhere, accommodation has often taken the form of proposing an amendment to the constitutional charter and leaving its fate to formally prescribed processes.

When we move from procedure to substance, difficulties increase in gravity and complexity.[20] To simplify analysis, let us restrict ourselves to constitutional amendments, though fully understanding that similar problems may also arise when constitutional change is attempted through other methods and that the original constitutional text may itself contain language that raises questions about legitimacy under democratic and/or constitutionalist theory.[21] As the German Constitutional Court carefully explained in its very first opinion: "That a constitutional provision itself may be null and void is not conceptually impossible. . . . There are constitutional principles that are so fundamental . . . that they also bind the framer of the constitution, and other constitutional provisions that do not rank so high may be null and void because they contravene these principles."[22]

---

20. For an argument against the possibility of an unconstitutional amendment, see John R. Vile, "Limitations on the Constitutional Amending Process," 2 *Con'l Comm.* 373 (1965). My argument has also been called both "poetic" and "astonishing": "poetic" by Lief H. Carter, *Contemporary Constitutional Lawmaking* (New York: Pergamon, 1985), p. 127; "astonishing" by Henry P. Monaghan, "Our Perfect Constitution," 56 *N.Y.U. L. Rev.* 353, 369 (1981). See also Paul Brest, "Accommodations of Majoritarianism and Rights of Human Dignity," 53 *So. Cal. L. Rev.* 761 (1980). I should add that in 1992 Professor Monaghan graciously told me that he no longer fully disagreed with my thesis.

21. The euphemistic language of the American text of 1787–88 left little doubt that slaves were not entitled to the rights the Declaration of Independence proclaimed belonged to "all men" and at least to this extent were not fully human. Furthermore, consistent American legal positivists, such as Hugo L. Black aspired to be, have had serious difficulty with the Ninth Amendment, which protects unlisted rights against governmental action. Their dilemma is analogous to that of a junior military officer whose commander says, "Disobey me!"

22. The SouthWest Case, 1 BVerfGE 14 (1951); trans. and reprinted in part in Walter F. Murphy and Joseph Tanenhaus, eds., *Comparative Constitutional Law* (New York: St. Martin's, 1977), pp. 208ff. The Court was quoting with approval the Bavarian Constitutional Court.

First to be noted about amendments is that some constitutional texts forbid certain kinds of changes. The American charter, for example, forbids reduction of a state's equal representation in the Senate without that state's consent. Similarly, the Australian document prohibits reapportioning a state's "representation in either house of parliament without the approval of a majority of voters in that state."[23] Article 4 of the Turkish charter forbids amendments that would alter the nature of the state as "democratic, secular, and social" or divide the nation's territory. The most well known of such "eternity clauses" have been those of Germany's Basic Law. Article 1, with its elevation of human dignity to the rank of the polity's preeminent value, and Article 20, with its designation of Germany as "a democratic and social federal state," are expressly declared to be unamendable, as is the division of the country into *Länder*.[24]

Eternity clauses do not end problems of substantive validity. Neither procedural purity nor absence of a specific prohibition always settles problems of constitutional legitimacy. The question could still arise: Would this amendment so violate the principles of constitutional democracy as to destroy the nature of the polity? It is conceivable that a dominant religious sect or ethnic group might push through an amendment that restricts the right to vote or to speak on issues of public policy to members of that sect or group. That sect might obtain an amendment that declared members of minority sects to be unworthy of other rights of citizenship. Furthermore, a dominant political party might secure an amendment that exempted from judicial or other oversight any actions the government might take after it proclaimed a

23. U.S. constitutional text, Article V; Aus. constitutional text, Article 128. In the latter case, the language used could trigger a constitutional controversy. The document speaks of the "approval of a majority of the electors" in the affected state. One could reasonably argue that that term means that what is needed is not a simple majority of those voting but a majority of those who are qualified to vote, that is, electors. I am not aware of any dispute's having actually arisen on this point. An amendment to sec. 91, subsec. 1, of the British North America Act, passed by Parliament at Westminster, forbade, inter alia, amendments that would affect the guarantees of the equal status of French and English or the right to establish religious schools. A Canadian amendment adopted in 1996 tightly structures the process for amendments that affect provincial power. If the proposal is not one that a province could veto, its introduction must be approved by a majority of the provinces that includes Ontario, Quebec, and British Columbia and at least two of the Atlantic provinces as well as two of the Prairie provinces (whose combined populations must equal at least half the total population of those provinces). The Atlantic provinces are New Brunswick, Newfoundland, Nova Scotia, and Prince Edward Island; the Prairie provinces are Alberta, Manitoba, and Saskatchewan.

24. There is an escape route from these clauses, but it seems sleazy: first repeal the clause that forbids repealing the protected clause(s), then repeal the now unprotected clause(s). The peculiarities of British-Canadian relations opens another possibility. Because the BNA and the Constitution Act of 1982 were mere statutes and no parliament can bind future parliaments, these charters are not entrenched in the United Kingdom's constitution. Thus, according to British constitutional interpretation, Canadian political structures exist at the sufferance of the Parliament at Westminster. It is doubtful, however, if this constitutional interpretation will ever be more than of academic interest.

state of emergency. As much as constitutional democrats might hope that these sorts of events would not occur, they are not mere academic nightmares. No one familiar with American history should doubt the possibility that a supposed constitutional democracy would impose a caste system or deny "normal" procedural safeguards to prisoners accused of being rebels or terrorists. Neither should people who hope to persuade Muslim countries to adopt at least a form of constitutional democracy doubt that, during the foreseeable future, Islamists would, either initially or after a few years, try to restrict the political or civil rights of other religious groups.

India supplies several additional examples. In 1975–1976, Indira Gandhi rammed through the Thirty-ninth and Forty-second amendments, which together stripped protection as a fundamental right freedom from preventive detention, assigned electoral problems to the exclusive oversight of the president or governor of a state, and pretty much eliminated judicial review of alleged violations of civil rights. Moreover, the Bharatiya Janata Party (BJP), with its enthusiastic pursuit of the Hindu-nationalist ideology of Hindutva, continues to pose a serious threat of imposing a religiously ordained hierarchy of citizenship. Given Hinduism's historic endorsement of a caste system, the social and political ramifications of Hindutva are enormous. Furthermore, its appeal in an overwhelmingly Hindu nation has been widespread, allowing the BJP to be the principal player in a governing coalition from 1998 until 2004. Even in defeat, it held on to 117 of Parliament's 288 seats, thus forcing the secularist Congress Party to govern through a coalition.[25]

At root is the gnawing question: can an amendment that has been adopted through proper procedures and does not violate any express limitation on amendments listed in the text[26] nevertheless be invalid because it wreaks violence on the principles of constitutional democracy?

Let us take a simple scenario first: A sometime constitutional democracy has fallen on hard times, and a charismatic leader seizes the moment to offer a society changes that promise more and better of whatever goods and services seem in short supply, whether jobs, wages, profits, religious piety, national pride, or protection from criminals, terrorists, or foreign invasion. He and his party compete in a free election and win control of the government. To carry out his program, he proposes—as during the campaign he promised he would—several constitutional amendments that would outlaw all politi-

25. For a discussion of the constitutional problems the BJP poses to the secularism of Gandhi and Nehru as embodied in India's constitutional text, see Gary Jeffrey Jacobsohn, *The Wheel of Law: India's Secularism in Comparative Constitutional Context* (Princeton, NJ: Princeton University Press, 2003), esp. chs. 5–7.

26. In 1970, Germany's Constitutional Court divided 4–4 on whether an amendment allowing wiretapping violated the Basic Law's recognition of human dignity, a clause that constitutional text declared unamendable. Privacy of Communications Case, 30 BVerfGE 1 (1970); abridged and reprinted in Murphy and Tanenhaus, eds., *Comparative Constitutional Law*, pp. 659ff.

cal parties except his own, turn elections into plebiscites with only a single candidate for each office, and make judges, legislators, and administrators dependent for appointment, pay, and retention on the new leader. This personage would bear the title Proconsul and would serve for renewable terms of fifteen years, commanding while in office the armed forces as well as the civil government. As a finishing twist, the last amendment in the bundle says that these amendments shall not be subject to alteration or repeal for fifty years.

After open debate, this package is ratified according to the rules laid down in the constitutional text. The political system is no longer democratic, because elections are abolished. It is no longer constitutionalist, because the only limitations on the proconsul's authority are his ruthlessness and skill in managing (or purging) his own party. At best, the new regime is authoritarian, at worst, totalitarian. In either case, it fits this book's definition of a tyranny.[27]

Question: Are these constitutional changes valid? Consistent legal positivists and constitutionists—that is, those who accept the terms of a constitutional text as providing the ultimate political norms—must give a clear, if appalled, yes. Just as a law is valid if enacted according to correct procedures, so a constitutional amendment must be valid if its adoption has followed prescribed procedures. These people, even if conscience-stricken, have only three basic options: exile, martyrdom through some version of self-immolation, or a peaceful (and perhaps fatal) struggle for a new constitutional convention to reconstitute the nation. On the other hand, committed, consistent, and courageous constitutional democrats must deny the legitimacy of the change.[28]

First, they would stress the difference between *amending* and *replacing* a constitutional text or constitutional order. The word *amend* comes from the Latin *emendere*, to correct. Thus an "amendment" corrects or modifies a system without fundamentally changing its nature—that is, an amendment operates within the boundaries of the existing constitutional order. Abolishing constitutional democracy and substituting a different system would not be an amendment at all, but a re-creation, a re-forming, not simply of political structures but also of the people themselves. This theme lies at the heart

27. See Chapter One, p. 16.
28. A series of my articles spell out my argument in greater detail than do these pages: "An Ordering of Constitutional Values," 53 *So. Cal. L. Rev.* 703 (1980); "Slaughter-House, Civil Rights, and Limits on Constitutional Change," 21 *Am. J. of Jurisp.* 1 (1986); "Privacy and the Constitution," in Shlomo Slonim, ed., *The Constitutional Bases of Social and Political Change in the United States* (New York: Praeger, 1990); "Consent and Constitutional Change," in James O'Reilly, ed., *Human Rights and Constitutional Law: Essays in Honour of Brian Walsh* (Dublin: Round Hall, 1992); and "Merlin's Memory: The Past and Future Imperfect of the Once and Future Polity," in Sanford Levinson, ed., *Responding to Imperfection: The Theory and Practice of Constitutional Amendment* (Princeton, NJ: Princeton University Press, 1995).

of the Indian Supreme Court's justification for declaring several amendments unconstitutional and that which the highest court of California used to strike down an amendment that would have required state judges, when interpreting the state constitutional text, to follow federal judicial interpretations of similar provisions in the national charter.[29]

An ancillary argument would contend that substituting a tyrannical constitutional order for constitutional democracy lies outside the authority of any set of governmental bodies, for all of them are creatures of the constitution of a constitutional democracy.[30] If governmental institutions destroy the constitutional order that legitimizes them, they destroy their own legitimacy.[31] So, too, if citizens destroy their own right to have rights, they destroy their authority to legitimize a political system.

29. Golak Nath v. Punjab [1967] was the first instance. It provoked a stream of criticism—some academic, e.g., H. C. L. Merillat, *Land and the Constitution in India* (New York: Columbia University Press, 1970)—but more importantly, much political. Because this decision, other rulings, and parliamentary opponents stymied Indira Gandhi's "reforms," she declared a state of emergency, imprisoned opponents, and pushed through a set of constitutional amendments that reversed *Golak Nath*'s doctrine. After the Indian electorate repudiated Gandhi's leadership, the Supreme Court, though rejecting *Golak Nath,* found new and stronger arguments for its own authority and invalidated some of Gandhi's amendments. Kesavananda Bharati's Case, [1973] S.C.R. 1 (Supp.) (Ind.), esp. the opinion of Justice H. R. Khanna; and Minerva Mills v. Union of India, [1980] S.C.R. 1789. See Upendra Baxi, *Courage, Craft, and Contention* (Bombay: Tripathi, 1985); and Lloyd and Suzanne Hoeber Rudolph, *In Pursuit of Lakshmi* (Chicago: University of Chicago Press, 1987), ch. 3.

Bangladesh's Supreme Court also invalidated a constitutional amendment, citing one of my papers as an authority for so doing. That paper reported (approvingly) the reasoning of the Indian Supreme Court. It was not admiration of my scholarship but political correctness that led the justices to pretend to follow an American scholar rather than the Supreme Court of a not-always-friendly neighbor. A shortened version of this paper was published in Douglas Greenberg, Stanley N. Katz, Melanie Beth Oliviero, and Steven C. Wheatley, eds., *Constitutionalism and Democracy: Transformations in the Contemporary World* (New York: Oxford University Press, 1993).

Raven v. Deukmejian, 801 P. 2d 1077 (1990), held that amendment would have made such a fundamental change in the state of California's status as a member of a federal union as to constitute a revision. And California's constitutional text provided that only a convention chosen for that purpose could "revise" the constitutional document.

30. Speaking of the American political system, Sotirios A. Barber puts it this way: "[T]here is no *constitutional* reason (i.e., a reason consistent with the Constitution) for accepting the supremacy of a scheme of government that has ceased to be what the Constitution expressly says is an instrument of justice and the other ends of government." *On What the Constitution Means* (Baltimore: Johns Hopkins University Press, 1984), pp. 51-52.

31. This reasoning might cast doubt on the validity of the American constitutional text of 1787–1788. The men at Philadelphia were also concerned about this question. Once ratified, the text of 1787–1788 abolished the Articles of Confederation and did so by a method *not* prescribed by the Articles. Furthermore, in 1866–1868 some opponents of the Thirteenth and Fourteenth amendments so contended. For discussions, see my "Slaughter-House, Civil Rights," and John E. Finn, *Constitutions in Crisis* (New York: Oxford University Press, 1991). Mark E. Brandon and I have had a continuing debate about whether these two amendments reconstituted the United States. He argues that they did. I contend that they did not do so, only removed some of the contradictions between the American constitutional text and constitutional democracy and put into that charter more of the terms of the second paragraph of the nation's founding document, the Declaration of Independence. However one decides this question, it is a close call. For Brandon's argument, see *Free*

More generally, constitutional democrats would argue, citizens' rights and dignity are not fundamental merely because the basic charter and the larger constitutional order recognize them as such; rather, the basic charter and the constitutional order protect those values because they are fundamental.[32] A constitutional order and its script draw their validity not simply from popular consent but also—some would argue primarily—from their roots in reason. One can hear echoes of arguments from natural law that an unjust law is not a valid law. Both rationales depend on a set of values and theories of right and wrong that transcend the commands of positive law. As Charles Evans Hughes said for the U.S. Supreme Court, "[B]ehind the words of the constitutional provisions are postulates which limit and control."[33] For natural law the basic postulates are reflected by the "right reason" of free and rational human beings. The origin of constitutional democracy's postulates are quite similar: they are contained in the overarching value of dignity and the necessity of effective but limited government. These principles "limit and control" the constitutional text and the entire constitutional order. For constitutional democrats the purpose of a charter and its amendments is to transubstantiate those norms into the political reality of a constitutional order.

Political Legitimacy and the Consent of the Governed

Let us change the scenario. After winning power through a free election, the new leader proceeds with a plan he announced and defended during the campaign: a referendum on whether to convene a constitutional convention to consider drafting a new constitutional charter to establish a tyrannical political system. After another vigorous campaign, a majority of voters opt for such a meeting. Later, again after free and open debates followed by fair elections, the voters select delegates who meet, discuss, and approve a basic document that creates a fresh political system whose core is the package of amendments described above. The convention then submits this text to another national referendum. It is debated and approved by a large majority of voters.

Our question about the validity of such a change recurs, but first we should narrow the issues. Let us assume that any regulations the old text lays down about how and when such a convention should take place have been met. Let us further stipulate that the new document allows dissenters to exit the country with all their tangible as well as intangible assets. Let us also

---

in the World: American Slavery and Constitutional Failure (Princeton, NJ: Princeton University Press, 1998), ch. 8, esp. pp. 200–203. James B. McPherson seems to agree with Brandon: "Antebellum Southern Exceptionalism," 29 *Civ. War Hist.* 230, 243 (1983).

32. I am, of course, paraphrasing Edward S. Corwin, "The Basic Doctrine of American Constitutional Law," 12 *Mich. L. Rev.* 247–48 (1914).

33. Monaco v. Mississippi, 292 U.S. 313, 322 (1934).

agree that the government commands the power to enforce the new constitutional text. Thus we focus attention on a single question: does the benediction of the people's consent legitimate this new constitutional text, even though that agreement demolishes both constitutionalism and democracy?

The case for validity is straightforward. The people are sovereign; therefore, they can adopt whatever political system pleases them. It also follows that they can modify an existing system as they wish, provided only that they allow real choice and follow the procedures to which they previously agreed. In short, the freely given consent of the people—their general will—is *the* great legitimator of government. With that consent, any political system is legitimate; without it no system is legitimate. In a pair of his more famous dissents, Oliver Wendell Holmes summed up this argument: the best test of "truth" is "the power of the thought to get itself accepted in the competition of the market."[34] "Freedom for the thought we hate" is not merely the ideal but also the operative constitutional rule for a democratic society: "If, in the long run, the beliefs expressed in the proletarian dictatorship are destined to be accepted by the dominant forces of the community, the only meaning of free speech is that they should be given their chance and have their way."[35]

An intelligent response requires an examination of the concepts of political legitimacy and of consent as well as of a temporal dimension of democracy.

Political Legitimacy

Political legitimacy refers to a people's acceptance of a regime as rightful, as having authority, not merely physical power.[36] When analysts discuss the criteria of legitimacy, they may be either describing the standards a particular people use at a particular time to validate a particular regime or referring to the general, intellectually defensible moral standards by which reasonable men and women can justify obligation to any political system. What, in fact, confers legitimacy on a political system varies from culture to culture and

34. Gitlow v. New York, 268 U.S. 562, dis. op., 673 (1925). For an analysis of Holmes's opinion, more sympathetic than mine, see Vincent Blasi, "Holmes and the Marketplace of Ideas," in Dennis J. Hutchinson, David A. Strauss, and Geoffrey R. Stone, eds., *2004 The Supreme Court Review* (Chicago: University of Chicago Press, 2005).

35. "Freedom . . ." is from United States v. Schwimmer, 279 U.S. 644, dis. op., 655 (1929). "If . . ." is from *Gitlow*, at 673.

36. Max Weber's analysis of legitimation is still among the most astute: "Politics as a Vocation," in *From Max Weber: Essays in Sociology*, ed. and trans. H. H. Gerth and C. Wright Mills (New York: Oxford University Press, 1946), esp. pp. 77–80. One can look on the corpus of John Rawls's writings as efforts to embed political legitimacy in, first, an overarching conception of justice and, later, several mutually compatible conceptions of "political" justice. Among the more interesting analyses of Rawls's evolving notions of the bases of political legitimacy are Frank I. Michaelman, "Justice as Fairness, Legitimacy, and the Question of Judicial Review," *73 Fordham L. Rev.* 1407 (2004); Samuel Freeman, "Public Reason and Political Justification," *72 Fordham L. Rev.* 2021; and Dennis F. Thompson, "Public Reason and Precluded Reasons," *72 Fordham L. Rev.* 2073.

perhaps from time to time within (what appears to be) a single culture: divine revelations, a bargain struck with the deity, magic, conformity to established processes, bravery in battle, proper ancestors, chrism administered by priest or prophet, the ability to extract a sword from a stone, and popular election have all forged political bonds.[37] That any or all of these are silly does not mean they were ineffective for their time and place. A more interesting question is how intelligent, self-reflective men and women have arrived at reasoned justifications for their political systems.

Consent

Since Hobbes used the fiction of a state of nature resulting in a social contract, the notion has spread in the West that societies and governmental systems are validated by agreements among inhabitants of a particular territory. From the Mayflower Compact of 1620 through state constitutional texts, the Articles of Confederation, and the constitutional document of 1787, Americans infused contracting into their politics.[38] Nevertheless, Jefferson's claim in the Declaration of Independence that governments derive

---

37. Divine revelation: According to Deuteronomy 1:16 and 16:18, Moses implied but did not explicitly claim that Yahweh inspired the system of judges Moses set up over the tribes of Israel. That system appears to have had its proximate origins in advice that Jethro, Moses's father-in-law, gave (Exodus 18:13–28).

Bargain with Deity: Abraham's covenant with Yahweh not only exchanged promises of worship and support but also established Abraham as the patriarchal ruler of what would become the nation of Israel. Many generations later, when the ancient Israelites tired of the rule of the judges whom Moses had instituted and were especially unhappy with the way Samuel's sons were running things, many of the elders wanted to install a king. But, being uneasy about their authority to amend the constitution that Moses, apparently with Yahweh's approbation, had given them, they persuaded Samuel, who was a prophet as well as a judge, to negotiate with Yahweh to transform their constitution. Yahweh was unhappy and told Samuel to warn the people of the costs kings imposed. The Israelites, however, persisted. When Samuel returned to the negotiating table, Yahweh, realizing, no doubt, the grief that Samuel felt because of the insult to his family and himself, displayed the talent of a great leader by reassuring His faithful servant that the Israelites were not rejecting him and sons so much as Yahweh Himself (1 Samuel 8–9). (Given Yahweh's propensity to jealousy [see esp. Deuteronomy 5:9], one might conclude that His acceptance of rejection did not come easily—or the narrator was a sensitive diplomat.)

Chrism: Again one might note the experience of Saul in ancient Israel. For him, of course, charisma was a sometime thing; Samuel made it clear that Yahweh taketh away as well as giveth. David, Saul's successor, fared somewhat better, though he, too, had difficult moments with Nathan and the Source of his authority. See 1 Samuel 9–31; 2 Samuel; and 1 Chronicles 10. From the time of the Merovingians, popes tried to make their anointing of the Holy Roman Emperor essential to his legitimacy. See Walter Ullmann, *The Growth of Papal Government in the Middle Ages* (New York: Barnes and Noble, 1954), and *Medieval Papalism: The Political Theory of the Medieval Canonists* (London: Methuen, 1949). When papal advisers had time to think matters through, they decided that the anointing should be of the large muscles in the ruler's back and shoulder, to symbolize that the gift the Church was imparting to the secular leader was physical, not spiritual, authority.

38. Daniel J. Elazar and his associates have produced a wealth of analyses of "constitutional covenanting." See, e.g., the symposium "Covenant, Polity, and Constitutionalism," 10 *Publius* 1 (Fall 1980).

"their just powers from the consent of the governed" was, outside of the colonies, revolutionary for its time. Although that assertion has become widely accepted, it is not self-evident why consent should serve as the ultimate legitimator for political systems.[39] To accept without reflection that claim is to substitute the myth of social contract for that of divine right of kings and to reject the value of a reasoned explanation for a political system. As Stephen Macedo has said: "We cannot honor our status as reasonable beings unless we remain open to a critical dialogue about the justifiability of our deepest political conceptions."[40]

Government by consent as a moral imperative does not lead ineluctably to constitutional or representative democracy. Belief in the legitimating power of consent reinforced Jefferson's devotion to representative democracy, but it did not inch Hobbes away from authoritarianism, and it led Rousseau toward populist totalitarianism.[41] Less philosophical men and women have made equally varied choices. Among the more naive assumptions of American officials who would transplant their political system to the Middle East is that these people would choose constitutional democracy's freedom over theocracy's strict moral code.

Proponents of consent might assert out that consent's legitimating power is "value free." Of itself, it posits no limits on the people who confer it. Problems flowing from a people's consent to tyranny lie not with consent but with the failure of constitutional democrats to convince others that theirs is the best form of government. This argument is necessary if consent is to play the role of great legitimator. For if consent's utility depends on other factors such as a capacity to produce power, efficiency, or a Rawlsian form of justice,[42] then it is the force of those factors, not consent itself, that begets legitimacy. And like legitimacy, consent is a plastic concept replete with

---

39. Which is not to say that the justification cannot be more or less persuasively made. See, for example, the efforts of Stephen Holmes, "Gag Rules or the Politics of Omission," and "Precommitment and the Paradox of Democracy," both in Jon Elster and Rune Slagstad, eds., *Constitutionalism and Democracy* (New York: Cambridge University Press, 1988); Michael Walzer, "Philosophy and Democracy," 9 *Pol. Th.* 379 (1981).

40. "Political Justification," 18 *Pol. Th.* 280, 288 (1990). Macedo was speaking as a good Kantian. See Immanuel Kant, *Critique of Pure Reason.* ed. and trans. Paul Guyer and Allen W. Wood (New York: Cambridge University Press, 1998), p. 643.

41. One might argue that although in *The Social Contract* Rousseau might have ended up a totalitarian, his concern for individualism expressed in *Émile* and for family reflected in *Julie* formed bulwarks against an all-powerful state.

42. Rawls, the great contractarian of the twentieth century, used the notion of justice, not consent, to justify constitutional democracy:

> Even the rule of promising does not give rise to a moral obligation by itself. To account for fiduciary obligations we must take the principle of fairness as a premise. Thus along with most other ethical theories, justice as fairness holds that natural duties and obligations arise only in virtue of ethical principles. These principles are those that would be chosen in the original position. (*A Theory of Justice* [Cambridge, MA: Harvard University Press, 1971], p. 348)

difficulties.[43] The first is definitional. *Webster's Third International Dictionary* initially defines consent as "Compliance or approval, espec. of what is done or proposed by another." This usage seems too broad to convey moral commitment. *Webster's* second definition is more useful: "Capable, deliberate, voluntary agreement to or concurrence in some act or purpose implying physical and mental power and free action." Now, capability, deliberation, voluntariness could create moral obligation, but each raises its own analytical as well as practical problems. I have discussed these elsewhere,[44] and once more, for the sake of simplicity, let us assume that in the current scenario these difficulties are not serious.

Recognition poses another set of problems. Even if we agree on what consent truly means, how do we know when a people have in fact consented to a political system? Referenda offer an obvious answer, but because they often present several issues, they do not invariably provide authoritative anointing. Besides, these processes are rather recent and still not universally used for either approval or amendment of constitutional charters.

Certainly consent makes life less dangerous and more productive. No intelligent person would quarrel with Madison's observation in *The Federalist* 49 that "the most rational government will not find it a superfluous advantage to have the prejudices of the community on its side." As far as internal national security is concerned, people who consent to a regime are less likely to subvert the political system than are those on whom it is imposed. Where regimes must rely largely on coercion, specters of coups and rebellions constantly prowl the corridors of power. We might paraphrase a fictional Greek merchant's comment about the harshness of Pontius Pilate's governance in Judea: eternal paranoia is the price of imposing rule on an unwilling people.[45]

A justification for consent based on efficiency is, however, vulnerable. One obvious weakness is that other means, including free mass distribution of drugs as in Aldous Huxley's *Brave New World,* may be more effective in securing obedience. More important, this argument turns the ultimate criterion into efficiency rather than consent itself. Consent needs a justification of

43. For critical analyses of the concept of consent, see Don Herzog, *Happy Slaves* (Chicago: University of Chicago Press, 1989); and Joseph Raz, "Government by Consent," in J. Roland Pennock and John W. Chapman, eds., *Authority Revisited* (New York: New York University Press, 1987). Economists, especially those concerned with "rational choice," have developed a huge literature relevant to consent. I mention only the work of the Nobel laureate James M. Buchanan particularly: *The Economics and the Ethics of Constitutional Order* (Ann Arbor: University of Michigan Press, 1991); with Geoffrey Brennan, *The Reason of Rules* (New York: Cambridge University Press, 1985); and with Gordon Tullock, *The Calculus of Consent* (Ann Arbor: University of Michigan Press, 1962).

44. "Consent and Constitutional Change," esp. pp. 129–33.

45. Quoted in Walter F. Murphy, *Upon This Rock* (New York: Macmillan, 1986), p. 221. For discussions of consent's producing a more law-abiding community, see above, Chapter Three.

its own as the ultimate political legitimator. Such an argument could run along these lines: All sane adults can understand much about themselves, perceive reality, analyze evidence, draw logical conclusions from those findings, and differentiate, if not perfectly, between demands of self-interest and general normative principles. Thus, at the most elementary level, they can also realize that they are capable of reasoning rather than being blind captives of emotions. Thus they understand that for others to force them to choose what reason says they should not offends their dignity and moral integrity.

Reasonable adults can extrapolate from their self-understanding to the realization that others have the same faculties. It is equally wrong, therefore, to force such choices on others except to avoid a greater harm to third parties or, perhaps, to themselves.[46] Furthermore. reasoning adults can understand that when choices are their own, they, as do other men and women, bear responsibility for the consequences, anticipated and unanticipated, those choices entail. Reason pushes toward moral autonomy; moral autonomy generates moral responsibility; and moral responsibility produces political obligation.

Alas, the concept of autonomy presents its own problems. In the modern world, physical autonomy is impossible unless a person is content with a life that is "nasty, brutish, and short." As Aristotle pointed out, because people cannot live as gods, they must live either as solitary beasts or as social human beings who participate in complicated, often convoluted divisions of labor. Moral autonomy is similarly impossible. No individual can count himself or herself as the ultimate authority in choosing a "life plan" or the means to achieve that plan, else selecting a career as a serial killer would be morally acceptable.[47] More positively, a life of reason requires that we accept the possibility that our judgments may be wrong and therefore we should keep our minds open to the arguments of others. And when we deeply love a mate, children, or friends, we cannot make important decisions without weighing their moral norms and their emotional commitments along with our own and sometimes surrendering our will to theirs. Only sociopaths, hermits, and autistics have the luxury of ignoring the feelings as well as the thinking of loved ones.

Nevertheless, if complete moral autonomy lies beyond the grasp of civilized men and women, understanding the difference between having a broad range of moral autonomy and being unrestrained by external (or objective)

46. "Perhaps" not because I join John Stuart Mill's concluding from his "harm principle" that we are never justified in protecting sane adults from their own choices, but to avoid a long digression. *On Liberty* (1854), ed. R. B. McCallum (Oxford: Basil Blackwell, 1948), ch. 4. For a perfectionist critique of Mill's argument, see Robert P. George, *Making Men Moral: Civil Liberties and Public Authority* (Oxford: Clarendon, 1993). He makes a much stronger case than do Mill and his apostles.

47. Even Eskimo groups who accepted homicide as more or less normal would, in effect, lynch a person who repeatedly killed. See E. Adamson Hoebel, *The Law of Primitive Man: A Study in Comparative Legal Dynamics* (Cambridge, MA: Harvard University Press, 1954), ch. 5.

moral rules or secular regulations is not. Reasonable men and women—a category that should include all self-reflective constitutional democrats—can distinguish between the two. Because constitutional democrats believe, or should believe, that all sane adults partake of the capacity to reason, they can debate and decide what sort of regime best suits their needs. It follows that they can *morally* bind themselves to each other, to general normative principles, and to the more specific regulations of a political order. This justification, however, limits consent's legitimating power. To entirely surrender one's capacity to make choices would be to commit moral suicide.[48] Consent to a political system that denies its citizens are rational, largely morally autonomous human beings is consent to a system that denies the basis on which the validity of consent itself rests.

No one has authority to destroy his or her own moral autonomy or that of others. John Stuart Mill made a similar argument about an individual's rights. "[B]y selling himself for a slave, he abdicates his liberty; he foregoes any future use of it beyond that single act. He therefore defeats, in his own case, the very purpose which is the justification of allowing him to dispose of himself. He is no longer free. . . . *The principle of freedom cannot require that he should be free not to be free. It is not freedom to be allowed to alienate his freedom.*"[49] Joseph Raz elaborates on and extends Mill's reasoning to include a whole people: "[T]o the extent that the validity of consent rests on the intrinsic value of autonomy it cannot extend to acts of consent that authorize another person to deprive people of their autonomy."[50]

And then there is the matter of future generations. Even were one to believe that it was rational for a people to accede to a regime that destroyed its subjects' moral autonomy, it would not follow that these people had a right to surrender the moral autonomy of future generations. In this sense Jefferson and Webster were correct: absent a serious, credible, and proximate threat, choosing to obliterate moral autonomy for those future generations cannot be justified.[51] Moreover, such a dire threat would vitiate the volun-

48. Anarchists, to be sure, argue that the case for moral autonomy destroys all claims to legitimate rule over others, even rule conferred by consent of the ruled. For a rebuttal, see Raz, "Government by Consent," pp. 78ff. Raz, however, concludes that the function of consent as a legitimator is very limited. He restricts it to a "modest" and "ancillary" role, valuable largely as an expression of trust, but an expression that, to bind the consenters, must be met by the political system's fulfilling the conditions of that trust—(1) to require or restrict citizens' action only in ways in which right reason would tell citizens they should or should not be acting, and (2) to require or restrict citizens' actions "only over matters regarding which acting according to right reason is more important than deciding for oneself how to act" (pp. 88–89).

49. *On Liberty*, p. 92; italics added.

50. "Government by Consent," p. 87.

51. James G. March and Johan P. Olsen, *Rediscovering Institutions: The Organizational Basis of Politics* (New York: Free Press, 1989). pp. 146-47.

tariness of consent.[52] At times, submission to force may be necessary for survival; but that sort of acquiescence does not transform power into authority. Mao may have been right that power comes out of the end of a gun, but authority must have additional sources. Thus despots have usually sought justification for their rule by appealing to such abstract notions as racism, ideology, and nationalism.

Omission of a temporal dimension also offends democracy's egalitarian norms. A current majority that decides to end self-government treats as less than equal not only their own future selves but also all other majorities that follow. As James G. March and Johan P. Olsen point out: "Unless a democratic system can solve the problem of representing the future, changing interests of the unborn, it violates a rather fundamental underlying premise of democracy—that those who bear the costs of decision should have their interests adequately reflected in the choice."[53] Including a temporal dimension extends democracy's objectives to include integrating current preferences with those, perhaps changed, preferences of succeeding generations. It is true that almost all choices a current generation makes inhibit future options—often painfully. A decision to wage war, for instance, has an enormous effect on the future by wiping out some gene pools. That cost is one of the many compelling reasons never to go to war unless absolutely necessary. Still, with that much said, a people may peacefully modify or repudiate most other policies that their predecessors have enacted, but only as long as democratic processes remain open.

At minimum, citizens acting democratically are obliged to leave to themselves as well as their successors a continuing right to self-government.[54] Therefore, because democratic theory must conceive of its political system as stretching across time, it cannot validate the current generation's depriving themselves and future generations of the right to make political choices.[55] As

52. For a discussion of the morally binding power of consent obtained through force, see my "Consent and Constitutional Change," esp. pp. 130–31, and sources cited.

53. *Rediscovering Institutions*, p. 146.

54. Although William F. Harris II rejects my reliance on constitutionalism, he argues that consent to tyranny obliterates the right of the people to determine their form of government and thus lies beyond the amending power. *The Interpretable Constitution* (Baltimore: Johns Hopkins University Press, 1993), ch. 4.

55. Complications abound. For instance, representation's refractions make it difficult enough to be certain of a people's current preferences. Calculating future preferences is, as Learned Hand would have put it, "shoveling smoke." Perhaps the preference we can identify with greatest assurance is that rational men and women would want to have some significant choices about the kind of society in which they would exist and the sorts of lives they could lead. Such preferences require some form of democratic governance. That conclusion rests, however, on several—typically unspoken—assumptions within Western secular societies that have achieved both large measures of economic development and constitutional democracy. The most obvious of these assumptions are that there are enough basic necessities available to sustain life and that most citizens agree that

Madison said during debate in the House of Representatives on the Bill of Rights: the people had retained an "indubitable, unalienable, and infeasible right to reform or change their Government, whenever it be found adverse or inadequate to the purpose of its institution."[56] And surrendering that right is precisely what agreeing to tyrannical rule entails. Democracy must mean more than one person, one vote, one time.

A viable argument for consent as the great legitimator thus transforms itself into a claim for a related but more fundamental value, that of citizens' great and equal dignity, with a consequent need for a wide ambit of moral autonomy. Consent may be a necessary condition for political legitimacy, but it cannot be the ultimate condition. Consent validates only insofar as it reflects the fundamental value of human dignity. Of itself, consent does not, as Hamilton maintained, constitute "the pure, original foundation of all legitimate authority."[57]

It also follows that a polity based on consent justified by human worth must—again continuously—acknowledge, as negative constitutionalism requires, certain substantive limitations on government's power as well as on the constitutive power of the people as whole. For example, the political system must recognize its citizens' inalienable rights to (1) treatment as being equal in worth to every other person, whether private individual or public official, and (2) enough physical privacy to permit freedom of reasonable use of their own bodies as well as some meaningful amount of psychic and physical space around their bodies.[58] More specifically, when the polity moves against any of its people, even those accused of crime, it must meticulously adhere to the procedures it has prescribed in advance to secure order and ensure fairness.

We are led back to the demands of positive constitutionalism. A consti-

---

religious differences should be tolerated. These assumptions might not hold in all areas of the world. In the Horn of Africa, where thousands of people are starving, survival would probably take precedence over all else. "Being," as Franklin Roosevelt once remarked, "comes before well being." And where people are deeply committed to particular religious beliefs, such as in parts of Saudi Arabia, Iran, Iraq, and the Bible Belt of the American South, sacred scripture may dictate hatred as *the* political choice. There are also cultural assumptions at work here (if we can separate culture and religion) about the desirability of individual autonomy. See Ashis Nandy, "The Political Culture of the Indian State," 118 *Daedalus* 1 (1989); and T. G. Vaidyanathan, "Authority and Identity in India," 118 *Daedalus* 147 1989).

The problem becomes even more complex when we add the dimension of the past. We might paraphrase Jefferson and simply say that life belongs to the living. Then, however, we risk muting "the mystic chords of memory" that unite a people and validate processes of decision making along with shared substantive values.

56. 1 *Annals of Congress* 110.

57. *The Federalist*, No. 22.

58. For fuller reasoning here, see my "The Right to Privacy and Legitimate Constitutional Change," in Slonim, *Constitutional Bases of Political and Social Change in the United States.*

tutional democracy worthy of its name must do its utmost to further its citizens' liberty *and* well-being. Each individual has a right to reasonable access to a certain amount of material goods to protect his or her status as an independent being. We recall Hamilton's claim that "*a power over a man's subsistence amounts to a power over his will*" (emphasis in original). Jefferson agreed that full citizenship under a "free government" required some economic autonomy: "Dependence begets subservience and venality, suffocates the germ of virtue, and prepares fit tools for the designs of ambition. . . . It is the manners and spirit of a people which preserve a republic in vigour."[59]

The system probably could not, and perhaps should not, go as far as Jefferson proposed for Virginia: give each citizen enough material goods to be economically self-sufficient.[60] Yet neither can a constitutional democracy let its citizens wallow in hunger or sickness. In this context, it is important to realize that public welfare takes many forms beyond helping the poor. The most commonly used measures range from offering direct subsidies to certain kinds of industries (including manufacture of arms, farming, education, and research), supporting trade by maintaining consular offices aboard, establishing tariffs to protect some kinds of economic activities, negotiating treaties to assist citizens who wish to engage in foreign trade, offering tax write-offs to encourage economic development, opening courts to those who feel aggrieved by competitors' business practices, enacting and enforcing laws to protect private property as well as personal safety, regulating entry into "public" professions such as the practice of law, and maintaining highways, harbors, and airports. To oppose public welfare on constitutional principle is to oppose much of what governments have historically done and continue to do. Even the night watchman guarded private property and so benefited the rich much more than the poverty-stricken.

The precise ways in which the polity must treat citizens equally, how much control over how much space citizens have a right to, how much and what kinds of property they can lawfully enjoy, how far they can control their own bodies without abusing the equal rights of others, what circumstances constrict or enlarge these ambits, the extent to which the unborn, the newborn, the elderly, and the terminally ill count as "others," the exact contours of procedural fairness, and the kinds of punishment that are inhumane—these issues will always remain controversial. An effective political system must periodically review its decisions on these sorts of problems as material

---

59. *Notes on Virginia* (1782), in *The Writings of Thomas Jefferson*, ed. Andrew A. Lipscomb (Washington, DC: Thomas Jefferson Memorial Association, 1903), 2:229.

60. "The Virginia Constitution: Third Draft of Jefferson," in *The Papers of Thomas Jefferson*, ed. Julian P. Boyd (Princeton, NJ: Princeton University Press, 1950), 1:358. For a discussion, see Stanley N. Katz, "Thomas Jefferson and the Right to Property in Revolutionary America," 19 *J. of L. and Econ.* 467 (1976).

conditions and conceptions change. But for any polity that takes seriously its claim to be founded on government by consent and offers a reasoned defense of consent as based on human worth, the general principle will always be crystalline, however controverted particular solutions to particular problems appear.

This principle restricts not only the forms that a polity may take at its founding but also the sorts of changes that will be legitimate. "Consent of the people" can justify a broad spectrum of choices; respect for human beings hardly demands one and only one specific political organization. But although that range is wide, it is not unbounded. Most fundamentally, consent cannot justify changing a constitutional (or representative) democracy to a system that treats human beings as mere means, either for the state or for individual citizens.[61]

Acceptance of such a principle does not mean that some citizens will not perceive certain public measures as depriving them of their rights, including the right to basic respect. Sometimes that perception will be false, sometimes it will be accurate. This sort of problem is inevitable in complex societies and speaks to a crucial practical need to construct peaceful institutional means to debate policies and to resolve not only clashes over tangible interests but also disputes about fundamental values. This problem also speaks to the necessity of devising processes to invalidate specific rules embodied in a constitutional text or constitutional history that violate the general principles of constitutional democracy. Two other limitations are relevant. First, if a system or its re-formed self does not receive the universal consent of its members, it must allow dissenters to exit. Second, citizens who later become fundamentally disaffected as the regime operates, develops, and incrementally changes must also be permitted to revoke their consent and leave. The polity may establish reasonable rules about what constitutes consent and withdrawal of consent; it may also require all who remain within its bounds to obey its ordinances. But in a system based on consent justified by human dignity, the right to expatriation is essential. To force people to join or remain members of a society whose policies violate their conscience gravely offends the system's basic value.

61. Sotirios A. Barber outlines a convincing case that people committed to reason can make only a provisional commitment to constitutional democracy or any specific constitutional democracy as the political system best suited to protect and promote justice and the general welfare. (I would include protection of "human dignity" within the concept of justice.) Such people must always be open to rational argument for radical political change to another sort of system that better guards and furthers the goals of government. A commitment to reason cannot, however, lead to acceptance of a political system that denies the primacy of reason. For a fuller development of this argument, see his *On What the Constitution Means*, pp. 59–60.

It is the invalidity of treating persons as mere means, I believe, that Michael Walzer is pointing to when he argues in "Philosophy and Democracy" about limitations democratic theory imposes on citizens of a democracy.

Who Determines the Validity of Constitutional Provisions?

If we agree that an amendment to or a clause within the constitutional text can be unconstitutional, a pair of mammoth problems arise: who determines constitutionality and by what processes? In its first decision, the Southwest Case, the German Constitutional Court assumed such authority. Because unlike their common law cousins, these justices answer questions rather than decide concrete cases, they can be quite flexible in their procedures, appointing counsel to argue specific matters, gathering evidence on their own,[62] and serving as triers of fact as well as of law. The common law's more rigid rules may not, however, impose insuperable barriers. Justices of India's Supreme Court operate much like common law judges elsewhere and, like the justices of California's Supreme Court, have found no procedural obstacles to invalidating constitutional amendments in the course of deciding ordinary cases.

Courts, then, provide one forum. Judges, however, may not have the expertise to function competently in this regard; they may lack the prestige to make their judgments stick; and despite occasional flashes of great courage, judges are not known as brave innovators. Equally important, absent a specific provision in a constitutional text, there is less reason to believe that judges should have a monopoly on constitutional interpretation here than there is for other issues. Executive officials and legislators as well as voters would have important interpretive roles (and authority) on these sorts of questions. But their participation raises other serious difficulties.

First, in a parliamentary system, the prime minister and cabinet members are very likely to have approved the questionable constitutional change; most of the upper echelons of the executive branch, then, are eliminated as challengers. In a presidential system, on the other hand, the possibility of a difference between the legislature and the executive is quite real, and it might be the president who declares a textual provision unconstitutional. Such action would probably aggravate a constitutional crisis—aggravate rather than provoke, because a constitutional crisis is exactly what a potentially unconstitutional change in the constitutional text creates. And in this case aggravation may be needed to rivet attention on the implications of such a quiet revolution.

The power and authority of individual legislative or officials to intervene is likely to be very limited except in nations that have a weak party system. Some middle-level administrators, however, may be well positioned to sabotage governmental operations and, if they are numerous and act collectively, could effectively publicize, if not block, the putatively unconstitutional change. Military officers may have the power to stop such a change,

---

62. See, for example, the Homosexuality Case, 6 BVerfGE 389 (1957), reprinted in Walter F. Murphy and Joseph Tanenhaus, eds., *Comparative Constitutional Law* (New York: St. Martin's, 1977), pp. 403ff.

but at the same time their intervention poses a great danger to constitutional democracy itself. In Latin America, soldiers have assumed a special role in protecting "the constitution,"[63] usually to assert their own selfish interests and/or those of their allies rather than to protect constitutional democracy. In the later years of the twentieth century, the Turkish military intervened on several occasions to thwart what they saw as threats from Islamists to change the secular state into a theocracy, a change the constitutional text expressly forbids.[64] Despite the results of these Turkish actions, thoughtful constitutional democrats would encourage military intervention only as a desperate last resort.

It is probable that whoever declares a portion of the constitutional document invalid would find it prudent to make a strong and immediate appeal to the electorate. If, however, we can extrapolate from the "bump" in public support American presidents get during crises,[65] the odds are against such an appeal's success—unless, of course, it is the chief executive who declares the change invalid. If there is no machinery in place to settle the issue, the result could be widespread civil disobedience or even anarchy. This sort of outcome would encourage the military to intervene, with all the dangers that generates. The possibility of these events would confront drafters of constitutional texts with a hard choice.[66] They might, as most have done, simply ignore the problem or rely on judges (or in France the Conseil Constitutionnel) to adjudicate such issues. The success of this institutional process would depend on courts' having a deep enough reservoir of public support to ensure governmental and public acquiescence. It would also depend on judges' courage.

On the other hand, framers who are worried about the possibility of unconstitutional change might conclude that neither their history nor their culture imbues judges with the necessary support and seek to build other machinery. Among the more interesting alternatives would be a variation on the French model: reference to a constitutional commission whose membership is not restricted to judges. For example, at the request of the chief executive in a presidential or mixed system, or a minority of parliament

63. Some constitutional texts in Latin America have explicitly authorized such a role. See Alfred Stepan, *The Military in Politics: Changing Patterns in Brazil* (Princeton, NJ: Princeton University Press, 1971), pp. 99–115. The closest the Turkish document comes is Article 125's exemption from judicial review of "acts of the President of the Republic on his or her own competence and the decisions of the Supreme Military Council."

64. The preamble to the Turkish constitutional text says, "[T]here shall be no interference whatsoever by sacred religious feelings in state affairs and politics." According to Article 2, "The Republic of Turkey is a democratic, secular, and social state . . . and based on the fundamental tenets set forth in the Preamble."

65. See Lee Epstein, Daniel E. Ho, Gary King, and Jeffrey Segal, "The Supreme Court during Crisis: How War Affects Only Non-war Cases," 80 *N.Y.U. L. Rev.* 1 (2005).

66. Realistically, the most likely course of action would be to ignore the problem and hope it would never occur, at least during the lifetime of any of the framers.

(perhaps one-third), or of either house if that body is bicameral, the question could be put before a special panel composed of a small but even number of judges, legislators, and academics with half chosen by either side in the dispute, with the panel to select from the same universe an additional voting member to serve as chair. This process is far from ideal. Its officials may lack the prestige or the courage to stand up against an ambitious executive or a stampeded legislature. Indeed, there is no easy solution to the problem. Perhaps there is no practical solution at all. The best hope is that the electorate would never be so short-sighted as to vote into office men and women who would destroy constitutional democracy. That hope, however, has not always been borne out.

More likely than a swift revolution by democratic means would be a set of gradual changes executed by a clique or political party that gained office under false colors and "by noiseless foot" moved unobtrusively toward a tyrannical system. This danger is especially real when a country faces external threats or perceived dangers from internal subversion or terrorism. Chipping away at constitutional safeguards in the name of national security can then be marketed as prudent rather than perilous, as means of "preserving freedom"—at least until a people become accustomed to their status as mere denizens. This possibility underlines the necessity of (1) active and intelligent governmental intervention in educational processes to ensure that citizens understand their constitutional order and the importance of their role as preservers of that political system and (2) government's adopting policies that in fact further a just society. A lazy, uninformed, uncommitted, and easily distracted electorate poses the ultimate danger to a polity, just as an attentive and informed electorate devoted to constitutional democracy's goals can be its strongest bulwark. As Walt Whitman put it, "Tyranny may always enter—there is no charm, nor bar against it—the only bar against it is a large resolute breed of men."[67] And women, we would add.

Parties and Political Speech

Yet another vital question arises. If some kinds of changes in the constitutional text or order can be unconstitutional, is it legitimate for a polity to outlaw a political party that advocates such changes and punish its leaders? Because keeping political processes open is essential to a viable democracy, does it not follow that a constitutional democracy cannot outlaw a political party or restrict freedom of political speech? As the ultimate judges of whom they shall choose as governors, the people have a right to hear *all* points of view. This claim of open popular access appears to rest on the same ground as that for consent as the ultimate legitimator, and it is subject to the same

67. "Notes for Lectures on Democracy and Adhesiveness," in *Walt Whitman's Workshop: A Collection of Unpublished Manuscripts,* ed. Clifton J. Furness (Cambridge, MA: Harvard University Press, 1928), p. 28.

difficulties. Indeed, one can turn the question around: Is it democratic (or constitutionalist) for a polity *not* to protect its citizens against parties that seek public office in order to destroy open political processes and limited governance? Does government lack authority to stop the people from alienating their fundamental rights as free citizens?

Three responses are obvious. First is that which consistent constitutionists and legal positivists should offer: It depends. The legitimacy of outlawing a political party and/or restricting speech depends solely on the wording of the constitutional text. If the basic document allows such action, then as a matter of constitutional law though not necessarily of wisdom, the issue is closed. And as the previous chapter pointed out, many charters expressly allow government to limit speech. Furthermore, a few constitutional documents permit banning supposedly subversive parties. For example, Article 3 (1) of the Hungarian text reads: "[P]olitical parties may be freely founded and may act in freedom provided they show respect for the Constitution and the statutes of constitutional law." Article 13 of Boris Yeltsin's constitutional document initially stresses protection of "ideological diversity" and a "multi-party system," then adds:

> The creation and activity of public associations whose goals or actions are aimed at forcibly changing the foundations of the constitutional system, violating the integrity of the Russian Federation, undermining the security of the state, creating armed formations or stirring up social, racial, national, or religious discord are prohibited.

The model for all such provisions is, of course, Article 21 of Germany's Basic Law, which recognizes a right to form parties, ordains them as organs of the state,[68] but also obliges them to conduct their internal operations democratically and authorizes the Constitutional Court to hold them unconstitutional if they "seek to impair or abolish the free democratic order or to endanger the existence" of the Federal Republic.

A second and very different response denies government authority to ban a party or punish political speech. The argument is essentially Holmes's in *Gitlow* and *Schwimmer*.[69] Freedom to speak, write, associate, and assemble is essential to democracy. The message of the words and the purposes of the association and assembly are irrelevant. As more recent U.S. justices have put it, any governmental regulations touching these matters must be "content neutral." Holmes's surrender to fate did not impress Karl Lowenstein, a refugee from Nazism. He spoke of "the treacherous belief that, in the long

---

68. As interpreted by the Federal Constitutional Court, the Basic Law raises parties "to the rank of constitutional institutions," making them "integral parts of [the] constitutional structure and [the] constitutionally ordered political life." The Socialist Reich Party Case, 2 BVerfGE 1 (1952), in Murphy and Tanenhaus, *Comparative Constitutional Law*, pp. 602ff.

69. Gitlow v. New York (1925) and Schwimmer v. United States (1929).

run, the inherent superiority of democratic values will assert itself over fascist ideology."[70]

Both the positivistic and the Holmesian responses are badly flawed. A positivistic answer may sometimes please but can never satisfy constitutional democrats. They cannot accept formal law as always being the final word, for what is written may not accord with the norms of constitutionalism or democracy. Besides, although most constitutional documents permit restrictions on speech, few explicitly allow governments to outlaw a political party. Thus a positivistic answer leaves a central part of the issue unresolved for most countries, forcing constitutionists in those nations to rely on norms of democratic or constitutionalist theory. That reliance wreaks havoc on constitutionism's (and positivism's) central claim that the system's basic norms are contained in the text and logical deductions from that text rather than in overarching political theories.

Holmes's contention is more seductive. His notion of a free exchange of ideas seems to fit democratic theory, which tends to equate "correct" political results with "the will of the people" as expressed through fair elections preceded by free debate. Thus, to a great extent, democratic theory embraces both positivism and moral relativism. As Michael Walzer has pointed out, what makes governmental decisions morally binding in a democracy is not their conformity to substantive [constitutionalist?] norms but their having been adopted through open political processes: the people choose representatives who debate and enact policies, then hold themselves accountable by standing for reelection in another open contest.[71]

We have already noted Holmes's neglect of democracy's temporal dimension and his naiveté in assuming the ineffectiveness of propaganda machines. And his claim has other major flaws. One is apparent in the last phrase of the previous paragraph: people who would substitute tyranny for constitutional democracy are *not* willing to stand for reelection in fair and open contests. They deny the validity of one of democracy's principal demands: public officials' accountability to an electorate free to speak its mind. History, not the voters, holds tyrants accountable.

The nub of a third, anti-Holmesian, response is that, because certain kinds of substantive political transformations are invalid, a constitutional democracy can legitimately ban organizations that strive for such changes and punish citizens who try to garner support for such organizations.[72]

70. "Legislative Control of Political Extremism in European Democracies: I," 38 *Colum. L. Rev.* 591, 593–94 (1938).

71. "Philosophy and Democracy."

72. For elaborations of my argument, see "Excluding Political Parties," in Paul Kirchhof and Donald P. Kommers, eds., *Germany and Its Basic Law* (Baden-Baden: Nomos Verlagsgesellschaft, 1993); and "May Constitutional Democracies 'Outlaw' a Political Party?" in John G. Geer, ed., *Politicians and Party Politics* (Baltimore: Johns Hopkins University Press, 1998). My argument

Neither democratic or constitutionalist theory requires that a polity quietly submit to assassination. The earlier argument regarding consent applies here as well: a people's agreeing to maintain democratic processes and constitutionalist values that allow them to live as free citizens stops them from either consenting to become slaves themselves or consigning later generations to that status.

American constitutionists might object that their constitutional system takes decisions regarding parties and speech away from government and rests it in the hands of the electorate. Unlike many texts, the First Amendment to their charter says Congress and, through the Fourteenth Amendment, the states can make *no* law abridging freedom of speech. This argument, insofar as it rests on the plain words of the text, fails. The First Amendment protects not "freedom of speech" but "*the* freedom of speech." "Freedom of speech" would refer to a broad concept; "the freedom of speech" refers to a specific conception of freedom of speech.[73] And there is no good reason to include a *right* to urge abolition of freedom of speech within a conception of freedom of speech that is compatible with constitutional democracy.

An American might, however, further contend that constitutional development has broadened the First Amendment's protection so as to turn its specific words into "markers"[74] of the underlying value of free communication of ideas. This approach to constitutional interpretation is appealing, going, as it does, beyond narrow textualism and clause-bound interpretivism to seeking a purpose not only for a particular clause but for the document as a whole. But granting that the purpose of this portion of the First Amendment (and of the entire charter) is to fortify a system of limited government responsible to a free electorate does not mean that, separately or together, the amendment, the full text, or the constitutional order imparts immunity to parties and persons who would destroy limited government responsible to a free electorate.

American judges, presidents, and legislators have burrowed twisted tun-

---

parallels that of "militant" or "fighting democracy," which Karl Loewenstein developed during the late 1930s. See esp. his "Militant Democracy and Fundamental Rights," 31 *Am. Pol. Sci. Rev.* 417, 638 (1937), and "Legislative Control of Political Extremism in European Democracies," 38 *Colum. L. Rev.* 591, 725 (1938). The opinion of the German Constitutional Court in the Socialist Reich Party Case (1952) offers a later exposition from *within* the framework of a "fighting democracy."

73. I do not pretend to know what was in the minds of the men who drafted and ratified the First Amendment. All of us can, however, read the words they wrote, know how those words have been interpreted (admittedly not always convincingly) during the past two centuries, and understand how those words fit into a scheme of constitutional democracy. For an effort to understand the background of the First Amendment, see Leonard W. Levy, *Legacy of Suppression: Freedom of Speech and Press in Early American History* (Cambridge: Belknap Press of Harvard University Press, 1960), and "The Legacy Reexamined," 37 *Stan. L. Rev.* 767 (1985).

74. See Abner S. Greene, "Constitutional Reductionism, Rawls, and the Religion Clauses," 72 *Fordham L. Rev.* 2089 (2004).

nels of sophisticated and sophistic reasoning to justify punishing certain kinds of political communication. Unfortunately, in so doing, these officials have never intelligibly explained—perhaps because they have never understood—the difference between a general concept of free speech and a specific conception of free speech necessary to maintain a political system that, while changing in many ways, remains both democratic and constitutionalist. As a matter of normative theory and practical politics, the question recurs: must government sit idly by and watch the system's destruction? If the answer is no, then government may outlaw parties and speech that aim to demolish the polity.

This discussion so far has been about the *legitimacy* of governmental regulation of parties and speech. In public as in private life, action that is permissible may be dysfunctional or even stupid. As Justice Frankfurter once noted, "Focusing attention on constitutionality tends to make constitutionality synonymous with wisdom. When legislation touches freedom of thought and freedom of speech, such a tendency is a formidable enemy of the free spirit."[75]

Restricting political speech or organization risks high costs.[76] Had the Federalists succeeded in crushing the Jeffersonians, the American political tradition—along with its constitutional order—would have been severely impoverished. Furthermore, allowing people who favor radical change to engage in open debate within the system may convert them, as illustrated by the transition of German Social Democrats from revolutionary Marxists to staunch constitutional democrats.[77] Otto von Bismarck's policies convinced them that incremental changes, possible even within imperial Germany's limited form of democracy, would achieve their goals more effectively than violent revolution. The founding of the Federal Republic turned that hope into near reality. Furthermore, American efforts to outlaw the Communist Party and to jail its leaders bordered on the silly. These people were, as William O. Douglas said, "miserable merchants of unwanted ideas."[78] Nevertheless, their criticisms of racism and economic injustices in American life were often on the mark.

There are, however, cases on the other side. The Nazis' participation in the democratic politics of Weimar only engorged their contempt for civil society. And after World War II, the possible resurgence of Nazism, the brutal communist takeovers in Eastern Europe, and communism's foothold within

75. Dennis v. United States, 341 U.S. 494, concur. op. (1951).

76. Tyrannical systems might find it expedient to dress their actions in constitutionist, if not constitutionalist, terms and abuse such authority, as Pinochet did under Article 8 of Chile's then operative constitutional text.

77. For this transformation during the last two decades of the nineteenth century and the first two decades of the twentieth, see Peter Gay, *The Dilemma of Democratic Socialism: Eduard Bernstein's Challenge to* Marx (New York: Columbia University Press, 1952).

78. Dennis v. United States, 341 U.S. 494, dis. op. (1951).

the Federal Republic left little reason to doubt that these parties would try to smother Germany's infant constitutional democracy in its crib.[79]

Questions of validity and wisdom blend with those of process. Practically speaking, it is almost impossible to separate these issues. Incumbents are often tempted to regard powerful rivals as subversives. Certainly in 1856–1861, southern Democrats believed that Lincoln and the Republicans would destroy their constitutional order. "We are upholding the true doctrines of the Federal Constitution," Jefferson Davis insisted. "We are conservative."[80] No less an historian than James B. McPherson believes that Davis and his confederates were constitutionally correct.[81] A century later, southern Democrats and conservative Republicans saw Earl Warren as a subversive who was ripping the very fabric of their social and political lives. Still later, Attorney General John Ashcroft branded as friends of terrorism citizens who thought that government should respect the Bill of Rights as it moved against terrorists within the United States. What is needed is a process that can protect the country against destruction without clamping off the circulation of ideas. The minimum requirement is that any governmental action against political writers, speakers, parties, or other organizations be transparent and carefully follow preset guidelines.

With good reason, constitutional democrats are wary of special tribunals to try people for political speech or association. The so-called Diplock courts that the British established in Northern Ireland set a horrific example of empowered hypocrisy. Prosecutors claimed to bring charges only for terrorist acts. Nevertheless, special police freely used torture to extract confessions from suspects, and special judges blithely imprisoned people for their words, thoughts, and sympathies rather than for their deeds.[82] Adjudicating British abuses of the rights of Irish prisoners formed a large part of

79. Kenneth H. F. Dyson has questioned whether the purpose of banning the Communist Party was "to protect the constitution's free democratic basic order or . . . to protect a particular economic and social system against criticism and reform." "Anti-communism in the Federal Republic of Germany: The Case of the 'Berufsverbot,'" 28 *Parl. Affrs.* 51 (1974). To look on the objectives Communist parties of Central and Eastern Europe during the 1940s and 1950s as criticism and reform seems to me the height or perhaps the depth of naiveté.

80. Quoted in McPherson, "Antebellum Southern Exceptionalism."

81. Ibid., p. 243 (1983):

when secessionists protested that they were acting to preserve traditional rights and values, they were correct. They fought to protect their constitutional liberties against the perceived Northern threat to overthrow them. The South's concept of republicanism had not changed in three-quarters of a century; the North's had. With complete sincerity the South fought to preserve its version of the republic of the founding fathers—a government of limited powers that protected the rights of property and whose constituency comprised an independent gentry and yeomanry of the white race undisturbed by large cities, heartless factories, restless free workers, and class conflict. . . . Therefore secession was a preemptive counterrevolution to prevent the Black Republican revolution from engulfing the South.

82. For an analysis of the Diplock courts, see Finn, *Constitutions in Crisis*, pt. 2.

the early work of the European Court of Human Rights. In the United States after 9/11, courts have overturned convictions of alleged domestic terrorists because of the government's use of tainted evidence. Whatever the upshot of the "trials" of alleged foreign terrorists held in military prisons, Gestapo-style torture has been commonplace in Guantánamo as well as Abu Ghraib.

The regular system of criminal justice may be able to handle matters pertaining to individuals' speech and acts, although in the United States it failed when Federalist judges applied the Alien and Sedition Acts, and during the Civil War Lincoln thought that civilian courts were inadequate and suspended the writ of habeas corpus. Moreover, the legal system was only barely effective during the McCarthy era. Dealing with organizations such as political parties poses additional difficulties, including problems of gathering and weighing evidence. Besides, a decision to outlaw a party can have an ex post facto effect and tar innocent people with guilt by association.

No process to outlaw allegedly subversive parties can guarantee fairness, but then neither can procedures in prosecutions for such "ordinary" crimes as fraud, larceny, and murder. Nevertheless, the German method of ascertaining the status of political parties comes reasonably close. Only outlined by the Basic Law, legislation and judicial decisions have woven detailed procedures. Professional procurators in effect indict a party and bring the case before the Constitutional Court.[83] The justices examine evidence and hear arguments presented by both sides, much as would a common-law trial court. In addition, on their own, the justices can direct production of further evidence and call for opinions from experts whom neither side summoned. Then the justices, guided by the criteria the Basic Law specifies, discuss the case, reach a decision, and publish an opinion justifying the result. All three branches of government are involved, and, except for the justices' conference, the proceedings are public. One modification might require judges to discuss the case much as the Swiss Constitutional Court does, that is, in a theater open to spectators so that what that the justices say is public.[84] Another modification might require an extraordinary majority of the court to ban a party, as does Article 149 of the Turkish charter.

83. Article 149 of the Turkish charter also allows the Constitutional Court permanently to dissolve a party that violates Article 68 4: "The statutes and programmes, as well as the activities of political parties shall not be in conflict with the independence of the state, its indivisible integrity with its territory and nation, human rights, the principles of equality and rule of law, sovereignty of the nation, the principles of the democratic and secular republic; they shall not aim to protect or establish class or group dictatorship or dictatorship of any kind, nor shall they incite citizens to crime."

84. Such apparent transparency may, of course, only drive the justices to private (and secret) discussions. Another modification might require a positive legislative vote to impeach, much as impeachment begins in the United States. The difficulty is that if the allegedly subversive party were well represented in Parliament, it might be able to block the action.

528 Maintaining a Constitutional Democracy

Is Constitutional Democracy Eternal?

Does the logic of this chapter require that once a people have adopted constitutional democracy, they as well as future generations are forever trapped in that sort of political system? Does it also follow that constitutional democracy may ban any party that is radical in the true sense of that term, that is, any party that advocates changes that go to the root of the system? The answer is largely, but not completely, no. That qualified response provides additional cause for worry. Let us back up a bit. The gist of the argument for constitutional democracy runs along these lines: Intelligent men and women believe that they can choose their form of government through "reflection and choice." Reason and experience have convinced them that constitutional democracy is the best form of government to achieve a satisfactory mix, on the one hand, of protections from fellow citizens as well as from public officials and, on the other, of governmental power to accomplish goals beyond the reach of individuals acting alone or in small groups.

This form of government, these people believe, best protects the values Benjamin N. Cardozo summed up under the rubric of "ordered liberty."[85] Not only do reason and experience lead them to try to create a constitutional democracy, but the legitimacy of such a system depends heavily on reasoned argument buttressed by experience, rather than on threats of violence. Thus constitutional democracy has a double appeal to people who treasure reason. Indeed, despite objecting to "perpetual constitutions," Noah Webster claimed that successful constitutional government would create an "empire of reason."

The primacy of reason, tested by experience, raises additional problems for constitutional democracy. Sotirios Barber maintains that a full commitment to reason allows only a provisional commitment to *any* constitutional order, because rational, self-reflective men and women must be open to intellectual persuasion about the moral desirability of a transformation of the polity.[86] That openness forbids opposition to political parties merely because they are radical. A plenary commitment to reason, however, does not permit *every* sort of systemic transformation, only the sort that will, at least as well as constitutional democracy, protect citizens' right to reason together about basic values and to carry out whatever political changes reason, informed by experience, indicates. Thus the justification for constitutional democracy would allow, in fact encourage, a shift to another system that would enlarge reason's empire or strengthen its reign. A move from constitutional democracy to a tyrannical system would, however, restrict reason's ambit for all

---

85. Palko v. Connecticut, 302 U.S. 319 (1937).
86. *On What the Constitution Means*, pp. 49–51, 59–61; *The Constitution of Judicial Power* (Baltimore: Johns Hopkins University Press, 1993), 60–61, 186–87, 232–34, 265n.

citizens except the ruler and his or her coterie—and it is far from obvious that such a system would push even that elite to rule by reason.

Tyrannical systems aside, what other kinds of transformations are validly open to a constitutional democracy? As the debate in Chapter Three indicated, representative democracy is a possibility, though it would have to operate within a political culture that imposed the same kinds of normative restraints as do constitutionalism's institutional checks. No other live options *yet* available offer alternatives. Certainly theocratic or secular dictatorships do not, nor, except perhaps for a brief transitional period for a developing nation, does guided capitalism.

Someday we may be able to imagine and create a kind of political system that better protects our capacity to reason together and more efficiently advances the value of individual human dignity than does constitutional democracy. Finality, as Disraeli said, is not in the language of politics. Yogi Berra put it more colloquially: "It ain't over till it's over." And "it" is never likely to be over until a wayward asteroid or an errant covey of H-bombs makes this planet uninhabitable. When—if—the day comes when we can envision a practically attainable political order that better protects those values, constitutional democracy's commitment to reason will demand that the change be made and that the polity encourage, not simply permit, individual citizens and political parties to adopt the new system. The crucial question involves our ability to discern the difference between a new system that would enhance our lives and one that would enslave us. Once again we enter the realm of practical wisdom; and human history suggests caution.

Epilogue

Midway in the journey of our life I found myself in a dark wood, for the straight way
was lost.   DANTE ALIGHIERI

In the natural sciences, scholars seldom assume that they are analyzing a
static world. It seems that the entire universe exists in a state of becoming.
We confront a similar situation in the study of politics. We cannot speak of
absolutely stable constitutional systems, only systems that are more or less
stable than others. More specifically, we cannot accurately speak of nations
that are constitutional democracies, only countries that *now* more or less
meet the relevant criteria. Even if we could achieve a hypostatic union between concept and reality, such a union would be only temporary. In the real
world of politics, we are apt to operate as if we were trapped inside Socrates'
cave. We can see shadows that approximate our ideals and can move closer to
(or farther from) them, although we likely will never be fully able to incar-
nate those ideals into political processes and institutions. Because we are
flawed, perfection always eludes us; but because we are educable, we may
be able to bring ideals and reality closer together. One need only think
of constitutional democracy as it existed in the United States before and
after the Thirteenth Amendment or as it existed before and after the long
struggles that followed Brown v. Board of Education or women's liberation.
Those and other battles go on and on and on; the results, alas, sometimes
move a polity away from rather than toward perfection. Change, as John
Randolph of Roanoke liked to say, does not always mean progress.

Thus Part II has, except where deposed despots are concerned, been
analyzing moving targets. Citizens are born, mature (or not), and eventually
die; during their life they may move back and forth among ideals, adequates,
and disaffected. For the sake of the polity, one hopes that they passed on the
political values of ideal or at least adequate citizenship to the next generation, but that outcome is never certain. And whatever values people of succeeding generations accept they are apt to modify, sometimes significantly.
So, too, people who staff judicial, bureaucratic, and military organizations
retire, if not die, and they also socialize their successors, who, in turn, are

likely to adjust their professional lore to fit their experiences more closely and to cope with new problems.

In constitutional interpretation the processes of change are most evident. To translate, Dante said, is to betray. Interpretation may not involve betrayal, but it often entails change from what the authors and ratifiers of a text meant to say as well as from what the builders of other parts of the constitutional order had in mind. One message of this book is that creating, maintaining, and changing a constitutional democracy are not separate and distinct operations. In many ways constitutional interpretation involves creativity, not in the sense of constructing something out of nothing, as traditional theologians postulate Yahweh did for the universe, but in the sense of exercising discretion to transform, usually incrementally, a constitutional order. If the interpreters, whoever they are, do their job well, the developing political system will conform more closely to the ideals of constitutional democracy. Insofar as interpreters err, the system's flaws will become more evident—as well as more serious.

Adding joy to the lives of those who operate the political system, there are limits to legitimate systemic change under a constitutional democracy. As the previous chapter argued, the processes of constitutional democracy cannot validate the establishment of tyranny, though they may permit, even encourage, the creation of a new regime that more effectively furthers the values of constitutional democracy.

Reprise

All things are enlinked, enlaced, and enamoured.   FRIEDRICH NIETZSCHE

Prudence, practical judgment, and luck often appear in these pages—and necessarily so. Establishing and maintaining a constitutional democracy are not tasks that can be reduced to mathematical formulas, scripted by thoughtful philosophers, or carried out by clever statesmen. At every turn, men and women who found or maintain a polity face choices that have to be made on the basis of incomplete, garbled, and perhaps erroneous information transmitted and processed by fallible minds. Intelligence, knowledge, experience, and memory are essential, but even when linked, these elements promise only a fair chance of success. Also essential is the courage to forge ahead knowing that choices may be tragically wrong. So, too, is good fortune, whether in the form of events in other countries, global economic moods, or technological change over which men and women who found and operate constitutional democracies have no control and of which they have perhaps small understanding. There is a myth about Napoleon's method of selecting generals: when presented with a candidate, he asked the officer's sponsors only one question: "Is he lucky?"

The advent of constitutional democracy is no more likely to mark the end of a nation's political development than is a coup that brings authoritarian rule. After decades of sweeping scholarship, William H. McNeill said that one thing struck him as "the principal unifying theme" of civilizations: "*Surprising new forms of collective behavior arise from what appear to be spontaneous appearances of increasing levels of complexity.*"[1] Constitutional democracies are conceived, they gestate, they are born, and perhaps they mature; sooner or later they will fall ill and, in all probability, will eventually die. The cause of death may be overthrow from within, dissipation of moral and material resources in foreign wars or in coping with domestic crises, conquest by an enemy power, or usurpation by an executive proclaiming a desperate need for emergency powers—powers he or she neglects to return. A people may also sacrifice freedom for what they believe will yield greater prosperity. And

---

1. "History and the Scientific World View," 37 *History and Theory* 1, 10 (1998). Italics in original.

534 Constitutional Democracy

there is no assurance that leaders will be sufficiently courageous, wise, or honest to operate such a fragile and complex political system or that a sufficient number of its people will continue to care enough about the polity to function as ideal or even adequate citizens. To paraphrase Thomas Fleming, constitutional democracy's life is "a churning mix" of conflicting lofty aspirations and personal ambitions, and individual and collective bouts of lethargy "over which leaders preside "only by constant effort."[2]

A constitutional democracy may also cease to exist because it is replaced by a more efficient political order. One theme that runs through this book is that the legitimacy of any such a change depends not only on its having followed prescribed procedures but also on whether the new constitutional order better guards the nation's security, more efficiently promotes economic prosperity, and more effectively protects the great and equal dignity of all its citizens and enables them to live the best lives possible, that is, in peace and justice with each other and the peoples of other nations. It is quite likely that this sort of change, if it ever comes, will require a people to move from being citizens of a nation-state to being citizens of a multinational union that will bear many of the marks of constitutional democracy.

This book has tended to look at constitutional democracy from the top down, that is, as the product of deliberate choice by persuasive leaders who try to build, or at least build on, a receptive culture not only to create peculiar political institutions and processes but also to instill and strengthen fellow citizens' commitment to norms that are congruent with and supportive of those institutions. We might contrast this approach with one that starts from the bottom and moves up, beginning with personal, perhaps religious, reform that constructs a base on which a different society forms, a society that results in a fresh political system. Such has been the path favored by some Islamist movements, most notably Egypt's Muslim Brotherhood.[3]

This dichotomy between reform from above and rejuvenation from below offers a false simplicity. In either situation, systemic political change does not simply happen. First, persuasive leaders must work long and hard to change their fellow citizens, their culture, and their institutions. Second, it is rare that a reform movement simply "catches on" without having leaders who create structures to spread the good news, weed out false messages, denounce heretics, and protect the group. All of these moves require discipline and obedience as well as organization to defend against established forces.[4] Whether leaders start at the top, the bottom, or somewhere in the

---

2. *Mysteries of My Father: An Irish-American Memoir* (New York: Wiley, 2005), p. 195.

3. See Anthony Shadid, *The Legacy of the Prophet: Despots, Democrats, and the New Politics of Islam* (Boulder: Westview, 2002), ch. 2, esp. p. 54.

4. Social and political reform through individual reform was the message of Hassan al-Banna, the most influential of the founders of the Muslim Brotherhood in Egypt during the late 1920s. The Brotherhood's next great leader, Sayyid Qutb, changed this message. No one who lived in a state

middle, to be successful they must change individuals, society, and institutions. The interactions here are circular and, leaders hope, synergistic. Individuals shape society, society shapes individuals, and both shape political institutions and processes, which in turn shape individuals and society.

In these processes, reason interacts with emotion and experience. And here we encounter the perennial problem of justifying constitutional democracy. Sotirios Barber contends that the case for constitutional democracy must be thin, because our commitment to reason is primary and only secondarily do we obligate ourselves to a constitutional order. This argument confronts us with an apparent dilemma. To be open to reason means to be willing to reexamine our most basic principles, premises, and values—to be open to change, even radical systemic change that would renounce constitutional democracy. But a commitment to reason would preclude some courses of action, most evidently adoption of a totalitarian political system, even by peaceful processes. Such a choice would not be rational, for it would prevent us and later generations from exercising our capacity to reason about the secular things that matter most.

One can, of course, argue—as I have—that a people cannot reasonably opt for totalitarianism or other forms of tyranny. But we often reason imperfectly, just as we often perceive imperfectly. The tendency to overestimate the worth of current over long-range benefits is near universal. Thus it may well seem to intelligent, decent human beings that they are following means, intermediate goals, or values conducive to the good life when, in fact, they are endorsing ideas whose actualization would destroy that people's notion of the good life. In this regard, one might ask oneself whether one would really like to be a citizen of Plato's Republic, a polity imagined by human reasoning simultaneously at its best and worst, both brilliant and flawed.

To restate the dilemma: On the one hand, a full commitment to reason allows only a provisional commitment to constitutional democracy, because we must be open to rational persuasion about the moral necessity, or at least desirability, of radical political change. On the other hand, a plenary commitment to reason does not allow *every* sort of political change, only a change to a system that will, at least equally as well as constitutional democracy, protect the capacity of humans to reason about basic values and about additional changes. So stated, the dilemma may become a problem of prudence exercised in a milieu of restricted choice. Most basically, one might avoid the dilemma by rejecting a primary commitment to reason. Although it is difficult to construct a persuasive argument that ignores or contradicts

---

that did not fully accept Islam could be a true Muslim. Each such person had to choose between God and the state. See ibid., ch. 2; Gilles Kepel, *Muslim Extremism in Egypt: The Prophet and the Pharaoh* (Berkeley: University of California Press, 1995); and Sayyid Qutb, *Milestones*, trans. S. Badrul Hasan (original 1964; Indianapolis: American Trust, 1990).

reason, to some extent such questioning is wise, because abstract reason may mislead us, as indeed it sometimes has. To command obedience, reason must be connected to the real world through experience. In that context, we are speaking of what Aristotle called practical reason, prudence. Alas, its efficacy can often be ascertained only long after its exercise.

In the end as in the beginning, we confront a clotted cluster of very troublesome facts. Constitutional democracy is an artifact. Its mix is fragile, its promises uncertain; only astute leaders can create it; only thoughtful leaders can justify it; only shrewd political leaders can maintain it; and they can do so only if supported by a mass of committed, concerned, and energetic citizens. In this regard at least, Nietzsche was largely correct: all political things may not be enamored, but they are certainly entwined and ensnarled.

General Index

This index does not list authors whose works are cited only (or mainly) in footnotes.

abortion: autonomy and, 375; Bathsheba and, 451n; Canada and, 135, 136; China and, 98; constitutional democracy and, 135–38; deliberative/representative democracy and, 139–40; divisive political issue, 134, 139, 140, 307, 315, 320, 336; as economic measure, 317; euphemisms for, 40, 375; fetus's rights and, 134–35, 137, 292, 315–16, 318–21; France, Italy, and Spain on, 139; Germany and, 135–37, 267, 503; human dignity and, 279, 315–16; human life and, 60, 106n, 134, 279; Ireland and, 136–38, 503; late term, 134; moral problems of, 140, 182; John Rawls on, 447n; religion and, 77; Peter Singer on, 318–19; United Kingdom and, 135n, 138; United States and, 135, 136; women's rights and, 134, 292, 319, 322
Adams, John, 54n, 355, 400
Adams, Sam, 70
Afghanistan, 69, 103, 356, 395, 405n, 409, 413–15, 423
Almond, Gabriel, 99, 347n
analytical jurisprudence. *See* legal positivism
Appiah, K. Anthony, 39
Aquinas, Thomas, 102, 197, 447, 448n, 452, 456, 457. *See also* Thomism/Thomists
Aristotle: on autonomy, 47, 513; citizen, definition of, 122, 346, 347n; citizen, excellence of, 342, 368; on constitution, expanding definitions of, 13; on elections v. lot as democratic, 4n, 346, 347n; on good life, 36, 105, 147, 449; on justice, 447n, 448n, 454n; on moral realism, 51, 101; politics, definition of, 3, 143; on punishment, 452, 457; on wisdom, practical, 489, 536
Austin, John, 249. *See also* legal positivism

autonomy: group or organizational, 84, 86, 125, 153–54, 157–59, 172, 353, 354, 375; individual, 43–48, 50, 53, 55–56, 86, 103, 173, 220, 320, 375, 408, 513–17

Barak, Aharon, and constitutional interpretation , 168n, 277, 461, 484–85
Barber, Sotirios A.: on constitutional aspirations, 198; on constitutional change, 518, 528; on constitutionalism and democracy, 10n; on moral realism, 447–48; on 9th amendment, 277n; on positive constitutionalism, 7n, 76, 113, 287n, 340n; on reason and political choices, 295, 300n, 377, 507, 518n, 528, 535
Beer, Lawrence Ward, 77
Black, Hugo L., 8, 191n, 277, 462, 498, 503n
Bork, Robert H.: and constitutional interpretation, 251; and 9th amendment, 277; and originalism, 475n, 480
bureaucracy/bureaucrats: Hannah Arendt on, 398; contact with citizens, 403; discretion of, 399, 401–6, 409; education for, 419; as essential to any political system, 398; as experts, 400–401; German, 409–11; ideal of, 399; Iraqi, 411; Japanese, 408–9; judicial personnel as, 402–3, 421–22; legislative personnel as, 402–3; political culture of, 399, 420, 421–24; representation within, 419–20. *See* also bureaucracy, staffing of; lustration
bureaucracy, staffing of: in Afghanistan, 413–15; in Africa, 413; in India, 415–16; cleansing of communists from, 412–13, 418; de-Nazification of, 408–11; Iraq and, 411; NGOs and, 416; UN and, 416–18. *See also* bureaucracy/bureaucrats; lustration
Burke, Edmund, 116, 497

Camus, Albert, on roles of intellectuals, 2
capitalism: and constitutionalism, 129, 335,

Index of Cases